THE ECONOMICS OF
SPORTS

fourth edition

Michael Leeds
TEMPLE UNIVERSITY

Peter von Allmen
MORAVIAN COLLEGE

Addison Wesley
Boston   Columbus   Indianapolis   New York   San Francisco   Upper Saddle River
Amsterdam   Cape Town   Dubai   London   Madrid   Milan   Munich   Paris   Montreal   Toronto   Delhi
Mexico City   Sao Paulo   Sydney   Hong Kong   Seoul   Singapore   Taipei   Tokyo

The Pearson Series in Economics

Abel/Bernanke/Croushore
*Macroeconomics**

Bade/Parkin
*Foundations of Economics**

Bierman/Fernandez
Game Theory with Economic Applications

Blanchard
Macroeconomics

Blau / Ferber / Winkler
The Economics of Women, Men and Work

Boardman / Greenberg / Vining / Weimer
Cost-Benefit Analysis

Boyer
Principles of Transportation Economics

Branson
Macroeconomic Theory and Policy

Brock/Adams
The Structure of American Industry

Bruce
Public Finance and the American Economy

Carlton/Perloff
Modern Industrial Organization

Case/Fair/Oster
*Principles of Economics**

Caves/Frankel/Jones
World Trade and Payments: An Introduction

Chapman
Environmental Economics: Theory, Application, and Policy

Cooter/Ulen
Law & Economics

Downs
An Economic Theory of Democracy

Ehrenberg/Smith
Modern Labor Economics

Ekelund/Ressler/Tollison
*Economics**

Farnham
Economics for Managers

Folland/Goodman/Stano
The Economics of Health and Health Care

Fort
Sports Economics

Froyen
Macroeconomics

Fusfeld
The Age of the Economist

Gerber
International Economics

Gordon
Macroeconomics

Greene
Econometric Analysis

Gregory
Essentials of Economics

Gregory/Stuart
Russian and Soviet Economic Performance and Structure

Hartwick/Olewiler
The Economics of Natural Resource Use

Heilbroner/ Milberg
The Making of the Economic Society

Heyne/ Boettke / Prychitko
The Economic Way of Thinking

Hoffman/Averett
Women and the Economy: Family, Work, and Pay

Holt
Markets, Games and Strategic Behavior

Hubbard
Money, the Financial System, and the Economy

Hubbard/OBrien
*Economics**

Hughes/Cain
American Economic History

Husted/Melvin
International Economics

Jehle/Reny
Advanced Microeconomic Theory

Johnson-Lans
A Health Economics Primer

Keat/Young
Managerial Economics

Klein
Mathematical Methods for Economics

Krugman/Obstfeld
*International Economics:
Theory & Policy**

Laidler
The Demand for Money

Leeds/von Allmen
The Economics of Sports

Leeds/von Allmen/Schiming
*Economics**

Lipsey/Ragan/Storer
*Economics**

Lynn
*Economic Development: Theory and
Practice for a Divided World*

Melvin
International Money and Finance

Miller
*Economics Today**
Understanding Modern Economics

Miller/Benjamin
The Economics of Macro Issues

Miller/Benjamin/North
The Economics of Public Issues

Mills/Hamilton
Urban Economics

Mishkin
*The Economics of Money, Banking,
and Financial Markets**
*The Economics of Money, Banking,
and Financial Markets,
Business School Edition**

Murray
Econometrics: A Modern Introduction

Nafziger
*The Economics of Developing
Countries*

O'Sullivan/Sheffrin/Perez
*Economics: Principles, Applications
and Tools**

Parkin
*Economics**

Perloff
*Microeconomics**
*Microeconomics: Theory and
Applications with Calculus*

Perman/Common/McGilvray/Ma
*Natural Resources and
Environmental Economics*

Phelps
Health Economics

Pindyck/Rubinfeld
*Microeconomics**

**Riddell/Shackelford/Stamos/
  Schneider**
*Economics: A Tool for Critically
Understanding Society*

Ritter/Silber/Udell
*Principles of Money, Banking &
Financial Markets**

Roberts
*The Choice: A Fable of Free Trade
and Protection*

Rohlf
*Introduction to Economic
Reasoning*

Ruffin/Gregory
Principles of Economics

Sargent
Rational Expectations and Inflation

Sawyer/Sprinkle
International Economics

Scherer
*Industry Structure, Strategy,
and Public Policy*

Schiller
*The Economics of Poverty and
Discrimination*

Sherman
Market Regulation

Silberberg
Principles of Microeconomics

Stock/Watson
Introduction to Econometrics
*Introduction to Econometrics,
Brief Edition*

Studenmund
*Using Econometrics: A
Practical Guide*

Tietenberg/Lewis
*Environmental and Natural Resource
Economics*
*Environmental Economics
and Policy*

Todaro/Smith
Economic Development

Waldman
Microeconomics

Waldman/Jensen
*Industrial Organization:
Theory and Practice*

Weil
Economic Growth

Williamson
Macroeconomics

*denotes myeconlab titles   Log onto www.myeconlab.com to learn more

Editorial Director: Sally Yagan
Editor in Chief: Donna Battista
Acquisitions Editor: Noel Kamm Seibert
Editorial Assistant: Laura Murphy
Director of Marketing: Patrice Jones
Senior Marketing Manager: Elizabeth A. Averbeck
Marketing Assistant: Ian Gold
Senior Manufacturing Buyer: Carol Melville
Managing Editor: Nancy H. Fenton
Senior Production Project Manager: Nancy
 Freihofer

Permissions Project Supervisor: Michael Joyce
Cover Designer: Jayne Conte
Cover Art: © Aflo/Corbis
Supplements Editor: Alison Eusden
Production Coordination, Text Design, and
 Composition: Laserwords
Printer/Binder: Hamilton Printing Co.
Cover Printer: Lehigh Phoenix
Text Font: 10/12 Palatino

Credits and acknowledgments borrowed from other sources and reproduced, with permission, in this textbook appear on appropriate page within text and on page 413.

Library of Congress Cataloging-in-Publication Data
Leeds, Michael (Michael A.)
  The economics of sports / Michael Leeds, Peter von Allmen. — 4th ed.
    p. cm.
  Includes bibliographical references and index.
  ISBN-13: 978-0-13-800929-8
  ISBN-10: 0-13-800929-5
1. Sports—Economic aspects.   I. Von Allmen, Peter.   II. Title.
  GV716.L44 2010
  338.4'3796—dc22

                                                           2009049033

10 9 8 7 6 5 4 3 2 1

Addison-Wesley
is an imprint of

www.pearsonhighered.com

ISBN-13: 978-0-13-800929-8
ISBN-10: 0-13-800929-5

In memory of Lawrence Hadley,
friend and mentor.

BRIEF CONTENTS

Detailed Contents   *vii*

Preface   *xiii*

PART ONE   Introduction and Review of Economic Concepts   1

CHAPTER 1   **Economics and Sports**   3
CHAPTER 2   **Review of the Economist's Arsenal**   13

PART TWO   The Industrial Organization of Sports   61

CHAPTER 3   **Sports Franchises as Profit-Maximizing Firms**   63
CHAPTER 4   **Monopoly and Antitrust**   107
CHAPTER 5   **Competitive Balance**   145

PART THREE   Public Finance and Sports   173

CHAPTER 6   **The Public Finance of Sports: The Market for Teams**   175
CHAPTER 7   **The Costs and Benefits of a Franchise to a City**   207

PART FOUR   The Labor Economics of Sports   241

CHAPTER 8   **An Introduction to Labor Markets in Professional Sports**   243
CHAPTER 9   **Labor Market Imperfections**   279
CHAPTER 10   **Discrimination**   311

PART FIVE   Sports in the Not-for-Profit Sector   345

CHAPTER 11   **The Economics of Amateurism and College Sports**   347

Works Cited   *389*

Index   *415*

CONTENTS

Preface   xiii

PART ONE   Introduction and Review of Economic Concepts   1

CHAPTER 1   Economics and Sports   3

Introduction   3
1.1 The Organization of the Text   4
1.2 Babe Ruth and Comparative Advantage   5
Opportunity Costs   6
Absolute and Comparative Advantage   6
BIOGRAPHICAL SKETCH   **BABE DIDRIKSON ZAHARIAS   8**
SUMMARY   10   DISCUSSION QUESTIONS   10   PROBLEMS   11

CHAPTER 2   Review of the Economist's Arsenal   13

Introduction   13
2.1 The Supply and Demand Model   14
Demand, Supply, and Equilibrium   14
Supply and Demand Curves and the Price of Baseball Cards   18
2.2 Price Ceilings and the Benefits of Scalping   27
2.3 Market Structures: From Perfect Competition to Monopoly   29
A Note on the Definition of Output   29
Perfect Competition   30
Monopoly and Other Imperfectly Competitive Market Structures   32
The Impact of an Increase in Costs   36
2.4 The Development of Professional Sports   37
BIOGRAPHICAL SKETCH   **SILVIO BERLUSCONI   40**
SUMMARY   42 DISCUSSION QUESTIONS   42 PROBLEMS   42

APPENDIX **2A**   **Utility Functions, Indifference Curves,
and Budget Constraints   44**
2A.1   Constrained Maximization   44
2A.2   Using Indifference Curves and Budget Constraints:
The Rise of Soccer and Baseball   50

APPENDIX **2B**   **Regression Analysis in Brief   53**
Multiple Regression and Dummy Variables   58

PART TWO   The Industrial Organization of Sports   61

CHAPTER 3   Sports Franchises as Profit-Maximizing Firms   63

Introduction   63

3.1 The Importance of Leagues   64
Setting the Rules   66
Limiting Entry   68
Controlling Entry as Cooperative Behavior   71
League Contraction   72
Marketing   73

3.2 What Are Profits and How Are They Maximized?   75
A Detailed Look at Revenue   76
Television Revenue   80
The Effects of Revenue Sharing   87
Cost   88
Opportunity Cost—Teams on the Move   89

3.3 Taxes, Profit, Owner Behavior, and Vertical Integration   90

3.4 Turning Losses into Profits: The Accounting Game   93
Using Sports to Maximize Profits Elsewhere   94
Operating Income, Book Profit, and Bill Veeck   94

3.5 Soccer's Alternative Business Model   97
Profit Maximization in Soccer   98
The Impact of Promotion and Relegation   99
The Financial Dangers of an Open System   101
The Single Entity Ownership Model   101

BIOGRAPHICAL SKETCH   **BILL VEECK   102**

SUMMARY   103   DISCUSSION QUESTIONS   104   PROBLEMS   104

CHAPTER 4   Monopoly and Antitrust   107

Introduction   107

4.1 What's Wrong with Monopoly?   108
Monopolists and Deadweight Loss   108
Promotion, Relegation, and Monopoly Power   111
Strategic Pricing and Price Discrimination   112
Consumer Surplus and Personal Seat Licenses   118
Monopoly Stood on Its Head: A Brief Introduction to Monopsony   120

4.2 What's Right with Monopoly?   121

4.3 Barriers to Entry   123

4.4 Society's Response to Monopoly and Monopsony: Antitrust Laws   124

4.5 An Important Anomaly: Baseball's Antitrust Exemption   126
The Economic Impact of the Antitrust Exemption   130
Limited Exemptions: The NFL and Television   131

4.6 The NCAA: An Incidental Cartel   132

4.7 Prisoner's Dilemma: How Rational Actions Lead
to Irrational Outcomes   136

BIOGRAPHICAL SKETCH   "PETE" ROZELLE   138

SUMMARY 140   DISCUSSION QUESTIONS 141   PROBLEMS 141

APPENDIX 4A   **An Alternative Application of Game Theory   142**

CHAPTER 5   **Competitive Balance**   **145**

Introduction   145
5.1 The Fan's Perspective   146
5.2 The Owners' Perspective   148
  The Effect of Market Size   149
5.3 Measuring Competitive Balance   151
  Within-Season Variation   151
  Between-Season Variation   155
  Illustrating Competitive Imbalance   157
  Competitive Balance in Major League Baseball   159
  Economic Theories of Competitive Balance   160
5.4 Attempts to Alter Competitive Balance   162
  Revenue Sharing   162
  Salary Caps and Luxury Taxes   164
  The Reverse-Order Entry Draft   165
  Schedule Adjustments in the NFL   168
  Promotion and Relegation   168

BIOGRAPHICAL SKETCH   **BUD SELIG   169**

SUMMARY 170   DISCUSSION QUESTIONS 171   PROBLEMS 171

PART THREE   **Public Finance and Sports   173**

CHAPTER 6   **The Public Finance of Sports: The Market for Teams**   **175**

Introduction   175
6.1 The Competition for Professional Sports Teams   177
  How Cities Underwrite Sports Facilities   177
  New Facilities and Attendance   181
6.2 How Teams Exploit Market Forces   182
  Leagues, Cities, and Market Power   183
  The All-Or-Nothing Demand Curve   185
  The Winner's Curse   187
6.3 How the Olympics and the World Cup Induce Overspending   188
6.4 The Form and Function of Stadiums and Arenas   191
  What's in a Name?   192
  The Size and Shape of Facilities   193

Location, Location, Location 199

BIOGRAPHICAL SKETCH   **AL DAVIS** 202

SUMMARY 204   DISCUSSION QUESTIONS 204   PROBLEMS 205

CHAPTER 7   **The Costs and Benefits of a Franchise to a City**   **207**

Introduction 207

7.1 Why Do Cities Do It? The Benefits of a Franchise 208
Privately Built Facilities 209
Publicly Built Facilities 210
Can Anyone Win at This Game? 222
The Impact of Special Events 225

7.2 A Public Choice Perspective 226

7.3 Stadium Costs and Financing 228
An Economic View of Taxes: Who Should Pay? 229
Sales Taxes 232
Incremental Financing 234
Taxes That Broaden the Burden 234
The Benefits of Debt 235

BIOGRAPHICAL SKETCH   **"MITT" ROMNEY** 237

SUMMARY 238   DISCUSSION QUESTIONS 238   PROBLEMS 239

PART FOUR   **The Labor Economics of Sports**   **241**

CHAPTER 8   **An Introduction to Labor Markets in Professional Sports**   **243**

Introduction 243

8.1 An Overview of Labor Supply and Labor Demand 245
Labor Supply 246
Labor Demand 248
Labor Market Equilibrium 251

8.2 The Economics of Tournaments and Superstars 255
An Exception to the Rule: NASCAR 259

8.3 Tournaments, Cheating, and the Distribution of Income 261
Too Much of a Good Thing 261
Performance-Enhancing Drugs 262
The Distribution of Income 265

BIOGRAPHICAL SKETCH   **SCOTT BORAS** 267

SUMMARY 268   DISCUSSION QUESTIONS 269   PROBLEMS 269

APPENDIX 8A   **The Labor–Leisure Choice Model of Indifference Curves**   **270**
The Labor–Leisure Model When Hours Are Fixed 275

CHAPTER 9   **Labor Market Imperfections**   **279**

Introduction 279
9.1 The Monopsony Power of Sports Leagues 280
   The Economics of Monopsony 280
   The Reserve Clause 281
   Salary Arbitration 284
   Salary Caps 286
   The Impact of Rival Leagues 290
   Measuring Monopsony Power 291
9.2 Unions in Professional Sports 292
   A Brief Introduction to the Economics of Unions 292
   Labor Conflict in Professional Sports 296
   Why Don't NFL Players Make More Money? 301
   Professional Tennis Associations 304

BIOGRAPHICAL SKETCH   **MARVIN MILLER**   **307**

SUMMARY 308   DISCUSSION QUESTIONS 309   PROBLEMS 309

CHAPTER 10   **Discrimination**   **311**

Introduction 311
10.1 Becker's Theory of Labor Discrimination 313
10.2 Different Forms of Discrimination in Professional Sports 315
   Employer Discrimination 315
   Does Anyone Win with Employer Discrimination? 320
   Employee Discrimination 326
   Consumer Discrimination 328
   Discrimination by National Origin in European Soccer 331
   Positional Discrimination or Hiring Discrimination 332
   Gender Equity—A Special Case? 336
10.3 Title IX and Discrimination in College Sports 338

BIOGRAPHICAL SKETCH   **BRANCH RICKEY**   **340**

SUMMARY 342   DISCUSSION QUESTIONS 342   PROBLEMS 343

PART FIVE   **Sports in the Not-for-Profit Sector**   **345**

CHAPTER 11   **The Economics of Amateurism and College Sports**   **347**

Introduction 347
11.1 The Troublesome Concept of Amateurism 348
   A Brief History of Amateurism and "the Olympic Ideal" 349
11.2 Amateurism, Profits, and the NCAA 352
   The Code of Amateurism: Academic Ideals or Monopsony Power? 353
   Pay for Play: The Grant-in-Aid 357

What's in a Name? The Lot of the "Student-Athlete"   358
Measuring the Net Value of Athletes to Colleges   358
Dividing the Profits: The NCAA as an Efficient Cartel   359

11.3 College as an Investment for the Student-Athlete   363

11.4 The NCAA and the Uneasy Coexistence of Athletics and Academia   368
Why Schools Promote Big-Time Athletic Programs   370
The Difficulty in Regulating College Sports   373
The Knight Commission on Intercollegiate Athletics   374
Academic Standards: Bulwarks of Integrity or Barriers to Entry?   375
Academic Standards as a Barrier to Entry   379

11.5 The Finances of College Athletics   380
Do Colleges Make a Profit from Athletics?   380
College Athletics and Profit Maximization   383

BIOGRAPHICAL SKETCH   **ANITA DEFRANTZ**   385
SUMMARY   386   DISCUSSION QUESTIONS   386   PROBLEMS   387

Works Cited   389

Photo Credits   413

Index   415

PREFACE

As *The Economics of Sports* enters its fourth edition, we remain as excited as ever about the events of the past and the possibilities for the future in sports economics. For economists, the relevance of the discipline within applied microeconomics continues to grow, as new research expands both our theoretical and applied knowledge of firm and individual behavior. Through the most tumultuous economic times in our lifetimes, the sports industry has not lost its relevance. It continues to serve as both a mirror and a lens; reflecting our broader culture and values, while at the same time bringing into focus such fundamental issues as fairness and the legitimacy of free markets. With the passing of each season, new events unfold in professional and amateur sports that deserve analysis and explanation. Finally, in the context of this book, sports economics remains a vital and interesting area of study for students of economics. Sports provides a seemingly endless set of examples from every area of microeconomics, giving students the opportunity to study public finance, industrial organization, and labor markets in a context that holds student interest like no other industry.

Over the many years that we have worked on this project, we have enjoyed continuous help and support from students and colleagues at colleges and universities across the United States and around the world. Our colleagues continue to offer encouragement, share classroom experiences, and suggest new and different coverage as the industry evolves. For all of this support and help, we are most grateful. And as we have said many times, we hope that our own enthusiasm, as well as the enthusiasm others have shared with us, is reflected in the text.

In recent years, many outstanding books that concentrate on specific sports or particular aspects of the economics of sports have been published. This text stands apart from the others in that it has the instruction of economic concepts as its central focus.

New to This Edition

In the fourth edition, we have retained the features from previous editions that made learning about sports economics meaningful as well as enjoyable, while at the same time incorporating many recent events in the sports industry and the broader economy.

- In order to capture students' interest earlier as well as reduce the quantity of material in Chapter 2, we have moved our discussion of opportunity cost and comparative advantage forward into Chapter 1.

- We have incorporated discussion of new profit-maximizing strategies of teams such as variable ticket pricing and ticket bundling.

- The most significant change for this edition is the reorganization of the chapters that cover labor markets. To help students focus on how labor markets differ from product markets and understand the nuances of these differences, we have substantially reorganized Chapters 8 and 9.

- In Chapter 8 we introduce the fundamental concepts required to study labor markets in team and individual sports markets, while in Chapter 9 we bring together all of the material on labor market imperfections that make these markets unique.

- We also have expanded our discussion of performance-enhancing drugs in a more comprehensive discussion of the economics of cheating.

- We have updated Chapter 11, which focuses on amateur and collegiate sports, to include discussion of the impact of important legal challenges to the status quo in the NCAA.

As with the first three editions, our goal for the fourth edition is to keep the text comprehensive yet accessible. The text is designed to serve as the foundation for undergraduate courses in sports economics. The nature of the subject matter makes this a unique challenge. Unlike area courses such as industrial organization or labor economics, which are self-contained fields in the broader area of economics, sports economics cuts across a wide array of economic disciplines. To deal with this problem, we have split the text into five parts, three of which are devoted to illustrating prominent areas of economics: industrial organization, public finance, and labor economics. We hope that this division provides students with an overview of much of economics and inspires them to pursue each field in its own right. Because we focus largely on professional sports in the first four parts of the book, we include a closing section devoted to amateur sports. This final part provides insights into theories related to the not-for-profit sector of the economy, such as the theory of bureaucracy. Each of the five parts of this text presents significant economic theory and recent evidence and research for that area of economics.

To make the text accessible, we assume that students have had one semester of microeconomics principles. Balancing exposition against an economist's desire for theoretical rigor presented a challenge that almost equaled that of providing a comprehensive text. In order to help the students understand the economics and to make the treatment more entertaining, we have included a generous component of sports history to place the events and economic theory in perspective.

Intended Audience

Economics of sports classes are taught at a variety of levels, ranging from undergraduate courses, with principles of economics as the only prerequisites, to the graduate level. This text is designed to offer a high level of flexibility to the instructor. All the material in the main body of the text should be accessible to students with a single semester of microeconomics principles. In order to enrich courses taught at a higher level, we have included appendices containing intermediate-level material at the end of several chapters. To ensure that all students begin the course with a common background, we provide a substantial review of principles-level material in Chapter 2. This material can either be covered explicitly with lecture support or left to the students to read on their own, as needed. For instructors interested in presenting the results of econometric research, Chapter 2 contains an appendix on the fundamentals of regression. In advanced undergraduate- and graduate-level courses, the text can serve as a foundation for common understanding of basic concepts.

Organization of the Text and Coverage Options

As stated previously, the text is divided into five parts. The first two chapters provide an introduction to sports economics, a review of principles-level tools, and an illustration of how economic principles apply to the sports industry. Chapters 3, 4, and 5 focus on the industrial organization of the sports industry. Here, we discuss the competitive landscape, the implications of monopoly power, profit maximization, and competitive balance. Chapter 4 focuses specifically on issues of anti-trust and regulation and how they have impacted the formation, success, and, sometimes, the failure of leagues. Chapter 5 describes why leagues are concerned about competitive balance, how competitive balance is measured, and how leagues might attempt to alter the balance of competition in a league. Chapter 6 and Chapter 7 focus on public finance. In this portion of the text, students learn the economics behind the financing of new stadiums in U.S. cities, why teams seem to have so much power over municipalities, and why municipalities fight so hard to keep the teams they have as well as court new ones. Chapters 8 through 10 focus on labor issues related to sports. Chapter 8 introduces the fundamental theories of labor markets, including human capital theory and tournament theory. Chapter 9 covers monopoly unions and monopsony, two labor market imperfections that profoundly impact the functioning of most sports labor markets. Chapter 10 discusses discrimination. Finally, Chapter 11 focuses on the economics of amateur sports, especially major collegiate sports. Because major college sports is really an industry itself, this chapter serves as a capstone to the text, incorporating the theories and concepts from many of the previous chapters.

Additional Resources

The text is accompanied by an online Instructor's Manual, updated for the fourth edition by Victor Matheson of the College of the Holy Cross. We are also pleased to provide PowerPoint slides, written by text author Michael Leeds, that contain all figures and tables in the text as well as lecture notes for classroom presentation. The Instructor's Manual and PowerPoint slides may be accessed via the Instructor's Resource Center at www.pearsonhighered.com/irc.

Students and instructors may also access the text's companion website at www.pearsonhighered.com/leeds. Updated for the fourth edition, the website features chapter quizzes, current web links, and additional sports data.

Acknowledgments

In a project such as this, the list of people who contributed to its completion extends far beyond those whose names appear on the cover. We owe personal and professional debts of sincere gratitude to a great many people. First, we thank our editorial team at Addison Wesley, including Noel Seibert, Laura Murphy, Denise Clinton, Nancy Freihofer, and Alison Eusden. Also thanks to Karen Berry at Laserwords for her work on preparing the manuscript. We also are grateful for the advice, encouragement, and suggestions from the ever-growing community of sports economists who use this book. Their input and support serve as a continuing source of motivation and assistance. We would particularly like to thank all of those who read and reviewed the manuscript as we prepared the fourth edition, including Norman Cloutier, University of Wisconsin–Parkside; Stacey Brook, University of Iowa; Greg Delemeester, Marietta College; Victor Matheson, College of the Holy Cross; Raymond Sauer, Clemson University; Karl Einolf, Mt. Saint Mary's University; Jason Winfree, University of Michigan; Amber Brown, Grand Valley State University; and Patrick Mason, Florida State University. Their suggestions for improvements were excellent, and we tried our best to incorporate them wherever possible. Finally, as always, we thank our families: Eva, Daniel, Melanie, Heather, Daniel, Thomas, and Eric, all of whom provided unwavering support.

Michael Leeds

Peter von Allmen

PART ONE
Introduction and Review of Economic Concepts

CHAPTER 1
Economics and Sports

CHAPTER 2
Review of the Economist's Arsenal

CHAPTER 1

Economics and Sports

All I remember about my wedding day in 1967 is that the Cubs dropped a double-header.

—GEORGE WILL[1]

Introduction

On October 31, 2008, the city of Philadelphia came to a complete halt. An estimated two million people—in a city of only 1.4 million—clogged the center of town. Schools were half-empty, and the city's subways stopped running because no one could get past the crowds to enter or leave the stations. This was not due to a homeland security exercise or a pre-election political rally. It was a celebration of the Philadelphia Phillies' recent World Series championship.

Sports occupy a unique position in the human psyche. They have even become a way by which institutions, cities, and nations define themselves. As early as the 19th century, universities have used football to give their students a sense of identity. Cities do not feel that they have achieved "big-time" status without a baseball, football, or basketball franchise. Entire countries have used Olympic performance as a way to justify their political and economic systems.

Sports can also serve as tools by which nations conduct foreign policy. They have been used to bring people together, as was the case in 1971 when a team of American table-tennis players and their "ping-pong diplomacy" marked the first step in the reopening of relations between the United States and China. They have also been used to keep people apart, as demonstrated by the boycotts that disrupted the 1976, 1980, and 1984 Olympics.

The clamor over sports would naturally lead one to think that the sports industry occupies a dominant position in the world economy. In fact, compared to many firms, let alone industries, it is a very small operation. According to *Forbes Magazine*, the total revenues generated by the four major North American

---

[1]George F. Will, *Bunts* (New York: Scribner, 1998), p. 22.

sports leagues (basketball, baseball, football, and hockey) totaled about $19.09 billion in 2008, which would not rank among the top 100 revenue generating companies. The sports' revenues are about one twenty-fourth those of Royal Dutch Shell's $458.36 billion and less than the $19.10 billion generated by CIGNA insurance, yet, unlike sports, the petroleum industry does not have its own section in any newspaper, and the local insurance company does not merit a segment on the evening news.

The disproportionate attention the public pays to sports provides economics professors with a way to present economic theory in a context their students can understand and enjoy. Students whose eyes glaze over at the thought of multipliers or tax incidence engage in impassioned discussions of the benefits of a new football stadium and how the city or state will pay for it. Classes that sit silently through discussions of marginal revenue product and wages jump to life when asked whether Alex Rodriguez or LeBron James is worth the money he is paid.

This book harnesses the enthusiasm that you bring to sports and uses it to introduce a variety of economic concepts. These concepts will help you to understand the business of sports, but they will also enable you to make sense of the wider world around you. Thus, understanding how sports leagues exercise monopoly power will give you deeper insight into the policies followed by OPEC or Microsoft. By the end of this book, you will have a deeper appreciation for sport as a business. You will also see more clearly how economic reasoning helps us understand the world around us.

1.1   The Organization of the Text

The text is divided into four parts. The remainder of this part will provide you with an extensive review of basic economic theory, particularly supply and demand and models of perfect competition and monopoly. All are presented as solutions to problems that people encounter in the world of sports.

The next three parts of the text are devoted to showing how three particular areas of economics provide insight into how sports function. Part Two presents the industrial organization of sports. **Industrial organization** is the study of how firms maximize profit. In Chapter 3, we discuss the purpose and structure of a variety of professional leagues. We also review the competitive and monopoly market structures and discuss the implications for profit maximization in each case. In Chapter 4, we extend the discussion of monopoly, including an extensive discussion of the challenges that concentrated markets create for consumers. Chapter 5 describes the desirability of competitive balance, how it can be measured, how it has changed over time, and how leagues have dealt with unbalanced competition.

Part Three contains two chapters on the public finance of sports. **Public finance** asks how and why governments provide goods and services and how they raise the funds to pay for them. In Chapter 6, we analyze how firms might get local municipalities to pay for new arenas and describe how fiscal and neighborhood constraints have helped to determine the shape of facilities over the years. In Chapter 7, we extend this analysis by asking why local governments would make such an investment and, if the investment is made, how to best fund it.

Part Four covers the labor economics of professional sports. **Labor economics** analyzes how markets determine the level of employment and compensation. In Chapter 8, we use labor markets to explain why professional athletes receive such high salaries. In doing so, we introduce basic labor market concepts, such as human capital. Chapter 9 explores labor market imperfections, such as the existence of labor unions, which also affect player salaries. In Chapter 10, we discuss the history and implications of discrimination in professional sports. From the informal yet strictly enforced "color lines" that marked the NFL and MLB until 1946 and 1947, respectively, to the possibility that hockey teams may view French Canadian defensemen as less productive than English Canadians, sports provide many examples of discriminatory behavior.

Finally, in Chapter 11 we broaden our study of sports to include amateur athletics at the Olympic and major college levels. We discuss the history of amateurism and the consequences that misperceptions about this history have had for the National Collegiate Athletic Association (NCAA). This chapter also examines the effects of recent changes in admissions and eligibility standards for schools and athletes. As part of this discussion, we include a section on the uneven racial impact of these rules.

As you progress through the course, we encourage you to make full use of the Internet as a powerful and easy-to-use source of further reading. First and foremost, the publisher of this text, Addison Wesley, maintains a Web site specifically designed to support the book. Log on to **www.aw-bc.com/leeds_vonallmen** and you will find a set of interesting links to other quality sites as well as information we provide directly to assist you. The site is updated regularly so that it contains links to sites and stories that are sure to be of interest.

In addition, virtually every major (and almost every minor) league team and individual sports league or association has its own Web site. These sites are continually updated with information about news (including economic events) from around the league. Finally, many sports magazines maintain Web sites that have current and archived information that can be very useful for term papers, projects, and general information. One caution: Beware of low-quality information that is rampant on noncommercial, individual blogs and private Web sites. The information they convey is often based on opinion rather than on fact and is of little or no value.

Let the games begin!

1.2 Babe Ruth and Comparative Advantage

We begin each chapter by posing a few puzzles that people have faced in the sports world. The material that we present in each chapter then helps us to solve the puzzles that we raise at the outset. This section provides a taste of what is to come. We will use the theory of comparative advantage, a concept normally used by specialists in international trade to explain why the Boston Red Sox stopped using the best left-handed pitcher in baseball in 1918.

Opportunity Costs

In 1915, a young left-hander for the Boston Red Sox emerged as one of the dominant pitchers in the game, helping the Red Sox to World Series championships in 1916 and 1918. In the 1918 World Series, he won two games and set a record for consecutive scoreless innings that stood until 1961. From 1915 through 1918, he won 78 games and lost only 40, and he allowed slightly over 2 runs per game. In 1919, he pitched in only 17 games and won only 16 more games in the rest of his career, yet no Boston fans complained. The reason was that the young pitcher was none other than George Herman "Babe" Ruth, who went on to redefine baseball as a power-hitting right fielder for the Red Sox and later for the New York Yankees.

Babe Ruth confronted the Red Sox with the classic economic problem of opportunity costs. An **opportunity cost** is the value of your best forgone alternative. We all face opportunity costs in our everyday lives. Our limited time, income, and energy constantly force us to choose between alternative actions. When you go to the movies on Saturday night, you no longer have the time or the money to go to a concert that evening. When the Red Sox used Babe Ruth as a right fielder, they gave up the chance to use him as a pitcher. (Because the main contribution of a right fielder is as a hitter, we will use the term "hitter" rather than right fielder from now on.) The games that the Red Sox would lose because they had to use a lesser pitcher are the opportunity cost of their using Ruth as a hitter. The games that they would lose because they had to use a worse hitter are the opportunity cost of using him as a pitcher.

Absolute and Comparative Advantage

It is usually easy to decide where to use a player, as only a few players make good pitchers, and pitchers are typically bad hitters. Babe Ruth, however, was an exception. He was the best pitcher *and* the best hitter on the team. Being the best at everything meant that Babe Ruth had an absolute advantage at both pitching and hitting. A person or country has an **absolute advantage** in an activity when it is more efficient at that activity than another person or country. If the United States can make cancer drugs using fewer resources than Japan can, it has an absolute advantage in making cancer drugs. Because Babe Ruth was a better pitcher and hitter than any other player on the Red Sox, he had an absolute advantage over all his teammates in both pitching and hitting.

The Red Sox decided to use Babe Ruth as a hitter because, although he had an absolute advantage as both a hitter and as a pitcher, his absolute advantage as a hitter was much larger than his absolute advantage as a pitcher. This meant that Babe Ruth had a comparative advantage as a hitter. A person or country has a **comparative advantage** when the opportunity cost of an activity is lower than it is for another person or country. Because Babe Ruth was such a good hitter, the opportunity cost of using him as a pitcher (the number of wins the team would sacrifice) was extremely high, much higher than for other players on the team. This meant that, even though Babe Ruth had an *absolute* advantage over his teammates as a pitcher, he did not have a *comparative* advantage as a pitcher.[2]

To see the gains from moving Babe Ruth from the pitcher's mound to the outfield more clearly, consider the situation facing the 1918 Red Sox. One can argue that Ruth's switch from pitcher to outfielder displaced Tilly Walker, arguably the worst of the Red Sox starting outfielders in 1917, and made room for Dutch Leonard, who had the highest earned run average (ERA) among the regular starting pitchers in 1918.[3] Ruth's last year as a pitcher—1917—was an amazing one; he won 24 games, lost 13, and gave up about 2 runs per game. His first year as an outfielder was even more amazing. He led the league in slugging percentage (the average number of bases advanced per at bat), and his 11 home runs not only led the league, they were almost twice as much as the 6 hit by the entire Red Sox starting outfield in 1917.

Table 1.1 shows that replacing Ruth, who had a 2.01 ERA in 1917, with Leonard, who had a (still low) 2.72, meant that the Sox gave up 0.71 more runs per 9 innings than they would have if Ruth had had an identical year in 1918. Over the 14 games that Leonard pitched, that meant that the Red Sox' opportunity cost of using Babe Ruth in the field was about 10 runs over the course of the 1918 season.[4] Using the formula for runs produced (runs scored + runs batted in − home runs), shows that Ruth produced 29 more runs in 1918 than Walker produced in 1917. Thus, the Red Sox came out 19 runs ahead from the switch.

TABLE 1.1

The Gain and Loss from Moving Babe Ruth

Player	Runs Sacrificed	Runs Produced
Babe Ruth	2.01 per game	105 per season
Dutch Leonard	2.72 per game	—
Tilly Walker	—	76 per season
Net change	+ 9.94 per season[a]	+ 29 per season

[a]Uses 14 starts for the 1918 season.
Source: Baseball Almanac, online at http://www.baseball-almanc.com

[2]For a more complete explanation of Babe Ruth's comparative advantage during his career with the New York Yankees, see Edward Scahill, "Did Babe Ruth Have a Comparative Advantage as a Pitcher?" *Journal of Economic Education*, vol. 21, no. 4 (Fall 1990), pp. 402–410.

[3]The earned run average is the average number of runs a pitcher gives up per nine innings, the normal length of a ballgame.

[4]The Boston Red Sox played only 126 games in 1918 because the season was terminated on September 1 due to the United States' entry into World War I.

At this point, you might ask why the Red Sox did not use Babe Ruth as a pitcher every four or five days and as a hitter every day in between. In baseball, the skills of pitching and hitting are so different that one cannot develop both at the same time. No player has ever managed to play every day and pitch every fourth or fifth day. More generally, one of the most important conclusions of the theory of comparative advantage is that individuals, firms, and nations gain from specializing. Professors employ research assistants and working parents hire day care providers because trying to do everything would take them away from the activities that they perform best. It is cheaper (more efficient) for them to pay other people to provide the goods or services than to try to do everything themselves.

At the national level, if the United States had a comparative advantage in the production of cancer drugs, it would be better off specializing in cancer drugs instead of TVs even if it had an absolute advantage over Japan in both products. The opportunity cost of sacrificing cancer drugs in order to make TVs ourselves is higher than the cost of sending cancer drugs to Japan in exchange for TVs. Like Babe Ruth, we are better off specializing in what we are relatively best at and leaving the rest to others.

BIOGRAPHICAL SKETCH

BABE DIDRIKSON ZAHARIAS

I knew exactly what I wanted to be when I grew up. My goal was to be the greatest athlete that ever lived.

—Babe Didrikson Zaharias[1]

The theory of comparative advantage tells us that athletes are better off when they specialize. A quick look at athletes from the professional ranks to middle schools seems to bear this hypothesis out. "Two-way" football players have become a rarity, and athletes who play more than one sport have all but disappeared. It is thus unlikely that the athletic world will ever see another Babe Didrikson Zaharias. Zaharias dominated the athletic world like no athlete before or since, achieving star status in the disparate worlds of basketball, track and field, and golf.

Mildred Ella Didriksen was born in 1911 to impoverished Norwegian immigrants in Port Arthur, Texas. The sixth of seven children and the youngest girl, Mildred got the nickname "Babe" while a young girl and still the "baby" of the family, though she later attributed the nickname to comparisons with baseball hero Babe Ruth. Her last name was changed to "Didrikson" as a result of a spelling error in her school records.

As a youth, Zaharias was drawn to sports at a time when sexual stereotypes still discouraged women from participating in "manly" sports. In this case, however, Zaharias' working-class upbringing freed her from many of the restrictions that would have constrained her development as an athlete. She did not participate in organized sports, however, until she left high school in 1930 to play basketball for the Employers Casualty Insurance Company.

It may seem odd today for an athlete to advance her career by taking a job as a secretary for $75 a month with an insurance company, but at that time, many colleges did not offer athletic programs for women, and the fledging NCAA was openly disdainful of women's athletics. Employers Casualty played in the 45-member Women's National Basketball League, which played under the auspices of the Amateur Athletic Union (AAU). The AAU was then the dominant athletic body; it oversaw competitions by a few schools and by companies that sponsored teams.

The Employers Casualty "Golden Cyclones" were one of the very best amateur teams in the nation. When the first All-American women's basketball team was announced in 1929, eight of its members were from Employers Casualty. Zaharias quickly established herself as a star among stars, being named an All-American for three straight years.

As good as she was on the basketball court, Zaharias found her greatest success in track and field. It was here that she recorded the greatest single performance in the history of track and field and perhaps of any athletic competition. The 1932 National Track and Field Competition served as the trials for the 1932 Los Angeles Olympic Games. Zaharias was the sole representative of the Employers Casualty team. In one afternoon, she ensured that Employers Casualty won the team championship by winning the shot put, the baseball throw, the javelin throw, the 80-meter hurdles, and the broad jump. She also tied for first in the high jump and finished fourth in the discus, an event in which she normally did not compete. In all, she won six gold medals and broke four world records in about three hours. Zaharias' performance was probably the greatest single day an athlete has ever known.

Zaharias hardly skipped a beat in the Olympics, setting world records in the javelin throw and the 80-meter hurdles. She also tied for first in the high jump, though her then-unorthodox style (the so-called Western Roll that soon became the dominant style) caused a controversy among some of the judges, who thought it illegal. As a compromise, she was declared the second-place finisher and given the only half-gold-half-silver medal in the history of the modern Olympics.

As the dominant performer and personality of the 1932 "Hollywood Games," Zaharias quickly became a national celebrity. Her publicity, however, came at a considerable cost. The public did not know what to make of a woman who defied sexual stereotypes of the time. Zaharias seemed destined to fade from public view when the AAU stripped her of her amateur status for being featured in an automobile advertisement (even though, apparently, she had not given permission for the firm to use her likeness). After a year or so of stunts and exhibition tours, she returned to work for Employers Casualty.

Over the next several years, Zaharias reconstructed her personal and athletic lives. Stung by her treatment in the press, she strove to develop a more feminine image, playing up her role as a wife following her marriage to professional wrestler (and later sports promoter) George Zaharias in 1938, but she was anything but a typical housewife. Having picked up golf as a teenager, Zaharias threw herself into her new, more socially accepted sport. In 1935, she won the Texas State Women's Golf Championship and was ready to enter full-time competition when the United States Golf Association banned her from amateur competition because of her appearance in the automobile advertisement. She responded by turning pro, but she quickly realized that professional golf provided neither adequate competition nor adequate remuneration. She succeeded in having her amateur status reinstated in 1943. Though she would have to wait until the end of World War II to enter the next stage of her athletic career, it was worth the wait.

Zaharias burst onto the women's golf tour in 1945, winning the Texas Women's Open and the

continued

Western Open, and being named "Woman Athlete of the Year" by the Associated Press (an award she had won 13 years earlier for her Olympic exploits). This proved merely a warm-up for 1946, when she won 14 straight tournaments. In 1947, Zaharias became the first American woman to win the British Women's Amateur golf championship in the 55-year history of the event.

After her victory in the British Amateur event, Zaharias again turned pro and a year later signed on as a charter member of the newly formed Ladies Professional Golf Association (LPGA—it chose the term "Ladies" to avoid conflict with the unsuccessful Women's PGA). Her talents led her to be a dominant figure in the LPGA—she won about two of every three events she entered for 1950 and 1951—and her showmanship, while not always appreciated by her competitors, helped market the new tour.

In 1953, Zaharias was diagnosed with cancer, and doctors told her family and friends (but not Zaharias herself) that she had less than a year to live. Within four months, however, she was back on the tour, finishing as the sixth-highest money winner for 1953. She did even better in 1954, winning five tournaments and having the lowest average on the tour. The cancer reappeared in 1955, and Babe Didrikson Zaharias, arguably the greatest athlete of the century, died in 1956.

[1]Susan Cayleff, *Babe: The Life and Legend of Babe Didrikson Zaharias* (Urbana: University of Illinois Press, 1995), p. 46.

Source: Susan Cayleff, *Babe: The Life and Legend of Babe Didrikson Zaharias* (Urbana: University of Illinois Press, 1995).

Summary

Sports occupy a unique place in the public psyche. Although sports generate less revenue than many other industries, sports results are predicted, reported, and analyzed in newspapers, magazines, books, and TV and radio programs. This text will present economic models from industrial organization, public finance, and labor economics to provide insight into the economics of sports. One of the most important economic models is that of comparative advantage. Despite having an absolute advantage as both a pitcher and an outfielder, Babe Ruth specialized in playing the outfield because that was where he had a comparative advantage. He had a comparative advantage in playing every day as an outfielder because the opportunity cost of his playing outfield—the additional runs that other teams would score against a lesser Red Sox pitcher—was less than the opportunity cost of his playing every four to five days as a pitcher—the lower number of runs the Red Sox would score from playing a lesser outfielder. Following the law of comparative advantage made Babe Ruth and the Red Sox better off.

Discussion Questions

1. Why do sports generate so much more news coverage than other industries that are much larger in financial terms?
2. The theory of comparative advantage predicts that athletes perform better when they specialize. Studies show that young athletes are increasingly focusing on a single sport. Do you think this is a good idea?

Problems

1.1 Why might Kobe Bryant employ someone to answer his fan mail even if he can read the letters and type the responses more quickly than the person he employs?

1.2 Is the following statement true or false? Explain your reasoning. "I am attending college on a full athletic scholarship, so the opportunity cost of attending college is zero for me."

1.3 From 1946 through 1967, the placekicker for the Cleveland Browns, Lou Groza, was successful on 54.9 percent of his field goal attempts. From 1999 through 2008, the Browns' kicker was Phil Dawson, who was successful on 82.8 percent of his attempts. Use the theory of comparative advantage to explain the massive improvement in the Browns' kicking game.

1.4 The term "figure skating" refers to the shapes that skaters used to trace in the ice as part of skating competitions. In the 1970s, this aspect of the sport was deemphasized and eventually eliminated. Use the theory of comparative advantage to show why eliminating this part of the competition has led skaters to perform much more difficult and sophisticated jumps and spins.

CHAPTER 2

Review of the Economist's Arsenal

To be a sports fan these days is to be taking a course in economics.
—ALLEN BARRA[1]

Introduction

As noted in Chapter 1, the sports business is full of puzzles. In this chapter we consider several.

- Collectors pay much more for Mickey Mantle baseball cards than for Hank Aaron baseball cards, even though Aaron had better career statistics.

- College football fans sometimes seek ways around antiscalping laws designed to protect them.

- The Chicago White Sox do not lower their ticket prices when doing so would allow them to sell out regularly like the Chicago Blackhawks do.

- Teams often claim that they have to increase ticket prices when they sign expensive new free agents, yet they do not raise prices when they re-sign those same players.

- The era of professional sports began at the same time in two different countries with two different sports.

Such behavior strikes the casual observer as unprofitable, self-defeating, even irrational. To the economist, however, such behavior is perfectly normal. All of the above puzzles can be easily resolved by appealing to basic economic theory. To resolve these and other puzzles, this chapter will reacquaint you with the concepts of supply and demand.

---

[1]Allen Barra, "In Anti-Trust We Trust," *Salon Magazine,* May 19, 2000, at http://www.salon.com/news/feature/2000/05/19/antitrust/index.html.

2.1   The Supply and Demand Model

The supply and demand model is the first and simplest model that we encounter. Recall that a **model** is a simplification of reality that allows economists to isolate particular economic forces. A good model allows economists to make predictions and provide explanations about the world quickly and easily.

Unlike physicists and chemists, economists and other social scientists find it difficult to conduct experiments. For example, it is far more difficult to control what people do than it is to control substances in a test tube. Even if economists were physically able to control what people do, ethical and legal considerations often limit what they are allowed to do. For example, it would be very hard—and certainly undesirable—for a person studying bankruptcy to force a person or firm to go bankrupt. Instead, economists rely on theoretical and statistical models of market structure to make reliable predictions about behavior.

For all its simplicity, the supply and demand model has remarkable power to explain the world around us.

Supply and demand show us how producers and consumers respond to price changes. Together, they determine how much of a good or service is produced and what value society places on it. In a different course, we might use these tools to analyze the financial meltdown of 2008 or the impact of a higher minimum wage on employment. In this section, we introduce the concepts of supply and demand and use them to show why Mickey Mantle cards cost so much more than Hank Aaron cards.

Demand, Supply, and Equilibrium

A consumer's **demand** for baseball cards (or for any good or service) is the relationship between the price of those cards and the number of cards that he or she is willing and able to buy. It is a sequence of answers to the question, "If baseball cards cost this much, how many of them would you buy?" Or, from the firm's perspective, "How many would we be able to sell?" Figure 2.1 shows that this relationship is invariably negative: as the price of cards falls, the number of cards that the consumer buys rises. The **demand curve** representing this relationship is thus downward sloping. Economists call the negative relationship between price and quantity the **law of demand**. A change in the price of a good causes a **change in quantity demanded**, moving quantity up along the demand curve when prices rise and down the demand curve when prices fall.

The relationship between price and quantity is negative for two reasons. First, as the price of baseball cards falls, consumers buy more baseball cards and less of other goods (such as football cards, comic books, or snack food). Just the opposite happens when the price of baseball cards rise. Economists call the switch to goods that have become relatively cheaper the **substitution effect** because consumers *substitute* baseball cards for items that they would have bought had baseball cards not fallen in price.

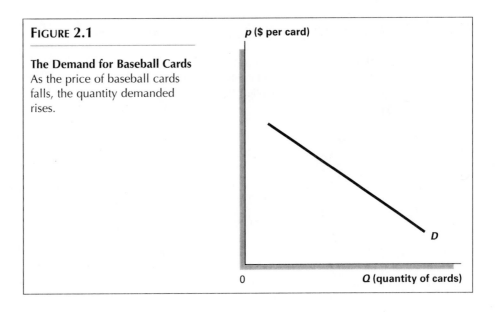

FIGURE 2.1

The Demand for Baseball Cards
As the price of baseball cards falls, the quantity demanded rises.

p **($ per card)**

D

0   *Q* **(quantity of cards)**

Second, when a good becomes less expensive, consumers can afford more of that good (and others as well), because their purchasing power rises even if their incomes remain fixed. For example, if the price of baseball cards falls, consumers can afford more baseball cards as well as more hockey cards. Since the lower prices make consumers' incomes go farther, economists call this impact the **purchasing power** (or **income**) **effect**. Normally—but, as we will soon see, not always—an increase in purchasing power causes consumers to buy more of a good or service.

The **supply** of baseball cards relates price to the number of cards that producers are willing and able to provide. As the price of baseball cards rises, each card producer has an incentive to produce more cards. At the same time, other producers have an incentive to stop what they are doing and start producing cards. Some economists call the positive relationship between price and quantity the **law of supply**.

Unlike consumers, who view the price of an item as the sacrifice they must make, producers view the price as a reward. As a result, higher prices encourage producers to make more, and the **supply curve** is upward sloping, as seen in Figure 2.2.[2] Again, if the price of cards changes, the quantity moves along the supply curve, a movement that economists call a **change in quantity supplied**.

Taken alone, demand tells nothing about the amount consumers actually buy or the price they pay. Similarly, supply alone does not tell the amount producers

---

[2]In the case of baseball cards, the number of cards from a previously manufactured set is fixed, yet the number of cards that owners will offer for sale will increase as the price rises. Thus, the supply curve is upward sloping.

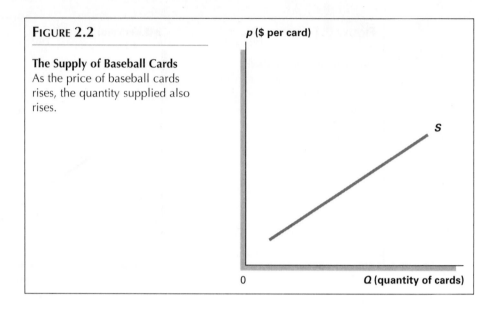

FIGURE 2.2

The Supply of Baseball Cards
As the price of baseball cards rises, the quantity supplied also rises.

sell or the price they receive. To find out what happens in the marketplace, you must look at supply and demand together. Figures 2.3a and 2.3b show that the two curves cross at the point labeled e. Economists call e the **equilibrium point** because at that point, the actions of consumers and producers are in balance. Consumers are willing and able to buy Q_e cards at the price p_e, which is exactly the quantity that producers are willing and able to sell at that price. As a result, neither consumers nor producers have any desire to alter their actions, the price stays at p_e, and the quantity at Q_e.

Figure 2.3a shows that, at a price higher than p_e (such as p_h) **disequilibrium** occurs, because producers want to sell Q_s while consumers want to buy only Q_d. Unable to sell all the cards they want, producers face a **surplus** or **excess supply**. Frustrated producers lower their prices in order to attract more customers. The lower price encourages consumers to buy more cards and discourages producers from selling them. As Q_d rises and Q_s falls, the excess supply falls until it equals zero, and equilibrium is restored at p_e.

Figure 2.3b shows that, at a price below the equilibrium (p_l), buyers want to purchase Q_d cards while sellers want to sell only Q_s. The **shortage** or **excess demand** for cards at p_l drives the price upward until the shortage disappears at p_e.

We cannot actually see the supply and demand curves of the products we consume. We do, however, observe equilibrium prices. For example, baseball trading card prices are published regularly in price guides. In 1955, the Bowman Company produced a set of cards known as the "TV set," with pictures of players appearing on the face of the card bordered by what appears to be a television set. Included in that set are the cards of Mickey Mantle, perhaps the greatest switch-hitting power hitter ever, and Hank Aaron, who was Major League Baseball's all-time home run leader from 1974 to 2007.

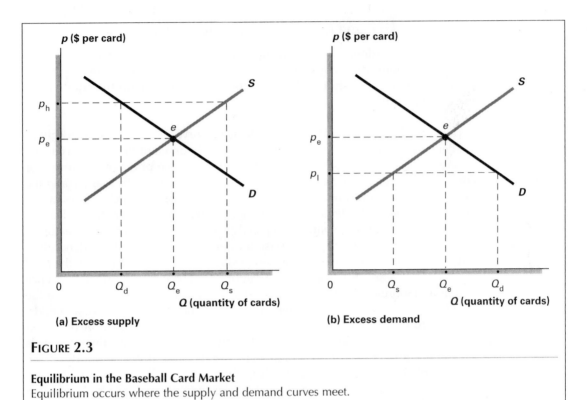

(a) Excess supply

(b) Excess demand

FIGURE 2.3

Equilibrium in the Baseball Card Market
Equilibrium occurs where the supply and demand curves meet.

According to Beckett's *Baseball Card Plus* price guide, which tracks card values, the June/July 2006 prices of Mantle and Aaron cards from the 1955 Bowman set were $800 and $250, respectively.[3] Such a large difference in price is difficult to justify, given that Hank Aaron had more home runs (HR), hits (H), runs scored (R), runs batted in (RBIs), and a higher batting average (Avg) than Mantle (see Table 2.1). We can use the simple supply and demand model as an analytical tool to investigate the difference in prices. Because the forces of supply and demand determine prices, the explanation must lie in differences in supply, in demand, or in both.

TABLE 2.1

Career Statistics of Hank Aaron and Mickey Mantle

	AB	H	R	HR	RBI	Avg	Card Price
Hank Aaron	12,364	3,771	2,174	755	2,297	.305	$250
Mickey Mantle	8,102	2,415	1,677	536	1,509	.298	$800

Source: Beckett's Baseball Card Plus, June/July, 2006.

---

[3]*Beckett's Baseball Card Plus*, June/July 2006, p. 16.

Supply and Demand Curves and the Price of Baseball Cards

The supply and demand relationships are not permanently fixed. They can change for many different reasons. This section reviews why the supply or demand curve might shift and the effects that shifts have on the equilibrium price and quantity.

Factors That Affect the Location of the Demand Curve Economists call a shift of the demand curve a change in demand. A **change in demand** stems from a change in any of five underlying factors: consumer income, the prices of substitutes or complements, consumer tastes, the number of consumers in the market, and the expectations that consumers hold. A change in the price of the item causes only a change in the quantity demanded, moving quantity along a given demand curve.

We have seen that consumers typically buy more of a good if their incomes increase, but frequent exceptions exist. If a hockey fan living in Providence, R.I., gets a raise, he might buy more hockey cards of the Providence Bruins, the local minor league team. Alternatively, he might buy fewer cards of the Providence Bruins and more cards of the NHL's Boston Bruins. If he buys more cards of the Providence Bruins as his income rises, then the cards are normal goods. **Normal goods** get their name because consumers normally buy more of a good or service when their incomes rise. If the fan buys fewer cards, then the cards are an inferior good. **Inferior goods** need not be undesirable or poorly made. One simply buys less of them as one's income rises.

If Providence Bruins fans buy fewer hockey cards when their incomes fall, it seems reasonable to conclude that they would go to fewer hockey games as well. Has the recent economic downturn had a negative impact on professional sports, or is sports somehow recession-proof? The evidence thus far is mixed. Attendance at the four major sports in 2008 and early 2009 is not significantly below previous levels, but all else has not been held equal as incomes have fallen. Some NBA teams sold tickets at significant discounts to prop up attendance. According to ESPN.com, the Memphis Grizzlies drew about as many fans in 2008–2009 (about 12,600 per game) as they did in 2007–2008 (12,770), but they sold their tickets so cheaply that the team's gross revenue per game was only $300,000, an average of less than $24 per fan.[4] Similarly, some Major League Baseball teams have discounted 2009 season tickets by up to 25 percent, and the New York Yankees were forced to cut the prices of some premium seats in the new ballpark by half.[5]

The major sports leagues have a safety net in the form of long-term TV contracts. As long as the recession does not outlast these contracts, the guaranteed

---

[4]Bill Simmons, "Welcome to the No Benjamins Association," ESPN.com, February 27, 2009, online at http://www.espn.go.com.

[5]Jon Birger, "Baseball Battles the Slump," CNNMoney.com, online at http://money.cnn.com/2009/02/18/magazines/fortune/birger_baseball.fortune/index.htm, February 19, 2009; and Richard Sandomir, "Yankees Slash the Price of Top Tickets," *The New York Times*, online at http://www.nytimes.com/2009/04/29/sports/baseball/29tickets.html?_r=1&scp=4&sq=+%20yankees%20+%20%22ticket%20prices%22&st=cse, April 28, 2009.

income of these contracts will help to sustain the teams. Sports and athletes that rely heavily on year-to-year sponsorships, such as golf and tennis, are in a more vulnerable position. Formula-1 and NASCAR have been particularly hard-hit by the downturn, as they rely heavily on sponsorships by car manufacturers that have been devastated by the recession.[6]

When the price of a substitute good increases, the demand curve shifts to the right. If a card collector views Mickey Mantle cards and Yogi Berra cards as reasonable substitutes, an increase in the price of Yogi Berra cards causes the demand curve for Mickey Mantle cards to shift to the right.

The opposite effect occurs when the price of a complement increases. For example, older cards need protection from bending and other mishaps that reduce the value of the card. The best way to prevent such mishaps is to keep the cards in protective sleeves. If the price of the sleeves rises, the demand for cards falls. This occurs because collectors tend to use the two products together and think of them as a single commodity. When the price of sleeves rises, the price of a card with a sleeve also rises, reducing demand for cards. Figure 2.4a

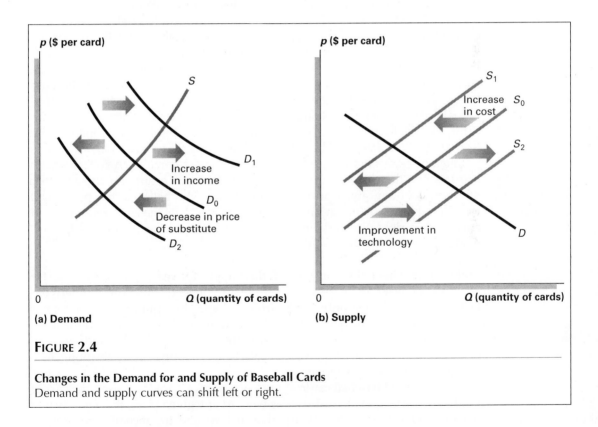

(a) Demand   (b) Supply

FIGURE 2.4

Changes in the Demand for and Supply of Baseball Cards
Demand and supply curves can shift left or right.

[6]Sean Gregory and Steve Goldberg, "Daytona Drag: NASCAR Tries to Outrace the Recession," *Time*, online at http://www.time.com/time/business/article/0,8599,1879136,00.html, February 12, 2009.

shows the impact of an increase in income and a reduction in the price of a substitute good on the demand curve.

In his book *The Blind Side,* Michael Lewis provides an interesting example of how tastes can affect the demand for a specific service.[7] Lewis notes that, until the 1980s, offensive linemen were regarded largely as interchangeable units and were among the lowest paid players on a football team. Today, left tackles are among the most highly paid players on the team. The premium paid to left tackles represents a change in tastes by football teams that have increasingly emphasized the forward pass.

The growing emphasis on the forward pass has made quarterbacks the stars of their teams and made protecting them a priority. It has become particularly important to protect quarterbacks from behind, their "blind side," where they cannot see oncoming defenders. This required players big enough to stand up to defensive ends but fast enough to move over to block linebackers. Left tackle (which protects a right-handed quarterback's blind side), thus became a unique—and highly paid—position.

Another example of the impact of tastes on prices can be found in ticket prices charged by Major League Baseball teams. Traditionally, teams have charged a fixed price for a given seat location, regardless of the opponent. Recently, they have started to behave more like European soccer teams or Japanese baseball teams by charging higher prices when more popular teams, such as the New York Yankees or the Boston Red Sox, come to town. Because the supply of seats is the same regardless of whom the visiting team is, differences in price must reflect changes in the demand curve. The demand curve for teams like the Red Sox and Yankees is farther to the right than for many other teams because of the greater taste of fans for seeing these teams play.

Finally, expectations of future prices can affect demand. A collector who believes that the prices of cards will rise in the near future is willing to buy more cards at any given price than a collector who believes that prices will remain stable. The expectation of a price increase shifts the collector's demand curve to the right. Similarly, if the collector believes that prices will fall, his demand curve shifts to the left.

Factors That Affect the Location of the Supply Curve   As was the case for demand, the position of the supply curve also depends on several underlying factors. A **change in supply** results from a change in input prices, technology, taxes, expectations held by producers, and natural events that destroy or promote products or resources. As was the case with the demand curve, a change in price causes a movement along the supply curve, resulting in a change in the quantity supplied.

In the case of baseball cards, if the price of paper products rises, the cost of producing each baseball card rises as well. At any given price, the net return to making and selling cards is lower than before, and the incentive to provide

---

[7]Michael Lewis, *The Blind Side: Evolution of a Game* (New York: W. W. Norton, 2006).

cards falls. Card manufacturers produce fewer cards at any given price, and the supply curve shifts to the left from S_0 to S_1 in Figure 2.4b.

A technological innovation that reduces the cost of making cards increases the profitability of making cards and encourages producers to make and sell more cards. The increase in technology shifts the supply curve rightward to S_2.

A sales tax on cards introduces a wedge between the price the consumer pays and the price the producer receives. The difference between what the consumer pays and what the producer receives means that the market has two supply curves, as seen in Figure 2.5. Figure 2.5 shows that the vertical difference between the two supply curves equals the amount of the tax. For example, a $0.10 per card tax on producers results in a new supply curve that lies $0.10 above the original. The price that consumers must pay (p_t) is determined by the intersection of the demand curve and the supply curve that includes the tax. Quantity decreases to Q_t because consumers are willing to purchase fewer units at the increased price. The price that sellers receive is the price for Q_t units on the original supply curve and is equal to the price that consumers pay minus the tax ($p_t - t$). The difference between the price that consumers pay and the price that sellers receive is the per-unit tax, t. Multiplying the per-unit tax by the number of units sold, Q_t, yields the tax revenue collected by the government. In Figure 2.5, this area is shaded gray.

Finally, if producers expect prices to rise in the future, they have an incentive to wait until prices rise before selling their product. At any price, producers

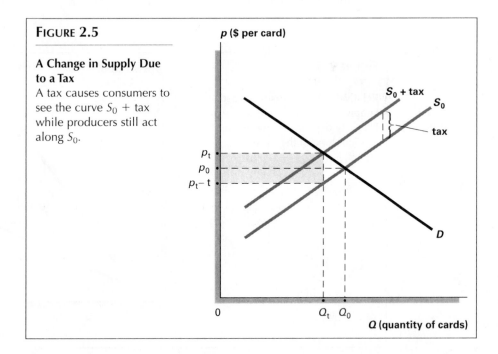

FIGURE 2.5

A Change in Supply Due to a Tax
A tax causes consumers to see the curve S_0 + tax while producers still act along S_0.

are willing to provide less today, thinking that they will be able to sell for more tomorrow, and the supply curve shifts to the left.

Elasticity of Supply   Economists are often less interested in how much producers produce than in how sensitive their production decisions are to changes in price. At first, one might be tempted to express this sensitivity in terms of slope. If the card producer had a steep supply curve, such as S_0 in Figure 2.6, then it appears that the firm does not respond very much to an increase in price. As price rises from p_0 to p_1, the firm's output grows from Q_0 cards to only Q_1. If the firm's supply curve is relatively flat (S_1), the producer responds to the price increase by expanding output from Q_0' to Q_1'. Slope, however, is a misleading measure of sensitivity.

Suppose, for example, that the price of a pack of baseball cards rises from $0.10 to $0.11 and that the company that produces them responds by printing 200 more packs of cards. The slope of the supply curve is the change in price divided by the change in quantity, or $0.01/(200 packs).

The problem is that 200 packs can represent a big change in the number of packs produced or a very small change, depending on how many packs it had been printing to begin with. Increasing production by 200 packs means much more to the producer if it expands from 1,000 packs to 1,200 than if it expands from 10,000 packs to 10,200. As a result, slope cannot tell us how meaningful the increase of 200 packs really is. Thus, while the supply of cards appears to be more sensitive to price changes at point B on supply curve S_1 because of its relatively flat slope, supply might actually be more sensitive at point A on curve S_0 because the initial quantity of cards is lower.

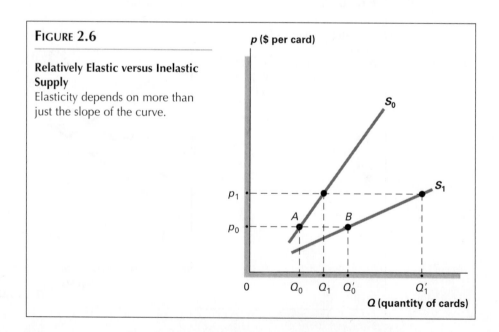

FIGURE 2.6

Relatively Elastic versus Inelastic Supply
Elasticity depends on more than just the slope of the curve.

Economists account for the producer's starting point by using percentage changes in price and output rather than absolute changes.[8] They use these percentage changes to measure the sensitivity of production to changes in price. We call this measure the elasticity of supply (which we denote as ε_s). The **elasticity of supply** is the percentage change in quantity that results from a given percentage change in price:

$$\varepsilon_s = \frac{\%\Delta Q^s}{\%\Delta p}$$

In the above example, the $0.01 increase in the price of a pack of cards corresponds to a percentage change of $0.01/$0.10 = 0.10, or 10 percent. If the company originally produced 1,000 packs of cards, then the percentage change in quantity is (1,200 − 1,000)/1,000 = 0.2, or 20 percent, and the elasticity of supply is ε_s = 0.2/0.1 = 2.0. When the price of a pack of cards rises by 10 percent, producers increase their output by 20 percent. The percentage increase in output is twice the percentage rise in price.

If the company originally produced 10,000 packs of cards, the percentage increase in output is (10,200 − 10,000)/10,000 = 0.02, or 2 percent, and the elasticity of supply becomes ε_s = 0.02/0.10 = 0.20. In this case, a 10 percent increase in the price of a pack of cards brings only a 2 percent increase in production, and the firm is much less responsive to changes in price.

Although the supply curve's location and elasticity are important for many of the issues we deal with later in the book, they cannot resolve our question about the relative prices of Mantle and Aaron cards. To simplify the analysis, we will make two weak assumptions and one strong assumption. A **weak assumption** is likely to be true in real life, while a **strong assumption** is often not true. Strong assumptions can be valuable, however, as long as the conclusions we draw are valid even when the assumption is not strictly true. In this case, our weak assumptions are that the Bowman Company produced the same number of Mickey Mantle and Hank Aaron cards and that the same number of Mantle and Aaron cards have survived in perfect (mint) condition. Our strong assumption is that the owners of these cards are willing and able to sell a fixed number of cards regardless of the price they receive. In this case, the supply curve is a vertical line. Because price changes do not affect the quantity supplied, the supply curve in Figure 2.7 is **perfectly inelastic.**

Elasticity of Demand   As with supply, we are often interested in the sensitivity of demand to changes in price rather than absolute levels of price and quantity. The **elasticity of demand** (ε_d) is the percentage change in quantity demanded for a given percentage change in price. The only difference between the

---

[8]We define the percentage change of the variable X ($\%\Delta X$) as $\Delta X/X = (X_1 - X_0)/X_0$. We use point elasticity rather than arc elasticity, which would replace the denominator with the mean of X_0 and X_1. If X_0 and X_1 are close together, the difference is negligible.

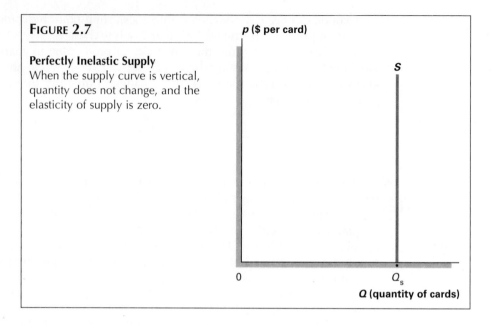

FIGURE 2.7

Perfectly Inelastic Supply
When the supply curve is vertical,
quantity does not change, and the
elasticity of supply is zero.

p ($ per card)

S

0   Q_s

Q (quantity of cards)

elasticity of demand and the elasticity of supply is that the elasticity of demand measures movement along the demand curve rather than the supply curve:

$$\varepsilon_d = \frac{\%\Delta Q^d}{\%\Delta p}$$

For example, if the price of a card increases from $0.10 to $0.11 and the quantity demanded falls from 1,000 to 750 cards, the elasticity of demand is

$$\frac{(1000 - 750)/1000}{(0.10 - 0.11)/0.10} = -2.5$$

Elasticities of demand fall between zero (perfectly inelastic) and minus infinity (infinitely elastic).[9] When the elasticity lies between 0 and −1, we say that demand is **inelastic**, because the percentage change in quantity is less than the percentage change in price. When the elasticity is less than −1, we say that demand is **elastic**.

Explaining the Difference in Card Prices   We can now use the simple supply and demand model to show that the difference in value between Mickey Mantle and Hank Aaron stems from economic forces rather than accident or error. We previously noted that there is no reason to believe that the supply curves of

---

[9]Some microeconomics textbooks eliminate the negative sign by taking the absolute value of the elasticity formula. We use the negative number because it reinforces the notion that price and quantity move in opposite directions along the demand curve.

Mantle and Aaron cards differ from each other. Because a fixed number of cards of each player were produced, we assume that supply is perfectly inelastic. As a result, differences in price must be the result of differences in demand. What factors might contribute to such a large difference in demand?

Mickey Mantle spent his entire career in New York, while Aaron spent his career in Milwaukee and Atlanta, which are much smaller cities. Even if Aaron and Mantle are equally popular with their hometown fans, the difference in population causes the demand curve for Mickey Mantle cards to lie far to the right of the demand curve for Hank Aaron cards. To see why, assume that a typical fan prefers players and memorabilia for his hometown team and that each Braves fan has the same individual demand for Hank Aaron cards that each Yankee fan has for Mickey Mantle cards. To simplify the example, assume that there are only two Braves fans—Ray and Roy—and that the supply of mint condition cards is fixed at 50.[10] Each has a demand curve for Hank Aaron cards, given by D_{Ray} and D_{Roy} in Figure 2.8, which tell us how many Hank Aaron cards Ray or Roy is willing and able to buy. We are not, however, interested in how many cards an individual Braves fan buys at each price. We want to know how many cards all Braves fans *combined* buy at each price. In this example, all we have to do is find how many cards Ray buys at each price and add that amount to the number that Roy buys at the same price. Thus, if Ray buys 22 cards at $250 while Roy buys 28, the market demand at $250 is 50 cards.

Suppose Ray and Roy have identical twins in New York who are just as rabid about Mickey Mantle as Ray and Roy are about Hank Aaron. Because

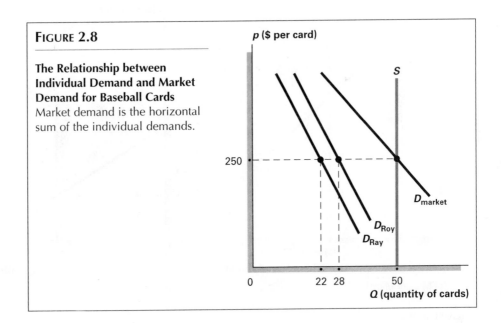

FIGURE 2.8

The Relationship between Individual Demand and Market Demand for Baseball Cards
Market demand is the horizontal sum of the individual demands.

---

[10]In practice, the process of determining market demand is the same whether there are two Braves fans or 2 million. Assuming there are only two fans just simplifies the illustration.

New York is a larger city, the twins in New York have several friends who also root for the Yankees. Adding all of the individual demand curves for Mickey Mantle cards pushes the market demand curve for his cards to the right, increasing their price relative to Hank Aaron cards.

In addition to having more people, the New York metropolitan area has fans who are, on average, wealthier than Braves fans in either Milwaukee or Atlanta. If baseball cards are normal goods, the higher level of income causes the demand curve for Mickey Mantle cards to shift out still farther relative to the demand for Hank Aaron cards.

Finally, one must account for the unfortunate possibility that the tastes of baseball fans for baseball cards reflect the prejudices of the population at large. As we shall see in Chapter 10, most economists regard discrimination as a taste or distaste for members of a particular group. If some card collectors prefer Mickey Mantle, who was white, to Hank Aaron, who is black, simply because of their races, the demand for Mantle cards would be greater than the demand for Aaron cards.

Figure 2.9 shows that the combined effects of the differences in market size, income, and tastes and preferences of individuals with a taste for discrimination result in greater demand for Mantle cards than for Aaron cards. The differences in demand coupled with the identical, perfectly inelastic supply curves create

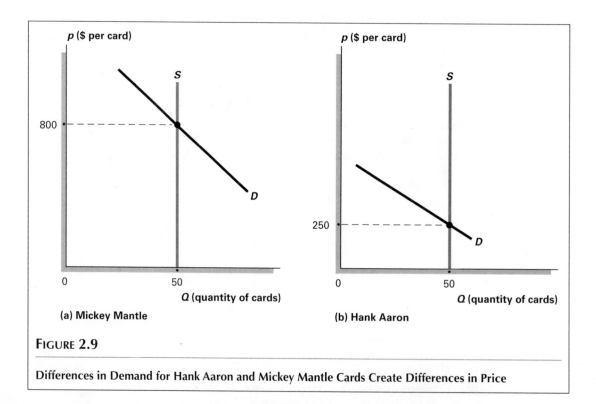

(a) Mickey Mantle

(b) Hank Aaron

FIGURE 2.9

Differences in Demand for Hank Aaron and Mickey Mantle Cards Create Differences in Price the difference in equilibrium price. Several studies of trading card prices have established that race plays a significant role in determining the price of playing cards. Nardinelli and Simon (1990) were the first to establish such a link. Gabriel, Johnson, and Stanton (1999) found that discrimination was less likely to occur for rookie cards, when the future performance of a player was unknown, but reappeared as the player's ability was revealed over the course of his career.[11]

2.2   Price Ceilings and the Benefits of Scalping

Today, fans wanting to buy or sell tickets to sporting events at the last minute can easily do so by accessing Web sites such as eBay or stubhub. In the past, however, a University of Michigan football fan who wanted to see the Wolverines play arch-rivals Ohio State or Michigan State often had to participate in a strange ritual. Students with tickets to the game could be found walking in front of the Michigan Student Union with their tickets in one hand and a pencil in the other. When someone offered to buy the ticket, the student would agree to do so—but only if the potential buyer also bought a pencil.

The key to understanding such an odd sales arrangement lies in the state of Michigan's antiscalping laws. According to the law, no one can sell tickets for more than the value printed on the ticket (its *face value*). The face value of the ticket, however, was well below what a free market would dictate. In economic terms, the law placed a **price ceiling** on tickets, keeping their price far below equilibrium. If the face value of a ticket is $15, and no sales are permitted above this price, the price ceiling (p^c) is $15. Such a ceiling is shown in Figure 2.10.

A price ceiling creates two problems for buyers and sellers. First, the price ceiling ($p^c = \$15$ in Figure 2.10) creates excess demand for tickets, since the quantity of tickets demanded (Q_d) is much greater than the quantity of tickets supplied (Q_s). To make matters worse, there is no guarantee that the people who place the greatest value on tickets will be able to get them. By limiting price to p^c, we know only that all buyers are willing and able to pay at least p^c to see the University of Michigan football team. If price does not serve as an allocation mechanism, someone who is just willing to pay the face value for a ticket might get one while someone who values it far more highly might not. Many colleges and universities set prices well below the equilibrium level. As a result, they have a persistent excess demand for tickets. This frequently leads to scenes of students camped outside the ticket office for days at a time to be sure that they have a seat for the big game. Thus, when prices do not ration tickets, some other limited resource, in this case time, typically does.

---

[11]Clark Nardinelli and Curtis Simon, "Customer Racial Discrimination in the Market for Memorabilia: The Case of Baseball," *Quarterly Journal of Economics*, vol. CV, no. 3, pp. 575–595; and Paul E. Gabriel, Curtis D. Johnson, and Timothy J. Stanton, "Customer Racial Discrimination for Baseball Memorabilia," *Applied Economics*, vol. 31, no. 11, pp. 1331–1335.

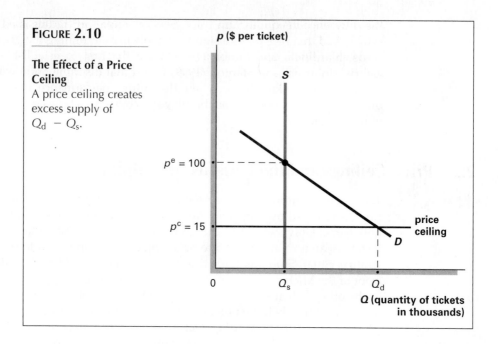

FIGURE 2.10

The Effect of a Price Ceiling
A price ceiling creates excess supply of $Q_d - Q_s$.

Universities set low prices for one of several reasons. For example, they might do so out of a sense of fairness to students with limited incomes. Recognizing that athletics are a student activity, athletic departments might want to be sure that all (or at least most) students can afford to see "their" team play.

If those with tickets could sell freely to those without, a mutually beneficial trade could be arranged. Suppose, for example, that Daniel is a rabid Michigan fan who is willing to pay $100 for a ticket to see Michigan play Michigan State. Melanie—the lucky recipient of a ticket—thinks a ticket is worth only $15. If Daniel pays Melanie $70 for the ticket, he would pay $30 less than the ticket is worth to him while Melanie would receive $55 more than the ticket is worth to her. Daniel and Melanie would both benefit from such an exchange, yet the law prohibits it. That is why Melanie can be found on State Street in Ann Arbor, offering her ticket for the face value of $15, but only to those who are willing to pay $55 for her pencil. That is why Daniel is there as well, happy to pay a premium price for a pencil![12]

Concluding that a school that sets the price of tickets at $15 rather than the equilibrium price of $100 creates excess supply is an example of positive economic reasoning. **Positive** economics is the study of "what is." It looks at economic actions from an objective viewpoint and requires no emotional or subjective judgments. An athletic director who concludes that charging the market price

---

[12]A note of caution: It is doubtful that this practice is legal in most areas—and thus it is not one that we would advocate or condone.

means that many students would not be able to afford tickets is using positive economic reasoning.

If we were to claim instead that selling tickets for more than their official price was morally wrong, we would be making a normative statement. **Normative economics** is the study of "what ought to be." It applies the values—the *norms*—of the individual or organization. An athletic director who concludes that setting prices that students can afford to pay is better than setting prices that they cannot afford to pay is using normative economic reasoning. Most of the discussion in this text focuses on developing the tools of positive economics, though we will sometimes apply economic reasoning to address normative issues.

2.3   Market Structures: From Perfect Competition to Monopoly

So far, we have implicitly made the unrealistic assumption that all goods are bought and sold in **competitive markets.** While this assumption may work for some goods, such as potatoes, it is not always accurate. As we will see in Chapters 3 and 4, it is usually inaccurate for professional and elite amateur sports markets. In this section, we review both competitive and monopolistic market structures. We then use these simple models to see why the Chicago White Sox do not lower their ticket prices even though they regularly fail to sell out. We also use them to explain why teams often raise ticket prices when they sign new stars to lucrative guaranteed contracts.

A Note on the Definition of Output

Before analyzing any market, economists must determine how to measure output. In some markets, such as the pizza market, defining output (Q) is easy. It is the number of pizzas produced in a given time period. In the sports industry, defining and measuring output is more complicated. If we think of output as that which the firm sells in order to obtain revenue, we could measure output as attendance or television appearances. If we focus on production, it may be more useful to measure output by the game, because the team must combine inputs to produce games throughout the course of the season. Finally, if a team's popularity, and hence its revenue, depend on its performance, the appropriate output is wins or winning percentage rather than simply games played. Our problem resembles the one facing those who study higher education. From the standpoint of revenue, a college or university may define output as the number of students enrolled. From the standpoint of input utilization, it may define output as the amount that its students learn, perhaps measured by their future incomes. Unfortunately, there is no simple resolution to this issue. To force a universal definition of output would cloud the issue as often as it would clarify it. In this text, we address this thorny issue by defining output according to the aspect of the market under consideration.

Perfect Competition

Competitive markets have many producers and consumers, all buying and selling a homogeneous product. Buyers and sellers are small compared with the overall size of the market, so no single firm or consumer can alter the market price unilaterally. We further assume that buyers and sellers have good information about prices. If a firm in a competitive market tries to raise the price it charges, consumers will purchase an equivalent product elsewhere at the market price.

Although the *market* demand curve for a good sold in a competitive market is still downward sloping, each *individual* competitive firm faces an L-shaped demand curve. The horizontal part of the curve shows the market price that is determined by market supply and demand. If a firm raises its price above that charged by its rivals in a perfectly competitive market, its sales fall to zero. The vertical part of the demand curve coincides with the vertical (price) axis and shows that the firm will not sell any output if it charges a price above the prevailing market price.

Figure 2.11 shows how a competitive market works for potatoes. Market demand and market supply dictate an equilibrium price of \$4/bag in Figure 2.11a. Each farmer thus faces a demand curve that is horizontal at $p = \$4$ in Figure 2.11b. If a farmer attempts to charge more than \$4, his sales fall to zero.

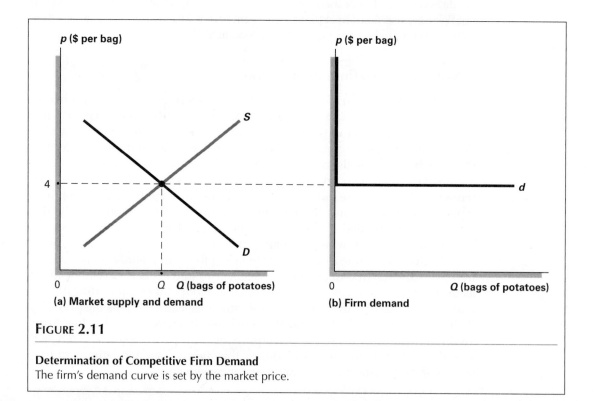

(a) Market supply and demand   (b) Firm demand

Figure 2.11

Determination of Competitive Firm Demand
The firm's demand curve is set by the market price.

Since each producer is so small relative to the size of the entire market, a farmer can sell all the bags he wants at the market price without causing the market price to fall. Economists call firms in this position **price-takers.**

Because the farmer can sell each additional bag of potatoes for $4, the extra revenue he receives from selling an additional bag—his **marginal revenue** (*MR*)—equals the price he charges for that last bag (*MR* = *p*). The farmer weighs the additional revenue received against the additional costs endured to produce an additional bag of potatoes, his **marginal cost** (*MC*). The farmer maximizes profits by producing and selling additional bags of potatoes until the extra revenue earned from selling the last bag equals the cost of producing that last bag (*MC*), as seen in Figure 2.12.

We can envision marginal revenue and marginal cost by imagining that the farmer keeps all of his money in a safe. When an additional bag of potatoes is produced and sold, the farmer must take some money out of the safe to pay the expenses associated with selling one more bag. The revenue from the sale goes back into the safe. If marginal revenue exceeds marginal cost, the total amount of money in the safe rises when the farmer sells another bag because he puts more money into the safe than he takes out. If selling an additional bag increases the total amount of money in the safe, the farmer wants to sell more potatoes. If marginal cost exceeds marginal revenue, selling more potatoes causes the farmer to take more money out of the safe than he puts in, and the farmer wants to cut back on the amount of potatoes grown and sold. When the farmer puts just as much money into the safe as he takes out of it, *MR* = *MC*, and there is no incentive to increase or reduce production.

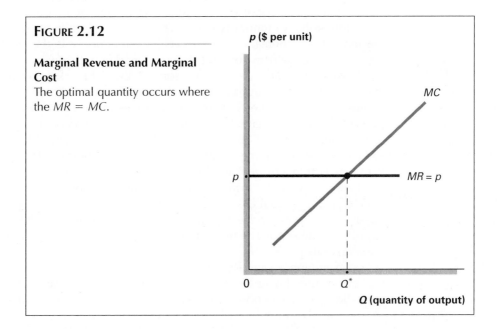

FIGURE 2.12

Marginal Revenue and Marginal Cost
The optimal quantity occurs where the *MR* = *MC*.

p ($ per unit)

MC

MR = *p*

0   *Q**

Q (quantity of output)

Finally, economists assume that competitive firms can freely enter and exit the market. Thus, if potato farmers are making large profits, more farmers will plant potatoes. The increase in the number of farmers growing potatoes shifts the market supply curve to the right. The rightward shift of the supply curve causes prices to fall, reducing individual firm profits. This result is probably the single most important outcome of the competitive market. When firms in a competitive industry are profitable, other firms enter, causing price and profits to fall.

Free entry by producers benefits consumers in two important ways. It ensures that firms in the industry cannot restrict output in order to drive up prices and earn excessive profits. More importantly, competitive markets are **economically efficient.** An economically efficient outcome maximizes society's gains from exchange. In this context, profits attract new farmers and stimulate production by existing farmers so that society's desire for potatoes is satisfied. We discuss the concept of economic efficiency extensively in Chapter 4.

Monopoly and Other Imperfectly Competitive Market Structures

In reality, most goods have some characteristics that distinguish them from other commodities. Consumers may have no clear preferences over the type of potatoes they buy, but they may prefer buying tickets to see the Colorado Rockies play baseball to buying tickets to see the Denver Broncos play football. If we measure output as the number of fans in attendance, and if sports fans in Denver feel that there are no perfect substitutes for a Rockies game, the Rockies have market power, which enables them to raise prices without losing all of their customers. As a result, the demand curve for Rockies games is downward sloping rather than L-shaped. If the Rockies had no competitors at all and consumers had the choice of seeing a Rockies game or seeing nothing, they would be a monopoly. A **monopoly** exists when a single firm is the sole producer in the market. The demand curve faced by a monopoly is the market demand curve, because the firm does not share the market with any other firms.

Most sports franchises exercise some degree of market power. This power stems from several sources. Baseball fans' preference for watching baseball games rather than other sporting events gives the Rockies a degree of market power. Moreover, potential competitors (i.e., teams competing for an audience against other forms of entertainment) often face substantial barriers to entry, such as access to playing facilities or a television contract. These barriers prevent new entrants from providing a reasonable alternative.

Like a competitive firm, a monopoly maximizes profit when marginal revenue equals marginal cost. Unlike a competitive firm, a monopolist does not passively accept the price and quantity that are dictated by the intersection of supply and demand. The monopolist can set price and output at the level that maximizes its profits.

As a monopoly, the Rockies face the downward-sloping market demand curve and must lower their ticket prices if they want to sell more tickets than they did last year. Since the Rockies cannot easily identify all the fans who bought tickets at a higher price last year, they will have to reduce the price of all the tickets they sell next year.[13] The extra revenue they receive from selling an additional ticket changes for two reasons. First, the team gains additional revenue from selling the extra tickets. Second, the team loses revenue because it must lower the price of all tickets in order to sell more of them. For example, suppose the Rockies sold 2 million tickets last year at $10 each and want to sell 3 million this year. If they attract the additional fans by charging $8 for all 3 million tickets, they gain $8 million in revenue from selling 1 million extra tickets at $8 apiece and lose $2 on each of the 2 million tickets they could have sold for $10 each. As a result, the additional revenue from increasing sales by 1 million tickets is only $4 million (new revenue = $8 × 3 million = $24 million less original revenue = $10 × 2 million = $20 million), not $8 million. As a result, the monopolist's marginal revenue curve lies below the demand curve, as seen in Figure 2.13.

As long as a team is not at capacity, the marginal cost of accommodating an extra spectator is close to zero. It costs the team relatively little to sell one more ticket and to admit and clean up after one more fan. As a result, economic analyses of ticket sales typically assume that the marginal cost of admitting an extra spectator equals zero. When ticket sales reach the capacity of the stadium, the marginal cost effectively becomes infinite since the team cannot sell any

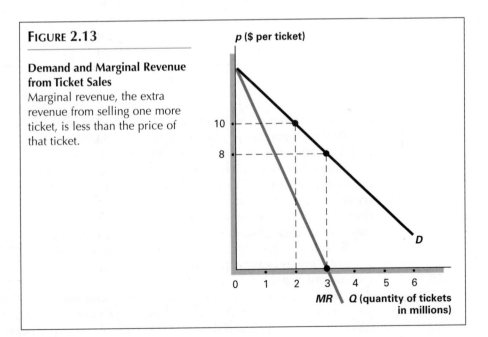

FIGURE 2.13

Demand and Marginal Revenue from Ticket Sales
Marginal revenue, the extra revenue from selling one more ticket, is less than the price of that ticket.

---

[13]For now we ignore the complication raised by season tickets and by price discrimination.

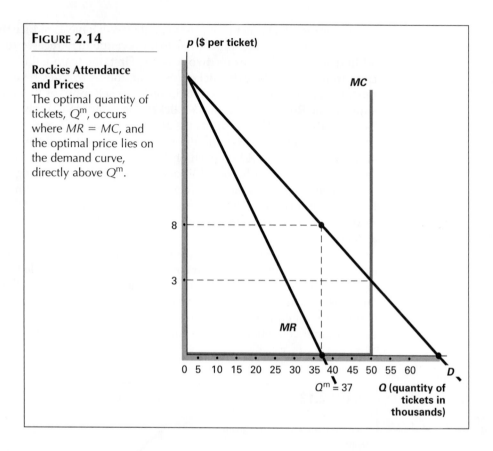

FIGURE 2.14

Rockies Attendance and Prices
The optimal quantity of tickets, Q^m, occurs where $MR = MC$, and the optimal price lies on the demand curve, directly above Q^m.

more seats at any price. Figure 2.14 illustrates the capacity constraint with a marginal cost curve that is effectively zero until 50,391 fans (the capacity of Coors Field) are admitted. At this point the marginal cost curve becomes vertical.

Figure 2.14 shows that monopoly power allows the monopoly to charge a higher price than would a competitive industry. A perfectly competitive industry operates where the market demand curve cuts the MC curve. It sells Q^c and charges $p^c = \$3$. The monopolist produces $Q^m < Q^c$ because the MR curve cuts the horizontal axis at a much lower level of output.

To find the highest price the team can charge and still sell Q^m (37,000 tickets per game in this example), we look at the demand curve. In addition to telling us how much people are willing and able to buy at a given set of prices, the demand curve tells us the maximum amount consumers are willing and able to pay for a given amount. The demand curve in Figure 2.14 tells us that the Rockies can sell 37,000 tickets if they charge no more than $8 per ticket.

We can now use this simple model of monopoly behavior to determine whether the Chicago White Sox or Chicago Blackhawks are irrational in their ticket policy. On the surface, it appears that someone is doing something wrong. After all, the Blackhawks regularly sold out the United Center during the 2008–2009 hockey season, while the White Sox rarely sold out U.S. Cellular Field during the 2008 baseball season.

In fact, both teams may be following optimal strategies. Having at least a degree of market power, both the White Sox and the Blackhawks face downward-sloping demand and marginal revenue curves. We continue to assume that marginal costs are zero, so their marginal cost curves lie along the horizontal axis at all attendance levels below full capacity. However, the teams reach full capacity at very different points. The White Sox home games at U.S. Cellular Field can accommodate slightly over 40,500 fans. Blackhawk games at the United Center, however, can hold only 20,500 per game. Because the United Center is so much smaller, the marginal cost curve for Blackhawks games becomes vertical much earlier than the marginal cost curve for the White Sox, as seen in Figure 2.15.

The different *MC* curves mean that the White Sox and the Blackhawks follow different pricing policies even if they have identical demand curves. Because the *MC* curve for the White Sox is horizontal over such a large range of attendance, the marginal revenue curve probably crosses the marginal

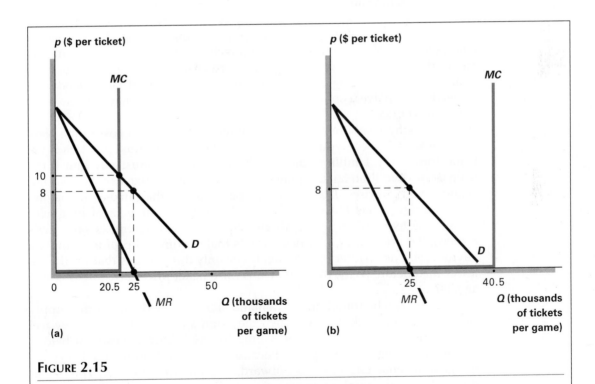

FIGURE 2.15

(a) Blackhawks Attendance and Prices; (b) White Sox Attendance and Prices
Stadium size dictates different policies.

cost curve along the horizontal axis, as seen in Figure 2.15b. This means that the White Sox were maximizing their profits from attendance even though they played in a stadium that was one-quarter empty. By contrast, the Black-hawks' marginal revenue curve is far more likely to cross the marginal cost curve on its vertical segment. The Blackhawks maximize their profits from attendance by charging a relatively high price and selling out the United Center.

The Impact of an Increase in Costs

We can also use the simple monopoly model to explain the puzzling response of ticket prices to player costs. Professional franchises typically blame increases in ticket prices on the spiraling salaries of their players. "Don't blame us," they say. "As our costs go up, we have to raise prices to keep pace." This explanation has been accepted without question by most fans and columnists. Unfortunately, the claim flies in the face of basic economic theory.

We have shown that teams determine how many tickets to sell—and how much to charge for their tickets—by equating the marginal revenue and marginal cost of selling an additional ticket. We have also shown that the marginal cost of providing an extra seat is generally very low until the team approaches the seating capacity of its venue. Perhaps surprisingly, the model completely ignores the cost of guaranteed player contracts. That is because such contracts are fixed costs. Like the name suggests, **fixed costs** do not vary with output, which we are measuring in this example as the number of fans attending a game. Because player contracts do not affect marginal costs, they have no bearing on ticket prices.

To see why Alex Rodriguez's salary represents a fixed cost to the New York Yankees, just ask yourself how much the Yankees must pay him if the team draws only 1 million fans and how much they must pay him if the team draws 4 million fans. A player's salary—like any fixed cost—does not change as output rises. The $33 million per year that the Yankees are paying Alex Rodriguez has the same impact that a $33 million legal judgment against the team might have. All else equal (or, as economists say, *ceteris paribus*), the price and quantity of tickets that maximized profits before the payment still do so after the payment. The only difference is that profits are lower than before. Why, then, do teams raise ticket prices after signing free agents?

The key can be found on the demand side of the ledger, not the supply side. Teams raise ticket prices when they sign a *new* free agent if they feel that the new player makes fans willing to pay higher prices than before. Teams charge higher ticket prices because the demand curve (and hence the marginal revenue curve) shifts outward, as seen in Figure 2.16. The higher demand and marginal revenue curves lead to a higher equilibrium price and (subject to capacity) quantity than before. In short, teams charge higher prices when they sign free agents because they *can* do so not because they *must*.

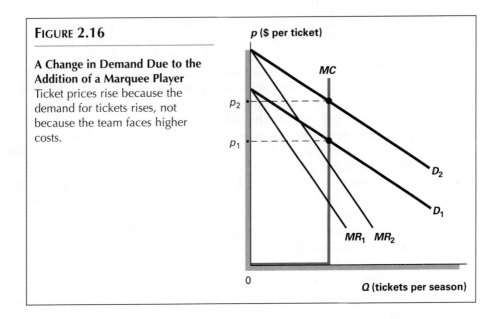

FIGURE 2.16

A Change in Demand Due to the Addition of a Marquee Player
Ticket prices rise because the demand for tickets rises, not because the team faces higher costs.

2.4   The Development of Professional Sports

While all "ball sports" have antecedents dating back to antiquity, baseball and soccer were the first sports to become widely popular, professional national pastimes.[14] Both sports developed and flourished when and where they did as the result of broad-based economic phenomena. Historians of sport determined early on that there was a link between the prosperity that came in the wake of the Industrial Revolution in the mid-19th century and the development of sport.[15] Specifically, for a society to have a pastime, it first must have time to pass.

To see why, we use the same marginal analysis that we used earlier in the chapter. We have seen that firms maximize profit by setting marginal revenue equal to marginal cost. The same basic principle holds for individual consumers who want to maximize their well-being. In this section, we will apply marginal analysis to the growth of leisure activity and then use this reasoning to show why spectator sports arose in the latter portion of the 19th century in England and the United States.

---

[14]The ancient sports were typically associated with religious festivals, whereas movements such as the *Turnverein* in the early 19th-century German states were more expressions of nationalism than entertainment.

[15]For a good historical overview, see William Baker, *Sports in the Western World* (Totowa, N.J.: Rowman & Littlefield, 1982); and Robert Burk, *Never Just a Game: Players, Owners, and American Baseball to 1920* (Chapel Hill: University of North Carolina Press, 1994).

Similar to a firm, a person spends an additional hour at an activity, whether it is work, studying, or leisure, until the benefit of an additional hour spent on that activity equals the cost of an additional hour. With a firm, benefits and costs were easy to understand and easy to measure: The revenue and expenditure related to the production process. For an individual, the concepts can be more abstract. While the reward for work might be easily measured in terms of wages and salaries, the reward for many activities is the utility we gain from them, where **utility** is another word for pleasure. We call the extra happiness we get from a little more of a good or an activity the marginal utility we receive from it. Similarly, the marginal cost of engaging in a little more of an activity might be monetary: the dollars we could have earned had we not studied economics or gone to a movie. They could also be the happiness we would have experienced by making a different choice.

Figure 2.17 shows typical marginal utility and marginal cost curves. The marginal utility curve slopes down, indicating that the more we engage in an activity to begin with, the less a little more means to us. The marginal cost curve slopes up, showing that, as we engage more in an activity, we have to give up increasingly valuable alternatives.

To see how this applies to the rise of spectator sports, consider what life was like for most people prior to the Industrial Revolution. Most people toiled in subsistence agricultural economies, meaning they spent all their waking hours growing enough food to survive. Anyone who did otherwise endangered his life and the lives of those around him. As Figure 2.17 shows, the marginal cost of leisure was therefore extremely high for most people. That meant that most people devoted no time to leisure. Thus, while a few 18th-century French aristocrats enjoyed playing *jeu de pomme*, an early form of tennis, a poor peasant had no time for such a luxury.

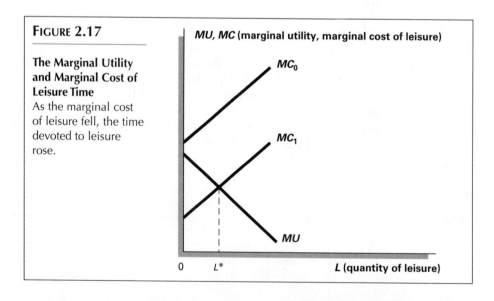

FIGURE 2.17

The Marginal Utility and Marginal Cost of Leisure Time
As the marginal cost of leisure fell, the time devoted to leisure rose.

MU, MC (marginal utility, marginal cost of leisure)

MC_0

MC_1

MU

0   L^* *L* (quantity of leisure)

Starting in the late 18th century, the Industrial Revolution significantly raised the living standards of large numbers of people in England. With larger incomes, people could spend time away from work without risking their lives. In terms of Figure 2.17, this meant that the marginal cost curve shifted down from MC_0 to MC_1. As a result, people could spend time pursing non-labor activities, such as schooling or leisure—or both at once.

The modern version of soccer developed in the elite "public schools" of England (e.g., Eton, Charterhouse, Westminster, Harrow, and Rugby). Starting from a vaguely defined primitive sport, soccer evolved at each of the public schools in much the same way that different species of animals evolve from a common ancestor when they live on separate islands. Each school developed its own version of soccer based on the unique characteristics of the terrain on which it was played. At most schools, rough or muddy grounds made violent contact impractical. Schools that had large, open fields, such as the Rugby School, developed much rougher versions of the sport. Soccer's popularity soon spread to Cambridge University and Oxford University and to clubs formed by public school and university graduates. It is no coincidence that one of the most popular of the early clubs called itself "The Old Etonians."

In the United States, baseball also first appeared among the more prosperous elements of society. An early form of baseball was an adaptation of English games played by the Puritan upper-middle class in New England in the late 18th century. The first organized game did not appear until 1842, with the formation of the New York Knickerbocker Club.

Though they lacked the social imprimatur of the British public school, baseball clubs also strove to establish or maintain the social positions of their members. Games between baseball clubs in the pre–Civil War era were less a competition than an exercise in "manly upright fellowship, harmony, and decorum. For them, excellence in performance meant exhibiting character as well as skill...."[16]

In the second half of the 19th century, the benefits of the Industrial Revolution began to spread to all segments of society in England and in the United States. The higher standard of living of working-class families led to a broader pursuit of leisure activities. As a result, soccer spread northward from the public schools around London into the industrial heartland of England and Scotland, and baseball spread south and west from New York. In addition, playing baseball became a way for members of immigrant communities to assert their "Americanness." Thus, by the turn of the century, in England, soccer clubs of working-class people had largely displaced "Old Etonians," while in America, first-generation Americans of German and Irish descent had largely displaced "Yankee" baseball players.

The most significant result of the popularity of soccer and baseball among the working class was the growing professionalization of the games.

---

[16]Burk, *Never Just a Game* (1994), p. 6. For an excellent summary and comparison of the origins of baseball and soccer, see *National Pastime*, by Stefan Szymanski and Andrew Zimbalist (Washington, D.C.: Brookings Institution Press, 2005).

Working-class athletes lacked the independent means of earlier participants, so they could not afford to play regularly without being compensated for the opportunity cost of their time. The upper-class sportsmen on both sides of the Atlantic saw their roles change from amateur participants to financial backers of professional teams. While they remained firmly in charge of the management and financing of the clubs, the old guard roundly condemned the "moral declension" that accompanied both the increasing professionalism of sports and the participation of working-class athletes. Their concern did not keep them from recognizing that they could profit from marketing a superior, professional product to a public that now had the money and leisure time to attend sporting events regularly. We will return to the discussion of the spread of sports activities to the working class in Chapter 11 in the context of the history of amateurism.

BIOGRAPHICAL SKETCH

SILVIO BERLUSCONI

We will make Italy like [AC] Milan.
—Silvio Berlusconi[1]

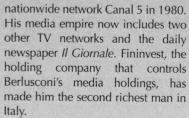

Take a little bit of Rupert Murdoch, add some Jerry Jones, sprinkle in a bit of George W. Bush, and you might just come up with Silvio Berlusconi. Like Murdoch, Berlusconi is a media magnate, dispensing much of the information flow received by Italians each day. His road to the top, while not quite a rags to riches story, had many twists and turns.

Berlusconi showed an entrepreneurial flair at an early age, working his way through college and law school by booking bands on cruise ships. When an act fell through, he sometimes filled in as a singer. Berlusconi's first major success came in real estate, as the developer of a luxury complex outside Milan.

Berlusconi created the TV station TeleMilano to provide entertainment for the luxury community's residents. The TV station was a big hit, particularly his pioneering of "Reality TV" in Italy. TeleMilano's success led Berlusconi to transform it into the nationwide network Canal 5 in 1980. His media empire now includes two other TV networks and the daily newspaper *Il Giornale*. Fininvest, the holding company that controls Berlusconi's media holdings, has made him the second richest man in Italy.

Despite his power and wealth, Berlusconi remained relatively unknown until he purchased AC Milan in 1986. Like Jerry Jones, who purchased the Dallas Cowboys three years later, Berlusconi purchased a storied franchise that had fallen on hard times. AC Milan, founded by English expatriates in 1899, is one of the oldest soccer clubs in Italy and one of its most successful. By 1986, however, AC Milan's fortunes were in steep decline. It had won the Italian Championship (the *Scudetto*) only once in the previous 18 years. In the early 1980s, it had been implicated in a series of scandals and had been relegated briefly from Serie A, Italy's top soccer league.

continued

Like Jones, Berlusconi thrilled in the limelight of owning and transforming a popular sports team. Berlusconi discarded the defensive style for which Italian teams were known and brought in many foreign players, including Ruud Gullit, a black player from Suriname. Integrating AC Milan was particularly controversial, as even today, Italian fans have a reputation for hostility to black players. Rather than simply call a press conference to introduce his new players, Berlusconi drew upon his media skills and flew his players into San Siro, the team's stadium, by helicopter to the strains of Wagner's *Ride of the Valkyries*.

Integrating the team and changing its style of play paid off, as AC Milan entered the most successful period in its history. It won the *Scudetto* in 1988, a feat it has repeated six times. It also won European soccer's (UEFA) Champions League in 1989 and four more times since, more than any other team.

Like George W. Bush, Berlusconi used his celebrity as a team owner to begin a career in politics, when he founded the political party *Forza Italia* ("Go Italy"), named for the cheer that Italian fans chant for their national soccer team, in 1993. Bush, once the part owner of the Texas Rangers, was elected Governor of Texas in 1994.

Berlusconi formed the party at an opportune time. The parties that had dominated Italian politics since the end of World War II, the Christian Democrats and the Communists, had both recently lost favor. Berlusconi exploited this vacuum, using sports metaphors to promote the message that he would bring a new energy and forcefulness to Italian politics. Berlusconi has ridden this message to three terms as Prime Minister. His first term lasted less than a year in 1994, but his second lasted from 2001 until a whisker-thin loss in 2006. This made his second administration the longest of any Italian government since World War II. In May 2008, Berlusconi was elected as Prime Minister a third time.

Berlusconi's political career has been stormy. He has been dogged by allegations of corruption since his time as a developer in Milan. Berlusconi's dominance of the press and TV are also cause for concern. Freedom House estimates that, between Berlusconi's private holdings and his power over state-run networks, he controls about 90 percent of the Italian media. Thus, during Berlusconi's second term, Freedom House rated Italy as the only nation in Western Europe not to have a free press. Berlusconi is also known for his often intemperate remarks, such as likening a German government official to a prison camp guard.

Most recently, Berlusconi has been caught up in a series of personal scandals. The first came when he behaved so flirtatiously toward a *Forza Italia* politician and former showgirl (since named to his new cabinet as Minister for Equal Opportunity) that his wife demanded an apology in a letter to a rival newspaper. The second, another flirtation with an 18-year-old model, has caused his wife of 28 years (for whom Berlusconi left his first wife in 1980) to file for divorce. The ongoing scandals and Italy's economic stagnation suggest that Berlusconi's political legacy will not be as storied as his legacy to Italian soccer.

[1]Franklin Foer, *How Soccer Explains the World: An Unlikely Theory of Globalization* (New York: Harper Collins, 2004).

Sources: "Answers Please," *The Economist,* August 2, 2003, pp. 23–27; "Silvio Berlusconi and Family," *The World's Billionaires,* online at http://www.forbes.com/lists/2009/10/billionaires-2009-richest-people_Silvio-Berlusconi-family_EEPT.html; Geoff Andrews, *Not a Normal Country: Italy After Berlusconi* (London: Pluto Press, 2005); Rachel Donadio, "Berlusconi's Wife Says She Wants a Divorce," *The New York Times,* May 4, 2009, online at http://www.nytimes.com/2009/05/04/world/europe/04iht-italy.html; Franklin Foer, *How Soccer Explains the World: An Unlikely Theory of Globalization* (New York: Harper Collins, 2004); Paul Ginsborg, *Silvio Berlusconi: Television, Power, and Patrimony* (London: Verso, 2004).

Summary

Supply and demand are among the simplest but most powerful tools in the economist's arsenal. Understanding most economic relationships requires a solid grasp of this framework. If you have a clear understanding of which external forces affect demand and supply, then you can make accurate predictions regarding the direction of change in prices and output.

When markets are competitive, prices are lower and output is higher than if a firm has monopoly power; not all economic activity, though, occurs in competitive markets. Monopoly power gives a firm the ability to set prices rather than simply accept the price as determined by the market. In most sports markets, teams have substantial market power. By setting ticket prices, teams have the ability to control attendance, subject to the capacity of their building.

Costs and the distinction between fixed and variable costs play a vital role in the determination of output and prices. For professional sports teams, players' salaries are often best treated as fixed costs, because they are unrelated to the number of games played.

Individuals also weigh marginal benefit and marginal cost when making decisions. People weigh the extra happiness, or marginal utility, that they get from leisure time and the marginal cost of an extra hour of leisure (the earnings forgone) when deciding how to allocate their time. The high marginal cost of leisure time prior to the Industrial Revolution explains why professional sports did not arise until the mid-19th century.

Discussion Questions

1. Does your college charge a higher price for football or basketball games against higher-profile opponents? If it does not charge different prices, do you think it should? Does it do anything else to differentiate games against more and less attractive opponents?

2. Who is made better off by sites such as stubhub.com? What reason do you have for your answer?

3. Governments in countries like China often provide substantial aid to their Olympic athletes. Do you think this is right?

4. The National Collegiate Athletic Association (NCAA) does not allow its members to play against schools that the NCAA does not certify. Is this a good idea? Why or why not?

Problems

2.1 Some cities have several teams in England's Premier League (the country's top soccer league). Explain how this affects the monopoly power of those teams.

2.2 The marginal cost of admitting an additional fan to watch the Sacramento Kings play basketball is close to zero, but the average price of a ticket to a Kings game is about $60. What do these facts tell you about the market in which the Kings operate? Justify your answer.

2.3 Suppose the St. Louis Cardinals sign Yu Darvish, a star pitcher in Japan, to a five-year contract worth $70 million.

   a. What is likely to happen to ticket prices in St. Louis? Why?

   b. Five years later, the Cardinals sign Darvish to another five-year contract, this one worth $100 million. What is likely to happen to ticket prices in St. Louis? Why?

2.4 The major North American sports leagues prohibit teams from locating within a specific distance of an existing team. Why do they have such a rule?

2.5 Use supply and demand to show why teams that win championships typically raise their ticket prices the next season.

2.6 Use a graph with attendance on the horizontal axis and the price of tickets on the vertical axis to show the effect of the following on the market for tickets to see the Vancouver Canucks play hockey.

   a. The quality of play falls, as European players are attracted to play in rival hockey leagues in their home countries.

   b. Vancouver places a C$1 tax on all tickets sold.

   c. A recession reduces the average income in Vancouver and the surrounding area.

   d. The NBA puts a new basketball franchise in Vancouver.

2.7 Suppose the market demand for tickets to see a University of Tennessee women's basketball game is $Q^d = 40,000 - 1,000p$, and the supply is $Q^s = 20,000$.

   a. What is the equilibrium price of a ticket to the game?

   b. What would happen to the market for tickets if the university set a price ceiling on tickets of $10 and if Tennessee had strict antiscalping laws?

   c. What would happen to your answer to (b) if the price ceiling were $30?

2.8 The New York Jets football team raises ticket prices from $100 to $110 per seat and experience a 5 percent decline in tickets sold. What is the elasticity of demand for tickets?

2.9 Since the 1990s, many Major League Baseball teams have moved to new stadiums that are far smaller than the ones they have replaced. Use the appropriate curves to show what this has meant for ticket prices.

2.10 Suppose the Tampa Bay Rays baseball team charges $10 bleacher seats (poor seats in the outfield) and sells 250,000 of them over the course of the season. The next season, the Rays increase the price to $12 and sell 200,000 tickets.

   a. What is the elasticity of demand for bleacher seats at Rays games?

   b. Assuming the marginal cost of admitting one more fan is zero, is the price increase a good idea?

A P P E N D I X   2A

Utility Functions, Indifference Curves, and Budget Constraints

This appendix reviews the basics of consumer theory. It contains an introduction to utility maximization, which involves the use of indifference curves and budget constraints. It then uses these tools to provide a more sophisticated account of the rise of spectator sports.

2A.1   Constrained Maximization

Sandy is a graduate student who loves to go to baseball games and read economics textbooks. In fact, tickets and books are the only things she buys.[18] Economists evaluate Sandy's feelings toward baseball and economics books using her utility function. Sandy's **utility function** is a mathematical representation of the happiness Sandy gets from her consumption decisions. In this example, Sandy's utility function contains only baseball tickets (T) and economics books (B), and so we can write her utility function as

$$U = u(B, T)$$

Since Sandy wants both books and tickets (they are "goods," as opposed to "bads" that she does *not* want), whenever the number of either books or tickets increases, Sandy's **total utility** increases as well.

Economists, like Freudian psychologists, believe that people are motivated by a desire for pleasure. Freudians call the pleasure impulse "the id." Economists call it "utility maximization." In this example, Sandy would maximize her utility by buying an infinite number of tickets and books.

Also like psychologists, economists see forces that hold the pleasure impulse in check. Rather than the internal, psychological barrier of Freud's superego, economists see external constraints in the limited resources that people have at their disposal. People have only so much money, time, and energy with which to satisfy their desires. As a result, they cannot have all things or engage in all activities that make them happy. Put simply, they have to make choices. They do not, however, choose randomly. Economists assume that people maximize their utility subject to constraint by making rational choices, the economic analogue to Freud's ego. Sandy makes a **rational choice** when she uses all available information to make the decision that maximizes her happiness.

---

[18]Sandy surely buys more than just two items, but this simplification allows us to use two-dimensional pictures rather than multivariate calculus.

Many noneconomists have seized on the idea of rational choice to claim that economists view people as walking calculators who carefully weigh all options and have no room for emotions of any kind. Such a characterization is unfair. In fact, rationality need not connote careful decision making—or even sanity. To an economist, actions that most people would regard as heinous or bizarre would still be rational as long as they maximized the decision maker's utility.

Indifference curves allow us to illustrate people's preferences in a world that contains two goods. Recall that Sandy likes to watch baseball games and buy economics texts. Sandy enjoys a certain amount of happiness from seeing 10 baseball games and buying four economics textbooks (a combination illustrated by point A in Figure 2A.1). If someone took away one of Sandy's books (moving her to point A'), she would not feel as happy as before. Sandy would not feel so bad, however, if the person who took away her book gave her a ticket to a ballgame in exchange. In fact, if the person gave her enough tickets (say three tickets, putting her at point B in Figure 2A.1), Sandy might feel just as happy as she did to begin with.

If Sandy feels exactly the same about the two combinations of ballgames and books, we say that she is **indifferent** between points A and B. There are typically many combinations of ballgames and books that make Sandy equally happy. Combining all these points yields an indifference curve, like the ones shown in Figure 2A.2.

Because every combination of ballgames and textbooks yields some level of utility, every point in Figure 2A.1 is on *some* indifference curve. As a result, drawing all of Sandy's indifference curves would require filling in the entire area of the graph. We therefore draw only a sampling of her indifference

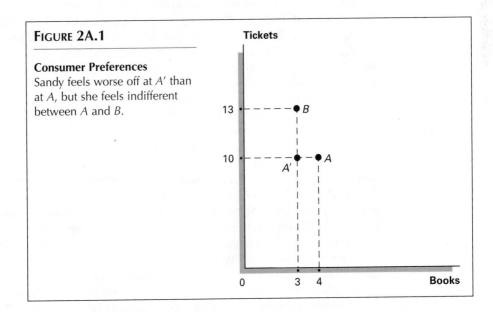

FIGURE 2A.1

Consumer Preferences
Sandy feels worse off at A' than at A, but she feels indifferent between A and B.

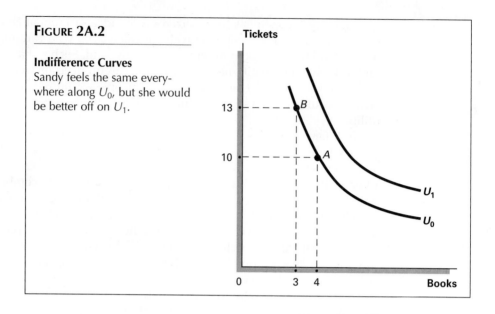

FIGURE 2A.2

Indifference Curves
Sandy feels the same everywhere along U_0, but she would
be better off on U_1.

curves. While indifference curves can come in many different shapes, most look like those in Figure 2A.2: They are downward sloping, convex, and cannot intersect.

Indifference curves slope downward any time we consider two products that the consumer likes. If we give Sandy more of a product that she likes, she is happier. To restore her initial utility level—and keep her on her original indifference curve—we have to take away some of something else that she values. More of one good means less of the other, and so the indifference curve slopes down. Having more of both goods makes Sandy happier, giving her a higher level of utility, shown by her being on a higher indifference curve in Figure 2A.2.

A convex indifference curve is typically very steep at first but becomes steadily flatter as one moves down and to the right. To see why, note that when Sandy sees many ballgames and reads few books, seeing one more or one less game means very little to her, but reading one more or one less book has a great impact on her happiness. As a result, she is willing to give up seeing a large number of ballgames in order to get only a few more books, as shown by the movement from point A to A' in Figure 2A.3. In this range, the indifference curve is steep. The same logic results in an almost flat indifference curve when Sandy has many books but sees only a few ballgames, as in the movement from B to B' in Figure 2A.3. Economists typically attribute Sandy's behavior to the principle of diminishing marginal rate of substitution. A **diminishing marginal rate of substitution** implies that, as consumers give up each successive unit of one good, they need increasing quantities of the other good in order to maintain the same level of utility. It is closely related to the law of diminishing marginal utility, which states that as a person consumes increasing quantities of one good, holding the consumption of all other goods constant, the marginal utility of the additional units consumed will eventually fall.

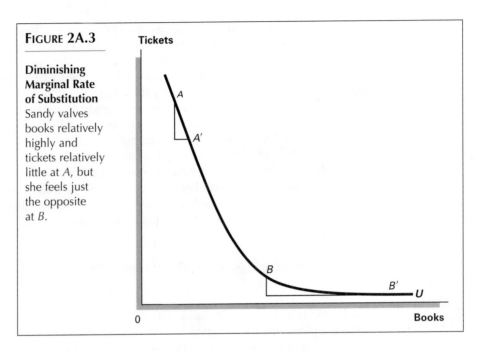

FIGURE 2A.3

Diminishing Marginal Rate of Substitution Sandy valves books relatively highly and tickets relatively little at A, but she feels just the opposite at B.

If indifference curves intersected, we would have to make some rather bizarre conclusions about how people behave. Figure 2A.4 shows what happens if two of Sandy's indifference curves, U_1 and U_2, cross at point A. Above point A, indifference curve U_2 lies to the right of indifference curve U_1. That means that Sandy can have more books without giving up any ballgames, leaving her better off. As a result, Sandy prefers all points on U_2 to all points on U_1. However, below point A, the positions of the indifference curves are reversed,

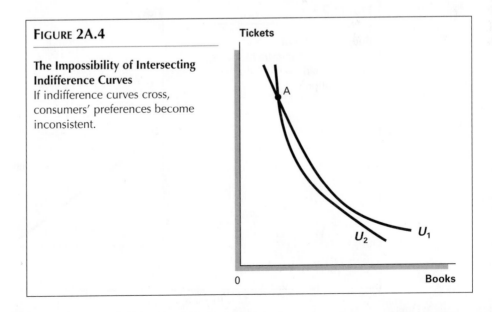

FIGURE 2A.4

The Impossibility of Intersecting Indifference Curves If indifference curves cross, consumers' preferences become inconsistent.

meaning Sandy prefers all points on U_1 to all points on U_2. To make matters still more confusing, since the two curves have point A in common, Sandy must get the same level of utility from both curves.

To maximize her utility, Sandy wants to be on the highest possible indifference curve. She is limited, however, by the amount of time, energy, and income at her disposal. For simplicity, assume that Sandy is constrained only by her income (I) of $800 and that tickets to a ballgame cost $10 while economics texts cost $20. Figure 2A.5 shows that she can buy 80 tickets if she buys only tickets and 40 textbooks if she buys only books. Since books cost twice as much as tickets, Sandy must give up two tickets in order to buy one more book. As a result, her budget constraint is a straight line with slope −2 that connects the points corresponding to 80 games and zero books, and zero games and 40 books.

We can write Sandy's constraint algebraically as

$$20B + 10T = 800$$

More generally, if p_b is the price of books and p_t is the price of tickets,

$$p_bB + p_tT = I$$

To see how changes in income and prices affect the constraint, consider what happens when we change the two. If the price of a ballgame doubles to $20, Sandy's opportunities fall. She can now see only 40 games if she spends all her money on tickets. Figure 2A.6 shows that the vertical intercept slides down to 40 games, and the budget constraint becomes flatter. Since ballgames and textbooks now cost the same amount, Sandy can get one more book by sacrificing one ballgame, and the slope of the constraint becomes −1. If the price of a ballgame falls to $5, Sandy can see 160 games, her opportunities expand, and the slope of her constraint becomes −4.

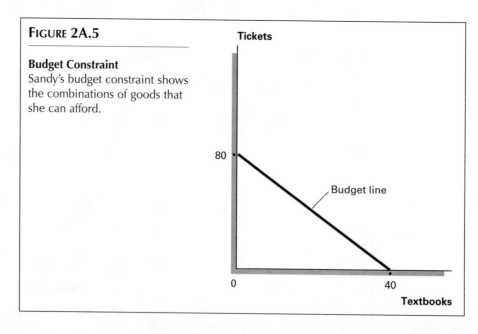

FIGURE 2A.5

Budget Constraint
Sandy's budget constraint shows the combinations of goods that she can afford.

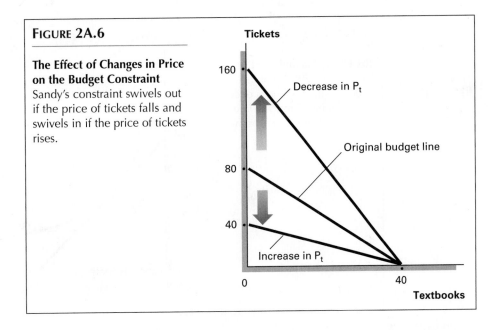

FIGURE 2A.6

The Effect of Changes in Price on the Budget Constraint
Sandy's constraint swivels out if the price of tickets falls and swivels in if the price of tickets rises.

If Sandy gets a raise so that she now has $1,000 at her disposal (and all prices stay at their original levels), her opportunities again expand. If she buys only tickets, she can go to 100 games. If she buys only textbooks, she can buy 50 books. Both intercepts in Figure 2A.7 increase, and the constraint shifts outward. Since the two prices have not changed, Sandy must still give up two ballgames to buy another book, and so the slope of her constraint remains −2.

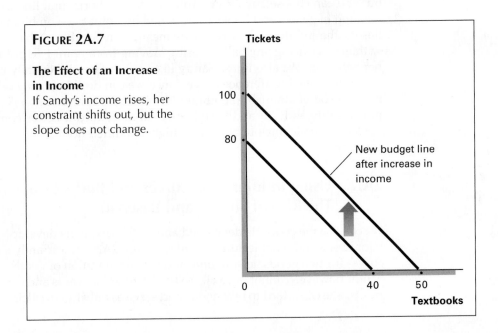

FIGURE 2A.7

The Effect of an Increase in Income
If Sandy's income rises, her constraint shifts out, but the slope does not change.

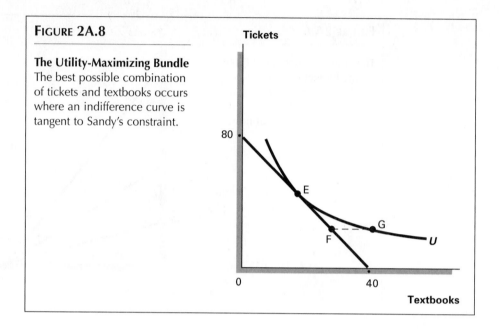

FIGURE 2A.8

The Utility-Maximizing Bundle
The best possible combination
of tickets and textbooks occurs
where an indifference curve is
tangent to Sandy's constraint.

Sandy's best possible choice of ballgames and economics texts comes on the highest indifference curve that still satisfies her budget constraint. This occurs where the indifference curve and the budget constraint are tangent, at point E in Figure 2A.8. To see that E is the best possible point, consider any other possible point on the budget constraint (we have chosen F in Figure 2A.8, but you can choose any other). You can draw a horizontal line from the combination of games and books represented by point F to combination G, which lies on the indifference curve. This means that Sandy can have more books without sacrificing any ballgames by moving from point F to point G, leaving her better off. We also know Sandy likes points G and E equally because they lie on the same indifference curve. Since we can do this for *any* other possible point, no other attainable combination of ballgames and textbooks provides as much utility as E. In addition, Sandy cannot afford a better combination of books and ballgames because any higher indifference curve lies outside her constraint.

2A.2   Using Indifference Curves and Budget Constraints: The Rise of Soccer and Baseball

We can use the concepts developed above to analyze the development of spectator sports and other leisure activities. Figure 2A.9 shows Sandy's indifference curves for two goods: leisure time and the consumption of goods and services. Sandy, however, cannot have all the leisure time she wants and consume all she wants. She can afford to buy goods and services only by sacrificing leisure time

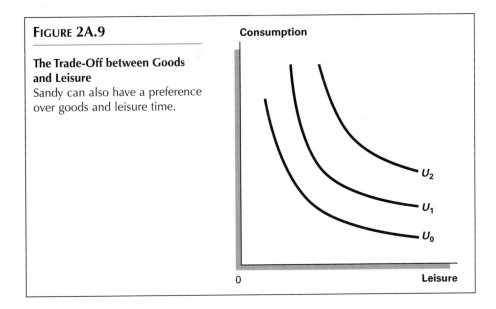

FIGURE 2A.9

The Trade-Off between Goods and Leisure
Sandy can also have a preference over goods and leisure time.

Consumption

U_2

U_1

U_0

0   Leisure

to work and earn income.[19] If, for example, Sandy earns $10 per hour, each hour of leisure that she sacrifices brings her $10 in added consumption. In this case, her budget constraint in Figure 2A.10 is a downward-sloping line connecting T hours, her maximal amount of leisure, with $10 \cdot T$, her maximal amount of consumption. As before, Sandy is best off at the point of tangency between an indifference curve and her constraint.

As noted in the chapter, prior to the Industrial Revolution, most societies could be characterized as subsistence economies in which people spent all their time generating goods they needed to survive. If Sandy must consume at least C_0 to survive, then she has an additional constraint. Her survival constraint is the horizontal line through C_0 in Figure 2A.11. Sandy cannot consume less and survive.

As an economy industrializes, workers become more productive, and their wages rise. A higher wage allows Sandy to generate more consumption for every hour of leisure she sacrifices. Her budget constraint swivels outward, and her maximum possible consumption rises from C_0 to C_1 in Figure 2A.12. Sandy now has several combinations of leisure and consumption that lie above her survival constraint. She can now afford to consume both goods and services and leisure time. The advent of leisure time allows Sandy to pursue nonproductive activities such as the participation in and attendance at athletic events.

---

[19]Economists acknowledge that people can allocate their time in other ways. One example is "home production," the unpaid work that goes into cooking, cleaning, and similar household activities.

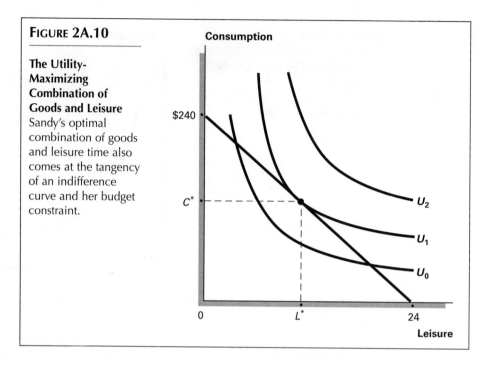

FIGURE 2A.10

The Utility-Maximizing Combination of Goods and Leisure Sandy's optimal combination of goods and leisure time also comes at the tangency of an indifference curve and her budget constraint.

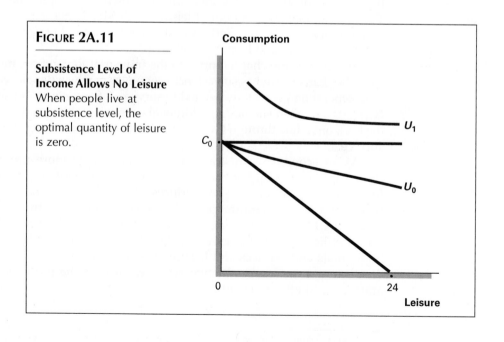

FIGURE 2A.11

Subsistence Level of Income Allows No Leisure When people live at subsistence level, the optimal quantity of leisure is zero.

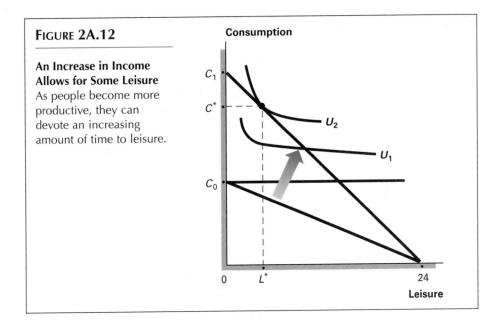

FIGURE 2A.12

An Increase in Income Allows for Some Leisure
As people become more productive, they can devote an increasing amount of time to leisure.

APPENDIX **2B**

Regression Analysis in Brief

How many times have you and your friends debated whether a player is worth the money his team pays him? Economists are not content to debate the monetary value of a player over lunch. They estimate a player's value based on a sophisticated statistical technique known as regression.[20] While we cannot make you an expert in a few short pages, by the end of this appendix, you should have an appreciation of the concept of a regression, a general idea of how economists use regressions, and a basic grasp of how to interpret regression output.

Suppose you want to figure out how much Sidney Crosby, a star center with the Pittsburgh Penguins, is worth to his team. Presumably, the Penguins pay him based on some measure of performance. (We shall discuss the precise measure in Chapter 8.) In a very simple world, teams may base the salaries of all players other than goalies on the number of goals they score:

$$\text{Salary} = f(\text{Goals})$$

---

[20]See G. S. Thomas, "Surhoff Proves to Be '99's Best Investment," in *Street & Smith's SportsBusiness Journal* (October 25–31, 1999), p. 1, for an article that uses a technique such as this.

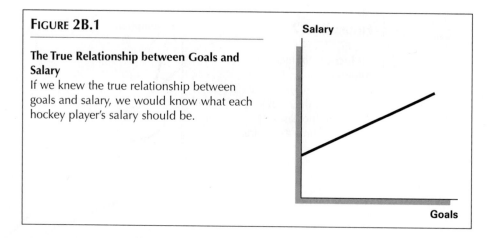

FIGURE 2B.1

The True Relationship between Goals and Salary
If we knew the true relationship between goals and salary, we would know what each hockey player's salary should be.

In the equation above a player's salary is a **dependent variable**, because its value depends on (is determined by) the number of goals a player scores. Because the number of goals does not depend on another variable in the equation above, we call it an **independent variable**. If the relationship between goals scored and a player's salary (the "functional form" of $f(x)$ in the equation above) was a straight line like that in Figure 2B.1, you would be able to compute how much Sidney Crosby was worth based on the number of goals he scored. Since you know that Sidney Crosby scored 33 goals in the 2008–2009 season, you could tell your friends how much he is worth to the team.

Unfortunately, life is not so simple. Salaries and goals scored do not line up perfectly along a straight line. Instead, the relationship is likely to be scattered around the line, as shown in Figure 2B.2. The points corresponding to players' goals and salaries may be scattered about the line for two reasons. First, there may be some error in measuring the variables involved. For example, Crosby's

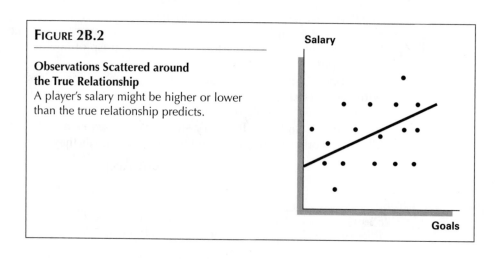

FIGURE 2B.2

Observations Scattered around the True Relationship
A player's salary might be higher or lower than the true relationship predicts.

official salary may not include a bonus he received for making the NHL All-Star Team. If so, the official statistics understate Crosby's full compensation, and the point corresponding to his goals and salary lies below the line.

Second, a player's salary and goals scored may not lie on the line because of some factor for which we have failed to account. For example, Crosby also had 70 assists—plays that led to goals scored by his teammates. If teams reward both players for both goals and assists, then Crosby's goal–salary combination may lie above the line in Figure 2B.2 because his salary also reflects a factor that our goal–salary relationship ignores.

Making matters more difficult still, in real life, we do not observe the line in Figure 2B.2. All we see is the scatter of points. From this scatter of points, we must estimate the relationship between goals and salaries before making a statement about a given player.

Economists who want to know the relationship between goals scored and salary in the NHL must first estimate the true relationship from the scatter of points that appear in Figure 2B.3. They do so through a process known as ordinary least squares (OLS). The name **ordinary least squares** indicates that we choose the line that minimizes the sum of the *squared* distances between the points and the line. If e_i is the distance (measured as a vertical line) between each point ($i = 1, \ldots, n$) scattered around the proposed line and the line itself, OLS minimizes the sum S, where

$$S = \sum_{i=1}^{n} e_i^2$$

While we do not bother with all the theory behind OLS estimation, it helps to see why economists prefer it to two alternative estimation methods. One alternative is to minimize the total error (Σe_i), in effect adding the signed distances of the points from the proposed line. Figure 2B.4 shows this method fails to distinguish between lines A and B, even though line A clearly gives the

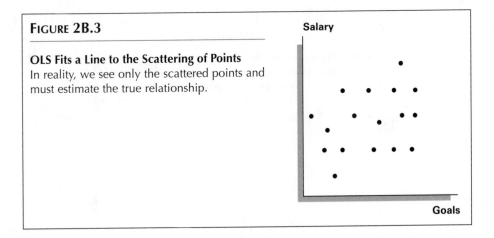

FIGURE 2B.3

OLS Fits a Line to the Scattering of Points
In reality, we see only the scattered points and must estimate the true relationship.

Salary

Goals

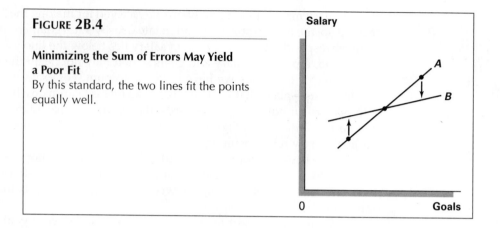

FIGURE 2B.4

Minimizing the Sum of Errors May Yield a Poor Fit
By this standard, the two lines fit the points equally well.

better fit. The problem is that the error for line B is also zero because the negative error offsets the positive error.

We can solve the problem of offsetting positive and negative misses by either squaring the errors or taking their absolute value ($\Sigma |e_i|$). The two methods, however, are not identical. If we added the absolute value of the error terms, we would conclude that either line C or line D in Figure 2B.5 fits the data equally well. By squaring the errors, OLS places greater weight on the large miss made by line D. OLS thus fits our intuitive notion that a line with several small misses fits the data better than a line with a few very large ones.

Economists call the OLS estimate of the line relating salary to goals a *simple regression,* because it assumes that there is a simple explanation for why some players make more than others: They score more goals. Here is the output from one such simple regression

$$\text{Salary} = 643{,}416 + 93{,}183 \cdot \text{Goals}$$

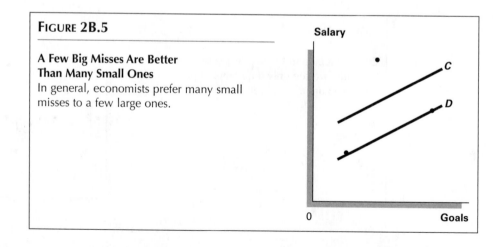

FIGURE 2B.5

A Few Big Misses Are Better Than Many Small Ones
In general, economists prefer many small misses to a few large ones.

In this equation, the coefficient 643,416 is the *intercept term*. It is the salary a player receives if he does not score any goals (Goals = 0). The coefficient 93,183 represents the *slope term*. It shows the impact that scoring an extra goal has on salary. It says that each goal scored adds a little over $93,000 to a player's salary. This model thus predicts that Sidney Crosby will make roughly 643,416 + 93,183 · (33) = $3.72 million.

We cannot, however, be certain that a player's salary will actually rise by about $93,000 per goal scored. Figure 2B.6 shows two different sets of points that both lead to the same slope term. While the estimate is the same for each, we are far more confident of our results in Figure 2B.6a. Statisticians measure their confidence in their estimates with a variable called the *standard error*. We shall not derive the formula for the standard error; we simply say that the closer the standard error of a coefficient is to zero, the more confident we are that our estimate accurately reflects the true value. A good rule of thumb is to look for a standard error that is no more than half the size of the coefficient. Computer programs generally compute the ratio of the coefficient to the standard error, a value called the *t-statistic*. Since we want the standard error to be no more than about half the value of the coefficient, we look for a *t*-statistic that is greater than 2.0. Most economics papers report the *t*-values in parentheses below the coefficients like this:

$$\text{Salary} = 643{,}415 + 93{,}183 \cdot \text{Goals}$$
$$(9.135) \quad (13.308)$$

In this case, we can be confident that the true values of both the constant and the slope terms are not zero and that goals actually do have an impact on salary.

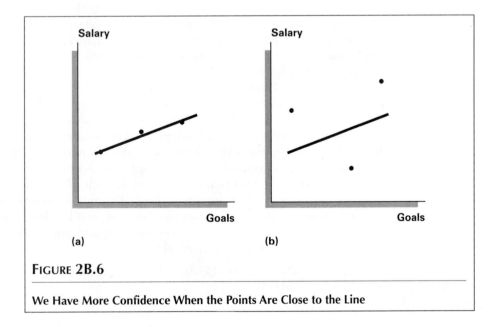

FIGURE 2B.6

We Have More Confidence When the Points Are Close to the Line

Multiple Regression and Dummy Variables

As noted earlier, we can probably make our measurement more accurate by including other variables that affect a player's salary. In fact, failing to include a key variable such as assists may cause our coefficient on goals to be off target, a problem statisticians call bias. We call a regression that has several explanatory variables a multiple regression, reflecting the fact that a dependent variable (in our case, salaries) may be affected by multiple factors. The results of a multiple regressions look very much like those of a simple regression. In this case, we find

$$\text{Salary} = 566{,}498 + 71{,}928 \cdot \text{Goals} + 19{,}946 \cdot \text{Assists}$$
$$(7.826) \quad (8.159) \qquad (3.895)$$

The interpretation of the coefficients becomes a bit more complex in a multiple regression. Now the coefficient on goals, 71,928, reflects the impact of an additional goal on a player's salary *holding the number of assists constant.* It allows us to say that if two players have the same number of assists (and any other factor one might include) but one of the players has 10 more goals than the other, we expect the player with more goals to earn about $720,000 per year more than the other.

While standard errors and *t*-statistics give a good idea as to how well specific variables explain the data, they do not tell how good a job the regression as a whole does. Fortunately, most regression packages provide several overall measures of the quality of the regression. The most intuitive measure of a regression's "quality of fit" is its R^2. The value of the R^2 tells us how much of the variation in the dependent variable can be explained by the explanatory variables in the regression. In the above regressions, for example, the R^2 rises from 0.222 to 0.241 when we add assists as an explanatory variable. This tells us that goals alone explain about 22 percent of the variation in salary, while goals and assists combined explain about 24 percent. Using both goals and assists improves the regression because the R^2 of the second regression is closer to 1, meaning it comes closer to explaining 100 percent of the variation in salary.

One additional variable we might want to include in our multiple regression is the player's position. Neither goals nor assists will be of as much importance to a defenseman, whose primary responsibility is to prevent scoring by the other team, as it is to an offensive player. We cannot add a player's position, however, in the same way that we would add the number of goals or assists he has. A player's position, like a worker's sex or race, is a qualitative variable; it does not have an obvious numerical value. To include position in our regression, we must first create a dummy variable. **Dummy variables** assign numerical values to qualitative variables. In this case, we let the dummy variable equal zero if the player was not a defenseman and one if the player was a defenseman. This changes the regression to

$$\text{Salary} = 261{,}128 + 91{,}569 \cdot \text{Goals} + 16{,}346 \cdot \text{Assists} + 585{,}560 \cdot \text{Defenseman}$$
$$(2.789) \quad (9.641) \qquad (3.301) \qquad (5.001)$$

Since the variable *Defenseman* equals zero for all players who do not play defense, the coefficient has no impact for them. We can think of the coefficient as the impact of playing defense, *ceteris paribus*—the impact of playing defense for a player who scores a given number of goals and who has a given number of assists. These results suggest that defensemen are paid a premium of over a half-million dollars. This does not mean that defensemen are more valuable to hockey teams. Defensemen are less likely to score goals or have assists than wings or centers. An offensive player who scores about six more goals than a defensive player makes up the half-million-dollar difference of the dummy variable. As expected, adding a player's position improves the quality of the regression—the R^2 rises to 0.270.

PART TWO
The Industrial Organization of Sports

CHAPTER 3
Sports Franchises as Profit-Maximizing Firms

CHAPTER 4
Monopoly and Antitrust

CHAPTER 5
Competitive Balance

CHAPTER 3

Sports Franchises as Profit-Maximizing Firms

For almost twenty years I owned and ran a National Football League team, the San Diego Chargers. When I bought the Chargers I believed I could apply to professional football the same principles of good business management that had enabled me to succeed in the corporate world. There was also a time when I believed in Santa Claus, the Easter Bunny, and the Tooth Fairy.

—GENE KLEIN[1]

Introduction

In 2009, two of America's largest corporations declared bankruptcy. General Motors and Chrysler, despite ads touting the high quality of their vehicles relative to their competitors', had lost so much money over the previous year, they simply couldn't continue without filing for bankruptcy. The management of both firms was vilified for the losses. Many American taxpayers were outraged at having to use public funds to subsidize the two automakers. Stockholders suffered massive losses as GM stock fell from over $41 per share in October of 2007 to less than $1 in June of 2009.

Sports fans, however, have a different attitude. They condemn team executives or owners whom they suspect of putting profit ahead of winning and have at times supported massive public subsidies unrelated to the profitability of the teams. Few owners are as popular as Mark Cuban, the owner of the Dallas Mavericks basketball team. In the 2007–2008 season, the Mavericks lost over $13 million, more than all but one other basketball franchise,[2] yet Cuban would probably say that it was worth every penny. Not only has he built a winning franchise, he is, in the words of one observer, "a *bona fide* sports star, better

---

[1]Eugene Klein, *First Down and a Billion: The Funny Business of Pro Football* (New York: Morrow), p. 12.

[2]"NBA Team Valuations," *Forbes Magazine* online at www.Forbes.com.

known and more popular than most of his players."[3] Cuban clearly views the Mavericks as a consumption good, a chance to have fun and to rub elbows with athletes, celebrities, and fans, rather than as a source of income.

While many owners have nonfinancial motives for owning a sports franchise—a factor we explore in Section 3.2—few of them show as much disregard for profit as Mark Cuban. Instead, their behavior often seems consistent with the standard principles of profit-maximizing behavior.[4] Teams that lose sight of the bottom line may share the fate of hockey's Ottawa Senators. The 2002–2003 hockey season marked a dual culmination for the Senators. The team rose to among hockey's elite, amassing the best regular season record in the NHL. As this was happening, the team fell over $100 million in debt and slowly slid into bankruptcy. The financial failure in Canada's capital was an embarrassment for the team, the NHL, and the country that gave birth to ice hockey. For most of this chapter, we shall explore how teams and leagues maximize profit and what happens when they fail to do so. Along the way, we shall examine the following points:

- The role that leagues play in the profits of individual teams
- The role that gate revenue, media revenue, and venue revenue play in the profits of a franchise
- How owners can manipulate their costs to make profits look like losses
- How alternative league structures affect teams' behavior

3.1 The Importance of Leagues

All major professional team and individual sports are organized into leagues or associations. Forming a league appears to be a prerequisite for the financial stability of a sport, yet the arrival of leagues did not coincide with the advent of professional teams.[5]

Baseball's National League, the oldest existing professional league in the United States, did not appear until 1876, seven years after the Cincinnati Red Stockings, the first openly professional team, began to play in 1869. It took another 20 years for the National League to establish a stable set of teams. The NFL took even longer to establish itself. The NFL formed in 1920, two generations after William Heffelfinger became the first professional football player in 1876, and it did not field a stable set of teams until 1936.[6] The same pattern held

---

[3]Chris Suellentrop, "Mark Cuban: How to Meddle with Your Sports Team—The Right Way," *Slate Magazine,* online at http://www.slate.com, December 4, 2002.

[4]See, for example, D. W. Ferguson et al. in "The Pricing of Sports Events: Do Teams Maximize Profits?" *Journal of Industrial Economics,* vol. 39 (March 1991), pp. 297–310.

[5]Leifer, *Making the Majors* (1995), p. 15.

[6]Quirk and Fort, *Pay Dirt* (1992), pp. 333–334.

in Europe, as a formal league structure for soccer arose in 1888, at least 12 years after the appearance of professional players, 25 years after the codification of the sport by the Football Association (FA), and decades after teams began playing the sport. Despite these delays, professional sports could not have survived without the formation of stable leagues.

Prior to the appearance of leagues, teams played each other on an informal, *ad hoc* basis. Until the latter part of the 19th century, most games involved teams from the same town. As transportation improved, matches were arranged between teams from different towns.[7] Informal trips to play teams in other towns, a practice known as barnstorming, became popular, but there was no guarantee that the opposition would show up or that the game would draw a sizable crowd. The experiences of the old Cincinnati Red Stockings illustrate this problem. During their grand tour of 1869, the Red Stockings drew large crowds from coast to coast while compiling a 56–0–1 record. The next year they lost only four games but disbanded when the season was over. The Red Stockings team resembled a strongman in a traveling carnival who offers to take on all comers. The sideshow may attract a crowd if it bills the strongman as "undefeated." A strongman who has won two-thirds of his matches (an enviable record for most teams today), however, would not generate much interest.

The typical fan regards a league as a collection of teams that agrees to play games against one another. This simple definition ignores the economic complexity of leagues. Leagues are by nature cooperative bodies. At one level, the teams are rivals that succeed at the expense of each other. At another level, each team's success depends on the success of the other teams in the league and on the success of the league as an institution. Leagues create a common set of rules, fix schedules, decide on revenue-sharing arrangements, stage championship tournaments, create a framework for the entry of new players and teams into the league, and conduct marketing campaigns.[8]

For much of this chapter, we will assume that teams share the goal of profit maximization and that leagues exist to help them meet this goal.[9] We will also see, however, that many teams—and some leagues—have not always shared this goal. In the remainder of this section, we focus on the how leagues

- Set rules

- Limit entry

- Promote competitive balance and share revenue

- Market their product

---

[7]See Michael Danielson, *Home Team: Professional Sport and the American Metropolis* (Princeton, N.J.: Princeton University Press, 1997), p. 20.

[8]Groups such as the Professional Golfers' Association and the United States Tennis Association perform much the same function for these more individual-based sports.

[9]See, for example, Gerald Scully, *The Market Structure of Sports* (Chicago: University of Chicago Press, 1995), pp. 3–40.

Setting the Rules

One of the most important—and most overlooked—functions of leagues is to establish and enforce a set of commonly accepted rules. For example, the many different rules by which 19th-century English football clubs played created conflict between clubs and stymied the growth of the game. In 1863, many clubs joined to form the Football Association (FA) to establish a single set of rules.[10] In addition to standardizing rules, the FA gave football the nickname it now enjoys in England and the United States. The approved version of the game was dubbed "Association Football," later shortened to "Assoc. Football" or "soccer."

In the early years of soccer, teams did not play a fixed schedule, and attempts to stage a championship series often resulted in dull, one-sided games. Recognizing the need to provide stable competition between evenly matched teams, 12 of the strongest clubs formed an elite grouping of teams in 1888 that called itself "the Football League" (FL). Despite the seeming conflict with the FA, the FL did not attempt to displace the FA to become the sole governing body of the elite teams. The members of the FL recognized that they were motivated by the interests of their individual clubs and not the welfare of the FL or the sport as a whole, and they chose to share power with the FA, allowing it to serve as an outside arbiter.[11]

Like soccer, baseball was played by different rules in different places. Two versions of the sport dominated, Massachusetts Rules and Knickerbocker Rules (also known as New York Rules). Knickerbocker Rules are the linear ancestor of modern baseball; Massachusetts Rules may seem bizarre to the modern observer. Under Massachusetts Rules, a team got an opposing player "out" by hitting him with a thrown ball, the bases were arranged in a square rather than a diamond, and winning a game required 100 runs or getting every member of the other team out, as in cricket. By the middle of the 19th century, the Knickerbocker Rules had become the norm.[12]

The earliest central authority in baseball, the National Association of Base Ball Players (NABBP), predates the FA, having formed in 1858. It did not arise out of a need to standardize rules, because the Knickerbocker Rules dominated the game played by the teams in the NABBP (largely in the New York area). Instead, it sought to combat professionalism and preserve the "gentlemanliness" of the game. The NABBP did not live up to expectations, and it succumbed to the growing professionalism of the sport. At first, individual players were paid "under the table." In 1869 the Cincinnati Red Stockings cast aside all

---

[10]Unhappy that the new rules did not allow their rougher version of football, devotees of the style developed at Rugby formed their own association, the Rugby Football Union, in 1871.

[11]Wray Vamplew, *Pay Up and Play the Game: Professional Sport in Britain, 1875–1914* (Cambridge, U.K.: Cambridge University Press, 1988), p. 125.

[12]See Harold Seymour, *Baseball: The Early Years* (New York: Oxford University Press, 1960), pp. 23–30; and Robert Burk, *Never Just a Game: Players, Owners, and American Baseball to 1920* (Chapel Hill: University of North Carolina Press, 1994), p. 14.

pretense and became an openly professional club.[13] Professional teams in Chicago, Boston, and elsewhere soon followed suit.

More recently, rules have been manipulated to create more excitement and fan interest. The NFL has continually tried to "open up" the game by limiting how much contact defenders can have with quarterbacks or receivers. It has also made teams kick off from deeper and deeper in their own territory in an effort to generate longer and more exciting kickoff returns. In an attempt to win back fans after the cancellation of the 2004–2005 season, the NHL instituted a number of changes designed to increase scoring. These included limiting the equipment and activities of goalies, allowing longer passes, and instituting "shootouts" to end tie games. After seeing how popular it had been in the rival American Basketball Association (ABA) and American Basketball League (ABL),[14] the NBA added the three-point basket to increase scoring and restore the value of outside shooting; more recently, they permitted teams to play "zone" defense. None of these changes was designed to increase the competitiveness or outcome of any specific contest. They were all made at the league level with the goal of making the game more spectator friendly.

Leagues establish and enforce a consistent set of rules off the field as well. Teams or players that do not obey the rules can be banished from the league. In its early years, the National League expelled teams for failing to play out their schedules. Individual players were also banned from baseball for intentionally losing games, as was the case for eight of the Chicago "Black Sox" following the 1919 World Series, or for betting on baseball games, as Pete Rose was in 1989. The NFL suspended Alex Karras of the Detroit Lions and Paul Hornung of the Green Bay Packers for one year in 1963 for betting on league games. Players may also be suspended for engaging in activity that may reflect poorly on the league, as witnessed by the numerous suspensions in all sports for drug use and Major League Baseball's suspension of the Dodgers' Manny Ramirez in 2009 for using a banned substance.

Leagues have also played a role in purging the crowds of "undesirable elements" that discouraged attendance. For example, Sunday beer sales at baseball games have been allowed only fairly recently. In the 1890s, the National League tried to present a wholesome image by expelling the Cincinnati Red Stockings for serving beer at all. Prior to the 1930s, games were not even played on Sundays in many cities. Currently, in the NHL, teams can be penalized during a game if fans repeatedly throw objects onto the ice and delay the game. In the NFL, the home team can be penalized if its fans are so noisy that the opposing team cannot hear the snap count.

---

[13]The team's payroll was $930. See Stefan Szymanski and Andrews Zimbalist, *National Pastime* (Washington, D.C.: Brookings Institution Press, 2005), p. 22.

[14]Terry Pluto, *Loose Balls: The Short, Wild Life of the American Basketball Association* (New York: Simon and Schuster, 1990), pp. 29–30.

Limiting Entry

Suppose you are very wealthy and want to try your hand at owning a professional football team. You name your team the Vultures, create a sharp-looking logo, and design eye-catching new uniforms. Now all you need are opponents, players, and a venue. The problem is, the only way to get them is to join the NFL, and the only way to join is to convince the other owners to admit you. Had you decided to open a shoe store, you would need only a storefront, a business license, a wholesale supplier, and a few employees. Can you imagine having to ask all the other shoe store owners in town for their permission to open? If you did, the retail shoe industry would certainly look quite different from how it does today.

All leagues place a limit on the number of teams they admit, though these limits sometimes vary. In North America, MLB, the NBA, and the NHL have all restricted themselves to 30 teams, while the NFL has 32 teams. In Australia, by contrast, the Australian Football League has only 16 teams. In Japan, the Nippon Professional Baseball League (NPB) has just 12 teams.

What forces determine how large a league becomes? The answer can be found in the work of Nobel laureate James Buchanan on the economics of clubs.[15] Buchanan reasoned that admitting a new member to a club—in this case a sports league—brings costs and benefits. Existing teams benefit from the admission fees that new teams pay to join the league and from the additional fan base and media outlets new teams bring.[16] Additional members also bring a cost. For example, admitting new teams to the league spreads any shared revenue over more members. It also reduces the ability of existing members to use the threat of moving to the new city as a bargaining chip when negotiating with their current home cities.

If the revenue from admitting one more team declines as the league grows—as one might expect if leagues admit cities from the most profitable cities first and then admit teams from less and less profitable cities—the marginal revenue curve would slope downward, as in Figure 3.1. Similarly, if the cost of admitting one more team rises, the marginal cost curve would slope upward. The equilibrium point occurs where the marginal revenue and marginal cost curves meet (e_0), which leads to optimal league size Q_0.

Figure 3.1 also shows the dangers that face leagues when they limit the number of teams. At the turn of the 20th century, the National League, then the only major professional league in North America, restricted itself to only eight teams. It failed to recognize, however, that rising populations and incomes in urban centers had shifted the marginal revenue curve rightward from MR_1 to MR_2. The shift caused the equilibrium point to shift to e_1 and the optimal

---

[15]James M. Buchanan, "An Economic Theory of Clubs," *Economica*, vol. 32, no. 1, February 1965, pp. 1–14; and John Vrooman, "Franchise Free Agency in Professional Sports Leagues," *Southern Journal of Economics*, vol. 64, no. 1 (July 1997), pp. 191–219.

[16]More generally, Buchanan assumes that members of a club produce "club goods" that members of the club share with one another but that outsiders cannot enjoy.

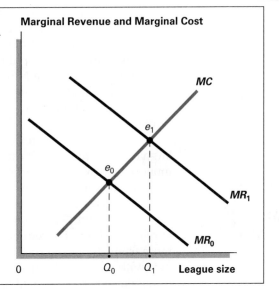

FIGURE 3.1

Determining the Optimal Size of a League
The optimal size of the league is set where the marginal revenue and the marginal cost from adding a new member are equal. This occurs at point e_0, which means that the optimal size of the league is Q_0. If the benefit of admitting a new member rises, the marginal benefit curve shifts to the right from MR_0 to MR_1, the equilibrium shifts to e_1, and the optimal number of new members rises to Q_1.

Marginal Revenue and Marginal Cost

league size to grow from Q_0 to Q_1. The failure of the National League to expand led Ban Johnson to found the American League.

Leagues not only limit the amount of entry, they dictate *where* entry can occur. Table 3.1 shows that, in 2009, each of the 10 largest metropolitan areas had several professional franchises. As expected, New York, the largest market, had almost twice as many franchises as any other area, with 11 franchises. Los

TABLE 3.1

Ten Most Populous Metropolitan Statistical Areas and Their Sports Teams in 2008

City (population)[a]	MLB	NBA	NFL	NHL	MLS	WNBA
New York (19.0)	2	2	2	3	1	1
Los Angeles (12.9)	2	2	0	1	1	1
Chicago (9.6)	2	1	1	1	1	1
Dallas (6.4)	1	1	1	1	1	0
Philadelphia (5.8)	1	1	1	1	1[b]	0
Houston (5.6)	1	1	1	0	1	0
Miami (5.4)	1	1	1	1	0	0
Atlanta (5.4)	1	1	1	1	0	1
Washington, D.C. (5.4)	1	1	1	1	1	1
Boston (4.5)	1	1	1	1	1	0

[a]Population in millions.
[b]Philadelphia's MLS team (Philadelphia Union) begins play in 2010.
Source: Metropolitan and Micropolitan Statistical Area Estimates, at www.census.gov/popest/metro/cbsa-est2008-pop-chg.html.

Angeles and Chicago, the second and third most populous metropolitan areas, were tied for the second most franchises with seven. MLB and the NBA had franchises in all of the 10 largest metropolitan areas. The NFL has placed all its teams in major metropolitan areas. These include almost all of the largest cities in the nation. The NFL was in every area top ten but Los Angeles, and the NHL was in every area except Houston. The WNBA had entered five metropolitan areas, while MLS was in seven, though they begin play in an eighth (Philadelphia) in 2010.

Placing franchises in the largest cities ensures that each team will have a large fan base to which it can market. Adding teams to a market dissipates the monopoly power of the existing teams. To have an effective monopoly, a firm must produce a good with no close substitutes. As the number of available substitutes increases, the demand curve facing the incumbent firm becomes more elastic. In Figure 3.2, the addition of a new, nearby team shifts the demand curve from D_0 to D_1, reducing the profit-maximizing price from p_0 to p_1. The more teams that exist in any given area, the more vigorously they must compete with one another in all areas of revenue generation, from luxury box sales to regular ticket sales to advertising. In terms of Figure 3.2, the more teams in the area, the more elastic the demand curve facing any individual team, and the weaker its monopoly power.

If teams in a league are making large profits, new teams will want to enter. The ability of new firms to enter an industry where profits exceed the normal rate of return ensures that competitive markets respond to the desires of their consumers. The threat of new entry puts constant downward pressure on

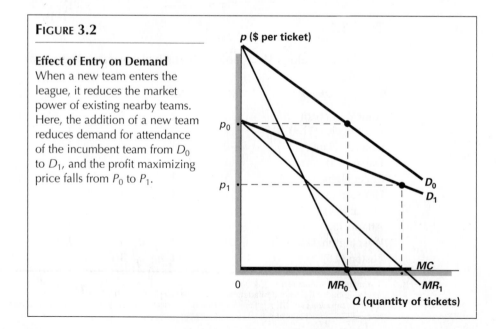

FIGURE 3.2

Effect of Entry on Demand
When a new team enters the league, it reduces the market power of existing nearby teams. Here, the addition of a new team reduces demand for attendance of the incumbent team from D_0 to D_1, and the profit maximizing price falls from P_0 to P_1.

prices and profits. The desire to escape this pressure gives incumbent firms the incentive to prevent new firms from joining the industry.

If potential owners cannot join an existing league, they have an incentive to create a new one. The viability of a new league is much less certain, however, if all of the most profitable locations already have teams in the existing league. The lack of profitable markets dogged the ABA, a short-lived rival to the NBA that lasted from 1967 to 1976. Many of the ABA's former players, coaches, and owners claim that ABA basketball was more exciting than the NBA game at the time. As proof, they point to the adoption of several ABA rules by the NBA and the excellent performance of ABA teams and players after the NBA absorbed four ABA teams.[17] To avoid direct competition with the NBA, the ABA chose mostly midsized cities for its franchises. A better product in a weak location, however, is often doomed to fail. Such was the fate of the ABA. When the league folded, only the Denver, New Jersey, San Antonio, and Indiana franchises survived to join the NBA.

There have been several recent attempts to form rival leagues in both football and ice hockey. The World Hockey Association (WHA) played from 1972 through 1979. After the 1978–1979 season, four teams from the WHA joined the NHL, two were compensated for not joining the NHL, and the remaining teams disbanded. All teams that attempted to compete head to head with NHL teams in the same large-city market failed. The only teams to survive played in midsized markets where no other team already existed, and three of those teams (Winnipeg, Hartford, and Quebec) eventually moved to more profitable markets (Phoenix, Charlotte, and Denver, respectively). Many of the original owners of American Football League franchises in the 1960s were wealthy people who had been unable to buy NFL teams. Other leagues followed, including the World Football League (WFL), the United States Football League (USFL), and the Extreme Football League (XFL). The WFL lasted less than two seasons in the mid-1970s, failing largely because of its inability to maintain a television contract. The USFL played from 1983 to 1985 but also folded due to a lack of stable ownership and rapidly falling TV revenues.[18] The XFL lasted only the 2000–2001 season due to poor TV ratings.

Controlling Entry as Cooperative Behavior

Some analysts regard leagues as multiplant monopolies. According to this view, a season of games is a "peculiar mixture: it comes in divisible parts, each of which can be sold separately, but it is also a joint and multiple yet divisible product."[19] For example, part of the excitement of attending a single game

---

[17]Julius ("Dr. J") Erving notes that in the first all-star game after the ABA folded, essentially merging its most promising locations with the NBA, 10 of the 24 players selected had come from the ABA. Pluto, *Loose Balls* (1990), p. 35.

[18]Jim Byrne, *The $1 League: The Rise and Fall of the USFL* (New York: Prentice Hall, 1986), *passim.*

[19]This view is expressed in W. Neale, "The Peculiar Economics of Professional Sports," *Quarterly Journal of Economics*, vol. 78, no. 1 (February 1964), pp. 1–14. The quote is taken from p. 3.

comes from how the outcome relates to league standings, which involves all teams in the league.

Leagues carefully coordinate the output (here measured as games played) and prices charged by member teams for the betterment of the league, even if such restrictions reduce the profits of some member teams. Major network television contracts are negotiated at the league level rather than by individual teams. Such cooperative behavior allows the most popular games to be aired on national television, and it prevents teams from competing with each other for broadcast rights, thereby keeping prices high. Such competition would inevitably lead to lower revenues for the league, because teams would have the incentive to reduce prices to networks for broadcast rights.

Restricting the number of teams (and the geographic locations they occupy) gives owners a guaranteed source of ticket and media revenue as well as a restricted market for apparel and other team-related enterprises. Leagues enforce territorial rights by setting a radius within which no other member of the league may locate. In the NFL, each team is given exclusive rights to an area with a radius measuring 75 miles from its home stadium. Territorial rights do not absolutely exclude other teams, but a team that moves into another's territory must compensate the existing team. For example, in the NBA, the Los Angeles Clippers had to pay the Los Angeles Lakers $6 million in 1984 for moving from San Diego into the Lakers territory without the league's permission.[20]

League Contraction

In the fall of 2001, MLB Commissioner Bud Selig announced that, after four decades of uninterrupted expansion, baseball had overextended itself and should contract. The blue-ribbon commission that he had appointed noted that the sport had become dangerously uncompetitive. When the commission divided the teams into four equal quartiles based on the size of the teams' payrolls, with Quartile I being the teams with the highest payrolls and Quartile IV being the teams with the lowest payrolls, it made a disturbing discovery. Over the five-year period of 1995 to 1999, during which there were 158 postseason play-off and World Series games, *"no club* from Quartiles III or IV won a DS [Division Series] or LCS [League Championship Series] game and *no club* from payroll Quartiles II, III, or IV won a World Series game."[21] Selig went on to claim that two teams, later revealed to be the Minnesota Twins and the Montreal Expos, were no longer financially viable and should be folded. Perhaps as a consequence of overexpansion, half of all baseball teams reported operating losses in 2002.[22]

Some critics of contraction were quick to point out that the blue-ribbon commission claimed that there was no need to eliminate teams. Others noted

---

[20]Gerald Scully, *The Market Structure of Sports* (Chicago: University of Chicago Press, 1995), p. 22.

[21]Richard C. Levin, George J. Mitchell, Paul A. Volker, George F. Will, "The Report of the Independent Members of the Commissioner's Blue Ribbon Panel on Baseball Economics," July 2000, online at http://www.mlb.com/mlb/downloads/blue_ribbon.pdf, p.i.

[22]"MLB Team Valuations," *Forbes Magazine*, online at http://www.forbes.com, April 28, 2003.

that the Minnesota Twins were not one of the teams that *Forbes* reported as having negative operating income in 2002. They also observed that the Twins' owner was embroiled in a battle with the Minnesota legislature to get a new state-funded stadium and that baseball's owners were in the midst of contentious negotiations with the players' union. The threat of shutting down the Twins, these critics argued, could only strengthen team owners' hands in both disputes. Finally, the success of low payroll teams in the 2002 playoffs led some to question the conclusions of the blue-ribbon commission's report. In 2002, the World Series featured the Anaheim Angels and the San Francisco Giants, both teams with payrolls in Quartile II. The Giants got to the World Series by beating the St. Louis Cardinals, another Quartile II club, while the Angels defeated none other than the Minnesota Twins, which had the third lowest payroll in baseball. Even the downtrodden Montreal Expos managed to finish second in their division. In light of 2002's results, one must ask which was the anomaly: 2002 or the five years considered by the blue-ribbon commission.

Some firmly believe that baseball's calls for contraction were part of a bargaining ploy by the owners, who were intent on driving a hard bargain with the players and with the residents of Minnesota. MLB resolved the crisis facing the Expos not by eliminating them but by moving them to Washington, D.C., where they were renamed the Nationals.

Marketing

While one team's marketing efforts may increase the profits of other teams, such spillovers are likely to be small. Teams run ads only in their home markets.[23] For example, because the NBA does not share gate or local media revenue, the Houston Rockets have an incentive to pay for advertisements that encourage fans to attend Rockets home games and to watch or listen to local broadcasts of their games. The rewards of fans' attending games in other cities accrue to other teams and the rewards from national broadcasts are shared evenly, so the Rockets have little reason to pay for more broadly focused ads. Individual team marketing is aimed at increasing local media ratings. If all marketing were done in this way, analyzing its impact on demand and profit would be straightforward. Marketing expenditures would appear as a fixed cost, and, if effective, they would shift the demand curve for the event to the right. Each team would advertise up to the point where the marginal benefit (*MB*) from the last dollar spent on advertising was equal to the marginal cost (*MC*) of the ad, as shown in Figure 3.3.

Leagues, in contrast, take a multilevel approach to marketing. As with traditional franchises such as McDonald's, professional teams contribute to joint advertisements run at the league level. In turn, the leagues work to create a specific image designed to increase demand for the sport as a whole. For instance, the WNBA spent $15 million on marketing in its first year. The league developed

---

[23]If a team broadcasts over a superstation, its "home" market may cover an extensive geographic area.

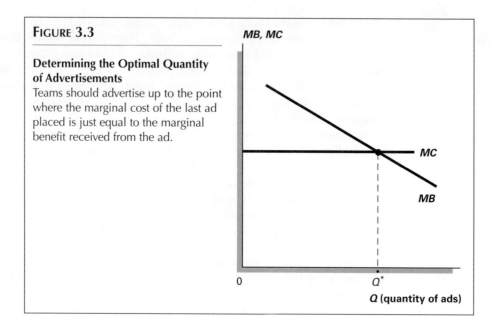

FIGURE 3.3

Determining the Optimal Quantity of Advertisements
Teams should advertise up to the point where the marginal cost of the last ad placed is just equal to the marginal benefit received from the ad.

a slogan ("We Got Next") and used it in a variety of ads designed to promote the league rather than any specific team.

Marketing at the league level promotes the welfare of all teams and thus is something of a **public good.** A public good is marked by **nonrivalry** in consumption. The benefit that one team receives from a league-wide marketing campaign does not diminish the benefit that any other team can receive from the same campaign. All teams receive equal amounts of the public good, even though they may value it differently. Public goods are also marked by **nonexclusion.** One team cannot prevent another team from receiving the benefits of the campaign. Asking teams to contribute voluntarily, however, creates a **free rider** problem. Free riding is an attempt to pay less than one's marginal benefit from a public good and to exploit the production by others. Thus, there are two challenges when trying to determine the optimal provision of such a good. The first is to determine the marginal benefit of the good to society, and the second is to ensure that each consumer (team, in this case) pays its share.

In a market for a private good, such as the market for apples, we arrive at the market demand by horizontally summing individual demand curves. If Amy buys 4 apples at $1 per apple and Pat buys 6 apples at $1 per apple, their combined demand is 10 apples at $1. With public goods, because consumption is nonrival, demand or marginal benefit curves are summed *vertically* rather than horizontally. Suppose that 60-second advertising slots on network television are available at a constant marginal cost of $50,000. Figure 3.4 shows that alone, no team in the NBA (or any sports league) may be willing to pay for such an advertisement. However, if the first 60-second preseason commercial is worth $10,000 to 15 smaller-market teams such as the Sacramento Kings, and

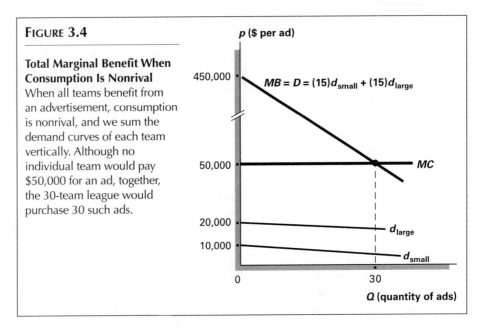

FIGURE 3.4

Total Marginal Benefit When Consumption Is Nonrival
When all teams benefit from an advertisement, consumption is nonrival, and we sum the demand curves of each team vertically. Although no individual team would pay $50,000 for an ad, together, the 30-team league would purchase 30 such ads.

$20,000 to 15 larger-market teams such as the Los Angeles Lakers, the first commercial is worth $450,000 to the 30 teams combined. Assuming marginal benefits decline as usual, so that the demand curves slope downward, the optimal number of commercials in Figure 3.4 is seen to be 30.

The second challenge, getting those who benefit from the good to contribute toward its production, can be very complex. Once built, public goods such as parks and roads can be used by anyone, so identifying the beneficiaries can be difficult. Because leagues provide marketing for a limited clientele, they have a much easier time identifying exactly who benefits. As a result, each team contributes to the league-wide marketing fund.[24]

3.2   What Are Profits and How Are They Maximized?

Economists define profits as total revenue minus total cost:

$$\pi = TR - TC$$

Total revenue is the sum of all revenues that the firm receives per period. In a typical market, total revenue is simply the price of the product times quantity sold. As we discussed in Chapter 2, though, there is no single, clear-cut definition of output in the professional sports market. Teams have numerous sources of revenue, not all of them directly related to attendance. Thus, total revenue in

---

[24]Craig A. Depken, David R. Kamerschen, and Arthur Snow, "Generic Advertising of Intermediate Goods: Theory and Evidence," *The Review of Industrial Organization*, vol. 20, no. 3, May 2002, pp. 205–220.

the above equation is the sum of several types of revenue: ticket sales, television rights, stadium revenues other than tickets (such as concessions and stadium-naming rights), licensing sales (jerseys, hats, etc.), shared or redistributed revenue from other teams, and subsidies from governments. An additional challenge for the study of team profits in professional sports is that profits—at least those profits reported using standard accounting rules—are easily manipulated. We discuss these difficulties in detail later in the chapter.

Like revenues, a firm's costs come in a variety of forms. Variable costs change with output. Most models of firm behavior consider the cost of labor to be a variable cost, since the firm must hire more labor in order to produce more output and can relatively easily change the number of workers that it hires. In professional sports, however, labor costs and most other costs are fixed (or variable over only a very narrow range) in a given season. The inability to vary labor costs over a single season stems from three factors. First, by agreement with the various player associations that represent the athletes, roster sizes are fixed in most sports. Thus, a team cannot save money simply by reducing the number of players on the team. Second, player contracts are set such that most pay is independent of performance or the amount of playing time a specific player receives. If a player on the Chicago Cubs has a contract for $1 million for the 2010 season, he receives that amount regardless of his batting average, fielding percentage, or even the number of at bats he has during the year. Finally, player contracts are often guaranteed in part or in full, meaning that the team must pay the player the salary specified in the contract for that year even if he is released from the team during the season.

A Detailed Look at Revenue

Professional teams generate revenue from four principal sources: ticket sales or gate receipts (R_G), local and national broadcasting rights (R_B), licensing income (R_L), and other stadium-related revenues, including luxury boxes, concessions, and stadium-naming rights (R_S):

$$TR = R_G + R_B + R_L + R_S$$

The proportion of total revenue generated from each source varies substantially from sport to sport and is determined by the level of demand for each. The sources of revenue have also changed dramatically over time. Table 3.2 shows revenue and cost data compiled by *Forbes Magazine* for several teams in each of the four major sports. While these revenue figures may seem large, a professional sports team is a relatively small firm within a large urban economy. For example, a professional sports team generates less annual revenue than a large department store.[25]

Table 3.2 shows estimates of the highest and lowest market value, revenue, player costs, and operating income for each of the major North American sports

---

[25]Roger Noll, "The Economics of Sports Leagues," in *Law of Professional and Amateur Sports*, ed. by Gary A. Uberstine, K. R. Stratos, and R. J. Grad (Deerfield, Ill.: The West Group, 1989), p. 17–2.

TABLE 3.2

Major League Franchise Revenue, Cost, and Valuations for 2008 (Millions $)

League/Team	Market Value	Revenue	Total Payroll	Operating Income
MLB				
Highest	Yankees: 1,500	Yankees: 375	Yankees: 209	Marlins: 43.7
Lowest	Marlins: 277	Marlins: 139	Marlins: 21.8	Tigers: −26.3
Median	403	122.5	80	17
NBA				
Highest	Knicks: 613	Knicks: 208	Knicks: 92.8	Bulls: 55.4
Lowest	Bucks: 278	Thunder: 82	Kings: 50.5	Nuggets: −26.3
Median	351.5	116.5	63.5	6.8
NHL				
Highest	Maple Leafs: 448	Maple Leafs: 160	Avalanche: 61.3	Maple Leafs: 66.4
Lowest	Coyotes: 142	Islanders: 64	Blue Jackets: 28	Hurricanes: −11.5
Median	202.5	88.5	45.2	1.2
NFL				
Highest	Cowboys: 1,612	Redskins: 327	Raiders: 152.4	Redskins: 58.1
Lowest	Vikings: 839	Vikings: 195	Chiefs: 83.6	Lions: −3.1
Median	1,024	214.5	112.7	22.6

Sources: Forbes data on market value, revenue, and operating income are compiled by Kurt Badenhausen, Michael K. Ozanian; and Kurt Badenhausen, Michael K. Ozanian and Christina Settimi (NBA). "NFL Team Valuations," at http://www.forbes.com/lists/2008/30/sportsmoney_nfl08_NFL-Team-Valuations_Rank.html; "NBA Team Valuations," at http://www.forbes.com/lists/2008/32/nba08_NBA-Team-Valuations_Rank.html; "MLB team Valuations," at http://www.forbes.com/lists/2009/33/baseball-values-09_The-Business-Of-Baseball_Rank.html; "NHL Team Valuations," at http://www.forbes.com/lists/2008/31/nhl08_NHL-Team-Valuations_Rank.html; Accessed June 12, 2009. Salary data are from "*USA Today* Salary Databases," at http://content.usatoday.com/sports/basketball/nba/salaries/default.aspx; http://content.usatoday.com/sports/baseball/salaries/default.aspx; http://content.usatoday.com/sports/football/nfl/salaries/default.aspx?Loc=Vanity; and http://content.usatoday.com/sports/hockey/nhl/salaries/default.aspx. Accessed June 12, 2009.

leagues in 2008 (2007–2008 for the NBA and NHL). It also shows the median values for each league. Note that the median value of an NFL franchise is more than double that of any other sport, usually an indication of greater profitability. While NFL teams do have the highest operating income at the median, the difference in operating income between the NFL and other sports is not as great as the difference in market value. **Operating income** is closely related (but not identical to) a firm's profits. It is the difference between a team's revenue and the costs of its day-to-day operations. It excludes costs not related to daily operations, such as interest payments on loans or wear and tear on its facility.

Table 3.2 shows great variability in profit, team payroll, and market value in MLB, the NFL, NHL, and NBA. In MLB, there is a huge difference between the $1.5 billion value of the Yankees and the $277 million value of the Florida Marlins. Perhaps even more striking, the Yankees are more than three times as valuable as the median MLB franchise. By contrast, the most valuable NFL franchise, the Dallas Cowboys, were only about 1.5 times as valuable as the median NFL franchise, and less than twice as valuable than the least valuable franchise (the Minnesota Vikings). In addition to a smaller dispersion of team values, NFL teams are more consistently profitable than any of the other sports. *Forbes* estimates that 12 NHL teams, 10 NBA teams, and 2 MLB teams lost money in 2007–2008, while the Detroit Lions were the only NFL franchise with negative operating income (which was much smaller than the losses of the least profitable team in the other leagues).

Perhaps the most striking feature of Table 3.2 is the mismatch between high (low) market value and high (low) operating income. None of the least valuable teams are the least profitable, and only the Maple Leafs stand as both most profitable and most valuable in their league. How can this be?

Some teams might have low operating income because the owners profit in ways that stretch beyond the boundaries of the team itself. For example, the Yankees, Red Sox, and Mets all own their own cable outlets. As we shall see later, a team owner might choose to maximize profits of the cable outlet at the expense of the team's bottom line.

High market value with low operating income may also reflect the investment strategy of the owner. Thus, a team might have high market value but low operating income if the owner is employing a strategy of building market value over a longer term at the expense of current profits. For example, as suggested at the beginning of this chapter in our discussion of Mavericks owner Mark Cuban, owners may have to choose between high wins and high profits in any given year. In contrast, other teams may be able to sacrifice wins in favor of profits in the short run. Consider that the two most profitable teams in MLB for 2008 were the Florida Marlins and the Washington Nationals, neither of which made the playoffs that year. Florida finished in third place in their division and the Nationals finished last. The Nationals' 2008 operating income of $42.6 million seems especially large when compared to the six division winners that year, which had a median operating income of $16.4 million, slightly below the median for the league as a whole.

If fans like to see their team win, it may be the case that in the long term, it will be able to increase demand for attendance only by building a successful team. Generally, this means obtaining or developing talented players, which, in turn, drives up the team's costs. Teams thus have two separate paths to short-term profitability: spending a lot of money with the hope of making even more revenue, or cutting costs and hoping that revenue does not fall even further. The NBA's Chicago Bulls have successfully followed both paths over the last 16 years. In the 1990s, the Bulls were a juggernaut both on and off the court, winning six NBA championships and serving as the marquee team of the NBA. Despite having one of the league's highest payrolls, topping out at over $61 million in their last championship year (1997–1998), the Bulls were among the most profitable teams in the NBA. In the four seasons that followed their last championship, the Bulls won only 66 games, four more than they won in 1997–1998. Despite their failures on the court, the Bulls remained profitable because of their lower payroll. In 2001–2002, the Bulls won only 21 games but led the league in operating income, garnering over \$20 million more than the champion Los Angeles Lakers.

Gate Revenue   Gate revenue (revenue from ticket sales) is an important source of income for all professional teams. While teams do not publicize gate revenue figures, one can easily form a rough estimate. For example, the average baseball ticket in 2008 cost \$25.40.[26] With 81 home games, and median attendance of about 30,000 per game, annual attendance revenue in MLB is likely to be around \$62 million for a typical team. One challenge that leagues face, however, is that gate revenue can vary widely from one team to another, affecting the stability of the league. For example, attendance revenue is much higher for high drawing teams like the Yankees and Mets, who averaged over 50,000 per game in 2008 and had average ticket prices well above the average. In contrast, the Florida Marlins and Kansas City Royals averaged less than 20,000 per game.[27] If some teams were unable to draw large crowds, they might not generate enough revenue to stay in business. For the first 16 years of its existence, 1920 through 1935, the NFL did not field the same set of teams in two consecutive years. Faced with such extreme instability, the NFL instituted what remains the most generous revenue-sharing policy of all the major professional sports in North America. Today, home teams in the NFL keep 60 percent of all gate revenue. The remaining 40 percent is put into a common pool that is distributed among all teams.[28] This sharing arrangement means that an NFL team's gate revenue is actually:

$$R_G = 0.6R_H + 0.4R_P$$

where R_H is a team's revenue from attendance at home games and R_P is the total amount of gate revenue generated by all NFL teams. This policy helped the league to survive its early, lean years and helps to explain why operating incomes and market values are so much closer in the NFL than in the other major U.S. leagues. It also set the stage for other revenue-sharing policies that would help make the NFL the most profitable of all the major sports in the United States.

The NHL does not explicitly share gate revenue, but instead has a complex system of revenue sharing based in part on total team revenues and playoff gate receipts. In contrast to the NFL, NBA teams do not share any gate revenue,

---

[26]"Major League Baseball average ticket price rises 10.9 percent to \$25.40," June 5, 2009, at http://sports.espn.go.com/espn/wire?section=mlb&id=3317969.

[27]"MLB Attendance Report—2008," June 5, 2009, at http://sports.espn.go.com/mlb/attendance?sort=home_avg&year=2008&seasonType=2.

[28]The NFL dates its founding from when the initial body, the "American Professional Football Association" took the name "National Football League" in 1922. See David Harris, *The League: The Rise and Decline of the NFL* (New York: Bantam Books, 1986), p. 12; and Eric M. Leifer, *Making the Majors: The Transformation of Team Sports in America* (Cambridge, Mass.: Harvard University Press, 1995), pp. 98–109.

so $R_G = R_H$. The less the gate revenue shared, the more important the home attendance, and so for NBA teams, the ability to draw fans at home is critically important for financial success. In addition, NBA teams with weak attendance figures are less financially stable, and less able to attract and pay for top players. We return to the relationship between salaries and wins in Chapter 8.

In the last two collective bargaining agreements, MLB teams have agreed to increase the amount of gate revenue that they share. Starting with the 2003 season, MLB teams have placed 34 percent of their net local revenues, including gate revenues, in a common pool that is divided equally among all teams.

Television Revenue

Few events have changed the finances of professional sports as much as the advent of television. All four major sports currently enjoy huge revenue streams from both local and national broadcasting rights. Table 3.3 shows, however, that TV benefits some sports more than others. The prosperity of the NFL depends on its huge network contract, the revenue from which the teams split evenly. The $117 million that the NFL's TV deal brings each team annually amounts to 60 percent of the Minnesota Vikings' 2007 revenue. The NBA, which also evenly shares TV revenue, agreed to a new TV contract in 2007 that extended their current agreement with ABC/ESPN and TNT for eight years, providing each team with $31 million per year in revenue. The network contract is responsible for over one-fourth of the median team's total revenue and over one-third of the total revenue of the Oklahoma City Thunder. The relative poverty of the NHL can be traced directly to its network contract, which is far

TABLE 3.3

Revenue from Broadcast Rights Agreements

Sport	Years	Stations	Total Fees[a]	Annual Average[b]
MLB	2006–13[c]	ESPN; Fox	$4.87	$713
NBA	2009–16	ABC/ESPN; TNT	$7.44	$930
NFL	2006–13[d]	ESPN; CBS; Fox; NBC; DirecTV	$23.9	$3,735
NHL[e]	2009–11	VERSUS; NBC	$0.21	$72.5
NASCAR	2007–14	Fox; Time Warner; ABC/ESPN	$4.4	$550

[a]In billions.
[b]In millions.
[c]ESPN: 2006–2013; FOX: 2001–2006.
[d]ESPN: 2006–2013; CBS, Fox, NBC: 2006–2011; DirecTV: 2006–2010.
[e]The contract with NBC provides no guaranteed revenue to the NHL; the contract value with Versus is set each year.
Sources: Street & Smith's Sports Journal; Andy Bernstein, "Flexibility a Key in New MLB-ESPN Deal," SportsBusiness Journal, online at www.sportsbusinessjournal.com; Leonard Shapiro and Mark Maske, "'Monday Night Football' Changes the Channel," Washington Post, April 19, 2005, p. A01; Rachel Cohen, "NBA extends TV deals with ESPN/ABC, TNT" June 27, 2007, at http://www.usatoday.com/sports/basketball/2007-06-27-3096131424_x.htm; and Mark Puko, "Hockey schedule a bow to NBC," June 4, 2009, at http://www.pittsburghlive.com/x/pittsburghtrib/sports/s_627457.html.

less than for any of the other major U.S. sports and is worth less than one-fifteenth of NASCAR's annual TV contract. To see the difference TV can make, consider what would happen if the NFL and NHL had each other's TV contract. The revenue of the median NFL team is $126 million more than the median NHL team. The NFL's TV contract pays each team $114 million more than does the NHL's contract. The NFL's prosperity and the NHL's poverty thus stem in large part from their respective TV deals.

The fact that the NFL and NBA split their revenue from network contracts evenly is a major reason why revenues are relatively evenly balanced in those leagues. The influx of TV money probably keeps several of these franchises from going bankrupt.

Major League Baseball's network contract for national broadcasts is far less lucrative than basketball's or football's, but unlike the NBA and NFL, some baseball teams have another major source of TV revenue: *local* TV contracts. To see the role that local TV revenue plays, consider the situation that faced the San Diego Padres and the New York Mets as they entered the 2006 season. In 2005, the San Diego Padres drew over 2.8 million fans, roughly 50,000 more than the New York Mets did. Despite virtually identical gate revenue ($67 million for the Padres; $69 million for the Mets), the Padres entered 2006 with a small-market $70 million payroll, while the Mets could afford a large-market payroll of $101 million. The reason lies in the convergence of three factors that all favor teams like the Mets. First, unlike network revenue, local media revenue is not evenly shared. While baseball teams now share roughly 34 percent of their local revenue, teams in larger media markets still enjoy a large advantage.

The second factor favoring the Mets is the growth of cable broadcasting. Cable rights are more valuable than the rights to over-the-air broadcasts because they provide an extra source of revenue to the broadcaster. In addition to the advertising revenue that both forms of broadcasting bring, a cable company receives a subscription fee from each cable user. Because cable contracts are more valuable, teams have been steadily switching to them from over-the-air broadcasts. As recently as 1996, almost 60 percent of all baseball broadcasts were still over-the-air telecasts. Today, most local broadcasts are seen on cable.

Finally, many teams, from the large-market Yankees and Mets to the small-market Minnesota Twins and Kansas City Royals, have formed their own cable companies. These companies allow the teams to eliminate the middleman and to capture the revenue streams from cable broadcasts. They also allow the teams to avoid league-wide revenue sharing by shuffling revenue from the team to the cable companies. Teams can do this by charging a low price for the broadcast rights. The low price hurts the team but helps the cable company, effectively taking money from one pocket and putting it in the other.

The relationship between teams, their leagues, and cable networks is not always so friendly. In June 2009, the NFL and NBA resolved a long-running and contentious negotiation with Comcast that placed their league networks on a digital classic tier rather than a premium tier. The agreement increases the number of households that will receive the broadcasts to 10.8 million, a big increase from the viewership on the premium service packages they were previously part of. In the case of the NFL, the dispute ended up in the courts as the NFL argued that it was being illegally shut out of a broader market, while Comcast argued that it was merely protecting subscribers from higher fees.[29] The battles over revenue from cable and satellite–based sports specific channels are contentious because the revenue they generate is enormous. The Baseball Channel revenues for 2007 were around $100 million.[30]

Because almost all of its TV revenue is shared equally (the major exception being local preseason broadcasts), the NFL has no disparity between large-market and small-market teams. Green Bay is smaller than any city hosting an MLB team, but its TV revenue is not significantly lower than that of NFL teams playing in New York or Chicago. With so much money coming from local cable broadcasts, MLB's Kansas City Royals are at a much greater disadvantage than the NFL's Kansas City Chiefs.

Baseball's disparities occur because big-market teams have such large local revenues. Hockey's disparities occur—at least in part—because its network revenues are so small. With only $2.4 million per team from the contract with VERSUS, NHL teams rely heavily on local TV revenues. Cities with small media markets, such as Edmonton and Ottawa, thus find it hard to compete financially with teams from larger markets such as Chicago or Toronto.

Like fixed costs in a profit equation, fixed revenues such as broadcast fees have no impact on how revenues or costs change with output. Ignoring for the moment the possible impact of televising games on gate receipts, a fixed revenue payment for broadcast rights (R_B) enters the profit function as a constant.

Television and Gate Receipts—Exposure versus Substitution   Broadcasting games is a double-edged sword to teams. To the extent that fans prefer to watch games on television rather than go to the stadium, televising home games reduces gate receipts. The first instance of this effect occurred in 1948, when the Philadelphia Eagles saw attendance drop by 50 percent after they decided to televise all their home games. This is why the NFL "blacks out" (forbids networks from showing in the local market) games that are not sold out. Blacking out the home team's game may not be enough if a New England Patriots fan in Boston prefers watching a televised game between the Cowboys and Dolphins to shivering at Gillette Stadium on a cold December day. On the other hand, if television stimulates fans' interest in the game, more broadcasts may increase attendance. The NFL owes a good deal of its popularity to its focus on nationally broadcast games and the "Sunday doubleheader," which allows fans to watch popular teams from other cities.

---

[29]Kelly Riddell, "Comcast, NFL Agree to New Contract, End Legal Fights," at http://www .bloomberg.com/apps/news?pid=email_en&sid=aOsV2TLja8jU; and Bob Fernandez, "Comcast to put NBA TV on 'Digital Classic' Tier," June 4, 2009, at http://www.philly.com/philly/business/ technology/46890407.html.

[30]Chris Isadore, "Baseball Close to Catching NFL as Top $ Sport," October 25, 2007, at http://money.cnn.com/2007/10/25/commentary/sportsbiz/index.htm. Accessed June 5, 2009.

Networks televise games when they profit from doing so. The demand by networks or local stations to televise games is a derived demand. The demand for a good or service is *derived* from the demand for another when the amount people are willing and able to buy depends on the market for a different product. For example, the demand for medical care depends in part on the demand for good health. In the case of broadcasting rights, the demand by TV networks for sporting events depends on—is derived from—the demand by sponsors for advertising time. A network's willingness to pay a league or team for the right to broadcast a game stems from its ability to sell advertising during the game. In the early 1980s, CBS paid $1 billion for the rights to broadcast the baseball "game of the week" largely due to a bidding war by the Anheuser-Busch and Miller Brewing Companies for advertising time.[31]

The exposure that broadcasts give a network and its advertisers explains why the NFL can charge so much more than the other sports. However, a network might pursue broadcast rights even though it knows that it will lose money as a result. Networks may be willing to overpay if they view football as a "loss leader." The broadcast itself might lose money, but if it attracts viewers to other shows on the network, it may still be consistent with overall profit maximization. Sports also give new entrants, such as Fox in 1998 or DirecTV in the latest NFL contract, an air of credibility with sponsors and potential affiliates. Lucie Salhany, chairperson of Fox Broadcasting when Fox first began broadcasting NFL games, argued, "We had to have it and it didn't matter what we paid for it. It put us on the map. It got us more affiliates. . . . Sales-wise, there were people we could never call on that we could call on once we got football."[32]

Television revenue has rivaled or surpassed gate revenue as the primary source of income for all major sports, and they have become so dependent on it that they have literally changed the way they play their games. Games are now interrupted by the infamous "TV time-out." Fans and players at the stadium wait while television viewers see advertisements, confident that play will not resume until the ads are over. Some sports, such as baseball, can easily accommodate such breaks. Other sports see stoppages in play extended for unnatural lengths. Football and basketball have gone so far as to introduce specific time-outs for no other purpose than to show commercials on TV. Fans at NHL games occasionally wait several minutes between face-offs to accommodate commercials. Football's two-minute warning came about as a concession to TV networks. The need to break for commercials represents a serious barrier to regular TV broadcasts of major league soccer, as play is continuous for long periods of time with no naturally occurring breaks.

Stadium Agreements   The Dallas Cowboys are the most valuable professional franchise in the United States. They held this position for most of the 1990s. At first, it is hard to see why. While the Cowboys were one of the most successful

---

[31]John Helyar, *Lords of the Realm* (New York: Villard Books, 1994), pp. 392–393.

[32]Eric Schmuckler, "Is the NFL Still Worth It?" *Mediaweek* (September 28, 1998), pp. 26–32.

teams in the NFL throughout the 1990s, the NFL did not give them much opportunity to capitalize on this success off the field. The Cowboys played in a stadium that was no larger than the NFL average, and the NFL's 60–40 split of gate revenues limits what they earn when they play before sell-out crowds. The Dallas media market is large, but it does not compare with those of New York, Los Angeles, and Chicago. Moreover, the Cowboys have to share all the revenue from their national telecasts equally with the other teams in the NFL. The key to the Cowboys' success in the 1990s was the team's extraordinarily profitable stadium agreement. The Cowboys' new stadium continues the tradition. It has 300 luxury boxes and 15,000 club seats, more than twice as many as at Heinz Field.

Venue revenue, or nonticket revenue from stadia (R_S), include revenue from parking and concessions, but, more importantly, they include revenue from luxury suites and other special seating, only a small portion of which counts as ticket revenue. Luxury seating has become particularly valuable in the NFL because teams share a substantial portion of ticket revenue with each other (and with their players as part of the salary cap, discussed in Chapter 8). For example, suppose a luxury suite in Texas Stadium rents for $500,000 per year and has 20 seats in it. If the Cowboys claim the value of the seats to be $50 each, they must share only $3,200 (0.4 × 20 × $50 × 8 games), and they keep the remaining $496,800 for themselves. Again, much of this revenue enters as a lump sum per season, because luxury boxes are typically leased on a per-season basis. Other attendance-related revenue, such as parking and concession, is directly connected to how many people come to the games, so it is more variable.

One of the newest sources of revenue in professional sports comes from teams selling the name of their facilities to the highest bidder. Stadium-naming rights are only one form of sponsorship. When you watch a NASCAR race, a European soccer match, or even a golf tournament, you can see the lengths to which companies go to associate their brands with a team, a player, or an event. Corporate names and logos adorn uniforms and equipment. The Phoenix Mercury of the WNBA have joined the trend and feature the Lifelock corporate logo on their uniforms.[33] One enterprising boxer even had an advertisement temporarily tattooed on his body.

Even against this background, naming rights stand apart. Rich Products, Inc., was the first company to purchase naming rights to a stadium when it purchased the name of the Buffalo Bills' new stadium in 1973 for $1.5 million over 25 years. For the next 20 years, professional sports in America largely ignored the revenue possibilities of naming rights. In 1990, only a handful of teams had sold such rights. Today, more than half of all baseball and football stadiums and over three-fourths of all basketball and hockey arenas have corporate names. Naming rights have even filtered down to the college level. University of Maryland fans can cheer on their basketball team at the Comcast Center

---

[33]Darren Rovell, "Branded Jerseys come to the WNBA," June 4, 2009, at http://www.cnbc.com/id/31034379/.

Advertisements have begun to appear in the oddest places.

(rights purchased for $20 million), while University of Louisville football fans root for their team at Papa John's Cardinal Stadium (rights purchased for $5 million).

Corporate executives and sports marketers clearly feel that naming rights are a great deal. In the words of Jeffrey Knapple, the president and CEO of Envision, "In a marketing landscape where corporations are continually striving to gain market share and 'share of mind' from their respective constituents, naming rights provides [sic] the ultimate opportunity to rise above the pack."[34]

The recent economic downturn has lent controversy to some naming rights purchases. Citi Group's record-breaking $400 million 20-year naming rights deal for the New York Mets' Citi Field has been particularly contentious in light of Citi Group's receiving $45 billion in support from the U.S. Treasury's Troubled Asset Relief Program.[35] Purchasing naming rights while receiving

---

[34]Jeffrey S. Knapple, "Naming Rights Industry" in *Naming Rights Deals* (Chicago: Team Marketing Report, 2001).

[35]Other companies with naming rights deals that have received TARP aid include Bank of America (Carolina Panthers), Comerica (Detroit Tigers), M&T Bank (Baltimore Ravens), and BB&T (Wake Forest University).

government aid would not be the subject of such debate if it were as profitable as its advocates claim. Unfortunately, evidence suggests that, while naming rights add millions each year to many teams' coffers, the purchases do little to a firm's bottom line. One recent study of 54 stadiums and arenas showed that only a handful of purchases had any impact on the company's profitability and that the effect was as likely to be negative as it was positive.[36]

Companies pay impressive sums to put their names on an NFL or MLB stadium, but these amounts do not come close to what companies pay to put their names on the jerseys of top soccer teams. Juventus (in Italy's Serie A), Bayern Munich (Germany's Bundesliga), Chelsea (England's Premier League), and Real Madrid (Spain's La Liga) all receive over $10 million each year in jersey sponsorships. The big winner, however, is England's Manchester United, which recently signed a deal with the Aon insurance brokerage that will pay the club $32.5 million per year.[37] With companies lining up to pay millions of dollars for sponsorships, it is little wonder that almost every major soccer team has seen its uniform become a mobile billboard. Only FC Barcelona of Spain's La Liga has chosen a different route. Unlike other uniforms, which tout everything from mobile phones to beer, "Barça's" uniforms promote the United Nation's Children's Fund (UNICEF). Moreover, UNICEF does not pay for this privileged position. Instead the team contributes over $1 million to the charity.[38]

Problems Created by Stadium Deals   Over the years, several NFL teams have moved away from their home cities to apparently illogical destinations. Both the Rams and Raiders left the Los Angeles market for far smaller markets in St. Louis and Oakland, respectively, leaving the nation's second largest market without a team. The Oilers abandoned what was then the nation's 10th largest metropolitan area in Houston for the 40th largest market in Nashville. Even the Cleveland Browns' move to Baltimore was from a larger city to a smaller one. On the surface, all these moves seem unprofitable, as they limit both the fan base and the media exposure for the teams. Why, then, do the teams move?

The answer can be found in the peculiar interaction of revenue sharing and stadium deals. Because the teams in the NFL split their national TV contract equally and their gate receipts almost equally, the consequences of a team's moving to a smaller city are spread over all the other teams. In baseball, where teams depend so heavily on local media revenue, a team in a media market the size of Los Angeles would never leave for a much smaller city. The Yankees, for example, might threaten to move from the Bronx to Manhattan or northern

---

[36]Eva Marikova Leeds, Michael A. Leeds, and Irina Pistolet, "A Stadium by Any Other Name," *Journal of Sports Economics*, vol. 8, no. 6 (December 2007), pp. 581–595.

[37]Associated Press, "Manchester United Signs Up Aon as New Jersey Sponsor," *USA Today*, June 4, 2009, online at http://www.usatoday.com/sports/soccer/europe/2009-06-03-manchester-united-aon-sponsorship_N.htm?csp=34.

[38]Paolo Bandini, "Barça Take the Moral High Ground," guardian.co.uk, September 13, 2006, online at http://www.guardian.co.uk/football/2006/sep/13/barcelona.

New Jersey, but they would never threaten to leave the New York metropolitan area. The Rams, who did not depend heavily on local media revenue, had no such qualms about leaving Los Angeles. The moves to smaller cities, however, may hurt the NFL's ratings in the nation's second-largest media market. This, in turn, could lead to worse TV contracts for the NFL—and less revenue for all teams, including the teams that moved—in the future.

The damage that an individual team's behavior can do to the NFL as a whole results in what economists call the **tragedy of the commons.** The "tragedy" gets its name from the problem that cities faced long ago when farmers all put their livestock out to graze on the town common. Because no one property owner had a claim on—or responsibility for—the town common, no one had any incentive to limit the amount of grazing that went on. As a result, the commons were overgrazed and eventually became worthless. Similarly, NFL teams do not worry about the consequences of leaving major media markets uncovered if they can get a better individual deal elsewhere.

While the costs of the Rams' move from Los Angeles to St. Louis are spread over the entire NFL, the Rams get to keep almost all the benefits for themselves. The stadium arrangement for the TransWorld Dome (since renamed the Edward Jones Dome) granted the Rams all revenues from the 124 luxury suites. As noted earlier, most of this revenue is not shared with other teams. In addition, the NFL does not count luxury suite revenue as revenue that must be shared with its players as part of its salary cap agreement. As long as municipalities continue to try to outbid one another for the right to host an NFL franchise, the league may continue to see teams move to smaller markets in pursuit of better stadium arrangements. We discuss this problem in detail in Chapters 6 and 7.

The Effects of Revenue Sharing

There are two fundamental, interrelated reasons that teams might want to share revenue. The first is to promote financial stability. If some teams have access to large pools of revenue and others do not, league stability will be jeopardized as the "have not" teams struggle to survive financially. Throughout the history of professional sports, leagues in which some teams are highly unstable financially have fared poorly. The other reason leagues may want teams to share revenue is to promote competitive balance. In this chapter, we focus on the financial ramifications of revenue sharing. We discuss competitive balance extensively in Chapter 5.

All leagues share revenues to some extent. In the NBA, revenue sharing does not extend beyond equally sharing licensing and national broadcast revenue. However, the size of each team's share of network revenue is so large relative to other revenue streams that it helps to smooth out the differences in gate and venue revenue. Because the NHL lacks a large TV contract, the differences in gate and venue revenue among the teams have more impact on the various teams' finances. As noted earlier, the NHL has recently adopted a complex revenue sharing system in an attempt to equalize teams' ability to compete. Under the agreement small-market, low-revenue teams receive transfer payments from large-market, high-revenue teams. In fact, the arrangement is so complex that "even some of the people who negotiated the deal confess that they don't understand it all."[39] Shared revenues come from playoff gate receipts, a portion of player salaries placed in escrow, and revenue from top grossing clubs. Only teams with fewer than 2.5 million television households and payrolls below the midpoint of league salaries are eligible to receive funds.[40]

As mentioned earlier, with the collective bargaining agreement that took effect in the summer of 2003, MLB sought to imitate the NFL's generous revenue sharing. While the NFL teams share 40 percent of their gate revenue equally and split all network revenue equally, baseball teams now share 34 percent of all net revenue from home attendance and local TV broadcasts. The huge differences in local TV revenue, however, ensure that MLB will continue to have much greater imbalances in revenue than the NFL.

From an economic standpoint, we could view revenue sharing as a tax on quality. Some team owners claim that revenue sharing—like any tax—penalizes teams for producing a higher quality product (spending more on salaries to field better teams) and reduces their incentive to do so. They argue that revenue sharing punishes teams that try to give their fans a better product and rewards owners for fielding bad teams with low payrolls. The profit statements of teams seem to support such cynicism. We demonstrated earlier in the chapter how the Bulls made mediocrity pay. Sadly, they are not alone. In the NFL, the Cincinnati Bengals, the worst team in the league for the 1990s (they averaged 11.5 losses per year from 1991 through 2002), did not suffer financial losses as a result of producing an inferior product. Thanks in part to shared gate and TV revenue, the Bengals' operating income exceeded that of the Buffalo Bills or Green Bay Packers, both of whom made multiple appearances in the Super Bowl over that period. In MLB, the transfers from wealthy teams to poor teams in 2002 meant that the Montreal Expos had higher operating income than seven other teams, despite drawing an average of only 10,000 fans per game (a figure exceeded by a few minor league teams) and having almost no local TV revenue. In 2005, the Tampa Bay Devil Rays, perhaps the worst team in baseball, played in a stadium that was more than two-thirds empty, but they had higher operating income than the Boston Red Sox, Chicago Cubs, Los Angeles Dodgers, and San Francisco Giants, all of which filled their stadiums to more than 90 percent of capacity.

Cost

When considering the cost side of the profit equation, we again see substantial differences between what costs mean to a professional sports franchise and what they mean to most other industries. The data in Table 3.2 show that, not surprisingly, players' salaries figure prominently in the total costs of professional franchises. Salaries, which include deferred payments, bonuses,

---

[39]Andy Bernstein, "Inside the Complex NHL Deal," June 4, 2009, at http://www .sportsbusi-nessjournal.com/index.cfm?fuseaction=article.printArticle&articleId=46287.

[40]Andy Bernstein, "Inside the Complex NHL Deal," June 4, 2009, at http://www .sportsbusi-nessjournal.com/index.cfm?fuseaction=article.printArticle&articleId=46287.

workers' compensation expenses, and pension contributions, make up over half a team's costs in every major sport. With a few exceptions, player costs vary little over the course of a single year.[41]

The remaining expenses include travel, marketing, administrative (both team and league), and venue expenses. For baseball, and, to a lesser extent, hockey, expenses also include player development. Travel expenses increase as the size of the team increases, with the number of away games, and with the distances traveled. Teams incur marketing and administrative costs at two levels. Each team does marketing specific to its own club and market, and each team has its own administrative costs, which include everything from office supplies to the salaries of the team executives. Marketing and administrative costs are also incurred at the league level. These costs include broad-based marketing campaigns designed to increase demand for the sport, and administrative costs such as the cost of paying a commissioner and maintaining league offices.

Total venue costs are highly variable. Some teams pay rent to local governments that own the venues in which they play, but those rents vary between what might be considered market values, and nothing at all. Among teams that own their own venues, some receive millions in public subsidies, while others receive little or no public funds. We explore these issues in detail in Chapters 6 and 7.

In MLB and to a lesser extent, the NHL, teams must also pay a portion of player development costs for players in their minor league systems. Each MLB team operates six minor league teams (AAA, AA, and three single A leagues). According to sports economist Andrew Zimbalist, the average MLB team spent more $20 million on player development in 2007.[42] These costs seem even greater when one considers that each minor league system generates only a few major league players per year. Thus, the development cost per major league player runs into the millions of dollars.

Opportunity Cost—Teams on the Move

Opportunity cost never appears on a team's balance sheet, yet it figures vitally in the strategic decision making of all teams. When franchises move from one city to another, they are driven by the prospect of higher profits in the new city. Research has shown that the greater the fan loyalty in a city, the more likely that city is to provide public funding toward a new stadium.[43] The opportunity costs of staying in a given city are the profits forgone by not moving to the new

---

[41]The exceptions include trades, waiving a player in midseason, very short-term contracts such as the 10-day contract in the NBA, and "two-way" contracts that allow the team to pay a player one salary if he is in the major leagues and a lower salary if he is sent to the minor leagues.

[42]Andrew Zimbalist, "There's more than meets the eye in determining players' salary shares," June 4, 2009, at http://www.sportsbusinessjournal.com/article/58351.

[43]Craig A. Depken, "Fan Loyalty and Stadium Funding in Professional Baseball, " *Journal of Sports Economics*, vol. 1, no. 2 (May 2000), pp. 124–138.

city. When a team contemplates a move, its owner usually cites the need for more skyboxes, lower lease payments, and better practice facilities. The implied threat in such statements is that some other city is offering such facilities, as seen in two of the most infamous franchise moves, baseball's Dodgers and football's Colts. For teams to exert their market power over cities, the league should not place teams in every viable location. The size of the league relative to the number of cities that want to host teams plays a key role in the bargaining strength of the teams within that league. The bargaining power of teams over cities is explored in detail in Chapter 6.

While many teams move because they are suffering losses in their current city, not all teams that move are losing money. When the Dodgers moved to Los Angeles in 1957, they ended a remarkably profitable run in Brooklyn. In the decade before they moved West, the Dodgers were the most profitable team in baseball, accounting for 47 percent of the profits of the entire National League. Similarly, in their last season before sneaking off to Indianapolis, the Baltimore Colts had an operating profit of $5.1 million, the third highest in the NFL.[44]

3.3 Taxes, Profit, Owner Behavior, and Vertical Integration

Most people complain that owners such as Jerry Jones of the Dallas Cowboys or Jerry Reinsdorf of the Chicago Bulls and White Sox fail to measure up to the "sportsmen" of a bygone era. Fans of all sports look back fondly to owners who nurtured the game and viewed it as more than a profit center or ego boost. Unfortunately, that image is largely fiction. As early as the 19th century, commentators were complaining that the spirit of sport had been lost in the clamor for profit. The Toronto Blue Jays and the Colorado Rockies may owe their origins to their owners' desire to sell beer (Labatt's in Toronto and Coors in Colorado),[45] but these owners had a role model about a century earlier in Chris von der Ahe, a brewer and the founder of the original St. Louis Browns, who used the ball club to boost his own beer sales.

While most baseball teams rely heavily on the money from local broadcast rights, the Atlanta Braves and Chicago Cubs, each of which broadcasts its "local" games nationally over cable superstations TBS and WGN, reported surprisingly little local income. However, when the teams revealed their TV revenue to Congress in 2001, the figures did not seem to add up. With revenue of $23.5 million, the Cubs made $6.5 less than their far less popular cross-town rivals, the Chicago White Sox. At only $20 million, the Braves trailed the Baltimore Orioles and barely beat out the Philadelphia Phillies and Detroit Tigers.

---

[44]Quirk and Fort, *Pay Dirt* (1992), p. 135; and Jon Morgan, *Glory for Sale: Fans, Dollars, and the New NFL* (Baltimore: Bancroft Press, 1997), p. 106.

[45]Some claim that the very name of the Blue Jays stems from the desire to promote one particular brand of beer, Labatt's Blue. See Helyar, *Lords of the Realm* (1994), p. 400.

At first glance, these figures look completely unjustified. On closer examination, they make perfect economic sense. While the owners of the Tigers or the White Sox had a strong incentive to charge as much as possible for the right to broadcast their teams' games, neither Time Warner, the owner of the Braves and TBS, nor the Tribune Company, then the owner of the Cubs and WGN, had an incentive to put broadcast rights up for competitive bidding. The Braves and the Cubs may not have generated as much revenue this way as they could have by selling the rights on the open market, but their parent companies were less interested in which subsidiary made a profit than in their overall profits.

As noted earlier in this chapter, sports teams have become increasingly entangled in the TV outlets that broadcast their games. The joint ownership of sports franchises and media outlets suggests that team owners see efficiency gains from **vertical integration,** the combination of different stages of production, and **cross subsidization,** the movement of revenues and expenses from one part of a company to another.

While integrating the team and the media outlet might increase the profits of the team owner, it seems like a losing proposition for the consumer. Alone, both the team and the broadcaster have monopoly power. Bringing the two together seems to create a "super monopoly" with even greater power to exploit consumers. Economic theory shows, however, that vertical integration of a team and a media outlet may actually improve the well-being of consumers.

To see why, consider two firms, each with monopoly power in its own market. One firm produces an item that the other uses to produce a finished product for consumers. Imagine that the two firms are located along a river. The **upstream firm** produces its output and floats it down the river to the **downstream firm,** which then floats the final output down the river to consumers. If the upstream firm has monopoly power, it can charge a monopoly price to the downstream firm. The downstream firm regards the price it pays as part of its marginal cost of production. It uses this inflated marginal cost to determine the price it then charges to consumers.

Figure 3.5 illustrates the impact of upstream and downstream monopolies. For simplicity, we assume that the upstream firm's marginal costs are constant, so that its MC curve is a horizontal line. We also assume that the downstream firm has no other costs so that its MC curve is a horizontal line at the price it pays the upstream firm. Figure 3.5b shows that the consumer faces a double whammy of two monopolies. The higher price charged by the upstream monopolist raises the costs of the downstream monopolist, which then raises prices still higher in exercising its own monopoly power.

If the downstream firm vertically integrates by buying the upstream firm, it has no reason to charge itself a high monopolistic price.[46] The cost of the upstream product to the downstream firm is now simply the marginal cost of production. The double whammy of Figure 3.5 now falls to a single whammy

---

[46]In fact, we shall show in Chapter 4 that charging a high price would harm the firm by creating a deadweight loss.

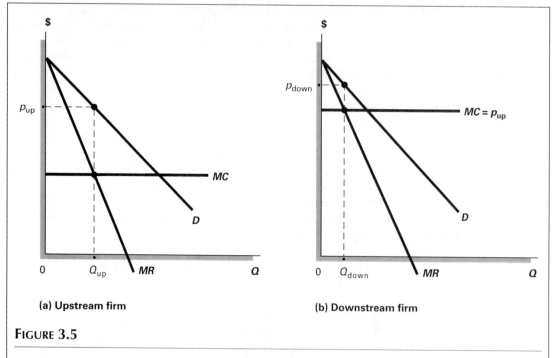

(a) Upstream firm

(b) Downstream firm

FIGURE 3.5

Monopoly Pricing by Upstream and Downstream Firms
When an upstream monopolist sells to a downstream monopolist, the downstream firm takes the price they pay the upstream firm (P_{up}) as marginal cost.

in Figure 3.6. While two separate monopolies apply their monopoly power twice, a single, vertically integrated monopoly applies its monopoly power only once. The result is a lower price and higher quantity for the consumer. In this case, it means more Braves games at a lower cost to the cable subscriber than would otherwise be the case.[47]

From the owner's perspective, an individual or group that owns two vertically integrated firms will seek to maximize total profits of the two combined enterprises. From a purely financial standpoint, the owner does not worry whether one firm shows a larger profit than the other. The price at which the upstream firm sells to the downstream firm is called the **transfer price.** Changes in transfer prices change accounting profits (those reported to the IRS), but not the overall profitability of the combined enterprises. Thus, the joint owner of a franchise and the cable station that broadcasts the franchise's games will set a low transfer price (i.e., broadcast rights fee) if tax or political considerations make it advantageous to do so. For example, if a team did not want to show high profits while seeking a public subsidy, or if the players were

---

[47] Although TBS is not a monopoly in the television broadcast market, it is a virtual monopolist in the market for broadcast of Braves games.

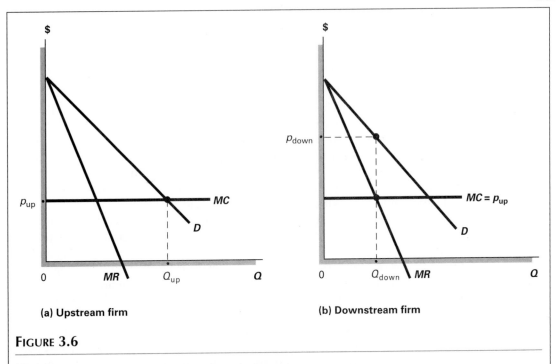

(a) Upstream firm

(b) Downstream firm

FIGURE 3.6

Vertical Integration with Competitive Pricing Upstream
When the upstream and downstream firms are vertically integrated, the downstream firm can purchase output at the competitive price ($MC = P_{up}$).

entitled to a given percentage of team profits, then the owner could keep more of the profits by having them transferred to his cable company through a low broadcast rights fee. Conversely, if the profits of the cable company were regulated, the owner may want to minimize earnings by charging a high broadcast rights fee. The moral of the story is that when firms are vertically integrated, as is becoming more and more common in the sports industry, one must view accounting profits with a skeptical eye.

3.4   Turning Losses into Profits: The Accounting Game

While teams worry about many different sources of revenues and costs, it still seems that one need only subtract the total cost from the various sources of revenue to calculate the profits. Unfortunately, nothing is simple in the finances of professional sports. Vertical integration is not the only tool that owners can use to manipulate profits. Paul Beeston, once the Toronto Blue Jays' vice president of business operations, put it best: "[A]nyone who quotes profits of a baseball club is missing the point. Under generally accepted accounting principles, I can turn a $4 million profit into a $2 million loss and get every national accounting firm to agree with me."[48] In this section, we explore how teams use the rules of accounting to manipulate their measures of profit.

Using Sports to Maximize Profits Elsewhere

Sometimes, team owners might take advantage of the high visibility that professional sports offers in order to increase profits in another industry. Perhaps nowhere is this practice more prevalent than in Japan, where all but two NPB teams are named for the corporations that own them, as opposed to the cities in which they play. As a result, the teams play an important role in marketing products unrelated to baseball. For example, the Seibu Lions, who play in Saitama, are owned by the Seibu group, where shoppers (and baseball fans) can ride the Seibu-Ikebukuro train from the game to a Seibu department store which, not coincidentally, celebrated with a major sale when the Seibu Lions won the 2008 Japan Series. An even more striking example is the Yomiuri Giants, owned by the Yomiuri Group, also owners of two newspapers and the NTV television network. In fact, pro baseball in Japan may have begun as a way to increase newspaper sales. The *Yomiuri Shimbun*, Japan's largest newspaper, sponsored a trip by the U.S. All Star team to play a series of games in Japan. The tour was so successful that the owner of the paper, Matsutaro Shoriki, decided to keep the team together and go on a tour of U.S. cities. Interestingly, it was at that time that the uniforms of the Japanese teams were changed to English on the front and Roman numbers on the back, a practice that continues today.[49]

Because of the ownership structure of the teams, profits are secondary to the teams' ability to market their sponsors. In fact, teams are regarded as marketing expenses by their parent companies, with front office positions often staffed from corporate headquarters rather than using baseball insiders.

While not as prevalent in American sports, one example from the NHL is striking. The Anaheim Ducks of the NHL were first named the Anaheim Mighty Ducks in 1993 and owned by the Walt Disney Corporation. The team's logo and colors were announced in June 1993 following the 1992 release of the *Mighty Ducks* movie from Walt Disney. According to the team Web site, team merchandise immediately became a top seller.[50]

Operating Income, Book Profit, and Bill Veeck

To this point, we have been using operating income, the net revenue from day-to-day operations, when discussing the profitability of sports franchises. When teams, or firms of any kind, report profits, however, they use **book profit,** the

---

[48]Quoted in Zimbalist, *Baseball and Billions* (1992), p. 62.

[49]Joseph A. Reaves, *Taking in a Game: The History of Baseball in Asia* (Lincoln, Neb.: University of Nebraska Press, 2002), pp. 69–77.

[50]"The Ducks Look," June 8, 2009, http://ducks.nhl.com/team/app/?service=page&page=NHLPage&id=16478.

difference between total revenue and total cost. Book profit differs from operating income in that it nets out interest expenses and depreciation as well as the day-to-day costs of production. Since corporate profit taxes are based on book profit, firms can deduct interest payments from their corporate profit taxes, while they must pay taxes on the profits that make up dividend payments. The asymmetric treatment of interest and dividends has led economists to conclude that firms generally prefer to raise funds by issuing debt (in the form of bonds and loans on which they must pay interest) rather than stock, which results in dividend payments. Moreover, most borrowing, and hence most interest payments, stem from the initial purchase of the team.

Depreciation allowances permit firms to estimate how much their plant and equipment have worn down as a result of the production process and to deduct this loss in value as an expense on their corporate taxes. Like other firms, sports franchises have often accounted for the decay of their physical plant. Unlike other firms, sports franchises have used this provision to write off the depreciation of their labor force by claiming that their players' skills erode just like machines wear out over time.

In 1949, Bill Veeck became the first owner to apply depreciation to his own players. Veeck's tenure as owner of the Cleveland Indians in the late 1940s was one of constant innovation. In 1947 he integrated the American League by signing Larry Doby. Not coincidentally, the Indians quickly became a contending team, winning pennants in 1948 and 1954, winning the World Series in 1948, and setting attendance records along the way. In his dealings with the Indians, Veeck introduced yet another innovation, a tax shelter that allowed an owner to make money by losing money.

The most flagrant use of this probably came in 1964, when a syndicate bought the Milwaukee Braves (and moved them to Atlanta a year later). The syndicate declared that only $50,000 of the $6.168 million it spent was for the team itself and that the remaining $6.118 million was embodied in the players. It also declared that the players were depreciable assets that wore out over a 10-year span, losing 10 percent of their original value each year. This method of estimating depreciation is called **straight-line depreciation** and is illustrated in Figure 3.7. The technique allowed the Braves' owners to write off $611,800 as depreciation expenses each year. At a 52 percent tax rate, the team reduced its tax burden by over $300,000 per year for 10 years. The total tax savings meant in effect that the new owners of the Braves were able to foist almost half the purchase price of the team onto the American taxpayer.

A team with a single owner could take the process one step further. Upon purchasing the franchise, the owner could reorganize the team as a *subchapter S corporation*. In a subchapter S corporation, all of the firm's profits are treated as the personal income of the owner. The income is thus taxed at the personal tax rate rather than at the corporate rate. At first, this seems illogical, since personal tax rates for people wealthy enough to own a franchise are higher than corporate rates. If the depreciation write-off is high enough, however, the owner can create a book loss for his team even though it has a positive operating income. The $300,000 depreciation write-off allowed the Braves to transform operating

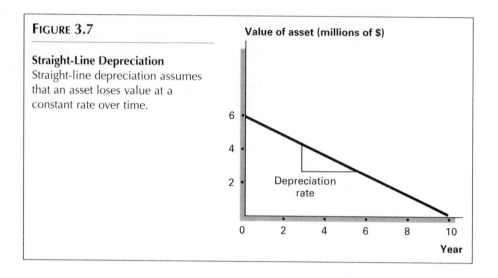

FIGURE 3.7

Straight-Line Depreciation
Straight-line depreciation assumes
that an asset loses value at a
constant rate over time.

Value of asset (millions of $)

Depreciation
rate

Year

income of $200,000 into a book loss of over $100,000. If the corporate tax rate
were 52 percent, then the corporate tax write-off would have been $52,000.
Since they were a subchapter S corporation, the Braves' losses were counted
against the owner's personal taxes, allowing him to reduce his taxes at the
higher personal tax rate. If the personal rate were 72 percent, then the write-off
would have been $72,000.

Owners who follow a subchapter S strategy face a problem when they have
fully depreciated their players, since they can no longer write off depreciation
to create paper losses. The owners can escape the higher tax burden in one of
two ways. They can sell the club, allowing the new owner to reorganize the corporation and begin the process all over again—even with the same players!
Alternatively, they can take advantage of a one-time opportunity to revoke
their subchapter S status.

The value of the aforementioned loopholes steadily decreased in the 50
or so years since Bill Veeck first used them. In the 1950s, the highest personal
tax rate was 72 percent, and the corporate income tax rate was a flat 52 percent. Since then, both rates have fallen by about half. In addition, IRS rulings
reduced the proportion of a team's value that the owner could attribute to
players from 90 percent to 50 percent. As a result, player depreciation and
Subchapter S corporations became less and less valuable to team owners.[51]
The American Jobs Creation Act of 2004, however, has reversed this trend.
One provision of the Act allows owners to attribute any proportion they
wish of a team's purchase price to players. With owners now able to write off
more revenue as depreciation, they have once again found these tax loopholes attractive.

---

[51]See Paul Weiler and Gary Roberts, *Sports and the Law: Cases, Materials, and Problems* (St. Paul,
Minn.: West Publishing, 1993), pp. 412–414.

3.5 Soccer's Alternative Business Model

Every four years, Americans are reminded that most of the world does not pay any attention at all to baseball or American football and that hockey and basketball are distinctly secondary diversions. Soccer dominates the world stage. As Table 3.4 shows, professional teams such as Manchester United, Real Madrid, and AC Milan have operating incomes and market values that rival those of the Dallas Cowboys and the New York Yankees. The sales of brand-name soccer merchandise exceed $3 billion, a figure that North American sports executives can only dream of. Despite this, a special issue of the *Journal of Sports Economics* has been devoted to "the crisis in football," while *Business Week* has asked "Can Football Be Saved?"[52] Given the data in Table 3.4, why does soccer need saving?

In fact, the financial picture facing many soccer teams is very bleak. While the top soccer teams compare very well with the top North American teams, operating income and market value drop off very quickly. The value of the Glaslow Rangers, the twenty-fifth most valuable soccer team in the world, is only $194 million. Thus, relatively few clubs prosper, while most of them struggle financially. Of the 25 most valuable franchises, 17 operate in just two countries, England and Germany.[53] Despite the passion for the sport and the outstanding performance of the national teams, no Latin American country has

TABLE 3.4

Soccer Club Values, Revenues, and Operating Incomes, 2009 ($ Millions)

Team	Country	Market Value	Revenue	Operating Income
Manchester United	England	1,870	512	160
Real Madrid	Spain	1,353	576	81
Arsenal	England	1,200	349	80
Bayern Munich	Germany	1,110	465	59
Liverpool	England	1,010	332	50
AC Milan	Italy	990	330	58
Barcelona	Spain	960	487	108
Chelsea	England	800	424	−13
Juventus	Italy	600	264	46
Schalke 04	Germany	510	234	41

Source: "Soccer Team Valuations," June 4, 2009, at http://www.forbes.com/lists/2009/34/soccer-values-09_Soccer-Team-Valuations_Rank.html.

---

[52]*Journal of Sports Economics,* vol. 7, no. 1 (February 2006); Jack Ewing, Laura Cohn, Maureen Kline, and Rachel Tiplady, "Can Football Be Saved?" *BusinessWeek Online* (July 19, 2004) online at www.businessweek.com.

[53]"Soccer Team Valuations," June 4, 2009, at http://www.forbes.com/lists/2009/34/soccer-values-09_Soccer-Team-Valuations_Rank.html.

a club in the top 25. Thus, European clubs employ almost all the top Latin American (and African and Asian) players.

The divide between rich and poor is not merely geographic. In England and Italy, for example, teams outside the top division (the Premier League and Serie A) have difficulty making a profit. Twenty-two of the seventy-two Football League clubs outside England's Premier League effectively declared bankruptcy at some point between 2000 and 2006.[54]

Profit Maximization in Soccer

As we saw earlier in this chapter, profit maximization is one of several possible motivations for a team owner in North America. The same can be said for European soccer teams. The Russian oligarch Roman Abramovich probably did not have profits on his mind when he bought a controlling interest in Chelsea of England's Premier League. Instead, his motivation was probably more in line with Mark Cuban's reasons for buying the Dallas Mavericks. Similarly, soccer enthusiasts from entertainer Elton John to Libyan dictator Muammar Qadafi have bought a financial interest in soccer teams (Watford and Juventus, respectively).

There are, moreover, broader social forces that have traditionally limited profit seeking by team owners. In England, the limits were remnants of the social hierarchy that surrounded the origins of the sport. As recently as 1982, the Football League, which oversees the four top divisions of soccer in England, prohibited teams from paying salaries to club directors.[55] Thus the business practices of English soccer teams have only recently begun to resemble those of North American teams. One example of the odd decisions that resulted from the lack of professional management came in 1967, when what is now the Premier League "rejected a BBC proposal of a million pounds for live broadcast of championship matches."[56] This is tantamount to the NFL's refusing to allow the networks to broadcast the Super Bowl.

In some countries, outside authorities limit the activities of teams. In France, the national soccer association strictly limits the teams' ability to borrow and spend. In Germany, the fact that loans must be personally guaranteed by team officials constrains the amount that teams will borrow.[57] Both sets of limitations have restricted the ability of teams to obtain top-flight players, but they have also kept teams from overextending themselves financially.

The greater role of government in European economies placed another limit on team profits by limiting broadcast revenue. Unlike the United States,

---

[54]Umberto Lago, Rob Simmons, and Stefan Szymanski, "The Financial Crisis in European Football," *Journal of Sports Economics*, vol. 7, no. 1, February 2006, pp. 3–12.

[55]Szymanski and Zimbalist (2005), p. 132.

[56]Wladimir Andreff and Paul D. Staudohar, "European and US Sports Business Models," *Transatlantic Sport*, Carlos Pestana Barros, Muradali Ibrahimo, and Stefan Szymanski, eds. (Cheltenham, UK: Edward Elgar, 2002), p. 25.

[57]Lago et al. (2006), p. 8.

European countries have only recently opened the airwaves to private broadcasters. With limited access to television, soccer broadcasts and broadcast revenues lagged badly behind those of the North American sports. For example, in the 1970s, when television had already become a dominant economic force for North American teams, teams in the top division of French soccer still derived over 80 percent of their revenue from ticket sales.[58]

With the growth of private TV stations, particularly on cable, television revenue has played an increasingly important role in the finances of European soccer teams. Today, French teams in Ligue 1 derive over 50 percent of their revenues from television. The same can be said for leagues in England, Italy, Germany, and Spain.[59] Aware of the value of integrating the game with the broadcast of the game, large cable companies have come to hold increasing stakes in teams themselves. Silvio Berlusconi's purchase of AC Milan through his broadcast company Fininvest is only one of many prominent cable broadcasters to invest in soccer teams.

The Impact of Promotion and Relegation

Unlike MLB, the NBA, the NFL, or the NHL, the membership in a typical soccer league is not fixed. Each year, the three worst teams in most soccer leagues are **relegated** to a lower division, while the three best teams in the next division are **promoted** to a higher one. Imagine baseball's Colorado Rockies' being sent down to the International League and replaced in the National League by the Columbus Clippers, and you have an idea of what promotion and relegation can do.

The fact that a team could move from one league to another and back again greatly complicates the structure of and relationship between leagues. At minimum, one needs an overall authority to oversee the relationships between the various leagues. Table 3.5 shows the various affiliations that exist in English soccer (other nations have similar structures).

In the English Premier League, television revenues are impressive. Their most recent contract with British Sky Broadcasting Group PLC covers the 2010

TABLE 3.5

Organizational Structure of English Soccer

Organization	Jurisdiction
Premier League	20 Best teams
Football League	92 Teams in top 4 leagues
Football Association	500 + Teams in all leagues
UEFA	Football clubs throughout Europe
Champions League	32 Best football clubs in UEFA
FIFA	Football clubs worldwide

---

[58]Andreff and Staudoher (2002), p. 25.

[59]Szymanski and Zimbalist (2005), p. 160.

through 2013 seasons and pays the teams a combined sum of $2.85 billion.[60] Historically, teams in Italy's Serie A went one step farther. They did not even share revenue with each other. As a result, Juventus and AC Milan had television revenues 20 times greater than smaller clubs. A recent vote of Serie A teams was 19–1 in favor of creating their own Premiership League, set to begin in 2010–2011. Under the new agreement teams would share revenue equally.[61]

The very best Premier League teams also have the chance to play in yet another league. Each year, the Union of European Football Associations (UEFA) holds a playoff among the top teams in each country to play in the Champions League, an elite group of 32 teams to determine the European Champion.[62] Teams earn substantial rewards if they advance far in the Champions League playoffs. According to Forbes.com the 32 clubs in the Champions League in 2008–2009 will share about $818 million, with the winning club receiving over $33 million in prize money. After including revenue from gate receipts, media rights, and increased value of the teams' players, winning the Champions League could be worth in excess of $150 million.[63]

Finally, continental organizations such as UEFA answer to the Federation International de Football Association (FIFA). FIFA is best known for the World Cup championship it stages every four years. In the World Cup competition, players return from their club teams to their home countries to compete as a nation.

One last source of revenue for soccer teams stems from the open system of relegation and promotion and explains how top Czech or Argentinean players wind up playing for Italian or Spanish teams. Many soccer teams keep themselves financially afloat by developing talented young players and then selling their rights to wealthier teams. Thus, a wealthy team such as Manchester United might purchase the rights to players from small "provincial" English teams, from teams from relatively poor countries such as Ukraine or Brazil, and from financially conservative teams such as many French teams (thanks in part to the strict regulation mentioned earlier). This practice is more acceptable in an open system of promotion and relegation than in a fixed, closed system because teams face a natural limit to the sales they are willing to make. If a relatively small team, such as Coventry, sells too many of its players, it will find itself relegated to a lesser league with a subsequent reduction in revenues. A team in a closed system faces no such disciplinary force. As we saw earlier in the chapter, the Chicago Bulls were able to pursue two different paths to high profits: high costs paired with higher revenues and low revenues paired with even lower costs. Few teams in an open system would be willing to take such a risk.

---

[60]Aaron O. Patrick and Dana Cimilluca. "English Soccer's Morning After," June 5, 2009, at http://online.wsj.com/article/SB124346762522860417.html.

[61]"Serie A Clubs Form Their Own Premiership," June 5, 2009, at http://www.footballeconomy.com/world.htm.

[62]This happens on each continent. For example, in South America the Confederacion Sudamericana de Futbol (CONMEBOL) stages the Copa Toyota Libertadores.

[63]Paul Maidment. "Rich Spoils from Soccer's Biggest Match," June 5, 2009, at http://www.forbes.com/2009/05/26/manchester-barcelona-uefa-business-sports-football.html.

The Financial Dangers of an Open System

Promotion brings a huge reward to the top teams in England's Premier League while relegation brings a huge penalty. This winner-take-all (or at least winner-take-most) structure provides a strong incentive for teams on the border of promotion or relegation to invest heavily in players who will ensure promotion or stave off relegation. If this effort fails, however, a team can find itself with a bloated payroll and diminished revenues.

The incentive to invest heavily in players does not apply just to teams at the bottom of the Premier League. Elite teams also face pressure to ensure inclusion in the Champions League. The dangers of spending heavily can be seen in the sad case of Leeds United (a team particularly close to one coauthor's heart). In the late 1990s the team's management spent heavily in an effort to win the European Championship. The team lost in the 2001 semifinals, however, costing the team about $18 million in lost revenue. Worse yet, Leeds failed to qualify for the Champions League the next season. With revenues far below expectations, the team had no choice but to sell off many of its high-price players. By 2005, the team had been relegated from the Premier League.[64] As of 2009, Leeds remains in League One, with no immediate prospect of moving back up to the Premier League.

The Single Entity Ownership Model

All of the leagues we have discussed so far have one thing in common: They operate based on what is known as a franchise model. Each team is owned by a different individual or corporation and is free to pursue its own strategy regarding profits and wins. These teams also make all of their own player personnel decisions such as who to draft, who to retain, and who to dismiss. Although this model of ownership is popular, especially among long-established sports, many of the newer leagues in sports that do not have the following of baseball or men's basketball have adopted a different ownership model: the single entity league.

In a single entity league, investors purchase a share in the league itself rather than purchase an individual team or share of a team. All operations of the league are made by the central league offices, including the allocation of players to teams.[65] This includes negotiation of player contracts, marketing and advertising decisions, and other expenditures. The advantage of this structure is the ability to manage costs across all teams—eliminating large market, small market disparities.[66] The challenge for single entity leagues is to be able to cater

---

[64]See Szymanski and Zimbalist (2005), p. 139.

[65]Roger G. Noll, "The Organization of Sports Leagues," *Oxford Review of Economic Policy*, vol. 19, no. 4, Winter 2003, p. 530.

[66]Tripp Mickle and Terry Lefton, "Several Leagues Later, Debate on Single Entity Model Still Lively," *Street and Smith's Sports Business Journal*," August 4, 2008, online at http://www .sportsbusinessjournal.com/index.cfm?fuseaction=article.printArticle&articleId=59720.   Accessed June 8, 2009.

to demand differences across local markets. The advantage of the franchise system is that individual team owners can make decisions that they believe are best for their own team rather than have to bow to a single decision that may be good for some teams, but not for others.

Interestingly, the new women's professional soccer league that began play in early 2009 is not a single entity league. The decision to structure the league using the franchise model may have been driven in part by the failure of the predecessor league, the WUSA. Some leagues are transitioning from the single entity model to a franchise model, such as MLS and the women's professional basketball (WNBA). Thus, while it seems clear that established leagues in well known sports prefer the franchise model, it appears that there is no single answer as to which league structure is best for emerging sports.

BIOGRAPHICAL SKETCH

BILL VEECK

People need people (who else is there to take advantage of?)

—*Bill Veeck*[1]

Many owners have won more games than Bill Veeck did with the Cleveland Indians (1946–1949), St. Louis Browns (1951–1953), and Chicago White Sox (which he owned twice, 1959–1961 and 1975–1980). It is safe to say, however, that no owner in the history of the game had nearly as much fun. Veeck was literally born into baseball—his father was president of the Chicago Cubs—and he never left. In the 1920s, young Bill helped plant the ivy that now covers the wall at Wrigley Field.

A self-described hustler, Veeck was a showman *nonpareil* who gave baseball such attractions as bat day and the exploding scoreboard, and such disasters as "disco demolition night," at which a sellout Chicago crowd went out of control after thousands of disco records were blown up. Veeck also proposed many innovations that

baseball adopted only after he had passed from the scene. In his 1969 memoir, *The Hustler's Handbook,* for example, Veeck proposed using the scoreboard to do a variety of things—to review disputed plays or to inform the fans about the type and speed of pitch that had just been thrown—that teams took decades to implement.

Bill Veeck had an innate sense of how the market and social justice come together. Between 1947 and 1964, only two American League teams other than the New York Yankees—the Cleveland Indians and the Chicago White Sox—won pennants, and only one won a World Series. Veeck was the owner of the Cleveland Indians when they won the 1948 World Series, and he built the team that appeared in the 1954 World Series. He was later the owner of the Chicago White Sox when they made it to the 1959 World Series, their first such appearance since the

continued

Black Sox scandal of 1919. One other factor that distinguished these teams was that they were among the leaders in integrating the American League. Veeck brought Larry Doby to the Indians in 1947, a few weeks after Jackie Robinson broke the color line with the Brooklyn Dodgers. Veeck was also responsible for bringing the legendary Satchel Paige, regarded by most as the greatest pitcher in the history of the Negro Leagues, to the major leagues while he owned the Indians. In 1943, the Philadelphia Phillies were one of the worst teams in baseball and one of the least popular. Veeck tried to integrate baseball when he sought to buy the sad sack Phillies and stock the team with players from the Negro Leagues. Veeck had long opposed baseball's color line on moral grounds, but he also felt that integrating the game made good business sense. He thought that bringing in star players from the Negro Leagues would build a talented, exciting team that fans would want to see. According to Veeck, MLB Commissioner Kenesaw Mountain Landis stepped in at the last minute and found another buyer for the Phillies, preventing his purchase of the team.

Veeck also showed a sense of fairness as an outspoken critic of baseball's reserve clause, which effectively bound a player to a team for life. He went so far as to testify against the reserve clause in Curt Flood's lawsuit against baseball in the 1970s.[2]

Needless to say, Veeck's unorthodox beliefs and promotions did little to endear him to the other owners. They went so far as to block his attempt to move the Browns from St. Louis to Baltimore, allowing the move only after Veeck had sold the team. In St. Louis, the Browns were poor relations of the Cardinals. In an attempt to boost interest in his team, Veeck tried such stunts as sending 3'7" Eddie Gaedel to the plate as a pinch hitter—he walked—and holding "You Be the Manager Day," in which fans were given the opportunity to make substitutions and determine strategy. Predictably, some owners attempted to block Veeck's attempt to get back into baseball in the 1970s.

Veeck's last go-round as an owner—his second stint with the Chicago White Sox—was not as successful as his previous efforts. The advent of free agency and the growing importance of TV and venue revenue did not fit his limited means and hustler mentality. He was forced to sell the team after seven years. Fortunately, Bill's son Michael, the part owner of several minor league teams, has kept the Veeck legacy alive. As owner of the St. Paul Saints, Michael Veeck staged such stunts as "Mime-O-Vision," in which mimes acted out the action on the field as a sort of living instant replay. The fans responded by pelting the mimes with hot dogs, a travesty trumpeted by headlines in all the local papers. Michael's father would have been proud.

[1]Bill Veeck, *The Hustler's Handbook*, p. 196.
[2]We discuss Flood's lawsuit in Chapter 4 and analyze the reserve clause in Chapter 8.

Sources: Bill Veeck, *The Hustler's Handbook* (Durham, N.C.: Baseball America Classic Books, 1996); and John Helyar, *Lords of the Realm* (New York: Ballantine Books, 1994).

Summary

This chapter describes how professional sports teams go about maximizing profits. Teams derive their revenue from ticket sales, other venue-related income, the sale of broadcast rights, and licensing income. The degree to which revenues are shared among teams varies from league to league, with the most sharing occurring in the NFL. An interesting finding with respect to revenue sharing is that while it may promote league stability, it does not appear to improve the competitive balance in a league.

In the sports industry, most sources of cost are fixed over the period of a single season. Primary sources of costs are player salaries, stadium leases, and administrative costs. In the NHL and MLB, subsidies to minor league affiliates for player development also add significantly to team total cost.

In addition to individual actions, teams use leagues to stabilize revenues and control costs. In some cases, it is more useful to view the league as the monopoly and teams as producers of a joint product. In the next chapter, we look in detail at the monopoly aspects of professional sports.

European soccer teams face a very different business climate than do North American sports teams. While some teams are highly profitable, most struggle financially. This is partly due to the fact that soccer has only recently been regarded as a business and partly due to the relegation and promotion system.

Discussion Questions

1. What do you predict about the popularity of PGA tour events if it was a virtual certainty that Tiger Woods would win every week?

2. How would professional leagues be different if teams only had corporate affiliation (e.g., the IBM Lions) rather than city or state affiliation?

3. Why aren't more teams separate, publicly traded corporations, as the Boston Celtics are, rather than held privately?

4. Why might a team not want to be too much better than its rivals?

5. Discuss the costs and benefits of expanding the NFL to include European teams.

6. Why do owners need to get the permission of the league to change cities?

7. What motivations were behind the proposal that MLB contract by eliminating two teams?

Problems

3.1 Suppose that you were the owner of a professional baseball team in a major city. If the league decided to allow a second team in your city, as long as you were compensated for this infringement, on what basis could the appropriate compensation be determined?

3.2 Draw a graph that shows the demand for seats at an NFL stadium. Show how demand for attendance at a given game would be affected if:

a. The prices of parking and food at the games increase.

b. Televised games switch from free TV to pay-per-view only.

c. A new league forms with a team that plays nearby.

d. The quality of the team decreases dramatically.

e. The length of the season is increased.

3.3 True or false; explain your answer: "If all teams are of equal quality, it doesn't matter whether they share gate receipts or not—revenue will remain unchanged."

3.4 Some researchers argue that revenue sharing is like socialism in that it removes the incentive to outperform rivals. Do you agree with this statement? Why or why not?

3.5 Suppose that each team in a league has a demand curve for generic advertising (a league-wide, nonteam–specific campaign) equal to $Q = 1,000 - 5p$. If there are 20 teams in the league, and ads cost \$175 each, how many ads will the teams want to purchase as a group?

3.6 Use the marginal revenue and marginal cost curves from the theory of clubs to explain why the NFL has 32 teams, while Bundesliga-1, the top German soccer league, has only 20 teams.

3.7 Suppose that most of the teams in a given league are owned by individuals, while two are owned by corporations. If the profits of the individually owned teams rise, but the corporate owned teams remains flat, is it fair to say that this is an inferior ownership structure? Why or why not?

3.8 Suppose an owner pays \$500 million to purchase a hockey team that earns operating profits of \$50 million per year. The new owner claims that \$200 million of this price is for the players, which he can depreciate using straight-line depreciation in five years. If the team pays corporate profit taxes of 40 percent, how much does the depreciation of the players save the owner?

3.9 How can it be that the Washington Nationals, one of the weakest teams in the National League from a wins-losses perspective, be one of the most profitable?

3.10 Why might a league favor a single entity ownership model? Explain the differences in the risks and rewards of such a system compared to a franchise owner system.

CHAPTER 4

Monopoly and Antitrust

Gentlemen, we have the only legal monopoly in the country, and we're [messing] it up.

—ATLANTA BRAVES OWNER, TED TURNER[1]

Introduction

Major League Baseball's National League is the oldest professional sports league in the United States.[2] Founded in 1876, it rested on two basic principles:

1. The exclusive right of member clubs to their home territory

2. A reserve system that bound players to member ball clubs for as long as the team wanted them

These rules proved so profitable that many succeeding North American sports leagues adopted them for themselves, often word for word. One need not look far to see why the system was so successful. The principle of "territorial rights" gave teams **monopoly power** in their host cities, as it precluded the entry of competing teams. The reserve system kept owners from bidding up salaries in order to lure away a rival team's players, giving each team **monopsony power** over its players. Baseball and all subsequent sports owe much of their early success to these two barriers.

While eliminating competition may be good for the teams, it imposes a cost on society. One of the themes of Chapter 2 was that competitive markets do a good job of allocating resources to their most appropriate use. Some segments of society may not like the resulting distribution of resources, but any attempt to override the forces of supply and demand typically leaves society worse off than before. The benefits of a free market, however, stem from the very

---

[1]Quoted in John Helyar, *Lords of the Realm* (New York: Villard Books, 1994), p. 268.

[2]The fact that it predates the American League by about 25 years has led to its nickname, "the senior circuit."

competition that leagues have always sought to suppress. This chapter will explore the nature and impact of monopoly and monopsony power in organized sports and how sports have frequently run afoul of our nation's attempts to rein in the power of monopolies and monopsonies. In the process, it will explain the following:

- Why teams sell personal seat licenses

- Why teams might charge fans more for tickets to some games than others

- Why the NFL has such a lucrative TV contract and why, until recently, European soccer leagues have not

- How the NCAA accidentally became a cartel, and why it was sued by its own members

This chapter explains how leagues have obtained and maintained their monopoly power. To keep the focus on output markets, we save most of the discussion of the economics of monopsony (the market in which there is only one buyer) for Chapter 8. However, because the legal challenges to the monopoly power of professional sports leagues have often been bound up with challenges to their monopsony power, we shall briefly introduce the notion of monopsony and chart the legal challenges to monopsony as well as monopoly power.

4.1 What's Wrong with Monopoly?

As we saw in Chapter 2, monopolies operate where marginal revenue equals marginal cost, whereas perfectly competitive firms set price equal to marginal cost. Figure 4.1 illustrates the profit maximizing attendance level for a monopoly team with a marginal cost curve that coincides with the horizontal axis, and downward-sloping demand and marginal revenue curves. A competitive industry would sell Q_c tickets, where price equals marginal cost.[3] The NFL's market power allows it to restrict output to Q_m, charging a higher price ($20 in this case) and selling fewer tickets.

Monopolists and Deadweight Loss

Most noneconomists dislike monopolies because of the high prices they charge. High prices, however, are a two-edged sword. They may hurt the consumers who have to pay them, but they benefit the stockholders, employees, and other stakeholders in the firms that receive them. In Figure 4.1, consumers pay an amount equal to the area *EFBG* because they pay a price per unit equal to segment *EF* on *EG* units of output. While this exceeds the competitive price (zero in this example), society—which consists of both consumers and producers—is

---

[3]Strictly speaking, the industry supply curve is the horizontal sum of all the individual marginal cost curves. For our purposes here, we ignore any complication raised by capacity constraints.

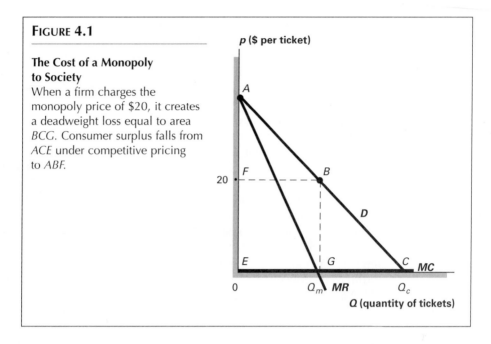

FIGURE 4.1

The Cost of a Monopoly to Society
When a firm charges the monopoly price of $20, it creates a deadweight loss equal to area *BCG*. Consumer surplus falls from *ACE* under competitive pricing to *ABF*.

not necessarily worse off, because producers receive *EFBG* more than if they charged the competitive price. Thus, higher prices reshuffle income without changing the total amount of income that society has. The higher price simply takes money from one pocket (the consumer's) and puts it in another (the monopolist's). Because one cannot say whether the higher prices that monopolies charge help or harm society, economists treat them as a transfer from consumers to producers, which brings no overall change in society's well-being.

Economists are much more concerned about the impact of the decline in output that accompanies monopoly. In particular, they worry about how monopoly affects the sum of consumer surplus and producer surplus. Consumer surplus stems from the fact that, despite our protestations to the contrary, we never would be satisfied "getting exactly what we paid for." In fact, if all we got out of an item was what we paid for it, we would be just as happy without it.[4] **Consumer surplus** is the net value that flows to consumers because not all consumers are charged the maximum that they are willing to pay. **Producer Surplus** is the net value that flows to producers because not all units are sold for the minimum that the producer would accept to sell them. It is straightforward to measure consumer surplus on a graph. It is equal to the area that lies under the demand curve and above the price up to the last unit sold. In Figure 4.1, at a price of $20, consumer surplus is the area *ABF*.

---

[4]Producer surplus is the extra revenue that a firm receives beyond what it requires to sell a given level of output. It is related to—but not identical to—profit. Economists calculate producer surplus as the area between the supply (or marginal cost) curve and the market price.

To see how consumer surplus arises, consider the case of four football fans. Debbie loves the Carolina Panthers and is willing and able to pay $40 for a ticket to see them play. Bill also likes to go to Panther games, though not as much as Debbie; he is willing and able to pay $20. Jeff is still less enthusiastic; he is willing and able to pay $10. Kathleen has no interest in seeing the Panthers play; she is willing and able to pay $0.

If consumers must pay the competitive price of $0 from Figure 4.1, all four consumers buy tickets to see the Panthers, but none of them feels the same way about his or her purchase. Since Debbie is willing and able to pay $40 for the ticket but pays $0, she gets a bonus—or consumer surplus—of $40 (the vertical segment YY in Figure 4.2). Similarly, Bill has a surplus of $20 (the vertical segment ZZ), Jeff has a surplus of $10 (the segment WW), and Kathleen has no surplus whatever. Kathleen is the only consumer who "gets what she pays for." She is willing and able to pay exactly what the Panthers charge her. Purchasing the ticket leaves her no better off—and no worse off—than before. Economists refer to a person in Kathleen's position as a **marginal consumer,** since she is indifferent between buying and not buying. She could just as easily pass up the ticket as buy it.

In fact, thousands of consumers, all with their own desires and abilities to pay, want Panthers tickets. As a result, there are hundreds or thousands of vertical segments indicating consumer surplus for the fans who buy tickets. Eventually, these segments fill up the triangle formed by the demand curve and the horizontal line representing the market price (the horizontal axis in Figure 4.2).

If the Panthers charged the monopoly price of $20, Kathleen would suffer a loss if she bought the ticket because she would pay $20 more than she was

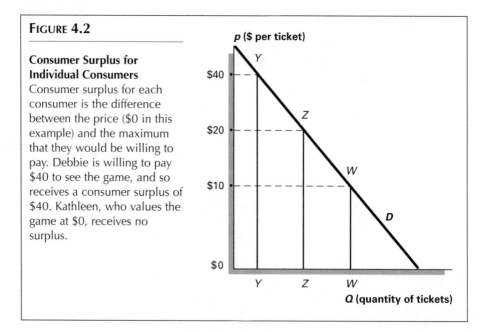

FIGURE 4.2

Consumer Surplus for Individual Consumers
Consumer surplus for each consumer is the difference between the price ($0 in this example) and the maximum that they would be willing to pay. Debbie is willing to pay $40 to see the game, and so receives a consumer surplus of $40. Kathleen, who values the game at $0, receives no surplus.

willing and able to pay. As a result, she no longer buys the ticket. Jeff, too, would suffer a loss and would not buy the ticket. Bill would now be the marginal consumer, because he is paying exactly what the ticket is worth to him. Only Debbie would enjoy a consumer surplus, though her surplus is much smaller than it had been ($20 instead of $40). More generally, when a monopoly serves the market, consumers buy fewer tickets, and consumer surplus shrinks. In terms of Figure 4.1, consumer surplus would be *ACE* if the market for tickets were perfectly competitive. Because the equilibrium price in this example is zero, consumer surplus is the entire area under the demand curve. When the same market is a monopoly, consumers pay an amount equal to *EFBG*. As a result, consumer surplus shrinks to *ABF*. In addition to the rectangle *EFBG*, consumers also lose the area of the triangle *BCG* because they buy less than before. This loss is not offset by gains elsewhere. Economists call losses that do not have offsetting gains elsewhere in the economy **deadweight losses.** The deadweight loss *BCG* that accompanies monopoly reduces the well-being of society.

Some economists, in particular those who belong to a particular school of thought known as **public choice,** believe that the social costs of monopoly exceed the deadweight loss of triangle *BCG* in Figure 4.1. These economists regard the expenditure the monopolist makes to obtain and protect its market position—behavior they call **rent seeking**—as an unproductive expenditure that adds to society's deadweight loss. They would claim that the $1.2 million that baseball spent lobbying Congress in 2001 represented an effort by baseball to protect its monopoly power.[5] As such, it imposed an additional cost on society, since that money could have been spent in more productive ways. In the limit, the monopolist would be willing to spend up to the total gains from its monopoly position, the area of the rectangle *EFBG*.[6] As a result, the total cost to society could be as large as the original deadweight loss plus the revenue of the monopolist (*BCG* + *EFBG*).

Promotion, Relegation, and Monopoly Power

In Chapter 3, we saw that the promotion and relegation system can cause soccer teams to behave differently from teams in the North American leagues. Perhaps the most important difference lies in the consequences of an open league for monopoly power. A closed league can create local monopoly power because it is limited to a fixed set of teams. New teams can enter the league only with the permission of the existing teams.[7]

---

[5]"Commissioner Spent $1.2 Million on Lobbying Congress in 2001," ESPN.com, at http://espn.go .com/mlb/news/2002/0515/1382924.html, May 16, 2002.

[6]See, for example, Richard Posner, "The Social Costs of Monopoly and Regulation," *Journal of Political Economy,* vol. 83, no. 4 (August 1975), pp. 807–827; Robert Tollison, "Rent Seeking," in *Perspectives on Public Choice: A Handbook,* ed. by Dennis Mueller (Cambridge, U.K.: Cambridge University Press, 1997); Associated Press, "Commissioner Spent $1.2 Million on Lobbying in 2001," ESPN.com, at http://www.espn.com, May 15, 2002.

[7]For a good discussion of open vs. closed leagues, see Noll (2003).

An open league has no such power. New teams can enter a low league, work their way up by being promoted to better leagues, and eventually compete at the highest level. Thus, while only the Giants and Jets were allowed to play the New York metropolitan area by the NFL, fourteen members of the Football League played in the London metropolitan area. Of these, five teams (Arsenal, Chelsea, Fulham, Tottenham Hotspur, and West Ham United) played in the premier league in 2008–2009. There is, moreover, no guarantee that this number could not rise even higher in the years ahead. Similarly, poor business or personnel decisions have caused some major metropolitan areas—such as Leeds, England or Florence, Italy—to go without a franchise in the top professional league. With no way to regulate entry or exit of competitors, it is very difficult for teams in open leagues to exercise local monopoly power.

Strategic Pricing and Price Discrimination

We know from Chapter 2 that monopolies have market power (the ability to set or control price). Unlike teams in open leagues with promotion and relegation, teams in U.S. leagues have substantial market power, which that stems from a lack of competition in their home markets, guaranteed by the structure of the league. Thus, teams are able to increase profits by setting price above marginal cost (the price that we would observe if the market were competitive). In this section, we describe ways in which a monopolist can increase its profits further by utilizing pricing strategies that are more sophisticated than simply using a single monopoly price for all games.

Variable Ticket Pricing   For a Red Sox fan, there is nothing like going to a game when the Yankees come to town. In the NHL, Chicago Blackhawk fans circle the date on the calendar when the always good (and popular) Red Wings visit. These are just two examples of what we intuitively know to be true: Some games are much more interesting to watch than others. Recall that the market demand curve is formed by adding the individual demand curves at each price. When individual fans have a greater desire to attend, the result is a market demand curve that lies farther to the right for desirable games than for undesirable games.

The quality of the opponent or the existence of a longstanding rivalry are not the only reasons for differences in demand. Differences may be due to the presence of a star player on the opposing team, promotional events such as giveaways and fireworks nights, the day of the week, and even the weather.[8] Rather than charge the same price for all games, teams can increase profits if they vary the price of tickets based from game to game. **Variable ticket pricing (VTP)** is the process of setting ticket prices in accordance with expected demand for a future game. When a team believes that demand for a given game will be lower, they can reduce the price to compensate. Conversely, they can

---

[8]Dan Rascher et al., "Variable Ticket Pricing in Major League Baseball," *Journal of Sport Management*, 2007, 21(3), pp. 407–437.

increase the price for a game they believe will be popular. For example, in 2009, the San Francisco Giants played a series against the New York Mets. For the first game, played on a cold Thursday night, upper deck prices were $1 off the usual $10 and bleacher seats were $2 off the usual $17. The next night, however, a weekend game with the Giants' best pitcher on the mound, those same seats went for $19 and $27. On Sunday, which featured a bobblehead doll giveaway, the Giants raised the price of a bleacher seat to $23. Some of these price adjustments were made very shortly before game day.[9] Variable ticket pricing appears to be gaining momentum across all professional sports. As of 2004, nine different MLB teams had variable pricing programs in place.[10]

Variable ticket pricing is also used in the NHL and NBA. The Buffalo Sabres, for example, have five different categories of prices for their games (not including the season ticket per game price). The highest category includes three games against nearby rival Toronto, plus a Friday night game against Montreal. The 2008–2009 price of a 200-level club seat for these "platinum" games was $233, while the same seat for a "value" (lowest) level game was just $99.[11] In the NBA, the Utah Jazz charged premium prices for certain seats at 10 select home games for 2008–2009, including games against Cleveland (with LeBron James) and against the Boston Celtics, one of the best teams in the NBA.[12] The NFL does not appear to make much use of variable ticket pricing, perhaps because with so few home games, relatively few empty seats exist for any given game regardless of opponent. Stephen Jones, Chief Operating Officer of the Dallas Cowboys, cited league parity and timing as reasons why variable pricing would be difficult in the NFL given that teams must finalize ticket prices long before they finalize rosters, moves that may alter team quality.[13]

From the team's perspective, differences in demand across games represent an opportunity to increase profits. When games are less popular, the team has an incentive to drop the price. With the marginal cost of attendance essentially zero, costs are about the same no matter how many fans attend. But, up to a point, revenues will increase as more fans buy tickets at lower prices. We can see the impact of variable vs. constant pricing in Figure 4.3. As usual, we assume that marginal cost is zero up to the point of stadium capacity (10,000). Demand for a less popular game is D_0, and demand for a more popular game is D_1. If the team uses a variable pricing strategy, it will set marginal revenue equal to marginal cost for each game ($MC = MR_0$ and $MC = MR_1$), resulting in prices of $6 and $10, respectively. The team will sell out the popular game

---

[9]Ken Belson, "Tickets Cost Too Much? Check Back Tomorrow," *The New York Times*, May 18, 2009. p. D-2.

[10]Rascher et al., 2007.

[11]"2008–09 Variable Pricing Schedule," June 10, 2009, at http://sabres.nhl.com/team/app/?service =page&page=NewsPage&articleid=369062.

[12]"Jazz Announces Variable Ticket Pricing Plan for Upcoming Season," June 9, 2009, at http://www .nba.com/jazz/tickets/0809_tickets_variablepricing.html.

[13]Darren Rovell, "Sports Fans Feel Pinch in Seat (Prices)," June 21, 2002, at http://espn.go.com/ sportsbusiness/s/2002/0621/1397693.html. Accessed June 10, 2009.

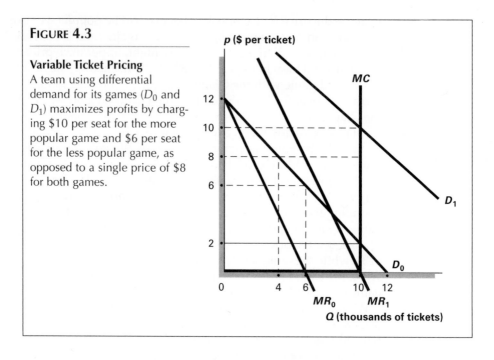

FIGURE 4.3

Variable Ticket Pricing
A team using differential demand for its games (D_0 and D_1) maximizes profits by charging $10 per seat for the more popular game and $6 per seat for the less popular game, as opposed to a single price of $8 for both games.

and sell 6,000 tickets to the less popular game. Total revenue for the two games is $136,000. You can see in the graph that if the team tried to sell tickets to the less popular game for $10, most of the seats would go unfilled. Similarly, if the team charged only $6 for the popular game, it would sell the same number of tickets as at the higher price but make 40 percent less in revenue. Suppose that instead of charging two prices, the team charged a single intermediate price, such as $8, for both games. We can easily show that such a strategy results in a price that is too high for the unpopular game, and too low for the popular game.[14] At a price of $8, the more popular game still sells out, but revenue falls from $100,000 to $80,000; for the less popular game, attendance falls to 4,000, resulting in revenue of just $32,000. Thus, overall revenue from charging a single price of $8 is $112,000, $24,000 less than the two-price scheme. This analysis is far from a theoretical abstraction. Rascher et al.'s results indicate that MLB teams would have increased ticket revenue by almost $600,000 in 1996 if they had charged variable prices.

In this story, teams maximize profit by maximizing ticket revenue. As Rascher et al. note, however, there are other revenue streams to consider. Parking and concessions are complements to tickets. As such, the team may do well to set ticket prices lower than would seem optimal because fans spend money on other goods once at the game.[15] There are limits to this strategy, however, as

---

[14]The equation for D_0 is $Q = 12 - P$. The equation for D_1 is $Q = 20 - P$.
[15]Rasher et al., 2007. They base this analysis on the work of Fort (2004).

total revenue from ticket sales begins to drop off quickly once marginal revenue becomes negative. For example, in the graph, at a price of $2 per ticket the less popular game will be a sellout. Lowering the price from $6 to $2, however, reduces ticket revenue from $36,000 ($6 × 6,000) to $20,000 ($2 × 10,000).

Bundling In addition to charging fans for individual games, teams can increase revenue by bundling games together. With **bundling,** a consumer who wants to buy good A must also buy good B (or perhaps many more goods, as in the case of season tickets.) With product bundling, firms take advantage of differing demand across products to capture some of the consumer surplus that might otherwise accrue to buyers. To illustrate this point, consider Joe, a huge Phillies fan who particularly likes to see them play their division rivals, the New York Mets. But because so many Phillies fans want to see the Mets game as well, and New York is close enough that many Mets fans can also see the game in Philadelphia, tickets can be hard to find. Fortunately for Joe, the Mets series is one that the Phillies have available as part of a "Grand Slam Four-Pack." The four-pack allows Joe to buy tickets to the Mets game as long as he also purchases tickets to three other games.[16]

To see how this pricing scheme benefits both Joe and the Phillies, let's assume that the tickets cost $30 per game for the Mets game. Joe is willing to pay $100 to see a Phillies–Mets game, but he would only pay $25 to see any other Phillies game. If the games were sold separately at the price of $30, he would go the to Mets game and receive a surplus of $70, but would not buy a ticket to the other games. Suppose, however, that Joe could see the Phillies–Mets game if he buys a four-pack of tickets. Unlike variable ticket pricing, bundling does not rely on setting different prices for each game. Instead, it relies on the large surplus consumers would receive from seeing a specific game. To see this, let's assume that all tickets are sold at the regular price, but must be purchased in a group of four (tickets to the four game set are priced at $120 [4 × $30]). Joe values the four tickets at $175 ($100 for the Mets game and $25 for the other three games). At a price of $120, he is better off making the purchase because he still receives a surplus of $55. Even though he experiences a loss of $5 on the three less popular games, the loss is more than offset by the surplus he receives from seeing the Mets game. The Phillies are better off as well because they sell tickets to four games instead of only one. With the marginal cost of Joe's attendance at these extra games at or close to zero, the Phillies' profits also increase.

Price Discrimination In our discussion of variable ticket pricing and bundling, teams used advanced pricing strategies based on differences in the perceived quality of the games by a given consumer. We now move on to a

---

[16]"Grand Slam Four Packs" at http://philadelphia.phillies.mlb.com/phi/ticketing/fourpacks.jsp. Tickets to the July and September 2009 Phillies–Mets series were offered as part of Grand Slam Four Packs. Accessed June 9, 2009.

different strategy that, as we'll see, relies on teams' identifying differences in willingness to pay *for the same game.*

Recall that in Figure 4.1, a single monopoly price led to a deadweight loss of area *BCG*, and left consumers with a surplus of area *ABF*. We know that consumer surplus is the extra benefit that consumers receive because the firm charges a single profit-maximizing price for all units it sells. Often, firms charge a single price to all consumers because they have no way to determine which consumers are willing to pay more, and consumers have no incentive to reveal their greater willingness to pay. If a monopolist could sort consumers by their willingness and ability to pay and set prices accordingly, it could capture some or perhaps even all consumer surplus. As we will see, such a pricing strategy also reduces or eliminates the deadweight loss associated with a single monopoly price. Economists call charging different prices to different consumers based on their willingness to pay **price discrimination.** Unlike the common use of the word *discrimination*, price discrimination has nothing to do with dislike for a particular demographic group. Instead, a firm price discriminates when it charges more to customers who are willing and able to pay more. On the surface, charging wealthy consumers a higher price than poor consumers sounds like the fair thing to do. We shall see, however, that firms that price discriminate seldom have such altruistic motives and that price discrimination does not leave consumers any better off.

If the Panthers know exactly how much Debbie, Bill, Jeff, and Kathleen are willing and able to pay, they can extract their consumer surplus by charging each person exactly what he or she thinks the ticket is worth. By charging Debbie $40, Bill $20, and Jeff $10, the Panthers turn all their consumers into marginal consumers.[17] All the consumers are now just willing to pay for the tickets because what was once their consumer surplus is now additional profit for the Panthers.

By treating each additional consumer like the marginal consumer, the Panthers no longer charge a lower price to everyone when they want to sell more tickets. The process of charging each consumer the maximum that he or she is willing to pay is known as **first-degree price discrimination.** By first degree (or perfectly) price discriminating, the Panthers' marginal revenue is the price of the last, cheapest ticket that it sells. The marginal revenue of selling a ticket to Bill is thus $20, while the marginal revenue of selling a ticket to Jeff is $10. In terms of Figure 4.1, if the Panthers can perfectly price discriminate, their *MR* curve coincides with their demand curve. The Panthers now sell the same number of tickets as a perfectly competitive industry, and total surplus grows to *ACE*. Social well-being is once again maximized, as the perfectly price-discriminating monopolist acts in an economically efficient manner. Consumers, however, do not receive any of the increase in social well-being. By charging all consumers exactly what the ticket is worth to them, the Panthers claim Debbie and Bill's consumer surplus for themselves. If the Panthers could perfectly

---

[17]Technically, the Panthers would have to charge $39.99, $19.99, and $9.99 to be sure that Debbie, Bill, and Jeff buy tickets. We round off for ease of exposition.

price discriminate, they would charge all of their fans exactly what they are willing and able to pay. This would enable the Panthers to capture all of the area *ACE* in Figure 4.1 as revenue.

Unfortunately for the Panthers, they have no way of perfectly discriminating among their consumers. They cannot figure out exactly how much each fan is willing and able to pay for a ticket to see them play. They can, however, make some reasonable guesses.

Even if the Panthers do not know how much Debbie, Bill, Jeff, and Kathleen are willing and able to pay, they can still practice **second-degree price discrmination** because they know that demand curves slope down. Second-degree price discrimination involves charging consumers different prices based on the quantity of the good they consume. The first form of second-degree price discrimination acknowledges that an *individual* demand curve slopes down. The Panthers know that the more games Debbie sees, the less she is willing or able to pay to see an additional game. They respond by charging Debbie less for season tickets than for separate tickets to each game.[18] Thus, second-degree price discrimination is similar to bundling, though it does not rely on differential quality of the good (game).

Figure 4.4 shows Debbie's individual demand curve (for simplicity, we assume that no game is inherently more attractive to her) and the impact of second-degree price discrimination on Debbie's consumer surplus. If the Panthers

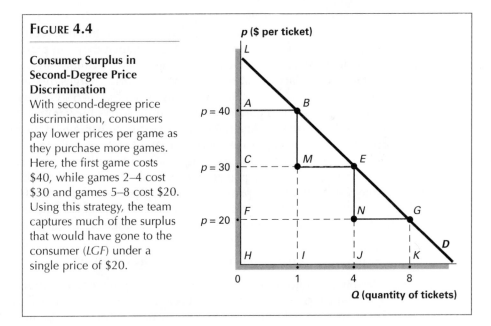

FIGURE 4.4

Consumer Surplus in Second-Degree Price Discrimination
With second-degree price discrimination, consumers pay lower prices per game as they purchase more games. Here, the first game costs $40, while games 2–4 cost $30 and games 5–8 cost $20. Using this strategy, the team captures much of the surplus that would have gone to the consumer (*LGF*) under a single price of $20.

---

[18]Debbie pays $130 = $40 + 3 games · $30/game for the four-game plan, and she pays $210 = $40 + 3 games · $30/game + 4 games · $20/game for the season ticket.

operate where marginal revenue equals marginal cost (Point *G* in Figure 4.4), they charge Debbie $20 for each ticket. In this example, Debbie buys tickets to eight home games, pays $160 for tickets, and enjoys consumer surplus *LGF*. Alternatively, suppose the Panthers offer a plan that charges $40 for an individual ticket, $130 for a four-game ticket plan, and $210 for a season ticket. In that case, the first ticket costs Debbie $40, the next three tickets cost her $30 each, and the last four tickets cost her $20 each. The rectangles *HABI, IMEJ,* and *JNGK* in Figure 4.4 show the cost of the incremental purchases as Debbie buys more tickets. They show that the Panthers can claim some of Debbie's consumer surplus if they charge her a price closer to her willingness and ability to pay. Some of Debbie's original consumer surplus (triangle *LGF*) is now taken up by the expenditure rectangles, reducing Debbie's consumer surplus to the sum of the three smaller triangles *LAB, BME,* and *ENG.*

The Panthers can also practice second-degree price discrimination by recognizing that *market* demand curves slope down. They may not know how much Debbie wants to pay, but they know that some members of her group are less willing or able to pay for tickets than others. The Panthers take advantage of this knowledge by offering group rates that are cheaper than tickets bought individually. Once a group is large enough, the individuals pay less for their tickets, inducing reluctant individuals to buy tickets.

Sometimes, the Panthers may know nothing about individuals, but they know that some groups are less willing or able to pay. For example, the Panthers may know that students on the whole have less disposable income and as a result are more sensitive to changes in price than are middle-aged adults.[19] If the Panthers can separate the student market from the adult market (e.g., by requiring students to show their university ID cards), then they can practice third-degree price discrimination by charging a higher price to adults than to students. **Third-degree price discrimination** occurs when a firm charges different prices for the same good in different segments of a market. Figure 4.5 shows what the Panthers can do if they can separate the demand by adults for Panthers tickets from the demand by students. Again ignoring capacity constraints, if the marginal cost of providing seats is approximately zero, the Panthers will maximize profit when the marginal revenue from selling to students and the marginal revenue from selling to adults both equal zero. Figure 4.5 shows that the $MR_s = MR_a = MC$ rule results in a lower price for students than for adults. In effect, the Panthers maximize profits by charging a lower price to consumers whose demand is more elastic and a higher price to those with less elastic demand.

Consumer Surplus and Personal Seat Licenses

Personal seat licenses (PSLs) are another way teams can extract consumer surplus and increase profits. PSLs became popular after the Carolina Panthers used them to help finance the construction of Ericsson Stadium (now Bank of America Stadium) in 1993. At first, the Panthers' use of PSLs had economists

---

[19]Senior citizens comprise another group that firms frequently feel is more sensitive to price.

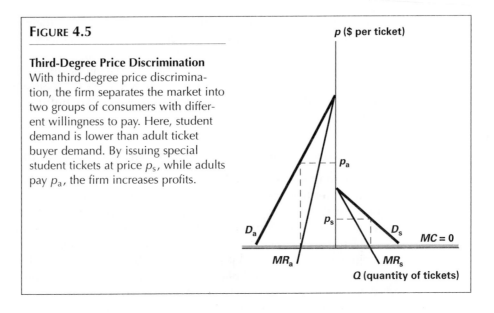

FIGURE 4.5

Third-Degree Price Discrimination
With third-degree price discrimination, the firm separates the market into
two groups of consumers with different willingness to pay. Here, student
demand is lower than adult ticket
buyer demand. By issuing special
student tickets at price p_s, while adults
pay p_a, the firm increases profits.

scratching their heads. The problem was that—on the surface—PSLs did not
make much sense.[20]

The idea of a PSL is very simple. A person pays a fixed fee for the right to
buy season tickets for a given period of time. One might naively conclude that
any additional fee enables teams to raise more money. Such reasoning, however, ignores the fact that when people decide to purchase tickets, they weigh
the benefits of seeing the ball games against the costs of seeing the games. The
benefits include the pleasure of spending an afternoon or evening at the ballpark, rooting for one's favorite team, while the costs include the price of tickets,
transportation, hot dogs, *and* PSLs. If teams charge an additional PSL fee, they
must either provide additional benefits to offset the higher costs or charge
lower prices for tickets. According to this argument, PSLs do not increase the
revenue flowing to the team; they simply change the way the team collects
money. Noll and Zimbalist justify the existence of PSLs by appealing to the
incentives provided by tax laws that allow teams to deduct revenues raised by
PSLs from their taxable income.

Teams might also use PSLs because they allow teams to claim the deadweight loss that ordinarily results from a monopoly. The Panthers could eliminate the deadweight loss by charging the competitive price for season tickets
and selling the competitive quantity. The lower price and higher quantity
restore consumer and producer surplus to their competitive levels. The
Panthers exert their monopoly power by charging the fixed PSL fee. The fee

---

[20]The argument that follows is based on Roger Noll and Andrew Zimbalist, "Build the Stadium—
Create the Jobs!" in *Sports, Jobs, and Taxes*, ed. by Roger Noll and Andrew Zimbalist (Washington,
D.C.: Brookings Institution Press, 1997), pp. 20–25.

allows them to claim some of the consumer surplus that their fans enjoy. If the Panthers knew exactly how much consumer surplus the typical fan enjoyed, they could charge a PSL fee that extracted almost all of his or her surplus. This would leave the fan just willing to buy the season ticket. The Panthers could thus keep all the benefits of a competitive market for themselves. Consumer surplus would expand to triangle *ACE* in Figure 4.6, but it would be claimed entirely by producers.

Monopoly Stood on Its Head: A Brief Introduction to Monopsony

Monopsony is essentially the mirror image of monopoly. Monopolists derive their power from being the only seller and use this power to drive up the price of what they sell. Monopsonists derive their power from being the sole consumer and use their power to drive down the price of what they buy.

Until the 1970s, sports leagues held monopsony power through specific language in the standard player contract, called the **reserve clause.** The reserve clause effectively bound players to the team that held their contracts for as long as the teams desired their services. Thus, a player such as Otto Graham, who had a Hall of Fame career with the Cleveland Browns in the 1950s, could not sell his services to any NFL team except the Browns. For Graham, playing

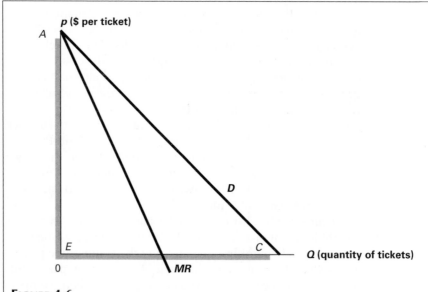

FIGURE 4.6

Consumer Surplus and Personal Seat Licenses
By charging season ticket holders a PSL fee, the team can increase profits by reducing the price to marginal cost ($0) in this example, and setting the PSL fee close the area *ACE,* which represents consumer surplus.

football in the NFL was indistinguishable from playing for the Browns. Facing no competition for Graham's services, the Browns could pay him a far lower salary than they would have if the Giants, Bears, or Rams could have bid for his services. We shall discuss the history and economics of the reserve clause in greater detail in Chapter 8.

Sometimes teams can also be the victims of monopsony power. As noted in Chapter 3, privately owned television stations are a relatively recent innovation in most countries. When only government-sponsored stations existed, sports leagues faced a single buyer for their broadcast rights. As a result, the revenues they received lagged badly behind those received by North American teams. In 1929, BBC radio went so far as to refuse to pay the Football Association for the right to broadcast the FA Cup Final.[21] The advent of private, pay TV broke the public stations' monopsony power and led to a dramatic rise in rights payment. In Italy, payments to Serie A and Serie B teams rose by almost 250 percent between 1993 and 1998.[22] While the payments to the NFL still dwarf those to soccer teams worldwide, television rights now bring teams in the major West European leagues tens of millions of dollars per year.

4.2   What's Right with Monopoly?

While monopolies often impose deadweight losses on society, the case against them is not always as straightforward as it may appear. First, it is not always so easy to identify a monopoly. For example, since Detroit has only one football team, the Lions, one might logically conclude that the Lions are a monopoly. The Lions, however, could plausibly claim that they are not a monopoly and that they actually operate in a very competitive environment. The key to this difference of opinion lies in the definition of the market in which the Lions operate. If the market is defined as one for an NFL team in the Detroit area, then the Lions are clearly a monopoly. The Lions could respond that such a definition is far too narrow. In the sports industry alone, the Lions must compete for attention with professional baseball, basketball, and hockey teams in and around Detroit. They also must contend with Football Bowl Subdivision (formerly Division I-A) football teams such as the University of Michigan and Michigan State University. If the market is expanded still further to include all possible leisure and cultural activities in the area, the market becomes very crowded, and the Lions begin to look like very small cats in a large jungle.

Even if the Lions fail to convince you that they are not a monopoly, they may be able to persuade you that their monopoly power arose from the natural functioning of the marketplace, not from any immoral or illegal actions on their part. In short, the Lions may claim that they are a **natural monopoly.** Natural monopolies result when large firms operate more efficiently than small firms do. If the

---

[21]Szymanski and Zimbalist (2005), p. 153.
[22]Baroncelli and Lago (2006), p. 17.

most efficient size of the firm is sufficiently large compared with the number of customers, there may be no room for competing firms to enter. **Large efficient size** generally results when firms face large start-up costs and low marginal costs.[23]

Figure 4.7a shows that a team such as the Lions may be a good example of a natural monopoly. As we illustrated in Chapter 2, a team's payroll is a fixed cost because the cost to the team will be the same regardless of its "output" as measured in tickets sold. Except for that part of rent that is tied to attendance, the expense of renting or building a stadium also adds to fixed costs. Because the marginal cost of accommodating an additional fan is effectively zero, the Lions' costs do not rise very much beyond this fixed amount until they reach the capacity of their stadium. Using these assumptions, we can approximate the **average cost,** or per-unit cost, of the Lions as

$$\text{Average cost} = \frac{\text{Total costs}}{\text{Quantity}} = \frac{\text{Fixed costs}}{\text{Number of tickets sold}}$$

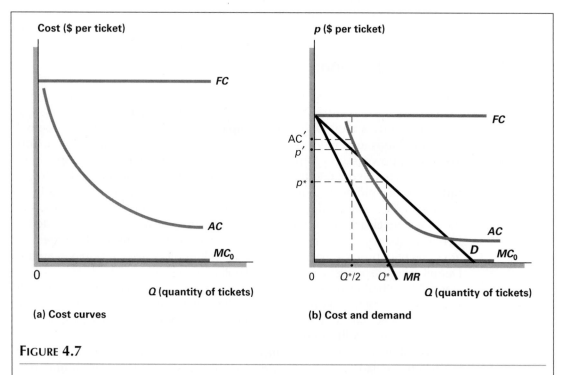

(a) Cost curves

(b) Cost and demand

FIGURE 4.7

Part (a) shows the cost curves for a natural monopoly. Average cost declines continuously. In part (b), the firm maximizes profits by setting price p^* and selling Q^*. If the firm were broken into two equal size smaller firms, each selling $Q^*/2$, both firms would suffer losses, as average cost (AC') exceed price (p').

[23]For a good discussion of natural monopoly and the general issue of antitrust policy as it applies to the NFL see Robert Heintel, "The Need for an Alternative to Antitrust Regulation of the National Football League," *Case Western Reserve Law Review*, vol. 46, no. 4 (Summer 1996), pp. 1033–1069.

As the number of tickets the Lions sell rises, their average cost gets closer and closer to MC_0. As a result, "bigger is better" to the Lions, since they can charge a lower price as their output rises and still cover their costs. Figure 4.7b again shows the cost curves for the monopolist and adds the demand and marginal revenue curves. The monopolist produces Q^* and charges p^*. Note that if another firm entered the market, and output were divided equally, neither firm would be profitable, as price (p') is less than average cost (AC). In such cases, as the term implies, the market structure naturally evolves to a single seller.

Leagues also claim that, while perfectly competitive markets increase the amount of the product and reduce its price, a league's monopoly power delivers other benefits to fans. One of the major benefits that MLB's monopoly power has conferred on baseball fans has been the relative stability of franchises. Owners who want to move their teams have traditionally had to seek the approval of the other owners. The failure of MLB's Pittsburgh Pirates and Chicago White Sox to secure approval was instrumental in preventing their moves to St. Petersburg. Leagues use these aborted moves as evidence that the monopoly power of leagues protects the interests of the hometown fans.

4.3 Barriers to Entry

Not all monopolies stem from the natural working of the market or from explicit governmental policy. Some monopolies owe their existence to the barriers created by the firms themselves. Sports leagues have become experts at erecting barriers to entry, and—when the barriers have failed to keep out competitors—at coopting the opposition.

In the 1960s, the battle lines in professional football reflected network battle lines. Fans of the National Football League tuned in to CBS, while devotees of the American Football League watched their games on ABC and then NBC. Today the NFL licenses its broadcasts to an alphabet soup of networks. In addition to providing a great source of revenue for the NFL, the variety of networks creates a crucial barrier to entry. Rival football leagues have long recognized that their livelihood depended on forming a lasting and profitable link with a television partner. The AFL owed its survival in the 1960s to the willingness of ABC and later NBC to pay for broadcast rights. The infusion of cash from network TV helped the AFL hang on through years of relatively low attendance. Much of the blame for the failure of the WFL in the 1970s and the USFL in the 1980s can be traced to their failure to get sufficient support from major television networks. The collapse of the XFL after only one season in 2002 stemmed largely from its steadily declining TV viewership.

As noted in Chapter 3, leagues can also forestall entry by locating franchises in the appropriate cities. In baseball, the American League found sufficient markets to enter thanks to the dogged refusal of the National League to admit more than eight franchises. The AFL tried to exploit a similar refusal to expand by the NFL in the late 1950s by planning flagship franchises for the rapidly growing cities of Dallas and Minneapolis. When the NFL got wind of these plans, it quickly convened an expansion meeting and awarded franchises to those same cities. This successfully prevented the AFL's entry into Minneapolis and doomed the Dallas entry to failure. The AFL sued, claiming that the NFL had awarded these franchises solely to monopolize professional football. Despite the admission by Redskins' owner George Preston Marshall that the NFL had awarded the franchises just to prevent the AFL from penetrating the markets, the AFL lost a bench verdict.[24]

4.4   Society's Response to Monopoly and Monopsony: Antitrust Laws

In 1890 the United States made its first concerted effort to combat monopolies and monopsonies with the Sherman Antitrust Act. The Sherman Act was later supplemented by the Clayton Act, which allowed private lawsuits to recover damages (which would then be trebled by the court) caused by subversion of the free market. The Sherman Act has two clauses:

1. Every contract, combination in the form of a trust or otherwise, or conspiracy, in restraint of trade or commerce among the several states, or with foreign nations is hereby declared to be illegal.

2. Every person who shall monopolize or attempt to monopolize any part of the trade or conspire with any other person or persons to monopolize any part of the trade or commerce among the several states or with foreign nations, shall be deemed guilty of a misdemeanor. . . . [25]

At first glance, the two clauses seem almost identical. The differences, while subtle, have been crucial in determining the course of antitrust suits against professional sports teams and leagues.

The first clause prohibits "independent entities that *ought* to be competing against one another from agreeing *not* to compete."[26] It prevents firms from joining together to form **cartels,** also known as *trusts* (hence the name of the act).

The second clause attacks monopolies themselves, regardless of how they are formed. It outlaws "conduct by a firm which creates, protects, or entrenches a dominant position in some relevant market."[27] Lawsuits brought under the second section, while well publicized, have generally had little impact on the sports industry.

---

[24]The AFL's Dallas Texans moved to Kansas City in 1963 to achieve great success as the Chiefs. See Gary Roberts, "Antitrust Issues in Professional Sports," in *Law of Professional and Amateur Sports*, ed. by Gary Uberstine (Deerfield, Ill.: Clark, Boardman, and Callaghan, 1992), pp. 19-8, 19-9; and James Quirk and Rodney Fort, *Pay Dirt* (Princeton, N.J.: Princeton University Press, 1992), pp. 346–347.

[25]Don E. Waldman, *Microeconomics* (Boston: Pearson Education, 2004), p. 340.

[26]Roberts, "Antitrust Issues" (1992), p. 19-10.

[27]Roberts, "Antitrust Issues" (1992), p. 19-4.

The courts have vacillated between two competing interpretations of the Sherman Act, which place very different standards on the litigants. The first standard, the *per se* standard, follows from a literal reading of the Sherman Act. It states that all monopolies are inherently bad and should be broken up. One need only establish that monopoly power exists for the *per se* standard to apply. The alternative reading of the antitrust laws, the "rule of reason," takes a more nuanced view of monopolies. According to this standard, society should be willing to tolerate monopolies if they have failed to exercise their monopoly power or if the benefits that flow from them (such as returns to scale or R&D) outweigh the costs of higher prices and lower output.

On the surface, leagues of any kind appear to violate antitrust legislation. By their very nature, leagues coordinate the actions of their member teams. The coordination can be relatively innocent, as in the establishment and enforcement of a common set of playing rules or the arranging of a commonly respected schedule. The coordination can also result in **collusion,** in which teams cooperate and act like one big monopoly. Critics say the result has been higher prices for tickets and broadcast rights and a restricted quantity of franchises due to limits on the entry of new teams and broadcast coverage of individual teams.[28]

As noted in Section 4.2, breaking up a natural monopoly sacrifices the economic efficiency that its size brings. Little is gained from antitrust action that creates many small, inefficient firms. Governments recognize this and try to retain the advantages that large size brings while limiting the ability of the natural monopoly to exploit its monopoly power. Governments try to **regulate** natural monopolies, requiring that they receive the approval of an oversight board before raising price. Those who feel that professional sports leagues are natural monopolies openly advocate regulating the sports industry to prevent it from earning monopoly profits.[29]

Sometimes governments allow monopolists to flex their muscle but limit the amount of time they have to do so. **Patents** give firms monopoly power over a specific process for 20 years (measured from the date the patent was filed). Similarly, copyright laws give monopoly power to those who produce intellectual property, such as movies or symphonies (or even catchphrases, such as when ex–Laker coach Pat Riley copyrighted the term "three-peat" when the Los Angeles Lakers seemed close to winning three consecutive NBA Championships in the 1980s).[30] When the patent or copyright expires, any firm may use the process or property free of charge. The government permits this limited monopoly to exist in order to promote innovation, experimentation,

---

[28]See, for example, Stephen Ross, "Should Congress Stop the Bidding War for Sports Franchises?", Hearing Before the Subcommittee on Antitrust, Business Rights, and Compensation, Senate Committee on the Judiciary, v. 4, November 29, 1994; "Academics," *Heartland Policy*, at http://www.heartland.org/stadps4.html.

[29]See, for example, Roberts, "Should Congress Stop the Bidding War for Sports Franchises?" (1994), pp. 4–5.

[30]See Todd Kantorczyk, "How to Stop the Fast Break: An Evaluation of the 'Three-Peat' Trademark," *UCLA Entertainment Law Review,* vol. 2 (1995), pp. 195–228.

and creative expression. The promise of monopoly power provides artists with the incentive to create and firms with an incentive to engage in costly and risky R&D.

Finally, the government explicitly rules out competition in some areas. For example, while competition may drive down costs, the United States government is unwilling to tolerate the existence of competing armies. At other times, the government may feel that other social aims merit granting a degree of monopoly power to producers. Most cities limit the number of vendors who may sell their wares outside. While this keeps prices higher than they would be if competing vendors could locate on city sidewalks, city governments are generally willing to tolerate the higher prices in order to improve the quality of urban life by avoiding congested sidewalks. In both cases, however, the government remains closely involved in the market. It carefully regulates licensed vendors and provides the military service itself.

4.5 An Important Anomaly: Baseball's Antitrust Exemption

Baseball occupies a unique place in the American economy. Unlike all other industries, it has long enjoyed an absolute exemption from all federal antitrust laws with no time limits, no governmental oversight, and no regulation of its pricing policies. Oddly, the courts and legislative branch recognized that baseball's exemption defies all legal and economic logic, yet they did nothing to terminate it for 75 years, and recent changes have been merely cosmetic, with no real effect.

Baseball owes its exemption to the last serious challenge to its monopoly position, the attempt by the Federal League to form a third major league in 1914 and 1915. The outlook for a third league seemed promising at the time. The successful entry by the American League to major league status in 1901 showed that a rival league could succeed, and the accommodation between the American and National Leagues prior to the 1903 season also caused considerable unrest among players, as salaries had been steadily falling since the leagues reached an agreement.[31]

As part of its assault on the two existing leagues, the Federal League filed an antitrust lawsuit against the 16 owners as well as the three members of the "National Commission" that oversaw the two major leagues. The lawsuit was based on both sections of the Sherman Act, as it charged the major leagues "with being a combination, conspiracy and monopoly."[32]

The Federal League filed its suit in the U.S. District Court of Northern Illinois before Judge Kenesaw Mountain Landis because Landis had acquired a reputation as a trustbuster. Unfortunately for the Federal League, he also

---

[31]Roger Abrams, *Legal Bases: Baseball and the Law* (Philadelphia: Temple University Press, 1998), pp. 53–60.

[32]The commission consisted of Ban Johnson, the president of the American League; John Tener, the president of the National League; and August Hermann, the owner of the Cincinnati (NL) team, who had been instrumental in brokering the peace between the National and American Leagues. See Harold Seymour, *Baseball: The Early Years* (New York: Oxford University Press, 1960), p. 212.

proved to be a rabid baseball fan. Landis scolded the Federal League's lawyers, saying that attacks on baseball "would be regarded by this court as a blow to a national institution."[33] After hearing the arguments, Landis refused to issue a ruling for over a year, by which time the major leagues had reached an agreement with all but one of the Federal League owners, driving the Federal League out of business.[34]

The one holdout was Ned Hanlon, the owner of the Federal League's Baltimore Terrapins. Hanlon was upset that his buyout offer of $50,000 was well below that offered to owners whose teams competed in cities with major league franchises.[35] He was also offended because Charles Comiskey, the owner of the Chicago White Sox, had called Baltimore a "minor league city, and not a hell of a good one at that," and that Charles Ebbets, owner of the Brooklyn Dodgers, had said that Baltimore was unfit to have a team because "you have too many colored population. . . ." Hanlon filed his own antitrust suit—*Federal Baseball Club of Baltimore, Inc.* v. *National League of Professional Baseball Clubs* (hereafter *Federal Baseball*)—and won an $80,000 settlement (trebled under the provisions of the Clayton Act to $240,000) in a Washington, D.C., Federal District Court. The judgment was overturned on appeal, whereupon Hanlon took his suit to the Supreme Court.[36]

In 1922 the Supreme Court ruled unanimously that baseball was not subject to antitrust laws. In his opinion for the court, Justice Oliver Wendell Holmes Jr. wrote that baseball was a "public exhibition, not commerce and that the interstate travel," which would have made baseball subject to federal legislation, was purely incidental to staging these exhibitions.

The rationale for this ruling has never been clear. Some claim that the Court feared that ruling against MLB would do irreparable damage in the wake of the "Black Sox" scandal in which eight members of the Chicago White Sox had been accused of conspiring with gamblers to throw the 1919 World Series. Others point out that Chief Justice William Howard Taft had played third base for Yale University's baseball team and was related to Philip Wrigley, the owner of the Chicago Cubs.[37]

Subsequent court decisions made baseball's exemption increasingly difficult to justify. The Supreme Court consistently denied other industries, particularly other sports, the right to use the *Federal Baseball* ruling as a precedent. Somehow, the Court maintained that other sports were commerce while baseball was not.

---

[33] Harold Seymour, *Baseball: The Golden Age* (New York: Oxford University Press, 1971), p. 212; and Abrams, *Legal Bases* (1998), p. 55.

[34] Seymour, *The Golden Age* (1971), pp. 212–213; and Andrew Zimbalist, *Baseball and Billions* (New York: Basic Books, 1992), p. 9.

[35] Some Federal League owners bought the Major League teams with which they competed. Wrigley Field was originally built for the Federal League's Chicago Whales. See Seymour, *Baseball: The Golden Age* (1971), pp. 215–243; and Zimbalist, *Baseball and Billions* (1992), p. 9.

[36] Abrams, *Legal Bases* (1998), p. 56; Seymour, *The Golden Age* (1971), p. 243; and John Johnson, "When a Professional Sport Is Not a Business: Baseball's Infamous Antitrust Exemption," in *Sports and the Law*, ed. by Charles Quirk (New York: Garland Publishers, 1996), p. 151.

[37] Abrams, *Legal Bases* (1998), p. 57; and Johnson, "Baseball's Infamous Antitrust Exemption" (1996), p. 151.

The Supreme Court's 1955 ruling in an antitrust lawsuit that the U.S. government had brought against the International Boxing Club is a prime example. The Supreme Court ruled that, while boxing matches occurred in a specific place and did not involve moving across state lines, deals for TV, radio, and motion picture rights did cross state boundaries. The Court acknowledged that this judgment contradicted previous rulings regarding baseball but declared that those rulings were "not authority for exempting other businesses merely because of the circumstance that they are also based on the performance of local exhibitions."[38]

Any question about the status of other sports was dispelled when the Supreme Court ruled on an antitrust lawsuit brought by George Radovich. Radovich challenged the right of the NFL to blacklist him for having played in the All American Football Conference (AAFC). A lower court dismissed Radovich's suit on the basis of the *Federal Baseball* decision. Radovich appealed to the Supreme Court, which reversed the lower court ruling by a 6–3 vote in 1957. The decision explicitly denied any form of exemption to any sport except baseball and expressed disapproval of the *Federal Baseball* ruling, though it let that ruling stand, leaving baseball's exemption intact.

Lacking exemption from antitrust laws, the NFL could not withstand legal challenges to its version of baseball's reserve clause. Initially, players were kept in place by a "gentlemen's agreement" among the owners not to pursue one another's players. When the agreement began to break down in the early 1960s, NFL Commissioner Pete Rozelle imposed a compensation system that effectively prevented players from switching teams. The "Rozelle rule" stipulated that a team that signed a free agent had to provide cash, draft choices, or players to the team whose player it signed. If the two teams could not reach an agreement on the appropriate compensation, the commissioner would impose an agreement. In 1972 John Mackey, the president of the National Football League Players Association (NFLPA) and star tight end for the Baltimore Colts, filed a lawsuit on behalf of himself and 31 other players.[39] The class action suit sought damages due to the Rozelle rule and other unfair labor practices. The U.S. District Court ruled that the Rozelle rule was a *per se* violation of the Sherman Act. An appeals court also ruled in favor of the NFLPA. Rather than file further appeals, the NFL chose to settle out of court with the NFLPA and to preserve a modified version of the Rozelle rule. Under the settlement, a team that signed a free agent now faced a fixed formula that dictated the cost of signing another team's player rather than submit to an uncertain ruling from the commissioner. While this removed the uncertainty associated with signing a free agent, the new rule continued to restrict player movement for over a decade.[40]

---

[38]Earl Warren writing for the majority. Cited in *U.S.* v. *International Boxing Club of N.Y.* Available online at http://www.ripon.edu/faculty/bowenj/antitrust/ibcofny1.htm.

[39]In a 1970 poll, Mackey was voted the best tight end of the NFL's first 50 years, but he was denied entrance to the Pro Football Hall of Fame until 1992, 20 years after he retired.

[40]See James Dworkin, *Owners Versus Players: Baseball and Collective Bargaining* (Boston: Auburn House, 1981), pp. 250–255; Quirk and Fort, *Paydirt* (1992), pp. 199–200; Roberts, "Antitrust Issues" (1992), pp. 19-31–19-33; and Richard Terry, "Tight End Mackey Blocks Commissioner Rozelle," in Sports and the Law, ed. by Charles Quirk (New York: Garland, 1996), pp. 187–189.

The tortured logic required to justify baseball's exemption from the antitrust laws was never more evident than in the early 1950s, when George Toolson, a player in the New York Yankees' system, resisted being sent back to the minor leagues. He then sued the Yankees, claiming that the reserve clause violated the antitrust laws. As Toolson's suit worked its way through the legal system, the House Subcommittee on the Study of Monopoly Power (chaired by Rep. Emmanuel Cellar and hence called the "Cellar Committee") began to hold hearings on baseball's antitrust exemption. When it became obvious that the Toolson case was going to the Supreme Court, the Cellar Committee postponed further action under the assumption that the courts would settle the matter. The Supreme Court seized upon this inaction, saying that Congress had signaled its approval of baseball's antitrust exemption by refusing to take any action against baseball. The "approval" granted by the Cellar Committee formed the basis of the Supreme Court's ruling in favor of the Yankees.[41]

Perhaps the most misunderstood legal case surrounding the reserve clause is Curt Flood's antitrust suit of the early 1970s. Most people incorrectly think of Flood as the man who single-handedly overthrew the reserve clause in baseball. In fact, Flood lost his case as well as his career. After the ruling against him, baseball players had to wait another four years before they were able to rid themselves of the reserve clause.

In the late 1960s, Curt Flood was a star outfielder for the St. Louis Cardinals. In 1968, after a particularly good season, Flood asked the team for a $30,000 raise. Not one inclined to tolerate such demands, Cardinals owner Augustus Busch traded Flood to the Philadelphia Phillies after the 1969 season. Curt Flood had many reasons for objecting to this trade. It sent him from a team that had won a World Series in 1967 and had come within one game of another championship in 1968 to a team that was a perennial also-ran. It also sent him to a town that had a history of bad relations with black ballplayers. Because of the reserve clause and baseball's exemption from antitrust regulations, however, Flood had no say in his own destiny. As a black man who had endured severe discrimination early in his career, Flood saw a parallel between his own position and that of enslaved blacks in America barely 100 years earlier. In asking Commissioner Bowie Kuhn to repeal the trade, Flood used words that Frederick Douglass might have used: "I do not feel I am a piece of property to be bought and sold irrespective of my wishes."[42]

In 1970, with the support of the Major League Baseball Players Association (MLBPA), Flood filed suit in U.S. Federal District Court against the commissioner's office, asking for $3 million (to be trebled) and for free agency. In language reminiscent of Kenesaw Landis's rhapsodies to baseball in the Federal

---

[41]See Abrams, *Legal Bases* (1998), p. 62; Quirk and Fort, *Pay Dirt* (1992), pp. 188–189; Roberts, "Antitrust Issues" (1992), pp. 19-33–19-36; and Zimbalist, *Baseball and Billions* (1992), pp. 12–15.

[42]While playing for a minor league town in the deep South early in his career, Flood was not allowed to mix his dirty laundry with that of his white teammates. White clubhouse attendants would not even handle his uniform. Flood's reference to slavery was not lost on Supreme Court Justice Thurgood Marshall, who also drew an analogy to slavery in his minority opinion.

League suit, the trial judge ruled in Kuhn's favor, arguing that baseball was on "higher ground" than mere commerce. An appeals court also ruled in Kuhn's favor, citing Congress's failure to act against the reserve clause, as the Supreme Court had argued almost 20 years earlier in its *Toolson* ruling.

The Supreme Court's decision, written by Harry Blackmun, was even more curious. Blackmun denied the basis for baseball's exemption by acknowledging that baseball was a business that engaged in interstate commerce. He called the exemption "an exception and an anomaly" and referred to the *Federal Baseball* and *Toolson* rulings as "aberration[s] confined to baseball." Despite these stinging condemnations of the reserve clause and of baseball's exemption from the antitrust laws, the Supreme Court ruled 6–2 (with one abstention) in Kuhn's favor in 1972. The Court based its decision on the principle of *stare decisis* ("let the old decision stand"), effectively saying that the original antitrust ruling was wrong but that too much now rested on the original decision for the Court to overturn it.[43]

In 1998, Congress finally placed limits on baseball's antitrust exemption by passing the "Curt Flood Act." The legislation, however, does little to change the status quo. The legislation limits baseball's powers only in the area of labor relations, granting players the right to file antitrust suits to resolve labor disputes. The players' right to sue, however, is limited by the Supreme Court's 1996 *Brown* v. *Pro Football, Inc.* ruling, which effectively stated that the players association would have to decertify itself before a player could sue on antitrust grounds.[44]

The Economic Impact of the Antitrust Exemption

Baseball's exemption from the antitrust laws has given it a greater ability to protect both its monopoly power and its monopsony power in the marketplace. It is no coincidence that the Federal League, whose antitrust suit was the basis for the antitrust exemption, was the last league to pose a serious challenge to Major League Baseball. Since then, baseball has faced only the feeble attempt to form a rival Mexican League in the 1940s and the stillborn attempts to form the Continental League in the late 1950s and the Union League in the mid-1990s.

Unlike baseball, all the other major professional leagues have endured serious challenges to their monopoly power. In each case, the existing league has had to absorb teams from a rival league and—in one case—to merge with a rival entrant. Quirk and Fort note, "a full 40 of the 103 franchises operating in major league pro sports in 1991 began life as members of rival leagues, and 7 or

---

[43]Blackmun's decision included the poems "He Never Heard of Casey," by Grantland Rice, and "Baseball's Sad Lexicon," by Franklin Pierre Adams. See Abrams, *Legal Bases* (1998), p. 62; Quirk and Fort, *Pay Dirt* (1992), pp. 188–189; Roberts, "Antitrust Issues" (1992), pp. 19-33–19-36; and Zimbalist, *Baseball and Billions* (1992), pp. 12–15.

[44]Gary Roberts, "Brown v. Pro Football, Inc.: The Supreme Court Gets It Right for the Wrong Reasons," *Antitrust Bulletin*, vol. 42, no. 3 (Fall 1997), pp. 595–639; and Sonya Ross, "Clinton Signs Bill Removing Baseball Antitrust Exemption for Labor Matters," Associated Press, October 28, 1998, at http://www.fl.milive.com/tigers/stories/19981028antitrust.html.

8 were created in direct response to the threats posed by rival leagues."[45] In 1976 the NBA ended a costly 10-year war with the American Basketball Association by allowing the Denver Nuggets, Indiana Pacers, New Jersey Nets, and San Antonio Spurs to join the NBA. Three years later, the NHL ended its own costly war with the World Hockey Association by absorbing the surviving WHA teams: the Edmonton Oilers, Hartford Whalers (now Carolina Hurricanes), Quebec Nordiques (now Colorado Avalanche), and Winnipeg Jets (now Phoenix Coyotes).[46]

Perhaps because it was the most consistently profitable enterprise, the NFL faced the most frequent and the most successful challenges. In the midst of a war with the second of four challengers to call themselves the "American Football League," the NFL persuaded the Cleveland Rams to join the NFL as a pseudo-expansion team in 1937. The AAFC, while it survived only from 1946 through 1949, had several lasting impacts on professional football. Of the four teams absorbed into the NFL in 1950—the Baltimore Colts, Cleveland Browns, New York Yankees, and San Francisco 49ers—two (the Browns and Colts) went on to become the dominant teams of the 1950s. More importantly, by allowing teams to employ black players, the AAFC helped force an end to the NFL's short-lived color line.

The most successful attack on the NFL's monopoly power came from the fourth and final iteration of the American Football League. After battling one another from 1960 through 1965, in 1966 the two leagues agreed to a full merger that was completed after the 1969 season.[47] In the 1980s, the USFL challenged the dominance of the NFL and precipitated perhaps the oddest antitrust decision of all. This suit alleged that the NFL had denied rival leagues access to television by reaching agreements with all three major networks. A jury found the NFL guilty of violating the antitrust laws but assessed damages of only $1 (trebled, of course, to $3). Opinions regarding this ruling vary. Some say that the jury found the problems faced by the USFL to be largely self-inflicted, while others assert that the jury was confused and assessed the penalty under the—incorrect—assumption that the trial judge could later increase it.[48]

Limited Exemptions: The NFL and Television

When Alvin "Pete" Rozelle became commissioner of the NFL following the death of longtime commissioner Bert Bell in 1959, professional football still lagged badly behind baseball and college football in the nation's consciousness. In 2006, the NFL began the most lucrative TV deal in the history of professional

---

[45]Quirk and Fort, *Pay Dirt* (1992), p. 297. The NFL's Yankees lasted for only a few years and played in Yankee Stadium.

[46]Interestingly, one man, a lawyer named Gary Davidson, was instrumental in the formation of both the ABA and the WHA.

[47]One sidelight to the agreement was the institution of an AFL–NFL Championship Game, later renamed the Super Bowl.

[48]See Byrne, *The $1 League* (1986), p. 346; Roberts, "Antitrust Issues" (1992); and Leifer, *Making the Majors* (1995), p. 142.

sports, an agreement that will generate almost $21 billion in revenue over eight years. The NFL's ingenious use of television, which we detail in Chapter 3, could never have been implemented, however, were it not for the limited exemption that the NFL obtained for its broadcasts. While we all take "the NFL on Fox" or "the NBA on ABC" for granted, professional sports—and Rozelle in particular—had to overcome serious obstacles to obtaining a league-wide contract.

The most significant obstacle was that such contracts were illegal. The NFL had been under an injunction since 1953 that expressly prohibited a league-wide contract.[49] Faced with a legal system that would not permit such "restraint of trade," Rozelle actively lobbied Congress to extend a limited exemption from antitrust laws to football, basketball, and hockey. The exemption would apply solely to these leagues' ability to negotiate league-wide broadcast rights. In 1962, Congress granted the exemption.[50]

The exemption had an immediate impact on the market for broadcast rights. NFL teams no longer had to negotiate local contracts (often in markets that overlapped one another, further depressing prices). By 1969, a mere seven years after the exemption was granted, the revenue from broadcast rights had risen by a factor of 5 for the New York Giants. The Green Bay Packers, with their much smaller media market, saw their revenues rise by a factor of 13. The merger of the NFL with the rival AFL in the late 1960s further increased the monopoly power of professional football, giving yet another upward boost to prices.

While professional sports in North America have generally succeeded in exercising monopoly power, European soccer leagues have had only mixed success. England's Premier League has been able to negotiate its own contract. In Italy, however, the courts ruled that the TV contract negotiated by Serie A and Serie B of the Italian soccer federation (Lega Calcio) violated antitrust laws. Teams must now negotiate their own contracts for broadcast rights. As a result, the TV revenue for teams like AC Milan is 10 times the revenue for the smaller clubs in Serie A.[51]

4.6   The NCAA: An Incidental Cartel

Supporters of the NCAA regard it as the guardian of integrity in collegiate athletics. Its foes see it as a money-grubbing cartel that ruthlessly exercises both monopoly and monopsony power. In fact, there may be elements of truth to both viewpoints. Former Executive Director Walter Byers described his job as "keeping intercollegiate sports clean while generating millions of dollars each

---

[49]Due to its exemption from antitrust laws, baseball faced no such prohibition, though it did little in the 1950s to exploit this advantage.

[50]One of the concessions that the NFL had to grant Congress in order to get its limited exemption was a promise not to compete with college or high school football. As a result, the NFL does not play Saturday games until the high school and college seasons end in early December.

[51]Alessandro Baroncelli and Umberto Lago, "Italian Football," *Journal of Sports Economics*, vol. 7, no. 1 (February 2006), p. 17

year as income for the colleges."[52] Yet high-minded ideals, such as keeping professionalism out of collegiate sports and limiting the number of games schools can play, coincide with the goal of a monopsony to drive down labor costs and the monopoly goal of limiting output to drive up prices. However, the NCAA is neither a monopoly nor a monopsony in the classic sense. Instead it is a collection of schools that have come together, for good or ill, to regulate intercollegiate athletics.

Economists call a group of firms that cooperate in order to exercise monopoly or monopsony power over a market a **cartel.** Members of cartels coordinate their activities so as to fix the market price, assign output levels to their members, divide profits, and erect barriers to entry by firms outside the cartel. The NCAA has—whatever its motives—done all these things, including erecting barriers to entry by driving out rival organizations. One example of the NCAA's predatory behavior came in the wake of federal legislation that vastly expanded funding for women's sports.[53] After first opposing the legislation because it might drain resources away from its traditional interests, the NCAA changed strategy and sought to extend its authority to cover women's sports. The only problem was that an oversight body already existed, the Association of Intercollegiate Athletics for Women (AIAW). In the early 1980s, the NCAA used its power over men's sports to cajole and coerce member schools to switch their affiliation from the AIAW to the NCAA. The NCAA also used its control over men's sports to guarantee superior media access for those schools that participated in NCAA-sanctioned events. By 1982, the AIAW had folded.

While the NCAA acts like a cartel, it differs from the classic image of a cartel in two important ways. First, it was not formed in order to monopolize (or monopsonize) a market. In fact, the colleges and universities formed the organization that evolved into the NCAA under duress. Their initial goal was to formulate rules of play on the football gridiron. From regulating behavior on the field, they quickly moved into regulating behavior off the field, eventually morphing into a multimillion dollar organization that carefully protects its financial interests. This gradual evolution into a collusive structure has led economists to call the NCAA an **incidental cartel.**

In addition, unlike classic cartels, the NCAA does not seek to maximize the profits of its members. In fact, the members of the NCAA explicitly reject the profit motive. Eschewing profits does not mean, however, that academia is averse to money. As is the case for their explicitly professional brethren, colleges find ways to turn profits into expenses. Expensive, luxurious weight rooms, coaches whose salaries exceed those of college presidents, and subsidies to less profitable sports are all time-honored examples of ways to dissipate profits earned by a few select teams.[54]

---

[52]Walter Byers with Charles Hammer, *Unsportsmanlike Conduct: Exploiting College Athletes* (Ann Arbor: University of Michigan Press, 1995), p. 5.

[53]This legislation, known as Title IX, will be discussed more thoroughly in Chapter 10.

[54]See James Koch, "Intercollegiate Athletics: An Economic Explanation," *Social Science Quarterly*, vol. 64, no. 2 (June 1983), pp. 360–374; and Arthur Fleisher et al., *The National Collegiate Athletic Association: A Study in Cartel Behavior* (Chicago: University of Chicago Press, 1992), pp. 73–94.

The origins of the NCAA are inextricably bound up with the development of football in America. At the start, American football resembled the rougher versions of football played in England. Football teams (and all other athletic clubs) were student-run organizations, so colleges often developed their own set of rules. The lack of consistent rules forced schools playing each other into negotiations that were sometimes comical. A football game between Harvard and McGill in Montreal was played under Harvard's rules for one half and McGill's rules for the other.[55] The transaction costs of negotiating rules on a game-by-game basis discouraged the spread of football.[56] The lack of consistent rules also made it difficult to enforce any one set of rules. As a result, football became an alarmingly violent game.

Events came to a head after the 1905 season, during which 18 students were killed and 159 suffered relatively serious injuries. In the wake of this carnage, President Theodore Roosevelt summoned representatives of Harvard, Yale, and Princeton—three major football powers of the time—to the White House, where he warned them to regulate the game or see it outlawed. In response, representatives of 13 colleges met to adopt an explicit set of rules and to establish an enforcement mechanism. The resulting organization, the Intercollegiate Athletic Association of the United States (IAAUS)—renamed the National Collegiate Athletic Association in 1910—succeeded where prior organizations had failed. Within a year, it had established a common set of rules that a large number schools could accept.

For the first several years, the NCAA was primarily concerned with standardizing rules in football and other intercollegiate sports. Soon, however, the NCAA turned its attention to rules for behavior off the field, passing numerous resolutions intended to discourage the professionalization of college sports. One can argue whether the NCAA's adherence to amateurism represented a high-minded stand in defense of the academic integrity of its members or an attempt to guarantee its members a cheap labor force. One cannot deny, however, that the NCAA was trying to serve as a coordinating body for its membership, urging them to cooperate on actions far beyond its initial mandate.

The NCAA quickly learned, however, that a successful cartel must be able to monitor the actions of its members and punish cheaters. In 1946 the NCAA finally tried to put an enforcement mechanism in place with the so-called Sanity Code. In the **Sanity Code,** the NCAA specified a set of principles designed to govern the behavior of member schools and recommended expulsion for members who failed to abide by its principles. However, seven schools—which came to be known as the "seven sinners"—announced that they would not abide by the Sanity Code's restrictions on financial aid.[57] In the first and only test of the Sanity Code, the NCAA membership failed to muster the necessary

---

[55]See Leifer, *Making the Majors* (1995), pp. 40–42.

[56]The most serious early attempt, the Intercollegiate Football Association, however, ended in failure in 1894 after 18 years.

[57]The seven sinners were Boston College, the Citadel, the University of Maryland, the University of Virginia, Virginia Military Institute, Virginia Polytechnic Institute, and Villanova University.

two-thirds majority it needed to expel the seven sinners. With no way to enforce coordinated action, the NCAA appeared dead as a cartel.

Ironically, the NCAA cartel was saved in the early 1950s by one of the most serious scandals in the history of collegiate athletics. In the postwar era, college basketball was enjoying an unprecedented surge in popularity. At the height of the boom, the sport was rocked by a series of point-shaving scandals. Point shaving was a way for unscrupulous gamblers to ensure that they beat point spreads. Gamblers typically get players to shave points by paying them to win by a smaller margin than bookies predict. The gamblers then bet that the team will not cover the point spread.

The scandal destroyed the basketball programs of several schools in the New York area in 1952, including that of former national champion City College of New York.[58] It also implicated several members of the national champion University of Kentucky basketball squad. The ensuing investigation brought to light evidence that the Kentucky coach, Adolph Rupp, had associated with Ed Curd, a gambler with links to organized crime (and who may have abetted the point shaving), and that Rupp had flagrantly violated NCAA regulations regarding payments to athletes.

Unable to enforce its own guidelines, the NCAA was powerless to take action against Kentucky. The Southeastern Conference (SEC), the group of schools with which Kentucky was associated, however, was so embarrassed by Kentucky's actions that Bernie H. Moore, the SEC commissioner, suspended Kentucky from the SEC for the ensuing year. Since none of the other SEC schools had a program that matched its own, Kentucky retorted that it would simply play schools outside of the SEC. The NCAA then stepped in to back the SEC by writing to all its member schools and urging them to honor the boycott. Rather than fight the boycott, Kentucky's faculty representatives accepted their punishment, an action that ex–NCAA Commissioner Byers feels would be unthinkable in today's litigious climate.[59]

The "death penalty" levied on Kentucky gave the NCAA a new lease on life. By mobilizing its members into a boycott of Kentucky (not, as is popularly believed, closing the program), the NCAA had stumbled upon a weapon with which to penalize cheaters and had—almost accidentally—shown a willingness to use it. Schools now accept lesser punishments in part because of the fear that failure to do so will result in the death penalty.[60]

---

[58]City College of New York is the only school ever to win the NCAA championship and the National Invitational Tournament (then the more prestigious event) in the same year. More recent point-shaving scandals have damaged programs from Boston College to Arizona State.

[59]See Murray Sperber, *Onward to Victory: The Crises That Shaped College Sports* (New York: Henry Holt and Co., 1998), pp. 330–343; Paul Lawrence, *Unsportsmanlike Conduct: The National Collegiate Athletic Association and the Business of College Football* (New York: Praeger, 1987), pp. 52–53; and Byers, *Unsportsmanlike Conduct* (1995), pp. 55–61.

[60]The most prominent recent imposition of the death penalty came against the football program at Southern Methodist University, which suspended its football program for the 1987 and 1988 seasons.

4.7 Prisoner's Dilemma: How Rational Actions Lead to Irrational Outcomes

As with many of the NCAA's anticompetitive actions, its restraint of trade in television began innocently. At a party in 1950, Dick Romney, the commissioner of the Mountain States Conference (now the Western Athletic Conference), approached University of Michigan coach Fritz Crisler and started discussing the TV package that the NCAA was then negotiating. He asked, half-seriously, if Crisler would be willing to set aside some games for the other schools so that schools such as Michigan would not get all the publicity and glory. To Romney's surprise, Crisler agreed and helped push through a limit on the number of games that each school could have on the network broadcast.[61]

As football became increasingly lucrative, the more powerful schools came to forget Crisler's spirit of fairness and wanted to increase their control over the flow of money. In 1976, 61 of the largest football powers in the NCAA formed the College Football Association (CFA), whose sole purpose was to lobby for greater control of television appearances and revenue. The NCAA responded in 1978 by recalculating its formula for dividing football programs. Previously, schools had been assigned to one of three divisions (Divisions I–III). These divisions were based on the size of their student populations in order to ensure competitive balance. In 1978 the NCAA split Division I, which consisted of the largest schools, into Divisions I-A and I-AA.

The two-tiered Division I arrangement increased the share of income flowing to the big-time programs, though not enough to satisfy the schools that had formed the CFA. In 1982, two members of the CFA, the University of Georgia and Oklahoma University, brought an antitrust suit against the NCAA. The suit alleged that the NCAA had conspired to prevent its own members from engaging in free commerce. Federal District Court Judge Juan Burciaga ruled against the NCAA in stinging terms. He called the NCAA "a classic cartel" and claimed that "[c]onsumer demand and the free market are sacrificed to the interests of the NCAA administration. . . . It is clear that [the] NCAA is in violation of Section 1 of the Sherman [Antitrust] Act."[62]

After a series of appeals, the case went before the Supreme Court in 1984. The majority of the court ruled that the television contract was not a *per se* violation of antitrust laws, since the "industry" of college football needed some restrictions in order to operate. The court ruled instead that the NCAA failed to meet the rule of reason and upheld Burciaga's initial ruling by a 7–2 vote. The dissenting opinion, written by Byron ("Whizzer") White, a former All-American at the University of Colorado, claimed that the majority had misapplied the

---

[61]Anecdote related in Byers, *Unsportsmanlike Conduct* (1995), pp. 81–82. Schools were limited to three appearances over a two-year period. Each of 12 football conferences also had to be represented over this period.

[62]Quoted in Murray Sperber, *College Sports Inc.* (New York: Henry Holt and Co., 1990), p. 51.

rule of reason by ignoring the noncommercial goals of the NCAA, a sentiment reminiscent of the *Federal Baseball* ruling.[63]

As expected, the ruling led to the flood of college games that we now see on television every fall. The separate deal between Notre Dame and NBC in 1991 even led some to say that the network's initials stood for "Notredame Broadcasting Corporation." Much to the surprise of the schools involved, their greater exposure did not make them any richer. In their haste to increase their TV exposure, the members of the CFA forgot that demand curves slope down. With more games on TV, the ratings for a typical broadcast fell by one-fourth. As a result, the fees schools could charge for broadcast rights plummeted. Four years after the decision, college football rights fees were only half of what they had been. In a crowning irony, Oklahoma, one of the plaintiffs in the case, saw its average revenue for a regional or national broadcast fall from over $425,000 the year before the Supreme Court ruling to less than $190,000 the season after.[64]

The members of the NCAA seemed to defy one of the central tenets of economic theory by taking an action that made them all worse off. Outside of the sports world, there are many examples of seemingly self-destructive behavior, such as wasteful arms races or advertising campaigns that the participants would like to avoid but for some reason cannot. Economists call the broad set of seemingly optimal actions that lead to suboptimal outcomes a prisoner's dilemma. **Prisoner's dilemma** is a specific example of a broader tool of analysis called **game theory.** While one can use game theory to analyze athletic situations such as whether a pitcher should throw a curveball or whether a chess player should sacrifice a queen, it also has much wider applications. Game theory can shed light on any situation involving three elements: players (individuals, organizations, or nations), strategies, and outcomes.

With a few simplifications, one can use game theory to explain why Georgia and Oklahoma engaged in such seemingly self-destructive behavior. For simplicity, we shall consider only two "players," Florida State University (FSU) and the University of Miami, and assume that each faces two possible strategies: limiting its broadcasts in accordance with its agreement, or breaking the agreement and broadcasting many games. Two players each with two strategies results in four possible outcomes, or "payoffs," as illustrated in the **payoff matrix** in Table 4.1.

---

[63]See Eric Seiken, "The NCAA and the Courts: College Football on Television," in *Sports and the Law*, ed. by Charles Quirk (New York: Garland, 1996), pp. 56–62; and Sperber, *College Sports Inc.* (1990), pp. 51–52.

[64]Sperber, *College Sports Inc.* (1990), p. 52; Francis Dealy, *Win at Any Cost: The Sell Out of College Athletics* (New York: Birch Lane Press, 1990), p. 150; and Roger Noll, "The Economics of Intercollegiate Sports," in *Rethinking College Athletics*, ed. by Judith Andre and David James (Philadelphia: Temple University Press, 1992), p. 202.

TABLE 4.1

College Football Broadcasts as a Prisoner's Dilemma

	Miami Televises Many Games	*Miami Limits Appearances*
FSU Televises Many Games	Miami gets $5 million FSU gets $5 million	Miami gets $3 million FSU gets $20 million
FSU Limits Appearances	Miami gets $20 million FSU gets $3 million	Miami gets $10 million FSU gets $10 million

If both schools limit their appearances on TV, then both schools make high profits, as was the case under the NCAA-negotiated contract. The member schools that sued the NCAA thought that they could increase their profits by broadcasting unlimited games. In terms of Table 4.1, unlimited broadcasts are a **dominant strategy,** because each school finds it the best strategy regardless of what the other school does. If FSU limits its appearances, Miami will gain an advantage over FSU (moving from parity at $10 million to a $17 million advantage) by televising many games. If FSU televises many games, Miami protects itself (moving from a $17 million disadvantage to parity at $5 million) by televising many games as well. The "dilemma" of the prisoners' dilemma stems from the fact that, while broadcasting many games is optimal for each individual school, it results in a suboptimal outcome if all schools decide on the same strategy. As a result, broadcasting many games leaves both Miami and FSU worse off than they were initially.

BIOGRAPHICAL SKETCH

"PETE" ROZELLE

If he were in private business and accomplished what he had
with the NFL, he'd be worth one hundred million dollars.
—*Anonymous corporate executive*[1]

Larry C. Morris/The New York Times

Paul Tagliabue, the NFL's previous commissioner, may have negotiated the NFL's recent $24 billion dollar mega-deal with the TV networks, and David Stern of the NBA may be professional sports' resident wizard, but none of the magic they worked would have been possible without the efforts of one man, Alvin Ray "Pete" Rozelle. As the NFL's commissioner from 1960 to 1989, Rozelle transformed football from an afterthought on the American sports scene to the most popular of our major team sports. In so doing, he also laid the groundwork on which the future success of other sports could be built.

Growing up just outside of Los Angeles, little about Rozelle's early life presaged a career in football. Like many young men his age, Rozelle entered the navy upon graduating from Compton High School in 1944. He returned in

1946 and entered Compton Junior College. In one of the remarkable coincidences that seemed to guide his career, the Cleveland Rams moved to Los Angeles that same year and selected Compton Junior College as their training camp. Rozelle found part-time work in the Rams' publicity department to help support himself at college until he left to attend the University of San Francisco, which he chose after a chance meeting with USF's legendary basketball coach Pete Newell, who promised him a part-time job as athletic news director. When he graduated in 1950, Rozelle became USF's full-time news director. Thanks to the high profile of USF sports at that time (an undefeated football team and a basketball team that won the then-prestigious National Invitational Tournament), Rozelle had the opportunity to meet many prominent sports figures, including Tex Schramm, the general manager (GM) of the Los Angeles Rams. When the Rams' public relations director abruptly left for another team in 1952, Schramm offered Rozelle the chance to come back to Los Angeles. Rozelle worked with the Rams until 1955, when he moved back to San Francisco to become a partner in a public relations firm.

Rozelle might never have had any further contact with football had it not been for the turmoil that engulfed the Los Angeles Rams in the late 1950s. Ownership of the team was equally divided between long-time owner Dan Reeves and two partners who shared a hatred for Reeves. The result was a paralysis that drove Tex Schramm to seek a job with CBS Sports and caused NFL Commissioner Bert Bell to seek a GM who could mediate between the two factions. Bell was a friend of Rozelle's partner in the PR firm and recalled Rozelle's previous attachment to the Rams as well as the work that he had done with the firm in marketing the 1956 Melbourne Olympic Games. In 1957, Rozelle once again headed south, to become GM of the Rams.

Two years later, fate again took a hand, when Bell died suddenly of a heart attack, leaving no clear successor. At their annual meetings the next January, the owners spent 10 fruitless days trying to agree on a new commissioner. Finally, during a break, Dan Reeves proposed his 33-year-old GM to Wellington Mara, the son of New York Giants'

owner Tim Mara, as a compromise candidate. When Mara suggested the owners consider Rozelle, the ensuing discussion was almost comical.

"What do you know about him?" [Steelers owner] Art Rooney asked.

"Reeves says he's good," Mara answered. . . .

"Rozelle?" Frank McNamee of the Philadelphia Eagles blurted out, "who's he?"[2]

Becoming "boy czar" of the NFL in 1960 was not the prize it would be today. The league had failed to capitalize on the popularity of its 1958 championship game between the Baltimore Colts and the New York Giants, and it remained a backwater. League offices were in the back room of a bank in Bell's hometown of Bala Cynwyd, Pa., and teams still struggled financially.

One of the main problems facing the NFL was the balkanized structure of its television dealings. With each team pursuing its own contracts, gross inequities in revenue resulted (the Baltimore Colts made $600,000 from television in 1959 while the Packers made only $80,000), though no team made very much. In the words of then-president of CBS Sports Bill McPhail, "Local stations made more money then by showing old movies than they did showing professional football games."[3]

Rozelle quickly responded to the challenge. To raise the profile and increase the marketability of the NFL, he immediately moved the league offices to Manhattan. He then set to work consolidating the league's television contracts. Rozelle faced two profound obstacles to his efforts. First, he had to instill a "league-think" mentality in owners who had previously had little ability or reason to look beyond their own survival. Using all the patience and marketing skills at his disposal, Rozelle convinced the owners of the big-city teams such as the Giants and the Chicago Bears to sacrifice their own short-term goals in favor of the long-term gains that would come from adopting a unified TV policy and sharing revenues equally.

Convincing the owners, however, was the easy part. Negotiating a league contract with the television networks was illegal for an entity that had lost any pretense of exemption from the antitrust laws with the *Radovich* decision of 1957. Rozelle spent the summer of 1961 lobbying Congress for a limited exemption that would

continued

allow the NFL to negotiate a single, league-wide TV contract. His efforts were rewarded that September with the Sports Antitrust Broadcast Act, which allowed football, hockey, and basketball leagues to pool their revenues from television.

Even then, Rozelle's work was not over. Unlike the lords of baseball, who steadily put obstacles in the way of television coverage, Rozelle actively courted the networks and their affiliates. The results of Rozelle's league-think mentality became readily apparent. In 1962–1963, the NFL's first contract with CBS paid approximately $330,000 per franchise per year. By 1964–1965, the payments had risen to about $1 million per franchise per year.

While such figures are far below current contracts, they broke new ground at the time and induced a sense of unity among the owners. This unity allowed Rozelle to create NFL Properties, which pooled the revenues from league licensing agreements. It also allowed the owners to withstand conflict with a restive players' union far better than the fractious lords of baseball.

In later years, Rozelle would see much of this unity of purpose fracture. The first major setback came with Al Davis's successful antitrust suit over the NFL's attempt to prevent his Oakland Raiders from moving to Los Angeles in 1980. The second came with the entry of a new breed of owners, best exemplified by the Cowboys' Jerry Jones, who—having paid huge sums for their franchises—were determined to maximize their own revenues, even if that meant scrapping the old league-think mentality. Still, the continued prosperity of the NFL and of all professional sports are a testament to the work of the one-time gofer for the Los Angeles Rams.

[1]David Harris, *The League: The Rise and Decline of the NFL* (New York: Bantam Books, 1986), p. 13.
[2]Quoted in Harris, *The League* (1986), p. 11.
[3]Quoted in Harris, *The League* (1986), p. 13.

Sources: David Harris, *The League: The Rise and Decline of the NFL* (New York: Bantam Books, 1986); John Hilyar, *Lords of the Realm* (New York: Villard Books, 1994).

Summary

Monopolies maximize profit by raising prices and reducing output. Economists regard the higher prices as a transfer from consumers to producers that does not affect the overall well-being of society. The lower output, however, creates a deadweight loss that does reduce social well-being. Firms may be able to increase profits beyond the level they can earn with a single price by charging variable prices or bundling games. In addition, monopolists may be able to capture some or the entire consumer surplus by engaging in different forms of price discrimination. Group discounts, season ticket plans, and personal seat licenses are three forms of price discrimination practiced by sports franchises.

Unlike North American leagues, soccer leagues in Europe have limited ability to exert monopoly power. The promotion-relegation system can undermine a team's local monopoly power or even remove it from a specific market.

Since the late 19th century, the U.S. government has opposed monopoly. The most famous antimonopoly legislation is the Sherman Antitrust Act, which has been applied against professional sports and the NCAA with varying degrees of success. Due to a series of bizarre court rulings early in the 20th century, baseball has enjoyed a blanket exemption from antitrust laws. It used the exemption to great effect, exerting monopsony power thanks to the reserve clause long after the clause was ruled illegal for other sports.

Some firms join together, forming cartels that exert monopoly power, almost accidentally. The NCAA is one example of an "incidental cartel." It was originally formed to establish rules of play for colleges. It soon learned, however, to cooperate for financial matters as well.

Discussion Questions

1. Do you think that all professional sports should share baseball's exemption from antitrust laws or that baseball should lose its exemption?
2. In professional soccer, teams that signed another team's player had to pay a "transfer fee" to compensate the player's original team. How does this affect the market for soccer players?
3. Is it fair to fans when teams create a bundle of more popular games and less popular games that must be purchased together?
4. Do you feel that leagues are better described as cartels made up of independent firms or as a single, multiplant firm?
5. What strategy would you follow if you were trying to create a rival basketball league?
6. Why do you think that antitrust lawsuits brought under the second clause of the Sherman Antitrust Act have generally been so unsuccessful?
7. Should major college sports powers be allowed to operate as cartels?

Problems

4.1 An athletic director was once quoted as saying that he felt his school spent too much on athletics but that it could not afford to stop. Use game theory to model his dilemma.

4.2 You are the commissioner of the National Hockey League. You have been called to testify at an antitrust case against the NHL. Argue that
  a. The NHL is not a monopoly.
  b. Even if it is a monopoly, it is a natural monopoly.

4.3 Why can't Premier League teams like Arsenal exert as much monopoly power as the NFL's Chicago Bears?

4.4 Suppose that the demand curve for tickets to see a football team is given by $Q = 100,000 - 100p$ and marginal cost is zero.
  a. How many tickets would the team be able to sell (ignoring capacity constraints) if it behaved competitively and set $p = MC$?
  b. How many tickets would it sell—and what price would it charge—if it behaved like a monopoly? (*Hint:* In this case the marginal revenue curve is given by $MR = 1,000 - .02Q$.)

4.5 Why was the limited exemption from antitrust laws so crucial to the development of the NFL?

4.6   Suppose that all St. Louis Rams fans feel the same as Jane, who values every game at $28, regardless of the opponent. Can the Rams increase profits by bundling the Rams–Bears game with three others? Why or why not?

4.7   Suppose that most fans prefer Sunday afternoon baseball games (regardless of opponent) to all other types of games. Describe two pricing strategies that a team could use to increase profits based on this difference in demand.

4.8   Suppose the typical Buffalo Bills fan has the demand curve for Bills football games: $p = 120 - 10 \cdot G$, where G is the number games the fan attends.

   a. If the Bills want to sell the fan a ticket to all eight home games, what price must they charge? What are their revenues?

   b. Suppose the Bills have the chance to offer a season ticket that is good for all eight home games, a partial season ticket that is good for four home games, and tickets to individual games. What price should they charge? What is their revenue?

4.9   Suppose the Arizona Cardinals have fans who are much more sensitive to price than the fans in Buffalo as described in the previous question. Their demand curve for Cardinals football games is: $p = 120 - 15G$. What is true about the prices they are able to charge and their revenue if they try to practice second degree price discrimination as the Bills did? Why does this happen?

4.10   Suppose that, in order to protect Ronaldo from his adoring fans, soccer teams that host Real Madrid must hire extra security, and security costs go up as the number of fans at the game goes up. When a team such as Arsenal hosts Real Madrid, how do these extra costs affect the price of a ticket for that game compared with the price of a ticket when they host any other team? Is this price discrimination by Arsenal? Why or why not?

APPENDIX   4A

An Alternative Application of Game Theory

The prisoner's dilemma is a particularly powerful and easily understood example of game theory and how it applies to economic settings. However, not all situations involving players, strategies, and payoffs result in a prisoner's dilemma, as the following example shows.[65]

---

[65]For a more formal take on the game theoretic basis of tennis serves, see Mark Walker and John Wooders, "Minimax Play at Wimbledon," *American Economic Review*, vol. 91, no. 5 (December 2001), pp. 1521–1538.

You are playing at Centre Court at Wimbledon, down 6–5 in the third set of the Ladies' Finals. Serena Williams awaits your serve. You know from bitter experience that Serena has a devastating forehand. As a result, in this most important match of your life, you serve... directly to her forehand?

Playing to an opponent's strength may seem like the height of folly, but athletes, generals, and CEOs do it all the time. They recognize that sometimes no single strategy dominates another and that their best hope lies in being unpredictable, following a **mixed strategy.**

Your match with Serena Williams is a perfect example of just such a strategy. It seems obvious to all that you should avoid Serena's forehand at such an important point in the game. Of course, one of those to whom this strategy seems obvious is Serena herself. As a result, she prepares herself mentally and physically for a serve to her backhand, leaving her vulnerable to a serve to her strength. The payoff matrix in Table 4A.1 clarifies the wisdom of this strategy. You have two choices when you serve: going to Serena's forehand or backhand. Serena, in turn, has two possible strategies: anticipating a serve to her forehand or backhand. If she correctly guesses that you are serving to her forehand, she wins the point 60 percent of the time. If she correctly guesses backhand, she wins 50 percent of the time. If she guesses forehand but you serve to her backhand, she wins 40 percent of the time. If she incorrectly guesses backhand, she also wins 40 percent of the time.

Unlike the prisoner's dilemma example, this situation has no single equilibrium outcome. Suppose, for example, that you consistently serve to Serena's forehand. Serena sees this. By always preparing for a forehand serve, she wins 60 percent of the points (the upper left portion). You realize that you can do better by fooling Serena, so you serve to her backhand and win 60 percent of the points (the lower left portion). Serena quickly recognizes your new strategy and begins to expect a serve to her backhand, winning 50 percent of the points (the lower right portion). You adjust again and now serve to Serena's strength. Because she still expects you to serve to her backhand, you manage to win 60 percent of the time (the upper right portion). Serena again catches on, however, and correctly anticipates the serve to her forehand, bringing us back to our starting point (the upper left portion), where you win 40 percent of the time.[66]

TABLE 4A.1

Mixed Strategies in Tennis

	Serena Guesses Forehand	*Serena Guesses Backhand*
You serve to her forehand	You win 40% Serena wins 60%	You win 60% Serena wins 40%
You serve to her backhand	You win 60% Serena wins 40%	You win 50% Serena wins 50%

[66]To see this problem carried out to comic extremes, see the confrontation between Vizzini and the Dread Pirate Roberts in *The Princess Bride*, by William Goldman (1974).

Since no strategy stays optimal for long, your greatest advantage comes from fooling Serena and hitting your serve "where she ain't." This means that you must follow a mixed strategy, serving sometimes to her forehand and sometimes to her backhand. When Serena guesses correctly, she may hit a devastating return. When she does not, you stand an excellent chance of winning the point. You must see to it that Serena does not guess correctly too often. Thus you must mix up your serves just often enough that Serena cannot gain any advantage by guessing that you will serve one way or the other.

Suppose your strategy is to serve to Serena's forehand with probability p (and hence to her backhand with probability $(1 - p)$). Suppose, further, that Serena's strategy is to anticipate a serve to her forehand with probability q (and a serve to her backhand with probability $(1 - q)$).[67] If Serena prepares for a serve to her forehand, then, from Table 4A.1, the probability that she wins the point is

$$\text{Prob}_{GF} = 0.6p + 0.4(1 - p)$$

because she wins 60 percent of the serves to her forehand and 40 percent of the serves to her backhand when she anticipates a serve to her forehand. By similar reasoning, the probability that she wins if she prepares for a serve to her backhand is

$$\text{Prob}_{GB} = 0.4p + 0.5(1 - p)$$

Your optimal strategy should be to serve to her forehand just often enough that Serena does not gain an advantage by guessing one way or the other. In other words, your best strategy is to choose p so that $\text{Prob}_{GF} = \text{Prob}_{GB}$. Setting these equations equal and solving for p, one finds that your optimal strategy would be to serve to Serena's forehand one-third of the time ($p = \frac{1}{3}$) and to her backhand two-thirds of the time. Then, no matter how she guesses, you will win 53.3 percent of the points.[68]

[67]We assume that both decisions are random and that each player knows only the probabilities of her opponent's actions (e.g., from previous matches).

[68]Similar reasoning will tell Serena her optimal guessing strategy—that is, what percentage of the time (q) she should prepare for a serve to her forehand. If either you or Serena deviates from your optimal strategy, the other will see this (i.e., you can tell how often Serena prepares for a forehand serve [q], and she can tell how often you serve to her forehand [p]). Then if, say, Serena sees you are not following the best strategy of serving to her forehand one-third of the time, she can adjust her strategy to reduce your winning percentage below .533.

CHAPTER 5

Competitive Balance

When you lose a couple of times, it makes you realize how difficult it is to win.
—STEFFI GRAF (GERMAN TENNIS PLAYER)[1]

Introduction

One of the oldest adages in professional football is that on any given Sunday, each team has a chance to beat the other. But what if, year after year, a few teams regularly won, while the rest almost always lost? No doubt, the games would be less interesting. As early as 1956, economists noted that successful leagues must be based on relatively even competition.[2] The degree of parity within a sports league can mean different things to different people. To some, it means close competition every year, with the difference between the best and worst teams being relatively small. To others, it means regular turnover in the winner of the league's championship. Whatever the measure, we refer to the degree of parity within a league as **competitive balance**. This chapter discusses competitive balance from the perspective of the fan and the owner. In addition, it explores how economists measure competitive balance, how leagues try to alter the competitive balance in a league, and why such efforts might not be successful. As we explain competitive balance, we will see the following:

- While the owners of Major League Baseball teams have been particularly vocal about competitive balance, baseball is not the sport with the least balanced competition.

- There is little evidence that free agency has harmed competitive balance.

- Many of the tools designed to promote competitive balance are not likely to succeed.

---

[1]www.famous-quotes-and-quotations.com/sports_quotes.html
[2]Simon Rottenberg, "The Baseball Players Labor Market," *Journal of Political Economy*, vol. 64, no. 3 (June 1956), pp. 242–258.

Fan's Perspective

Suppose you are an exchange student to the United States, and your host family takes you to see your first baseball game; it's between the Washington Nationals and the New York Yankees. The game quickly gets boring because the talent on the two teams is very uneven. The Yankees score on the hapless Nationals over and over again, and you notice that most fans leave by the seventh inning. The final score is 11–0. "That's OK," your host says, "the Nationals lose all the time, and the Yankees always win." If that were your only exposure to baseball, you would probably leave America thinking baseball was a waste of time. If instead you had seen the Philadelphia Phillies beat the St. Louis Cardinals in a wild 5–4 game after a home run in the bottom of the ninth, and you learned that almost all games are like this, you might become a lifelong fan.

From the fan's perspective, an uncertain outcome is much more interesting than a foregone conclusion. Historically, fans have shown their displeasure with unbalanced competition, even when their own team did most of the winning. An often-cited example is the Cleveland Browns of the late 1940s; their dominance of the All-American Football Conference caused them to become less popular with their home fans. In baseball, the Yankees may have had the same kind of negative effect on attendance at their own games and across the American League when they won eight League pennants and six World Series between 1950 and 1958. Table 5.1 shows that between 1950 and 1958, a period generally marked by prosperity and economic growth, attendance at both Yankee games and those of the entire American League either stagnated or fell as the Yankees dominated the league. The effect was especially pronounced in the late 1950s, as National League attendance grew substantially while American League attendance fell.

TABLE 5.1

New York Yankees' Success and American League and National League Attendance, 1950–1958

Year	AL Champion	World Series Champion	Yankees Attendance	AL Attendance	NL Attendance
1950	Yankees	Yankees	2,081,380	9,142,361	8,320,616
1951	Yankees	Yankees	1,950,107	8,888,614	7,244,002
1952	Yankees	Yankees	1,629,665	8,293,896	6,339,148
1953	Yankees	Yankees	1,531,811	6,964,076	7,419,721
1954	Cleveland	NY Giants	1,475,171	7,922,364	8,013,519
1955	Yankees	Brooklyn	1,490,138	8,942,971	7,674,412
1956	Yankees	Yankees	1,491,784	7,893,683	8,649,567
1957	Yankees	Milwaukee	1,497,134	8,169,218	8,819,601
1958	Yankees	Yankees	1,428,438	7,296,034	10,164,596

Source: Attendance data are from Rodney Fort and James Quirk, *Pay Dirt* (1992). Performance data is from the official MLB Web site http://www.MLB.com.

Fans enjoy a contest with an uncertain outcome even though they root for their team to win every game. Research shows that fans are most interested in games in which the home team has a 60 to 70 percent chance of winning.[3] This does not mean that fans want their teams to lose 30 to 40 percent of the time. They just want them to have a chance of losing. If fans were certain that their team would win every week, they would lose a major source of excitement from the game.

Competitive imbalance is not a new problem for professional sports leagues. In MLB, the New York Yankees have been a dominant franchise since the 1920s, when they won six American league championships between 1921 (the year after they acquired Babe Ruth) and 1928. It was even more pronounced when they won five straight World Series between 1949 and 1953.

Two of the three other major sports have similar histories. The Boston Celtics won every NBA championship but one between 1959 and 1969. Between 1965 and 1979, the Montreal Canadiens won the NHL's Stanley Cup 10 times. The Canadiens' dynasty was followed by that of the New York Islanders, who won the Cup the next four years in a row. Only in the NFL has no team ever won the league championship—the Super Bowl—more than twice in a row, but

The San Antonio Spurs celebrate winning their fourth NBA championship since 1998–1999.

---

[3]See Glenn Knowles, Keith Sherony, and Mike Haupert, "The Demand for Major League Baseball: A Test of the Uncertainty of Outcome Hypothesis," *The American Economist*, vol. 36, no. 2 (Fall 1992) pp. 73–80; and Mark McDonald and Daniel Rascher, "Does Bat Day Make Cents? The Effect of Promotions on the Demand for Major League Baseball," *Journal of Sport Management*, vol. 14, no. 1 (January 2000), pp. 8–27. For a different view, see Babatunde Buraimo and Rob Simmons, "Do Sports Fans Really Value Uncertainty of Outcome? Evidence from the English Premier League," *International Journal of Sport Finance*, vol. 3, no. 3 (August 2008) pp. 146–55.

even the NFL has several franchises that have been consistently uncompetitive, such as Cincinnati and Detroit.

Internationally, unbalanced competition in the elite European soccer leagues is even more skewed toward a few dominant teams. Since the 1999–2000 season, FC Barcelona and Real Madrid have combined to win seven of ten La Liga championships in Spain, while Bayern Munich and Manchester United have each accounted for six of ten championships in Germany's Bundesliga and England's Premier League, respectively.[4]

Competitive imbalance also appears at the amateur level. For example, since the formation of the college football's Big 10 Conference in 1896, the University of Michigan has won or shared 42 titles, more than one-third of the total. In contrast, Indiana University has won only two titles, five fewer than the University of Chicago, which gave up football in 1939.

Changes in the relative importance of the various revenue sources and the growth of the sports industry in general have increased the concerns that the financial consequences of unbalanced competition are becoming more severe. Accordingly, we must consider the owners' perspective on equalizing competition.

5.2   The Owners' Perspective

In Chapter 3 we saw that leagues often perform functions that individual teams either cannot do or have no incentive to do. Ensuring competitive balance is one of the most important—and most difficult—of those duties. Leagues develop policies to promote competitive balance because individual teams often lack the means or the motivation to do so. As noted in Chapter 3, teams with large fan bases and media markets frequently have much higher revenues than other teams. The deeper pockets of the big-market teams give them an advantage when pursuing talented players. In addition, some teams prefer success on the field to high profits. The Philadelphia Flyers in the NHL, the Dallas Mavericks in the NBA, and the New York Yankees in MLB all have low operating income despite operating in relatively large markets. For either or both of these reasons, some franchises develop into dynasties that dominate their divisions or leagues for years on end. The negative impact of dynasties on overall attendance gives leagues an incentive to limit the ability of individual teams to pursue players.

If it is in the best interest of leagues to have relatively close competition between their member teams, they have an incentive to promote competitive balance. Leagues and professional associations, such as NASCAR do not need to take specific action if they tend naturally toward equal strength. If, however, a few teams flourish while most teams languish, the league has an incentive to act. For example, in auto racing, organizations such as NASCAR go to great lengths to promote equal competition between cars. Each car in a NASCAR

---

[4]Results for Italy's Serie A have been confounded by a game-fixing scandal that saw Juventus stripped of the 2004–2005 and 2005–2006 championships and relegated to Serie B.

race is measured using a series of 30 or more templates and scales for height, weight, length, width, air displacement, and overall shape. In addition, engines must meet an exacting set of criteria and are even restricted to reduce horsepower on larger tracks where speeds are greatest. To further ensure fair competition, some cars are retested at the conclusion of the race. By placing so many restrictions on the cars, racing leagues hope to ensure close competitions decided by the skills of the drivers and their teams.

Chapters 3 and 4 explained how teams in larger, more populous markets generally have a larger fan base and higher gate and television revenues. They can thus afford to hire better players in a free market. In addition, successful teams are likely to have an advantage in attracting players, thereby creating self-perpetuating dynasties.

Even without intervention by the league, teams have an incentive to limit their pursuit of star players because of the law of diminishing marginal returns. **Diminishing marginal returns** refers to the fact that the value of the last unit of an input eventually declines, as the firm uses more and more of that input. Diminishing returns to labor are found in every industry. In the short run, as a firm adds units of labor, the marginal product (the additional output) of the last unit of labor must eventually fall, even if the labor is homogeneous. The reason is straightforward: In the short run, capital is fixed. Thus, eventually, the additional workers have insufficient capital to work with, so they are not as productive.

In the context of sports, diminishing returns may set in very quickly, especially in basketball, where only five team members play at a time, player substitution is relatively limited and, as the saying goes, "there is only one ball." Once a team has even two players who shoot frequently, adding a third shooter to the roster is likely to add very little to team quality, certainly less than the addition of the first two scorers. The Los Angeles Lakers would not dispute that Dwayne Wade is a great player, but his value to the Lakers is surely less than the price a team without a top scorer would pay, given that the Lakers already have Kobe Bryant.

Diminishing returns act as a brake on team behavior because they reduce the incentive any one team has to stockpile talent. It does not make economic sense for a team to spend large sums of money acquiring all the best players at each position when some, perhaps many, of them will contribute very little.

The Effect of Market Size

Differences in market size across the league provide an additional challenge to team owners. If, as research shows, the dollar value of a win is greater to teams in large cities than to teams in smaller ones, maximizing competitive balance and maximizing total league profits may not be consistent goals.[5] Even if fans

---

[5]For more on this topic, see Eric M. Leifer, *Making the Majors* (Cambridge, Mass.: Harvard University Press, 1995). See also John D. Burger and Stephen J.K. Walters, "Market Size, Pay, and Performance: A General Model and Application to Major League Baseball," *Journal of Sports Economics,* vol. 4, no. 2 (May 2003), pp. 108–125, for research supporting the relationship between market size and performance.

desire some level of uncertainty, a profit-maximizing league prefers to have the teams in the largest markets win more often than teams elsewhere. In a 30-team league, perfect parity would mean that the Yankees and Dodgers—teams in the two largest markets—would win the World Series only once every 30 years. If championships were allocated so that they were distributed equally on a per-fan basis, rather than a per-team basis, the large-market teams would win more frequently than once every 30 years because they have so many more fans than small-market teams. The tension here between individual team profits and overall league profits is similar to that of a cartel. Each individual team can increase its profits by improving relative to the rest of the league, but from the league perspective, it is better if some teams are more successful than others.

To see why big-market teams benefit more from winning than small-market teams do, assume that each team gets its revenue only from tickets and local television revenue. Assume further that teams benefit from having a higher winning percentage, but the additional benefits of increasing the winning percentage become smaller as it approaches 1.000. The logic here is that increasing a team's winning percentage from .470 to .500 increases revenues more than increasing it from .870 to .900. Thus, the marginal revenue curve from additional wins is positive but downward sloping. Because teams in larger cities enjoy greater increases in fan support from an additional win than teams in small cities, an additional win will generate more gate revenue, more media revenue, and more venue revenue for a team in Los Angeles than it will for a team in Indianapolis. Figure 5.1 illustrates the greater value of wins for a team in a large market. It shows the additional (marginal) revenue from one more win for a team in a small market (MR_s) and a team in a large market

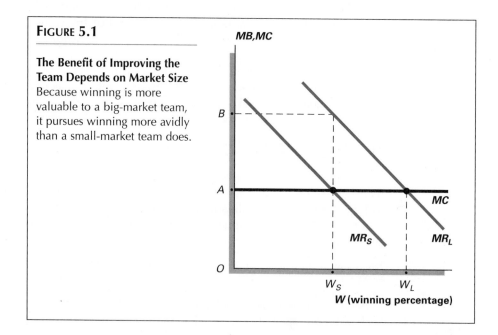

FIGURE 5.1

The Benefit of Improving the Team Depends on Market Size
Because winning is more valuable to a big-market team, it pursues winning more avidly than a small-market team does.

(MR_L). If both teams win W_S games, the value of one more win for the small-market team is OA. The value of an additional win for the large-market team is much greater (OB).[6]

If all firms maximize profits then they will operate where the marginal revenue of wins equals the marginal cost of wins. To keep the focus on revenue, assume that the marginal cost of a win is constant and equal for all teams. For the small-market team, this occurs at W_S wins. However, at W_S the marginal revenue of another win for a large-market team is much higher. The large-market team thus has an incentive to acquire more talent and wins $W_L > W_S$ games. Thus, even in a world without Mark Cubans or Jerry Joneses, where all teams maximize profit, economic theory predicts that teams from big cities will win more frequently than teams from small cities.

5.3 Measuring Competitive Balance

There are two approaches to measuring competitive balance.[7] The first approach focuses on team performance over the course of a given season. To examine this, economists have developed measures of dispersion in single-season performance. A wide dispersion in winning percentages means that some teams are much better than others in a given season. The second approach looks across several seasons. It measures the concentration of championships over a given period or turnover in the league's standings. Leagues with a high concentration of championships have a small set of teams winning year after year. No single approach is necessarily better than the other. In fact, to fully evaluate the competitive balance in a league, it is necessary to consider both types of variation. Fans and owners are likely to desire both tightly contested seasonal competition and regular turnover in champions.

Within-Season Variation

Believe it or not, sports fans resemble opera or classic rock buffs. Both are attracted by the absolute quality of the performers. Thus, the demand to see a big-time college football game between Texas and Oklahoma far outstrips the demand to see a game between Ivy League powers Harvard and Brown. In addition, at any level of absolute quality, the demand for a sporting event

---

[6]This model first appeared in Mohamed El-Hodiri and James Quirk, "An Economic Model of a Professional Sports League," *Journal of Political Economy*, vol. 79, no. 6 (November/December 1971), pp. 1302–1319.

[7]For more sophisticated views of some of the techniques presented here, see Craig A. Depken II, "Free-agency and the competitiveness of Major League Baseball," *Review of Industrial Organization*, vol. 14, no. 3 (May 1999) pp. 205–217; Brad Humphreys, "Alternative Measures of Competitive Balance," *Journal of Sports Economics*, vol. 3, no. 2 (May 2002), pp. 133–148; and P. Owen Dorian, Michael Ryan, and Clayton R. Weatherston, "Measuring Competitive Balance in Professional Team Sports Using the Herfindahl-Hirschman Index," *Journal of Industrial Organization*, vol. 31, no. 4 (December 2007), pp. 289–302.

depends upon the relative quality of the opposing players or teams. Fans might therefore prefer to see a tightly contested game between Harvard and Brown over a 49–0 shellacking of Oklahoma by Texas. Within-season variation in winning percentage focuses on the evenness of competition over the course of a season.

Most measures of within-season variation start with the standard deviation of winning percentage. The **standard deviation** measures the dispersion of the observations around the mean; it is the distance of the typical observation from the sample mean. In the case of professional sports, there is a loser for every winner, so the mean winning percentage for a league must be 0.5.

The formula for the standard deviation of winning percentages within a single season is

$$\sigma_{w,t} = \sqrt{\frac{\sum_{i=1}^{N}(WPCT_{i,t} - .500)^2}{N}},$$

where $WPCT_{i,t}$ is the winning percentage of the ith team in the league in year t, .500 is the average winning percentage of all teams for the year, and N is the number of teams in the league. The larger the standard deviation, the greater the dispersion of the winning percentages. For example, consider the final standings for the NBA's 2008–2009 season. Table 5.2 shows the final standings for the Atlantic Division of the Eastern Conference and the Pacific Division of the Western Conference. One can get a first impression of how balanced the two divisions were by looking at the highest and lowest winning percentages. In the Atlantic Division, the Boston Celtics won 75.6 percent of the time, while the New York Knicks won only 39.0 percent of the time. The Pacific Division was even less balanced, as the Los Angeles Lakers won 79.3 percent of their games, and the Sacramento Kings won only 20.7 percent of their games. Computing the standard deviation confirms this impression. The standard deviation of winning percentage in the Atlantic Division was 0.153, meaning that the typical

TABLE 5.2

Winning Percentages for the NBA Atlantic and Pacific Divisions 2008–2009

Atlantic	Winning Percentages	Southeast	Winning Percentages
Boston	0.756	LA Lakers	0.793
Philadelphia	0.500	Phoenix	0.561
New Jersey	0.415	Golden State	0.354
Toronto	0.402	LA Clippers	0.232
New York	0.390	Sacramento	0.207
σ	0.153	σ	0.247

Source: http://www.nba.com/standings/2004/team_record_comparison/conferenceNew_Std_Div.html.

observation varies by 0.153 from the mean winning percentage.[8] The standard deviation in the Pacific Division is 0.247, much greater than in the Atlantic Division. This means that the typical deviation of teams in the Pacific Division from the mean performance is much greater than in the Atlantic Division.

The standard deviation of winning percentages is a useful summary of competitive balance, but it has significant limitations. In particular, the standard deviation of winning percentages varies with the number of games in a season. To see why, try flipping a fair coin—one with an equal chance of coming up heads or tails—four times. This is the equivalent to two equally matched teams playing one another four times, with only random factors determining the outcome. More than 12 percent of the time (about once in eight tries), you will get an extreme outcome of all heads or all tails.[9] As you increase the number of flips to 40, 400, or 4,000, the chance of an extreme outcome becomes more and more remote. This experiment tells us that, even if a league were perfectly balanced, we might very well see some teams with many more wins than others in a short season. As the season gets longer, however, winning and losing streaks begin to offset one another, just like runs of heads and tails with coin flips.

Table 5.3 shows that the standard deviation of winning percentage in the NFL was about three times the standard deviation of winning percentage in MLB in 2008. This finding might reflect greater competitive balance in MLB, or it might result from the fact that the NFL has only a 16-game season while MLB has a 162-game season. To account for the fact that the standard deviation is larger for sports with shorter seasons, we do not directly compare standard deviations. Instead, we first compute what the standard deviation of winning percentage would be for a league that had completely equal teams. The ratio of

TABLE 5.3

Dispersion of Winning Percentages

League	2008 Actual	Ideal	2008 Ratio
MLB	.068	.039	1.75
NFL	.207	.125	1.66
NBA	.172	.056	3.07
NHL	.084	.056	1.50
English Premier League	.160	.081	1.97

Sources: 2008 data are generated from the ESPN Web sites http://espn.go.com. Soccer and NHL data are from 2008–2009. Because teams receive one point for overtime losses, winning percentage in the NHL is computed as the percentage of possible points. English Premier and Bundesliga statistics are standard deviations of points rather than winning percentage.

---

[8]Because the Atlantic Division teams play teams from other divisions in the NBA, the average winning percentage here does not have to equal 0.5. In this case, the average was 0.493. The mean winning percentage in the Pacific Division was 0.429.

[9]This is a straightforward application of the binomial distribution.

the actual standard deviation to this "ideal" standard deviation tells us how far out of balance the league was. Because the ratios for MLB and the NFL account for the length of the season, we can use them to compare competitive balance in the two leagues.

The standard deviation that corresponds to a world in which each team has a 0.5 chance of winning each game is

$$\sigma_I = \frac{0.5}{\sqrt{G}},$$

where 0.5 indicates that each team has a 0.5 probability of winning, and G is the number of games each team plays.[10] Because each MLB team plays 162 games per season, the ideal is 0.039. Because NFL teams play only 16 games, a randomly occurring string of wins or losses has a greater impact on a team's final winning percentage, so the ideal standard deviation is much larger, 0.125. In the NHL and NBA, where teams play 82-game schedules, the standard deviations are 0.056.

To measure competitive balance within a single season, we use the ratio (R) of the actual standard deviation of winning percentages (σ_w) to the ideal standard deviation (σ_I).[11]

$$R = \frac{\sigma_w}{\sigma_I}.$$

Thus, for the NBA in 2008–2009,

$$R = 0.172/0.056 = 3.07.$$

Based on this result, we see that the standard deviation of winning percentages in the NBA is more than three times what it would be in a world with absolutely balanced teams. Again, this result is consistent with our casual observation that competition appears unbalanced in the NBA, as four teams had winning percentages of over .700, while five teams had winning percentages of less than .300.

Table 5.3 presents the actual and ideal standard deviations for five major sports leagues. It shows that the NHL was the most equally balanced league in 2008–2009, with an R-value of 1.50. The NFL and MLB followed with R-values of 1.66 and 1.75. The English Premier League in soccer was somewhat less balanced, with an R-value of 1.97. The NBA, with a ratio of 3.07, is by far the least balanced of the five leagues.

---

[10]This results from the fact that the variance of the binomial distribution is $\sigma^2 = \frac{p*(1-p)}{N}$, where p is the number of successes, and N is the number of trials.

[11]See Scully (1989) for an early application of this method to professional baseball. We can use the same idea to evaluate competitive balance over many seasons by calculating the average value of the standard deviation over several years and using that value as σ_w when computing R.

The data in the table clearly show the NBA to be the least balanced league in North America. In *The Wages of Wins*, Dave Berri, Martin Schmidt, and Stacey Brook discuss why this might be so.[12] Their theory is based on the old adage "you can't teach height." In basketball, taller players have a distinct advantage over shorter ones. There are good players who are not tall, but if we compare two players of equal skill but substantially different heights, the taller player will be more effective. The number of very tall people who are also very gifted athletes—and whose athletic skills are well suited for basketball—is extremely small. Thus, a team lucky enough to get an unusually gifted player, such as Dwight Howard, has a competitive advantage.

Between-Season Variation

For baseball fans everywhere, spring is a special time of year that brings the promise of a new baseball season and the chance that "this could be the year" that their team wins it all. Across seasons, competitive balance implies that each team has the opportunity to move up in the standings each year and compete for playoff berths. This type of competitive balance is called turnover, or team-specific variation. It is different from within-season variation in that it considers the change in the relative positions of the teams in the standings each year rather than the distance between teams in a given season. Brad Humphreys (2002) defines team-specific variation for a team as

$$\sigma_{i,T} = \sqrt{\frac{\sum_{i=1}^{T}(WPCT_i - \overline{WPCT})^2}{T}},$$

where T is the number of seasons, and $\overline{WPCT}$ is the team's average winning percentage over the T seasons.[13] The larger σ_T becomes, the more a team's fortunes change from year to year. If every team always finished with the same record, σ_T would be zero. The more a team's fortunes change from year to year, the greater the standard deviation. If fans support a team only if it has a reasonable chance of winning its division or conference, variation across seasons is vital to maintaining fan interest over long stretches of time. If σ_T were zero for all teams, we would know how all teams would perform before the season even started. Such a situation would surely reduce demand for all teams.

One frustrating aspect of using the variation between seasons is that, unlike the within-season standard deviation, there is no obvious standard of comparison.

---

[12]Dave Berri, Martin Schmidt, and Stacey Brook, *The Wages of Wins* (Stanford, Calif.: Stanford University Press, 2006). The arguments presented here are based on a previous paper by Berri et al. titled "The Short Supply of Tall People: Explaining Competitive Imbalance in the National Basketball Association," *Journal of Economic Issues*, vol. 39, no. 4 (December), pp. 1029–1041.

[13]If you are interested in reading about the debate over which measures are most appropriate, see the articles by Brad R. Humphreys and E. W. Eckard in *Journal of Sports Economics*, vol. 4, no. 1 (February 2003).

It is not possible to say whether fans or owners care more about how much their team's winning percentage varies across the years or how their team's position changes relative to other teams. For example, would Philadelphia hockey fans feel better if the Flyers had a very good record instead of a mediocre record but finished second to the New Jersey Devils every year? Though turnover is certainly important, the absence of an absolute standard means that team-specific variation is useful only as a relative measure of dispersion (when comparing one time period with another or one sport with another).

Frequency of Championships It is also possible to evaluate competitive balance by looking at the frequency with which teams win successive championships. On one hand, if the Yankees win the World Series every year, then the winning percentages of the teams in the league do not matter as much, since the league is clearly unbalanced. On the other hand, if different teams win the American League and National League pennants every year, then one can argue that competition in each league is balanced, regardless of how bad the worst teams are relative to the best teams. This criterion is similar to the turnover criterion discussed above, but it relates to championships rather than regular season standings.

Table 5.4 shows that the NBA is also the least balanced North American league in terms of how often teams win championships. Just 2 of 30 teams won seven of 10 championships between 1999 and 2008. No other North American sports league shows such imbalance. The English Premier League, however, is even more imbalanced, as Manchester United alone accounts for six of the last ten championships. The NHL is far more balanced, with seven different teams winning championships, while eight teams each from the NFL and MLB have won championships.

TABLE 5.4

Distribution of Championships: 1998–1999 to 2007–2008

NBA	NHL[a]	NFL	MLB	Premier League
Spurs—4	Red Wings—3	Patriots—3	Red Sox—2	Manchester United—6
Lakers—3	Devils—2	Broncos—1	Yankees—2	Arsenal—2
Celtics—1	Avalanche—1	Bucs—1	Angels—1	Chelsea—2
Heat—1	Ducks—1	Colts—1	Cardinals—1	
Pistons—1	Hurricanes—1	Giants—1	Diamondbacks—1	
	Lightning—1	Rams—1	Marlins—1	
	Stars—1	Ravens—1	Phillies—1	
		Steelers—1	White Sox—1	
HHI = 0.28	HHI = 0.18	HHI = 0.16	HHI = 0.14	HHI = 0.44

[a]Hockey championships start with 1997–1998 because there was no champion in 2004–2005.

The Herfindahl-Hirschman Index   Counting the number of championships shows that the NBA and the Premier League are less balanced than the NFL, the NHL, or MLB. Unfortunately, it does not tell us whether the Patriots' winning three Super Bowls makes the NFL more or less balanced than MLB, in which the Yankees and Red Sox won two World Series each. The Herfindahl-Hirschman Index (*HHI*) gives us a metric with which we can make such comparisons. The *HHI* was originally developed to measure the concentration of firms in an industry, but we use it to measure the concentration of league championships.

We calculate the *HHI* by counting the number of championships (c_i) team i won within a given period, dividing by the number of years in the period (T), squaring this fraction, and adding the fractions for all teams:

$$HHI = \sum_i \left(\frac{c_i}{T}\right)^2$$

The minimum value of the *HHI* is $1/N$, where N is the number of teams in the league. This corresponds to a completely balanced league in which all teams alternate championships. The maximum, 1, indicates perfect imbalance. To see this, consider two leagues, each with five teams. In one league each team has won two championships over the last 10 years. In the other league, one team has won all the championships. The *HHI* for each league is:

$$HHI_1 = \left[\left(\frac{2}{10}\right)^2 + \left(\frac{2}{10}\right)^2 + \left(\frac{2}{10}\right)^2 + \left(\frac{2}{10}\right)^2 + \left(\frac{2}{10}\right)^2\right] = \frac{20}{100} = \frac{1}{5}$$

$$HHI_2 = \left[\left(\frac{10}{10}\right)^2 + \left(\frac{0}{10}\right)^2 + \left(\frac{0}{10}\right)^2 + \left(\frac{0}{10}\right)^2 + \left(\frac{0}{10}\right)^2\right] = \frac{100}{100} = 1$$

The last line in Table 5.4 shows the *HHI* for the five leagues. As expected, the *HHI* for the Premier League is far greater than for any other league. This is followed by the *HHI* for the NBA. The *HHI* for the NHL, NFL, and MLB are substantially smaller and are relatively close together, with MLB being the smallest. Thus, by this metric, MLB has been more balanced than any of the other four major North American leagues from 1998–1999 to 2007–2008.

Illustrating Competitive Imbalance

Thus far, we have measured competitive balance with sometimes complex algebraic formulae. In this section, we show how to express competitive balance graphically. To do so, we use an economic tool known as the Lorenz curve. The **Lorenz curve** illustrates how evenly distributed a resource or characteristic is in a population.

To see how the Lorenz curve works, let's consider the NBA's 2008–2009 regular season. Because the NBA has 30 teams that play an 82-game schedule, there are 1,230 games—and hence 1,230 possible wins—over the course of the season. The three weakest teams (the Sacramento Kings, Los Angeles Clippers, and Washington Wizards) combined to win only 55 games. Thus, the bottom 10 percent of the NBA population accounted for about 4.5 percent of the NBA's total wins. The combination (10, 4.5) corresponds to point *A* in Figure 5.2. The next three teams combined for 71 wins, or almost 5.8 percent of the total. In terms of Figure 5.2, we move another 10 percent to the right and 5.8 percent up to point *B*. Point *B* shows that the bottom 20 percent of the NBA population accounted for slightly less than 10.3 percent of all wins. As we add better teams, we account for more and more wins, so the Lorenz curve becomes steeper as we move to the right. Finally, the three best teams (the Boston Celtics, Los Angeles Lakers, and Cleveland Cavaliers) won 193 games, 15.7 percent of all wins. Going the final 10 percent to the right and the final 15.7 percent up accounts for all teams and all possible wins, so we end up at the point (100, 100).

The value of the NBA's Lorenz curve becomes apparent when we compare it to the curve that would result in a world of complete equality, in which each team won 41 games and lost 41 games. In this case, it does not matter which three teams we choose first because any three teams combine for 123 wins, or 10 percent of the total. Thus, adding 10 percent of the population always adds 10 percent of the total wins. In this case, the Lorenz curve is a straight line from the origin to the point (100, 100).

The actual Lorenz curve lies below the "ideal" Lorenz curve because the three weakest teams account for far less than 10 percent of the wins, causing the actual Lorenz curve to sag below the ideal. When all teams and all wins are counted, the actual curve rejoins the ideal curve at the point (100, 100). As competitive imbalance grows, the weak teams account for a lower percentage

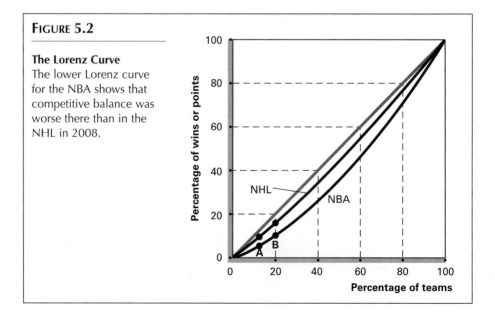

FIGURE 5.2

The Lorenz Curve
The lower Lorenz curve for the NBA shows that competitive balance was worse there than in the NHL in 2008.

of wins, the strong teams account for a greater percentage of wins, and the Lorenz curve sags farther below the ideal. Thus, performing the same exercise for the NHL yields a Lorenz curve that lies between the NBA's Lorenz curve and the ideal.[14] This shows that the NHL is not perfectly balanced, but it is more evenly balanced than the NBA is. Figure 5.2 thus reinforces the statistics in Table 5.3, which showed that the ratio of the actual to the ideal standard deviation of winning percentages was 1.50 for the NHL and 3.07 for the NBA.

In sum, there are many ways to measure competitive balance, and no single method should be regarded as most appropriate. To fully grasp the state of competitive balance in a league requires consideration of intraseason balance—the spread of winning percentages across teams—as well as interseason balance, the turnover of teams in the standings, and the frequency of championships. Leagues must be concerned about all these forms of competitive balance because fan interest—and correspondingly attendance, television ratings, and league profits—is likely to be affected by each.

Competitive Balance in Major League Baseball

Many team owners in Major League Baseball have bemoaned what they see as a severe competitive imbalance between teams in big markets like New York and teams in small markets like Kansas City. In 2000, the owners established a Blue Ribbon Panel, which supported their claim that big-market teams can afford to pay much higher salaries, thereby attracting the best players. They assert that big-market clubs can afford more talent than the small-market clubs and, as a result, win championship after championship. The owners maintain that the imbalance has become particularly acute since 1976, when baseball players won the right to **free agency,** which allows a player to sell his services to the highest bidder.

Contrary to the owners' claims, the metrics we have developed in this chapter suggest that baseball does not have particularly severe competitive imbalance. Table 5.3 shows that the dispersion of winning percentages in MLB is only slightly worse than that in the NHL or NFL, but it is much better than the dispersion in the NBA and the English Professional League. In addition, Table 5.4 shows that, over the last ten years, the *HHI* for championships in MLB is lower than for any of the other four leagues.

Contrary to the owners' assertion that free agency has harmed competitive balance, there has been greater turnover in champions in the free agency era. In the 31 years prior to free agency (1946–1976), the Yankees dominated, winning 11 World Series. They were followed by the Dodgers, who won 4, and the Athletics and Cardinals, who won 3 each. The *HHI* for the pre–free agency period that we consider is 0.176. The Yankees again dominated the 31 seasons that followed the advent of free agency, but they won only 6 championships

---

[14]Because the NHL distinguishes wins from "overtime wins," we use the total number of points (two points for a win in regulation time, one for an overtime win) rather than wins for the NHL.

over this period, and no other team won more than 2.[15] The *HHI* for 1977–2008 is only 0.078. While much else in MLB has changed since 1976—it has expanded from 24 to 30 teams, gone from two to three divisions, and added a "wild card" team to the playoffs—championships in the free agency period have been spread much more evenly across the league.

Economic Theories of Competitive Balance

Economists are not surprised that free agency has not harmed competitive balance. In fact, economic theory predicts that freely functioning markets distribute resources to where they are most highly valued. Changing **property rights**—the ownership or control of resources—affects who gets paid but not where the resources go. The fact that the allocation of resources does not vary when property rights change is known as the **invariance principle**.[16]

To see how the invariance principle works, consider the problem facing Brazilian President Luis Inácio Lula da Silva. "Lula" has to figure out how to allocate tickets for the 2014 World Cup, which Brazil will host. Brazil is such a soccer-mad country, and its citizens are so confident about their national team, that Brazilian fans would fill the stadium several times over if they could. In this hypothetical example, suppose the stadium holds 100,000 people and, as seen in Figure 5.3, the final game would sell out if tickets cost $150. (For simplicity, we assume that all seats are equally valuable.) Lula decides that $150 is too much to charge and declares that tickets will cost only $10. At a price of $10, however, 500,000 people are willing to buy tickets. At that price, the Brazilian government must ration the tickets in some way. To solve this problem, the government institutes a lottery in which 100,000 people are chosen at random. Those lucky winners can buy tickets for $10.

The invariance principle says that, as long as people are free to transact with one another, the final allocation of tickets will be the same under both the free market and the lottery. Suppose, for example, that Barry is willing to pay $300 for a ticket, while Ann won a ticket, which she values at $20. As we saw in Chapters 2 and 3, Barry and Ann can become better off if Barry buys the ticket at a price between $20 and $300. For example, if Barry pays Ann $150, he enjoys a consumer surplus of $150. In addition, Ann enjoys a producer surplus of $130.

More generally, if people are free to transact with one another, there are two results. First, the market price of a ticket rises from the official price of $10 to $150. Second, because the market price is now $150, all ticket holders will place a value of at least $150 on their tickets. By transferring the property rights to the

---

[15]There was no World Series in 1994 due to the labor stoppage, so the 31 championships span 32 years.

[16]The invariance principle is frequently attributed to 1991 Nobel Laureate Ronald Coase. However, Coase's contribution was to apply the invariance principle in the context of externalities, a concept we cover in Chapter 7. See Ronald Coase, "The Problem of Social Cost," *Journal of Law and Economics*, v. 3 (October 1960), pp. 1–44.

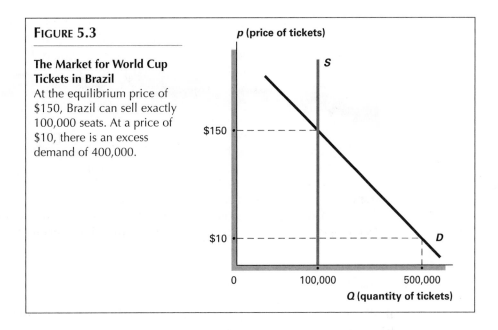

FIGURE 5.3

The Market for World Cup Tickets in Brazil
At the equilibrium price of $150, Brazil can sell exactly 100,000 seats. At a price of $10, there is an excess demand of 400,000.

ticket holders, the Brazilian government has not altered the ultimate distribution of tickets. It has simply changed who gets paid for them.

In the context of professional sports, consider the hypothetical case of LeBron James, star player for the NBA's Cleveland Cavaliers. As one of the best players in the NBA, James is a popular draw and adds greatly to the gate and media revenue of any team for which he plays. In a mid-size city like Cleveland, he might generate $25 million per year in additional revenue. However, in a much larger, wealthier city, such as New York, James would add considerably more, perhaps $50 million. In a world of unrestricted free agency in which James could freely sell his services to the highest bidder, Cleveland would lose out to the New York Knicks because it is willing to pay James up to $25 million, while the Knicks are willing to pay him up to $50 million.

Consider now what happens in a world in which players are not free to move but owners are free to sell the rights to players' services for cash or payment in kind. The Knicks still get LeBron James because they are willing to pay the Cavaliers more than James is worth in Cleveland but less than he is worth in New York. As a result, both teams profit. Such a transaction sent Babe Ruth from the Boston Red Sox to the New York Yankees in 1920. An avid fan of musical theater, Red Sox owner Harry Frazee sold the rights to Babe Ruth to the Yankees for $100,000 so that he could finance the Broadway production of the musical *No, No, Nannette*.

This example shows that property rights do not affect where LeBron James plays. They do, however, determine whom New York pays to obtain his services. Under free agency, LeBron James owns the rights to his services. In such a world, New York lures James from Cleveland to New York by offering him a higher salary. If James is unable to move freely, the Knicks do not have to worry about enticing James to New York. Instead, they must pay the Cavaliers.

In some situations, the invariance principle fails to hold. For our purposes, the most important situation occurs when there are substantial transactions costs. As the term suggests, a **transaction cost** is the expense of dealing with a buyer or seller in a market *in addition to* the price one pays for the good or service. If, for example, Barry had to take out a $200 advertisement in the newspaper to find Ann, he would face a market price of $150 plus a transaction cost of $200. Because the ticket is worth only $150 to Barry, the transaction cost would discourage Barry from buying the ticket. More generally, when there are substantial transaction costs, resources might not flow to their most valued use. In the next section, we analyze several ways in which leagues have imposed transaction costs that prevent the free flow of players to their most valued positions.

5.4 Attempts to Alter Competitive Balance

All the major sports leagues have developed policies designed to promote competitive balance. All these policies—revenue sharing, salary caps and luxury taxes, and the reverse-order draft—are designed to limit the advantages of big-market teams by reducing the benefits or increasing the costs big-market teams face when pursuing talent. Whatever impact these policies have on competitive balance, many players believe that the true goal is to depress salaries. We analyze the impact of these policies on salaries in Chapter 9. In this section, we focus on their impact on competitive balance.[17]

Revenue Sharing

As we showed in Chapter 3, a primary outcome of revenue sharing is a leveling of teams' profits. Some team owners also claim that revenue sharing is necessary to equalize the demand for talent. Teams from large cities like New York or Los Angeles have two advantages. First, their access to larger fan bases and media markets means that they can afford to pay more for talented players. Second, as we saw in Figure 5.1, winning generates more revenue for big-market teams, which gives them a greater incentive to bid for talented players.

Revenue sharing reduces both these inequalities. The transfer from high-revenue to low-revenue teams equalizes the ability to pay for talent. In addition, the transfer reduces the marginal revenue of winning to big-market teams. In terms of Figure 5.1, revenue sharing shifts MR_L to the left because the team gets

---

[17]For a more detailed account of how leagues use these tools to promote competitive balance see Michael A. Leeds, "Salary Caps and Luxury Taxes in Professional Sports Leagues," in *The Business of Sports,* edited by Brad R. Humphreys and Dennis R. Howard, vol. 2 (Westport, Conn.: Praeger, 2008), pp. 181–206.

to keep less of the revenue a star player generates. In the limit, if teams share all revenue equally, the curves MR_L and MR_S coincide, and their demand for winning and talent is equal.

As noted in Chapter 3, all the major North American sports leagues have adopted some form of revenue sharing, though they vary greatly in the form and degree of sharing. They all share the revenue from league-wide broadcast rights equally, though the lucrative contracts signed by the NFL and NBA do much more to equalize revenue than do the contracts for MLB and the NHL. Chapter 3 also showed that the NFL shares a larger portion of its gate revenue than any other sport. Starting in 2002, MLB significantly increased its revenue sharing, as teams now pay 34 percent of their net local revenue into a central pool. Part of this pool is paid equally to all teams, while part is paid only to teams with below-average local revenue. The NHL recently adopted a complex formula that makes transfers from high-revenue teams to low-revenue teams to equalize payrolls.

Economic theory and empirical evidence suggest, however, that revenue sharing does not equalize talent.[18] If the teams in the league maximize their profits, the big-market teams acquire more talent even if MR_L and MR_S coincide. To see why, assume that all teams share revenue equally, so that the value of winning is equal for all teams. In effect, all teams put their revenue in a big pot and take out an equal share. The fact that big-market teams generate more revenue from winning means that if they win more often, more money goes into the pot, and each team's share of income rises. Thus, even under a system that equalizes revenue, leagues have a financial interest in allocating talent disproportionately to large-market teams. This will maximize the amount of money in the pot and hence the share going to each team.

In addition, equalizing the ability to pay will equalize the distribution of talent only if all teams pursue talent equally. However, as we showed in Chapter 3, not all teams do so. Consider, for example, MLB's two most profitable teams, the Florida Marlins (operating income: $43.7 million) and Washington Nationals (operating income: $42.6 million).[19] In part, the Marlins' high profits in 2008 were due to a payroll of less than $22 million. This was only one-tenth of what the New York Yankees paid and was less than half the payroll of the Tampa Bay Rays, who had the second-lowest payroll in MLB. The Washington Nationals, who have not fielded a team with a winning record since 2002, when they played in Montreal, had the fifth-lowest payroll but showed huge profits. Profits seem to be more of a priority for these clubs than winning.

---

[18]For more on the impact of revenue sharing, see Stefan Kesenne, "Revenue Sharing and Competitive Balance: Does the Invariance Proposition Hold?," *Journal of Sports Economics*, vol. 6, no. 1 (February 2005) pp. 98–106.

[19]Operating income data comes from Forbes.com, "The Business of Baseball" on line at http://www.forbes.com/lists/2009/33/baseball-values-09_The-Business-Of-Baseball_MetroArea.html, April 22, 2009. Payroll data from USAToday.com, "USA Today Salaries Database," on line at http://content.usatoday.com/sports/baseball/salaries/default.aspx, consulted June 10, 2009.

Salary Caps and Luxury Taxes

Of the major North American sports leagues, only MLB does not have a salary cap. A **salary cap** is a direct restriction on the amount a team is allowed to pay its players. Here, we focus on their impact on competitive balance. The term "salary cap" is a misnomer for two reasons. First, with the exception of the NBA (which we discuss later), the cap applies to payrolls rather than to individual salaries. Second, all salary caps are bands, setting both a maximum and a minimum that a team may spend on player salaries in a given year. In the 2008 (2008–2009) season, the maximum payrolls were $116 million in the NFL, $56.7 million in the NHL, and $55.63 million in the NBA.

Salary caps are effectively a new form of revenue sharing, not among teams but between teams and players. They are set by identifying two factors: a revenue base and a player share. The NFL, for example, sets aside 59.5 percent of its designated gross revenue for player salaries. Designated gross revenue (DGR) does not consist of all team revenue. It is made up of:

- Gate revenue from preseason, regular season, and postseason games
- Broadcast rights
- Other licensing agreements
- The ticket revenue portion of income from luxury boxes and premium seating

The NFL deducts nonsalary benefits from this total and then allocates the amount equally among all 32 teams. The cap formula is thus:

$$CAP = 0.595 * (DGR - B) \div 32$$

In 2008, the cap for NFL teams was $116 million. The minimum salary was 85.2 percent of the cap, or $98.8 million. Although revenue and share are different for the NBA and the NHL, the basic formula is similar for both leagues.

The big difference between the NFL and the NBA is that NFL payrolls have a hard cap, while NBA payrolls have a soft cap. A **hard cap** is an absolute limit. NFL teams must stay within the limits of the cap. A **soft cap** has numerous exceptions to the limits that the cap imposes. The three most important exceptions to the NBA's cap are the mid-level exception, the rookie exception, and the Larry Bird exception. The mid-level exception allows each team to sign one player to the average NBA salary even if the team is already over the salary limit or if signing a player to such a contract would put the team over the limit. Under the rookie exception, a team can sign a rookie to his first contract even if doing so puts the team over its cap limit. The Larry Bird exception permits teams to re-sign players who are already on their roster even if doing so would exceed the cap limit. This rule got its name because its first use permitted the Boston Celtics to re-sign their star player in 1983. In 1983, the Celtics were loaded with stars, and a hard cap would have forced the Celtics to break up this very popular team to re-sign Larry Bird. To avoid this, the NBA softened the cap, permitting the Celtics to keep their team intact. The result was that team payrolls routinely exceeded the salary cap, and competitive balance remained a problem. In fact, the within-season standard deviation of winning percentages has risen consistently over this period, indicating a decline in competitive balance.

Because all of the exceptions have undermined the soft cap approach, the NBA has had to develop a number of supplemental measures to reinforce it. These include caps on salaries that teams can pay individual players and a luxury tax. The cap on individual salaries classifies players according to their years of experience and specifies maximum and minimum salaries that a team can pay players with a given amount of experience.

A **luxury tax** has nothing to do with luxury boxes; it is a surcharge the league imposes on teams whose payroll exceeds a specified level. The luxury tax in the NBA is very strict, as teams must pay $1 to a central fund for every $1 by which its payroll exceeds the salary cap.

Baseball's luxury tax also charges teams for paying more than a prespecified threshold ($155 million in 2008). Unlike other sports, MLB charges a different tax rate depending on how many times a team has exceeded the threshold. Thus, in 2008, the Detroit Tigers paid the 22.5 percent levy charged to all first-time violators on a payroll that exceeded the limit by $5.8 million. The Tigers thus paid a $1.3 million penalty. The New York Yankees, the only other team charged a tax, paid $26.9 million. Their tax was much higher than the Tigers' because they exceeded the threshold by $67.2 million and because, having exceeded the threshold for the sixth consecutive year, they paid the maximum 40 percent tax rate. Since the luxury tax was implemented in 2003, the Yankees have paid a total of $148.3 million in penalties.[20] While the Yankees' 2009 payroll is less than their payroll for 2008, their continued willingness to exceed the threshold indicates that the luxury tax has had a limited impact on their behavior.

The Reverse-Order Entry Draft

The reverse-order entry draft allows teams to choose incoming players in reverse order from their finish of the previous season. The team with the worst record chooses first, the second-worst team chooses second, and so on, until the team that won the previous season's championship chooses last. The same procedure is followed through subsequent rounds. All players who have not been chosen in the draft are free to sign contracts with any team.

The origin of the draft can be traced to 1934, when two NFL teams—the old Brooklyn Dodgers and the Philadelphia Eagles—bid against each other for the services of Stan Kostka, an All-American player at the University of Minnesota. The resulting bidding war drove salary offers to the then unbelievable level of $5,000 (what Bronko Nagurski—the greatest player of the era—made).

---

[20]Tom Singer, "Yankees, Tigers Hit with Luxury Tax," Yankees.com. online at http://mlb.mlb .com/news/article.jsp?ymd=20081222&content_id=3726222&vkey=news_nyy&fext=.jsp&c_id=nyy& partnerId=rss_nyy, December 22, 2008.

At the next league meeting, Bert Bell, the Philadelphia Eagles owner, proposed a unique way to avoid future bidding wars. Teams would select the rights to unsigned players, with the order of selection determined by each team's performance in the previous season. All the major North American leagues now have a reverse-order draft. Partly because NBA rosters are so small—each team has only 12 players on its active roster—the NBA draft lasts only two rounds. Because other leagues have larger squads and because success at the professional level has traditionally been harder to predict, they have longer drafts, with the NHL draft lasting five rounds, the NFL draft lasting seven rounds, and the MLB draft continuing until teams decide to stop drafting players.

Evaluating the Reverse-Order Draft   Reverse-order drafts can, in theory, promote competitive balance by allocating the best new players to the weakest teams. However, its success in equalizing talent depends on the ability of teams to identify and develop talented players, and every draft has busts and unexpected successes. More significantly, some teams (such as the NFL's New England Patriots) seem consistently able to find talented players despite having poor draft picks, while other teams (such as the NFL's Detroit Lions) regularly fail to find good players despite having excellent draft positions.[21]

Because the reverse-order draft rewards failure with high draft picks, it can worsen competitive balance. As teams fall out of competition, they could begin to lose deliberately in order to improve their position in a future draft.[22] In response to teams' intentionally losing, the NBA and NHL have instituted lottery systems in which teams with the worst records have the best chance of securing the top draft pick but are not sure to get it. While a lottery reduces the incentive to lose games intentionally, it also reduces the possibility that the weakest teams will benefit most from the draft. For example, the NBA's Orlando Magic won the 1993 draft lottery despite having just missed the playoffs the previous season and having the best record of any teams eligible for the lottery.

The dubious impact of drafts on competitive balance and the clear limitations drafts place on the market power of drafted players have led critics to claim that the reverse-order draft is nothing more than a tool to keep players' salaries low. It might be no coincidence that Bert Bell's Eagles were a last-place team when he proposed the draft. Still, some teams gave up a considerable advantage by agreeing to the draft. The New York Giants and the Chicago Bears, two teams from the biggest markets of all at the time, dominated the NFL's early years. Giving up the right to bid against other teams was not in their immediate self-interest. However, the owners of the Giants and Bears recognized that a larger issue was at stake. In the words of Tim Mara, the owner

---

[21]Perhaps the best selection by the Patriots came in 2000, when they chose future Hall of Fame quarterback Tom Brady in the sixth round of the draft, meaning that all other NFL teams had five or more chances to select Brady before the Patriots chose him.

[22]See Beck A. Taylor and Justin G. Trogdon, "Losing to Win: Tournament Incentives in the National Basketball Association," *Journal of Labor Economics*, vol. 20, no. 1 (January 2002), pp. 23–41.

of the Giants at the time, "People come to see a competition. We could give them a competition only if the teams had some sort of equality."[23]

Evaluating Talent: The Oakland Athletics and *Moneyball*   In the early 2000s, the Oakland Athletics baseball team seemed to have found a new way to evaluate talent. Despite being a quintessential small-market team that regularly had among the lowest revenues and payroll in MLB, the Athletics were a consistent winner. They finished first in their division four times between 2000 and 2006 and finished second the other three years.[24]

Michael Lewis analyzed the Athletics' astonishing run in the best-selling book *Moneyball*.[25] Lewis attributes much of the Athletics' success to their General Manager, Billy Beane. According to Lewis, Beane stood much of the conventional wisdom regarding player evaluation on its head. Teams traditionally looked for players with good physical tools, players who could run fast, throw far, and hit the ball hard. The standard yardstick for this type of performance was slugging percentage, which relates a player's total bases per at bat. A player who hits a lot of home runs will, all else equal, have a much higher slugging percentage than a player who hits a lot of singles. Beane felt that the key to success lay in a team's getting on base as often as possible, which is best measured by a player's on-base percentage.[26] Lewis asserts that, while traditional scouts look for physically gifted athletes, Beane looked for players who were disciplined and received a lot of bases on balls, even if they were not much to look at in a uniform.

In their economic analysis of *Moneyball*, Hakes and Sauer find evidence to support Lewis's claim that Beane had found an unexploited imperfection in the market.[27] Using multiple regression analysis, they show that increasing a team's on base percentage contributes more to wins than increasing its slugging percentage. Using salaries to measure the value that teams place on a player's characteristics, they also show that teams generally value slugging percentage more highly than on-base percentage. Emphasizing on-base percentage allowed Beane to acquire players whose contribution to success had been undervalued by other teams. This gave the Athletics a competitive advantage and allowed them to win consistently with far lower payrolls than other teams.

Unfortunately, as in any competitive market, the first mover enjoys a relatively brief advantage. Hakes and Sauer point out that the relative

---

[23]Michael MacCambridge, *America's Game* (New York: Random House, 2004), p. 44.

[24]They finished second in 2001 despite winning 102 games because the Seattle Mariners won an American League record 116 games.

[25]Michael Lewis, *Moneyball* (New York: Norton, 2003).

[26]Slugging percentage is computed as $(1B + 2*2B + 3*3B + 4*HR)/AB$, where $1B$ is the number of singles a player hits, $2B$ is the number of doubles, $3B$ is the number of triples, HR is the number of home runs, and AB is the number of at-bats. On-base percentage equals $(H + BB + HBP)/(AB + BB + HBP + SF)$, where H is the number of hits, BB is the number of bases on balls ("walks"), HBP is the number of times the player was hit by a pitch, and SF is the number of sacrifice flies. Appearances that result in BB, HBP, or SF are not counted as an AB.

[27]Jahn Hakes and Raymond Sauer, "An Economic Evaluation of the *Moneyball* Hypothesis," *Journal of Economic Perspectives*, vol. 20, no. 3 (Summer 2006), pp. 173–185.

valuation of slugging percentage and on-base percentage had begun to shift by 2004. With other teams now applying the lesson learned by Billy Beane, the Athletics were relegated to also-ran status by 2007.

Schedule Adjustments in the NFL

The NFL has a unique method for introducing an additional element of parity across seasons that is unrelated to the movement or acquisition of players. Each team's schedule is determined in part by the team's performance in the previous season. The scheduling formula requires that each team play 14 of its 16 games against opponents that are common to all members of a division. Each team plays the other three teams in its own division twice, plus all four teams in one other division within the conference, plus all four teams from one division in the other conference, for a total of 14 games. The relevant portion of the schedule for this discussion is that for each team, the remaining two games are played against opponents determined based on performance in the previous season. The first-place team in each division plays the first-place teams in the two divisions that the team is not scheduled to play; the second-place team plays the other two second-place teams, and so on. As a result, stronger teams play stronger schedules the following year, and weaker teams play weaker schedules the following year, creating a natural tendency toward parity.

Promotion and Relegation

The promotion and relegation system provides an additional incentive mechanism that may increase competitive balance. We saw that top European leagues such as the English Premier League and the Bundesliga have actual to ideal competitive balance ratios that are not far from the NFL, North America's most balanced league. Yet, if we consider frequency of championships as the measure of balance, Table 5.3 provides strong evidence that these same leagues are among the least competitive. The promotion and relegation system may help to provide an explanation to this puzzle.

When a team in a North American league is having a bad season and stands to finish near the bottom of the standings, it may not have much incentive to win. Once eliminated from the playoffs, the team may instead use the remaining games to try out new players in its minor league system, or raise capital by selling off some of its top players to playoff-bound teams that are in search of that "missing piece" needed to make them a championship contender. Thus the winning percentage of the poor team may erode further, increasing the standard deviation of winning percentage. In a promotion and relegation league, teams near the bottom of the standings have no such luxury. If they allow their performance to continue to slide, they may end up being relegated to the next lower league. Teams that are near the bottom of the standings have an incentive to continue to play to win right to the end. Thus, promotion and relegation may not create turnover of the league champion, but it could well decrease the standard deviation of wins within the league.

BIOGRAPHICAL SKETCH

BUD SELIG

Selig listened and questioned and murmured empathetically, all of the things he did best.

—*John Helyar*[1]

Perhaps no person symbolizes the struggle over competitive balance more than baseball Commissioner Alan H. ("Bud") Selig. Selig's Wisconsin roots run deep. Born in Milwaukee, he graduated from the University of Wisconsin at Madison in 1956 and, after serving in the military for two years, joined his father's automobile business. Business proved so good that, when major league baseball came to Milwaukee, Selig was able to act on his love of baseball by becoming a stockholder in the Milwaukee Braves. Selig's ties, however, were to the *Milwaukee* Braves. When the team moved to Atlanta in 1965, Selig promptly sold his stock and formed a group dedicated to bringing a new team to Milwaukee. His efforts bore fruit when the Seattle Pilots, a badly financed expansion team, went bankrupt after the 1970 season. Selig immediately bought the team for $10.8 million and moved it to Milwaukee.

With Selig as their president, the Brewers gained a reputation as an exemplary organization, and the team came within a game of winning the 1982 World Series. The Brewers' performance on and off the field led Selig to play a growing role in the governance of Major League Baseball's affairs. When the owners forced Fay Vincent to resign as commissioner in 1992, Selig, as chairman of the owners' executive council, effectively took over the duties of commissioner. For the next six years, Selig walked a tightrope, serving the interests of all of baseball while working to advance the interests of his own Milwaukee Brewers. Finally, in July 1998, Selig's fellow owners elected him as commissioner. Selig then put his holdings in the

Brewers into a blind trust and turned operations of the Brewers to his daughter Wendy Selig-Preib.

Selig's popularity with his fellow owners and his insistence on consensus has brought the owners unprecedented cohesion. That has enabled him to introduce a variety of innovations designed to bring greater excitement to the game. Under his tenure, baseball raised the number of divisions per league from two to three, increasing the number of teams in the postseason. The number was further increased by the introduction of a "wildcard" playoff team (which won both the 2002 and 2003 World Series). He also oversaw a greater consolidation of the American and National Leagues, whose war of the early 1900s did not fully end until Selig brought both leagues under the authority of the commissioner's office in 2000.

Most importantly, by bringing the often-fractious owners together, Selig reversed a trend of over 20 years. All labor stoppages prior to Selig's becoming commissioner had effectively ended with the owners' capitulating. The 1994–1995 strike effectively ended in a draw, with neither side achieving its aims. In the near strike of 2002, the ownership succeeded in forcing the players association to blink and to approve a revenue-sharing plan and luxury tax that it had bitterly opposed. This marked ownership's first outright victory in negotiations since the first dispute in 1972. Sadly, the 1994–1995 strike caused the cancellation of the 1994 World Series, something two world wars had failed to do. The willingness of owners to forgo the rest of the season severely tarnished the game's reputation. The resurgence of baseball's popularity in the late 1990s has since

continued

been marred by allegations that many of the period's greatest stars used performance-enhancing drugs. The allegations of drug use and of the weak antidrug stance by MLB led to a series of congressional hearings at which Selig, union representatives, and star players were subjected to embarrassing questions on national television.

Because of his controversial record, some see Bud Selig as a man who saved the game. Others feel that he was ill suited to be anything other than the owner of a small-market team. Whatever one's opinion of him, few can deny that he has had a major impact on the game.

[1]John Helyar, *Lords of the Realm* (1994), p. 505.

Sources: Associated Press, "MLB Official Says 'Nothing Improper' About 1995 Loan," ESPN Baseball at http://espn.go.com/mlb/news/2002/0108/1307601.html, January 9, 2002; Anonymous, "Bud Selig," BaseballLibrary.com at http://www.baseballlibrary.com/baseballlibrary/ballplayers/S/Selig_ Bud.stm; Anonymous, "Alan H. 'Bud' Selig" Commissioners at http://mlb.mlb. com/NASApp/mlb/ mlb/history/mlb_history_people_ profile.jsp?section=bio&person-type=com&personid=9.

Summary

For a league to be financially successful in the long run, there must be a semblance of even competition among teams. Given that the value of a win is much greater in large cities, it is unlikely that leagues would maximize revenue from perfect parity across teams, and would likely do better to have better teams in cities where demand for the sport is greatest.

Fans and owners both have an interest in competitive balance. Fans enjoy contests that have uncertain outcomes. If the home team wins too much or too little, attendance will decline. The fact that fans are less likely to follow a team that wins or loses too often gives owners a financial stake in maintaining competitive balance. Because teams typically try to win as often as possible, moves to assure competitive balance typically originate from the central league office.

There are several ways to measure competitive balance, no one of which is necessarily better than the others. A popular way to measure within-season balance is to take the ratio of the standard deviation of winning percentages to the "ideal" standard deviation that would prevail if all teams were equally talented. A popular way to measure across-season balance is to use the Herfindahl-Hirschman index, which shows how narrowly concentrated the champions have been over a given time period. By both measures MLB is relatively competitive compared to other sports. This contradicts the claims of MLB owners that baseball has had a competitive balance crisis since the advent of free agency.

Economic theory predicts that free agency will not affect the distribution of talent in a sport as long as the team owners maximize profit, players maximize income, and transaction costs are low. Sports leagues have implemented a number of policies—such as revenue sharing, salary caps, luxury taxes, and the reverse-order draft—to increase transaction costs and limit the movement of players from small-market to big-market teams. These measures have met with uneven success.

Discussion Questions

1. How far should leagues go to ensure parity among teams?
2. What do you believe means more to fans, winning the championship once in a while or being competitive every year?
3. Should Major League Baseball adopt a system of promotion and relegation?

Problems

5.1 Suppose, as an owner, you could leave the highly competitive league (in terms of closeness of contests) that you currently play in and enter a league that assured that your team would never lose again. Would you want to do so? Why or why not?

5.2 Explain how the law of diminishing returns provides a natural tendency toward competitive balance.

5.3 Suppose in a six-team league, the winning percentages were as follows at the end of the season—Team A: .750, Team B: .600, Team C: .500, Team D: .500, Team E: .400, Team F: .250. Compute the standard deviation of winning percentages.

5.4 In question 3, suppose each team plays a 50-game schedule. Compute the "ideal" standard deviation based on equal playing strength, and the ratio of the actual to the ideal.

5.5 If the NFL increased its schedule from 16 games to 36, what would the new benchmark ideal standard deviation be (assuming equal playing strength)?

5.6 Why do many economists believe that free agency has not affected competitive balance?

5.7 Draw the Lorenz curves from Figure 5.3. Based on what you know from this chapter, add a Lorenz curve for the NFL and a Lorenz curve for the English Premier League. Why did you place them where you did?

5.8 Suppose that over five seasons, the order of finish for five teams in the West League and the East League are as follows. Use the *HHI* to determine which league has better competitive balance across seasons.

West League Season					*East League Season*				
1	2	3	4	5	1	2	3	4	5
A	A	A	E	E	A	B	C	D	E
B	B	D	D	D	E	A	A	A	A
C	C	C	C	C	C	B	D	E	D
D	D	B	B	B	B	D	B	B	B
E	E	E	A	A	D	E	E	C	C

5.9 If you were a fan of Team A, which set of distributions shown in the previous question (West or East) would you prefer? Why?

5.10 Go to the NFL regular season standings for 2009 (http://sports.espn.go .com/nfl/standings) and compute the standard deviation of winning percentage and the ratio of actual to ideal standard deviation. Was competitive balance in 2009 better or worse than it was in 2008?

PART THREE
Public Finance and Sports

CHAPTER 6
The Public Finance of Sports: The Market for Teams

CHAPTER 7
The Costs and Benefits of a Franchise to a City

CHAPTER 6

The Public Finance of Sports: The Market for Teams

*[T]hey ain't going nowhere 'cause they're the **Brooklyn** Dodgers.*

—USHER AT EBBETS FIELD[1]

In sports today the Phoenix Cardinals, who used to be the St. Louis Cardinals, took a seemingly insurmountable three-touchdown lead into the fourth quarter of their game against the Indianapolis Colts, who used to be the Baltimore Colts— not to be confused with the Baltimore Ravens, who used to be the Cleveland Browns—only to see the game slip from their grasp when, with three seconds left in the game, the Colts announced that they were moving to Albuquerque to become a professional hockey team.

—DAVE BARRY[2]

Introduction

One day in the late 1950s, Jack Newfield and Pete Hamill, both reporters for New York newspapers, discussed writing an article called "The Ten Worst Human Beings Who Ever Lived." On a whim, each wrote the names of the three people he regarded as "the all-time worst" on a napkin. To their amazement, they listed the same three names: Adolf Hitler, Joseph Stalin, and Walter O'Malley.[3]

Since Newfield and Hamill lived in a nation with fresh memories of the Second World War and new worries over the Cold War, their inclusion of Hitler and Stalin was not a surprise, but their both naming O'Malley was. Unlike his companions on the list, O'Malley's crime against humanity did not involve

---

[1]Quoted in Michael Danielson, *Home Team: Professional Sport and the American Metropolis* (Princeton, N.J.: Princeton University Press, 1997), p. xvii.

[2]Dave Barry, *Dave Barry Turns 50* (New York: Random House, 1999), p. 62.

[3]Geoffrey Ward and Kenneth Burns, *Baseball: An Illustrated History* (New York: Alfred A. Knopf, 1994), pp. 351–352.

mass murder or show trials. Instead, he changed the landscape of professional sports forever by moving the Dodgers from Brooklyn to Los Angeles.

While the Dodgers' move was the most notorious, they were not the first team to change cities. Nor was baseball the only sport to experience such moves. Teams entered, exited, and moved so frequently in the early years of all professional leagues that they were reluctant to erect permanent facilities. As a general rule, the moves were from small towns to large ones. The NFL likes to reminisce about its small-town, midwestern origins, but professional football did not become financially stable until teams like the Decatur Staleys and Portsmouth Spartans had moved to larger cities and had become teams like the Chicago Bears and Detroit Lions.[4] Sports leagues generally achieved financial stability only after they located franchises in the nation's largest cities. Unfavorable locations proved the undoing of entire leagues, as seen by the demise of baseball's American Association in the 1890s, the National Basketball League in the 1940s, and the women's American Basketball League in the 1990s.

The "Golden Age" of baseball marked the longest period of franchise stability. Between 1903, when the Baltimore Orioles left for New York to become the Highlanders (and later the Yankees), and 1953, when the Braves left Boston for Milwaukee, no Major League Baseball team entered, left, or changed cities. Baseball's growing prosperity led to the construction of its historic ballparks, starting with Shibe Park in Philadelphia and Forbes Field in Pittsburgh in 1909 and followed a year later by Comiskey Park in Chicago. The construction boom effectively ended with Yankee Stadium in 1923. Between the 1920s and the 1950s, only one new baseball stadium was built, Cleveland's Municipal Stadium.

The Braves' move to Milwaukee did not necessarily signal the end of MLB's Golden Age. The Boston Braves; the Philadelphia Athletics, who moved to Kansas City in 1954 (and then to Oakland in 1968); and the St. Louis Browns, who moved to Baltimore and were rechristened the Orioles in 1953, were all neglected stepsisters in cities whose hearts belonged to the Red Sox, Phillies, and Cardinals, respectively. When the Braves left Boston, few fans noticed and fewer still mourned their loss. In their first nine games in Milwaukee, the Braves drew as many fans as they had attracted in the entire preceding year.[5]

Unlike the franchises that moved in the early 1950s, the Brooklyn Dodgers played second fiddle to no one. In the 11 years prior to their move, from 1947 to 1957, the Dodgers were the most successful and most profitable team in the National League. The value of the Dodgers, however, cannot be measured solely in dollars and cents. They were "a cultural totem" for the residents of Brooklyn, a rallying point for those who felt scorned by the wealthier, more sophisticated Manhattanites.[6] It was this sense of loss—and the sense of powerlessness that

---

[4]See Danielson, *Home Team* (1997), pp. 20–24; and Charles Euchner, *Playing the Field* (Baltimore: Johns Hopkins University Press, 1993), p. 4. The NFL Hall of Fame is in Canton, Ohio, home of the long-defunct Canton Bulldogs.

[5]Neil J. Sullivan, *The Dodgers Move West* (New York: Oxford University Press, 1987), p. 42.

[6]See Sullivan, *The Dodgers Move West* (1987), p. 15; and Danielson, *Home Team* (1997), p. 9. Manhattan was the home of the Dodgers' archrivals, the New York Giants, who, ironically, moved to San Francisco when the Dodgers left for Los Angeles.

accompanied it—that prompted the sportswriters to elevate O'Malley to the elite company of Stalin and Hitler.

To O'Malley, the issue was a simple matter of economic profit. While the Dodgers did well in Brooklyn, he realized that the Dodgers would earn even more if they had Los Angeles and, at the time, all of Southern California to themselves. O'Malley recognized the difference between accounting and economic profits. **Accounting profits** are what we typically think of as profit, the revenue a firm makes minus its cost of production. **Economic profit** equals revenue minus all opportunity costs of the firm's production decision. Opportunity costs include the explicit costs of the resources used in the production process *plus* the profits that could have been earned in the firm's best alternative activity. Because economic profits include forgone profits from its best alternative, a firm could have negative economic profits even when its accounting profits are very high. The Dodgers thus had very high accounting profits, but the profits they sacrificed by playing before 1.5 million fans each year in Brooklyn when they could have played before more than 3 million fans in Los Angeles were too great to ignore.

In this chapter, we explore the power that team owners have over cities and the impact of that power on the decisions that cities and teams make. Along the way, we will discover:

- How cities sometimes spend great sums on "free" facilities

- Why some cities gladly spend more than a team or event is worth to serve as a host city

- Why people who want to build stadiums downtown "the way they used to be built" are misremembering history

6.1   The Competition for Professional Sports Teams

The move by the Dodgers altered the relationship between cities and sports teams. If the highly profitable Dodgers could move, so could any team. Cities without teams believed that luring a team would bring tangible benefits, such as jobs and tax revenue, as well as intangible benefits, such as the pride of living in a "big league" city. Bidding wars thus developed between cities hoping to attract a team and cities that were just as determined to keep "their" team.

How Cities Underwrite Sports Facilities

The bidding wars between cities differ from normal auction markets in two important ways. First, unlike a normal market, a city's successful bid for a team does not bring ownership rights. In fact, professional leagues have gone to considerable lengths to prevent cities from owning franchises. MLB owners, for example, blocked Joan Krock's attempt to give the Padres to San Diego after she inherited the team from her late husband. The NFL's bylaws specifically require that teams have an individual majority owner. The Green Bay Packers are a frequently cited exception to the rule against public ownership. Contrary to popular opinion, however, the Packers are not owned by Green Bay; they are a publicly held corporation. As such, they once threatened to leave Green Bay if the city did not accede to their demands for stadium improvements.[7]

Leagues oppose municipal ownership because a municipally-owned team is by definition an immobile team. The city can provide facilities on its own terms, thereby undercutting much of the market power that teams hold over cities. In addition, city ownership makes the finances of the team a matter of public record, something that teams and leagues strongly oppose.

The second unique characteristic of the bidding for teams comes in the form of payment by the winning city. Unlike an auction, which results in a cash transaction, cities do not pay directly for the team they have "won." Their payment is actually a form of barter in which cities provide teams with facilities. In a few cases, the city effectively gives the facility to the team. More often, the city owns the facility and charges a rent that is far below market value.

Table 6.1 shows the total cost and public share of facilities built for professional sports teams since 2000. Adding up the figures in Table 6.1 shows that $11.34 billion has been spent since 2000 to construct new facilities for the major North American sports leagues. More than half this amount, about $6.1 billion, has come from state and local governments. Sometimes, the spending on sports facilities comes when the city has other pressing needs. Over the course of the 1990s, Cleveland, a city whose school system had gone into receivership, committed over a billion dollars to new facilities for its baseball, football, and basketball teams.

The data in Table 6.1 suggest that some cities have driven much harder bargains than others. For example, Columbus, Ohio, paid nothing for the Blue Jackets' new hockey arena, while St. Paul paid almost three-fourths of the bill for the Xcel Center.

The data in Table 6.1, however, tell only a part of the story. Using these data alone can lead analysts to misstate the full burden of a facility on a team. Construction costs are not the only expenditure that a city makes on a sports facility. It also pays for infrastructure, such as roads and utilities, and for support services, such as police and sanitation. In addition, a facility might impose significant opportunity costs on a city. For example, cities frequently donate the land on which the facility is built, thereby sacrificing revenues that could have been made from using, renting, or selling the property. If the stadium is owned by the state or local authority or by a public–private partnership, the city could also lose tax revenue, as a local government cannot tax itself. Offsetting these

---

[7]The Packers are, however, the only NFL team that does not have a single managing partner. See Joanna Cagan and Neil deMause, *Field of Schemes* (Monroe, Maine: Common Courage Press, 1998), pp. 93–94 and 191–192; Richard Jones and Don Walker, "Packer Boss Warns of Move If Stadium Doesn't Get Upgrade," *Milwaukee Sentinel Journal*, March 1, 2000, at http://www.jsonline.com /packer/news/feb00/lambeau01022900.asp; and Barry Lorge, "Kroc Wanted to Give Padres to City," *San Diego Union-Tribune*, July 29, 1990, p. H1.

TABLE 6.1

Facilities Built between 2000 and 2009

Year	League	City	Facility	Construction Cost[a]	Public Expenditure[a]	Percent Public
2000	MLB	Houston	Minute Maid Park[b]	$269	$217	80.7
2000	MLB	San Francisco	AT&T Park[b]	$343	$15	4.4
2000	MLB	Detroit	Comerica Park	$365	$116	31.8
2000	NFL	Cincinnati	Paul Brown Stadium	$475	$377	79.4
2000	NHL	St. Paul	Xcel Energy Center	$131	$96	73.3
2000	NHL	Columbus, OH	Nationwide Arena	$152	$0	0.0
2001	MLB	Pittsburgh	PNC Park	$262	$239	91.2
2001	MLB	Milwaukee	Miller Park	$357	$207	58.0
2001	NBA/NHL	Dallas	American Airlines Arena	$380	$125	32.9
2001	NFL	Pittsburgh	Heinz Field	$233	$196	84.1
2001	NFL	Denver	Invesco Field	$510	$310	60.8
2002	NFL	Detroit	Ford Field	$300	$260	86.7
2002	NBA	San Antonio	SBC Center	$186	$186	100.0
2003	MLB	Cincinnati	Great American Ballpark	$325	$280	86.2
2003	NBA	Houston	Toyota Center	$175	$175	100.0
2003	NFL	Philadelphia	Lincoln Financial Field	$512	$212	41.4
2004	MLB	Philadelphia	Citizens Bank Park	$346	$174	50.3
2003	NHL	Phoenix	Jobing.com Arena	$180	$180	100.0
2004	MLB	San Diego	PETCO Park	$457	$304	66.5
2004	NBA	Memphis	FedEx Forum	$250	$250	100.0
2006	MLB	St. Louis	Bush Stadium III	$365	$45	12.3
2006	NBA	Charlotte	Charlotte Arena	$265	$265	100.0
2006	NFL	Phoenix	University of Phoenix Stadium	$455	$455	100.0
2007	NHL	Newark	Prudential Center	$375	$210	56.0
2008	NFL	Indianapolis	Lucas Oil Stadium	$720	$626	87.0
2008	MLB	Washington, D.C.	Nationals Park	$611	$611	100.0
2009	MLB	New York	Citi Field	$600	$164	27.0
2009	MLB	New York	Yankee Stadium II	$1,300	$220	17.0
2009	NFL	Arlington, Tex.	Cowboys Stadium	$1,000	$350	35.0

[a]In millions of current dollars.
[b]Originally named Enron Field and Pacific Bell Park, respectively.
Sources: Data for facilities built from 2000–2002 come from Judith Grant Long, "Full Count: The Real Cost of Public Funding for Major League Sports Facilities," *Journal of Sports Economics,* vol. 6, no. 2, May 2005, pp. 119–143. Data from 2003–2006 come from Paul Munsey and Cory Suppes, *Ballparks,* at http://ballparks.com, 2007. Data for Lincoln Financial field also used information from National Sports Law Institute, "Sports Facility Reports: Appendix 3—National Football League," vol. 6, Summer 2005, online at http://law.marquette.edu/cgi-bin/site.pl?2130&pageID=2203. Nick Baker, "New Indianapolis Stadium May Already Need Bailout," The Heartland Institute, online at http://www.heartland.org/publications/budget%20tax/article/24305/New_Indianapolis_Stadium_May_Already_Need_Bailout.html, January 1, 2009; and Andrea Ahles, "Dallas Cowboys Stadium Funding from a Variety of Sources," Star-Telegram.com, online at http://www.star-telegram.com/stadium/story/937327.html, September 28, 2008.

expenses are a variety of revenues, including the city's share of parking, concession, and luxury box revenue, as well as rent payments by the team that occupies the facility. Judith Grant Long calculated the full net cost of stadiums built prior to 2002 to local governments.[8] Table 6.2 shows the full net cost of the facilities listed in Table 6.1 that were built in 2000 and 2001.

Comparing Tables 6.1 and 6.2 shows that construction costs alone can significantly understate—and, in a few cases, overstate—a city's true financial commitment. For example, if we consider only the cost of construction, it seems as though the city of Columbus drove a great deal with its hockey team. However, the end result does not seem so great when one includes all costs. According to Long, the full net cost of the Nationwide Arena to Columbus was $62 million, making it much less of a bargain than it first appeared. In contrast, the Xcel Energy Center returned about $14 million of the initial outlay to St. Paul. Sometimes the cost of a facility is simply understated. New York City's comptroller claims that the estimates of the city's contribution to Yankee Stadium in Table 6.1 are more than $100 million less than its true commitment.[9]

TABLE 6.2

Total Public Support for Sports Facilities in 2000–2001

League	City	Facility	Construction Cost[a]	Public Expenditure[a]	Added Expenditure[a]	Percent Public
MLB	Houston	Enron Park[b]	$269	$217	$33	92.9
MLB	San Francisco	Pacific Bell Park[b]	$343	$15	$127	41.4
MLB	Detroit	Comerica Park	$365	$116	−$2	31.2
NFL	Cincinnati	Paul Brown Stadium	$475	$377	$203	122.1
NHL	Minneapolis/ St. Paul	Xcel Energy Center	$131	$96	−$14	62.6
NHL	Columbus, OH	Nationwide Arena	$152	$0	$62	40.8
MLB	Pittsburgh	PNC Park	$262	$239	$64	115.6
MLB	Milwaukee	Miller Park	$357	$207	$229	122.1
NBA/NHL	Dallas	American Airlines Arena	$380	$125	$95	57.9
NFL	Pittsburgh	Heinz Field	$233	$196	$75	116.3
NFL	Denver	Invesco Field	$510	$310	$153	90.8

[a]In millions.
[b]Enron Park and Pacific Bell Park have since been renamed Minute Maid Park and AT&T Park.
Source: Long (2005).

---

[8]Judith Grant Long, "Full Count: The Real Cost of Public Funding for Major League Sports Facilities," *Journal of Sports Economics*, vol. 6, no. 2, May 2005, pp. 119–143.

[9]Sewell Chan, "Comptroller Assails Mayor on New Yankee Stadium," *New York Times*: City Room, online at http://cityroom.blogs.nytimes.com/2009/01/13/comptroller-assails-mayor-on-new-yankee-stadium, January 13, 2009.

Table 6.2 shows that some cities paid more than 100 percent of the construction cost. This means that the value of the direct expenditure, infrastructure, and services the city has provided and the opportunity costs that the city has borne add up to more than the total construction cost of the facility. In effect the citizens of Cincinnati, Milwaukee, and Pittsburgh have given the Bengals, Brewers, and Steelers tens of millions of dollars beyond the cost of a new stadium.

New Facilities and Attendance

In addition to creating new sources of revenue—what we called *venue revenue* in Chapter 3—new stadiums and arenas invariably lead to increases in attendance in the years following their construction. The Baltimore Orioles and the Cleveland Indians, the two teams whose new stadiums in 1992 and 1994 touched off the boom in "retro" stadiums in the early 1990s, saw their average attendance rise by 40 percent and 31 percent in their first year in Oriole Park and Jacobs (now Progressive) Field.

Over time, however, the novelty of a new ballpark fades. Attendance at Oriole Park and Progressive Field have fallen in recent years as the Orioles and Indians, which fielded powerful teams in the 1990s, have fallen back to also-ran status in the 2000s. In 2008, attendance at Oriole Park was only 25,000 per game, while attendance at Progressive Field was 27,122.[10] Both of these figures are well below the attendance when their ballparks first opened. More significantly, they are below the attendance in the teams' last year in their old ballparks.

Because many state and local governments now have a large stake in the financial success of sports facilities, the impact of a new facility on attendance—the "honeymoon effect"—has received increasing attention.[11] Studies have shown that a new facility has the greatest impact on baseball teams, increasing attendance by about one-third. As the experience of the Orioles and Indians suggests, the increase does not last forever. All else equal, attendance falls back to its original level after about 10 years.

Over time, a new facility cannot disguise the quality of the team that plays there, as the experience of the Milwaukee Brewers has shown. When Miller

---

[10]Attendance figures are from "Baltimore Orioles Attendance Analysis" and "Cleveland Indians Attendance Analysis," *Baseball Almanac*, online at www.baseball-almanac.com, viewed June 18, 2009.

[11]See Christopher M. Clapp and Jahn K. Hakes, "How Long a Honeymoon? The Effect of New Stadiums on Attendance in Major League Baseball," *Journal of Sports Economcis*, vol. 6, no. 3 (August 2005), pp. 237–263; John C. Leadley and Zenon X. Zygmont, "When Is the Honeymoon Over? National Basketball Association Attendance 1971–2000," *Journal of Sports Economics*, vol. 6, no. 2 (May 2005), pp. 203–221; John C. Leadley and Zenon X. Zygmont, "When Is the Honeymoon Over? Major League Baseball Attendance 1970–2000," *Journal of Sport Mangement*, vol. 19, no. 3 (July 2005), pp. 278–299; and John C. Leadley and Zenon X. Zygmont, "When Is the Honeymoon Over? National Hockey League Attendance 1970–2003," *Canadian Public Policy*, vol. 32, no. 2 (June 2006), pp. 213–232.

Park first opened in 2001, attendance rose by 80 percent, going from 19,427 to 34,704 per game. Attendance fell quickly, however, as fans were turned off by poor performance on the field. By 2003, attendance had fallen to 20,992, nearly pre–Miller Park levels. Since then, an improving team has attracted more and more fans. In 2008, the Brewers made their first appearance in the postseason since 1982 and drew a record 37,882 fans per game.

New hockey and basketball arenas have a smaller, shorter-lived effect on attendance. Perhaps due to the smaller capacity of such arenas, attendance rises by only 15 to 20 percent in the facility's first year. In addition, the honeymoon effect quickly diminishes. Hockey attendance falls back to previous levels within five to eight years, while basketball attendance returns to previous levels by year nine.

Team owners in all sports justify municipal support by pointing to improved performance by teams like the Brewers. Teams and leagues draw a direct causal relationship between the revenues gleaned from a new facility and the ability to field a competitive team. Such reasoning has a number of flaws. First is the fallacy of composition. The **fallacy of composition** states that a policy that works for a small group of people need not work if everyone does it. The most famous application of the fallacy of composition is the paradox of thrift, which states that an individual who saves more can be better off, but an entire economy will be worse off (at least in the short run) if everyone saves more. In the context of sports facilities, the fallacy of composition says that the Sacramento Kings might win more games if they have a new arena, but neither the Kings nor any other team will win more often if all teams get one. Quinn et al. (2006) find a positive relationship between a new facility and team performance only in baseball.

6.2   How Teams Exploit Market Forces

Three market forces play into the hands of professional sports franchises, each of which gives them an advantage in their dealings with cities. We have already encountered one of the forces at work, monopoly power. In Chapter 4, we explained how professional sports leagues and the NCAA exercise the market power that comes with being the only provider of their sport and the only buyer of athletic talent for that sport. We now look more closely at how teams and leagues use their monopoly power when they deal with cities.

The second market force also stems from a familiar source. In Chapter 4, we showed that most fans enjoy a consumer surplus when they attend a sporting event and that teams can use price discrimination or personal seat licenses to claim a portion of this surplus for themselves. Like fans, cities can enjoy a surplus from hosting a franchise or event. Leagues and event coordinators try to extract the surplus that cities enjoy by confronting them with the choice of buying more than they would ideally choose or buying nothing at all. The third market force arises when leagues exploit the uncertainty of cities that bid to host franchises. Leagues often use this uncertainty to charge the "winning" city a price that exceeds the value of the team to the city.

Leagues, Cities, and Market Power

For over 100 years, sports leagues have limited the number of teams as a way to ensure financial viability. They have believed that admitting too many teams would lead to competitive imbalance, as some teams have little chance of winning. As we saw in Chapter 5, a predictable outcome discourages attendance. In the late 19th century, the proliferation of teams threatened the financial stability of baseball leagues. Teams regularly folded, sometimes in the middle of the season. In 1900, the National League, the sole major league, set a strict limit of eight teams. The fear of instability also contributed to the reluctance of the other major sports leagues to expand until the 1960s.

Financial instability is not the only reason to restrict the number of teams. Leagues with monopoly power have an incentive to keep the number of teams below the level that ensures economic viability. Limiting the number of teams is a way monopoly leagues assert their market power and maximize their members' monopoly profits. By restricting the number of teams that are available, leagues can drive up the price cities pay to attract or retain a team. Donald Fehr, then the executive director of the Major League Baseball Players Association (MLBPA), summed up this point of view when he explained the White Sox threat to move to Tampa if Chicago did not build a new stadium: "[I]f you put a team in Tampa [White Sox owner Jerry] Reinsdorf can't extort money from the city of Chicago by threatening to move to Tampa."[12]

As early as the 1930s, demographic changes and falling transportation costs began to put pressure on Major League Baseball to expand. Although the Great Depression and World War II precluded any moves, by the mid-1940s the distribution of teams made little financial sense. At that time, for example, Los Angeles had no major league teams, while Boston had two baseball teams and a hockey team.[13]

After the war, both MLB and the NFL placed teams on the West Coast, but neither sport did so by increasing the number of teams. The NFL's Rams left Cleveland for Los Angeles in 1946, a move prompted by the creation of the Cleveland Browns of the new All-American Football Conference.[14] Baseball had an explicit offer to expand westward when the Pacific Coast League (PCL), a high minor league that had sent stars such as Joe DiMaggio and Ted Williams to MLB, broached the idea of becoming a third major league. The negotiations fell through, when MLB, which regarded its own reserve clause as sacrosanct, refused to honor the PCL's contracts with its own players. Instead, MLB chose to allow the Giants and Dodgers to move west, establishing a beachhead on the West Coast and reducing the PCL to truly minor league status.[15]

---

[12]Quoted in Euchner, *Playing the Field* (1993), p. 24.

[13]See Danielson, *Home Team* (1997), p. 25.

[14]The Rams feared the popularity of a new team headed by the legendary Ohio State coach Paul Brown, who gave his name to the new team. See Jon Morgan, *Glory for Sale: Fans, Dollars, and the New NFL* (Baltimore: Bancroft Press, 1997), p. 59.

[15]See Sullivan, *The Dodgers Move West* (1987), pp. 90–94.

MLB seemed perfectly content to respond to demographic pressures by rearranging franchises until it undertook the first systematic expansion by a professional sports league in 1961. The new policy, however, did not reflect a change of heart. Instead, it was a direct response to pressure from Congress. Faced with the highly unpopular moves of the Dodgers and Giants and aghast at the impending loss of the Washington Senators to Minneapolis–St. Paul (where they became the Twins), Congress had once again begun to investigate baseball's antitrust exemption. In addition, Branch Rickey, the man who built the great Cardinal teams of the 1930s and Dodger teams of the late 1940s and 1950s, was looking into forming a new league, with two of the flagship teams planned for Houston and New York. Not surprisingly, three of MLB's first four expansion teams were located in Houston, New York, and Washington, D.C.[16] Creating these three teams placated Congress and prevented the rival league from forming. The fourth team, the Los Angeles Angels, gave the American League the West Coast presence that it had long coveted.

The NFL's first several expansions also came under duress. As noted in Chapter 4, the NFL had no intention of expanding in the early 1960s until it learned that the fledgling AFL planned to put teams in Dallas and Minneapolis. The AFL also spurred the NFL's second expansion in 1967. This time, however, the motive was peace, not war. The NFL and AFL recognized that their impending merger would run afoul of the antitrust laws and requested special legislation that would allow them to merge. In their path stood two powerful legislators from Louisiana, Representative Hale Boggs and Senator Russell Long, who could have delayed or derailed the legislation. Fortunately for the NFL, both men were keen to have an NFL franchise in New Orleans. Not surprisingly, less than two weeks after Congress passed the legislation granting the NFL and AFL the right to merge, the NFL approved the creation of the New Orleans Saints.[17]

Cities sometimes contribute to the monopoly power of teams by committing themselves to projects despite having no corresponding guarantee from the franchise. For example, in May 1990, the residents of Cuyahoga County, which includes Cleveland, voted to approve the construction of a new baseball stadium for the Indians and a new basketball arena for the Cavaliers, who were playing in the Richfield Coliseum in a nearby suburb. Unfortunately for Cuyahoga County, the Indians did not agree to lease terms until December and the Cavaliers did not agree until even later. Worse still, the teams had not even agreed on architectural plans for the new facilities. Having committed themselves to new facilities, the civic leaders forfeited any bargaining power with the franchises. The teams were able to insist on such added features as stadium suites, office complexes, and restaurants, all at no extra charge to them. These add-ons led Jacobs Field to cost about $48 million more than estimated and

---

[16]See Zimbalist, *Baseball and Billions* (1992), pp. 16–17; and James Miller, *The Baseball Business: Pursuing Pennants and Profits in Baltimore* (Chapel Hill: University of North Carolina Press, 1990), pp. 78–84.

[17]Morgan, *Glory for Sale* (1997), p. 89; and David Harris, *The League: The Rise and Decline of the NFL* (New York: Bantam Books, 1986), p. 17.

Gund (now Quicken Loans) Arena to cost $73 million more, almost double the arena's estimated cost.

Sometimes leagues reduce their monopoly power by overexpanding, as MLB has done, or by locating their franchises in an unbalanced manner. Of the 16 teams in the Australian Football League, 9 are located in Melbourne, with a 10th located in nearby Geelong. While the fans of the Western Bulldogs might be upset if the team threatens to move to Canberra, Melbourne itself is not likely to suffer. As with baseball, bidding wars for Australian Football franchises is unlikely.

Cities in England, Italy, Spain, or other European countries do not face the same pressures from their top-league soccer clubs. The promotion and relegation system for soccer franchises reduces a team's ability to threaten it will move. Every potential location is already likely to have a franchise in the team's league or with the potential to be in its league. In addition, unlike the case in North America, local governments have gained some managerial control over franchises in exchange for their investment in the franchise, further reducing the chance of a move.[18]

The All-Or-Nothing Demand Curve

When NASCAR sought a host city for its Hall of Fame, it did not offer cities a choice of how much material they wished to house. Cities had to host the entire NASCAR collection or none at all. The **all-or-nothing** choice gave NASCAR an advantage that even the most powerful monopoly seldom has. While a monopoly has the power to set the price it charges or the quantity that it sells, it generally cannot do both simultaneously. For example, if a monopolist sets the price of its product, its sales are limited by the demand curve. Consumers respond to the monopoly price by buying as much of the good or service as they want. The monopoly's power is thus limited by the demand curve that it faces. As we saw in Chapter 2, if the monopoly raises its price, its sales will fall. Even the most powerful monopolist generally cannot tell consumers how much to pay *and* how much to buy.

Under certain circumstances, a monopolist can dictate both price and quantity. Foot-long hot dogs at the ballpark or one-pound boxes of Milk Duds at the movie theater may have become something of a tradition, but they are also far bigger than most consumers want to buy. They are, instead, part of an attempt by producers to extract consumer surplus by getting consumers to buy more than they would choose. By not allowing consumers to bring in their own candy, the theaters establish local monopoly power over the sale of candy.[19] Similarly, sports teams, sports leagues, or institutions such as the International Olympic Committee or NASCAR exploit their monopoly power by auctioning off teams or events to an array of eager cities. They confront

---

[18]See Szymanski and Zimbalist, *National Pastime* (2005), p. 130.

[19]For an alternative interpretation of the behavior of vendors at theaters or arenas, see Steven Landsburg, *The Armchair Economist: Economics and Everyday Life* (New York: Free Press, 1993), pp. 157–167.

cities with an all-or-nothing choice. Since the city cannot choose to host a franchise or event for a smaller part of a season at a lower overall cost, it must pay the full price or host nothing at all.

If NASCAR had acted like a typical monopolist, it would have charged cities the monopoly price of p_1 per unit (where, to make matters concrete, we let one unit be a room in the Hall) and let them "buy" as much of the Hall of Fame as they wanted. As seen in Figure 6.1, a city would choose to "buy" Q_1, and its residents would enjoy the consumer surplus AEC. Figure 6.1 shows that NASCAR could take some of this surplus by telling the city that if it wanted to host any of the Hall at all, it had to build all Q_2 rooms. Buying more rooms than it wants at the price p_1 results in a "consumer loss" equal to EFG, because residents of the city must pay more than the additional quantity is worth to them. The city will accept this loss as long as the surplus that residents enjoy on the first Q_1 rooms is greater than the loss residents suffer on the next $Q_2 - Q_1$. That is, as long as consuming "too many" rooms is preferable to consuming none, the city will choose to consume too much. The franchise can push the city to build more rooms until the size of the loss (EFG) catches up with the size of the surplus (AEC).

In the real world, cities do not look at hypothetical demand curves to decide how much a team, stadium, or event is worth to them. Instead, they compute the item's present value. The **present value** (or the present discounted value) of a good or service tells us what a stream of future benefits is worth today. To see how cities, firms, or consumers compute present value, we make three simplifying assumptions. First, suppose that all costs to host the Olympics are paid the moment the city wins the bid. Second, suppose that the revenue the city receives from the Games (e.g., revenue from the Games themselves and future use of the facilities built for the Games) comes in annual lump sums.

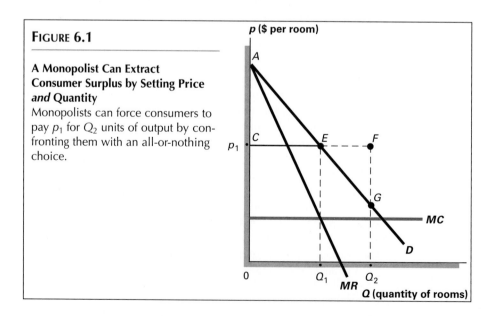

FIGURE 6.1

A Monopolist Can Extract Consumer Surplus by Setting Price and Quantity
Monopolists can force consumers to pay p_1 for Q_2 units of output by confronting them with an all-or-nothing choice.

Third, assume that cities know exactly how much they must spend and exactly how much revenue they will receive, so that expected revenue always equals actual revenue. The first two assumptions make our analysis much neater without straying too far from reality. We shall eventually replace the third assumption with a less restrictive one. Under these assumptions, if the city receives benefits of B_t for each of T years after it wins the bid, then it is willing to pay the price V, where V equals the value of the future stream of returns.

One might expect V to equal the sum of payments the city receives $(B_1 + B_2 + B_3 + \cdots)$, but reality is a bit more complicated. The city must compare a *present* cost with a *future* stream of benefits. Because one can save the dollar that one receives today and earn the market rate of interest, r, a dollar today actually equals $1 + r$ dollars a year from today, $(1 + r)^2$ dollars two years from today, and so on. The **future value** that \$1 today will have in t years is thus $\$(1 + r)^t$, while the **present value** of \$1 that one will receive t years from today equals $\$1/(1 + r)^t$. The present value of the stream of benefits to the city equals

$$V = \frac{B_1}{(1 + r)} + \frac{B_2}{(1 + r)^2} + \frac{B_3}{(1 + r)^3} + \cdots + \frac{B_T}{(1 + r)^T}$$

The Winner's Curse

Even the pressures created by the all-or-nothing demand curve understate the power of sports leagues or teams to extract consumer surplus. They often can solicit bids that exceed the value of the franchise to the winning city. In any auction in which the bidders do not know the value of the prize with absolute certainty, the winner may well overpay for what has been won, falling victim to the **winner's curse.** The winner's curse was first applied to oil leases, when researchers sought to explain why investments by oil companies in the oil-rich Gulf of Mexico "paid off at something less than the local credit union." Since then, it has been applied to contexts as diverse as advances paid to authors and the salaries paid to baseball players.[20]

To see how the winner's curse works, consider the fact that Charlotte had to outbid several other cities (e.g., Daytona and Atlanta) to host the NASCAR Hall of Fame. Suppose each competing city based its bid on how much it expected the Hall to be worth.[21] The competing cities would hire experts to evaluate the benefits of a new franchise. Based on these estimates, each city would submit bids to NASCAR. Charlotte won the auction by bidding more than any other city. It might have won for any of three reasons. First, it might have been able to make more profitable use of the Hall than any other city. For

---

[20]Richard Thaler, "The Winner's Curse," *Journal of Economic Perspectives*, vol. 2, no. 1 (Winter 1988), pp. 191–202. For an application to sports, see James Cassing and Richard Douglas, "Implications of the Auction Mechanism in Baseball's Free Agent Draft," *Southern Economic Journal*, vol. 47, no. 1 (July 1980), pp. 110–121.

[21]Since cities have much greater access to capital than individuals do, we ignore the question of the city's ability to pay.

example, the Hall might have created synergies with other attractions in Charlotte that did not exist elsewhere. Second, if Charlotte had overestimated the benefits that the Hall would bring, it might have overbid for the Hall and won the auction even though it would have been better off losing. Finally, the auction process itself might have led Charlotte to bid more than the Hall was worth by making winning the auction more important than the value of the prize.

The key to the winner's curse lies in the fact that not all cities have the same expectations and that only the most optimistic bidder wins the prize. In addition to any objective advantages it may have over other cities, Charlotte's winning bid also reflects its optimism about the uncertain value of the Hall. Charlotte's optimism might not be justified. It might have overstated the value of the Hall and submitted a bid that was higher than the true return to hosting the NASCAR Hall of Fame.

Finally, Charlotte might have gotten caught up in trying to win the right to host the Hall of Fame, independent of expected benefits. Empirical studies and clinical experiments of bidding behavior have shown that, on average, bidders accurately assess the value of uncertain prizes. The winning bid, however, consistently overstates the value of the prize. Moreover, the degree to which a winner overbids, and hence the degree of loss, generally rises with the number of bidders. This has led some economists to conclude that participants get caught up in the action and begin to set winning the auction as a goal in itself. As a result, bids by cities and individuals alike may reflect both the value of the prize and the desire to win the prize regardless of its inherent worth.

6.3 How the Olympics and the World Cup Induce Overspending

The International Olympic Committee (IOC) and soccer's World Cup organizer, the Federation Internationale de Football Association (International Federation of Association Football, better known as FIFA), may be the ultimate franchise monopolists. With one Summer Olympics, one Winter Olympics, and one World Cup held every four years, cities see each event as a chance to attract hordes of tourists and generate international attention. The high price of staging these events and the corruption that has tainted the Olympic site selection process form a case study of the three forces outlined earlier. Cities that wish to host one of these events must purchase the right from a monopoly. Moreover, they cannot purchase part of an event. Cities therefore face an all-or-nothing decision. Finally, the winning city might be overly optimistic about the benefits of being a host city or might be led by the auction process to overbid. In this section, we show how the IOC and FIFA have exploited the market forces outlined earlier in this chapter.

Over the years, there have been numerous entrants into the market for multisport athletic competition, making for about 40 Olympic-style events. These generally consist of regional competitions, such as the Pan American Games, or events focused on specific sets of competitors, such as the Commonwealth or World University Games. While the Olympics have soccer competition, the

IOC goes out of its way to avoid conflict with FIFA. The Olympics impose a complex age limit on its competitors, with only three players per team allowed to be older than 23. Unlike other events, which seek to attract the world's best athletes, Olympic soccer is intended as a preview of future stars.[22] Similarly, many of the regional events avoid competing with the Olympics. Instead, they serve as warm-ups or even as qualifying rounds for the Olympics.

Only the Goodwill Games have competed directly with the Olympics, inviting top athletes from around the world to a festival of athletic competition. The Goodwill Games were established by Ted Turner in response to what he saw as the increasing politicization of the Olympics. They held competitions in 1986, 1990, 1994, 1998, and 2001 before finally folding.[23]

The failure of the Goodwill Games might be evidence that the demand for broad-based athletic competition is not great enough to sustain two such events. If that is the case, then the Olympics would be a natural monopoly, as defined in Chapter 4. It is also possible, however, that the IOC's monopoly is not entirely natural. It has, for example, repeatedly gone to court to protect its trademark rights over the term "Olympics."[24] In addition, after 1992, the IOC shifted from offering the Winter Olympics to a different cycle, occurring midway between Summer Games. The IOC cited the logistical concerns of staging Summer and Winter Games in one calendar year. However, it is also true that offering Olympic competition every two years instead of every four years narrowed the window for alternative athletic competitions.

Massive spending by cities seeking to host the Olympics has long been a part of its history. Los Angeles spent about $1 million to build the Coliseum in an unsuccessful attempt to attract the 1924 Games and spent almost another $1 million (for a total of over $28 million in 2009 dollars) to refurbish the Coliseum in its successful bid for the 1932 Games. Cleveland spent even more, roughly $3 million (about $47 million in 2009 dollars), to build the mammoth Municipal Stadium—when completed, it had the largest seating capacity of any outdoor arena in the world—in its unsuccessful bid to host the 1932 Games. Germany spent huge sums as part of its successful effort to outdo the 1932 "Hollywood Olympics" and to present the world with a positive image of the Nazi regime during the 1936 Berlin Games. One of the cities Berlin beat out was Barcelona, which housed much of the 1992 Games in the stadium it built in 1929 in an attempt to host the 1936 Games.[25]

---

[22]Sam Stern, "Olympic Soccer Limits Age, Not Talent," *New York Sun*, August 5, 2008, online at http://www.nysun.com/sports/olympic-soccer-limits-age-not-talent/83209/.

[23]See, for example, "History of the Goodwill Games," *Courier Mail* (Queensland, Australia), July 17, 2001, p. H4; and "AOL Kills Goodwill Games after $150 Million in Losses," *Wall Street Journal*, December 21, 2001, p. B7.

[24]See, for example, James Grimaldi, "Olympics File Suit over Web Domain," *Washington Post*, July 14, 2000, p. E4.

[25]Raymond Keating, "Sports Pork: The Costly Relationship Between Major League Sports and Government," *Policy Analysis*, no. 339 (Washington, D.C.: Cato Institute, 1999), p. 4; Mark Rosentraub, *Major League Losers* (New York: Basic Books, 1997), pp. 253–254. The propaganda value of the 1936 Olympics and the elaborate preparations for the Games are described in Duff Hart-Davis, *Hitler's Games* (London: Century, 1986); and R. Mundell, *The Nazi Olympics* (New York: Ballantine Books, 1972).

In more recent years, the cost of attracting and staging the Games has reached truly Olympian heights. The Greek government spent about $9 billion to stage the 2004 Summer Olympics, more than three times the amount spent by Montreal to stage the 1976 Games. Ironically, Montreal did not finish paying off its Games until two years after the Athens Games.[26] Greece's spending paled, however, compared to the 2008 Summer Games. Initially estimated to cost "only" $16 billion, the Beijing Games had a final price tag of over $40 billion.

While the Olympics are the most expensive athletic event, other competitions also come at a heavy price. To host the 2002 World Cup, Japan and Korea spent huge amounts to build and upgrade facilities. Japan spent about $4.5 billion on constructing 7 new stadiums and refurbishing 3 others for the World Cup finals, while South Korea spent $2 billion on 10 new facilities. Most of these are now white elephants for the communities that had them built. The Japanese district of Saitama built a 64,000-seat stadium for the preliminary rounds of the World Cup at a cost of $667 million. Saitama must now spend $6 million per year to maintain the facility for a local professional team that draws barely 20,000 fans.[27]

Officials in Japan and Korea appear to have been victims of the winner's curse. They vastly overstated the benefits of hosting the World Cup finals. Prior to the tournament, a Japanese research group predicted benefits of over $26 billion to the Japanese economy. The Korean organizing committee was also very optimistic, predicting benefits of over $5 billion. In their study of the actual impact of the World Cup on the Japanese and Korean economies, Robert Baade and Victor Matheson found that hosting the games actually *cost* the two countries a combined total of $5.5 billion.[28]

The IOC's power grew dramatically after the 1984 Los Angeles Games. In the wake of Montreal's financial disaster in 1976, no other city volunteered to host the 1984 Games. Using largely existing facilities and tapping for the first time into corporate sponsorships, the Los Angeles Games generated a surplus of $232.5 million.[29] In response, the IOC began to treat the selection process as

---

[26]That figure does not include the estimated $500 million per year that Greece now spends on upkeep for the facilities. Athens News Agency, "Cost of 2004 Olympics," *Hellenic Republic Embassy of Greece,* online at http://www.greekembassy.org/Embassy/content/en/Article.aspx?office=3&folder=200&article=14269, November 13, 2004; Nicole Itano, "As Olympic Glow Fades, Athens Questions $15 Billion Cost," *Christian Science Monitor,* July 21, 2008, online at http://www.csmonitor.com/2008/0721/p04s01-wogn.html; Andrew Malone, "Abandoned, Derelict, Covered in Graffiti and Rubbish: What Remains of Athens' £9 Billion Olympic 'Glory'?", *Mail Online,* July 18, 2008, online at http://www.dailymail.co.uk/news/worldnews/article-1036373/Abandoned-derelict-covered-graffiti-rubbish-What-left-Athens-9billion-Olympic-glory.html; and CBC News, "Quebec's Big Owe Stadium Debt is Over," CBCnews.ca, online at http://www.cbc.ca/canada/montreal/story/2006/12/19/qc-olympicstadium.html, December 19, 2006.

[27]Doug Struck, "Hosts Left to Foot World Cup Bill," *Washington Post,* June 29, 2002, p. A1; and Robert A. Baade and Victor A. Matheson, "The Quest for the Cup: Assessing the Economic Impact of the World Cup," *Regional Science,* vol. 38, no. 4, June 2004, pp. 343–354.

[28]Struck (2002) and Baade and Matheson (2004).

[29]"1984 Los Angeles Olympic Games Surplus Continues to Benefit Southern California Youth," *LA84 Foundation,* June 23, 2004, online at http://www.la84foundation.org/10ap/NewsRelease06232004_frmst.htm.

an auction and the chance to host the Games as an asset to be sold to the highest bidder. With cities seeing a greater return to hosting the Olympics, the bids began to feature increasingly elaborate facilities, luxurious accommodations for IOC officials, and for a time, outright payments to the IOC site selection committee.

An auction combined with the uncertain payoff of hosting an Olympic competition raises the possibility of the winner's curse, a result the IOC sometimes seems to encourage. The competition among the cities hoping to host the 2008 Summer Olympics—Beijing, Paris, Istanbul, and Osaka—exemplified the pressure on the cities to win the auction. From the outset, the rival sites viewed the bidding process as "a high-level competition between cities and countries."[30] Consciously or not, the IOC structures the selection process as a tournament, with cities advancing from preliminary rounds to "the finals," with the ante rising at each stage. Even the terminology used by journalists and bid officials resembled that of the athletic competition they hoped to stage. The official Chinese news source pictured Beijing as being in a "neck-in-neck [*sic*] competition" to host the 2008 Games, while Osaka officials cited the need to catch their breath before moving forward. Toronto officials were even more explicit, saying, "We've made the play-offs . . . [b]ut there are a bunch of rounds coming up and we've got to make sure that we're the last survivor at the end of the day." The emotion and self-esteem invested in such competition makes winning the competition an end in itself, beyond the financial merits of the actual prize.[31]

In sum, the Olympics present a very challenging problem for cities that would like to host the Games. Potential hosts face a monopolist offering an all-or-nothing choice in an environment with highly uncertain costs and benefits. Moreover, the decision is made in an auction process seemingly designed to promote the winner's curse. Cities in this situation must take particular care to avoid spending more than the event is worth to them.

6.4 The Form and Function of Stadiums and Arenas

The ability of leagues and event organizers to exploit their market power has had a major impact on the nature of the facilities themselves. Over the years, facilities have changed names, location, even size and shape, as the source of funding has shifted from team owners to the public sector. In this section, we examine how the growing involvement of municipal governments gave rise to

---

[30]Beijing's Vice-Mayor Liu Jingmin, deputy director of the Chinese Olympics Bidding Committee, quoted in "Bejing Enters Play-offs to Be Olympics Host," *People's Daily Online*, March 24, 2000, at http://english.peopledaily.com.cn/200003/24/eng20000324S101.html.

[31]See *People's Daily Online* (2000); Channel Sports, "Beijing Welcomes Inclusion on Shortlist to Hold 2008 Olympics," *China Daily Information*, August 29, 2000, at http://www.chinadaily.net/cover/storydb/2000/08/29/sp-beiji.829.html; Reuters, "Osaka Vows to Battle On to Host 2008 Olympics," August 28, 2000, at http://web4.sportsline.com/u/wire/stories/0,1169,2712403_15,00.html; and Dan Ralph, "Toronto Among Finalists to Host 2008 Olympics," *Canadian Press*, August 29, 2000, at http://www.herald.ns.ca/stories/2000/08/29/f161.raw.html.

large, multipurpose stadiums in the 1960s and to more specialized facilities in the 1990s. Along the way, we encounter the economic theory of location and learn why the skyline in Crookston, Minnesota, does not resemble the skyline in Manhattan and why central business districts are indeed central.

What's in a Name?

At the risk of some oversimplification, one can divide the history of sports facilities into three broad eras. Like a paleontologist identifying dinosaur bones, one can discern one era from another by looking for certain telltale signs in each facility. The first era was dominated by baseball stadiums, largely because baseball was the only organized professional sport for most of the period in question. These stadiums had names like Forbes Field, Wrigley Field, or Shibe Park.[32] The second era was marked by facilities that housed multiple sports and had such names as Texas Stadium, the Kingdome, and Oakland–Alameda County Stadium. The third era saw a multiplying of facilities, each housing a specific sport. Typical facilities in this era were Ford Field, the Honda Center, and National Car Rental Arena.

The first era covered the first two decades of the 20th century. All of the facilities built during this time have two common features. First, none has the word *Stadium* in its title. The universal use of the word *Park* or *Field* reflects the pastoral origins of baseball. In baseball's formative years, prior to the enclosure of games in private structures, games were played in open fields or parks. The term *stadium* was not used until Jacob Ruppert applied the name to his new "Yankee Stadium" in 1923 in a deliberate attempt to recall the grandeur of classical architecture. (*Stadium* comes from the Greek word *stadion*, which originally meant a specific distance, later referred to a race of that distance, and eventually came to mean the seats for spectators who watched the race.) Second, most of the ballparks, with exceptions like Fenway Park, bear the name of the owner of the baseball team for which the stadium was built. During this era, teams typically built ballparks to prevent bystanders from seeing ballgames for free.[33]

The unparalleled stability that baseball enjoyed during its "Golden Age" kept teams in the same facilities. Prior to 1950, Cleveland's Municipal Stadium and the Los Angeles Coliseum were the only major publicly built facilities, and—as noted earlier in this chapter—they were built with the Olympics in mind, not baseball or football. Eventually, the aging of the facilities, the changing face of American cities, and the growing ability and willingness of franchises to use the market forces described earlier in this chapter has led to the gradual disappearance of facilities built in the first era. Of these ballparks, only Wrigley Field and Fenway Park still exist.

---

[32]Wrigley Field was originally named Weeghman Field for the owner of the Chicago Whales of the Federal League. When Philip Wrigley bought the team and the stadium, he renamed it for himself.

[33]In 1936 Connie Mack went so far as to erect a "spite fence" behind right field of Shibe Park to prevent fans from viewing the game from the roofs of nearby apartment buildings.

While there were some antecedents in the 1950s—such as Milwaukee's County Stadium and Baltimore's Memorial Stadium—the second era of stadium construction ran from 1962 to 1991. The first stadium in this new era, Dodger Stadium in Los Angeles, was one of the key lures that brought the Dodgers west. While "Dodger Stadium" was named for the team that occupied the facility, most of the new stadiums were named for the cities or counties that funded them. Several, such as Three Rivers Stadium, were identified with distinctive local geographical features. Still others, such as Veterans Stadium in Philadelphia, took on patriotic names.

The third era began in 1992 and has been marked by continued public funding combined with the sale of naming rights to private sponsors. The Toyota Center, FedEx Forum, and Jobing.com Arena were all completely financed by the state and local government. The names of these facilities bear no trace of the cities that paid for them (Houston; Memphis; and Glendale, AZ), as the teams occupying these arenas all sold the naming rights to private enterprises.

The Size and Shape of Facilities

In 1999, their last year in the Astrodome, the Houston Astros filled their home park to 61.0 percent of capacity. In 2008, the Astros filled 82.7 percent of the seats of Minute Maid Park. One might conclude from these figures that fans flocked to watch a much more attractive team or revel in a more attractive stadium in 2008. However, the Astros' average attendance in 2008 (34,741) was only marginally larger than a decade earlier (33,408). The percentage rose because Minute Maid Park has only 42,000 seats, while the Astrodome had almost 55,000. The Astros were not the only team to move to a smaller facility. During the second era of sports facilities (1962–1991), stadiums grew. The new stadiums' distinctive, round shape and their close resemblance to one another led critics to call them "cookie-cutter stadiums." In the third era (1992–present), baseball stadiums have become much smaller and have adopted almost self-consciously quirky shapes. In this section, we examine why the size and shape of stadiums has changed so dramatically.

Baseball, Football, and Multipurpose Facilities   Until the 1960s, baseball team owners built ballparks specifically to house the teams they owned. Like the hockey owners who rented their arenas to basketball teams, baseball owners allowed football teams to rent the facilities in the off-season to gain more revenue.[34] By the 1960s, when cities began to build multipurpose stadiums, football had begun to draw large crowds. With football teams pressing for more seating, stadiums began to grow.

---

[34]NFL teams even adopted variants of the names of MLB teams whose facilities they used (e.g., the Chicago Bears, who rented Wrigley Field from the Cubs) or took on the names of the teams themselves (e.g., the New York Giants of the NFL, who rented the Polo Grounds from MLB's Giants). Ironically, college football enjoyed a building spree during the early decades of the century, when classic facilities such as Michigan Stadium and the Yale Bowl were built.

Stadiums also began to change shape in the 1960s. While the ballparks of the early 20th century were built solely for baseball, the new, multipurpose facilities were built in part for football. Unfortunately for the fans of either sport, the ideal seating arrangements for football and baseball look nothing alike. Football teams play on a standardized, rectangular field. Teams score by going to one end of the field or the other, but the bulk of the action takes place in the middle of the field. A football stadium's least desirable seats are therefore located in either end zone. Such seats give little perspective on the action and provide a poor view of what is happening on much of the field. They are typically the cheapest and last to sell. By contrast, most of the action on a baseball field takes place within the diamond that forms the infield. Early baseball stadiums thus consisted of grandstands that extended outward from home plate around the foul lines and did not encompass the outfield. Figure 6.2 shows the design of Reliant Stadium, which was built for the NFL's Houston Texans. It maximizes the number of fans who can sit along either sideline and has relatively few seats far from the action. By contrast, most

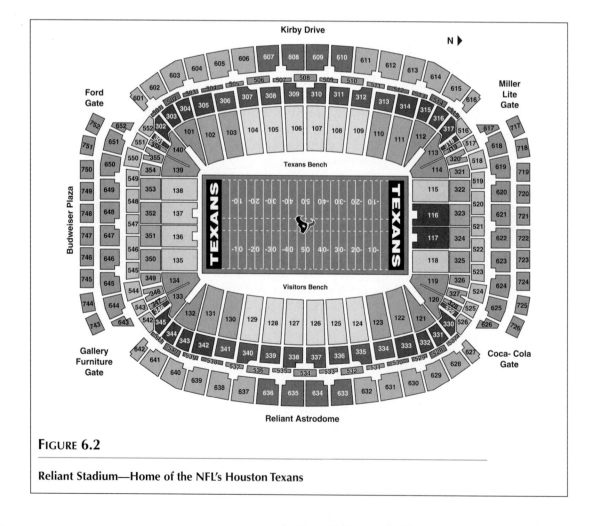

FIGURE 6.2

Reliant Stadium—Home of the NFL's Houston Texans

of the action on a baseball field takes place within the diamond that forms the infield. Early baseball stadiums thus consisted of grandstands that extended outward from home plate along the foul lines and did not encompass the outfield.

The new "fan friendly" baseball stadiums have returned to the original pattern. Figure 6.3 shows the design of Houston's baseball-only facility, Minute Maid Park. Like older ballparks whose memory it seeks to evoke, Minute Maid Park maximizes the number of seats near home plate and the infield and has relatively few seats far from the action in the outfield.

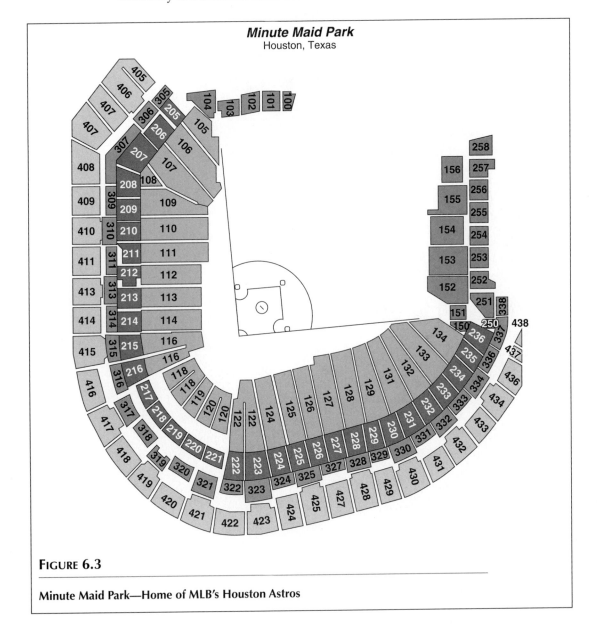

Minute Maid Park
Houston, Texas

FIGURE 6.3

Minute Maid Park—Home of MLB's Houston Astros

Architects charged with designing the new multipurpose facilities faced an unavoidable conflict. The ideal design for football seating is parallel lines of seats on either side of the football field, while the ideal design for baseball is a horseshoe shape with the bottom of the "U" behind home plate. The resulting compromise was the circular, cookie-cutter stadium, which provided poor sight-lines for both sports. Figures 6.4a and 6.4b show Houston's

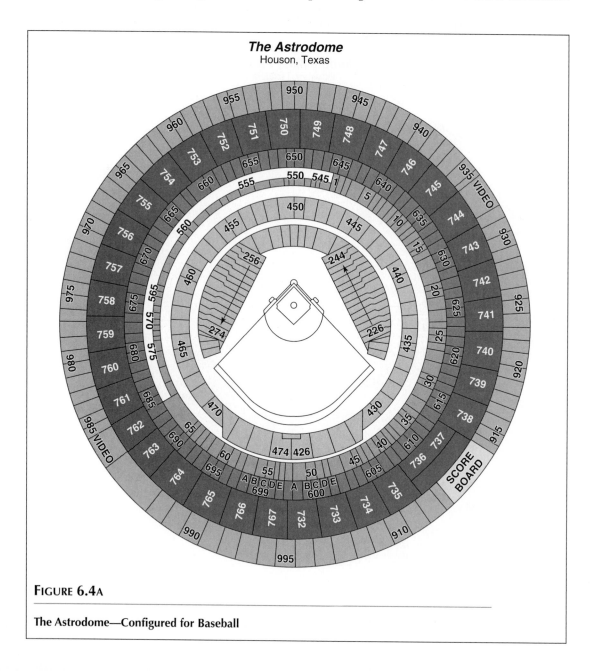

FIGURE 6.4A

The Astrodome—Configured for Baseball

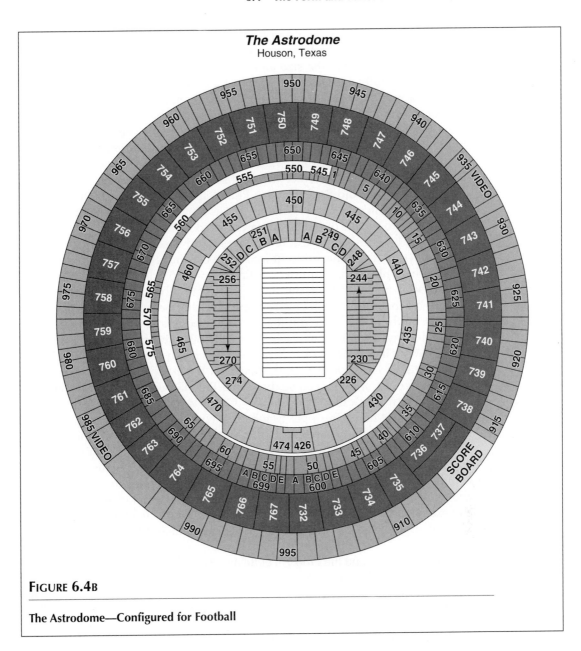

FIGURE 6.4B

The Astrodome—Configured for Football

Astrodome when it was configured for baseball and football. In both cases, the stadium had many seats in the least desirable locations. When arranged for football, the Astrodome had a lot of seats in the end zone and many of the seats near midfield were far from the action. When arranged for baseball, the Astrodome had a lot of seats in the outfield. As a result, many baseball and football fans had poor views of the action, and teams had trouble selling large blocks of tickets.

The cookie-cutter shape of the second era's facilities also imposed uniformity on baseball, which had previously been characterized by idiosyncratically shaped ballparks. While the size and shape of a football field and a baseball infield are carefully specified, the shape of a baseball outfield has few restrictions. As a result, the first era of facilities contained stadiums in a dizzying array of sizes and shapes. Some were shaped around the particular strengths or weaknesses of the home team. Yankee Stadium may have been the "house that Ruth built," but it was also built to order for Babe Ruth, a left-handed batter who hit prodigious home runs. Yankee Stadium accommodated Ruth with a short right field fence and left-center field so deep that it came to be known as "Death Valley." The old Baker Bowl in Philadelphia so favored left-handed hitters that Red Smith, the famed columnist, was moved to comment, "It might be exaggerating to say the outfield wall casts a shadow across the infield. But if the right fielder had eaten onions at lunch, the second baseman knew it."[35]

Other fields were shaped to fit into a pre-existing city plan. Center field in Philadelphia's Shibe Park came to a distinctive point 515 feet from home plate so that the stadium could fit in the square block grid. Two of the most dramatic plays in baseball history—Bobby Thompson's "shot heard round the world," a dramatic ninth-inning home run that beat the Dodgers in a 1951 play-off game, and Willie Mays's miraculous catch of a mammoth drive by the Cleveland Indians' Vic Wertz in the 1954 World Series—had as much to do with the configuration of the Polo Grounds as with the talents of the two players. With one of the oddest shapes of any baseball stadium, the Polo Grounds, named for an area north of Central Park that the New York Giants shared with polo teams before moving to their home in upper Manhattan, could be a very easy place or an incredibly difficult place in which to hit a home run, depending on where one hit the ball. The left field wall was only 258 feet away, with an overhang that reduced the effective distance of the left field seats—where Thompson hit his home run—to only 250 feet. Center field was a different story. The stands in left-center field and right-center field were about 450 feet away, with a cutout in dead center field that extended the distance to about 480 feet.[36] In almost any other stadium, Willie Mays would have been staring at the ball Vic Wertz hit as it sailed out of the park.

The NBA, the NHL, and the Problem of Being a Secondary Tenant   NBA and NHL teams have often shared arenas without the same tension that marks baseball and football co-tenants. The reason is that hockey and basketball are played on surfaces that have roughly the same size and shape. Like football teams, both basketball and hockey teams move up and down rectangular surfaces and shoot at goals or baskets that are at opposite ends of the rectangle. The optimal shape of basketball and hockey arenas are thus about the same. Because both sports play 82-game schedules and have roughly comparable fan bases, the optimal seating capacity should not differ as much as for baseball and football.

---

[35]Quoted in Rich Westcott, *Philadelphia's Old Ballparks* (Philadelphia: Temple University Press, 1996), p. 32.

[36]Stew Thornley, *Land of the Giants: New York's Polo Grounds* (Philadelphia: Temple University Press, 2000), p. 3.

Conflict has arisen because NBA teams have typically been the primary tenants of the arenas that they share with NHL teams, and hence have benefited much more from their facilities. NHL teams have suffered from their role as secondary tenants in facilities that cater to NBA teams. Hockey's second-class status is ironic given that the relationship between hockey and basketball once resembled the relationship between baseball and football. Decades ago, hockey team owners frequently owned or controlled the facilities in which they played. When there was no hockey game scheduled, they rented the facilities to basketball teams as a way of making extra money.

A hockey team that is a secondary tenant generally faces worse financial arrangements than the basketball team with which it shares the arena.[37] It is no surprise that the most profitable teams in the NHL—the Toronto Maple Leafs, New York Rangers, Montreal Canadiens, Detroit Red Wings, and Philadelphia Flyers—are all primary tenants in their facilities. The Rangers and Flyers have arrangements with Madison Square Garden and the Wachovia Center that are equal or superior to those of their co-tenants, the NBA's Knicks and 76ers, while the Maple Leafs, Canadiens, and Red Wings have their own arenas.

Location, Location, Location

Nostalgia buffs and urban planners delight in the fact that all the ballparks built since the early 1990s, starting with Baltimore's Oriole Park at Camden Yards, have a "retro" feel. Not only are they built to look like the old ballparks (both Miller Field in Milwaukee and Citi Field in New York deliberately evoke memories of the Brooklyn Dodgers' old Ebbets Field), but they are also frequently in downtown areas, reminiscent of the old parks' locations.

The warm and fuzzy feeling associated with the downtown location of many of the newest stadiums is proof that nostalgia is not what it used to be. When they were first built, the old ballparks were no more urban than the multipurpose facilities of the 1960s and 1970s. When Shibe Park (later renamed Connie Mack Stadium) was built at 21st and Lehigh Streets in North Philadelphia in 1909, it stood near the site of a recently demolished hospital for communicable diseases. Given the state of medical knowledge at the turn of the 20th century, society tended to deal with communicable diseases by locating the patients as far from town as possible. For several years after Shibe Park was built, Philadelphians complained about the distance they had to travel to reach it.[38] Similarly, Yankee Stadium in the South Bronx was not always associated with urban congestion. It was built on an empty 10-acre lot, bordered by unpaved roads, in a part of town known as "Goatville," hardly a metropolitan setting.[39] Brooklyn's Ebbets Field was not much different. By the mid-1950s, it may have come to epitomize the urban ballpark, but in 1913, the neighborhood

---

[37]See Robert La Franco, "Profits on Ice," *Forbes*, May 5, 1997, pp. 86–89.

[38]See Bruce Kuklick, *To Everything a Season: Shibe Park and Urban Philadelphia, 1909–1976* (Princeton, N.J.: Princeton University Press, 1991), pp. 21–25; and Westcott, *Philadelphia's Old Ballparks* (1996), pp. 104–105.

[39]W. Nack, "This Old House," *Sports Illustrated*, June 7, 1999, pp. 100–116.

in which it was built bore the nickname "Pigtown . . . where poor Italian immigrants lived in miserable shanties amidst goats and dandelions."[40]

As time went on, urban areas developed and then decayed around many of the old ballparks. As the old stadiums began to decay, team owners and cities turned their attention to the outskirts of town and the suburbs for sociological, technological, and economic reasons. An increasingly suburbanized fan base was more and more reluctant to attend games in the crumbling inner city.

The movement to the suburbs also brought a need to accommodate fans who drove to the game. Any new ballpark would have to come packaged with acres of parking lots, and this vastly increased the space required for a stadium. Space, however, costs money and becomes increasingly expensive as one moves toward the center of town. Consider, for example, the case of two bookstores, Barnes and Noble and Borders, that are trying to figure out where to locate in the circular city shown in Figure 6.5. If the population is evenly spread over the city, then the best place for the stores to locate is in the very center of the circle. To see why, assume that the stores initially consider locating at the edge of town, along the diameter *AA* in Figure 6.5. Since the stores are identical in every way but convenience, customers base their purchases on how close they are to each store. In this case, half the city's population is closer to Barnes and Noble and half is closer to Borders. As a result, each store gets an equal share of the city's business. The managers of the Barnes and Noble quickly learn how customers decide to shop and recognize that they can capture some of Borders' business by moving to a more convenient location. They can do so by moving along the diameter toward the center of the circular town. The managers at Borders also recognize this and try to do Barnes and Noble one better by moving still closer to the center of the circle. The process continues until both stores compete for space in the center of town. The tendency of businesses to locate in the center of a city has given rise to the term **central business district.**

The competition for space also explains why property values are so much higher toward the center of town. Urban economists call the rise in property values as one moves toward the center of town the **rent gradient.** Figure 6.6 shows a typical rent gradient. As the price of land rises, people seek out ways to

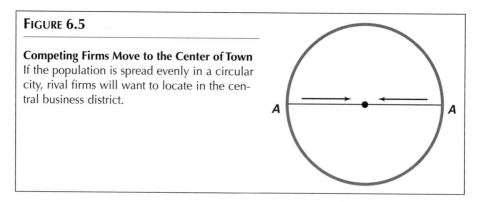

FIGURE 6.5

Competing Firms Move to the Center of Town
If the population is spread evenly in a circular city, rival firms will want to locate in the central business district.

A A

---

[40]Harold Seymour, *Baseball: The Golden Years* (New York: Oxford University Press, 1971), p. 52.

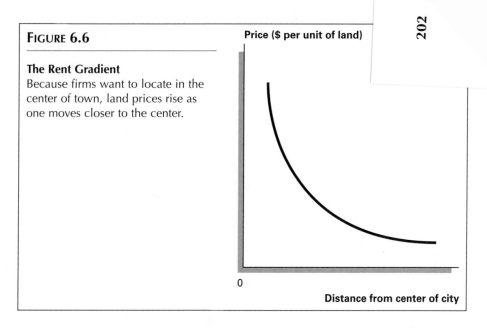

FIGURE 6.6

The Rent Gradient
Because firms want to locate in the center of town, land prices rise as one moves closer to the center.

Price ($ per unit of land)

0

Distance from center of city

economize on their use of it. If the cost of land rises high enough, developers will find it cheaper to build vertically—high-rise offices and apartment buildings—than to build horizontally. Buildings therefore tend to become taller as one moves toward the center of town, and Figure 6.6 could illustrate the heights of buildings as well as the cost of land. A stadium surrounded by parking facilities requires so much space that the cost of land can make locating in the center of town prohibitively expensive.

Teams moved to the outskirts of town in the 1960s and 1970s, in part because the cities could afford the land they needed for large stadiums and parking lots. Stadiums in these outlying locations became virtual islands in "seas of asphalt or concrete."[41] Fans drive to these isolated stadiums on highways designed to take them to the stadium from their suburban enclaves with minimal contact with the center of town and its attendant traffic jams. Largely built with public funds in order to attract consumer spending and income, the multipurpose cookie-cutter stadiums were designed and located in a way that minimized any spillover of consumer spending into the surrounding community. Since fans have found it inconvenient to go into town to enjoy restaurants, taverns, and other forms of entertainment, the stadium has taken on many of those functions itself, further isolating the stadium and its income flows from the host area. In the words of Robert Baade, "[I]n many cases the modern sports facility resembles a small walled city."[42] In moving stadiums back to the center

---

[41]Robert Baade and Allen Sanderson, "Field of Fantasies," *Intellectual Ammunition,* March/April 1996, at http://www.heartland.org/01maap96.htm, p. 2.

[42]Robert Baade, "Should Congress Stop the Bidding War for Sports Franchises?" Hearing Before the Subcommittee on Antitrust, Business Rights, and Compensation, Senate Committee on the Judiciary, vol. 4, November 29, 1995, "Academics," *Heartland Policy,* at http://www.heartland.org/stadps4.html, p. 16.

of town, cities are expressing a willingness to spend more in order to generate greater spillovers for the community. With both greater benefits (in the form of consumer spending at local businesses) and higher construction costs, there is little reason to believe that the new trend in building stadiums downtown will result in substantial benefits for the cities that fund the stadiums.

BIOGRAPHICAL SKETCH

AL DAVIS

To me, professional football is a business and an avocation. I never wanted to hurt anybody. To Davis, it is a war.

—Gene Klein[1]

Sometimes an individual finds a niche that suits him so perfectly that he becomes completely identified with the position he occupies or the era in which he works. For about 30 years, Al Davis was the public face of one of the most successful and distinctive teams in professional sports. Al Davis *was* the Raiders, serving as their head coach, general manager, team owner, even—briefly—the commissioner of the league in which they played. In so doing, he infuriated his fellow team owners, as well as the residents of Northern and Southern California as his team moved from Oakland to Los Angeles and back again.

While he was an undergraduate at Syracuse University in the early 1950s, Davis became enchanted by the innovative offensive schemes of the team's new football coach, Ben Schwartzwalder. Despite the fact that he had no official position with the team, Davis became a fixture at strategy classes and team practices. Never one to let the lack of credentials get in his way, Davis talked his way into a job as an assistant coach at Adelphi University immediately after graduating from Syracuse. Later stops at the Citadel and the University of Southern California confirmed Davis as a first-rate offensive mind and a brilliant recruiter. These qualities, however, also had a downside, as Davis could

not fit into the hierarchy of a coaching staff. He constantly battled with fellow assistant coaches and never hid his desire to become a head coach. To make matters worse, his aggressive recruiting practices often ran afoul of NCAA regulations.

Tainted by scandal and unable to move up to a head coaching position, Davis found himself adrift in 1960. Fortunately for him, that was the year that the fledgling AFL opened up a realm of new opportunities, and he soon found a position on the staff of the Los Angeles (later San Diego) Chargers. Under the tutelage of head coach Sid Gillman, a widely acclaimed offensive genius, Davis refined the concept of an attacking, pass-oriented offense. He also applied his marketing skills to stealing players from the NFL and rival AFL clubs. The Chargers' dominance of the AFL put Davis in position to grab the chance of a lifetime—though it hardly seemed such at the time.

For the first three years of its existence, the Oakland Raiders was the laughingstock of the nascent AFL. They were, in fact, something of an accidental franchise. As noted in Chapter 4, the AFL had originally hoped to locate a flagship franchise in Minneapolis. Caught unprepared when the NFL hastily expanded to Minneapolis, the AFL awarded the Minnesota franchise to Oakland even though no one in Oakland had expressed an interest in owning a franchise. A group led by developer Wayne Valley eventually stepped forward, but the Raiders reflected their slapdash origins, compiling an appalling record in front of minuscule crowds. In 1963, desperate for a respectable team, the Raiders hired Davis as head coach. Within a year, Davis made the Raiders competitive, and within five years, they were playing in the Super Bowl. By that time, however, Davis had already moved beyond the coaching ranks.

In 1966, the AFL's owners narrowly approved Davis as the league's second commissioner. Six months later, they negotiated a merger with the NFL behind his back. This experience confirmed Davis's low opinion of football's owners and inculcated a deep dislike of NFL Commissioner Pete Rozelle, whom Davis—Rozelle's opposite in upbringing and temperament—felt had undermined him during the merger talks. Some even believe that Davis felt that he should have been named commissioner of the expanded league.

His term as commissioner quickly over, Davis again was a man without a team until Wayne Valley agreed to bring Davis back in 1966 as a "managing general partner" with a one-tenth interest in the team. Valley's move came as a surprise to many who had seen the growing friction between Valley and Davis. Valley soon regretted bringing Davis back to Oakland. In 1972 Davis masterminded a coup that reduced Valley to a figurehead position and—after four years of bitter legal battles—gave Davis control of the team.

As effective owner of the Raiders, Davis quickly became a pariah among the other owners, who were deeply committed to the "league-think" approach of Commissioner Rozelle. Whether out of principle or personal animosity, Davis repeatedly challenged the rest of the league. Unlike his peers, he welcomed free agency, declaring, "Just cut all the players and make everybody a free agent." He testified on behalf of the USFL in its antitrust suit against the NFL. (In return, the USFL pointedly sued only 27 of the existing 28 teams in the NFL.) He even refused to sign over the Raiders' share of profits from NFL Properties to the NFL Charities Foundation, claiming that the Raiders did their charity work locally.

Davis's biggest challenge to Rozelle and the NFL came in March 1980, when he sought to move the Raiders to Los Angeles. Davis had long coveted a larger stage than Oakland afforded, and he was among the first owners to see that favorable stadium deals would affect the balance of power in the NFL. The other owners, however, forbade him from moving the team, citing the league's constitution, which barred a team from moving into another's home territory without the league's unanimous consent. Davis responded by filing an antitrust suit against the NFL. After a series of trials that were finally settled in 1989, the NFL dropped its objections to the move and agreed to pay the Raiders $18 million. The impact of the judgment, however, went far beyond the courtroom. Never again would the NFL invoke its bylaws to block a franchise from moving. This opened the door for later moves by the Colts, Rams, Browns (now Ravens), Oilers (now Titans), and the Raiders themselves—back to Oakland—in 1995. Davis had quickly become disenchanted with his agreement with the authorities in Los Angeles. The rush to an agreement had left much of the language open to multiple interpretations, and Davis soon saw that his move would not bring the financial benefits that he had anticipated.

The return to Oakland has not been a joyous homecoming. Perhaps because of their many moves, the Raiders have not been the dominant team that they were in the 1970s and 1980s. Almost constant litigation since the mid-1970s has absorbed much of Davis's time and energy. In addition, the rest of the league has finally caught on to Davis's tactics. Perhaps even worse for Davis, the new breed of owner—best personified by Cowboys' owner Jerry Jones—has come to imitate his persona. No longer the rebel, Davis is now the role model, a position he cannot relish.

[1]Eugene Klein, *First Down and a Billion: The Funny Business of Professional Football* (New York: Morrow, 1987). *Sources:* Glenn Dickey, *Just Win, Baby: Al Davis and His Raiders* (New York: Harcourt, Brace and Jovanovich, 1991); David Harris, *The League: The Rise and Decline of the NFL* (New York: Bantam Books, 1986); and Mark Ribowsky, *Slick: The Silver and Black Life of Al Davis* (New York: Macmillan, 1991).

Summary

Since the 1950s, cities and states have played a major role in the financing of sports facilities. Several characteristics of the market in which sports leagues and cities operate explain the large expenditures cities have made to attract or keep teams. Leagues have exploited their monopoly power by keeping the number of teams below the level needed for the league to remain financially viable. This has driven up the price cities have to pay to attract and keep a team.

Teams and leagues have also confronted cities with all-or-nothing situations, in which the city must "consume" more than it desires or risk not being able to host a franchise at all. In the limit, teams can use the all-or-nothing threat to extract a city's entire consumer surplus. Finally, because teams and leagues effectively auction off the right to host a team, the host city might fall victim to the winner's curse by paying more than the team is worth. Teams and leagues are not the only possible beneficiaries of these three forces. Organizations such as the IOC have also exploited them.

Stadiums and arenas have gone through three phases. The first phase, which lasted into the 1920s, was marked by baseball stadiums that were built for baseball teams and financed by team owners. The second phase saw the construction of multipurpose stadiums and arenas, designed to house several sports teams. The names of the facilities generally reflected the municipal funding source. The final phase has seen the re-emergence of single-purpose facilities. These facilities are still largely publicly financed, but teams now sell the naming rights to private sponsors. The move from single purpose to multipurpose facilities has affected the size and shape of baseball stadiums. Because of the NFL's shorter schedule, the typical football game attracts far more fans than the typical baseball game. The multipurpose stadiums are thus generally larger than the single purpose facilities. The shape of multipurpose facilities is also a compromise between the ideal shapes of football and baseball stadiums. Because the playing areas for basketball and hockey are roughly the same size and shape and because they play similar schedules, the joint arenas do not have the same tension. NHL teams in joint arenas often suffer from being secondary tenants and having worse deals than the NBA teams.

Discussion Questions

1. Suppose the New York Jets decide they want to move to Los Angeles. As a football fan, would you approve of this move? Would you feel differently if you were the commissioner of the NFL?

2. Suppose your city (or the nearest city housing an NBA franchise) is trying to decide where to build a new arena. Think of two or three possible sites and describe the pros and cons of each. Which site do you think is best?

3. Do you think that China's expenditure of over $40 billion on the 2008 Summer Olympics was worthwhile? Why?

Problems

6.1 Use the all-or-nothing demand curve to explain why the IOC is unlikely to accept a bid by Los Angeles to host only the track and field events in its bid for the 2020 Summer Olympics.

6.2 Use the rent gradient to show why New York did not build a new stadium for the Yankees in midtown Manhattan.

6.3 Critics of referenda often complain that this method of determining expenditure often results in the community spending more than it really wants to. Do they have a point? Explain your answer.

6.4 Suppose New York wants to build a new facility to replace Madison Square Garden. Assume that the cost of building a new arena in midtown Manhattan is $2 billion and that all the costs occur right away. Also assume that New York will receive annual benefits of $100 million for the next 30 years, after which the new arena becomes worthless. Does it make financial sense to build the new facility if interest rates are 5 percent?

6.5 While football and baseball teams have gone from multipurpose to football- and baseball-only facilities, basketball and hockey teams continue to share arenas. Why?

6.6 Suppose that Phoenix wants to host the Super Bowl. Arrange the following in order of their impact on the price that Phoenix is likely to pay:

   a. The monopoly power of the NFL

   b. The NFL's use of the all-or-nothing demand curve

   c. The winner's curse

6.7 Why does the fact that the NFL does not have a franchise in Los Angeles give its teams greater leverage with their host cities than teams in the other sports have?

6.8 If a new baseball stadium has only a very short-term impact on a team's attendance, why do MLB teams still pursue them?

6.9 Suppose the International Olympic Committee announced that it would hold all of its Summer Games in Athens and all of its Winter Games in Sapporo. What is the likely impact on the monopoly power of the IOC, the IOC's ability to exploit an all-or-nothing demand curve, and the winner's curse?

6.10 Suppose a city is laid out along a major highway, so the city is shaped like a straight-line segment rather than a circle. If the city wants to build a sports arena, where along the segment should the city build the arena? Why?

CHAPTER 7

The Costs and Benefits of a Franchise to a City

The pride and the presence of a professional football team is far more important than 30 libraries.
    —Art Modell, former owner of the Baltimore Ravens[1]

Introduction

"Build it, and they will come." The mantra worked such wonders for Kevin Costner in *Field of Dreams* that cities adopted it as their own. Many state and local officials see sports facilities as the anchors around which their cities can revive their decaying downtown areas.[2] They have visions of tourists drawn to their towns to attend sporting events, of residents staying in center city areas for entertainment and shopping rather than heading for the suburbs, and of local merchants relocating to prosperous downtown sites. When they propose building sports facilities based on these projections, however, state and local officials enter a political minefield. Like any other economic entity, municipalities face constraints. They cannot do everything and must choose among alternatives. Thus, the decision to build professional sports venues is bound up with the decision of how to finance their construction. There are opportunity costs to providing public funds. Citizens may legitimately ask why their tax dollars are going toward building facilities that are owned and used by millionaires rather than improving public schools or repairing local roads.

This chapter explores the pros and cons of the public sector's involvement in subsidizing facilities for professional sports franchises. It then considers what the most economically efficient method of financing a facility would be

---

[1]Quoted in Joanna Cagan and Neil deMause, *Field of Schemes* (Monroe, Me.: Common Cause Press, 1998), p. 137.

[2]Mark Rosentraub, "Stadiums and Urban Space," in *Sports, Jobs, and Taxes*, ed. by Roger Noll and Andrew Zimbalist (Washington, D.C.: Brookings Institution Press, 1997), pp. 178–180.

and compares the ideal system to what states and municipalities have actually done. Along the way the chapter also discusses the following:

- Why cities might regard expenditure on facilities as worthwhile even though they do not turn a profit

- How a dollar of expenditure creates ripple effects in a local economy

- Why governments sometimes aid the few at the expense of the majority

- What an optimal tax system should look like

Chapter 6 explained how professional franchises have benefited tremendously from public sector funding. This chapter shows that the reality of building and then operating facilities may not justify the enthusiasm with which local officials embraced the concept of doing so.

7.1   Why Do Cities Do It? The Benefits of a Franchise

Critics of stadium projects often complain that if a new stadium is such a good idea, then the team should pay for it. In fact, under certain circumstances, substantial public funding for a stadium may be justified. By their very nature, governments evaluate projects by different criteria than do private firms. The private sector's pursuit of profit generally does a good job of allocating resources, but the private sector sometimes fails to provide the socially desired amount of a good or service. The market may fail because the firm does not account for the full costs or benefits of the good or service it provides. Economists often justify the existence of government by appealing to its role in correcting such market failure. **Market failure** occurs when private markets fail to allocate goods and services in the way that is most valued by the members of that economy. More precisely, market failure occurs when, for a particular activity, the marginal benefits and marginal costs to the society rather than just the individual firms or consumers, are not equalized.

This section explores two common sources of market failure: public goods and externalities. Recall from Chapter 3 that a public good is non-excludable and non-rival in consumption. Non-excludability means that once the good is available to anyone, it is available to everyone because one cannot prevent some consumers from using it. If a good is non-rival in consumption, it means that one person's consumption does not impact another's. An **externality** occurs when a party not directly involved in a transaction receives unintended benefits (a positive externality) or bears unintended costs (a negative externality) as a result of that transaction. The rationale for public funding of a stadium or arena stems from the belief that sports franchises are public goods and that they have positive externalities for the community. Examining why cities subsidize sports facilities gets at the heart of the difference between the motives and actions of the private and public sectors. Before we continue, it is important to note that not all stadium ownership arrangements are alike. There are probably as many different arrangements as there are venues. That said, it will be useful to understand a few general categories of ownership structure before proceeding.

Typically, local governments (through a combination of state and local funds) pay for construction and maintenance of the facility, and charge rent to the team(s) that plays there. Such venues are usually either owned by the city itself (such as the FedEx Forum in Memphis) or a local stadium authority (as in the case of Oriole Park). Going forward, we refer to these as publicly owned facilities. While the teams that play in these venues do pay rent, the value of the relationship to the city depends highly on the terms of the lease, a topic we address in detail later in the chapter. Sometimes, venues are privately owned, such as Citi Field in New York. In such cases, local municipalities subsidize the cost for a stadium that is ultimately owned by the team or a related corporate entity. Finally, a venue may be jointly owned by the team and the city, as in the case of Miller Park in Milwaukee, 64 percent of which is owned by the Southeast Wisconsin Professional Baseball District and 36 percent by the Brewers.[3] As we will see, the nature of the ownership relationship has a powerful impact on the incentives of the team.

Privately Built Facilities

A team will build a new facility if it expects the project to generate positive economic profits. That occurs if the net expenditures by fans on tickets and on related activities at the facility exceed the cost of building and maintaining it. The pressure to maximize profit—the difference between revenue and cost—will tend to keep the expenditures on the facility in check. Foxboro (originally Schaefer) Stadium, home of the NFL's New England Patriots from 1971 to 2001, is one example of how economic pressures can keep the cost of a facility down. With no one to bankroll them, the Sullivan family—who owned the Patriots at the time—found a number of creative ways to minimize cost, including exchanging free advertising for a scoreboard and acquiring free artificial turf from a firm that was seeking to break into the industry. All told, they built the stadium for only $6.7 million, roughly one-eighth of what Kansas City spent on its municipally funded football stadium a year later and about one-fiftieth of what the Patriots' new home, the publicly funded Gillette Stadium, cost in 2002. When team owners do not spend their own money, it seems that they are less likely to seek low-cost solutions.[4]

When owners do not keep their impulses in check, they often face severe consequences. Constructed in 1913, Ebbets Field was a wonder of its day. Fans entered through an 80-foot rotunda enveloped in Italian marble and walked under a chandelier with 12 baseball-bat arms that held 12 globes

---

[3]Munsey and Suppes, "Miller Park," at http://www.ballparks.com/baseball/index.htm. Accessed June 22, 2009.

[4]Raymond Keating, "Sports Pork," *Policy Analysis*, no. 339 (Washington, D.C.: Cato Institute, 1999), pp. 6, 13; and James Quirk and Rodney Fort, *Pay Dirt* (Princeton, N.J.: Princeton University Press, 1992), p. 158.

shaped like baseballs. The cost of the stadium put Charles Ebbets so badly into debt that he had to offer half his interest in the team to two local contractors.[5] This split the ownership of the team into two warring factions, which doomed the Dodgers to mediocrity for three decades. More recently, the new Yankee Stadium opened in 2009 at a total cost of approximately $1.3 billion. As one of the most expensive stadium projects ever constructed, the team was counting on selling top quality seats—those closest to the field—for top dollar. Faced with the worst recession since the 1930s, the team unexpectedly had to discount many of the front row seats by as much as 50 percent, and offer free tickets to those customers who had paid full price for tickets they already owned.[6]

Publicly Built Facilities

When facilities are publicly owned, it may seem a simple matter to compare the lease payments made by the team to the cost of building and maintaining the stadium. Suppose, for example, a new stadium is constructed at a cost of $500 million using funds raised by issuing 30-year bonds at 3.5 percent. The formula for the annual payment on a bond is

$$P = \frac{V}{\dfrac{1 - (1 + r)^{-t}}{r}}$$

Where V is the value of the bond issue ($500 million), r is the interest rate (0.035), and t is the length of the loan (30 years). The payment, P, would be $27.2 million per year. Thus, for the city to cover the cost of the bonds using only lease payments from the team, it would have to charge the team more than $2.2 million per month. If the team were to completely self-finance the building, it would have to expect revenues from the venue to exceed these annual payments. In practice, teams rarely pay what might be considered fair market rents. The history of stadium arrangements includes teams that have paid no rent at all, such as the Baltimore Ravens, Phoenix Suns, and Milwaukee Bucks, or a token rent of $1 per year (the White Sox). Worse yet, in 1995, the NFL's San Diego Chargers signed a contract with the city that paid them more for not selling tickets than for selling them. As part of their lease agreement with Qualcomm Stadium, the Chargers kept 90 percent of all ticket revenue (40 percent of which they then shared with the rest of the NFL). San Diego agreed, however, to reimburse the Chargers for 100 percent of the value of all tickets that the team failed to sell. The Chargers thus gained $27 from the sale of a $50 ticket,

---

[5]Harold Seymour, *Baseball: The Golden Years* (New York: Oxford University Press, 1971), p. 52; and P. Munsey and C. Suppes, *Ballparks*, 1999, at http://www.ballparks.com.

[6]"Yanks Cut Some Premium Ticket Prices," at http://sports.espn.go.com/espn/print?id=4108293 &type=HeadlineNews&imagesPrint=off. Accessed June 22, 2009.

while they gained $50 if they did not sell that same ticket.[7] To make matters worse, the lease gave the Chargers an incentive to lose football games, which drives away fans but increases revenue.[8]

Even if payments from teams do not come close to covering the bond payments, such funding might still be a good idea. Cities and states often build parks and recreation areas even though they do not generate profits because of the recreational value they confer to residents. Similarly the benefits that a city realizes from hosting a team may extend beyond the rental fees received if residents feel better with a team than without. We must carefully consider all of the potential costs and benefits before making a decision about the wisdom of public financing.

Direct Benefits   The direct benefits that a franchise brings to a city stem from the new spending generated plus any externalities that it generates. This includes expenditures by local residents on tickets, souvenirs, meals at (or before or after) the game, and parking revenue.

A common error in valuing such benefits is ignoring the fact that much of the money spent by fans would have been spent anyway. As such, the expenditures substitute spending on one leisure activity for spending on another. For example, in 2003, the New York state comptroller released a report on the impact of the Buffalo Sabres hockey team on the Buffalo–Niagara region that asserted that the Sabres brought direct benefits of $43.6 million to the region. This figure consists of "$31 million in gate receipts, $8.6 million in concessions revenue, and $4 million in broadcast and advertising revenue."[9] However, these figures vastly overstate the actual direct benefit. Keep in mind that the direct benefits stem only from the *new* spending that the Buffalo Sabres generate. Substitution spending by local residents does not increase economic activity. New spending can take one of two forms. First, a franchise might cause the residents to spend more—and save less—of their incomes; this increases their **average propensity to consume** (APC). A person's APC is the ratio of his or her expenditure on consumption goods to his or her total income. Thus, if Rachel earns $40,000 and spends $30,000, her APC is $30,000/$40,000 = 0.75. If the team's presence in town causes Rachel to increase her spending from $30,000 to $32,000, her APC will increase from .75 to .80.

Second, and more significantly, a franchise can stimulate **net exports** by the city. International trade economists define net exports as the difference between the value of goods and services a nation exports and the value of goods and services it imports. While Buffalo and Detroit are not separate countries, they resemble separate countries in that they buy and sell goods from one another

---

[7]Darren Rovell, "What's the Lease You Can Do?" *ESPN: Sports Business*, September 20, 2002, at http://ESPN.com.

[8]Cagan and deMause, *Field of Schemes* (1998), pp. 59–60; and Caitlin Rother, "Tab Climbs in Charger Ticket Deal with City," *San Diego Union-Tribune*, September 12, 2000, p. B1.

[9]Figures taken from Gene Warner, "Hockey Team Has $65 Million Impact, Hevesi Says," *Buffalo News* online, February 26, 2003, at http://www.Buffalo.com.

and other cities. Buffalo exports the services of its hockey team, the Sabres, to the surrounding region if the team attracts fans from the surrounding area to its games in Buffalo. The Sabres also increase Buffalo's net exports by reducing the city's imports from other cities. Buffalo's imports fall if residents attend Sabres games in Buffalo rather than spend their money in the surrounding area.

Accounting only for the expenditures of Sabres fans, however, overstates the impact the Sabres have on Buffalo's net exports. One must look at the Sabres' expenditures as well, because they might stimulate imports as well as exports. Coaches or athletes who play for the Sabres but live outside of Buffalo count as inputs that must be imported. Unfortunately for Buffalo, most of the full-time jobs and most of the income generated by the Sabres go to the team's athletes, coaches, front-office staff, executives, and owners, relatively few of whom live year-round in Buffalo. The Sabres thus serve as a conduit, transferring money from one set of out-of-town residents to another set of out-of-towners.

Even if all the personnel associated with the Sabres lived in Buffalo, counting all the expenditures that the team generates as new revenues would still overstate the Sabres' direct impact on Buffalo. If it is true, as Baade and Sanderson claim, that "Hollywood enjoyed its best September ever during the [1994 baseball] players' strike,"[10] then the money fans spend on hockey games could just as easily have gone to some other form of local entertainment without increasing overall expenditure, causing the impact of the Sabres to be highly overstated.

Substitution may also occur on the supply side. If Buffalo's economy is close to full employment, then expanding one sector of the economy comes at the expense of another sector of the city's economy. The **production possibilities frontier** (PPF) in Figure 7.1 shows the impact of expanding expenditure on a sports franchise. The PPF shows the combinations of sports facilities and other goods that Buffalo can offer. It can provide any combination of sports facilities and other goods inside (point A) or on (point B) the frontier. Buffalo does not have enough resources, however, to produce at a point outside the frontier (point C). If Buffalo is not at full employment—at point A—then expanding the sports sector can increase the total level of spending and production. If, however, resources are already fully employed, as at point B on the PPF, then Buffalo can expand the sports sector only by reducing the output of the other goods such as by moving to point D.

Finally, despite their high profile, sports franchises are really a rather small business. In the words of one expert, "the sales revenue of Fruit of the Loom exceeds that for all of Major League Baseball."[11] Table 7.1 shows the importance of sports in three large cities. Denver and Philadelphia both have four major

---

[10]Robert Baade and Allen Sanderson, "The Employment Effect of Teams and Sports Facilities," in *Sports, Jobs, and Taxes,* ed. by Roger Noll and Andrew Zimbalist (Washington, D.C.: Brookings Institution Press, 1997), p. 97.

[11]Robert Baade, "Should Congress Stop the Bidding War for Sports Franchises?" Hearing Before the Subcommittee on Antitrust, Business Rights, and Compensation, Senate Committee on the Judiciary, November 29, 1995, vol. 4, "Academics," *Heartland Policy,* at http://www.heartland.org/stadps4.html, p. 19.

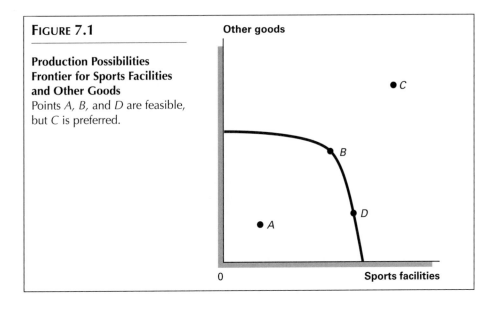

FIGURE 7.1

Production Possibilities Frontier for Sports Facilities and Other Goods
Points A, B, and D are feasible, but C is preferred.

sports teams, one from each of the four major North American sports, within their city limits. Chicago, with two MLB teams, has five. As we have seen earlier, revenues do not always translate into incomes, so these figures, if anything, overstate the importance of sports to the local economy. Despite this, we see that the revenues of all major sports teams combined make up less than one-half of one percent of local incomes. The impact of sports franchises on specific cities is thus very small.

To put these numbers in perspective, *Forbes* listed the gross revenues of the Buffalo Sabres in 2004 as about $51 million. Compare this with the revenues of Haverford and Bryn Mawr, two small Quaker-affiliated colleges in suburban Philadelphia. The total revenues of the two colleges from tuition alone (disregarding, for example, research grants or consulting revenue earned by the faculty) accounted for about $105.5 million. By this reasoning, Buffalo would

TABLE 7.1

Importance of Sports Teams in Local Metropolitan Areas in 2007 (in millions)

MSA	Sports Revenue[a]	Personal Income	Ratio
Chicago area	$809	$416,357	.0019
Denver area	$546	$114,466	.0048
Philadelphia area	$606	$264,937	.0023

[a]Sports Revenue is revenue from MLB, the NFL, NBA, and NHL for 2007 based on *Forbes* estimates. Metropolitan Statistical Area (MSA) includes the city plus surrounding communities.
Sources: Personal income data from Bureau of Economic Analysis, "Personal Income and Per Capita Personal Income by Metropolitan Area, 2005–2007," June 23, 2009, at http://www.bea.gov/newsreleases/regional/mpi/mpi_newsrelease.htm. Total sports revenue from Forbes.com various team report pages.

generate more than twice as much income if it let the Sabres move but induced the two colleges to move to town. The evening news, however, has no reports of cities trying to lure colleges to town.[12]

The benefits of the direct increase in spending may not be enough to justify using public funds to attract or host a team. Unlike directors of a private firm, however, public officials must account for costs and benefits beyond those attributable directly to the facility. They must also account for costs and benefits that the team and facility bring to people who never attend a game. A private firm such as the franchise has no reason to account for these indirect costs and benefits. It may even be unaware that such costs and benefits exist. Recall that economists call the benefits conferred on third parties **positive externalities,** and the costs that producers impose on third parties who do not buy from or sell to the firm **negative externalities.** One of the major justifications for the existence of government is to account for the benefit or harm done by positive or negative externalities.

Like monopoly and monopsony power, positive and negative externalities interfere with the market's ability to allocate resources. Consider, for example, the negative externalities the Buffalo Sabres would create if there were no government. In addition to whatever direct costs and benefits the Sabres convey on the residents of Buffalo, they also create negative externalities such as congestion, noise, and perhaps crime each time they play a game. In deciding how much to produce, the Sabres and the NHL as a whole are concerned only with the private cost of operation—how much they must spend on salaries, travel, and a host of other inputs. They do not consider—and may not even be aware of—the external costs of the health problems and inconvenience they create for people affected by the congestion, pollution, and crime. The private costs that form the basis of the Sabres' and NHL's profit maximization decisions understate the full social costs, which include both private costs and the costs imposed on third parties.[13] If the Sabres or any firm considered all costs, the net rewards associated with any given price—and the incentive to produce—would be lower. As a result the "private" supply curve (S_p) in Figure 7.2, which includes only private costs experienced directly by the firm, lies to the right of the "social" supply curve (S_s), which includes all private and social costs.

The market equilibrium that results from the private decisions of producers and consumers in Figure 7.2 is Q_p, while the "social equilibrium" is only Q_s

---

[12]The Sabres' revenue comes from NHL team valuations online at http://www.forbes.com. The tuition revenue for Haverford and Bryn Mawr were simulated by using the bills for tuition and room and board for the 2006–2007 academic year (roughly $44,000) and the enrollment of the two colleges (about 1,100 for Haverford and 1,300 for Bryn Mawr). There is at least one example of cities competing for colleges. In the mid-1950s, Winston-Salem, North Carolina, paid for Wake Forest University to move from its original site to help create a middle class in town.

[13]Some teams have tried to reduce or eliminate negative externalities. The Chicago Cubs provide shuttle buses to reduce traffic, and cleanup crews to reduce litter in the surrounding community. See Christopher Hepp, "Near Fabled Park, Ambience a Lure," *Philadelphia Inquirer* (September 29, 1999), pp. A1, A6.

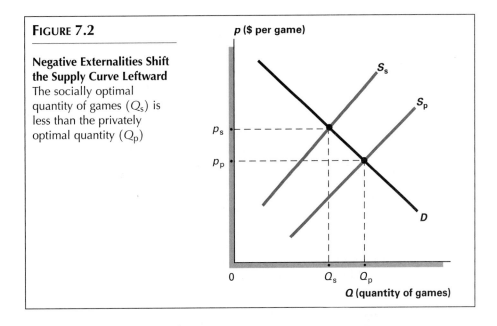

FIGURE 7.2

Negative Externalities Shift the Supply Curve Leftward
The socially optimal quantity of games (Q_s) is less than the privately optimal quantity (Q_p)

games. The difference ($Q_p - Q_s$) shows that the negative externality causes the Sabres to schedule too many games when left to their own devices. Similarly, the difference between the price that the Sabres charge and the price that society would like them to charge ($p_p - p_s$) shows that a negative externality causes the Sabres to charge their fans too little.

That the Sabres do not actually pay for the negative externality makes them better off. Fans who attend Sabres games benefit because they can see a game more cheaply, since the Sabres need not account for all the costs of production. Buffalo as a whole suffers, however, because costs more appropriately borne by the Sabres and the NHL are imposed on city residents.

Surprisingly, Buffalo generally would not want to entirely eliminate the negative externalities that the Sabres impose on it. The only way to ensure that the Sabres impose no negative externalities on Buffalo would be for the Sabres to play no games there. Negative externalities, however, are not all bad; they are negative by-products of a process that gives people something they want. In general, people would be worse off without the output even if it meant a cleaner, safer environment. In this example, the people of Buffalo want to see the number of games reduced to Q_s, where the benefits and social costs of one more hockey game are equal, but they do not want to eliminate the games entirely.

Oddly, the negative externalities associated with sports facilities seem to apply most to newly proposed facilities. Although residents of neighborhoods where a structure will be built often complain bitterly about the problems it will bring, residents are almost rhapsodic about many existing structures. In the words of baseball historian Harold Seymour, a ballpark is "a landmark, an asset to city life—especially to the lives of those who live in the neighborhood."[14]

One major reason for the difference in attitudes comes from the fact that most of the costs that an old ballpark such as Wrigley Field imposes on its neighbors have already been internalized, so fans who live near Wrigley Field have been compensated for any inconvenience the Cubs may impose in the form of lower housing costs. To the extent that proximity to Wrigley imposes costs on residents of the neighborhood, newcomers will pay less for homes or apartments. The prices and rents compensate residents for any costs imposed on them by the Cubs, thereby internalizing the externality. The only ones to be hurt would be the original homeowners and landlords, few—if any—of whom are still alive. By contrast, the negative externalities generated by newer facilities, such as Chicago's United Center, which was built in 1994, have yet to be fully internalized. People who own nearby housing may see the value of their property decline. Unlike the residents near Wrigley Field, they did not pay a discounted price for their property.

Most local politicians believe that the negative externalities associated with franchises are dwarfed by the positive externalities they convey. They believe that professional sports franchises bring benefits to the city for which the team is not rewarded. Just as the costs that a negative externality imposes cause the supply curve to be too far out in Figure 7.2, the benefits a positive externality conveys cause the demand curve to be too far to the left. Figure 7.3 shows that, in the absence of government intervention, a positive externality would cause

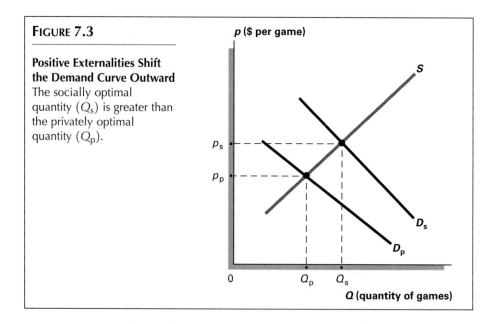

FIGURE 7.3

Positive Externalities Shift the Demand Curve Outward
The socially optimal quantity (Q_s) is greater than the privately optimal quantity (Q_p).

p ($ per game)

Q (quantity of games)

[14]See the Foreword to Michael Betzold and Ethan Casey, *Queen of Diamonds: The Tiger Stadium Story* (West Bloomfield, Mich.: Northfield Publishing, 1992).

the Sabres to play too few games. Buffalo would like the Sabres to play Q_s games, but the Sabres would play only Q_p. Because the Sabres' revenues understate the total benefit to the residents of Buffalo, the city must provide an additional incentive for the Sabres to play games in Buffalo rather than elsewhere. In the case of professional sports franchises, these incentives often take the form of public funding of sports facilities.

The impact of a professional sports franchise on a city or region goes far beyond a strict dollars and cents accounting. As noted above, states, cities, or neighborhoods can derive a sense of identity from having a professional franchise in their midst.[15] A successful team, in particular, may contribute to a city's self-image. As Bill Veeck said of his 1948 Cleveland Indians, "[T]here is that feeling of reflected glory in a successful baseball team. Cleveland is winning the pennant. The eyes of the whole country are upon Cleveland, upon us, upon me and you. *We're looking pretty good, aren't we, Mac?*"[16] All the residents of a community can share in the reflected glory of their hometown team without having to pay for the privilege. A franchise thus has aspects of a public good in that those who consume it do not prevent others from enjoying the team's presence, further justifying a role for government in providing it. The nonrivalry and nonexclusion allow people to free ride by passively following the team rather than buying tickets. The free rider problem means that fans do not compensate teams fully for the benefits they provide. As a result, teams produce less of the good than they would if they were compensated for generating the positive externality. In Chapter 3, we saw that in the case of league-wide marketing efforts, teams solve their own free rider problem by forming a larger collective known as a league. The league resolves the free rider problem by forcing teams to contribute to activities that benefit all teams. Society deals with the free rider problem by forming a larger collective known as government. The government forces people to contribute to collectively consumed public goods by imposing taxes and providing the good.

Small to midsized cities, in particular, generate a sense of being a "big-time" city from having a major league franchise. Indianapolis may not be able to compete with New York in terms of economic or cultural clout, but it derives a sense of superiority to New York whenever *our* Indiana Pacers defeat *their* New York Knicks. It may therefore come as no surprise that a survey of residents of Indianapolis in the 1990s found that the Indiana Pacers were a close second to the city's museums as a source of civic pride, with the Indianapolis Colts placing third.[17]

---

[15]Michael Danielson, *Home Team: Professional Sport and the American Metropolis* (Princeton, N.J.: Princeton University Press, 1997); Rosentraub, *Major League Losers* (1997), pp. 30–73; and David Swindell and Mark Rosentraub, "Who Benefits from the Presence of Professional Sports Teams? The Implications for Public Funding of Stadiums and Arenas," *Public Administration Review*, vol. 58, no. 1 (January/February 1998), pp. 11–20.

[16]Bill Veeck and Ed Linn, *Veeck as in Wreck* (Chicago: University of Chicago Press, 1962), p. 121.

[17]Mark Rosentraub, "Stadiums and Urban Space" (1997), pp. 189–190; and Swindell and Rosentraub, "Who Benefits from the Presence of Professional Sports Teams?" (1998), pp. 11–20.

City officials often claim that, in addition to improving the self-esteem of residents, having a professional franchise gives the city a higher profile, which in turn attracts business that would otherwise not locate there. However, this is disproved by the experts. From the pathbreaking work of Robert Baade and Richard Dye to more recent work by Ian Hudson and by Dennis Coates and Brad Humphreys, economists have consistently found no evidence that facilities and teams have an impact on the level of employment, incomes, or wages in a city.[18] They uniformly conclude that neither sports franchises nor new facilities bring appreciable financial gain to the communities where they are located.

The links between sport and society can sometimes run far deeper than good feelings about one's hometown. Local sports teams sometimes reflect the aspirations of rival ethnic groups. For example, the Glasgow Rangers and Celtic play out the rivalry between Protestants and Catholics in Glasgow in the Scottish Football League. The Montreal Canadiens and FC Barcelona have been symbols of something even larger: the nationalist yearnings by ethnic minorities. French Canada has long identified with the Canadiens. In fact, some regard the "Richard Riot"—a response to the suspension of hockey great Maurice Richard for several games at the end of the 1954–1955 NHL season and the ensuing playoffs—as a seminal event in the social and economic development of Quebec and in the separatist Quebecois movement. While some Canadiens fans speak of separation, FC Barcelona fans actually fought for it during the Spanish Civil War. During the four decades of fascist rule that followed the civil war, "[o]nly the Camp Nou [FC Barcelona's home field] provided Catalans a place to yell and scream against the regime in their own, banned vernacular."[19]

Because they are so closely integrated into their communities, the Glasgow Rangers and Celtic, the Montreal Canadiens, and FC Barcelona can count on municipal support to keep them solvent even in the worst of times. This added solvency, however, does not mean that the teams have a blank check. As noted earlier, Canadian cities do not give teams the same sort of tax breaks that many U.S. cities do. European and Latin American cities often go a step further and take an active role in the management of the team, something the North American leagues do not permit. Perhaps as a result, governmental contributions to soccer franchises in Europe have actually fallen in importance over the last several decades.[20]

Multiplier Effects   While the New York state comptroller finds that fans spend $43.6 million on the Buffalo Sabres, he concludes that the team has a $65 million

---

[18]Robert Baade and Richard Dye, "The Impact of Stadiums and Professional Sports on Metropolitan Area Development," *Growth and Change*, vol. 21, no. 2 (Spring 1990), pp. 1–14; Ian Hudson, "Bright Lights, Big City: Do Professional Sports Teams Increase Employment?," *Journal of Urban Affairs*, vol. 21, no. 4 (1999), pp. 397–407; and Dennis Coates and Brad Humphreys, "The Effect of Professional Sports on Earnings and Employment in U.S. Cities," *Regional Science and Urban Economics*, vol. 33, no. 2 (March 2003), pp. 175–198.

[19]Franklin Foer, *How Soccer Explains the World: An Unlikely Theory of Globalization* (New York: Harper Collins, 2004), p. 195.

[20]See Andreff and Staudohar (2002).

impact on the local economy. Where does the extra money come from? The difference lies in the fact that any new spending that the Sabres cause in Buffalo has an indirect benefit, or **multiplier effect.** That is, each new dollar spent on the Sabres generates additional expenditures, increasing the overall impact of the Sabres on spending and incomes in Buffalo.

To envision the multiplier process, think of Buffalo's economy as a still pond. Attracting the Sabres to town is like throwing a pebble into the pond. The direct impact of the Sabres is the splash caused by the pebble's hitting the water. A series of ripples quickly spreads out from the initial point of impact. As they spread out, the ripples become fainter and fainter, until they are indistinguishable from the flat pond. The multiplier effect is like those ripples, spreading the direct impact that the Sabres have on Buffalo throughout the entire city. To illustrate this, the income that Donna, a Buffalo resident, earns from working as an accountant for the Sabres is part of the direct impact the Sabres have on income in Buffalo. Her salary is thus part of the initial splash the pebble makes in the pond. Donna saves some of her income and spends some, perhaps on a new condominium in town. Her expenditure on the condo becomes part of the first ripple. Her purchase, in turn, increases the income of the local builder (and realtor and others). The builder then saves some of his additional income and spends some, perhaps buying a new computer from a local computer outlet, forming yet another ripple, and so on.

The ripples get smaller because people do not spend all their additional income. Economists call the fraction of an additional dollar of income that consumers spend the **marginal propensity to consume** (MPC). They call the fraction of an additional dollar that they save the **marginal propensity to save** (MPS). Consumers must spend or save that entire additional dollar, so

$$MPC + MPS = 1.$$

Most economists believe that Americans spend more than nine-tenths of each additional dollar that they earn. Assuming for simplicity that the $MPC = 0.9$, if Donna earned \$100,000, then she would spend

$$(0.9)(\$100,000) = \$90,000.$$

The \$90,000 that Donna spends is additional income to other people, who then spend nine-tenths of that income, or

$$(0.9)[(0.9)(\$100,000)] = \$81,000.$$

The process continues in steadily decreasing ripples until the additional expenditure becomes indistinguishable from zero and the ripples effectively disappear.

The total impact of Donna's \$100,000 income on the Buffalo economy is

$$T = \$100,000 + \$90,000 + \$81,000 + \$72,900 + \cdots.$$

While the numbers in this sum decline steadily to zero, it is not clear what the total impact is. We can, however, solve this infinite sum. Using what we know about the numbers in the sum, we can rewrite T as

$$T = \$100,000 * S$$

where

$$S = 1 + 0.9 + 0.9^2 + 0.9^3 + 0.9^4 + \cdots$$

It is not hard to solve for S, which in this case is approximately equal to $\dfrac{1}{1 - 0.9}$ or 10. The total impact of Donna's salary is thus $\$100,000 * 10$, or $\$1,000,000$. Because we multiply the initial expenditure by the sum S, we call S the **multiplier.** Of course, the MPC need not equal 0.9. More generally, we compute the multiplier as:

$$S = \frac{1}{1 - MPC} = \frac{1}{MPS}.$$

Clearly, the size of the multiplier has major implications for the value of a franchise to a city. A relatively small direct impact can lead to a huge increase in incomes and the well-being of the city. The simple multiplier, however, vastly overstates the multiplier that is applicable to professional sports teams. Research by Siegfried and Zimbalist shows that the multiplier for NBA player salaries is much smaller than the traditional multiplier.[21] There are several reasons for this. First, because professional athletes' salaries are much higher than for most workers, they are taxed at a higher rate, leaving less of their income available for consumption. Second, as income increases, workers have a greater tendency to save. Because professional athletes' careers tend to be relatively short, they have an additional incentive to save more of their current income than spend it. Finally, as Siegfried and Zimbalist note, most players do not live in the area where they work. For example, they report that while 93 percent of average employees live near where they work, only 29 percent of NBA players do so. In all, they estimate that, while over 58 percent of income is injected into a local economy for an average employee, for an NBA player the same percentage is only about 10 percent. As a result, use of a traditional multiplier based on average employees will overstate the first round of spending by almost 485 percent.[22] Their research supports the findings of many other economists, who find that the multiplier is unlikely to be in excess of 1.0; that is, there is no multiplier effect. That said, economic impact studies sponsored by local city governments typically ignore or understate these leakages. For example, by predicting a total impact of $65 million when direct expenditures are only $43.6 million, the New York state comptroller implicitly assumes that the multiplier for Buffalo is 1.5.

---

[21]John Siegfried and Andrew Zimbalist, "A Note on the Local Economic Impact of Sports Expenditures," *Journal of Sports Economics*, vol. 3, no. 4 (November 2002), pp. 361–366.

[22]Siegfried and Zimbalist (2002), p. 365.

Even if the multiplier exceeds 1, the overall financial impact of a franchise seems small. A study by Deloitte and Touche of the economic impact of the Arizona Diamondbacks on the state's economy found that the state gained about 340 full-time jobs at a cost of $240 million.[23] While $706,000 per job created may be higher than for most cities, it is not extraordinarily high for the cost of jobs created by a sports facility. In its analysis of the new stadium it was building for the Baltimore Ravens, the Maryland Department of Business and Economic Development projected economic benefits of $111 million and 1,394 new jobs from the Ravens. Other analysts claim that these estimates are too high and put the true impacts at $33 million and 534 jobs. As a result, the estimates of the cost to the state of Maryland per job created range from $127,000 to $331,000. While this figure is better than for Arizona, it is still far higher than other job-creation projects. Compared with the 5,200 full-time jobs created by Maryland's Sunny Day Fund for economic development, which cost taxpayers only $6,250 per job, the Ravens seem like a poor choice as a spur for economic development.[24]

The simple truth is that a professional franchise cannot be an engine for regional or local growth when its facility is empty more than 200 days a year. Because their primary tenants do not use football stadiums more than 350 days per year, football in particular is a poor vehicle for growth. In fact, some studies find that, because a sports franchise often drains resources from more productive expenditures, spending money to attract or retain a team can actually inhibit municipal growth.

Although there is little evidence that a team or a facility brings financial benefits, a city may still be willing to go to the expense of hosting it. As Bill Veeck and others have suggested, the main benefits a sports franchise brings a city are intangible feelings of well-being.[25] In one study, Rappoport and Wilkerson claim that such benefits could make a sports franchise worthwhile for a city even if they do not bring financial gain. Because they are intangible, however, these benefits are difficult to measure. Coates and Humphreys attempt to capture the intangible value of a franchise by looking at the impact of a team on property values, holding housing and other community characteristics constant.[26] All else equal, they find that housing located within a half-mile of the team does have higher value, though the effect quickly declines at greater distances. They conclude that a professional sports franchise makes the

[23]Baade and Sanderson, "The Employment Effect of Teams and Sports Facilities" (1997), p. 101.

[24]Dennis Zimmerman, "Subsidizing Stadiums: Who Benefits, Who Pays?" in *Sports, Jobs, and Taxes,* ed. by Roger Noll and Andrew Zimbalist (Washington, D.C.: Brookings Institution Press, 1997), p. 122. These figures agree with the finding that the jobs created by the new basketball and baseball facilities in Cleveland cost $231,000 per job. See Ziona Austrian and Mark Rosentraub, "Cleveland's Gateway to the Future," also in *Sports, Jobs, and Taxes,* p. 382.

[25]Others include Danielson (1997) and Swindell and Rosentraub (1998).

[26]Jordan Rappoport and Chad Wilkerson, "What Are the Benefits of Hosting a Major League Sports Franchise?" *Federal Reserve Bank of Kansas City Economic Review,* First Quarter, 2001, pp. 55–85; Dennis Coates and Brad R. Humphreys, "Professional Sports Facilities, Franchises and Urban Economic Development," *UMBC Working Paper 03–103,* 2003.

immediate community more attractive to potential homebuyers but that it has little effect on the city as a whole.

Can Anyone Win at This Game?

Although the consensus among economists is that cities do not come out ahead in what Shropshire calls "the sports franchise game,"[27] some cities clearly do better than others. Some of the determinants of success have more to do with accidents of geography and history. The difficulties experienced by midsized American cities such as Hartford, which lost its NHL team in 1997 and more recently tried unsuccessfully to attract an NFL team, as well as the "skate drain" that slowly drew hockey franchises out of Canada, demonstrate the problems some cities face. Still, by carefully incorporating sports franchises in a broader economic development plan, local politicians can increase the benefits a franchise brings to their city.

Larger cities have a natural advantage at attracting and retaining franchises. As noted in Chapter 3, leagues that placed franchises in midsized cities all lost out to leagues that placed teams in larger cities. Larger cities have more people who benefit, directly or indirectly, from having a team in town. While their fans may be more rabid and more knowledgeable, towns such as Winnipeg or Quebec cannot generate the same fan base or media market as a team in Phoenix or Denver can. Bigger cities also have larger multiplier effects because their employees are more likely to live in town or in surrounding communities.

While franchises benefit greatly from locating in a large local market, larger cities do not necessarily benefit more from hosting them. The size and diversity of the local economy has an ambiguous effect on the value of a franchise to a city. Larger, more diverse economies give residents more opportunities to spend their money with local proprietors. If the local economy can capture more of the ripple effect, the multiplier effect rises, making a franchise more valuable to a city. A more diverse economy also increases the substitution effect, since people are likely to spend their money on more types of other local activities if they do not have a local sporting event to attend.[28] This, in turn, makes a franchise less valuable.

In sum, cities such as Denver have a big advantage over cities such as Hartford when it comes to attracting franchises. Denver is a large city surrounded by smaller cities that offer little competition for entertainment dollars. It can therefore draw fans from a sizeable geographic area. Hartford, by contrast, is a midsized city that is squeezed between New York and Boston. As a result, Hartford had a much harder time creating a fan base and capturing the direct and indirect benefits of a professional franchise. Local politicians can try to offset this disadvantage, but they cannot eliminate it.

Similarly, Canadian cities have struggled mightily to retain franchises for their national game. In the 1990s, teams left Quebec for Denver and Winnipeg

---

[27]Kenneth Shropshire, *The Sports Franchise Game* (Philadelphia: University of Pennsylvania Press, 1995).

[28]See Noll and Zimbalist, "The Economic Impact of Sports Teams and Facilities" (1997), pp. 79–80.

for Phoenix. Both cities were doomed by their small fan base, limited gate revenue, and low local media revenue. Although the NFL can support small-market cities such as Green Bay, thanks to generous gate revenue sharing and a large national TV contract (which is shared equally among all teams), the NHL has a minimal safety net: Though it shares some revenue sources, it gets much less revenue from its network contract than does the NFL.

In addition, the Canadian franchises have been badly stung by the relatively high tax rates in Canada. Because high tax rates reduce the disposable income available to hockey players on Canadian teams, Canadian teams and cities are less attractive to play for. As players have won more control over where they can play and as the NHL increasingly draws players from around the globe who lack personal ties to Canada, players are choosing to leave Canadian teams and play on American teams. High tax rates also reduce the after-tax profits of Canadian franchises relative to franchises in the United States, making it more difficult for franchises to offer attractive salaries and compete for players in free agent markets.

There was, however, an even more pervasive threat to Canadian franchises, one that led some to speculate that eventually Canada might be left with only the Toronto Maple Leafs and Montreal Canadiens.[29] That threat was the exchange rate between Canadian and U.S. dollars. The weak Canadian dollar of the late 1990s and early 2000s seriously damaged the ability of Canadian teams to compete with their U.S. rivals because Canadian teams' revenue streams were largely in Canadian dollars, but they paid salaries that matched those paid by teams in the United States. Local and provincial governments have attempted to subsidize their hockey franchises to prevent them from moving. Canadian voters, however, were reluctant to approve taxes that would be earmarked for privately owned sports teams. An attempt to establish a wage tax on visiting hockey players was opposed by both the NHL and the NHLPA.

To show the impact of exchange rates on Canadian franchises, we make the simplifying assumption that a Canadian team pays its team in U.S. dollars. Since its revenues are all in Canadian dollars, the team must buy U.S. dollars before it can pay its players. It does so by buying dollars on a **currency market.** Currency markets treat dollars, yen, or francs like any other commodity. Figure 7.4 shows the market for U.S. dollars. The "price" of U.S. dollars is the number of Canadian dollars it takes to buy US$1. This price is called the **exchange rate,** because it determines how many Canadian dollars must be exchanged to get US$1. In January 2003, the Canadian dollar fell to its lowest point, requiring C$1.55 to exchange for US$1.

At this exchange rate, the Canadian hockey teams' expenses were magnified 55 percent by the exchange rate with the U.S. dollar. This created an "exchange rate deficit" of up to C$8 million for some teams, despite tax breaks of up to C$4 million given by some Canadian provinces. Team owners could escape this burden—and lessen their tax burden as well—by moving south of the border. Players, too, were discouraged from choosing to sign with Canadian

---

[29]Michael Farber, "Giant Sucking Sound," *Sports Illustrated* (March 20, 1995).

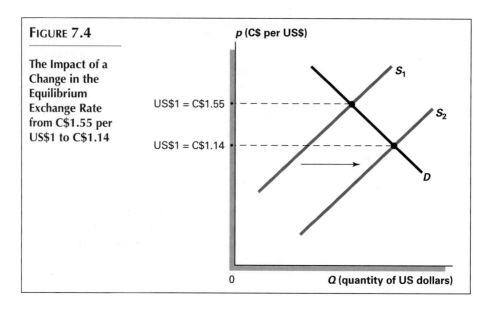

FIGURE 7.4

The Impact of a
Change in the
Equilibrium
Exchange Rate
from C$1.55 per
US$1 to C$1.14

p (C$ per US$)

US$1 = C$1.55

US$1 = C$1.14

S_1

S_2

D

0

Q (quantity of US dollars)

franchises, which discouraged attendance and put further economic pressure on Canadian franchises to relocate. Since January 2003, the increasing U.S. trade deficit has steadily weakened the U.S. dollar. Because it is buying more from abroad than it is selling abroad, the U.S. supplies dollars to currency markets, shifting out the supply curve in Figure 7.4. The exchange rate has fallen as a result, reaching C$1.14 per US$1 in July 2009. While still penalizing Canadian teams, the smaller differential has eased the financial pressure on Canadian hockey teams.

What can local officials do to maximize the benefits of hosting a sports franchise? Some experts claim that a city gains more from attracting or retaining a franchise—and hence can afford to make a more attractive offer to a franchise—if it has integrated the facilities into the urban fabric.[30] According to these analysts, many cities waste their chance to benefit from hosting a franchise by making their decisions at the last minute under threats by teams to move if their demands are not satisfied. Members of the Illinois legislature literally had to stop the clock to prevent the White Sox from leaving Chicago for St. Petersburg.[31] Chicago's lack of planning showed in the decision to locate the "New Comiskey Park" (now U.S. Cellular Field) across the street from the old one with little attention paid to incorporating the stadium into broader plans for economic development.

By contrast, Baltimore, Cleveland, and Indianapolis all undertook extensive efforts to incorporate the new facilities into their plans for urban

---

[30]Thomas Chema, "When Professional Sports Justify the Subsidy," *Journal of Urban Affairs*, vol. 18, no. 1 (1996), p. 20; and Baade and Sanderson, "The Employment Effect of Teams and Sports Facilities" (1997), pp. 94–95.

[31]Shropshire, *The Sports Franchise Game* (1995), p. 11.

revival. Baltimore sought to capitalize on the success of its efforts in the Inner Harbor, anchored by the Baltimore Aquarium, by building Oriole Park at Camden Yards and M&T Bank Stadium (home of the Ravens) close by. In Cleveland, Jacobs Field (now Progressive Field), which kept the Indians in town, and the Gund Arena (now Quicken Loans Arena), which brought the Cavaliers back to Cleveland from suburban Richfield, were all part of a broader Gateway Project designed to revitalize downtown Cleveland. In the 1980s, Indianapolis also decided to redevelop its downtown by extensive construction of a wide array of athletic facilities, including the Hoosier (later RCA) Dome. It linked this construction to the expansion of nonsports facilities such as the campus of Indiana University–Purdue University at Indianapolis.

All three projects have been loudly proclaimed as successes in creating jobs and revitalizing downtown areas. A closer look suggests that even a carefully planned sports complex may not have much of an impact. Indianapolis had only moderate, short-term success in retarding the relocation of employment to the suburbs.[32] While Cleveland did experience job growth following the construction of the sports facilities, the growth was actually lower downtown than elsewhere in the region and was slower than in the years immediately preceding the project.[33] Despite the fanfare surrounding the "best case" scenario of Camden Yards, estimates show that Orioles Park has created fewer than 600 jobs and has left the typical household roughly $12 poorer through the taxes they must pay to support the construction. Preliminary estimates show that, if anything, M&T Bank Stadium does an even worse job.[34] In sum, it appears that regardless of the approach they take, cities do not gain significantly from attracting a franchise.

The Impact of Special Events

Even if cities do not gain much from hosting a sports franchise, they may profit from hosting a special event, such as the Super Bowl, the Olympics, or the World Cup finals. Special events like these differ from the typical game played by local franchises in that they do not appeal specifically to local fans. While much of the money spent by local fans on a baseball game or a regular season football game may just replace money they would have spent on something else, special events attract people from all over the world who would not have come to the host city had the event not taken place. The impact of special events would therefore be expected to be significantly larger than those of a franchise over a similar period of time.

As shown in Chapter 6, however, the benefits of the 2002 World Cup came nowhere near the projected $31 billion. Similar overoptimism seems to

---

[32]Rosentraub, "Stadiums and Urban Space" (1997), pp. 178–207.

[33]Austrian and Rosentraub, "Cleveland's Gateway to the Future" (1997), pp. 355–384.

[34]Bruce Hamilton and Peter Kahn, "Baltimore's Camden Yards Ballparks," in *Sports, Jobs, and Taxes*, ed. by Roger Noll and Andrew Zimbalist (Washington, D.C.: Brookings Institution Press, 1997), pp. 245–281.

accompany the Super Bowl. Here, though, even the findings after the fact are subject to dispute. In his study of the economic impact of the Super Bowl, Philip Porter notes that studies conducted by host committees or the NFL on the Super Bowls held in Tampa (1991), Miami (1995), and Phoenix (1996) show an impact ranging from almost $120 million to over $160 million.[35]

Porter examined the impact of the Super Bowl on Miami, Tampa, and Phoenix by estimating the impact of the Super Bowl on the dollar value of sales in each city's county (Dade, Hillsborough, and Maricopa Counties, respectively) for the 1979, 1984, 1989, 1991, 1995, and 1996 Super Bowls. He found little evidence that the Super Bowl had a major financial impact on the local economies. He found a statistically significant impact only for the 1984 Super Bowl in Tampa, and even this indicated that local sales increased by only $1.3 million during the month of the Super Bowl.

How can one reconcile Porter's findings with the huge returns detected by the NFL and the host committees? The key seems to be analogous to our finding that spending by city residents on local sports franchises crowds out other local spending. In this case, the NFL and host committees seem to have assumed that all spending on the Super Bowl was new expenditure by additional tourists. Porter concluded that spending on a Super Bowl largely displaces spending by tourists who would have gone to these cities but could not do so because of the influx of football fans. The net impact of a Super Bowl in such a situation is essentially zero.

7.2 A Public Choice Perspective

If cities do not gain significantly from sports franchises, then their spending millions of dollars on facilities for these franchises seems to defy all economic logic. A relatively new area of economic thought—known as **public choice theory**—provides an economic framework that makes it possible to understand why cities do what they do.

Public choice theory stems from the work of Nobel laureate James Buchanan, Gordon Tullock, William Niskanen, and others in the 1960s. The basic premise rests on the notion that decision makers in the public sector do not automatically act to resolve the market failures of public goods and externalities. Instead, public officials are subject to many of the same temptations and constraints facing consumers and producers in the private sector.

According to the public choice perspective, the interests of politicians and the owners of sports franchises come together very neatly. Politicians have an interest in attaining, maintaining, and advancing their political standing. They therefore undertake actions that they feel will ensure their re-election or get them elected to higher office. To do so, they respond to the interests of the electorate.

---

[35]Philip Porter, "Mega-Sporting Events as Municipal Investments: A Critique of Impact Analysis," in *Sports Economics: Current Research*, ed. by John Fizel, Elizabeth Gustafson, and Larry Hadley (Westport: Praeger Publishers, 1999).

Since it is costly to determine the specific interests of large numbers of disparate voters, politicians are most responsive to organized group interests; the more highly organized the group, the more influence it wields over officeholders.[36]

Team owners, often in alliance with business and labor interests, have sought to use their organized influence over the political process. At times, the groups may actually improve the efficiency of the political process. By expressing the intensity of their desires, interest groups may—through a process known as **logrolling**—induce politicians to pass legislation that the electoral process would deny. To see this, suppose a legislature consists of three equal groups, each representing one-third of the state (i.e., East, Central, and West). The state is considering building two stadiums, one each in the East and West of the state. Suppose each new stadium would greatly benefit the region in which it is located but mildly hurt—through higher taxes that everyone in the state must pay to fund the stadiums—the other two portions of the state, as seen in Table 7.2. If the representatives voted according to the impact of the stadium on their constituents, they would defeat both stadium proposals, because each proposal hurts two-thirds of the state. According to the payoffs in Table 7.2, however, the benefits of each proposal benefit the host constituency so much that majority rule leaves the state worse off. By expressing the intensity of their desires, group interests may induce legislators from the East and West to vote for each other's proposals and improve social well-being by passing both proposals. The proposals would therefore pass by a 2–1 margin, despite the fact that each facility benefits only one region.[37]

Generally speaking, group interests do not have such a positive impact on society. This is particularly true when groups use their political influence to pursue rents. Chapter 4 explained how rent-seeking behavior by firms in the private sector may increase the deadweight loss due to monopoly. In the public sphere, rents result from the monopoly right to provide an output. Rent-seeking

TABLE 7.2

How Logrolling Can Improve Social Well-Being

Region	Payoff to Proposal #1	Payoff to Proposal #2
East	+$10 million	−$ 2 million
Central	−$ 2 million	−$ 2 million
West	−$ 2 million	+$ 10 million
Overall impact	+$ 6 million	+$ 6 million

[36]See, for example, Arthur Seldon, "Public Choice and the Choices of the Public," in *Democracy and Public Choice*, ed. by Charles Rowley (London: Basil Blackwell, 1987), pp. 122–134. In Chapter 10 we explore the role played by bureaucrats who are not directly answerable to voters.

[37]See, for example, Thomas Stratmann, "Logrolling," in *Perspectives on Public Choice: A Handbook*, ed. by Dennis Mueller (Cambridge, U.K.: Cambridge University Press, 1997), pp. 322–341.

behavior in the public sector thus consists of a two-step process. First, the rent seeker must control the political process that determines the distribution of rights or output. Second, once in control of the political process, the rent seeker then exploits his or her monopoly position.

It is possible to see such a two-stage process in the expenditures well-organized interests make to pursue their political ends. Pro-stadium forces in Cleveland raised over $1 million to pay for their 1990 referendum effort; this included payments of over $300,000 from the Indians and Cavaliers. In a more extreme example, Paul Allen, who used some of the fortune he made from Microsoft to purchase the Seattle Seahawks football team, paid the state of Washington $4.2 million to cover the costs of the referendum on financing a new football stadium. This move neatly sidestepped the state's requirement that the team demonstrate sufficient support for a publicly funded referendum by gathering petitions. Allen also spent $5 million during the campaign to convince voters to support the proposal to spend $300 million on the new Seahawks stadium. The effort proved successful, as Washington voters narrowly approved the proposal. The $300 million return on a $9.2 million investment proved to be one of Allen's most profitable moves since joining with Bill Gates to form Microsoft.[38]

7.3 Stadium Costs and Financing

Cities bear two types of costs when attempting to lure or retain a franchise: initial venue construction costs and maintenance costs. As we saw from Chapter 6, a city's expenditure for a venue can range from a relatively modest share of the total cost, as in the recent cases of the Mets and Yankees, to the full cost of the building, as in the case of the Washington Nationals. The annual costs that are borne by the city also depend on the lease agreement between the team and the city, but could include staffing the venue, insurance, maintenance and upkeep, and ongoing improvements. To get a sense of the magnitude of these costs, consider the case of the new football-only stadium in Indianapolis. According to the *Indianapolis Business Journal*, the city's Capital Improvement Board expects that Lucas Oil Stadium, which cost $720 million to build, will also cost $27.7 million in operating expenses for 2009, $20 million more than the city's share of revenue from stadium events.[39]

While the size of the expenditures seem extraordinary to those of us not familiar with large-scale budgeting, the real cost must be measured against alternatives. Recall from our discussion of financing costs in Chapter 6 that one of the most fundamental—and important—concepts in economics is the notion of opportunity costs. When cities decide to pay for all or part of a new stadium and its operating costs, it is at the same time deciding *not* to pursue other

[38]Cagan and deMause, *Field of Schemes* (1998), pp. 16, 44, 166–168.
[39]Jennifer Whitson, "Lucas Oil Stadium Begins in the Red," *Indianapolis Business Journal*, August 9, 2008, at http://www.ibj.com/html/detail_page_Full.asp?content=18441. Accessed June 23, 2009.

projects for which it could have used the same funds. Even if the venue is paid for with new taxes or bonds, as opposed to existing sources of revenue, it is still the case that the same funds might have been raised to build libraries, zoos, parks, or schools.

Section 7.1 showed that state and local governments can—at least in theory—justify subsidizing franchises, if the city or state benefits from the public good aspect of the franchise or from the positive externalities it conveys upon the city. Because the local team is not rewarded for all the benefits it provides to the community, it may not have enough of an incentive to locate in the city without a public subsidy. The subsidy, however, has to come from somewhere. State and local governments have two basic sources of revenue: taxes and debt. Both sources have their advantages and disadvantages. Even if the community borrows, however, eventually it will have to raise taxes in order to repay the loan. Since governments cannot escape imposing a tax, they should pay careful attention to the form of tax they impose, as different taxes have significantly different impacts on subgroups in the population. In the first part of this section, we present several criteria by which economists evaluate tax plans. We then use these criteria to evaluate methods that cities have chosen to finance new facilities. Finally, we look at why governments prefer using debt to finance new facilities.

An Economic View of Taxes: Who Should Pay?

We have seen that negative externalities cause society to produce and consume too much of a good and that positive externalities cause it to produce and consume too little. Governments typically try to resolve the problems that externalities cause by forcing firms to *internalize* them. In the case of negative externalities, taxes raise the cost of production, causing firms to produce less. In the case of positive externalities, subsidies increase the rewards from production and encourage firms to produce more.

Using a subsidy to eliminate a positive externality raises a crucial question: Where does the government get the money to provide the subsidy? Economic theory explains that governments maximize the well-being of their residents if they finance the subsidy by imposing taxes or fees based on the benefits each person receives from the positive externality. Unfortunately, the nature of positive externalities often makes it difficult to identify exactly who benefits. Fortunately, it is possible to establish some general principles for determining who should pay how much for a sports franchise.

One such principle—known as the **Ramsey rule**—dictates that sales taxes should be levied in inverse proportion to the price elasticity of demand for the good or service on which the government places the tax. Such a tax is more efficient than alternative tax schemes in the sense that it minimizes the deadweight loss.

For example, suppose Charlotte, North Carolina, considered two ways to raise money for the NASCAR Hall of Fame: a tax on hotel stays and a tax on kidney dialysis.[40] Assume, for simplicity, that the city feels it can raise all the

---

[40]In fact, it has imposed a 2 percent hotel tax.

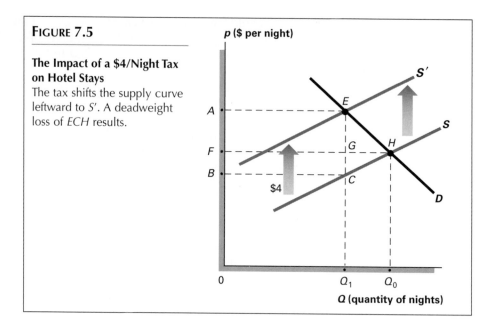

FIGURE 7.5

The Impact of a $4/Night Tax on Hotel Stays
The tax shifts the supply curve leftward to S'. A deadweight loss of *ECH* results.

p ($ per night)

Q (quantity of nights)

revenue it needs by imposing a $4 tax on either. Figure 7.5 shows the impact of a tax on hotel stays. As shown in Chapter 2, a $4 sales tax causes consumers to see a supply curve that is $4 higher than the true supply curve.

Since the equilibrium number of nights spent at local hotels falls from Q_0 to Q_1, the deadweight loss imposed by the tax equals the area of the triangle ECH. This burden consists of lost consumer surplus for hotel guests (EGH) and lost producer surplus for hotel operators (CGH). The implications of this shared burden are explored later in the chapter.

Contrast the deadweight loss from a hotel tax with the deadweight loss from a tax on kidney dialysis, as seen in Figure 7.6. A $4 tax on dialysis shifts the supply curve (which, for simplicity, we assume to be identical to the supply curve in Figure 7.5) up by $4, just like before. Unlike hotel stays, kidney dialysis has no good substitutes. The demand for dialysis is therefore much less sensitive to changes in price than the demand for hotels. Since the demand curve is so inelastic, the quantity of dialysis hardly changes and the price increases by almost the full amount of the tax. Because the tax on dialysis causes little loss of output, there is very little deadweight loss (the area of the triangle ECH).

If Charlotte wants to impose a tax that minimizes deadweight loss, then a tax on dialysis may be just the thing. Most people, however, would not choose to impose a greater burden on people who are unfortunate enough to require dialysis.

Society must often choose between policies that are efficient and policies that satisfy some notion of fairness or *equity*. Tax analyses frequently apply two forms of equity: **horizontal equity** and **vertical equity.** Economists say that a policy satisfies vertical equity if it takes account of people's ability to pay. More generally, one can say that a vertically equitable tax does not fall particularly

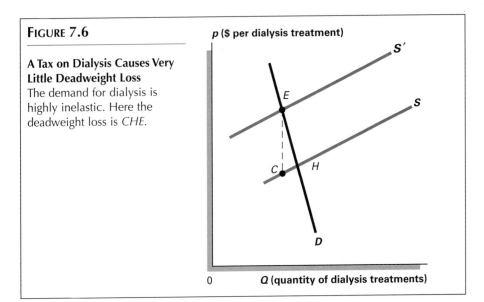

FIGURE 7.6

A Tax on Dialysis Causes Very Little Deadweight Loss
The demand for dialysis is highly inelastic. Here the deadweight loss is *CHE*.

p ($ per dialysis treatment)

S'

S

E

C   *H*

D

0   *Q* (quantity of dialysis treatments)

heavily on those with an already low level of income. Since hotel stays are generally either part of a vacation by relatively well-to-do households or underwritten by businesses while dialysis is an undesired burden borne by people from a variety of income groups, a hotel tax is more vertically equitable than a dialysis tax.

While vertical equity applies across income or utility levels, horizontal equity refers to fairness at a given level. A tax is horizontally equitable if it treats equals equally. Since public expenditure often confers unequal benefits on the population, the pursuit of horizontal equity leads governments to levy taxes in proportion to the benefits received from the expenditure. In this example, the hotel stay and dialysis tax appear to do equally well by this criterion.[41]

Some economists feel that governments should rely on **user fees** rather than public taxation to fund facilities. They believe that the public good aspects of a professional franchise are dwarfed by the private consumption that takes place. The emphasis that teams now place on luxury boxes and prime seating has made it difficult for middle- or low-income fans to attend the major professional sports games on a regular basis.[42]

The growing reliance of many teams on cable television has also made it increasingly difficult for low- and middle-income fans to follow the team at

---

[41]For more on these—and other—criteria for evaluating taxes, see, for example, Harvey Rosen, *Public Finance* (Chicago: Irwin, 1995).

[42]For an interesting example, see John Pastier, "Diamonds in the Rough: Two Cheers for the New Baseball Palaces," *Slate Magazine*, July 31, 1996, at http://slate.msn.com/feature2/96-07-31/feature2.asp; and John Siegfried and Andrew Zimbalist, "The Economics of Sports Facilities and Their Construction," *Journal of Economic Perspectives*, vol. 14, no. 3 (Summer 2000), pp. 95–114.

home. While all the citizens of New York may take pride in the success of the Yankees, much of the city benefits only from having something to talk and feel proud about since they can afford neither tickets nor cable fees. Poor and minority residents, in particular, must content themselves with radio broadcasts or newspaper accounts of their home team.[43]

In fact, many of the consumption benefits of a major league franchise flow out of the city to the residents of the relatively wealthy suburban ring. The suburbs disproportionately house the people who can most afford tickets to sporting events. They also disproportionately house corporate executives who use the luxury boxes and other premium seating that now account for so much of the cost of a facility. In addition, as explained earlier, most cities get only a small fraction of the revenue from luxury boxes. Taxes that fall on residents of the city that houses the team therefore allow suburbanites to free ride, while those who pay the most may enjoy the least consumption value from the team.

Sales Taxes

In addition to creating a deadweight loss, sales taxes often place a burden on groups that the government does not wish to target. Depending on the products subject to tax, the burden may fall upon people who do not benefit from the new facility, thereby violating horizontal equity. The merits of sales taxes on items directly related to sports facilities are considered later in the chapter. This section explores the problem posed when the burden of a sales tax does not fall solely on the people who ostensibly pay the tax. The tax burden shifts because people respond to the world around them. Governments that impose a tax expecting people to behave the same way they did before the tax was levied are in for a rude awakening.

The Dallas Cowboys stirred up a major controversy when they proposed raising a portion of the $1 billion for a new stadium with a three percentage point increase (up to 18 percent total, among the highest in the nation) in the tax on hotel stays in the Dallas–Fort Worth area. Such a tax would seem to be a very popular way to raise funds. After all, the tax was designed to fall on out-of-town visitors, thereby exporting the burden of paying for a new stadium to taxpayers from other states. The proposed tax, however, drew a firestorm of protest from the local Visitors Bureau and—of all groups—Mary Kay Cosmetics.[44]

Mary Kay's opposition was understandable. The company holds its annual convention in the area and did not want to see its expenses rise. Why, however, did the Visitors Bureau, which represents the local hospitality industry, object to having out-of-towners pay?

---

[43]See, for example, Roger Thurow, "Thrown for a Curve," *Wall Street Journal* (August 28, 1998), pp. A1, A6.
[44]See Hugh Aynsworth, "Owner of Dallas Cowboys Seeks $1 Billion in Tax Funds," *Washington Times*, February 2, 2004, online at http://www.washingtontimes.com/national/20040202-120350-8901r.htm.

To see why local hotels might object, let's first simplify the problem and again assume that the hotel tax is a flat $4 for each person spending an evening in a local hotel. Let us further assume that 1 million people spent an average of 5 nights each in hotels in the Dallas-Fort Worth area in a typical year. One might initially conclude that the tax would raise $20 million ($4 per night × 1 million people × 5 nights per person) per year. This naïve calculation, however, assumes that visitors do not respond to the higher cost of staying in a local hotel.

Recall from Figure 7.5 that the tax causes the price of a night in a hotel room to rise—though by less than $4—and the number of nights spent at hotels to fall. The higher price that people pay per night spent at a hotel (segment AF in Figure 7.5 is the portion of the $4 tax that they bear. Since the government has imposed a $4 tax but the price of a night at a hotel has risen by less than $4, hotel operators receive a lower price per night than they did before the tax was imposed. The lower price that hotel operators receive (segment FB in Figure 7.5) is the portion of the $4 tax that customers have passed on to the local hotel industry.

The total tax burden equals the $4 per night tax (segment AB in Figure 7.5) times the number of rooms rented (segment AE). This product, the total tax revenue, equals the area of the rectangle ABCE in Figure 7.5. The portion of this rectangle that lies above the original price of the room (the rectangle AFGE in Figure 7.5) is the burden borne by people who stay at hotels. The rectangle below the original price, the rectangle (FGCB in Figure 7.5) is the burden borne by local hotel operators. Since customers respond to the higher price of hotel stays in Charlotte with fewer or shorter stays there, the tax revenue falls short of the target.

Cleveland applied a different kind of sales tax to help fund the facilities it built. It imposed a 15-year **sin tax** on residents of Cuyahoga County. Like most sin taxes, these taxes consisted of sales taxes on tobacco products and alcohol. They are popular with many citizens because they impose a burden on people who engage in or cater to "sinful" behavior. Much of the public thus views sin taxes as a way to raise revenue by taxing other people and as a way to discourage undesirable activity. Unfortunately, sin taxes cannot achieve both of these ends. As shown in Figure 7.5, if a tax discourages behavior, it creates a large deadweight loss and fails to raise the anticipated amount of revenue. To the extent that drinking and smoking are addictive behaviors, the demand for them is highly price inelastic. Figure 7.6 showed that taxes on goods for which demand is inelastic create very little deadweight loss and come much closer to raising the desired revenue. However, because the change in quantity due to the tax is so small, the tax fails to discourage the sinful behavior.

Public choice theory helps to explain why Cleveland's sin taxes stirred less organized opposition than the Dallas area's proposed hotel tax. The deadweight loss of a tax adds to the burden on the group that pays the tax and hence subsidizes the publicly funded facility. A larger burden makes that group more likely to organize opposition to the tax. Since the demand for cigarettes and alcohol are far less price elastic than the demand for hotel stays, a smaller deadweight loss and less opposition arose to the sin tax. Since the tax falls most heavily on the poor and minorities, who are less likely to enjoy the benefits of the new ballpark, the tax and stadium policies fail on grounds of both vertical and horizontal equity.[45]

Incremental Financing

Some cities, most notably San Francisco and San Diego, hope to finance their new facilities (AT&T—originally Pacific Bell—Park and PETCO Park) through a new technique that tries to avoid raising taxes. **Incremental financing** does not impose a new tax. Instead, it earmarks increased tax revenue to pay the city's debt to its bondholders. The idea behind this is that the new facility will stimulate tourism. The additional tourists will increase hotel occupancy rates, increase patronage at local restaurants, and generally increase expenditure in the community. This added expenditure will lead to higher revenues from existing sales taxes and hotel taxes without the city's having to increase tax rates at all. The city just commits to using this additional tax revenue to pay its bondholders.

If it succeeds, incremental financing minimizes the burden on both tourists and local merchants. To succeed, however, the new facility must cause tourist expenditure to rise for a sustained period. Recall from Table 6.3, however, that the honeymoon period for a new stadium is not very long. Just four years after opening, attendance at AT&T Park was down almost 200,000 from the first year it was open, and attendance at PETCO park in San Diego was down over half a million. While San Francisco maintained attendance above three million through 2007, much of that might be due to its 2002 World Series appearance and to Barry Bonds's pursuit of Hank Aaron's home run record. For San Diego, incremental financing looks even more risky. With neither a recent World Series nor a superstar to sustain them, the Padres' attendance has fallen dramatically.

Taxes That Broaden the Burden

None of these funding mechanisms does a particularly good job of meeting the criteria set out at the beginning of this section. Some are inefficient; others fail on equity grounds. We now turn to two funding sources that, while flawed, do a better job of meeting the criteria. Each tries explicitly to allocate burdens more equitably, though they do so in different manners.

The first mechanism is exemplified by the way that the Milwaukee Brewers have funded the new stadium, Miller Park: by thinking big. They instituted a sales tax on Milwaukee and the surrounding five-county region. The broader geographic reach of this tax accounts for the regional impact of a stadium and thus reduces the vertical and horizontal inequities that result when inner-city taxpayers finance a facility that benefits wealthy suburbanites. While the regional tax reduces inequities, it does not eliminate them entirely. In addition, while the sales tax does a better job of targeting the beneficiaries of the stadium,

---

[45]See Gary Becker, "A Theory of Competition Among Pressure Groups for Political Influence," *Quarterly Journal of Economics,* vol. 98, no. 3 (August 1983), pp. 371–400.

it remains a rather broad brush, as it is based on a person's purchases of goods and services and not on a person's benefits from having the Brewers in town.[46]

The second mechanism is demonstrated by the way that Seattle and the state of Washington are funding Safeco Field: by thinking small. They have tried to target the funding of the new ballpark directly at the beneficiaries of the public expenditure with a special sales tax of 0.5 percent on restaurants, bars, and taverns in King County and a tax of up to 5 percent on admissions to Safeco Field. They have also sought to export some of the burden with a 2 percent tax on rental cars. This sales tax makes an attempt to match burdens to benefits by placing the greatest tax burden on those who benefit from having the Mariners in town, though it does not get things quite right. By charging a five-star French restaurant at the opposite end of the county the same tax that it charges a bar across the street from the stadium, the government does not match costs to benefits particularly well. The government tax on admissions does a far better job of matching costs and benefits. The tax on car rentals has the same imperfect impact as the hotel room tax example discussed earlier.[47]

Despite each mechanism's drawbacks, these plans appear to do the best job of minimizing deadweight loss while averting horizontal and vertical inequities.

The Benefits of Debt

According to economic theory, borrowing to finance a new stadium does not lessen the tax burden on a community. It simply delays the inevitable. Since David Ricardo first stated his famous "equivalence theorem," economists have known that borrowing and taxation have the same impact on residents, at least in theory.[48] State and local governments, however, face several institutional factors that lead them to prefer debt funding to direct taxation.

While people and small firms typically borrow money by taking out a loan at a bank, large corporations and governments often want to borrow more money than a single lender is willing to provide. As a result, they typically borrow by issuing **bonds.** A bond is a promise to pay the person who owns the bond a fixed amount—the **face value** of the bond—at some future point in time. Few people are willing to lend money without some form of additional compensation, and so bonds also promise to make periodic **interest** payments as well.[49] Consumers can compare two bonds with different face values and interest payments by computing the **interest rate.** The interest rate equals the ratio of the interest payment to the price of the bond. This provides a common

---

[46]See Zimmerman, "Subsidizing Stadiums: Who Benefits, Who Pays?" (1997), p. 137.

[47]MSC Sports, "New Park Financing: How the Deals Got Done," 1999, at http://www.wcco.com/sports/stadiums.html.

[48]For a more complete treatment, see N. Gregory Mankiw, *Macroeconomics* (New York: Worth, 2000), pp. 419–424.

[49]Lenders demand interest because they are sacrificing the chance to use that money by letting someone else have it. The interest payment is compensation for that lost consumption.

yardstick for comparing the value of two different bonds to lenders and the cost to borrowers.

Bonds issued by state or local governments have an advantage over otherwise identical bonds offered by corporations. Tax laws allow bondholders to deduct the interest they earn from state and local bonds from their federal taxes. The higher preference for municipal government bonds drives up the demand for them and causes their price to rise from p_0 to p_1, as shown in Figure 7.7.

If the price of the municipal bond rises, then the interest rate falls. Bonds offered by state and local governments are then cheaper to the state and local governments because of federal tax laws. The lower tax revenues mean that taxpayers elsewhere will have to pay higher taxes, that federal programs will have to be cut, or that the federal government will have to borrow more and drive up interest rates. No matter what, the deductibility of municipal bonds imposes costs on the rest of the nation. Municipalities thus like the idea of debt finance because it imposes some of the cost of a stadium on residents of other municipalities.

Even if debt did not export the burden geographically, it could export the burden intertemporally. If future generations enjoy the benefits of the new facility, then economic theory says that society is better off if they pay some of the burden. Debt financing allows a city to impose some of the burden of a new facility on future generations. Unfortunately, one result of the increasing exercise of monopoly outlined in Chapter 6 has been the steady decreasing of a facility's economic life. Structures that could stand for 40 to 50 years now become economically obsolete in only 10 or 20. Future generations may therefore be stuck with the bill for a facility that their teams have already abandoned.

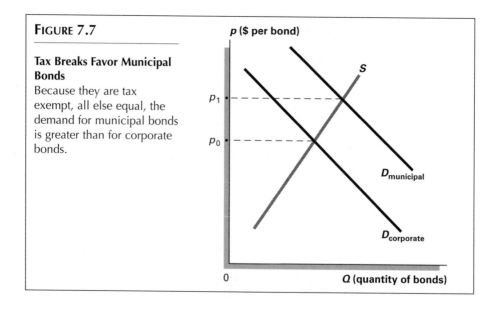

FIGURE 7.7

Tax Breaks Favor Municipal Bonds
Because they are tax exempt, all else equal, the demand for municipal bonds is greater than for corporate bonds.

BIOGRAPHICAL SKETCH

"MITT" ROMNEY

"He felt like he was walking into an empty elevator shaft."
—*Fraser Bullock, describing Romney's reaction to learning
the financial state of the Salt Lake Organizing Committee*[1]

Seldom have politics and sports been more intertwined than in the recent career of Willard ("Mitt") Romney. Mitt Romney was born and raised in Michigan; his father, the late George Romney, had served as the state's governor and had once been a presidential candidate. A practicing Mormon, Romney graduated with highest honors from Brigham Young University in 1971, and in 1974, he received both a JD and an MBA from Harvard. After spending two years on a Mormon mission to France, Romney went to work at Bain and Co., a Boston management consulting firm. In 1984, he founded Bain Capital, a venture capital firm that invested in hundreds of companies, including Staples, Domino's Pizza, and The Sports Authority.

In 1994, Romney entered the political arena by challenging Senator Edward Kennedy's reelection bid. The election's outcome was a foregone conclusion. Kennedy soundly defeated Romney, garnering 60 percent of the vote. This might have been the end of Romney's political career were it not for a surprising move he made five years later.

In late 1998, the Salt Lake Organizing Committee (SLOC), the body charged with organizing and financing the 2002 Winter Olympics, was facing a severe crisis. With the Olympics just three years off, the SLOC was almost $400 million in debt, having badly underestimated the costs of the Games. To make matters worse, fundraising was at a standstill, with no new sponsors secured in over a year. Voluntarism was also lagging, and the leadership of SLOC was under investigation by the U.S. Justice Department for giving alleged bribes exceeding $1 million to International Olympic Committee officials in order to secure the Games for Salt Lake City. SLOC was in desperate need of a person who could combine business connections and savvy with unquestioned integrity *and* who would not mind moving to Utah for the next three years. The job requirements seemed to fit Romney perfectly, and he soon showed why.

In February 1999, Romney took over as CEO and president of the SLOC and quickly began putting his personal stamp on the process. Recognizing that the allegations of corruption had demoralized workers and frightened off donors, Romney insisted on strict ethical standards in all SLOC's activities. He opened all meetings and records to the public. He also demanded that all employees and board members report any possible conflicts of interest and complete annual surveys of ethical conduct.

Ethics would help, but morality alone would not balance the budget. Romney cut the Games' budget by about $200 million and vigorously pursued his political and business connections. The results were impressive. Romney's governmental contacts helped secure an estimated $1.5 billion from the federal government. That total is almost ten times more than the amount of federal support per athlete provided at the 1996 Summer Olympics Games in Atlanta. Between the government support and private sponsorships, the SLOC managed to dig out of its financial hole and wind up slightly in the black. The citizens of Utah were

continued

also energized, as 67,000 people volunteered for 23,000 volunteer positions.

Although the Games did little to revive the flagging business community in Salt Lake City, they were a public relations triumph. As head of the Games, Romney had become a celebrity. Less than six weeks after the Olympic flame had been extinguished, Romney had become the Republican standard bearer in the race for governor of Massachusetts, despite his having spent most of the previous three years across the country. In November of 2002, Romney was elected governor.

Romney may well turn his Olympic experience into a springboard to the presidency. If he does, he will not be the first person to use sports that way. After all, President George W. Bush first entered the public eye as a member of the ownership group of the Texas Rangers baseball team.

[1]Cathy Harasta, "Romney Shows His Mettle," *Dallas Morning News,* February 17, 2002,

Sources: Donald Bartlett and James Steele, "Snow Job," *Sports Illustrated,* December 10, 2001, pp. 79–97; Paul Foy, "Romney Just Glad Olympics Worked," *2002 Winter Olympic Games* on line at http://olympics.hiasys .com/olympics_main/news/ap_olynewsscene 02252002 .htm; "Governor Mitt Romney," *Massachusetts Office of the Governor* online at http://www.mass.gov/portal/ index.jsp?pageID= agccagid=govagca=biographiesagcc =mittromneybio; Paula Parrish, "Leap of Faith: Mitt Romney Embraces Challenges, and This Might Be His Biggest One," *Rocky Mountain News,* February 4, 2002, p. 8S; Lewis Rice, "Games Saver," *Harvard Law Bulletin,* Spring 2002, on line at http://www.law.harvard.edu/ alumni/bulletin/2002/spring/feature_1-1.html.

Summary

In this chapter, we examined why cities might be willing to make such huge payments to help build facilities for sports teams. Cities do not—and should not—operate with the same goals as a private firm. Building and maintaining a stadium may not be profitable for the city, but may generate enough positive externalities to justify the expense. The externalities reflect benefits to people or businesses that have no direct contact with the franchise. Many of these perceived benefits come from the argument that a substantial multiplier effect is operating on spending in the local economy. However, most evidence shows that the financial benefits of a facility do not outweigh the costs.

Cities must also find the appropriate funding mechanism for a facility. Economic theory indicates that the tax burden should reflect the benefits that a person or business receives from the expenditure. Most cities, however, do not adhere to this principle when they fund their facilities.

Discussion Questions

1. What kinds of promises might a city ask a team to make about a stadium-funding deal to increase the size of the indirect benefits that the facility yields?

2. Which is better for a city, a stadium right in the downtown area or one on the outskirts of town? Which is better for the team?

3. Describe the externalities associated with a football stadium compared with an amusement park. Which would have greater positive externalities? Negative externalities?

4. Think of some taxes that would be highly progressive. Why are such taxes difficult to pass?

5. If an urban municipality decides to assist in the funding of a baseball stadium, what other types of public spending will likely need to be increased as well?

6. Which do you believe is more important in taxing the public to provide funds for stadiums—horizontal equity or vertical equity? Why?

7. Would the opportunity cost of constructing a stadium in a relatively poor city be greater or less than the opportunity cost for a relatively wealthy city? Why?

Problems

7.1 Evaluate the following taxes from the standpoint of vertical and horizontal equity:
   a. A 25-cent per-gallon tax on milk
   b. A tax on stock market transactions
   c. A sales tax on men's clothing
   d. A tax on cigarettes

7.2 Suppose the demand for toothbrushes is perfectly inelastic, at $Q_d = 3,000$. The market supply curve is perfectly elastic and is equal to $p = 2.00$. What would be the deadweight loss associated with a $0.20 tax on toothbrushes? Based on the Ramsey rule, would this be a good product to tax or not?

7.3 If the marginal propensity to consume in a municipality is 0.8, what is the value of the simple multiplier? If a new stadium that adds $30 million in new consumption expenditures is built, what is the impact on the economy based on this multiplier?

7.4 True or false; explain your answer: "The new stadium was entirely privately funded because all the city contributed was a 50-acre site on which to build it."

7.5 You own a team in San Francisco. What does public choice theory say about what you will do if Los Angeles presses the California legislature to underwrite a new stadium in Los Angeles?

7.6 Why is the multiplier effect for the Los Angeles Lakers likely to be greater than the multiplier effect for the Sacramento Kings, when they are both teams in the NBA?

7.7 Your city is committed to raising $100 million for a new arena. The mayor suggests putting a tax on taxicab rides since out-of-towners disproportionately use taxicabs. Evaluate the wisdom of this policy decision.

7.8 Under what circumstances would a city government want to contribute funding for a stadium even if it knows that the revenue it receives will not cover the city's share of operating expenses?

7.9 Why might a city want to go into debt as a way to fund a new stadium?

7.10 Why would a Super Bowl played in Detroit probably have more of an impact than a Super Bowl played in Miami, even if both were to draw the same amount of fans? Why would a Super Bowl at Ford Field in Detroit have more of an impact on Detroit than a regular season Detroit Lions game that draws the same number of fans?

PART FOUR
The Labor Economics of Sports

CHAPTER 8
An Introduction to Labor Markets in Professional Sports

CHAPTER 9
Labor Market Imperfections

CHAPTER 10
Discrimination

CHAPTER 8

An Introduction to Labor Markets in Professional Sports

After my fourth season I asked for $43,000 and General Manager Ed Barrow told me, 'Young man, do you realize Lou Gehrig, a 16-year-man, is playing for only $44,000?' I said, Mr. Barrow, there is only one answer to that—Mr. Gehrig is terribly underpaid.

——Yankees outfielder Joe DiMaggio[1]

Introduction

Joe Louis and Oscar de la Hoya were among the best—perhaps *the* best—fighters in the history of boxing. Joe Louis was heavyweight champion for 12 years (1937–1949) and successfully defended his title 25 times (still a record for the heavyweight division). Louis was so dominant that people took to calling his opponents "The Bum of the Month Club." De la Hoya won an Olympic gold medal in the 1992 Barcelona Olympics and went on to win 10 titles in 6 different weight classes.[2]

In addition to sharing glorious careers, both staged less than glorious comebacks. Louis re-entered the ring almost two years after retiring but lost a title fight to Ezzard Charles in 1950. In 1951, Louis's career finally ended when he was knocked out by future champion Rocky Marciano. De la Hoya's comeback, also after almost two years away from fighting, met with initial success, when he won the middleweight title in 2006. However, de la Hoya then lost two of his next three fights before retiring in 2009.

While Louis and de la Hoya both attempted comebacks, their motivations for doing so could not have been more different. Louis started fighting again

---

[1]"Cot's Baseball Contracts" online at http://mlbcontracts.blogspot.com/. Accessed March 20, 2007

[2]De la Hoya won the super flyweight, lightweight, light welterweight, welterweight, junior middleweight, and middleweight titles.

out of poverty. In his 12 years as heavyweight champion, Louis was paid $800,000 (roughly $10 million in 2008 dollars), a large sum to most people at the time, but small change by today's standards for heavyweight champions.[3] Moreover, mismanagement of Louis's funds and tax problems with the IRS left him with almost nothing to live on after retirement. With no skills other than his fading boxing talents, Louis had no choice but to fight again.[4]

De la Hoya had no such money worries. His nickname, "Golden Boy," might have referred to his prodigious skills, but it could just as easily have applied to his extraordinary earnings.[5] De la Hoya earned over $600 million in his career and earned more than twice the value of Joe Louis's lifetime earnings for just one fight (about $23 million for a 2007 loss to Floyd Mayweather). He has also parlayed his success in the ring into a variety of business ventures, most notably Golden Boy Enterprises, which generates about $100 million per year in revenue.[6]

The motivation for Joe Louis's attempted comeback is clear. His savings were so low that he could not afford to stop fighting. Oscar de la Hoya had no such monetary worries, but he also could not afford to turn down the offer to return to ring. The monetary rewards for fighting were too high for him to turn down.

The salaries paid to professional athletes in all sports have risen greatly in recent decades. In 2008, the average weekly earnings in the NBA were more twice the average annual earnings of nonathletes in the United States. In this chapter, we analyze the forces that have caused the incomes of professional athletes to reach such levels. This analysis will also place the earnings of professional athletes in perspective and show that, in some cases, professional athletes might actually be underpaid for what they do. Along the way, we will discover:

- How Michael Jordan caused the pay of other, marginal players in the NBA to rise

- Why minor league players are paid less than they are worth

- Why close doesn't count in tennis and golf tournaments

- Why some athletes jeopardize their reputations and health by taking performance enhancing drugs

---

[3]"Joe Louis (Barrow)," Arlington National Cemetery Web site, online at http://www.arlingtoncemetery.net/joelouis.htm, accessed July 27, 2009.

[4]See, for example, Chris Mead, "Triumphs and Trials," *SIVault*, September 23, 1985, online at http://vault.sportsillustrated.cnn.com/vault/article/magazine/MAG1119926/4/index.htm.

[5]It is probably no coincidence that *Golden Boy* is also the title of a play (later made into a musical) about a prizefighter.

[6]Tom van Riper, "Boxing's Last Golden Boy?" Forbes.com, January 15, 2009, online at http://www.forbes.com/2009/01/14/boxing-oscar-de-la-hoya-biz-sports_cx_tvr_0115delahoya.html?partner=whiteglove_google.

8.1   An Overview of Labor Supply and Labor Demand

As noted in the introduction, Oscar de la Hoya earned more for one fight than Joe Louis earned his entire career. Similarly, the salaries paid to professional athletes in the four major North American sports were not always as high as they are now. Figure 8.1 shows that much of the rise in pay for the four major North American sports leagues has occurred over the last three decades. In 1978, football players and baseball players both earned $100,000 on average. Hockey players earned somewhat less, about $92,000, while basketball players earned about $139,000. To put this in perspective, in 1978, nominal GDP per capita was about $10,000, roughly one-tenth the average earnings in MLB.

In 2008, salaries in football and hockey were almost 20 times their 1978 levels. Salaries in baseball and basketball rose even faster; by 2008, they were over 30 times their 1978 levels. In contrast, nominal GDP per capita in the United States rose by a factor of only 4.6. As a result, in 2008 the average salary in MLB was over 66 times nominal GDP per capita. There are many reasons for the increasing gap between the earnings of professional athletes and the earnings of "regular" people. This chapter examines the role played by supply and demand in the labor market.

In this section, we discuss both sides of the labor market. On the supply side, individual players offer their services to professional sports teams in order to maximize their utility. Teams demand labor in order to maximize profits. Chapter 3 showed that profit maximization may lead to a variety of personnel decisions, including fielding a low-quality team. Unless we state otherwise, for the remainder of this chapter we assume that team quality and profits are directly related. The interaction of labor supply and labor demand determines the labor market for professional athletes.

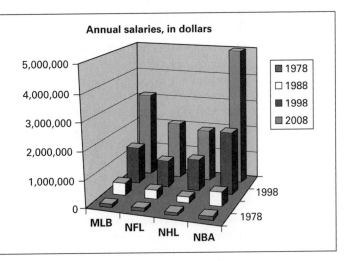

FIGURE 8.1

Average Player Salaries in 1978, 1988, 1998, and 2008
The average salaries of athletes in the four major North American Leagues have all risen significantly since 1978.
Source: MLB data from "USA Today Salaries Data Base," USAToday.com, online at http://content.usatoday.com/sports/baseball/salaries/totalpayroll.aspx?year=2008, viewed August 8, 2009. Other data can be reached from that site.

Labor Supply

In many ways, a worker's labor supply decision resembles a firm's supply decision. As Figure 8.2a shows, the labor supply curve looks like the supply curve for a product.[7] There are, however, several important differences. One important difference occurs in the units of measurement. The horizontal axis of a product supply curve refers to the amount of output the firm provides and is typically measured in physical units (e.g., the number of shoes or automobiles), and the vertical axis denotes the cost per unit of the firm's output. Labor markets do not use physical units; people do not buy and sell workers. Instead, they buy and sell the time that people offer. Thus, the quantity axis in Figure 8.2a refers to the hours of work that a person is willing to provide. Similarly, the vertical axis is now the cost per unit of time. In most cases, economists use the worker's hourly pay, his **wage,** as the unit price of a worker's time.[8] The upward-sloping labor supply curve thus tells us that a worker typically responds to higher wages by offering more of his time to employers.

In professional sports, we cannot use hours as the unit of labor because almost all athletes contract for a fixed amount of time, be it a football or baseball season, a tennis or golf tournament, or a boxing match. Figure 8.2b modifies the standard labor supply curve to reflect this fact. The horizontal axis now measures the quantity of fights a boxer has over the course of his career, and the vertical axis tells us the boxer's earnings per fight (which, for simplicity, we assume to be uniform). In team sports, the quantity of labor provided by a player is again typically set for a given season.[9] The price variable is thus the amount paid per season (or salary). The quantity variable depends on what one wants to evaluate. If one wants to analyze the labor market in a given season, it can refer to the number of players employed in that season. Alternatively, if one wants to look at a typical player's career, it can refer to the number of seasons that player plays.

Returning to our boxing example, moving from point A to point B shows us that a boxer will be induced to take on more fights as his pay increases, as was the case for Oscar de la Hoya. By this reasoning, the lower pay that Joe Louis received should have led him to fight less. As noted earlier, lower pay was not the only problem facing Louis. After retiring, Louis discovered that his manager had mishandled his funds and that he owed the IRS hundreds of thousands of dollars in back taxes. The lower savings—and hence the lower income that Louis would have received in retirement—meant that Louis had to fight more to maintain his standard of living. His labor supply curve shifted right to S', moving him from point A to point A'.

---

[7]For a more complete treatment of the labor supply curve and the labor–leisure choice model, see Appendix 8A.

[8]Using the wage can significantly understate the unit price of labor, as it ignores many other factors, such as taxes, and fringe benefits. Still, it is a useful first approximation.

[9]While the actual number of minutes or innings played may vary, the players make themselves available for the full season.

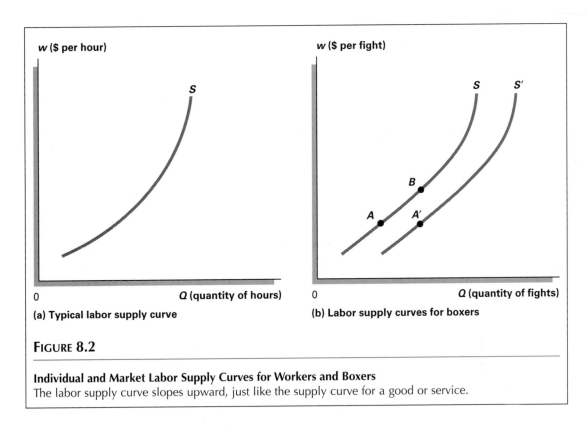

FIGURE 8.2

Individual and Market Labor Supply Curves for Workers and Boxers
The labor supply curve slopes upward, just like the supply curve for a good or service.

To see why the labor supply curve looks and shifts the way it does in Figure 8.2b, we must recognize that people choose how much to work based on the wage and the alternative to work—leisure. At first, such a model seems ill-suited to professional sports, an industry in which the personnel are referred to as *players* rather than workers. This distinction suggests that professional athletics is a leisure activity rather than a way to make a living, but such a conclusion would be a mistake. While most, if not all, professional players might still play "for fun" if they could not play professionally, playing professionally requires a level of dedication from the players that goes well beyond what they would choose for pure recreation.

To understand the shape of the individual labor supply curve, consider a person's options at various wages. When wages are low, the opportunity cost of not working is low. As wages increase, the cost of not working rises, because workers must sacrifice higher earnings when they choose to "purchase" leisure. As Chapter 2 explained, the substitution effect causes workers to shift away from the now more expensive leisure and to work more when wages rise, creating the positively sloped supply curve.

Changes in the wage also affect a worker's income, touching off an income effect as well. If leisure is a normal good, then the worker buys more leisure—and works less—as his or her income rises. In this case, the income effect counteracts, rather than reinforces, the substitution effect.

In general, the substitution effect is stronger than the income effect, so higher wages lead workers to supply more labor and the labor supply curve slopes upward.[10] When a person's nonlabor income falls—as might happen if one's spouse loses her job—or when the value of one's assets collapses—as has happened to many people's home values in 2008–2009—the demand for all goods and services falls. One such good is the quantity of leisure. A decline in the demand for leisure is equivalent to an increase in the supply of labor. Thus, Joe Louis's tax troubles led him to fight more frequently than he otherwise would have.

Labor Demand

Much of the debate among sports fans regarding athletes' salaries stems from a failure to understand the demand for labor. Armchair quarterbacks might spend Sunday afternoons yelling at their televisions, complaining about overpaid athletes. If these same fans understood the factors underlying the demand for labor and combined labor demand with labor supply, they would discover that many highly paid professional athletes are actually underpaid.

Marginal Revenue Product   We begin our analysis by assuming that firms produce a single output using two inputs, capital (K) and labor (L). We also assume that the firm is operating in the short run, so capital is fixed and the firm can alter output (Q) only by changing the labor input. Finally, we assume that all markets are perfectly competitive, so firms cannot affect the market price of their output. In such a setting, firms maximize profit by choosing L to maximize the difference between revenue and cost. This occurs where the marginal revenue from employing one more worker equals the marginal cost of employing that worker.

Ignoring all employment costs except for a worker's pay, the marginal cost of one more hour of labor is the worker's wage, w. The benefit of adding a worker is the extra revenue that worker generates. Economists call the extra revenue generated by an additional worker the **marginal revenue product.** Since marginal revenue equals price in a competitive market, marginal revenue product is simply the price per unit of output times the additional output produced:

$$MRP_L = MR \cdot MP_L = p\left(\frac{\Delta Q}{\Delta L}\right).$$

If, for example, the 10th worker produces an additional 20 units that can be sold for $5 each, the value of the 10th worker to the firm is $100 = 5×20.

As noted earlier, the profit-maximizing firm balances marginal benefits and marginal costs. This means that it hires just enough workers so that the marginal cost, w, equals the marginal benefit, MRP_L:

$$MRP_L = w.$$

---

[10]At high wage rates, it is possible that the income effect becomes stronger than the substitution effect. This would cause higher wages to reduce the number of hours worked, leading to a "backward-bending" labor supply curve.

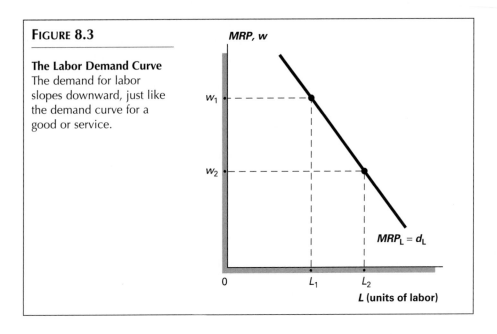

FIGURE 8.3

The Labor Demand Curve
The demand for labor
slopes downward, just like
the demand curve for a
good or service.

Figure 8.3 shows a firm's marginal revenue product curve. Suppose the wage w_1 equals the MRP_L at the employment level L_1. If the wage falls to w_2, the revenue generated by the last worker exceeds his cost to the firm, and the firm responds by hiring more workers until $w = MRP_L$ is restored. If we relabel the vertical axis with the wage, the curve shows that the unit price of labor and the quantity of labor demanded by the firm are negatively related, just like the demand curve for a good or service.

Measuring a Player's MRP   While the theory behind a player's value is quite simple, determining what a particular player is worth can be quite complex. One major reason for the complexity is the fact that players are not homogeneous inputs that can be increased or reduced at will. Another is the difficulty in measuring output. Players do not directly produce a saleable good. Instead, players are an important input in the production of wins. If teams maximize profits, we must then further establish the relationship between wins and profits. Economists have produced numerous estimates of the value of professional athletes' output since Simon Rottenberg's pioneering work in 1956.[11] We present one relatively intuitive measure developed by David Berri,

---

[11]See, for example, Simon Rottenberg, "The Baseball Players' Labor Market," *Journal of Political Economy,* vol. 64, no. 3 (June 1956), pp. 242–258; Gerald W. Scully, "Pay and Performance in Major League Baseball," *American Economic Review,* vol. 64, no. 5 (December 1974), pp. 915–930; Andrew Zimbalist, "Salaries and Performance: Beyond the Scully Model," in *Diamonds are Forever: The Business of Baseball,* ed. by Paul M. Sommers (Washington, D.C.: Brookings Institution, 1992), pp. 109–133; Anthony C. Krautmann, "What's Wrong with Scully's Estimates of a Player's Marginal Revenue Product?," *Economic Inquiry,* vol. 37, no. 2 (April 1999), pp. 269–381.

Martin Schmidt, and Stacey Brook. They have calculated the marginal revenue product for several players in the NBA.[12] They start by assuming that teams produce wins using players as inputs. The value of a player is thus

$$MRP_{ij} = MR_{win} * \Delta wins_{ij}$$

where MRP_{ij} is the marginal revenue product of player i when he plays for team j, MR_{win} is the value of an additional win to a team, and $\Delta wins_{ij}$ is the additional number of wins that team j can attribute to player i. Berri et al. estimate that the monetary value of a win to a team is about $1.67 million. In his blog, Berri uses an equation from *The Wages of Wins* to calculate how many wins each player produces[13]

$\Delta wins$ = points + total rebounds + steals + $\frac{1}{2}$*(blocked shots + assists)
 − field goal attempts − turnovers − $\frac{1}{2}$*(free throws + personal fouls)

This equation (from which we have deleted subscripts for simplicity) rewards players for positive contributions, such as scoring and rebounding, and penalizes them for negative contributions, such as turnovers and fouls. It subtracts the number of field goal and free throw attempts on the theory that a player who requires more shots to score a given number of points is not contributing as much to his team.

Berri reports that this methodology shows Chris Paul to have been the NBA's most valuable player in 2007–2008. He estimates that the 25.4 wins that Paul contributed to the New Orleans Hornets made him worth $42 million to the team. The value of a star player does not end with his contributions to his own team. Because NBA star players attract many fans to other teams' home arenas and NBA teams do not share gate revenue, economists have found that star players in the NBA generate substantial positive externalities. In each of his last two seasons, for example, Michael Jordan generated over $50 million in revenue for other NBA teams.[14]

Imperfect Competition and Labor Demand   While the competitive model forms a useful baseline, the labor markets in professional sports frequently violate its underlying assumptions. We examine many labor market imperfections in Chapter 9. One imperfection, however, comes not from the labor

[12]David J. Berri "What Do Chris Paul, Dwight Howard, LeBron James, and Tim Duncan have in Common?," *The Wages of Wins Journal*, May 22, 2008, online at http://dberri.wordpress.com/2008/05/22/what-do-chris-paul-dwight-howard-lebron-james-and-tim-duncan-have-in-common/.

[13]See David J. Berri et al., *The Wages of Wins* (2006).

[14]Jerry A. Hausman and Gregory K. Leonard, "Superstars in the National Basketball Association: Economic Value and Policy," *Journal of Labor Economics*, vol. 15, no. 4 (October 1997), pp 586–624; and David J. Berri and Martin B. Schmidt, "On the Road with the National Basketball Association's Superstar Externality," *Journal of Sports Economics*, vol. 7, no. 4 (November 2006), pp. 347–358.

market but from the product market. Recall from Chapters 3 and 4 that a monopoly sets a price that exceeds marginal revenue because the marginal revenue curve lies below the demand curve. As a result, the MRP_L curve for the profit-maximizing monopolist lies to the left of the MRP_L curve of the competitive industry, and the monopolist hires fewer workers and pays lower wages than it would if the industry were competitive. Figure 8.4 shows that if demand were based on competitive markets, teams would pay higher salaries and hire more players. However, because demand is based on a monopoly in the output (games) market, MRP is below and to the left of the competitive market labor demand curve.

Labor Market Equilibrium

Recall from Chapter 2 that market demand (supply) is the horizontal sum of all individual demand (supply) curves. The same principle applies to labor markets. Figure 8.5 shows the market supply (S_L) and market demand (D_L) of players to a sports league. As was true for the product markets described in Chapters 2 and 3, the equilibrium quantity of labor (L^e) and the equilibrium level of compensation (w^e) are given by the intersection of the supply and demand curves.

Figure 8.6 shows what happens to pay when market conditions change. When basketball became much more popular in the 1980s thanks to the arrival of charismatic stars such as Magic Johnson, Larry Bird, and Michael Jordan, the demand to see professional basketball both in person and on TV rose. This, in turn, increased the value of each player's contribution to the product provided by the NBA. As a result, the marginal revenue product of all NBA players rose.

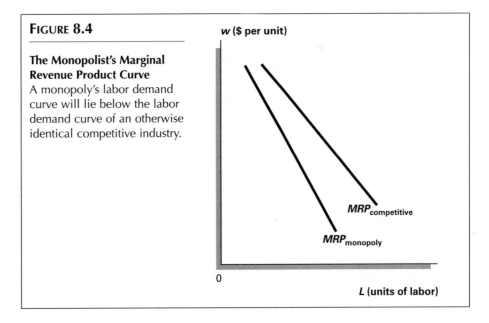

FIGURE 8.4

The Monopolist's Marginal Revenue Product Curve
A monopoly's labor demand curve will lie below the labor demand curve of an otherwise identical competitive industry.

w ($ per unit)

$MRP_{\text{competitive}}$

MRP_{monopoly}

0

L (units of labor)

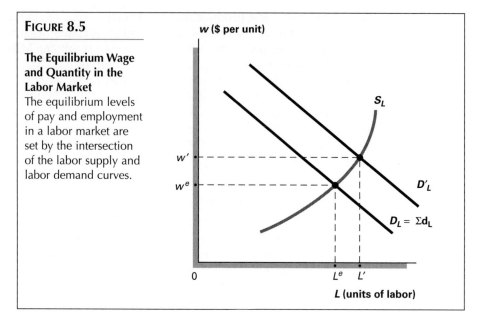

FIGURE 8.5

The Equilibrium Wage and Quantity in the Labor Market
The equilibrium levels of pay and employment in a labor market are set by the intersection of the labor supply and labor demand curves.

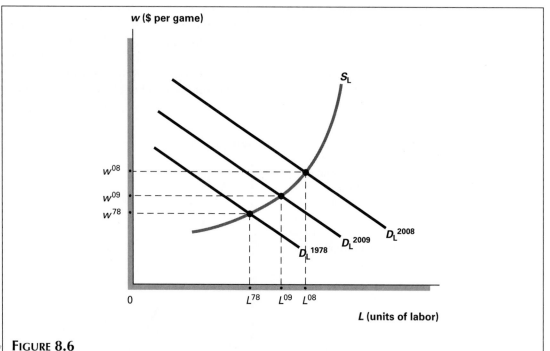

FIGURE 8.6

Wages Increase in the NBA Due to Increases in Demand
As basketball became more popular, the MRP of basketball players rose, shifting the labor demand curve to the right. This increased the pay and the level of employment. When attendance fell in 2008–2009, team revenues fell, and the MRP curve shifted left.

The increase was not due to higher productivity. Instead, it was due to the rise in the marginal revenue that resulted from greater fan interest. A higher MR_{win} led to a higher MRP, which, in turn, caused the demand for labor to shift to the right and led to higher pay. Declining economic conditions in 2008 reduced the demand for tickets to NBA games.[15] This, in turn, caused the MRP of players in the NBA to decline. As a result, salaries in the NBA for the 2009–2010 season fell slightly from their 2008–2009 level.

The number of teams also affects the overall demand for players. The number of teams can vary with the entry of rival leagues (a factor we revisit in Chapter 9) or with the expansion or contraction of a given league. Increasing the number of teams increases the number of teams in the horizontal sum in Figure 8.5. This shifts the demand for labor from D_L to D_L' and causes the equilibrium quantity of labor to rise to L' and the equilibrium level of pay to rise to w'. The impact of the number of teams explains why players associations oppose any form of contraction. In 2004, for example, baseball players in Japan staged their only strike, a two-day job action to protest the proposed merger of the Kintetsu Buffaloes and the Orix Blue Wave.[16]

Human Capital and Player Compensation   If workers are more productive, the MP_L and MRP_L rise, and wages rise as well. It follows that if people can increase their productivity, they can increase their earnings. **Human capital** is the set of skills that contribute to a person's productivity. The term implies that each person has a stock of skills that can be increased by investing in additional skills.

According to Nobel laureate Gary Becker, who developed the theory of human capital in the 1960s, a person investing in human capital resembles a business investing in physical capital. When a firm purchases a drill press, it makes a one-time expenditure in return for an expected stream of benefits over the life span of the equipment. Similarly, a student who spends four years studying economics in college or a hockey player who spends four years developing his skills in the minor leagues endures an up-front cost to acquire skills that he can use for his entire career.

Unlike physical capital, human capital tends to depreciate with age or disuse rather than with use. Many of the skills an athlete acquires, such as learning the basic rules of play, will not depreciate until long after retirement. Although physical abilities depreciate with age, an athlete's knowledge of the game may increase throughout his or her career. An important difference between human and physical capital is that a firm can generally transfer physical capital to another simply by selling the asset. Human capital, however, is embodied in the worker who cannot sell his skills to another player.

Human capital theory divides training into two types: **general** and **specific.** General training increases the worker's productivity regardless of the

---

[15]Because the NBA contract was still in force, TV revenues had not declined.

[16]The two teams did merge to form the Orix Buffaloes, but the owners agreed to keep the number of teams at 12 by admitting the Rakuten Golden Eagles as an expansion team.

setting. For example, learning to read increases one's productivity no matter where one works. General training in hockey includes learning the rules of the game, how to pass or shoot the puck accurately, and how to check (stop) an opposing player. The more a hockey player can master these skills, the more valuable he is to all teams.

Specific training increases a person's MRP in a specific context. At the most extreme, it is applicable only at the firm that provides the training. For example, learning the plays in a team's playbook helps a player only as long as he or she is part of that team. Training often provides a mix of both general and specific skills.

Who Pays for Training?   Because workers and firms both gain when the workers are more skilled, both groups have an incentive to provide training. However, the benefits to each group, and the incentive to pay for training, vary with the skills that are imparted.

Becker concluded that the nature of the training a worker receives determines who pays for it. When a player receives specific training, he is more valuable to his current team than to other teams. The team can therefore capture at least some of the returns to the training it provides because it must pay the player only enough to prevent him from moving to another team.

When a person receives general training, his or her productivity rises at all firms. If the team has no way to restrict player mobility, such as with the reserve clause, it is unwilling to pay for the training. Suppose, for example, the Toronto Maple Leafs of the NHL pays for a player's training costs by hiring coaches and providing training facilities while the player plays for the Maple Leafs' minor league team. With no restrictions in place, the player could simply leave the Leafs for another team when his contract expires, taking his human capital with him. The Maple Leafs would end up paying for the training without receiving the benefit of the player's increased productivity. Because all teams recognize this potential loss of investment, they force players to pay for general training in the form of low minor league salaries. We can formalize the model a bit to see why this is so.

For simplicity, assume that a player's career lasts only two seasons. In the first season, he costlessly receives skills, which he can then apply in the second season. Using the concept of present value that we introduced in Chapter 6, we can show that the player's value over the two seasons is his value in the first season (MRP_1) plus the present value of his MRP in the second season (MRP_2). If the interest rate is r, the player generates benefits (B):

$$B = MRP_1 + \frac{MRP_2}{1 + r}$$

In the first period, the team pays him $w_1 = MRP_1$ and in the second period, it pays him $w_2 = MRP_2$. If the team must pay training costs, T, it faces a problem, as the player's costs exceed his contribution to the team

$$w_1 + \frac{w_2}{1 + r} + T > MRP_1 + \frac{MRP_2}{1 + r}$$

To restore equality, the team must somehow reduce the player's pay. If the team training provides team-specific skills, the team can capture a return on its investment by paying the player less than he is worth to them but more than he is worth to other teams. If the training increases the player's general skills, the player can apply his new skills equally well for any other team. Any attempt to reduce w_2 will induce the player to leave for another team. The team will provide training only if the player pays for the training costs (usually in the form of lower pay) in the first period.[17]

For example, minor league hockey and baseball salaries are very low compared to the NHL and MLB. By accepting relatively low salaries while in the minor leagues and during their first several years in the major leagues players are helping to pay for the training they need.

8.2 The Economics of Tournaments and Superstars

The theory of labor market equilibrium implies that players who are slightly more productive than other players should receive slightly higher rewards. Sometimes, however, small differences in performance translate into huge differences in compensation. For example, Roger Federer won the 2009 "Gentlemen's Singles" Championship at Wimbledon in a grueling five-set match with Andy Roddick that lasted more than four hours and took 77 games to complete (the equivalent of playing more than two 6–4, 6–4, 6–4 straight-set victories). It is hard to imagine a closer match. For winning the tournament, Federer received £850,000 (almost $1.41 million), while Roddick received only half that amount. The huge difference in payoffs seems even more drastic considering that a player who was eliminated in the second round earned just £7,000 more than a player who was eliminated in the first round. The return to winning a match increases dramatically as a player advances through the tournament. Similar conclusions hold for golf, bowling, and most other individual sports.

In such cases, *relative* productivity rather than *absolute* productivity matters. Roger Federer would have received the same prize for winning Wimbledon regardless of his margin of victory. Winning is all that matters. The only objective is to beat the other player.[18] Because the order of finish is the only performance criterion, such contests are known as **rank-order tournaments.**

Why would the organizers of a tournament set prizes based on rank order rather than absolute quality of performance? In all individual sports, the quality of any single performance depends on a long list of factors that have nothing to do with individual ability, such as the quality of the playing surface,

---

[17]In a world of uncertainty, where neither the player nor the team is sure that the training will result in higher skills and higher pay, there is an incentive for the two to share the costs of training.

[18]Two men were being chased by a grizzly bear when one of them stopped and began to put on track shoes. The other stopped and said, "You don't think track shoes are going to help you outrun a grizzly, do you?" The first man looked up and replied, "It's not the grizzly I'm trying to outrun."

the weather conditions, or the ability of the opponent.[19] To determine the absolute level of a player's marginal product, judges would have to account for all these factors, a difficult and expensive task. Moreover, if tournament organizers cannot measure marginal product, they cannot provide a reward based on the players' *MRP*. They must devise a new way to distribute prize money and provide appropriate incentives for participants. Fortunately, relative performance is more readily measured. The highly uneven distribution of the purses appeals to the most basic of economic tenets: self-interest.

We start by assuming that participants maximize utility and that their utility increases with income and leisure and, hence, decreases with effort. We also assume that the organizers of the tournament want players to give their maximum effort thereby providing fans with the most exciting contest. If all players are paid the same regardless of performance, then players do not have an incentive to work hard to win. Because effort is not perfectly observable, the organizers must award prize money so that players have the incentive to play their best.

Figure 8.7 shows how a player determines the optimal level of effort to expend in a tournament. Casual observation is enough to show that the marginal cost of effort is positive, which means that there are costs associated with trying harder to win (more hours of practice, learning to handle pressure

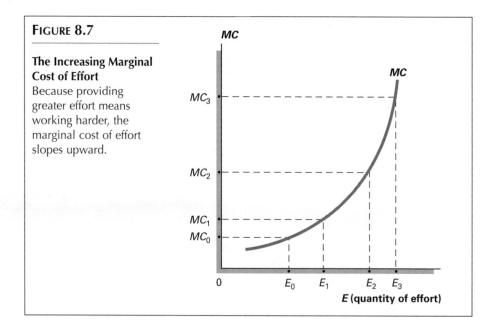

FIGURE 8.7

The Increasing Marginal Cost of Effort
Because providing greater effort means working harder, the marginal cost of effort slopes upward.

---

[19]In one famous example, the course of the 1960 World Series was changed when a ground ball to the Yankee shortstop hit a pebble, took an unexpected bounce, and sustained a key Pirate rally in the seventh and deciding game.

situations, and extra effort in the contest itself). Thus, the marginal cost curve slopes upward in Figure 8.7. The marginal cost curve also becomes steeper (increases at an increasing rate) as the amount of effort rises. The increasing slope means that changes in effort level become costlier as effort level rises. For example, moving from E_0 to E_1 adds little to the player's cost. In contrast, increasing effort from an already high level, such as from E_2 to an even higher level, E_3, comes at a great cost.

If the tournament's organizers (reflecting the desires of the fans who buy tickets and the advertisers who sponsor broadcasts) want to see the players try their hardest, they must make sure that the differences between the prizes increase for players who reach the top of the rankings. Figure 8.8 shows why. In a contest with one winner and one loser, such as the finals of a tennis match, and with contestants who are roughly equal in ability, the difference between winning and losing may come down to random factors such as playing conditions.[20] The increasing marginal cost of effort is MC^I. Organizers want to stage the most exciting (and thus marketable) possible contest, so they want the players to give their maximum effort (E_1). A player's marginal benefit is the additional revenue he gets from moving up one position (e.g., from second to first). By creating a large difference between first and second prize, MR_1, the players have an incentive to expend much more effort than if the difference were small (MR_2). If the marginal cost of effort is linear, as shown by the line

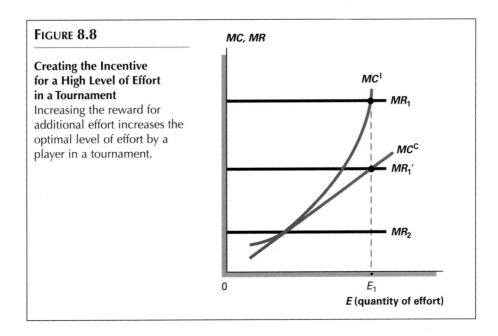

FIGURE 8.8

Creating the Incentive for a High Level of Effort in a Tournament
Increasing the reward for additional effort increases the optimal level of effort by a player in a tournament.

---

[20]If the contestants are not equal in ability, the resulting tournament may be poor entertainment. If the weaker opponent knows he or she has no chance to win, there is no incentive to try.

MC^C, the organizers can elicit the same level of effort with a much smaller difference between prizes (MR'_1).

Table 8.1 lists the five highest-paid celebrities and five highest-paid athletes in *Forbes* magazine's "Celebrity 100."[21] While most people in the entertainment industry struggle to make ends meet, the table shows that becoming a star brings a huge reward. With the exception of Tiger Woods, these rewards dwarf the compensation of professional athletes. Kobe Bryant, the second-highest paid athlete on the list, is tied for 28th in overall income. (The highest-paid female athlete on the list, Maria Sharapova, is 71st.) The extreme rewards for winning an economic contest can be further seen by the fact that George Lucas's position is due largely to continued sales of *Star Wars* merchandise and earnings from one film in 2008 (*Indiana Jones and the Kingdom of the Crystal Skull*), and that Michael Jordan tied Bryant as the second-highest paid athlete on the *Forbes* list eight years after his retirement from basketball.

Economic contests apply more generally in the corporate world. The salary of a top executive in a large corporation is likely to be at least twice that of his or her nearest rival. This does not mean that the *MRP* of the top-ranked executive is twice that of his or her nearest rival. In fact, the value of their marginal product is very difficult to determine, because they do not produce output that

TABLE 8.1

The Five Highest-Paid Celebrities and Athletes in the *Forbes* 2009 "Celebrity 100"

Rank/Name	Occupation	Earnings (in millions)
Celebrities		
1. Oprah Winfrey	Personality	$275
2. George Lucas	Director/Producer	$170
3. Steven Spielberg	Director/Producer	$150
4. (T) Madonna	Musician	$110
4. (T) Tiger Woods	Athlete	$110
Athletes		
1. Tiger Woods	Golf	$110
2. (T) Kobe Bryant	Basketball	$45
2. (T) Michael Jordan	Basketball (retired)	$45
2. (T) Kimi Raikkonen	Formula One	$45
5. David Beckham	Soccer	$42

Source: Matthew Miller, Dorothy Pomerantz, and Lacey Rose, "The Celebrity 100," Forbes.com, June 3, 2009, online at www.forbes.com/2009/06/03/forbes-100-celebrity-09-jolie-oprah-madonna-land.html.

---

[21]This list is technically of the most "powerful" celebrities, but income is an important factor in *Forbes*'s rating system.

can be readily measured. To ensure that second-tier executives give their best effort, tournament-style wages create disproportionately large rewards for increases in rank.

An Exception to the Rule: NASCAR

The reward scheme used in NASCAR racing is an interesting exception to both the standard model of wage determination and the highly nonlinear rewards used in golf and tennis.[22] Although stock car racing appears to satisfy the basic conditions for a rank-order tournament, the reward scheme on a per-race basis is nearly horizontal. Figure 8.9 shows the NASCAR prize money for a single race and, for comparison, the prize structure for a single PGA tournament. The 12th-place finisher in either event receives roughly the same prize (around $132,000). Moving down to 42nd in the golf tournament reduces the prize to $20,125. In the race, however, drivers who finished as low as 43rd earned as

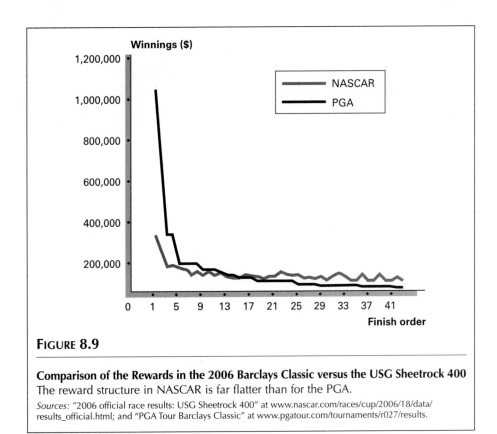

FIGURE 8.9

Comparison of the Rewards in the 2006 Barclays Classic versus the USG Sheetrock 400
The reward structure in NASCAR is far flatter than for the PGA.

Sources: "2006 official race results: USG Sheetrock 400" at www.nascar.com/races/cup/2006/18/data/results_official.html; and "PGA Tour Barclays Classic" at www.pgatour.com/tournaments/r027/results.

---

[22]This section is based on Peter von Allmen, "Is the Reward System in NASCAR Efficient?," *Journal of Sports Economics,* vol. 2, no. 1 (February 2000), pp. 62–79.

NASCAR drivers battle for position.

much as $76,500. Finishing first increases the payout in the golf tournament to $1,035,000 but only to $327,761 in the race. While one might initially expect the same winner-take-all pressure in NASCAR as in figure skating or gymnastics, several unique features of racing work against the use of tournament-style rewards.

As noted earlier, in most individual sports, the competitors have no way to prevent their opponent from succeeding. In racing, however, where drivers all compete on the same track at the same time, tournament-style wages may lead to reckless driving—with catastrophic results. The risk of a severe accident raises the probability that high social costs may exist with a win-at-all-cost strategy that would not be present in other individual sports. In addition, in NASCAR racing, teams that sponsor cars have relatively complex revenue and profit functions that include revenue from sponsors, year-end prize money, and a wide variety of bonuses that drivers can win during races. The accumulation of on-air time for sponsors and season championship points give drivers a powerful incentive to remain on the track for the entire race rather than risk crashing in order to achieve a greater share of the purse for that race. Thus, highly nonlinear reward schemes for individual races would likely do more harm than good.

8.3 Tournaments, Cheating, and the Distribution of Income

While tournaments might provide athletes with an incentive to do their best, a large spread in rewards can have negative effects on athletes' behavior in both individual and team sports. When teammates feel they are competing for individual rewards, the result can sometimes be selfish play that undermines the cooperation that teams need to succeed. The inability of Kobe Bryant and Shaquille O'Neal to cooperate was widely blamed for the breakup of the great Los Angeles Lakers teams of the late 1990s and early 2000s, while the later success of the Lakers was frequently attributed to the maturation of Kobe Bryant into a team player.

In extreme cases, a tournament can lead to outright sabotage. The most famous such case might be that of Tonya Harding, a former national champion figure skater who admitted to "hindering prosecution" in the plot to injure fellow skater Nancy Kerrigan prior to the 1994 Winter Olympics. Kerrigan was attacked during the National Championships, at which the Olympic team was to be chosen. Harding's ex-husband and an accomplice confessed to carrying out the attack and claimed that Harding herself was involved in planning it.[23] Harding's primary motivation behind the attack was to remove Kerrigan as the preeminent U.S. woman figure skater so that Harding could assume that role, thus providing her "ticket to fame and fortune."[24]

Too Much of a Good Thing

The disproportionate rewards that accompany even small differences in performance sometimes induce coaches, trainers, and athletes to push themselves and others too hard.

Possibly the most frightening example of the potential for undesirable outcomes in tournaments comes from a surprising yet familiar source. Imagine a country in which selected children are put to work full-time. School, friends, a normal childhood are all denied them as they perform hours of backbreaking work. When they try to get away, they are subjected to physical and emotional abuse, sometimes at the hands of their own parents. By the time they reach adulthood, many of them are physically broken—some even killed—by the arduous demands of their supervisors. Still others bear permanent emotional scars. Unable to form normal relationships with their peers, some take solace in drugs and others in self-abusive behavior. The country is the United States, and the abused children are the same ones we cheer on at events such as the Olympics, Wimbledon, and the NCAA championships.[25]

---

[23]Sonja Steptoe and E. M. Swift, "A Done Deal," *Sports Illustrated* (March 28, 1994), pp. 32–36.

[24]E. M. Swift, "Anatomy of a Plot: The Kerrigan Assault," *Sports Illustrated* (February 14, 1994), pp. 28–38.

[25]Joan Ryan, *Little Girls in Pretty Boxes* (New York: Doubleday, 1995), catalogs the horrors confronting many young female gymnasts and figure skaters.

These youths are victims of a reward system in which first place counts for everything and second place for next to nothing. Adolescent girls take to the ice for the Olympic figure skating championship with greater individual rewards at stake than for any single event except, perhaps, a heavyweight boxing championship.[26] A gold medalist may get TV specials and starring roles in skating exhibitions. Her name will be entered in record books, and fans will remember her performance fondly for years to come. In contrast, all but a few relatives and friends will soon forget the performance of the fourth-place finisher.

As a result of the highly skewed reward structure, young girls are willing to work extremely long hours, some in excess of 45 hours per week. Their coaches and gyms, which stand to benefit mightily from the publicity these girls bring them, would be violating child labor laws if they paid the girls for their efforts. The long hours of training can bring permanent physical and psychological damage. Hoping to please their parents and coaches and yearning for a chance to stand on the Olympic podium, young gymnasts suffer through severe injuries that they do not allow to heal for fear of missing a championship or an Olympics before they become too old. One elite coach discouraged girls from having casts put on fractured limbs because "he feared it would hurt their muscle tone."[27] Some take an array of "laxatives, thyroid pills, and diuretics to lose the weight brought on by puberty."[28] The obsession with weight can become so serious that eating disorders can develop. Surveys show that almost a third of female college athletes—and up to two-thirds of female gymnasts surveyed—admit to some sort of eating disorder. One young gymnast, Christy Henrich, literally starved herself to death. The eating disorders can have long-term effects, leading to menstrual dysfunction and osteoporosis.[29]

Performance-Enhancing Drugs

In recent years, professional sports seem to have been plagued by the widespread use of performance-enhancing drugs (PEDs). PEDs present sports with a dilemma. Sports celebrate athletes who push themselves to their absolute limits. The swimmer who shaves his head and body, the high-jumper who finds a new way to clear the bar, and the running back who comes back from knee surgery are all seeking an edge that will propel them to (or keep them at) the top of their fields. While some changes, such as Babe Didrikson's use of the "Western Roll" high jump in the 1932 caused controversy at first (and cost her an Olympic gold medal), the advantage that such innovations bring quickly dissipate as they become widely adopted.

---

[26]Ryan, *Little Girls in Pretty Boxes* (1995), p. 193.

[27]Merrell Noden, "Dying to Win," *Sports Illustrated* (August 8, 1994), pp. 52–59.

[28]Robert Frank and Phillip Cook, *The Winner-Take-All Society* (New York: The Free Press, 1995), p. 132.

[29]See S. Gilbert, "The Smallest Olympians Pay the Biggest Price," *New York Times* (July 28, 1996), p. E4; Noden, "Dying to Win" (1994), pp. 52–59; Ryan, *Little Girls in Pretty Boxes* (1995), pp. 17–54; Ian Tofler, Barri Katz Stryer, Lyle Micheli, and Lisa Herman, "Physical and Emotional Problems of Elite Female Gymnasts," *New England Journal of Medicine,* vol. 335, no 4 (July 25, 1996), pp. 281–283.

We perceive PEDs as somehow different from shaving one's body, finding a new way to jump, or having career-extending surgery. One reason for this difference is that many of the drugs that athletes take are controlled substances that are not used legally without a prescription. Another reason is that, unlike different jumping techniques, one cannot be sure that athletes are doping just by looking at them. Perhaps most important, though, is the danger that PEDs present. The risks associated with PEDs is not new; the first documented doping-related fatality came during a bicycle race in 1879. More recently, the fall of the Berlin Wall in 1989 and the resulting publication of state secrets showed the high cost of East German Olympic success. Physical disabilities, birth defects, even a change in sexual identity were all attributed to the "vitamins" that unsuspecting East German girls were given as part of their training regimen. In the United States, some estimates show that as many as one million high school students have used anabolic steroids, a popular PED. Researchers claim that the use of steroids causes heart and liver damage, violent mood swings ("roid rage"), and psychological dependency.[30]

The dangers of PEDs have not deterred athletes from using them. Some insight into the mindset of elite athletes can be found in a survey of almost 200 sprinters, swimmers, powerlifters, and other athletes. The survey confronted the athletes with a hypothetical situation:

You are offered a banned performance-enhancing substance that comes with two guarantees:

1. You will not be caught.

2. You will win every competition you enter for the next five years, and then you will die from the side effects of the substances.

Would you take it?

More than half the athletes surveyed said they would accept such an offer.[31]

Such attitudes among athletes have led economists to model PED use as a prisoner's dilemma.[32] Figure 8.10 provides a simple model of PED use. It begins with the simplifying assumption that we have only two athletes, Mark and Sam, each of whom has the choice of using PEDs or not using them. Using PEDs positively impacts performance and gives each player an advantage if the other does not use them.

The payoffs (expressed as units of happiness experienced by Mark and Sam) in the upper left diagonal entry occur when neither athlete takes PEDs, while the

---

[30]See Aleksander Berentsen, "The Economics of Doping," *European Journal of Political Economy*, vol. 18 (2002), pp. 109–127; Steven Ungerleider, *Faust's Gold: Inside the East German Doping Machine* (New York: Thomas Dunne Books, 2001); and Jane Weaver, "Steroid Addiction a Risk for Young Athletes," MSNBC, April 5, 2005, online at http://www.msnbc.msn.com/id/7348758.

[31]Michael Bamberger and Don Yaeger, "Over the Edge," *Sports Illustrated* (April 14, 1997), pp. 61–70.

[32]For more detailed treatments of doping as a prisoner's dilemma, see Berentsen (2002) and Kjetil K. Haugen, "The Performance Enhancing Drug Game," *Journal of Sports Economics*, vol. 5, no. 1 (February 2004) pp. 67–86.

FIGURE 8.10

PED Use as a Prisoner's Dilemma

		Mark	
		Doesn't use PEDs	*Uses PEDs*
	Doesn't use PEDs	(2,2) No advantage/No harm	(5,0) Mark wins/Sam loses
Sam			
	Uses PEDs	(0,5) Mark loses/Sam wins	(1,1) No advantage/harm

---

payoffs in the lower right occur when both do. In both situations, neither Sam nor Mark has an advantage over the other. The only difference is that both athletes are risking their health if they both take PEDs. As a result, the payoffs in the upper left square are superior to the outcomes in the lower right square. The off-diagonal payoffs reflect the fact that, as the survey suggests, an athlete's happiness heavily depends on his winning. If one athlete takes PEDs and the other does not, then the athlete taking PEDs wins (by setting a world record, winning the home run title, or becoming world champion) and the other loses. The payoff structure in Figure 8.10 reflects the results of the survey cited earlier, that athletes place greater emphasis on success in their chosen field than on a long and healthy life. Such preferences can, as in Figure 8.10, cause taking PEDs to be a dominant strategy. The result of the game is a prisoner's dilemma because both players take PEDs despite the fact that they would be better of if neither did.

Although PED usage is not new, many major sports have recently experienced embarrassing scandals involving PEDs. Perhaps the best-known scandal involves the Bay Area Laboratory Co-Operative (BALCO), whose founder, Victor Conte, served a short prison sentence after pleading guilty to steroid distribution and money laundering in June 2005. When the government seized BALCO's records, it found evidence that many well-known athletes had used steroids, human growth hormones, and other PEDs.

The track star Marion Jones was probably the most prominent athlete caught up in the BALCO scandal. She was stripped of the five medals that she had won at the 2000 Sydney Olympics (gold in the 100- and 200-meter sprint and the 1600-meter relay, and bronze in the long jump and the 400-meter relay). Jones was also sentenced to six months in prison for lying to federal prosecutors about her steroid use.

The BALCO scandal has also implicated MLB's all-time home run champion Barry Bonds. Although it is not yet clear whether Bonds knowingly used PEDs, the allegations made Bonds's pursuit of Hank Aaron's home run title an embarrassing episode.[33] Later allegations have severely damaged the chances

---

[33] Aaron declined the offer to attend games at which Bonds might break his record. See also Mark Fainaru-Wade and Lance Williams, *Game of Shadows: Barry Bonds, BALCO, and the Steroids Scandal That Rocked Professional Sports* (New York: Gotham Books, 2006).

that potential Hall of Famers as Roger Clemens, Mark McGwire, Raphael Palmiero, Manny Ramirez, Alex Rodriguez, and Sammy Sosa will ever be voted into the Hall.

No other sport has been as severely damaged by PEDs than bicycling. The credibility of the sport was in doubt following the embarrassment surrounding the 2006 Tour de France. Just days before the race was to begin, nine riders, including prerace favorites Jan Ullrich and Ivan Basso, were barred from the race for suspicion of doping. The race itself proved to be one of the most dramatic ever. Floyd Landis, who was in 11th place after the 16th stage of the race, came back to win the 17th stage by almost six minutes, an unheard-of margin, and went on to win the race. A few days later, however, all the good will generated by Landis's comeback was dashed. A drug test administered after the 17th stage had found abnormal levels of testosterone. Landis was subsequently stripped of his title and banned from competitive cycling for two years. Despite efforts at improving testing, professional cycling has had difficulty regaining its standing and remains under a cloud.

The ongoing scandals reveal how widespread the incentive to cheat has become, and how difficult it is for sports leagues and international antidoping agencies to keep up with the development of new and increasingly sophisticated PEDs. Perhaps nothing reflects the times as well as the fact that FIDE, the World Chess Federation, now requires that participants in international chess tournaments undergo drug testing after their matches.[34]

The Distribution of Income

Because financial rewards for individual victories are so heavily weighted in favor of top performers, the distribution of income in individual sports is highly skewed. For example, through July, the top three prize winners on 2009 WTA tennis tour (Serena Williams, Dinara Safina, and Svetlana Kuznetsova) accounted for 26.5 percent of the total winnings of the top 100 players.[35] As in Chapter 5, we can illustrate the inequality on the women's tennis tour with a Lorenz curve. As in Chapter 5, the horizontal axis in Figure 8.11 shows the cumulative percentage of the population (trivial here because each player accounts for 1 percent of the population). The vertical axis shows the cumulative percentage of earnings. The Lorenz curve sags below the straight line, as the bottom 10 percent of the money winners on the tour account for less than 3 percent of total winnings (point A), and counting the 94 percent of the players accounts for less than two-thirds of the earnings on the tour.

---

[34]Vassiliy Ivanchuk, the third-ranking chess player in the world, was in danger of receiving a two-year suspension from international competition after he refused to submit to a drug test after the 2008 Dresden Chess Olympiad. A FIDE panel ruled that he had misunderstood the request because of language difficulties and the fact that he was distraught after a loss.

[35]A similar situation holds for team sports as well. In 2008, the average salary for the New York Yankees was over $5 million, while the median salary was less than $2 million.

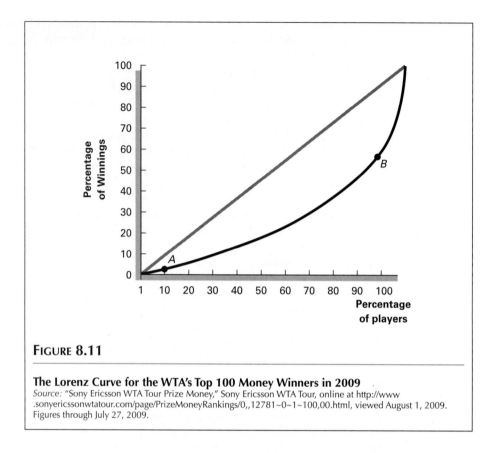

FIGURE 8.11

The Lorenz Curve for the WTA's Top 100 Money Winners in 2009
Source: "Sony Ericsson WTA Tour Prize Money," Sony Ericsson WTA Tour, online at http://www
.sonyericssonwtatour.com/page/PrizeMoneyRankings/0,,12781~0~1~100,00.html, viewed August 1, 2009.
Figures through July 27, 2009.

The salary structure in all sports is highly uneven due to the earnings of superstars. Even at the highest levels of competition, a few players often have abilities and charisma that set them apart from the rest.[36] Players such as Sidney Crosby, LeBron James, Tom Brady, and Ryan Howard stand at the extreme right end of the talent distribution. The extraordinary performances of which these athletes are capable vastly increase the demand to see games in which they play. Most fans would rather see a matchup of two of a sport's top stars than to see five games played by teams stocked with mediocre players. Fans' desire to see the very best players causes the demand for their services, and hence their earnings, to be much greater than those of players of only slightly lesser ability.

---

[36]For a detailed description of the nonlinear returns to ability, see Sherwin Rosen, "The Economics of Superstars," *American Economic Review,* vol. 71, no. 5 (December 1981), pp. 845–858.

BIOGRAPHICAL SKETCH

SCOTT BORAS

Talking to Boras about baseball executives is like talking to a lion about red meat.

——*Matt Taibbi*[1]

While players like Alex Rodriguez, Mark Teixeira, and Barry Zito would be millionaires no matter who represented them, there can be little question that they, and dozens of other baseball players, have benefited significantly from their association with Scott Boras. In securing high earnings for his clients, Boras has earned the universal hatred of owners. In the words of one reporter, they regard Boras as "Shiva god of destruction, sent to Earth to wreck all that is holy." Boras has proven so successful, and so popular with players, however, that few teams can afford not to deal with him.

Unlike many other agents, Boras did not set out to become an agent. When he was a young man, it looked like he might be a baseball player instead. Boras grew up on a farm in northern California and played baseball at the University of the Pacific, eventually becoming team captain. He was not, however, the stereotypical "jock," majoring in chemistry and taking Ph.D.-level classes in industrial pharmacology. This sometimes forced Boras to schedule private labs, some of which lasted until midnight, after baseball practice.

Boras was good enough at baseball to sign a contract with the St. Louis Cardinals in 1974. He did not let his professional career derail his graduate studies, as he would offer his coaches beer to proctor exams for him while he was with the team. A series of knee injuries ended Boras's hopes of making the major leagues, and he left baseball in 1978. At the same time, he began studying for a law degree at Pacific's McGeorge School of Law. After graduating from law school, Boras continued to use his background in chem-

istry, defending drug companies against class-action suits for a large law firm in Chicago, hardly the type of work one would expect of a man who would soon take on the moguls of baseball.

In 1985, Boras helped Bill Caudill, a former minor-league teammate, negotiate a contract with the Toronto Blue Jays. The result, a five-year, $7 million contract that made Caudill the second-highest-paid relief pitcher in baseball, caught the baseball world's attention and led to Boras's switch full-time to representing players. (Boras insists that he acts as players' legal representative and is not their agent.)

Today, Boras is the head of the Scott Boras Corporation. The company has about 45 employees, including a 14-person research staff, and represents more than 60 players. He has negotiated some of the most lucrative contracts in baseball history, including Alex Rodriguez's 10-year, $252 million contract with the Texas Rangers and Barry Zito's 7-year $126 million deal with the San Francisco Giants. At the time, these contracts were records for a position-player and pitcher.

Boras has achieved these results by adopting tactics that neutralize or reverse the traditional monopsony power of MLB owners. He has, for example, effectively used the fact that he can speak with multiple teams while the teams are legally forbidden from speaking to each other about player negotiations. Boras used this asymmetric information to convince Texas Rangers majority owner Tom Hicks that other teams were interested in Rodriguez. Hicks responded by increasing his offer despite the fact that no other team was willing to surpass his previous offer. The

continued

end result was a contract whose monetary value was greater than the sum Hicks's partnership, which included George W. Bush, had paid for the entire team.

Boras has also used the draft to obtain leverage for his clients. Traditionally the draft has been a source of monopsony power for teams, as they have exclusive rights to negotiate with the players they draft. Boras, however, convinced Tim Belcher, a top draft choice of the Minnesota Twins to return to college rather than sign with the Twins (Belcher could do so because his college—Mount Vernon Nazarene—belonged to the NAIA and not the NCAA). He later convinced J. D. Drew, the first overall choice of the 1997 draft, to play with the St. Paul Saints, an independent minor league team, rather than sign with the Philadelphia Phillies. Both Belcher and Drew signed much more lucrative contracts with different teams a year later.

At times, Boras's techniques have backfired. Boras's hardball tactics in negotiating a new contract for Alex Rodriguez were so aggressive—he announced that Rodriguez would opt out of the remaining three years of his contract during game 4 of the 2007 World Series—that Rodriguez distanced himself from Boras during the negotiations and eventually dropped him as an agent. It has also become clear that many of the contracts Boras has negotiated have resulted in compensation far greater than the players' value to the teams that signed them. For example, Bill Caudill had only one good season for the Toronto Blue Jays, and Barry Zito's first two years with the San Francisco Giants (a 21–30 record and a 4.83 earned run average) are hardly the stuff of a player Boras described as "one of the best left-handed pitchers of all time."[2] Still, these negatives did not prevent Stephen Strasburg, the top overall pick of the 2008 amateur draft, from naming Boras as his agent.

[1]Mattt Taibbi, "The Devil's Doorstep: A Visit with Scott Boras," *Men's Journal,* February 23, 2009, online at http://www.mensjournal.com/the-devil%E2%80%99s-doorstep.
[2]Quoted in Bob Nightengale, "Boras Is Baseball's Bigger Deal Man, *USA Today,* November 14, 2006, online at http://www.usatoday.com/sports/baseball/2006-11-14-boras-cover_x.htm.

Sources: Ben McGrath, "The Extortionist," *The New Yorker,* October 29, 2009, online at http://www.newyorker.com/reporting/2007/10/29/071029fa_fact_mcgrath; Bob Nightengale, "Boras Is Baseball's Bigger Deal Man, *USA Today,* November 14, 2006, online at http://www.usatoday.com/sports/baseball/2006-11-14-boras-cover_x.htm; and Mattt Taibbi, "The Devil's Doorstep: A Visit with Scott Boras," *Men's Journal,* February 23, 2009, on line at http://www.mensjournal.com/the-devil%E2%80%99s-doorstep.

Summary

In this chapter, we examined how labor markets work in professional sports. The forces of labor supply and labor demand do a good job of explaining why the salaries of professional athletes have grown so much over the last several decades. Increasing demand by fans for the sport translates into higher demand for labor by teams. Athletes can increase their own earnings by investing in human capital. To the degree that the skills they acquire are general skills, the athletes will have to pay for the training by accepting lower salaries.

The distribution of income in professional sports is highly skewed toward those with the most talent. Tournament organizers and teams provide disproportionate rewards to get players to provide more effort. This reward system has some dangers, as it can lead to poor teamwork, sabotaging one's opponents, and carrying effort to unhealthy extremes. The unhealthy extremes include levels of practice that lead to permanent disability later in life or to the abuse of performance-enhancing drugs.

Discussion Questions

1. Has the recent focus on measuring individual performance harmed professional sports?
2. Should baseball and football follow the example of the IOC and disregard records set by players who have used PEDs?
3. If PEDs do not cause irreparable harm to an athlete's health, should they be permitted?
4. Are disproportionately high rewards to star athletes a bad thing for team sports?

Problems

8.1 Suppose that the market demand for baseball players is perfectly inelastic (vertical) at 750 players. If the market supply increases due to an increase in the number of available international players, show using a graph how wages will change as a result.

8.2 Suppose that there are two types of players, good and medium. The team demand curve for top-quality players is $Q = 27 - 5w$, and the market supply of top players is $Q = 4w$, where w is the wage in millions of dollars. How many top-quality players will the team hire? What will they be paid?

8.3 Use a graph similar to Figure 8.5 to show the effect on league salaries of

   a. An increase in the number of players available

   b. A decrease in television revenues due to fan preferences for drama shows

   c. A minimum salary set above the equilibrium wage

8.4 Based on the following player statistics, compute the Win Score values. Assuming the players have equal star power to attract fans and players are rewarded only based on Win Score values, which player deserves to be paid the most? Who should be paid the least? How would your answer change if players were only rewarded for scoring?

| | Players | | | |
Statistic	Joe	Bob	Fred	Jim
Points	17	25	10	20
Total rebounds	7	5	10	6
Steals	3	0	4	2
Blocks	2	2	0	0
Assists	3	4	6	8
Field goal attempts	18	28	8	13
Free throw attempts	10	9	4	5
Turnovers	2	3	2	4
Personal fouls	4	5	3	3

8.5 Go to the web site http://www.basketball-reference.com and find the statistics and salary of your favorite NBA player. Use the equation on p. 250 for additional wins and the value of a win to determine what he is worth and compare it with his actual salary. Is he overpaid, underpaid, or accurately paid?

8.6 Use a labor supply and labor demand to show why salaries in the NBA went down in 2009–2010. Explain why the curves moved they way they did.

8.7 Explain and show using a graph why, at any given wage, a monopoly firm will hire less labor than the total employment if the industry were competitive.

8.8 Using a graph, show what happens to player effort in a tournament if the marginal cost-of-effort curve shifts upward.

8.9 Show what would have happened to the Lorenz curve in Figure 8.11 if Serena Williams, Darina Safina, and Svetlana Kuznetsova had all lost in the first round of the U.S. Open in September 2009.

8.10 Use the supply and demand model to explain why top athletes are paid less than top celebrities.

APPENDIX 8A

The Labor–Leisure Choice Model of Indifference Curves

Like all decisions in economics, the decision to work is one of choosing among alternatives. In the simple labor–leisure choice model, a person chooses between working for pay and not working (consuming leisure). Each person possesses a **utility function** as defined in Appendix 2A. Labor economists typically assume that utility results from consuming goods (X) and leisure (Z), both of which are normal goods, as shown in the following equation:

$$U = u(X, Z)$$

We can illustrate the utility function using indifference curves, as shown in Figure 8A.1. Each curve represents a specific level of utility, and utility increases as we move northeast, away from the origin (i.e., $U_2 > U_1$). The slope of an indifference curve, also called the **marginal rate of substitution,** represents the rate at which the person is willing to exchange one good for the other, holding

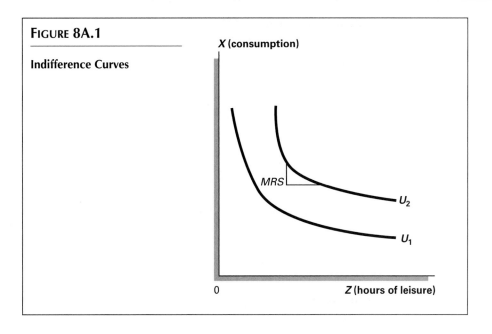

FIGURE 8A.1

Indifference Curves

X (consumption)

MRS

U_2

U_1

0

Z (hours of leisure)

utility constant. Recall that the negative slope of an indifference curve implies a trade-off: The person must receive more of one good if he or she receives less of the other in order to hold utility constant. The convex shape of the indifference curves reflects the diminishing marginal utility associated with consuming more and more of any single commodity.

Consumption is limited by an **income constraint** and a **time constraint**. A person's income consists of his or her earnings from working h hours at wage w, and exogenous income V, which consists of all nonlabor income such as dividends, inheritances, and so on:

$$X = wh + V$$

The time constraint reflects the fact that there are only so many hours in a day (T) that must be allocated to either work or leisure.

$$T = h + Z$$

The time constraint implies that the opportunity cost of consuming one additional hour of leisure equals the hourly wage. In Figure 8A.2, the time constraint mandates that a person cannot spend less than zero hours working and more than T hours at leisure (and vice versa). Because many people receive some exogenous income even if they do not work, the budget constraint begins from a point \$$V$ directly above T. The constraint has a slope equal to $-w$ since the person must give up \$$w$ for every hour of leisure he or she consumes.

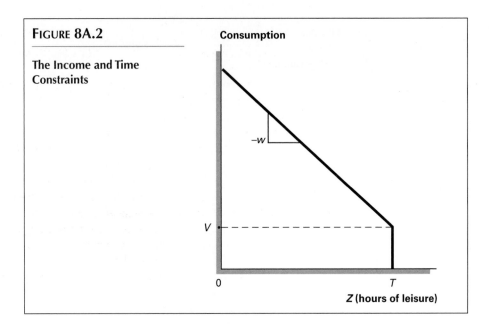

FIGURE 8A.2

The Income and Time
Constraints

We can combine the person's utility function with his or her budget
constraint to determine the person's utility-maximizing choice. Suppose a local
golf pro, Bill, can earn income by giving golf lessons for $20 per hour. In addi-
tion, he receives $100 per day in dividend income.[37] His constraints are

$$X = 20h + 100$$
$$24 = h + Z$$

Bill can teach all the lessons he wants, but each hour that he spends teaching requires that he give up one hour of leisure. Conversely, the opportunity
cost of consuming an extra hour of leisure is $20. Bill's utility maximizing solu-
tion is shown in Figure 8A.3. He maximizes his utility by teaching 8 hours per
day and consuming 16 hours of leisure. His total daily income is $260, and his
utility level is U_2. At the utility-maximizing point, S, the marginal rate of substitution (the slope of the indifference curve) equals the wage rate, the slope of
the budget constraint:

$$MRS = w$$

If Bill had a strong preference for leisure, we could illustrate his preferences
with the dashed indifference curve U_1. In this example, Bill does not want to

---

[37]We could alter the model by assuming that Bill needs to devote a certain portion of each day to
personal needs such as sleeping and eating, but the framework would be the same. With such an
allowance, T would simply shift to the left by the amount of personal time, p, per period
$(T - p = h + Z)$.

work at all. The indifference curve U_1 touches the budget line at Z, which means that $h = 0$, and all time is devoted to leisure. Economists refer to such an outcome as a **corner** solution.

By varying Bill's wage rate, we can derive his labor supply curve. Figure 8A.4 shows Bill's initial optimal point from Figure 8A.3 and the effect of a decrease in

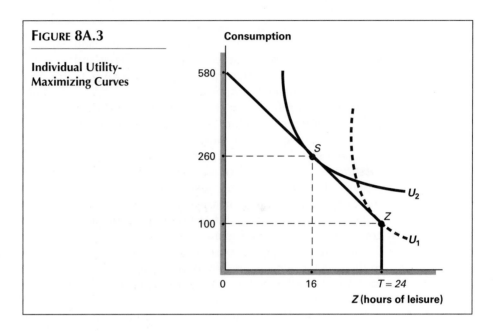

FIGURE 8A.3

Individual Utility-Maximizing Curves

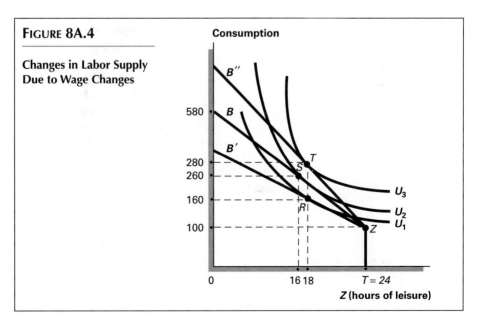

FIGURE 8A.4

Changes in Labor Supply Due to Wage Changes

his hourly wage to $10 per hour. When Bill's wage rate falls to $10 per hour, his budget line becomes flatter (ZB') and his utility level falls to U_1 at point R. At the new, lower wage, Bill works 6 hours per day and consumes 18 hours per day of leisure. His total income is now $160 per day. Finally, Bill responds to an increase in his wage to $30 per hour (which shifts the budget line to ZB'') by choosing the consumption–leisure combination, labeled T on the indifference curve U_3. Again Bill decides to work 6 hours per day, giving him an income of $280, and he consumes 18 hours per day of leisure.

From Figure 8A.4 we can easily derive Bill's labor supply curve. Like any supply curve, a labor supply curve shows the quantity (of hours in this case) that Bill supplies at various prices. In Figure 8A.5, points R', S', and T' correspond to the tangencies R, S, and T in Figure 8A.4. The line ll that connects these points is Bill's labor supply curve. The difference between this supply curve and a typical product supply curve is that it bends backward at wages above $20. To see why, we must look further into the labor–leisure decision.

Labor supply curves sometimes bend backward because of the *income* and *substitution effects* we described in Appendix 2A. The substitution effect causes a person to shift his or her consumption away from goods that have become more expensive. Because the opportunity cost of leisure is the wage rate, when Bill's wage rate increases, it increases the cost of leisure, which will lead him to consume less leisure and work more.

If leisure is a normal good, then an increase in income results in an increase in the demand for leisure. When Bill's wage rises, his ability to obtain income increases as well, which increases his demand for leisure, leading him to work fewer hours. In effect, he "buys" time away from work with his increased earning power. The substitution and income effects work in opposite directions

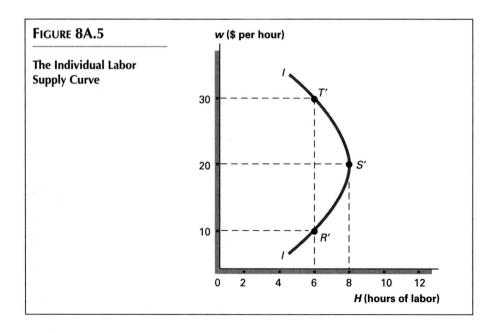

FIGURE 8A.5

The Individual Labor Supply Curve

in this case. Whether Bill's labor supply curve slopes upward or backward at any given point depends on which effect is stronger. When the substitution effect is larger than the income effect, Bill works more as his wage increases. When the income effect dominates, he works less in response to a wage increase. Figure 8A.5 shows that Bill's substitution effect dominates at wages below $20 per hour, but his income effect dominates at wages above $20 per hour.

Because of the intense level of training and dedication required at the professional level, players or coaches sometimes walk away from the game despite still being able to compete at the highest level in order to pursue other activities, such as spending more time with their families. Dick Vermeil, coach of the 2000 Super Bowl champion St. Louis Rams, had become a classic case of burnout almost two decades earlier. While coaching the Philadelphia Eagles from 1976 to 1983, Vermeil worked so many hours that he noticed a growth spurt of his second oldest son only while watching game film with his assistant coaches and seeing his son standing on the sidelines.[38] He left coaching at the end of the 1982–1983 season after working himself to the point of complete physical exhaustion. Although he worked after that as a broadcaster and motivational speaker, he did not return to coaching again until 1997, when he took over as head coach of the Rams. For Vermeil, a change in his preferences away from work toward leisure led him to leave the game.

We can also show how an increase in wealth affects the decision to work using the labor–leisure model. Consider the example of Oscar de la Hoya described in the text. In the case of de la Hoya and other highly paid athletes, the vertical portion of the income constraint becomes very large over time due to endorsement and accumulated past income. As the exogenous income segment increases, so does the income effect, because a person can achieve greater and greater utility levels without working, as shown in Figure 8A.6.

The Labor–Leisure Model When Hours Are Fixed

The labor supply model assumes that a person can choose the number of hours that he or she would like to work. In many occupations, people cannot choose the number of hours they work. For example, some production workers may prefer to work part-time but must work a full 40-hour week in order to keep their jobs. The same is true in sports. Athletes face two possible constraints when they play in a professional league: The season may be either shorter or longer than they prefer. For example, Nikki McCray originally chose to play in the ABL because she preferred to play a longer season.[39] At the time, the ABL played a 40-game season, while the WNBA played only a 28-game season. When the ABL folded and her only option was the WNBA, her hours were set at a level below the level she would have chosen. We illustrate the effects of the shorter season on her utility maximization problem in Figure 8A.7 by imposing

---

[38]Gary Smith, "A New Life," *Sports Illustrated* (March 28, 1983), pp. 60–67.

[39]Steve Lopez, "They Got Next," *Sports Illustrated* (June 30, 1997), pp. 44–47.

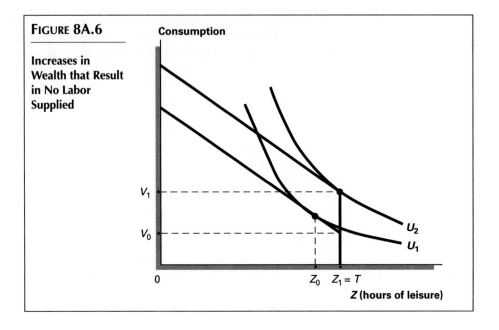

FIGURE 8A.6

Increases in Wealth that Result in No Labor Supplied

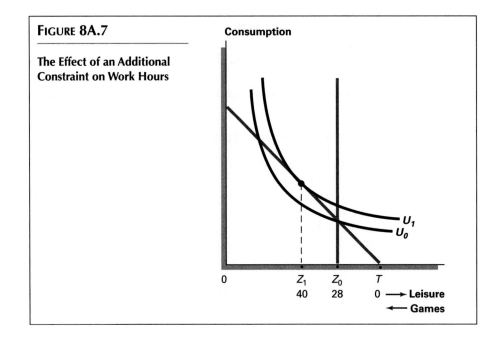

FIGURE 8A.7

The Effect of an Additional Constraint on Work Hours

another constraint, fixing hours (or games in this case) along the vertical line set at Z_0. In the absence of this constraint, McCray maximizes her utility on U_1 by playing 40 games. In the presence of the games constraint, however, she cannot play more than 28 games (WNBA players are contractually forbidden to play in other leagues or for other teams). Thus, she maximizes her utility by playing only 28 games and consuming more leisure than she would like. While some leisure is a good thing, when a person consumes very large quantities of any good, leisure included, the marginal utility received from the last hour becomes very small.

Athletes who play individual sports typically do not face such stringent quantity constraints. For example, a professional golfer with a newborn child may elect to take several weeks away from the tour.[40] For athletes involved in team sports, part-time play is generally not an option. For them, when family needs dictate time away from the game, retirement may be the only option. Such was the case with Mark Rypien, who retired from the Atlanta Falcons in order to care for his terminally ill son. In other cases, players leave the labor force temporarily. For example, Buffalo Bills linebacker Chris Spielman left the team for a full season to care for his critically ill wife.

---

[40]The LPGA now maintains a day care center that travels with the tour, allowing golfers to keep their small children with them rather than be forced to choose between playing and staying home.

CHAPTER 9

Labor Market Imperfections

The squabbling within baseball, the finger-pointing, the tendency to see economic issues as moral ones ... all of these are contributing to our joint fall from grace.

—FORMER MLB COMMISSIONER FAY VINCENT[1]

Introduction

As we saw in Chapter 8, the salaries paid to professional athletes have grown significantly since the 1970s. Moreover, salaries have grown more rapidly in some sports than in others. For example, in 1978 the average salary in MLB was virtually identical to the average salary in the NFL. By 2008, salaries in MLB were more than 50 percent higher than in the NFL. The more rapid growth of salaries in baseball is surprising for two reasons. First, revenues in football have grown more rapidly than in baseball. Rising revenues should increase the *MRP* of players and their salaries. In addition, thanks largely to baseball's exemption from the antitrust laws, baseball players were not able to challenge the owners' monopsony power in court. The answer lies in the relative power of the sports' players associations. Baseball owners have been far less successful in exerting monopsony power because the Major League Baseball Players Association (MLBPA) has been far more adept at overcoming the monopsony power of the owners than the National Football League Players Association (NFLPA).

In this chapter, we examine how professional sports leagues have exerted monopsony power. We then show how the different sports unions have tried to exert countervailing monopoly power by controlling the labor input. Along the way we see:

- Why a Chicago businessman created MLB's National League

- Why the best running back in NFL history found no takers as a free agent

- Why strikes occur even though they are economically inefficient

---

[1] Quoted in *Cot's Baseball Contracts* online at http://mlbcontracts.blogspot.com/, viewed March 15, 2007.

9.1 The Monopsony Power of Sports Leagues

The labor markets in all the major North American sports are marked by deviations from the assumptions of the competitive model. As we saw in Chapter 4, the reserve clause gave teams considerable monopsony power over their players. In this section, we take a closer look at the reserve clause, the advent of free agency in professional sports, and how monopsony power continues to repress the salaries of players who are not yet eligible for free agency. For players who have earned free agent status, leagues have used other mechanisms to reduce salary growth. For example, salary caps have affected pay in professional basketball, football, and hockey.

The Economics of Monopsony

A monopsony is the sole buyer of a good or service. Firms that sell their goods or services in a monopsonistic market can sell them to no one except the monopsony. A monopsony exerts its market power like a monopoly, though its impact is the mirror image of a monopoly. While a monopolist uses its power to drive up the price it can charge consumers, a monopsonist uses its market power to drive down the prices it pays producers or workers. A monopsonist and a monopolist are identical in one respect. Both restrict the quantity of transactions relative to a perfectly competitive industry. The resulting reductions in output and consumption impose a deadweight loss on society.

Figure 9.1 shows that, since the monopsonist is the only buyer in a market, its supply curve is the market supply curve (just as the monopolist's demand curve

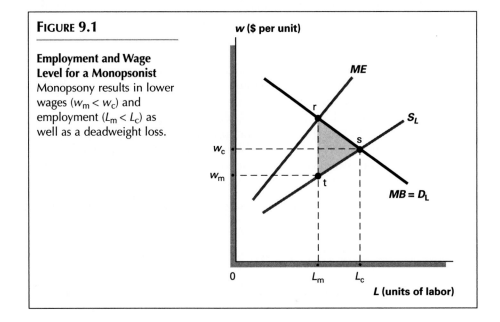

FIGURE 9.1

Employment and Wage Level for a Monopsonist
Monopsony results in lower wages ($w_m < w_c$) and employment ($L_m < L_c$) as well as a deadweight loss.

is the market demand curve). Because the supply curve is upward-sloping, the monopsonist can buy more only if it is willing and able to pay more. Since a monopsonist usually cannot tell exactly which seller is willing to sell for how much, it generally must pay a higher price for all the items it buys—not just for the additional items. The cost of buying a little more, the **marginal expenditure,** is thus greater than the cost of the additional purchases, because the monopsonist must spend more on both the marginal unit and all preceding units. As a result, the monopsonist's **marginal expenditure curve** lies above and to the left of the supply curve (just as the monopolist's marginal revenue curve lies below the demand curve). The monopsonist maximizes its profits when it buys just enough that its marginal benefit equals its marginal expenditure.

In Figure 9.1 the demand curve shows the monopsonist's marginal benefit (recall that the demand curve for labor is derived from the additional revenue it generates for the firm). The monopsonist hires workers until marginal benefit equals marginal expenditure. Just as the monopolist determines the price it charges by looking up to the demand curve, the monopsonist determines the price it pays by looking down to the supply curve. Thus, the monopsony price in Figure 9.1 is w_m, not the competitive wage w_c. In the graph, the marginal expenditure curve cuts the marginal benefit curve at point r, and the monopsony level of employment is L_m. If the labor market were competitive, firms would hire L_c workers, which is where the marginal benefit of the last worker equals the competitive wage (w_c). Thus, monopsony results in lower wages and lower employment than in a competitive market. It also results in a deadweight loss (the area rst). Monopsony power was once one of the cornerstones of professional sports. As noted in Chapter 4, the formation of the National League in baseball can be traced directly to its exerting monopsony power, through the creation of the reserve clause.

The Reserve Clause

Prior to the reserve clause, professional baseball players moved freely from team to team, sometimes jumping contracts in the middle of the season.[2] This changed in 1876. Envious of the success of the Boston Red Stockings, William Hulbert, the financial backer of the Chicago White Stockings, lured away four of Boston's star players (and one from Philadelphia) late in the 1875 season. In a remarkable display of chutzpah, Hulbert then appealed to the other backers to create a new system that would—among other things—stop the bidding war for players. This *coup d'état* overthrew baseball's existing structure, the National Association of Professional Base Ball Players. The name of the new organization—the National League of Professional Baseball Clubs—was highly significant. Prior to Hulbert's coup, players' associations had run baseball.

---

[2]One of the institutional weaknesses of the Negro Leagues was the teams' inability to maintain stable rosters. See Robert Peterson, *Only the Ball Was White* (New York: Gramercy Books, 1970), pp. 95–98.

Now the clubs—and their owners—reigned supreme, and the players occupied a secondary position.[3]

Just how secondary became apparent in 1887, when the owners unveiled what had been an implicit "gentlemen's agreement" for the previous decade. With the formation of the National League, each owner had reserved the rights to five players' services for as long as he wanted them.[4] By 1889 the system of reserving players had expanded to the entire roster and had been installed as a clause in the standard player's contract:

> [I]f, prior to March 1, ... the player and the club have not agreed upon the terms of such contract [for the next playing season], then on or before ten days after said March 1, the club shall have the right to renew this contract for the period of one year on the same terms except that the amount payable to the player shall be such as the club shall fix in said notice.[5]

On the surface, the clause seemed fairly innocuous. It restricted a player to a team for the length of the contract plus, if the team renewed the existing contract, one additional year of service. The catch lies in the fact that the owners interpreted the right to "renew this contract ... on the same terms" as renewing all the terms of the contract, including the reserve clause, thus binding the player to the team for yet another year. Using this recursive system, a team could restrict a player from selling his services for as long as it wanted to keep him. Leagues in other sports saw the value of the reserve clause in keeping down costs and copied this clause almost word for word in their standard contracts.

With no alternative employer able to bid away the services of their players, teams drove down their players' salaries to levels that just kept them in the sport. While players today can afford to support small entourages, even stars of an earlier time had to hold second jobs. Imagine walking into an appliance store and buying a washing machine from Albert Pujols. In 1951 you could have done just that from Jackie Robinson.[6]

The Advent of Free Agency   Baseball players initially viewed being "reserved" as an honor because it formally recognized them as one of the top players on the team. Once the impact of the reserve clause on salaries became clear, players in all leagues became implacably opposed to it. Eventually, the unions in all four sports were able to overturn the reserve clause. Three unions did so through the court system, and, as we will see, one union did so by outmaneuvering MLB's owners and commissioner.

Football players were the first to achieve free agency, though they were not the first to take advantage of it. The Supreme Court's 1957 *Radovich* v. *National Football League* concluded that, football—unlike baseball—was interstate

---

[3]Harold Seymour, *Baseball: The Early Years* (New York: Oxford University Press, 1960), p. 80.

[4]Perhaps not surprisingly, this was exactly the number that Hulbert had signed away in 1875.

[5]Quoted from James Quirk and Rodney Fort, *Pay Dirt* (Princeton, N.J.: Princeton University Press, 1992), p. 185.

[6]John Helyar, *Lords of the Realm* (New York: Villard Books, 1994), p. 12.

commerce and therefore was subject to the antitrust laws. In particular, the decision formally rejected NFL teams' right to reserve players.

Despite this resounding court victory, players would have to wait another 35 years for true free agency. At first, NFL team owners responded by entering into an informal "gentlemen's agreement" not to pursue each other's players. When this broke down in the early 1960s, NFL commissioner Pete Rozelle unilaterally imposed the "Rozelle rule."

> Whenever a player, becoming a free agent in such manner thereafter signed a contract with a different club in the league, then unless mutually satisfactory arrangements have been concluded between the two League clubs, the Commissioner may name and then award to the former club one or more players from the Active, Reserve, or Selection List (including future selection choices of the acquiring club as the Commissioner in his sole discretion deems fair and equitable); any such decisions by the Commissioner shall be final and conclusive.[7]

The Rozelle rule thus recognized the players' right to free agency in theory but effectively killed it in practice. The rule turned signing a free agent into a trade in which the team had no control over the players it would lose. A form of the Rozelle rule survived until 1992, when a U.S. District Court ruled in *McNeil et al.* v. *NFL* that it violated antitrust laws.[8]

The reserve clause in professional hockey and basketball were both overturned as the result of competition from rival leagues. In 1972, the World Hockey Association (WHA) sued the NHL for violating antitrust laws when the NHL tried to block players from jumping to the WHA. The resulting ruling (*Philadelphia World Hockey Club* v. *Philadelphia Hockey Club)* struck down the NHL's reserve clause.

In the NBA, the antitrust lawsuit was brought by players rather than by the rival league. Oscar Robertson, a star player and president of the National Basketball Players Association (NBPA), sued the league (*Robertson* v. *NBA*) in response to the NBA's attempt to end a costly war with the rival American Basketball Association through a partial merger. Faced with an unfavorable court ruling and the prospect of continued rivalry with the ABA, the NBA dropped its appeal of the Robertson case in 1976 and agreed to phase in free agency.

Unlike the players in other sports, baseball players could not resolve their problem through the courts. The 1922 Supreme Court decision in the *Federal Baseball Club* v. *National League* gave MLB blanket exemption from antitrust laws. Even though subsequent rulings recognized the absurdity of the *Federal Baseball Club* decision, they repeatedly upheld the monopsony power of baseball teams (e.g., *Toolson* v. *New York Yankees* in 1953 and *Flood* v. *Kuhn* in 1971).

The Major League Baseball Players Association (MLBPA) was able to overthrow the reserve clause by outsmarting the owners rather than by suing them. Prior to 1970, all grievances by players were filed with the Commissioner, who typically sided with the owners. In the 1970 negotiations, Marvin Miller, the MLBPA's Executive Director, got the owners to agree to replace the commissioner

---

[7]Quoted from the standard player contract in Dworkin, *Owners Versus Players* (1981), p. 250.
[8]See, for example, Staudohar (1996), pp. 82–83.

with a three-person panel, with one member appointed by the owners, one member appointed by the union, and one member drawn from a mutually agreed upon list. The owners agreed to the commission after Miller assured them that the panel would deal only with trifling monetary matters. Then-Commissioner Bowie Kuhn would have the final say in all overarching matters that affected the integrity of the game. By couching its challenge to the reserve clause as a financial matter, the MLBPA was able to force the issue into the hands of an outside arbitrator, who ruled in favor of the players (and who was promptly dismissed by the owners).[9]

Forms of Free Agency   While the idea of free agency—the right of a player to sign with any team that offers him a contract—is universal, different sports leagues have placed different restrictions on when and how a player becomes a free agent. To begin with, some sports have two different levels of free agency. Most fans who discuss free agents are actually thinking of unrestricted free agents. An **unrestricted free agent** is a player with no strings attached; he is free to sign with any team that makes him an offer. In MLB, a player can become an unrestricted free agent after six years of service at the major league level.

Restricted free agents are free to solicit offers from other teams but not to sign with them. His original team has the **right of first refusal,** meaning it can retain the player if it matches the other team's offer. In the NFL, a player with three years of experience can become a restricted free agent after his contract has expired. He can become an unrestricted free agent after four years if his contract has expired.

In the NBA, a first-round draft pick can become a restricted free agent after his fourth year. Players can become unrestricted free agents after four years if they are not first round draft picks or if they are first-round picks and their team does not exercise its right of first refusal.

The National Hockey League has a dizzying array of categories related to a player's age and level of experience. For example, a player whose contract has expired, who first signed a contract when he was 18–21 years old and who has three years of experience can become a restricted free agent. The experience requirement is shorter for players who signed their initial contracts when they were older. Hockey players can become unrestricted free agents when their contracts expire if they have at least seven years of experience or if they are at least 27 years old. The restrictions fall to three or more seasons and 25 years old for those who have played in fewer than 80 NHL games (fewer than 28 games for goalies) over the course of their contracts.

Salary Arbitration

Before players become free agents, teams can exert monopsony power, confronting them with "take it or leave it" contract offers. Athletes in MLB and the NHL, however, have an intermediate stage that gives them some recourse. Players in these two sports have the opportunity to submit disputes for salary

---

[9]For a complete account, see Helyar, *Lords of the Realm* (1994).

arbitration. **Arbitration** occurs when parties to a dispute submit proposals to an **arbitrator,** a third party who then suggests or imposes a resolution. Both baseball and hockey have **binding arbitration,** in which both sides commit to accepting the ruling of a third party. Outside the sports world, binding arbitration is particularly popular in the public sector. Fearful of the consequences of a strike by police or firefighters, municipal officials often offer binding arbitration in exchange for the unions' accepting laws that prohibit them from striking. However, the NHL and MLB have different forms of arbitration.

Arbitration in the NHL   Salary arbitration is open to NHL players who are eligible for restricted free agency (typically those with at least four years of experience). The players who file for arbitration and the teams for which they play both submit proposals based on a variety of factors. These factors include the performance of the player, his contribution to the overall performance of the team, and the performance and pay of comparable players in the NHL. The arbitrator then has 48 hours to choose one of the proposals or to impose a decision of his own. A recent study has shown that arbitration rulings are roughly equivalent to what regression analysis predicts the players are worth to their teams.[10] Thus, arbitration appears to aid efficiency by bringing players and teams to a resolution that they would otherwise have trouble achieving.

Arbitration in MLB   MLB uses a different process, known as final offer arbitration. In **final offer arbitration (FOA),** arbitrators cannot impose their own solutions; they must choose one of the two proposals submitted to them. The goal of FOA is to prevent the two parties from becoming addicted to arbitration. Arbitration addiction often results from the incentives that the parties to binding arbitration face. Arbitrators, who are generally well-compensated, do not wish to jeopardize their employment by appearing prejudiced toward one side or the other. As a result, they have an incentive to "split the difference" of any two offers put in front of them. If the two parties to the negotiation recognize this tendency, they have little reason to compromise, as any moderation of their stance would lead the arbitrator to impose a less favorable ruling.[11] FOA reverses this incentive. The goal of each party is to convince the arbitrator that its proposal is the more reasonable one. This forces the two sides to adopt moderate positions. Ideally, the two positions will move so close together that the two sides reach an agreement without recourse to arbitration. FOA is open to all players with at least three years of major league experience. The criteria on which a judgment is based are very similar to those used in hockey.

The results of the 2009 arbitration proceedings support this view of FOA.[12] Of the 111 players who filed for arbitration, 65 settled with their teams before

---

[10]See James Lambrinos and Thomas D. Ashman, "Salary Determination in the National Hockey League: Is Arbitration Efficient?," *Journal of Sports Economics*, vol. 8, no. 2 (April 2007), pp. 192–201.

[11]For more on the addictive nature of binding arbitration, see Ronald Ehrenberg and Robert Smith, *Modern Labor Economics* (Boston: Addison Wesley, 2008).

[12]See Maury Brown, "2009 MLB Salary Arbitration Vital Stats," *The Biz of Baseball*, February 20, 2009, online at http://www.bizofbaseball.com/index.php?option=com_content&view=article&id=2974:2009-mlb-salary-arbitration-vital-stats&catid=66:free-agency-and-trades&Itemid=153.

the time came to file briefs with the arbitrator. Of the remaining 46, only three actually went forward with arbitration. In two of the three cases, the arbitrator ruled in favor of the player, making 2009 the first year since 1996 that players won a majority of the hearings. Overall, owners have won close to 60 percent of the arbitration cases (280 of 487).

Despite the players' losing record in arbitration hearings, FOA has had a significant impact on player salaries. Former MLBPA Executive Director Marvin Miller has gone so far as to say that FOA has done more for player salaries than free agency. The evidence from 2009 suggests that Miller might be correct in his assessment of FOA. The 111 players who filed for free agency received an average salary increase of 143 percent over the previous year.

Salary Caps

The four major North American sports leagues have sought salary caps as a countermeasure to free agency. As we will see, they appear to have kept salaries lower and compressed the differences in team payrolls. Three of the four major sports leagues now have salary caps. MLB owners have tried but failed to impose a cap for three decades. In Chapter 5, we described the impact of salary caps on competitive balance. Here we examine their impact on team payrolls.

The Salary Cap in the NBA The NBA was the first league to create a salary cap. Unlike the reserve clause, the salary cap arose out of weakness rather than strength. During the 1970s, the salary war with the ABA and free agency had pushed payrolls in the NBA to 70 percent of the league's gross revenues.[13] Prior to the 1984–1985 season, desperate team owners convinced the players to accept a salary cap as part of a revenue-sharing agreement that gave players a percentage of league revenues. NBA owners credit the cap with saving the league in the 1980s.

Team owners were so convinced of the value of the cap that they were willing to suffer a work stoppage that canceled half the 1998–1999 season to tighten it. The tightening took two forms: a cap on individual salaries as well as on overall payrolls, and an escrow tax on salaries. The individual cap sets a salary scale for players based on their years of experience in the league. For example, in 2008–2009, an NBA rookie had to be paid between $442,000 and $13.76 million. A player with seven years of experience had to be paid between $1.07 million and $16.51 million.[14] The escrow system further tightened the salary cap. Under this system, the league sets aside 9 percent of each player's salary.[15] If

---

[13]For a discussion of salary caps in the NFL and the NBA, see Staudohar (1996).

[14]Rookies drafted in the first round were paid more, according to a rookie salary scale. The maximum salaries were set according to prespecified formulae. A player with fewer than 7 years of experience could make up to the greater of $9 million or 25 percent of the team cap. A player with 7–10 years of experience could be paid up to $11 million or 30 percent of the team cap. See Larry Coon, "NBA Salary Cap FAQ," http://members.cox.net/lmcoon/salarycap.htm, viewed August 8, 2009.

[15]This percentage will fall to 8 percent in 2010–2011.

player salaries and benefits—regardless of the exceptions mentioned in Chapter 5—exceed 57 percent of basketball-related income (6 percentage points over the limit set by the cap), then the funds in escrow are remitted to the league until the total is reduced to 57 percent. Otherwise, players receive the funds held in escrow at the end of the season.

The Salary Cap in the NHL   NHL owners felt so strongly about a salary cap that they locked out their players for the entire 2004–2005 season to gain a salary cap. Like the NBA and NFL, the NHL's cap guarantees the players a share of league revenue. Unlike the other two leagues, the NHL players' share is set by a sliding scale. Players receive 54 percent when "hockey-related" revenue is below $2.2 billion, and up to 57 percent when revenue exceeds $2.7 billion.

The NHL has a hard cap, which includes all salaries, signing bonuses, and performance bonuses. The NHL cap has also adopted limits similar to those that had been imposed by the NBA in 1999. It limits individual player salaries to be no more than 20 percent of the team's allowable payroll, and it uses an escrow system to ensure that payments stay within the salary cap limits. In the 2008–2009, players put 13.5 percent of their salaries (increased to 25 percent in midseason) into escrow.

The Salary Cap in the NFL   The NFL negotiated a salary cap in 1994 with the National Football League Players Association (NFLPA) in response to the 1992 court ruling that had granted players free agency. Like the NHL, the NFL has a hard cap, in which almost all payments to players count against the cap.

The formula for the NFL's salary cap closely resembles the NBA's formula, but the two differ in several important ways.[16] For the 2009 season, the NFL set aside 62.24 percent of its "designated gross revenues" (DGR) for player salaries and benefits. While the NFL guarantees its players a much higher percentage of revenue than the NBA or NHL, it counts less income in the base than the NBA or NHL. For example, the NFL's DGR counts only the ticket portion of luxury box revenue, while the other leagues count all luxury box revenue. This has a significant impact on DGR because most luxury box revenue is counted as concession revenue, and teams do not share concession revenue.

Two other factors complicate the NFL's salary cap computations. First, although NFL teams have 53 players on their active rosters, the salary cap applies only to the 51 highest-paid players. Second, the bonuses a team pays might or might not count toward its salary cap.

Bonuses have become an important part of player contracts in the NFL because football players generally do not have guaranteed contracts. A player who has signed a multiyear contract that is not guaranteed will not be paid if he

---

[16]The NFL's salary cap can be found in its CBA, which is available at National Football League Players Association, "CBA Complete," online at http://www.nflpa.org/CBA/CBA_Complete .aspx, 2002; and the 2006 extension at National Football League Players Association, "CBA Extension," online at http://www.nflpa.org/CBA/CBA_Extension.aspx, 2006.

does not make the team. This has led some teams to cut players with multiyear contracts and then sign them to much lower salaries a few days later. A large signing bonus or easily obtained incentive bonus can protect a player with a long-term contract by providing a source of guaranteed income. Signing bonuses, roster bonuses (paid if a player makes the team roster), workout bonuses (paid if the player attends off-season team workouts), and any bonus paid for meeting conditions that the player had also satisfied the previous year are all considered *likely to be earned* (LTBE) bonuses and count against the salary cap. However, the NFL allows teams to prorate them over the length of the contract rather than count them at the time they are paid. Thus, for cap purposes, a contract that pays a player $35 million dollars in equal $7 million increments over five years is indistinguishable from one that pays the player a $15 million signing bonus and $4 million over five years.[17] Bonuses for meeting previously unmet goals (e.g., a running back running for more yards than he has before) count as *not likely to be earned* (NLTBE) and do not count against the cap.

The Impact of Salary Caps   For all the importance placed on salary caps, the caps do not always limit what teams actually pay in a given year. Using the most recent payroll data from *USA Today*,[18] 5 of 30 NHL teams exceeded the $50.3 million salary cap, and 12 of 32 NFL teams were over the $116.7 limit. In the NBA, only 2 of 30 teams were below the $58.68 salary cap. Some teams were far over the limit. Both the NFL's Oakland Raiders and the NBA's New York Knicks had payrolls that were more than $35 million over the limit.

Despite the fact that many teams exceed the salary cap in any given year, the cap seems to have had an effect. Figure 9.2 illustrates the payrolls of the teams in the four major North American sports.[19] The graph shows that the payrolls of teams in the three leagues that have salary caps are far more equal than the payrolls in MLB.

Even discounting the New York Yankees, whose payroll is exceptional even by MLB standards, MLB has far greater variation than any other league. The highest (non-Yankee) MLB payrolls rival those of the highest NFL payrolls despite the fact that MLB rosters are less than half as large as NFL rosters, while the lowest payroll is lower than for any other sport. By setting bands within which teams are supposed to operate, salary caps seem to have equalized payrolls.

Figure 9.3 shows payrolls for the 30 NHL teams from 2003–2004 through 2007–2008 (recall that the 2004–2005 season was lost to a lockout).

---

[17]If a player is released or traded, bonus payments that have not yet been counted are counted in the year in which the player was released. Because such payments go for players who are no longer with the team, they have come to be called "dead money."

[18]Data are from the 2007–2008 hockey season, the 2008 football season, and the 2008–2009 basketball season. Data for the NHL can be found on line at *USA Today*, "USA Today Salaries Databases," online at http://content.usatoday.com/sports/hockey/nhl/salaries/totalpayroll.aspx?year=2007–08, viewed August 8, 2009. Data for the other sports are available at analogous sites and can be accessed from this site.

[19]Because all the other sports have 30 teams, we show only the top 30 payrolls for the NFL.

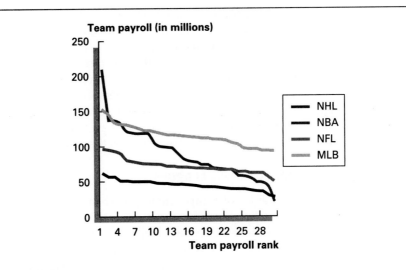

FIGURE 9.2

Payrolls for Teams in the Four Major Leagues
Payrolls in baseball, which does not have a salary cap, vary far more than payrolls in the three other major sports.

Source: MLB data from "USA Today Salaries Data Base," USAToday.com, online at http://content
.usatoday.com/sports/baseball/salaries/totalpayroll.aspx?year=2008, viewed August 8, 2009. Other data can be reached from that site.

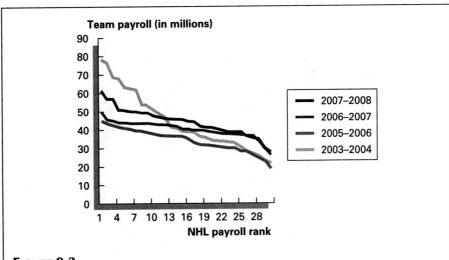

FIGURE 9.3

NHL Team Payrolls from 2003–2004 to 2007–2008
The salary cap lowered and compressed salaries in the NHL.

Source: Data for the 2007–2008 season can be found at "USA Today Salaries Data Base," USAToday.com,
online at http://content.usatoday.com/sports/hockey/nhl/salaries/totalpayroll.aspx?year=2007–08, viewed
August 8, 2009. Other data can be reached from that site.

This figure looks remarkably like Figure 9.2. In this case, the outlier is the NHL's 2003–2004 season. The figure shows that team payrolls varied far more in 2003–2004 than in the years following the implementation of the cap. Although several teams exceeded the cap, the cap did significantly reduce salaries. The average payroll in the NHL was $44.40 million in 2003–2004. It fell to $34.31 million in 2005–2006 and did not reach its pre-cap level until 2007–2008, when it hit $44.37 million. One potential cause for concern, however, is the fact that the payroll curve became significantly steeper in 2007–2008, as the high-payroll teams began to separate themselves from the rest of the league.

The Impact of Rival Leagues

The periodic entry of competing leagues has also caused player salaries to rise. As we saw earlier, the appearance of rival leagues was an important factor in undermining the reserve clause in professional basketball and hockey. Rival leagues can also directly undermine a sports league's monopsony power. Figure 9.4 shows how a rival league affects wages in employment. Initially the monopsony hires L_m workers and pays the monopsony wage w_m. When the rival league enters, the teams must compete for players. Even if the increase in demand is relatively small, total employment increases to L_c, and the competition for players forces the wage up to w_c.

Salary increases caused by the startup of rival leagues have occurred in all major U.S. sports leagues. The appearance of the American League as a rival to the National League in 1901 caused the salaries of baseball players to rise sharply. The fear of higher salaries attending the entry of the Federal League led Connie Mack to sell off the star players from a powerful Philadelphia

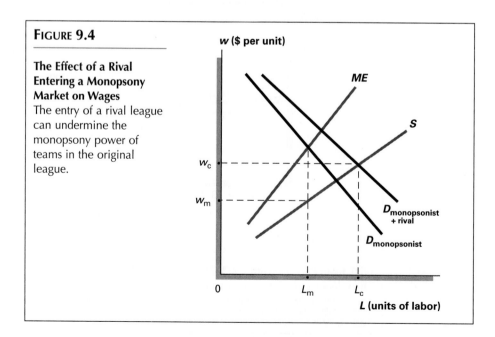

FIGURE 9.4

The Effect of a Rival Entering a Monopsony Market on Wages
The entry of a rival league can undermine the monopsony power of teams in the original league.

Athletics baseball club in 1915, an act from which it took the team over a decade to recover.

Since its merger with the American Football League in 1969, the NFL has faced down several rival leagues. The most serious challenges were posed by the World Football League, which operated in 1974 and 1975, and the United States Football League (USFL), which operated from 1983 through 1985. The XFL played only one season in 2001 and most likely had no major impact on NFL salaries. Between 1982 and 1986, the average salary in the NFL almost doubled as a direct result of the USFL's attempt to lure away players.

Similar "wars" drove up salaries when the ABA challenged the NBA in the 1960s and 1970s and when the WHA opposed the NHL in the 1970s. Between 1970 and 1976, the time period in which the WHA actively competed against the NHL for players, salaries in the NHL more than tripled. One study found that the pay in the NHL rose so much that players received more than their marginal revenue product.[20]

Measuring Monopsony Power

We have seen that, despite the end of the reserve clause, teams can still exert a degree of monopsony power, particularly for players who have relatively few years of experience. Economists measure the degree to which teams exploit their monopsony power by comparing the estimated value of a player (as measured by his MRP) with his wage. As we saw in Chapter 8, computing a player's MRP can be a complicated task. Today, most studies use a methodology first proposed by Anthony Krautmann.[21] Krautmann assumes that the salary received by a free agent reflects his marginal product. This changes the equation

$$MRP_i = \beta_0 + \beta_1 Perf_i + \beta_2 Z_i + \varepsilon_i$$

into

$$w_i = \beta_0 + \beta_1 Perf_i + \beta_2 Z_i + \varepsilon_i,$$

where $Perf_i$ is a vector of performance measures for player i, Z_i is a vector of control variables, w_i is player i's salary, and ε_i is a random error term. This change transforms an equation in which the key variable is unobservable (MRP) into one in which the key variable is readily observable (w_i). One can then estimate the coefficients of the equation using regression analysis. Applying the resulting estimated coefficients to data for players who are not free agents allows us to see whether the "restricted" players also receive salaries that equal their marginal revenue products. Recently, Krautmann, von Allmen,

---

[20]J.C.H. Jones and W.D. Walsh, "The World Hockey Association and Player Exploitation in the National Hockey League," *Quarterly Review of Economics and Business*, vol. 27, no. 2 (Summer 1987), pp. 87–101.

[21]See Anthony Krautmann, "What's Wrong with Scully Estimates of a Player's Marginal Revenue Product?" (1999).

and Berri have used this methodology to measure the degree of monopsony power exercised by teams in baseball, basketball, and football. They find that considerable monopsony power remains, particularly for players with the least amount of experience. These players, whom they call "apprentices," are not eligible for arbitration or restricted free agency. They find that, on average, such players receive 66 percent of their *MRP* in the NBA, 50 percent of their *MRP* in the NFL, and only 19 percent of their *MRP* in MLB. "Journeyman" players, who are eligible for arbitration in baseball or restricted free agency in football,[22] did much better. In the NFL, such players received 77 percent of their *MRP*. The impact of arbitration, or at least the threat of arbitration, was strongly felt in MLB, as journeyman players received 86 percent of their *MRP*.

9.2 Unions in Professional Sports

Unions have occupied a steadily decreasing role in the private sector of the U.S. economy. In 2007, only 7.5 percent of all employed wage and salary workers were union members, less than half their representation in the early 1980s. American unions have been in steady decline since the early 1950s, when they represented about one-third of the U.S. labor force. Globalization, technological advances, and demographic changes of the workforce (particularly the growing participation of women) have all contributed to the decline. By contrast, unions in professional sports have continued to thrive. Union representation of the major sports leagues remains at or near 100 percent. In this section, we examine the impact that unions have had on the labor market for professional athletes.

A Brief Introduction to the Economics of Unions

Unions typically fall into one of two categories: craft unions and industrial unions. **Craft unions** are by far the older of the two. Their origins can be traced back to the medieval guilds, groups of skilled artisans who joined together to prevent others from entering the city to undercut their prices. Modern craft unions consist of workers who share a common skill. For example, it is easy to guess what the members of the International Brotherhood of Electrical Workers do or what task the members of the Screen Actors Guild perform.

Industrial unions are much younger than craft unions. Workers first formed these unions in response to the harsh conditions they confronted as a result of the rise of large employers in the nineteenth century. Partly because they opposed the entrenched interests of their employers, organizers of industrial unions faced greater hostility than did craft unions. Industrial unions take their names from the types of output they produce, such as the United Auto Workers or the United Steel Workers.

---

[22]The authors find that almost no players were restricted free agents in the NBA. See Anthony C. Krautmann, Peter von Allmen, and David Berri, *International Journal of Sport Finance*, vol. 4, no. 3, (August 2009), pp. 75–93.

The different organizational structures of the two types of unions cause them to use different tactics on behalf of their members.[23] Craft unions increase wages by limiting access to the union and to skills. Firms do not hire workers in a craft union. Instead, the union assigns workers to employers through a (literal or figurative) hiring hall. In effect, they shift the labor supply curve leftward, as seen in Figure 9.5. The result is a union wage (w^u) that exceeds the competitive wage.

Industrial unions represent workers with many different skills. As a result, they leave hiring and firing to the employer. Like craft unions, industrial unions push up wages, but they do so through collective bargaining. In **collective bargaining,** unions meet with employers to produce an collective bargaining agreement that specifies pay and other working conditions. Industrial unions induce employers to increase pay by engaging in or threatening to engage in strikes. A **strike** occurs when workers act together to remove the labor input from the production process. In contrast, a **lockout** occurs when the management of the firm does not permit the labor input to operate. The need to state or threaten a damaging strike means that industrial unions derive their

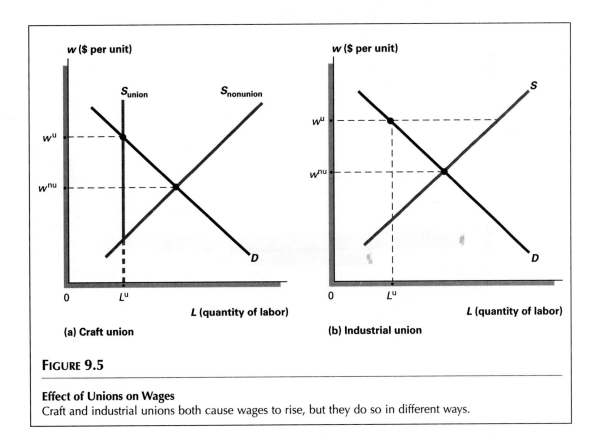

FIGURE 9.5

Effect of Unions on Wages
Craft and industrial unions both cause wages to rise, but they do so in different ways.

---

[23]While workers and unions negotiate over many different aspects of the job, we simplify the analysis by focusing solely on wages.

strength from being inclusive. The union cannot succeed unless the firms' employees remain loyal to the union during a strike. This contrasts with craft unions, whose power comes from being exclusive and keeping out competing workers. Figures 9.5a and 9.5b show the different ways in which the two unions achieve the goal of higher wages.[24]

Opponents of unions assert that unions create inefficiency in the economy. They say that unions limit employment and production, thereby harming the economy. Higher wages mean higher costs of production, which puts domestic producers at a competitive disadvantage and encourages producers to relocate abroad.

Union supporters feel that the opponents of unions paint an unnecessarily harsh picture. They claim that unions provide an important outlet for workers that improves efficiency. They point out that unions formalize grievance procedures by workers, giving them a way to express their concerns to employers and allowing employers to respond to the needs of their workforce, thereby reducing conflict in the workplace. By making workers more productive, unions increase their MRP and cause the demand for labor to shift to the right. The higher MRP thus increases the equlibibrium level of employment and justifies the higher wage that union workers receive.

Union supporters also point out that there is no clear evidence that unions either reduce productivity or slow productivity growth. Finally, some economists suggest that unions serve as a countervailing force against the monopsony power of employers, forcing employers to pay workers their marginal revenue product and—perhaps—making the labor market more closely resemble a competitive market.[25]

Figure 9.6 shows that a monopsony drives down the wage from the competitive level, w^c, to the monopsony level, w^m. It also drives down employment from L^c to L^m, creating a deadweight loss. By setting a wage above w^m, a union may actually increase employment and reduce or eliminate the deadweight loss. For example, setting the wage at w^c makes the marginal expenditure curve a horizontal line at that level and forces the monopsony to act like a competitive industry.

When a monopoly union confronts a monopsony employer—a situation that economists call **bilateral monopoly**—the wage falls into an indeterminate range between the union wage and the monopsony wage. In Figure 9.7, the union would like to set its wage where the marginal revenue of union members (MR) equals the supply of labor (S). The monopoly wage w^u is determined by looking up from this intersection to the demand curve for labor. The monopsonist would like to set the quantity of labor where the marginal expense of the

---

[24]The NFLPA had difficulty maintaining unity during a strike due to racial divisions among players. See Cynthia Gramm and John Schnell, "Difficult Choices, Crossing the Picket Line During the 1987 National Football League Strike," *Journal of Labor Economics*, vol. 12, no. 1 (January 1994), pp. 41–71.

[25]See Richard Freeman and James Medoff, *What Do Unions Do?* (New York, Basic Books, 1984) for a good example of this more positive view of unions.

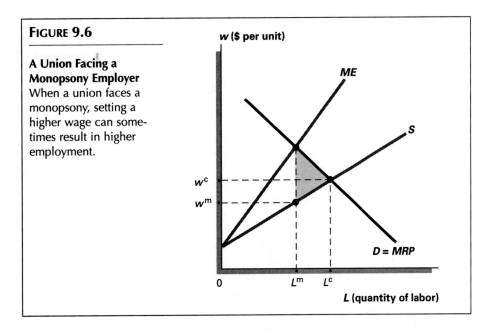

FIGURE 9.6

A Union Facing a Monopsony Employer
When a union faces a monopsony, setting a higher wage can sometimes result in higher employment.

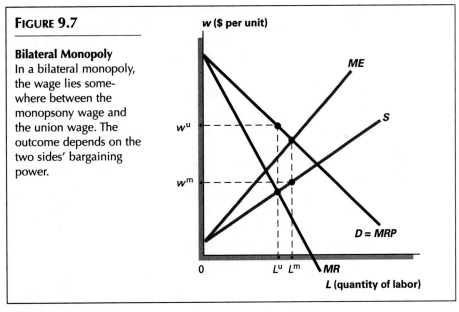

FIGURE 9.7

Bilateral Monopoly
In a bilateral monopoly, the wage lies somewhere between the monopsony wage and the union wage. The outcome depends on the two sides' bargaining power.

last worker (ME) equals the marginal revenue product ($MRP = D$) of the last worker. The monopsony wage w^m comes from looking down to the supply curve of labor. The precise settlement lies somewhere between w^u and w^m in Figure 9.7 and depends on the bargaining strength of the two sides.

In 1950, Nobel laureate John Nash developed a model to solve these types of bargaining problems that has served as the basis for much of the work on bargaining. One of the Nash model's central findings was that a group's bargaining power stems from its ability to walk away from the bargaining table. Nash calls the value of each side's alternatives its **threat point.** The more valuable the threat point for either side, the greater its bargaining power and the more favorable a solution it can achieve.

If, for example, the employer has a readily available source of labor (perhaps due to high unemployment rates), the benefits of permanently dissolving its relationship with the union may be very high. All else being equal, this will allow the firm to drive a harder bargain and reach a lower wage settlement. Alternatively, if union workers have high-paying jobs awaiting them elsewhere, their threat point and the resulting wage both rise.

Unions in professional sports do not readily fit into any of the categories outlined above. On one hand, they clearly represent workers with similar and distinct skills, like a craft union. On the other hand, they engage in collective bargaining with employers who do the hiring and firing, like an industrial union.

More important, unlike other unions, sports unions do not engage in wage negotiations. Instead, they bargain over the general framework within which individual players and their agents negotiate with teams.[26] Finally, the major sports unions and the leagues with which they negotiate sometimes advocate positions that are unlike those of other unions or firms. For example, during the 1998–1999 lockout, the NBA advocated a fixed salary scale for players while the union championed the free market. These stances are diametrically opposed to the stances taken by most firms and unions. Typically, the union pushes for salary scales, and the firm that wants salaries set by the market.

Labor Conflict in Professional Sports

Compared to the rest of the economy, labor relations in professional sports have been particularly contentious.[27] From 1972 through 1994, every renewal of the collective bargaining agreement in MLB was accompanied by a strike or lockout. As Table 9.1 shows, each of the four major North American sports has experienced a work stoppage since 1980.

At first glance, labor conflict seems inconsistent with the economic assumption that workers and firms behave rationally. Like wars and lawsuits, strikes and lockouts seem willfully to waste resources. For example, the NHL's 301-day lockout in 2004–2005 is widely credited with the imposition of a salary cap. The settlement came, however, only after the cancellation of the entire season and the attendant loss of team revenue and player salaries. Both team owners and players would have been better off if they had agreed to implement a salary cap at the beginning of the season and avoided the loss of income.

---

[26]The NFLPA has reserved the right to conduct salary negotiations in its collective bargaining agreement, but it has never exercised this right. See Staudohar, *Playing for Dollars* (1996), p. 67.

[27]For a direct comparison, see James Quirk and Rodney Fort, *Hardball* (Princeton: Princeton University Press, 1999), p. 68.

TABLE **9.1**

Labor Unrest in Professional Sports Since 1980

Year	MLB	NBA	NFL	NHL
1981	50-day strike			
1982			57-day strike	
1985	2-day strike			
1987			24-day strike	
1989	32-day lockout			
1992				10-day strike
1994–1995	232-day strike			103-day lockout
1998–1999		191-day lockout		
2004–2005				301-day lockout

In 2004, owners entered negotiations determined to install a salary cap, while the players were equally determined to avoid one. Thus, in the words of Paul Staudohar, "[T]he dispute was more about each side's philosophical approach than numbers."[28] As we have seen, when the parties disagree over such broad issues, they are less flexible in their positions and more uncertain about the implications of their positions. Seeking to avoid a strike during the post-season, when the players' leverage would be greatest, the owners locked out the players at the start of the 2004–2005 season. With neither side willing to budge, the standoff resulted in the cancellation of the season.

Economic Theory and Labor Conflict Economists reconcile strikes with rational behavior by acknowledging the role played by uncertainty. Uncertainty affects negotiations in one of two ways. If one side is overly pessimistic—either because it underestimates its own bargaining power or because it overstates the power of its opposition—it may settle for a less favorable agreement than it could have reached. If the participant errs on the side of optimism—overestimating its own bargaining power or understating the power of its opposition—conflict may result. Unduly optimistic perceptions of reality can prevent one or both parties from making the necessary concessions in time to prevent conflict. Uncertainty might be aggravated by a mistrust of the other side. If one party has reason to mistrust its counterpart, then it runs the risk of disregarding a truthful position.

If both labor and management know exactly how far they can push the other side, they can typically reach a settlement without resorting to conflict. Figure 9.8 illustrates how this might come about. In the figure, the union wants to push wages higher while the employer wants to drive wages lower. Unless labor and the employer are better off separating permanently, each side will be

---

[28]Paul Staudohar, "The Hockey Lockout of 2004–2005," *Monthly Labor Report,* December 2005, p. 26.

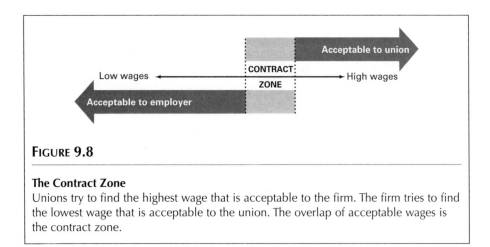

FIGURE 9.8

The Contract Zone
Unions try to find the highest wage that is acceptable to the firm. The firm tries to find the lowest wage that is acceptable to the union. The overlap of acceptable wages is the contract zone.

willing to accept a range of wages or salaries that is also acceptable to the other side. We have labeled this range of wages the **contract zone.**

The precise position of the contract zone depends on the two sides' threat points. If the union has strong alternative opportunities, then its threat point corresponds to a higher wage and the lower end of the contract zone moves to a higher wage, as shown in Figure 9.9a. If the firm has better alternatives, the upper end of the contract zone moves to a lower wage, as shown in Figure 9.9b.

The precise settlement depends on the bargaining strength of the two parties. A problem arises when workers, firms, or both do not know how far they can push the other side—or even how far they are willing to go themselves. When they are overly pessimistic, they are likely to concede too much and reach an unfavorable settlement.[29] When they are overly optimistic during negotiations, neither side proposes a settlement in the contract zone, and conflict results, as illustrated in Figure 9.9c.

Labor Conflict and Professional Sports   The unique position that sports unions play in negotiating broad frameworks rather than dollars and cents issues such as wages and salaries naturally leads to greater uncertainty and hence conflict. Most unions are legally prohibited from negotiating over "basic entrepreneurial decisions," which are the responsibility of management. Entrepreneurial decisions, such as revenue sharing and league expansion or contraction, however, are often at the heart of negotiations in professional sports.[30] For example, the NFLPA staged two strikes in the 1980s in an attempt to get the NFL to agree to

---

[29]See, for example, Beth Hayes, "Unions and Strikes with Asymmetric Information," *Journal of Labor Economics,* vol. 2, no. 1 (January 1984), pp. 57–84; and Michael A. Leeds, "Bargaining as Search Behavior Under Mutual Uncertainty," *Southern Economic Journal,* vol. 53, no. 3 (January 1987), pp. 677–684, for two different perspectives on the role uncertainty may play.

[30]Robert N. Covington, "(How Much) Is the Law To Blame for Baseball's Turbulent Labor Relations?," *Journal of Sports Economics,* vol. 4, no. 4 (November 2003), pp. 357–361.

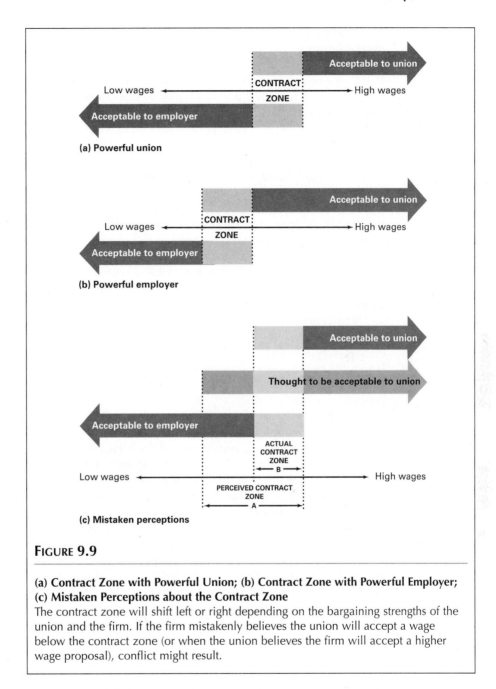

FIGURE 9.9

(a) Contract Zone with Powerful Union; (b) Contract Zone with Powerful Employer; (c) Mistaken Perceptions about the Contract Zone
The contract zone will shift left or right depending on the bargaining strengths of the union and the firm. If the firm mistakenly believes the union will accept a wage below the contract zone (or when the union believes the firm will accept a higher wage proposal), conflict might result.

free agency, which would have revolutionized the way in which salaries were determined. The high stakes involved led both sides to take more extreme positions than they otherwise would have. They also caused both sides to be less certain about the implications of their bargaining positions than would have been the case if they had been haggling over whether starting quarterbacks should be paid $5 million or $6 million per year.

Baseball's MLBPA often faced a unique source of uncertainty. Because baseball teams rely so heavily on local revenue, the owners often disagreed among themselves on the goals and strategies in their negotiations with the MLBPA. Big-market teams, such as the Yankees and Dodgers, were reluctant to implement changes designed to level the financial playing field. Because they played in such large markets, the big-market teams also lost much more gate and media revenue from a labor stoppage. As a result, they were eager to avoid prolonged conflict. Small-market teams, such as the Kansas City Royals or Milwaukee Brewers, had very different incentives. They pushed heavily for limits to the financial advantages of big-market teams and were willing to endure long work stoppages to implement such limits. The conflicting goals of the teams made it hard for MLB ownership to present a coherent bargaining position, which made it hard for the union to know where the other side stood.[31] The relative peace in MLB since the strike of 1995–1995 is due in part to the harmony that MLB Commissioner Bud Selig has been able to instill among the owners.

Strikes are particularly likely if the parties do not trust one another. Unfortunately, mistrust has been a frequent feature of labor relations in professional sports. Jerry McMorris, the former owner of the Colorado Rockies, once said of baseball's negotiations, "I never would have believed the level of mistrust and lack of confidence in each other. . . . It made it very difficult for people to compromise or experiment."[32]

The mistrust can sometimes be well-founded. For example, the NHL's 103-day work stoppage in 1994–1995 was due in part to the ill will created by one man: Alan Eagleson. As director of the NHLPA since its inception in 1967, Eagleson was responsible for representing the interests of the players. At the same time, Eagleson was director of a foundation that oversaw international hockey exhibitions, such as the Canada Cup series. Eagleson convinced NHL players to participate in these exhibitions without pay by assuring them that a percentage of revenue had been earmarked for the NHLPA pension fund. However, a 1989 investigation showed that the owners had misappropriated the funds with Eagleson's knowledge and approval. The NHLPA successfully sued the NHL for $50 million, and Eagleson, who resigned under fire from the NHLPA in 1992, was imprisoned on fraud and mail fraud charges.[33]

Negotiations between NHL players and owners in the mid-1990s were doomed from the beginning. First, the two sides were negotiating large,

---

[31]See Paul Staudohar, "Why No Baseball Work Stoppage?" *Journal of Sports Economics,* vol. 4, no. 4 (November 2003), pp. 362–366; Andrew Zimbalist, "Labor Relations in Major League Baseball," *Journal of Sports Economics,* vol. 4, no. 4 (November 2003), pp. 332-355; and John Helyar, *Lords of the Realm* (New York: Villard Books, 1994).

[32]Helyar (1994), p. 602.

[33]Jane O'Hara, "In the Name of Greed," *Maclean's* (January 19, 1998), pp. 22–24; and Staudohar, *Playing for Dollars* (1996), pp. 140–141.

defining issues, such as the creation of a salary cap. Second, both sides faced increased uncertainty due to the recent naming of Gary Bettman as new NHL Commissioner and Bob Goodenow as new executive director of the NHLPA. Finally, the players entered the negotiations still bitter over their betrayal by Eagleson and mistrustful of owners who had misallocated their pension funds. The two sides were unable to reach an agreement, and the 1994–1995 season began without a contract in place. Fearful that the players would strike on the eve of the playoffs, when their leverage would be greatest (and when they had held a 10-day strike in 1992), the owners staged a preemptive lockout.

Why Don't NFL Players Make More Money?

As we saw in Chapter 8, the average salary in the NFL was slightly higher than the average in MLB in 1978. By 2008, however, it fell to about two-thirds that of MLB. In part, NFL salaries have fallen behind because of factors beyond the players' control. However, the National Football League Players Association (NFLPA) has also made several missteps that it is still trying to overcome.

Structural Problems Facing the NFLPA As noted, in the 25 years that followed the granting of free agency in 1976, MLB owners had difficulty presenting a united front. One result of this disunity was the frequent strikes and lockouts that plagued MLB. In addition, the Major League Baseball Players Association was able to exploit these divisions to get its own way in negotiations. In contrast, the NFLPA faced a united ownership bloc. The "league-think" mentality instilled by Pete Rozelle in the 1960s and the leveling impact of the league-wide TV contract encouraged owners to adopt common goals and enabled them to work together to achieve them. The players, on the other hand, have often been a fractious group, forcing Gene Upshaw, Executive Director of the NFLPA from 1983 to 2008, to bridge gaps among the players while negotiating with the owners. In part, this is due to the sheer size of the union. NFL squads are more than twice as large as baseball and hockey teams and more than four times as large as basketball teams, making it more difficult for the NFLPA to adopt a common position and ensure unity in support of it.

The differences among players were exacerbated by a star system that favored players at the "skill positions" (players who touched the ball, such as receivers, running backs, and particularly quarterbacks) over other players. Unfortunately, for the union, the union leaders sometimes responded to this system in ways that inadvertently pitted players against one another.[34] The

---

[34]Unlike the leaders of the MLBPA, who stressed unity, Ed Garvey, the Executive Director of the NFLPA in the 1970s and 1980s, said that the union was "for the guards and tackles. The quarterbacks can take care of themselves." Quoted in Helyar, *Lords of the Realm* (1994), p. 311. See also Harris, *The League* (1992), pp. 165–166.

disunity of the players and the unity of the owners were crucial factors in the unsuccessful players' strike of 1987, the last job action in the NFL.[35]

Missteps by the NFLPA   In addition to some unavoidable obstacles, the NFLPA has inadvertently created some of its own. In 1976, the NFL players successfully sued the NFL for antitrust violations. The *Mackey* v. *National Football League* ruling unequivocally struck down the unilaterally-imposed Rozelle rule as a violation of the principles of collective bargaining.[36]

The NFLPA promptly fumbled away its victory, however, when it allowed the NFL to restore a modified form of the Rozelle rule in exchange for the NFL's agreeing to automatic payment of union dues from players' paychecks.[37]

Restoring the Rozelle rule, which replaced the whim of the commissioner with a fixed compensation formula, effectively reversed the *Mackey* ruling. Between 1977 and 1988, an average of more than 125 players per year filed for free agency. Only two of those players changed teams. The owners' unwillingness to bid for players is perhaps best exemplified by Walter Payton's experience. In 1981, Payton was on his way to becoming the NFL's all-time leading rusher, yet he found no takers except for his old team, the Chicago Bears.[38]

Recognizing its error, the NFLPA tried to win back free agency at the negotiating table and in the courts. It failed in both arenas. Seeing what free agency was doing to salaries in baseball and basketball, the owners had no intention of relaxing their grip on the Rozelle rule. While the courts were sympathetic to the players, they found that they could no longer intervene on the players' behalf. They ruled that, while the original Rozelle rule violated the collective bargaining agreement because the commissioner had imposed it unilaterally, the modified rule was the result of collective bargaining. The only way the union could win back free agency was through collective bargaining. Unsuccessful strikes in 1982 and 1987, however, showed that the union would not win free agency there either.

The only way out was for the NFLPA to disband, which it did in 1988. With no union, there was no collective bargaining agreement, and players were again free to sue the NFL on antitrust grounds.

This policy paid off in the 1992 *McNeil* v. *Pro Football, Inc.* decision, in which running back Freeman McNeil and seven other litigants were declared free agents.

---

[35]See Staudohar, *Playing for Dollars* (1996), p. 149; Paul Staudohar, "The Football Strike of 1987: The Question of Free Agency," *Monthly Labor Review*, vol. 111, no. 8 (August 1988), p. 27; Paul Staudohar, Professional Football and the Great Salary Dispute," *Personnel Journal*, vol. 61, no. 9 (September 1982), p. 675.

[36]An earlier lawsuit by former Minnesota Vikings quarterback Joe Kapp resulted in a bizarre court ruling that found that the Rozelle rule violated antitrust laws, but did not impose any damages on the NFL.

[37]Paying for Mackey's lawsuit had come close to bankrupting the NFLPA. See David Harris, *The League: The Rise and Decline of the NFL* (New York: Bantam Books, 1986) for an account of the *Mackey* decision's aftermath.

[38]James Quirk and Rodney Fort, *Pay Dirt* (Princeton, N.J.: Princeton University Press, 1992), p. 201.

In the wake of the ruling, the NFLPA quickly recertified and negotiated a new agreement with the league in 1993. Surprisingly, this agreement placed severe limits on free agency. It allowed players to become free agents only if they had at least four years of experience. It also permitted each team to designate one "franchise player" whom it could "reserve" as long as it paid him no less than the average of the top five salaries at his position.

Most significantly, the agreement instituted a salary cap. The salary cap agreement guaranteed players at least 58 percent of designated revenue (estimates have put designated revenue at about 95 percent of total revenue) in 1994. While this forced a few low-budget teams to increase their payrolls, it actually reduced the share of revenue going to labor. In 1993 the players had received 67 percent of league revenues. As a result, despite the presence of the rival WFL, USFL, and XFL, and despite being the most profitable of the major sports over the last two decades, average salaries in the NFL have lagged behind those in baseball and basketball.

Resurgent Ownership   Over the last three decades, players unions have won numerous victories over the leagues that employed them. However, in recent negotiations, owners have managed to insert limits on many sports. We have already seen that, following the lockout of 1998–1999, the NBA hardened the cap and placed limits on individual compensation as well as on team payrolls. In 2005, hockey owners were able to impose a salary cap that significantly lowered payrolls. Even baseball players saw some rolling back of the gains that their powerful union had won.

Until 2002, the MLBPA had never lost a job action. All previous strikes and lockouts had ended with the players either securing significant concessions or successfully defending previous gains. In 2002, however, the players faced several factors that they had never confronted. First, as noted earlier, the ownership was far more united than it had ever been. Second, after decades of steady expansion, the possibility of contraction was in the air, as owners had threatened to disband both the Montreal Expos and the Minnesota Twins. The negotiations ended with a clear victory for the owners, as they were able to institute a luxury tax and significantly increase revenue sharing. The 2006 bargaining agreement again avoided conflict and left management's gains largely intact.

Surprisingly for the league that has had the longest period of labor peace, the NFL entered the 2009 season facing the significant possibility of a strike. The owners had opted out of an extension to the 2006 agreement, which could have lasted until 2012, and the parties had to reach an agreement by 2010, or the salary cap would disappear. Unfortunately, the owners did not foresee two events when they chose to end the contract early. First, long-time NFLPA executive director Gene Upshaw died unexpectedly in 2008, and the new executive director, DeMaurice Smith, was not named until the spring of 2009. Second, the new contract would be the first for a major North American sports league since the advent of the 2008 financial crisis and resulting economic slowdown. The uncertainty caused by these two events created what one expert calls a "perfect

Strikes and lockouts have alienated many sports fans.

storm for a work stoppage."[39] Only time will tell whether the two sides can to find common ground without conflict.

Professional Tennis Associations

Individual sports, such as tennis or golf, also have associations that represent the interests of the players. These unions, however, differ from those in the team sports in several important ways. This section examines the unique aspects of the unions representing men and women tennis players. It also points out some differences in the goals of the men's and women's unions.

In 1968, the first year of "open" tennis, in which professionals and amateurs could both compete, the prize for winning the men's singles at Wimbledon was only £2,000. By 2008, the prize had risen to £750,000, an increase of 37,400 percent. The prizes in women's tennis had finally become as

---

[39]Gary Roberts, quoted in Tom van Riper, "Strike Risk Grows for NFL," Forbes.com, June 9, 2009, online at http://www.forbes.com/2009/06/09/nfl-players-union-business-sports-football.html.

large as for men, so their increase was even more spectacular, growing from £750 to £750,000.[40] Much of the increase can be attributed to the presence of two organizations, the Association of Tennis Professionals (ATP) and the Women's Tennis Association (WTA).

These two associations differ significantly from the associations we have discussed thus far. First, they are relatively young. Until the late 1960s the Grand Slam events—the Australian, French, and U.S. Open and Wimbledon—were known as Championships (Wimbledon's official name is the "All England Lawn Tennis Championship") and were restricted to amateurs. The participants were largely well-to-do men and women who played tennis for a few years before going on to what they regarded as their adult lives.[41] When these tournaments welcomed professional players, a wider array of people sought to make a living by playing tennis.[42] While recognition by the Grand Slam tournaments conveyed prestige on professional tennis, even today only a few tennis players could make a living on their winnings from that handful of major events. The players needed a body that would represent their interests to venues and sponsors who sought to hold professional tournaments. Unfortunately, the tournament committees at the time had been created by and for amateur players and were either inexperienced at dealing with professionals or outright hostile toward them. To fill this void, the men formed the ATP in 1972, while the women formed the WTA a year later.

Unlike the unions we have encountered so far, the ATP and WTA fairly closely resemble craft unions. Like craft unions, the ATP and WTA define who is and who is not a qualified employee. As we saw in Figure 9.5, craft unions increase the pay of their members by restricting the supply curve of labor. Like firms that come to a hiring hall to obtain labor, venues that wish to establish tournaments obtain different classes of labor by applying to the unions for a tournament of a given status. Higher-status tournaments with higher payments and better benefits then receive higher-quality players. Because they sanction the events in which players take part, the ATP and WTA have become synonymous with the men's and women's professional tennis tours. In fact, since 2005, the WTA has been known as The Sony Ericsson WTA Tour, though for brevity we shall refer to it as the WTA.

Like other unions in team sports, the ATP and WTA do not specify how much tournaments pay specific players. They do, however, establish the reward structure of the tournament so that all players know what they will earn from a particular performance. They also negotiate all aspects of the "working

---

[40]Figures from "Prize Money" at *Wimbledon: The Official Site,* online at http://aeltc.wimbledon.org/en_GB/about/history/prizemoney_history.html.

[41]See E. Digby Baltzell, *Sporting Gentlemen: Men's Tennis form the Age of Honor to the Cult of the Superstar* (New York: The Free Press, 1995), for a highly entertaining, if very opinionated, history of men's tennis.

[42]By the 1960s, many of the tournaments were offering so many benefits and side payments to players that detractors called the participants "shamateurs." See Baltzell, *Sporting Gentlemen* (1995), pp. 335–336.

conditions" of each tournament, from the types of hotel rooms the players occupy, to the uniforms of the "ballpersons," to the nature of the bathroom facilities in the locker rooms. The ATP and WTA rulebooks, which specify these regulations, are themselves significant. Unlike the major North American team sports, tennis players have a rulebook rather than a collective bargaining agreement. The source of this difference lies in the fact that the ATP and WTA do not engage in negotiations with a single management group. Instead, they set rules for employers who wish to hire tennis players for a tournament, much like construction unions (a typical craft union) set rules for developers who wish to construct offices or apartment buildings.

Also unlike most other unions, the ATP and WTA are strictly segregated by sex. In part, this is because men and women do not play against one another (except in mixed doubles). In fact, except for the Grand Slam and a few other similar events, men and women do not even compete in the same venues. Moreover, the needs of women who play tennis professionally differ significantly from the needs of men. These needs are reflected in the differing regulations spelled out in the organizations' rulebooks. The differences between rules that govern the men's and women's tennis tours range from vitally important—the WTA, for example, specifies how long a woman may retain her status on the tour after having a child, while the ATP rulebook makes no mention of children—to the seemingly trivial—the WTA rulebook mentions "changes of attire" fifteen times, while the ATP rulebook mentions it only once.[43]

---

[43]ATP Tour, Inc. "The 2006 ATP Official Rulebook," on line at http://www.atptennis.com/en/common/TrackIt.asp?file=/en/players/ATP_Rulebook.pdf}; Sony Ericsson WTA Tour, "The Sony Ericsson WTA Tour 2006 Official Rulebook," online at http://www.sonyericssonwtatour.com/global/pdfs/shared/thewtatour/officialrules/rules.pdf.

BIOGRAPHICAL SKETCH

MARVIN MILLER

*Man, don't the owners know that there's going to be a whole generation of ballplayers'
sons who grow up with the middle name Marvin?*
—New York Yankees pitcher Rudy May[1]

When reporters first asked Marvin Miller why he had gone from being chief economist of the United Steelworkers (USW), one of the nation's foremost unions, to heading a ragtag players association that did not even have a permanent office, he had a simple response for them: "'I grew up in Brooklyn,' I said, 'not far from Ebbets Field.' . . . Heads nodded. No further explanation was required."[2] Further explanation *is* required, however, of a man who almost single-handedly overthrew the powers of one of the most powerful monopolies in America and transformed the face of professional sports. In so doing, Marvin Miller evolved from a man who might be the subject of an occasional dissertation on the history of unions to one of the towering figures in professional sports.

Miller did grow up in the shadow of Ebbets Field, the son of a storekeeper and a teacher in the New York public school system. He got his first taste of labor relations during World War II when he worked at the National War Labor Board, which adjudicated union–management disputes as part of labor's pledge not to impede the war effort by going on strike.

After the war, Miller worked at a variety of jobs with little clear direction when, in 1950, Otis Brubaker, the research director at the United Steelworkers and an acquaintance from the National War Labor Board, asked Miller to join his staff at the USW. Miller found a home at the USW and worked his way up to becoming the USW's chief economist and assistant to the union's president,

David J. McDonald. Ironically, Miller's most notable accomplishment at USW was the creation of a "productivity sharing plan" at Kaiser Steel that became a model for promoting good union–management relations and preventing conflict.

In 1965, however, I. W. Abel defeated McDonald in a hotly contested union election that centered on McDonald's reliance on "technicians," such as Miller, rather than elected officials. With his future at USW uncertain, Miller was intrigued when several player representatives approached him about becoming the first full-time executive director of the Major League Baseball Players Association.

The road to becoming director, however, was not smooth. In a full vote, the player representatives chose their part-time director, Robert W. Cannon, instead. When Cannon attached additional conditions to becoming full-time director, refusing, for example, to move from his office in Milwaukee to New York, the players turned to Miller as their second choice. Even then, Miller's selection was far from certain, as he had to secure the approval of the full membership. Egged on by owners who viewed him as a rabble-rousing union boss, the players were skeptical. The Cleveland Indians' manager, Birdie Tebbetts, openly asked Miller, "How can the players be sure you're not a Communist?" After a rocky start—Miller was voted down by the players at the Arizona spring training facilities 102–17 before being approved overwhelmingly by the players at the Florida camps—Miller quickly earned the players' approval and then their fierce devotion.

continued

Miller viewed the MLBPA as a chance to practice principles of democratic unionism that would have been so hard to implement in a huge union such as the USW. He won the players' confidence not by using the sophisticated arguments that Ed Garvey used with the football players or by intimidating the players like Alan Eagleson did in hockey, but by listening. He made a point of meeting every player during spring training and meeting every team's player representative at least four times a year. These meetings, moreover, were not intended to rubber stamp prearranged positions. The meetings were often lengthy, untidy affairs with players arguing with Miller and each other at great length. The one rule that Miller imposed was that the players had to leave the

meeting unified. "'Anything less than 100 percent is unacceptable,' was his unshakable motto."[3] The result was a union that managed to do what many thought impossible, overturn the reserve clause when it lacked any legal standing to do so.

[1]Quoted Helyar, *Lords of the Realm* (New York: Villard Books, 1994), p. 239.
[2]Quoted in Marvin Miller, *A Whole Different Ballgame* (New York: Carol Publishing Group, 1991). pp. 11–12.
[3]Helyar, *Lords of the Realm* (1994), p. 84.

Sources: James Dworkin, *Owners versus Players:* Baseball and Collective Bargaining (Boston: Auburn House, 1981); Korr, "Marvin Miller and the New Unionism in Baseball" (1991); Miller, *A Whole Different Ballgame* (1991); and Helyar, *Lords of the Realm* (1994).

Summary

Labor markets in the four major North American sports leagues were marked by significant monopsony power for most of the 20th century. As the sole buyer, a monopsony can drive down the price it pays. The reserve clause, the main source of monopsony power, bound players to the team that held their contract for as long as the team wanted them. By 1976, however, all four sports had discarded the reserve clause and had adopted some form of free agency. Leagues have tried to limit the impact of free agency in a number of ways. Salary caps have proven effective at both limiting player salaries and at reducing the differences in team payrolls.

Unlike unions elsewhere in the economy, unions in professional sports have proven remarkably successful at organizing their workforce. The sports industry has also experienced far more labor conflict than have other labor markets. Economists have difficulty explaining conflict, as it seems to defy rational behavior. When one accounts for uncertainty, however, one can explain strikes as a mistake by one or both of the negotiating parties.

Some unions have proven more successful than others at promoting the interests of their players. The NFLPA has had trouble keeping pace with other unions, notably the MLBPA. Some of these problems have been unavoidable, while others have been the result of mistaken policies by the union.

Professional tennis players have established their own associations. These unions resemble craft unions in that they set out rules for players that limit the supply of labor and rules for employers (tournaments) that seek to hire players. Unlike most craft unions, the tennis unions are strictly segregated by sex.

Discussion Questions

1. Are salary caps good for professional sports? Would you want to have a salary cap in your job? If your answers differ, how do you justify the different answers?
2. Are unions good or bad for professional sports?
3. Should the government step in when there is a strike or lockout in professional sports?

Problems

9.1 Give an economic interpretation of the deadweight loss in Figure 9.1.

9.2 How did the Rozelle Rule subvert free agency in the NFL?

9.3 Would a craft union or an industrial union be more inclined to argue against the designated hitter? Why?

9.4 Suppose that Congress repeals MLB's exemption from the antitrust laws. How might this affect the contract zone between MLB and the MLBPA?

9.5 MLB has adopted final offer arbitration because it fears that regular binding arbitration is addictive. In what way can binding arbitration be addictive? Why isn't FOA addictive?

9.6 Explain how each of the following would affect the NHLPA's bargaining position.
   a. A new professional league is formed in Russia.
   b. A change in the tax laws increases the profitability of owning stock and decreases the profitability of owning a sports franchise.

9.7 In what way are sports unions like craft unions? In what way are they like industrial unions? In what way do they differ from both?

9.8 Use what you have learned in this chapter to explain why "journeymen" in MLB earn 86 percent of their *MRP* while "apprentices" earn only 19 percent.

9.9 Why has labor conflict been much more common in hockey in recent years than in baseball?

9.10 Use supply and demand curves to show how the ATP and the WTA increased the prize money offered on the men's and women's professional tennis tours.

CHAPTER 10

Discrimination

The biggest thing I don't like about New York are the foreigners. I'm not a very big fan of foreigners. How the hell did they get in this country? I'm not a racist or prejudiced person, but certain people bother me.

—JOHN ROCKER, FORMER MAJOR LEAGUE PITCHER[1]

I was raised on the beliefs of my father, my uncle, and Dr. Martin Luther King which, in essence, are "Don't do me any favors. Let's agree on what the rules are, and then judge me fairly."

—ARTHUR ASHE[2]

Introduction

On April 18, 1946, in a minor league game between the Montreal Royals and the Jersey City Little Giants, Jackie Robinson crossed the color line and became the first African American baseball player since the 1880s to play professional baseball in the "major leagues." His first at bat, a ground ball to the Jersey City shortstop, ended more than 50 years of segregated professional baseball in the United States.[3] Almost exactly one year later, on April 15, 1947, he took the field as a Brooklyn Dodger. Over the objections of many fans, players, and owners, Dodgers' president Branch Rickey had reintegrated baseball. Three months after Robinson broke the color barrier in the National League, Larry Doby became the first black to play in the American League when Bill Veeck signed him to a contract with the Cleveland Indians. Doby suffered much of the same treatment as

---

[1]Jeff Pearlman, "At Full Blast," *Sports Illustrated* (December 27, 1999–January 3, 2000), pp. 62–64.

[2]Francis Dealey, *Win at Any Cost: The Sell Out of College Athletics* (New York: Birch Lane Press, 1990), p. 101.

[3]He did, however, hit a home run later in the same game. From Robert Peterson, *Only the Ball Was White: A History of Legendary Black Players and All-Black Professional Teams* (New York: Gramercy Books, 1970), p. 194.

Robinson, including endless streams of insults from fans and players alike, death threats, and segregated hotels and restaurants that prevented him from staying and eating with his teammates. It is remarkable that Robinson and Doby flourished despite the tense atmosphere in which they played. While baseball's history of discrimination against black players is surely the most widely known case of discrimination in sports, it is by no means the only one. Just as discrimination has long been a source of concern in almost every walk of life, it has been an issue in virtually every sport. The purpose of this chapter is to show how economists study and measure discrimination and to discuss a few instances when those methods have uncovered significant evidence that discrimination exists in the sports industry. Thus, there is a chance you may come away from this material with the perception that discrimination in professional sports is widespread. In fact, most current research finds that players' opportunities are remarkably free from discrimination.[4] For example, the *Racial and Gender Report Card*, which is published annually by The Institute for Diversity and Ethics in Sport at the University of Central Florida, gives the NFL, NBA, MLS (Major League Soccer), WNBA, and MLB straight A+'s for their performance in racial equity among players (the report did not include the NHL).[5] Although the report generally graded the leagues lower in areas such as coaching and management, these grades indicate that widespread systemic discrimination against players is a thing of the past.

As we explore discrimination in professional and college sports, we need to distinguish between prejudice, which is a feeling or emotion, and discrimination, which is an action. A simple economic definition of discrimination is the "unequal treatment of equals."[6] This chapter focuses solely on the economic effects of discrimination in the labor market. Thus, we use human capital theory and productivity data to discuss the existence, measurement, and changes in discrimination over time. The underlying question for all studies in this area is whether people of different demographic groups are evaluated and rewarded solely on the basis of their productivity.

Economists who study discrimination usually focus on two areas of inquiry. The first is whether equally qualified people have equal access to labor markets. This issue can be summarized as *equal access to work*. For example, if only whites are allowed to play quarterback in the NFL, or if only men are allowed to work as referees in the NBA, we would say that blacks and women

---

[4]A good overview of studies of discrimination in sports can be found in Lawrence M. Kahn, "The Sports Business as a Labor Market Laboratory," *Journal of Economic Perspectives*, vol. 14, no. 3 (Summer 2000), pp. 75–94.

[5]The Institute for Diversity and Ethics in Sport, Richard Lapchick, Director. Richard Lapchick, et al., *The 2008 Racial and Gender Report Card: Major League Soccer; The 2008 Racial and Gender Report Card: The National Football League; The 2009 Racial and Gender Report Card: Major League Baseball; The 2009 Racial and Gender Report Card: National Basketball Association;* and *The 2008 Racial and Gender Report Card: The Women's National Basketball Association,* all online at http://www.tidesport.org/racialgenderreportcard.html. Accessed July 20, 2009.

[6]*MIT Dictionary of Economics,* 3rd edition, ed. by David W. Pearce (Cambridge, Mass.: The MIT Press, 1986), p. 109.

do not have equal access to these labor markets. The second issue, *equal pay for equal work,* asks whether equally qualified workers in identical positions are paid equally. For example, if French-Canadian hockey players were paid less than English-speaking Canadian players of equal ability, our second criterion would be violated.

This chapter explains the following:

- Why an owner who discriminates against black players suffers economically for his actions

- How discrimination in sports may stem from owners, players, fans, or all three at once

- Why black players in the NBA might be the victims of discrimination even when they earn more than white players

- How laws protect and encourage women's sports at the collegiate and scholastic level.

Nobel Prize–winning economist Gary Becker, whose work on human capital is discussed in Chapter 8, also made major contributions to the way economists view discrimination. We focus much of our attention on his model. The next section describes how Becker's model approaches and measures discrimination. Section 10.2 applies the Becker model to discrimination in professional sports, introduces a method by which economists measure discrimination, and reviews some of the important empirical studies. Section 10.3 discusses discrimination at the collegiate level and recent legislation designed to increase athletic opportunities for women.

10.1 Becker's Theory of Labor Discrimination

Before focusing on the economics of discrimination, we should acknowledge that economics is not the only lens through which one can view discrimination. The economic approach to discrimination is relatively new. In fact, before Gary Becker introduced the neoclassical theory of discrimination in his groundbreaking book, *The Economics of Discrimination,* in 1957, economists had generally left the field to other disciplines.[7] Psychologists and sociologists have spent a great deal of time studying discrimination and its roots. From the perspective of social psychology, discrimination is the result of a three-part process that begins with prejudice. Prejudice is a multifaceted form of group identification, based on an attitude not supported by facts. It has an *affective* component, meaning that it is based on feeling or emotions—an irrational feeling of negativity toward another group. To say that you are part of one group, say African Americans, and someone else is not, makes them somehow different from you.

---

[7]Gary S. Becker, *The Economics of Discrimination,* 2nd edition (Chicago: University of Chicago Press, 1971).

The affective component is not rational because of the assumption that "different" is "inferior." The *cognitive* component is the assignment of a single set of characteristics to all members of a group, creating a stereotype. To say, for example, that all blondes are dumb is a stereotype. Finally, the *behavioral* component translates prejudices based on stereotypes into actions. To disallow all Jews membership in a club is a discriminatory action.[8] The economic approach to the study of discrimination we discuss here is consistent with this multifaceted approach. However, economists focus much more on the outcome of discrimination than its origin. A more radical political–economic theory is the Marxist view, which regards discrimination as a tool used by capitalists to divide the working class.

The theory Becker developed differs from the social–psychological approach and the Marxist approach in that he saw neither irrationality nor plots. Instead, he introduced the concept of a **taste for discrimination.** Tastes are one of the basic building blocks of economic theory. As such, they are generally not questioned. It is possible, however, to alter people's decisions regardless of their tastes.[9] To see the futility of challenging tastes, ask a friend what his favorite flavor of ice cream is. When he responds, ask him why he chose that flavor (say, peach). He will probably say something like, "Because peach tastes good." Now try asking him why peach tastes better than chocolate chip. Odds are he will shrug his shoulders and say he does not know why, or he will offer a variant on "because it tastes good."

Your friend's inability to explain the reasons behind his tastes does not mean that you cannot alter his actions. If you offer your friend a large enough cash payment along with the chocolate chip ice cream or charge a high enough price for the peach ice cream, you might convince him to eat the flavor that he does not most prefer. Becker's central insight was that people could have a taste for discrimination just like they can have a taste for a specific flavor of ice cream. People have a taste for discrimination if they act as if they are willing to pay to associate with one group rather than another.

Rather than wrestle with the complexity of the roots and mechanics of prejudice, Becker's theory allows economists to focus directly on behavior. It uses money to measure a person's taste for discrimination, avoiding problems associated with uncovering why someone discriminates. With this definition, testing for the presence of and measuring the results of discrimination are fairly straightforward. In addition, Becker's theory enables analysts to predict how discrimination affects the people who practice it and who are victimized by it.

---

[8]For a more complete introduction to discrimination and prejudice from the perspective of social psychology, see, for example, Eliot Aronson, Timothy D. Wilson, and Robin M. Akert, *Social Psychology: The Heart and Mind* (New York: HarperCollins, 1994).

[9]A classic treatment of tastes and how economists regard them can be found in George Stigler and Gary Becker, "De Gustibus Non Est Disputandum," *American Economic Review,* vol. 67, no. 1 (March 1977), pp. 76–90.

In labor markets, the payment a discriminator makes to avoid associating with another group can take many forms, such as lower profits, higher prices, or lower wages. We distinguish among these payments because the source of discrimination and the nature of the payment depends on which party (if any) gains and which party loses.

10.2 Different Forms of Discrimination in Professional Sports

This section describes how employers, employees, and consumers practice discrimination. Although in each case we use money to measure discrimination, we shall see that the Becker model is based on utility maximization. As people with a taste for discrimination maximize their utility, their willingness to pay in order to indulge their tastes has a variety of effects on the market. In addition, the structure of the market has important implications for both the discriminator and the groups that are discriminated against.

Employer Discrimination

Because it is based on utility maximization, Becker's model takes a broader view of the firm than simple profit maximization. For example, an employer may be willing to sacrifice profits in order to avoid associating with a group of people that reduces his or her utility. Because a firm may be willing to sacrifice profits in order to satisfy the owner's taste for discrimination, we can make specific predictions regarding firms that discriminate in both competitive and monopoly or monopsony markets. We discuss this outcome below in greater detail, as it has a significant bearing on the persistence of discrimination in the marketplace.

Most people associate labor market discrimination with employers who refuse to hire women or minorities or who do not pay them wages commensurate with their abilities. In this case, employers have a set of preferences regarding employees with whom they do and do not want to associate. For example, there is an ongoing debate in the sports economics literature regarding discrimination against French-speaking hockey players (Francophones).[10] Many studies claim that whether a team discriminates depends in part on the players' positions—whether they are forwards or defensemen—and where the team is located. One study found evidence of employer discrimination against French-speaking defensemen but not forwards.[11] Another study found evidence of

---

[10]One study is Neil Longley, "The Underrepresentation of French Canadians on English Canadian Teams," *Journal of Sports Economics*, vol. 1, no. 3 (August 2000), pp. 236–256. Marc Lavoie, Gilles Grenier, and Serge Columbe have written several papers that support the hypothesis of discrimination. Several appeared in the journal *Canadian Public Policy—Analyse de Politiques*: issues vol. 13, no. 4 (December 1987), pp. 407–422; vol. 15, no. 1 (1989); and vol. 18, no. 4 (December 1992), pp. 461–469.

[11]J. C. H. Jones and W. D. Walsh, "Salary Determination in the National Hockey League: The Effects of Skills, Franchise Characteristics, and Discrimination," *Industrial and Labor Relations Review*, vol. 44, no. 4 (July 1988), pp. 592–604.

French Canadian Maxim Lapierre

discrimination only by teams based in the English-speaking provinces of Canada.[12]

There is general agreement among researchers that French-speaking Canadians have a different style of play than English-speaking Canadians. Many believe that French-speaking Canadians are more offense oriented and are less likely to engage in fights during the game than their English-speaking Canadian counterparts. The disagreement over whether teams discriminate stems from differences in the samples chosen and the measurement of defensive ability.

To simplify matters, assume that there are only two groups of players, English-speaking (E) and French-speaking (F). To keep the focus on discrimination, assume for the moment that although the players' styles may be different, they are equally

---

[12]Neil Longley, "Salary Discrimination in the National Hockey League: The Effects of Location," *Canadian Public Policy—Analyse de Politiques*, vol. 21, no. 4 (December 1995), pp. 413–422. Others dispute these claims, criticizing the statistical analysis. See William D. Walsh, "The Entry Problem of Francophones in the National Hockey League: A Systematic Interpretation," *Canadian Public Policy—Analyse de Politiques*, vol. 18, no. 4 (December 1992), pp. 443–460, for a critique of Lavoie, Grenier, and Columbe. See Michael Krashinsky and Harry D. Krashinsky, "Do English Canadian Hockey Teams Discriminate Against French Canadian Players?" *Canadian Public Policy—Analyse de Politiques*, vol. 23, no. 2 (June 1997), pp. 212–216, and Longley's reply that immediately follows in the same issue (pp. 217–220).

productive. This way, in the absence of discrimination, demand for the two types of players would be equal. Becker measures the distaste that owners have for French-speaking players with a **discrimination coefficient** (d_F). The discrimination coefficient is greater than zero if an owner feels that he pays an emotional (or *psychic*) cost in addition to the wage when he employs a French-speaking player. When hiring, he acts as if the wage were w for all E workers and $w(1 + d_F)$ for all F's. If NHL owners have a taste for discrimination and prefer hiring English-speaking Canadians to hiring French-speaking Canadians, the demand for English-speaking Canadians (D_E) will be greater than that for French-speaking Canadians (D_F). In Figure 10.1a, we assume that there is an equal supply of each type of player ($S_E = S_F$). The difference in demand based on employer preferences, however, leads to a difference in wages as well as a difference in the number of players hired.

If the supply of English-speaking Canadians is greater than that of French-speaking Canadians, or the taste for discrimination (that creates the differences in demand) is great enough, teams may hire no French-speaking Canadians. That is, there would be unequal access to work. To use an example from other sports, the National and American Leagues in baseball hired no blacks at all between 1890 and 1947. Alternatively, if there were no discrimination at all, we could simply add the two supply curves in Figure 10.1a to arrive at the market

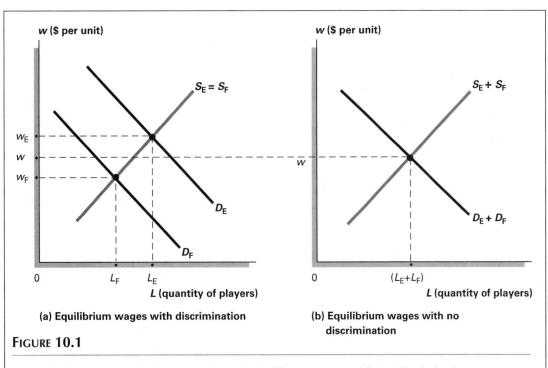

(a) Equilibrium wages with discrimination

(b) Equilibrium wages with no discrimination

FIGURE 10.1

(a) Equilibrium Wages with Discrimination; (b) Equilibrium Wages with No Discrimination
Panel (a) shows that, with an equal number of both groups of players but differential demand based on discrimination, wages for French-speaking players will be lower than for English-speaking players. In Panel (b), owners have no taste for discrimination and wages. Thus, w is the equilibrium wage for all players.

supply and add the two demand curves (which would be identical) to get the market demand, and players would be hired from the market supply without regard to race, as in Figure 10.1b.

Suppose that Jake, the owner of an NHL club, is evaluating, drafting, and signing players. Two players, Eddie and François, perform identically on every skill test, play the same position, and have identical past experience. From a productivity standpoint, they are perfect substitutes. Either player would sign a contract for $500,000 per season. However, during the interview process, Jake discovers that, although François has no trouble communicating with his English-speaking teammates, his primary language is French. Jake now separates the prospects into two groups: Eddie is an E, and François is an F. Because he has a taste for discrimination against all F's, Jake's discrimination coefficient is a positive number, say 0.2. Thus, when making his final decision, Jake feels as if he were paying Eddie $w_E = \$500,000$, and François $w_F = \$500,000(1 + 0.2) = \$600,000$. Jake does not actually pay the extra $100,000, but his desire to not be associated with French-speaking players makes him feel as though he were paying the extra, psychic cost.[13]

Jake does incur additional cost, however, if the increase in demand for E's increases their wages above $500,000. If enough owners have a taste for discrimination against F's, the market for players will be similar to that shown in Figure 10.1a, and owners with a taste for discrimination will pay higher wages than those without.

Discriminating clearly makes the team owner worse off financially. If Jake's taste for discrimination against F players makes the psychic and monetary wage of group F players greater than w_E, he will not hire any players from group F. Jake is happier paying w_E to fill his roster with English speakers than he is paying a mixed team the competitive wage w. The economic cost of employing only English speakers depends on the elasticities of supply and demand or, more simply, the relative slopes of the supply and demand curves. For example, if the supply of E players is perfectly elastic (a horizontal line), then owners will not have to increase w_E at all when they hire more of them.

However, even prejudiced owners may employ F players if the players are willing to work for wages that are low enough. For example, in the previous example, Jake's discrimination coefficient makes him feel that he is paying a wage premium of 20 percent. If the F's are willing to work for 20 percent less than E's, Jake would be willing to hire them. In this case, the result would be unequal pay for equal work.

If the market for players is not competitive because players are not homogeneous, Jake may also end up with a mixed team. For simplicity, suppose E's and F's consist of good players (E_g and F_g) and bad players (E_b and F_b). If the E_g's are relatively scarce, Jake may exhaust the supply of E_g's, and he must choose between the less productive E_b's and the more productive F_g's. In such a case, Jake may maximize his utility by hiring some F_g's.

---

[13]As noted above, the Becker model does not address the issue of *why* the owner feels this way. We discuss later the question of why people might develop tastes for discrimination.

Discrimination clearly makes players in group *F* worse off. *F*'s receive no offers as long as employers feel they pay *F*'s more than the wage of players in group *E*. Even if *F*'s are hired, they receive lower offers than equally productive *E*'s. *E* players are better off as a group because their chances of making the team, and their pay if they do, both increase. Although owners avoid associating with group *F* players, they pay for the privilege in the form of reduced profits. We stress that owners are worse off *financially* and not that they are worse off overall. Owners who discriminate do so in order to maximize utility. In this case, utility maximization comes at the cost of reduced income.

Statistical Discrimination It is also necessary to admit that differences in average performance across groups may exist. For example, it may be the case that, on *average,* French-speaking Canadian players have better offensive statistics and lesser defensive statistics in college or junior hockey (the stepping stone to the NHL for most Canadian players) than their English-speaking Canadian counterparts. The problem is that group averages are just that. They mask the individual variation *within* groups. Thus, each player must be judged on his own merits, rather than those of the group to which he belongs. The use of group averages to judge individual productivity levels is called **statistical discrimination.**[14] Statistical discrimination differs from discrimination that stems from tastes and preferences, because it is based on incomplete information rather than on the utility-maximizing choices of people with accurate information.

While it does not result from prejudice, statistical discrimination can have a very strong impact on a team's hiring practices. Consider, for example, a team that believes that a young French Canadian player has a 49 percent chance of being a successful player in the NHL, while a young English-speaking Canadian has a 51 percent chance of success. That team would not seek to have an almost equal split of French-speaking and English-speaking players. Because the team believes that any one English-speaking player is more likely to be good than any one French-speaking player, it will seek to hire only English speakers, at least until the pay differential becomes so great that the team is willing (in its eyes) to take on worse players.

Statistical discrimination is troublesome for two reasons. First, it may be profit-maximizing behavior on the part of firms. Even though assuming that each French-speaking Canadian player is weaker defensively than each English-speaking Canadian is not always accurate, teams may be correct on average if they always use this assumption when choosing players. Thus they may feel justified in acting as discriminators. Second, statistical discrimination

---

[14]In the case of ethnicity, players are not able to switch groups. In some cases, however, employees may be able to switch from a less preferred group to a more preferred group in an attempt to signal to potential employers that they are highly productive. For example, a college degree may signal to employers that a person is highly productive. Employers would want potential employees to send this signal if it is costly to find out the truth about whether they are highly productive. For a detailed explanation of signaling, see Michael A. Spence, "Job Market Signaling," *Quarterly Journal of Economics,* vol. 87, no. 3 (August 1973), pp. 355–374.

can become a self-fulfilling prophecy. If offensive-minded French-speaking Canadian forwards are drafted and defensive-minded ones are not, over time, league statistics will reflect that French-speaking Canadians are offensive minded. Unfortunately, this means that statistical discrimination and its consequences can occur even if the initial difference in offensive versus defensive ability stemmed from inaccurate perceptions.

Does Anyone Win with Employer Discrimination?

As noted above, one group that certainly loses from the presence of discrimination is the employees who are the victims of discrimination. Employers lose profits but do so willingly in order to maximize utility. To see if any groups benefit economically from the employers' taste for discrimination, consider the case of racial discrimination in Major League Baseball. Blacks were effectively barred from organized baseball from 1888 to 1947 by a "gentlemen's agreement." Many black players who were good enough to play in the major leagues—some of them good enough to be admitted to baseball's Hall of Fame—were relegated to the Negro Leagues, which lasted until the late 1950s.[15] Such players were certainly worse off.

One group that benefited from discrimination was white players of that era. Because blacks were excluded, more white players played in the major leagues than would have been possible otherwise. For purposes of illustration, we begin by assuming that all players are equally productive (homogeneous) and subsequently consider the more realistic case of variation in player quality. If all labor was equally productive, and 30 percent of the available labor force was black, in the absence of discrimination, 30 percent of the players would be black. If there was a very large pool of available labor, the market supply curve of players would have been a horizontal line, as shown in Figure 10.2. Players' wages would be set at the market level at w. In this case, the labor force is so large relative to demand that the labor supply curve for white players only (S_w) still results in the same wage. Because employers have a taste for discrimination, no blacks will be hired and employment of whites will be much greater than if there were no discrimination.

In practice, players are not homogeneous. Players vary greatly in ability. If an employer has a taste for discrimination against black players, and the quality of players of both races varies, that team owner will choose marginal white players over blacks of greater ability to fill out their rosters. In this case, white players of marginal ability would be the beneficiaries of the owners' taste for discrimination. Even with no formal or informal color line, as long as the decrease in marginal revenue product that results from hiring a less-skilled white player is less than the wage premium, an owner would feel that he or she is paying a black player more based on his or her taste for discrimination, and the white player would be hired.

---

[15]For an excellent history of the Negro Leagues, see Peterson, *Only the Ball Was White: A History of Legendary Black Players and All-Black Professional Teams* (1970).

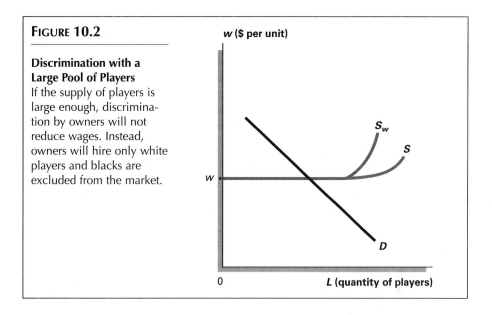

FIGURE 10.2

Discrimination with a Large Pool of Players
If the supply of players is large enough, discrimination by owners will not reduce wages. Instead, owners will hire only white players and blacks are excluded from the market.

While white players would be expected to benefit and black players to be hurt by the color line, one set of beneficiaries may come as a surprise. The color line allowed owners of Negro League baseball teams—themselves largely African American—to draw on a large pool of captive talent.[16] In addition, demand for Negro League baseball was much greater than it would have been with integrated major leagues. Figures 10.3 and 10.4 show that black fans' desire to see black players reduced their demand for major league baseball and increased their demand for Negro League baseball. In each case, D_S represents the level of demand for tickets when the leagues were segregated, and D_I represents the demand for tickets when leagues were integrated. If each league plays a set schedule, the supply curve is a vertical line. Integration brings higher prices in the major leagues and lower prices in the Negro Leagues.

To see the Negro Leagues' reliance on segregation, one need look no further than the demise of the Negro Leagues after Robinson and other Negro League stars jumped leagues. Attendance dropped sharply, and in 1947, nearly every team lost money. By 1950, all but five major league teams had integrated. As Negro League teams lost increasing numbers of talented young players to the major leagues, gate receipts dwindled, teams folded, and a chief source of revenue became the sale of rights to their players to the major leagues. Player salaries for those that remained in the Negro Leagues dropped by about 50 percent, to as low as $200 per month. Despite valiant efforts to keep the league going, in 1960 it finally folded.[17]

---

[16]While the word *Negro* is no longer used to describe African Americans, historians and economists still use the term *Negro Leagues* to describe the collection of all-black teams that competed in the era when baseball was segregated.

[17]Peterson, *A History of Legendary Black Players and All-Black Professional Teams* (1970), pp. 203–204.

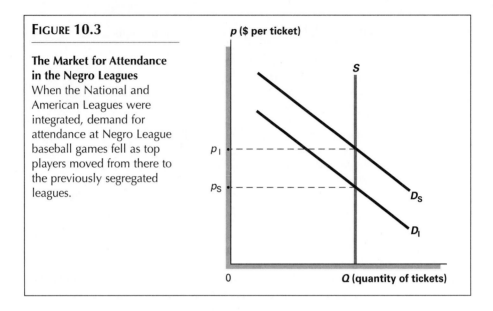

FIGURE 10.3

The Market for Attendance in the Negro Leagues
When the National and American Leagues were integrated, demand for attendance at Negro League baseball games fell as top players moved from there to the previously segregated leagues.

How Competition Can Eliminate Discrimination Becker's theory implies that less discriminatory employers will be more successful than highly discriminatory employers. Suppose, for example, that because of their taste for discrimination, discriminatory employers are willing to pay blacks $10 per hour and whites $15 per hour. A potential employer who does not have any prejudice ($d = 0$) can enter and undercut any employer who uses white labor

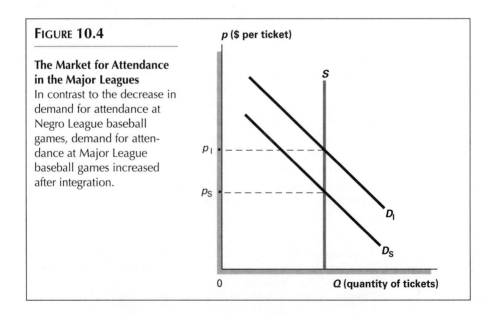

FIGURE 10.4

The Market for Attendance in the Major Leagues
In contrast to the decrease in demand for attendance at Negro League baseball games, demand for attendance at Major League baseball games increased after integration.

by hiring only blacks and paying them $11 per hour. Continued entry by unprejudiced employers increases the wage paid to black workers, driving down the profits available to potential entrants. If there are enough unprejudiced employers, black workers' wages rise until the wages of blacks and whites are equal. At this point, all prejudiced employers either stop acting on their prejudices or are driven from the market. In professional sports, although the markets are not perfectly competitive, the competition to win games and championships can be viewed as a powerful motivating force for owners to overcome their prejudices in order to maximize team quality. Allen Barra relates an example of how the pressure to win can overcome prejudice in his biography of legendary Alabama football coach Paul "Bear" Bryant. After reading a news account of Bryant's claim that African Americans would eventually play for Alabama, a fan remarked, "Well, I hope there're some Negro linebackers available. We need linebackers."[18]

A quick review of baseball's history supports the hypothesis that discriminators pay a price measured in wins for indulging their tastes. Historically, employers that integrated their teams more quickly have generally won more games than those that were slower to integrate. For example, the Dodgers, who led the way to racial integration of the National League, won NL pennants in 1947 and 1949, and five pennants in the 1950s. The Giants, who ranked second, won pennants in 1951 and 1954. In fact, over the course of the 1950s, five of the six most successful teams (in terms of winning percentages) were the five teams that integrated most quickly.[19] Only the Yankees stood among the top teams in the 1950s with a relatively low percentage of black players.

While most owners were aware of the large pool of talent in the Negro Leagues before the color line was broken, only a few were willing to act on this knowledge. Bill Veeck attempted to purchase the Philadelphia Phillies in 1943 and planned to stock the team with stars from the Negro Leagues (for more information on Veeck, see his biographical sketch in Chapter 3 on pages 102–103). Major league owners blocked him by selling the team to someone else for much less than Veeck was willing to pay.[20]

More formally, Stefan Szymanski has demonstrated the presence of discrimination in a sample of teams from England's Football League over the period 1978 to 1993. Using a multiple regression model that holds team payroll constant, he has shown that teams with more black players during this period also won more frequently. Thus, a nondiscriminatory team could "buy" wins more cheaply than a team that wished to hire only white players.[21]

---

[18]Allen Barra, *The Last Coach: A Life of Paul "Bear" Bryant* (New York: W. W. Norton, 2005), p. 330.

[19]These teams were the Brooklyn (Los Angeles) Dodgers (0.592), Cleveland Indians (0.588), Boston (Milwaukee) Braves (0.554), Chicago White Sox (0.550), and New York (San Francisco) Giants (0.532).

[20]James A. Gwartney and Charles Haworth, "Employer Costs and Discrimination: The Case of Baseball," *Journal of Political Economy*, vol. 82, no. 4 (July/August 1974), pp. 873–881.

[21]Stefan Szymanski, "A Market Test for Discrimination in the English Professional Soccer Leagues," *Journal of Political Economy*, vol. 108, no. 3 (June 2000), pp. 590–603.

When Markets Are Not Competitive   Becker's theory also applies when workers are not homogeneous—and hence not perfect substitutes for one another—and when markets are not competitive, as is the case in professional sports. As in competitive markets, monopsonistic employers with a taste for discrimination treat the wage of the less-preferred group as though it were the wage $\times (1 + d_i)$. Unlike competitive markets, however, where there are many employers, monopsonistic employers will not be driven from the market if workers have nowhere else to sell their services. If employers discriminate, players with lesser abilities can end up making more than players with greater abilities. Perhaps more difficult to see, a discriminatory monopsonist may end up paying the "victims" of his prejudice more than players he ostensibly favors. For example, suppose that E's value to the team is $1,000 per game, and F's value to the team is $1,500. The employer has no taste for discrimination against E and thus sets the monopsony wage at $w = \$800$ in Figure 10.5. Note that in Figure 10.5, the demand curve is also labeled as the marginal revenue product (MRP). Recall from Chapter 8 that the MRP is the value of an additional unit of labor to the firm. By setting the ME equal to MRP, the firm equates the marginal benefit and cost of additional labor.

Figure 10.6 shows the wages paid to F players by both a nondiscriminating employer and one with a taste for discrimination. For the nondiscriminating employer, the relevant demand curve is D, which, again, is also MRP. As in Figure 10.5, the nondiscriminating monopsonist sets ME equal to the MRP and then takes the wage of $1,200 from the supply curve for the more productive F workers. The discriminating employer has a taste for discrimination against F

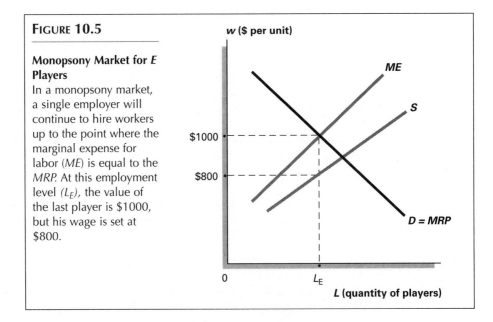

FIGURE 10.5

Monopsony Market for E Players
In a monopsony market, a single employer will continue to hire workers up to the point where the marginal expense for labor (ME) is equal to the MRP. At this employment level (L_E), the value of the last player is $1000, but his wage is set at $800.

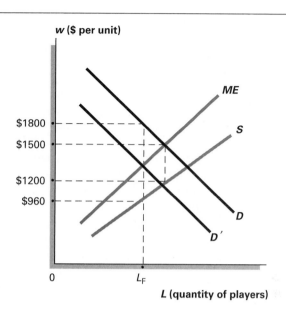

Figure 10.6

Monopsony Market for *F* Players
When a monopsonist also has a taste for discrimination, the wage of the group that is discriminated against may still receive higher wages than the preferred group. In this case, *F* players are more productive than *E* players, but the monopsonist employer has a taste for discrimination against *F*'s. They receive a wage of $960 ($160 more than the wage offer to *E*'s in Figure 10.5), but would have received $1,200 with no discrimination.

players that is 0.2. This reduces the employer's demand curve from D to D' in Figure 10.6. Because the employer is a monopsonist, he forces F to accept $w/(1 + d_i) = \$960$ per game or be excluded from the market. As F's cannot earn more than $960 in any other labor market, they accept the offer. Thus, despite earning 20 percent more than E, who earns $800, F is discriminated against. The actual MRP of F's is $1,800, and they receive only $960 because of the combined forces of monopsonistic exploitation and discrimination. As such, they are paid $840 less than their contribution to the team, whereas E's are paid only $200 less than their contribution to the team. Thus, F's are paid more but also are exploited to a much greater extent than E's.

In addition, unlike the competitive firm, a monopsonist who discriminates is not necessarily driven from the market. If players are bound to a team by a reserve clause, they cannot use the force of the market to increase their wage. If they have no employment opportunity outside the league that can offer the same wage or greater, they will stay, and the employer will profit from the players' inability to change teams.

Employee Discrimination

Discrimination is not limited to employers. Prejudiced employees can also discriminate against their coworkers. Employees with a taste for discrimination regard the market wage w as $w(1 - d_j)$ if they must work with members of a group they do not like. As before, d_j represents the coefficient of discrimination.

In the 1880s, a small number of black baseball players played in the American Association, then a "major" league. The first was Moses Fleetwood Walker, who played for Toledo in 1884. Fleetwood's brother Weldy also played part of one season with Toledo. A somewhat larger number of blacks played in the International League, which was a minor league. Some white players refused to play for teams that also hired blacks. Others played only grudgingly. In 1887, Douglas Crothers was suspended from the Syracuse Stars of the International League for refusing to appear in a team photo with Bob Higgins, a black pitcher on the team. Cap Anson, a star white player of the same era with a well-known dislike for black players, gained much notoriety from his refusal to play against blacks (though he did play when he learned he would not be paid otherwise) and his opposition to the New York Giants' desire to sign black pitcher George Stovey.[22] Such behavior persisted even though the few blacks who were in the game, such as Fleetwood Walker and Frank Grant, were among the top players in their leagues. It is a sad footnote on baseball history that the origin of the feet-first slide was from attempts of white players to spike Grant, a second baseman; he eventually invented the shinguard to protect himself from their spikes. Discriminatory behavior toward blacks continued when the major leagues were reintegrated in 1947.

During their first season, Larry Doby and Jackie Robinson were subjected to employee discrimination by several opposing teams and even by their own teammates. When Doby was introduced to his new team, several players refused to shake his hand. When the other Dodger players learned that Robinson was to begin the season with their club, several of his teammates, including such prominent players as Dixie Walker, Carl Furillo, and Eddie Stankey, circulated a petition opposing the decision. Dodger manager Leo Durocher's response was to call a team meeting at 1:00 in the morning in which he told his players, in part:

> Boys, I hear that some of you don't want to play with Robinson. Some of you have drawn up a petition. Well you know what you can use that petition for. . . . I'm the manager and I'm paid to win and I'd play an elephant if he could win for me and this fellow Robinson is no elephant. You can't throw him out on the bases and you can't get him out at the plate. This fellow is a great player. He's gonna win pennants. He's gonna put money in your pockets and mine. . . . Unless you wake up, these colored ball players are gonna run you right outa the park. I don't want to see your petition. . . . The meeting is over. Go back to bed.[23]

---

[22]Peterson, *Only the Ball Was White: A History of Legendary Black Players and All-Black Professional Teams* (1970), p. 28.

[23]From Roger Kahn, *The Era: 1947–1957* (New York: Ticknor and Fields, 1993), p. 36.

Ironically, Pee Wee Reese, a Kentucky native and shortstop who ran the risk of losing his position to Robinson, refused to sign.[24] Early in the 1947 season, both the Philadelphia Phillies and St. Louis Cardinals threatened to strike rather than play against Robinson when he came to town.[25] They relented only when faced with forfeiture and suspensions for not playing. In Robinson's first game in Philadelphia, however, the Phillies, led by their manager, Ben Chapman, hurled such savage abuse and obscenities at Robinson throughout the game that even those Dodgers who had opposed Robinson rallied around him.

The extent of the economic harm prejudiced workers do to others and themselves depends on the nature of the labor market. If players are perfect substitutes for one another and the labor market is competitive, the Becker model predicts that prejudiced employees would never accept employment on a team that is integrated because they perceive the market wage, w (that is offered to all employees), to be $w * (1 - d_j)$. Thus, they require a wage of $w/(1 - d_j)$ in order to feel as though they have received the market wage. However, no such offers exist in a market with a perfectly elastic supply of players (horizontal supply curve). Crothers and others who refused to play alongside black players were simply replaced by those who would. If a prejudiced player with a taste for discrimination was traded to an all-white team, he would no longer require a wage premium. Thus, one possible outcome of employee discrimination is segregation. Although segregation is usually considered to be employer driven, in this case, the taste for discrimination by employees creates the segregated market.[26]

As with employer discrimination, the results of the model are different when markets are not competitive. If players have different playing abilities, more than one market wage will exist, and prejudiced employees may end up as teammates of players they dislike. For example, an owner may be willing to pay the wage differential demanded by a top player with a taste for discrimination because there are no viable substitutes of equal quality. Sometimes, workers are so necessary that employers cannot substitute for them. For instance, a title boxing match must, by definition, include the reigning champion. No black boxer fought for the world heavyweight championship between Jack Johnson's loss of the title in 1915 and Joe Louis's winning the title in 1937. The reason was not a lack of good black boxers. Instead, one could not substitute away from the white champions, and the white champions had such a strong distaste for fighting blacks (such a large d_j) that no match was possible.[27]

If markets cannot be segregated, and players of different groups are perfect substitutes for one another, those with a taste for discrimination will be driven from the market. The players who discriminate, not the players discriminated

---

[24]Ken Burns, *Baseball* miniseries, PBS (1994), "Bottom of the Sixth" episode.

[25]Peterson, *Only the Ball Was White: A History of Legendary Black Players and All-Black Professional Teams* (1970), p. 199. Neither strike occurred after the league threatened suspensions.

[26]Becker, *The Economics of Discrimination* (1971), p. 56.

[27]See David Margolick, *Beyond Glory: Joe Louis vs. Max Schmeling, and a World on the Brink* (New York: Alfred A. Knopf, 2005), p. 11.

against, end up suffering the most. Becker argued that this should eliminate employee discrimination from the market in the long run. Although employer and/or employee discrimination may have significantly depressed salaries of minorities as recently as the mid-1980s, most recent studies find that in the NFL, NBA, and MLB, wage differentials based on race have been eliminated.[28] If Becker's theory is correct, there are two explanations for why this has happened. The competition between teams could have driven discriminatory owners or players from the market. Alternatively, the utility derived from the economic gains could be so much greater than the utility derived from discriminating that those with a taste for discrimination choose to stay in the market and bear the disutility of playing with groups they do not like.

Consumer Discrimination

Research on salary differentials among black, white, and Latino baseball players indicates that neither race nor ethnic background affects salaries.[29] However, evidence from both baseball and basketball indicates that discrimination still exists among consumers in the sports industry.

Consumers have a taste for discrimination if they prefer to not purchase goods or services from members of a specific group. For example, if a basketball fan has a taste for discrimination against black players, he or she perceives the price of admission to a game involving only white players to be p and the price of admission to a game in which blacks also play to be $p(1 + d_k)$.

Consumer discrimination can be difficult to isolate in a typical product market because product characteristics, particularly product quality, can cause variations in demand that are not the result of discrimination. One study did find that Nielson television ratings of basketball games are higher when white players play more.[30] Some also suggest that the recent influx of players from Europe and Latin America, such as Pau Gasol and Manu Ginobili, to the NBA

---

[28]Orn B. Bovarsson, "A Test of Employer Discrimination in the NBA," *Contemporary Economic Policy,* vol. 17, no. 2 (April 1999), pp. 243–256, cites several recent studies that find no statistical evidence of employer discrimination. In addition, Jeffrey A. Jenkins, "A Reexamination of Salary Determination in Professional Basketball," *Social Science Quarterly,* vol. 77, no. 3 (September 1996), pp. 594–608; and Matthew S. Dey, "Racial Differences in National Basketball Association Salaries: A New Look," *American Economist,* vol. 41, no. 2 (Fall 1997), pp. 84–90, find no significant differences in NBA salaries by race. Lawrence M. Kahn, "The Effects of Race on Professional Football Players' Compensation," *Industrial Labor Relations Review,* vol. 45, no. 2 (January 1992), pp. 295–310, finds that as early as 1989 racial differences between blacks and whites were no more than 4 percent. In a survey article, Kahn also discusses his own work using 1989 data that show no significant discrimination against blacks or Latinos in major league baseball. See Lawrence M. Kahn, "Discrimination in Professional Sports: A Survey of the Literature," *Industrial and Labor Relations Review,* vol. 44, no. 3 (April 1991), pp. 395–418.

[29]For more study results and discussion on this point, see Kahn, "Discrimination in Professional Sports" (1991).

[30]Mark T. Kanazawa and Jonas P. Funk, "Racial Discrimination in Professional Basketball: Evidence from Nielson Ratings," *Economic Inquiry,* vol. 39, no. 4 (October 2001), pp. 599–608.

reflects the desire of fans to see more white players.[31] By contrast, Preston and Szymanski find no evidence that consumers have driven discrimination by professional soccer teams in England.[32]

To conclude that consumers discriminate, one must isolate the effect of players' race or ethnicity from other factors that affect consumer demand, such as the quality of the team or the facility in which it plays. To do this, some researchers have turned to the market in trading cards.[33] The results of these studies are mixed; however, a study by Nardinelli and Simon finds that cards for white pitchers were 13 percent more expensive than the players' performances would justify and that nonwhite hitters (i.e., nonpitchers) cards were about 10 percent too expensive. They found that the difference was particularly great for Latino players. A study by Anderson and La Croix, however, found little evidence of discrimination against Latino players but that black players were the victims of discrimination.[34]

Fort and Gill posited that some of the confusion stems from consumers' confusion regarding race. They developed a continuous measure of race by showing people pictures and names of players and asking them "how black" and "how Hispanic" the players appeared to be.[35] Fort and Gill used these ratings to evaluate the impact of race and ethnicity on the price of the cards. They found that consumers discriminate more against players who, in the eyes of the respondents, appeared to be "more black" or "more Hispanic."

Consumer discrimination can affect attendance in several ways. First, consumers could show their taste for discrimination by supporting teams that have fewer players from the group that they dislike. Second, consumers could follow teams that are integrated but do so with less intensity—going to fewer games, buying fewer jerseys, watching the team less on television. Perhaps most extreme, they could stop following the sport altogether if too many players come from the group they dislike.

Consumer discrimination is also reflected in advertising firms' choices of athletes as sponsors. Demand for athletes as endorsers is driven by consumers' desire to emulate people they admire. If audiences are predominantly white, and consumers have a taste for discrimination, firms may in turn discriminate against black athletes.

---

[31]Dan McGraw, "The Foreign Invasion of the American Game," *The Village Voice Online,* May 28–June 3, 2003, online at http://www.villagevoice.com/news/0322,mcgraw,44409,1.html.

[32]Ian Preston and Stefan Szymanski. "Racial Discrimination in English Football," *Scottish Journal of Political Economy,* vol. 47, no. 4 (September 2000), pp. 342–363.

[33]For a different approach to consumer discrimination, see Daraius Irani, "Estimating Consumer Discrimination Using Panel Data: 1972–1991," in *Baseball Economics: Current Research,* ed. by John Fizel, Elizabeth Gustafson, and Lawrence Hadley (Westport, Conn.: Praeger, 1996).

[34]See Curtis Nardinelli and Clark Simon, "Customer Discrimination in the Market for Memorabilia: The Case of Baseball," *Quarterly Journal of Economics,* vol. 105, no. 3 (August 1990), pp. 575–595; and Torben Anderson and Sumner J. La Croix, "Customer Discrimination in Major League Baseball," *Economic Inquiry,* vol. 29, no. 4 (October 1991), pp. 665–677.

[35]Rodney Fort and Andrew Gill, "Race and Ethnicity Assessment in Baseball Card Markets," *Journal of Sports Economics,* vol. 1, no. 1 (February 2000), pp. 21–38.

Evidence suggests that consumer discrimination still existed in the NBA until the early 1990s. Wage differentials between blacks and whites persisted in professional basketball, and discriminating consumers seemed to be the source of the differential.[36] Kahn and Sherer found that blacks in the NBA earned about 20 percent less than equally productive white players in the mid-1980s.[37] A follow-up study by Hamilton found that the average salaries of black and white players had become virtually identical by the 1994–1995 season. However, Hamilton also found large differences between blacks and whites at both very high incomes and very low incomes.[38] Hamilton controlled for differences in attendance that resulted from the quality of the team, population and average income in the metropolitan area, and the fraction of the population in the local area that was black. Once all the variation that could be explained by these factors was removed, he was able to zero in on the variation in attendance that could be attributed to the number of players on the team that were white. His results indicate that white players were more likely to be at the bottom end of the pay scale, near what was then the league minimum of $150,000. This appeared to indicate discrimination against whites. However, at the upper end of NBA salaries, whites earned 19 percent more than equally productive blacks. Thus, even though blacks earned more than whites on average, black players were discriminated against overall. Again, evidence supports the prediction that the more contact the consumer has with the athlete, the more intense the discrimination will be. In this case, highly paid stars are much more visible than bench players who earn the NBA minimum.

Evidence of consumer discrimination also exists in the men's college Division I basketball market. Regression techniques similar to those described above show that fans spend an additional $121,000 (as measured by home-gate revenues) if an additional white player is added to the team.[39] It is encouraging to note that research on consumer discrimination using the results of fan voting for all-stars in baseball shows that this type of discrimination has declined sharply since the 1970s and that a study on salaries of NBA players using data from the 1995–1996 season found no evidence of discrimination, contradicting Hamilton's findings from just one year earlier. The lack of clear evidence of the presence of discrimination is itself a good indication that it is less prevalent than in the past.[40]

---

[36]Lawrence M. Kahn and Peter Sherer, "Racial Differences in Professional Basketball Players' Compensation," *Journal of Labor Economics*, vol. 6, no. 1 (January 1988), pp. 40–61; and Barton H. Hamilton, "Racial Discrimination and Professional Basketball Salaries in the 1990s," *Applied Economics*, vol. 29, no. 3 (March 1997), pp. 287–296.

[37]Kahn and Sherer, "Racial Differences in Professional Basketball Players' Compensation" (1988), p. 51.

[38]Hamilton, "Racial Discrimination and Professional Basketball Salaries in the 1990s" (1997).

[39]Robert W. Brown and R. Todd Jewell, "Is There Customer Discrimination in College Basketball? The Premium Fans Pay for White Players," *Social Science Quarterly*, vol. 75, no. 2 (June 1994), pp. 401–412.

[40]Andrew F. Hanssen and Torben Anderson, "Has Discrimination Lessened over Time? A Test Using Baseball's All-Star Vote," *Economic Inquiry*, vol. 37, no. 2 (April 1999), pp. 326–352; and Mark Gius and Donn Johnson, "An Empirical Investigation of Wage Discrimination in Professional Basketball," *Applied Economics Letters*, vol. 5, no. 11 (November 1998), pp. 703–705.

Unfortunately, consumer discrimination differs from other types of discrimination in one important regard: Market forces do not eliminate it over time. In fact, if consumers have a taste for discrimination against a particular group, and employers maximize profit, the employers will not hire any members of that group. It is the only form of discrimination that harms the group that is discriminated against without in turn damaging those with the taste for discrimination.

Discrimination by National Origin in European Soccer

Civil rights legislation the world over outlaws discrimination on the basis of "race, color, religion, sex, or national origin." Discrimination on the basis of national origin, however, is at the heart of a dispute among the Union of Economic Football Associations (UEFA), the governing body of European Football; FIFA, the international governing body; and the European Union. The problem lies in the conflicting motivations facing European club teams. Collectively, teams in each country worry that an influx of foreign players will diminish interest in their product. Individually, however, each team wants to put the best team it can afford on the field, regardless of where the players come from. This is particularly true of the premier league teams in the major countries: England, Germany, Italy, and Spain, who are constantly under pressure to advance to the Champions League. As a result, foreign players have long been a major factor on club rosters. Only once in the ten years from 1999 to 2008 has the winner of the "Golden Ball," which is awarded to the European player of the year, played for a club in his native country.[41] While star players have long crossed national—and continental—boundaries, until 1991 UEFA rules had strictly limited the number of foreign players, allowing only two per team. Such a policy, however, ran contrary to the letter and spirit of the Treaty of Rome, the agreement that has formed the groundwork of the European Union (EU) since 1957. In 1991, UEFA and the EU reached a compromise known as the "3 + 2 rule."[42] This rule limited each team to three starting players from other countries. Two more starters could be foreign citizens if they had lived in the club's country long enough.

Like many landmark lawsuits, the incident underlying the suit that brought down both the 3 + 2 rule as well as the transfer system in Europe was not momentous. Jean-Marc Bosman played for Liege, a second-division team in the Belgian League. Liege blocked a move by Bosman to a French team in Dunkerque because it felt the French team did not offer a sufficient transfer fee. Bosman sued the Belgian league, claiming that the transfer system blocked the free flow of resources across European boundaries, a key element of the Treaty of Rome. In December 1995, the European Court of Justice ruled in Bosman's favor. It declared that the transfer system applied only when a player was

---

[41]That was Michael Owen, playing for Liverpool in 2001.

[42]Lindsey Valaine Briggs, "UEFA v. The European Community: Attempts of the Governing Body of European Soccer to Circumvent EU Freedom of Movement and Antidiscrimination Labor Law," *Chicago Journal of International Law,* vol. 6, no. 1 (Summer 2005), pp. 440–441.

under contract with a team and could not be applied at the end of the contract. It went on to declare that the 3 + 2 rule also blocked resources and was illegal.[43]

Because the Court of Justice did not accept its argument that soccer should be exempted from the Treaty of Rome, UEFA changed its tack. It instead asked European club teams to abide by the "Homegrown Rule." This rule replaced strict numerical quotas with a limit based on player development. It required teams to carry at least four players who have been trained in the team's player development program and four more who have trained with another team in the same nation. The rule also limited the number of players a team can carry on its roster (teams previously had no limit) to 25, increasing the chance that the eight players who meet the Homegrown Rule will actually play.[44]

FIFA policy on the use of foreign players changed again in 2008 (with the change planned to take effect in 2012–2013). The new policy, reminiscent of the 3 + 2 rule, is known as the 6 + 5 rule. Despite concerns of conflict with the EU, the 6 + 5 rule reinstates limitations on foreign-born players, mandating a maximum of five foreign players in the starting eleven.[45] Given that FIFA cannot actually impose conditions on individual clubs (which are governed by their national associations), the implications for top teams that employ a large number of foreign players are unclear, though it seems likely that this controversy will remain active for years to come.

Positional Discrimination or Hiring Discrimination[46]

Given the high percentage of athletes of differing races and ethnic groups in the major leagues and the results of recent research, such as Hamilton's study of the NBA, there is little evidence of discrimination that affects access to professional leagues. However, this ignores the question of whether minorities have equal access to all positions. For example, since about two-thirds of the players in the NFL are black, one would expect about two-thirds of the players at each position to be black. One would also expect the racial balance of the coaches in the league to be similar to that of the players. As it turns out, however, these expectations are not realized.

Historically, positional discrimination, also known as **stacking,** has been an issue in both the NFL and MLB. Even today, whites dominate at some positions while blacks dominate at others. As recently as 2006, 82 percent of the

---

[43]Andreff and Staudohar, "European and US Sports Business Models" (2002), p. 41.

[44]Briggs, "UEFA v. The European Community" (2005), pp. 441 and 448.

[45]"FIFA thumbs-up for 'six-plus-five' player rule," May 30, 2008. http://soccernet.espn.go.com/news/story?id=540901&cc=5901; and Andrew Hodgson, "Blatter bid to put limit on foreign players wins FIFA backing," May 30, 2008. *London Evening Standard (Standard.co.uk)*, http://www.thisislondon.co.uk/standard-sport/article-23488572-details/Blatter+bid+to+put+limit+on+foreign+players+wins+FIFA+backing/article.do. Accessed August 4, 2009.

[46]Data in this section, unless otherwise noted, are from *The 2008 Racial and Gender Report Card* available at http://tidesport.org/RGRC/2008/2008_MLB_RGRC_PR.pdf.

quarterbacks in the NFL were white, as were 70 percent of the centers and 54 percent of the tight ends. At the opposite end of the spectrum, 88 percent of the running backs and 91 percent of wide receivers were black, as were 96 percent of the cornerbacks. In general, white players are more likely to be found on offense than on defense.

Economists call the systematic steering of minorities to specific positions on the field and within the coaching ranks **role discrimination.** For example, if a player must have a strong arm and quick reactions in order to be a quarterback and if coaches erroneously assume that blacks do not possess these attributes at the same level as whites, then coaches will discourage young black players from investing in the skills required to play quarterback.[47]

Table 10.1 shows the racial and ethnic breakdown of major league baseball players for 2004. It shows that although Latinos made up 26 percent of the league overall, 64 percent of shortstops and 32 percent of second basemen were Latino. In contrast, blacks were much more likely to be outfielders than their overall percentage would suggest, and whites were much more likely to be pitchers. *The Racial and Gender Report Card* does not separate players into specific infield positions after 2004, but in 2007, there were no African American catchers and only 3 percent of pitchers and 7 percent of infielders were African American, compared to 28 percent of outfielders. Thus, while opportunities for all races to play exist in the major leagues, positional segregation appears to be an ongoing concern.

There is simply not enough evidence to discuss race and positional segregation in hockey, as there are only a few players of color in the entire league. The most significant change in the makeup of hockey personnel in recent years is the large influx of European—particularly Eastern European—players since the fall of the Berlin Wall in 1989. The large influx of star players such as Peter Forsberg, Jaromir Jagr, and others improved the quality of play in the NHL.

TABLE 10.1

Racial and Ethnic Breakdown of MLB Players in 2004 at Selected Positions (%)

	Total	Pitchers	Catchers	First Base	Second Base	Third Base	Shortstop	Outfield
White	63	72	65	64	53	75	28	46
African American	9	3	2	15	15	5	7	26
Latino	26	22	33	20	32	19	64	25
Asian	3	3	0	2	0	0	1	3

Source: Richard E. Lapchick, Nikki Bowey, and Ray Matthew. 2008 *Racial and Gender Report Card*, The Institute for Diversity and Ethics in Sport. Online at http://tidesport.org/RGRC/2008/2008_MLB_RGRC_PR.pdf. accessed August 3, 2009.

---

[47]The same argument is frequently used to explain why women are overrepresented in certain occupations and underrepresented in others.

Although not all European players have enjoyed immediate success in the NHL due to the differences in the size of the ice surface and style of play, some teams have thrived after successfully signing top players from former Eastern Bloc countries such as Russia and the Czech Republic.

Role discrimination is a form of statistical discrimination. For example, if on average women do not know as much as men about sports, they could be systematically discouraged from pursuing roles as officials or broadcasters. The problem is that uncertainty causes the employer to attribute the characteristics of the average person in the group to each member of the group. There is no way to determine without testing whether a specific woman has the knowledge to officiate a game. Unfortunately for women, if the discrimination occurs early in the application screening process, they may never get the opportunity to reveal their skills. The same is true in positional discrimination. If, for example, black potential quarterbacks are never given the opportunity to try out, they cannot demonstrate their skills to coaches and prove they are capable of playing the position.

Recent research by Berri and Simmons finds evidence of both role discrimination and employer discrimination against black quarterbacks in the NFL.[48] They note that, while about two-thirds of the players in the league are black, 73 percent of the quarterbacks who attempted 100 or more passes between 2000 and 2006 were white. In addition, they find that wage differences across race exist in portions of the salary range. They construct a performance measure of quarterbacks that includes both running and passing productivity and show that, controlling for productivity, black quarterbacks at the upper half of the salary scale are compensated less than white quarterbacks of equal productivity. Thus, while wages and playing opportunities have increased, Berri and Simmons' results indicate that there is more work to be done to completely close the racial divide at the quarterback position.

Discrimination in Coaching and Administrative Ranks If blacks had only recently entered professional sports in significant numbers, one might not expect to find many black head coaches. However, the racial composition of the NFL has been relatively constant for the last 10 years (as mentioned above, it is roughly one-third white and two-thirds black). Since most coaches are former players, one might expect two-thirds of the coaches to be black as well. However, in 2007, 81 percent of head coaches in the NFL were white and only 19 percent were black. While far below the percentage of players, this represents an all-time high for the NFL and more than a doubling of the percentage of black coaches since 2003.

Latino and black baseball players are also less likely to become coaches than whites. The data in Table 10.2 show that, while the percentage of MLB managers that are black has decreased substantially in the last few years, the

[48]David J. Berri and Rob Simmons. "Race and the Evaluation of Signal Callers in the National Football League," *Journal of Sports Economics,* vol. 10, no. 1 (February, 2009); pp. 23–43.

TABLE 10.2

Percentage of Black and Latino Head Coaches and Managers in the NBA, NFL, and MLB in 1991 and 2005

	1991	2000	2007
NBA	7	34	40
NFL	7	10	19
MLB			
Black	13	13	7
Latino	<4	3	13

Sources: Richard E. Lapchick, Stacy Martin, Danielle Kushner, and Jenny Brendan, *2005 Racial and Gender Report Card.* The Institute for Ethics and Diversity in Sport. Online at http://www.ncasports.org/FINAL%20RGRC.pdf. Accessed March 23, 2007.

increase in the number of Latino managers is even larger. It is also encouraging to see the upward trend in minority head coaches in the NBA, especially given that it has the highest percentage of black players of any of the major professional sports leagues.

While women have had little more than a token role in the NBA and NHL and have not appeared at all as players in MLB or the NFL, they do work in administrative positions in all sports. The obstacles facing women in such positions vary with the nature of the jobs they hold. The value of having previously played the game is different for different jobs. General managers, for example, evaluate talent and work with the coach, so people who have played the game have a significant advantage in obtaining these positions.[49] Thus, it is no surprise that none of the major sports teams has a woman in charge of personnel decisions.

The hiring records at the collegiate level are very similar to those at the professional level. In both coaching and administrative positions, Division I athletic programs are dominated by white males, but colleges' hiring records vary widely by sport. *The 2008 Racial and Gender Report Card* gives Division I basketball programs an "A" for providing opportunities to black basketball coaches, as 22.9 percent of all Division I coaches are black. However, it gives Division I Football Bowl subdivision football programs an "F" because only 5.1 percent of major football coaches are black.[50] Over 52 percent of Division I women's sports teams have white male head coaches. Perhaps more disappointing is that even in Division II and III, the percentages of minorities and

---

[49]It may also be the case, however, that having prior playing experience does not yield any significant advantage. For example, it seems likely that a top-caliber women's basketball player would also be an effective evaluator of male basketball talent. If this is the case, then the absence of women as general managers in basketball would also represent role discrimination.

[50]Richard Lapchick, et al. *The 2008 Racial and Gender Report Card: College Sports,* online at http://www.tidesport.org/RGRC/2008/2008CollegRGRC.pdf. Accessed August 3, 2009.

women are similar, and in some cases worse. In fact, blacks are so underrepresented as head coaches in Division II male sports that they outnumber women head coaches of male sports by less than two percentage points. Given these figures, it should not come as a surprise that at the highest administrative level, 82.8 percent of Division I athletic directors are white males.

We will return to the question of discrimination in collegiate athletics in Section 10.3. For now, we simply note that the imbalance at the collegiate level is likely to slow changes at the professional level, because top-level collegiate programs often serve as training grounds for future professional coaches. Thus, the argument that the absence of minority professional coaches is simply a "pipeline" problem (that is, that the data will improve over time as more top-level candidates become available) seems misguided. If increases in the number of black NFL head coaches must be preceded by increases in Division I minority representation, it appears that the status quo will continue for some time. In addition, research by Janice Madden shows that between 1990 and 2001, minority head coaches in the NFL have been significantly more successful than their white counterparts, raising the question of whether a double standard is in force in which blacks must have higher qualifications to reach the level of head coach than whites.[51]

Gender Equity—A Special Case?

Women rarely attempt to enter traditionally male professional or college sports leagues such as football. Gender differences in size, weight, and strength make such occurrences unlikely in the future as well. Annika Sorenstam and, more recently, Michelle Wie have provided the rare exceptions by their participation in men's golf tournaments. The only sports where men and women routinely compete against one another at the professional level are mixed doubles in tennis, auto racing, and as jockeys in horse racing. Mixed doubles (with one man and one woman per team) is a somewhat contrived event at major professional tournaments. Only in auto racing and thoroughbred horse racing do men and women compete against one another under a common set of rules. Thus, those sports provide a unique opportunity to test for the existence of gender discrimination. A 1993 study of thoroughbred racing showed that, holding performance and experience constant, female jockeys receive significantly fewer racing opportunities. As a result, they have significantly fewer winnings than similarly qualified male jockeys.[52]

No systematic research has investigated the economics of gender discrimination in auto racing. Although Shirley Muldowney is one of the most successful drag racers of all time, she is still one of the only women ever to win a National Hot Rod Association (NHRA) national title event in the professional

---

[51]Janice Fanning Madden, "Differences in the Success of NFL Coaches by Race, 1990–2002: Evidence of Last Hire, First Fire," *Journal of Sports Economics*, vol. 5, no. 1 (February 2004), pp. 6–19.

[52]Margaret A. Ray and Paul W. Grimes, "Jockeying for Position: Winnings and Gender Discrimination on the Thoroughbred Track," *Social Science Quarterly*, vol. 74, no. 1 (March 1993), pp. 46–61.

category.[53] The relatively small number of successful female race drivers such as Danica Patrick raises the question of whether so few women are found in the sport because of low demand or low supply. If no evidence exists that women are inferior race drivers or that they lack the human capital needed to become professional drivers, a lack of demand for women drivers represents employer discrimination. If the small number of drivers is the result of a lack of supply (not many women pursue this career), it could be caused by role discrimination or not be discrimination at all.

Recall from Chapter 3 that television rights are a derived demand, driven by the demand of advertisers that are in turn determined by ratings. If the demand for women's sports is as high as that for men's sports, and no other cost differences exist, then in the absence of discrimination, there should be equal prize money.[54] Sponsors should have the same willingness to pay for advertising time regardless of gender.

Unfortunately for the players, owners, and fans of women's sports, it appears that there are significant differences in the public demand for professional teams across gender. The demise of the U.S. women's professional soccer league (the WUSA) serves as a case in point. Although the league was unquestionably the preeminent league in the world, employed top stars from the Women's World Cup team such as Mia Hamm, and had benefited from over $100 million in initial investments, there simply was not enough demand from fans and sponsors to keep the league from folding in 2003.

Historically, women have fared better when it comes to individual sports. A striking example of how players can raise not only awareness but also wages comes from the world of tennis. Open tennis tournaments began in the late 1960s. Today, both amateurs and professionals can qualify to play in an open tournament through a series of local and regional competitions. Initially, men's prize money was approximately 10 times that of women. In November 1972, the Women's U.S. Open champion, Billie Jean King, threatened to lead a boycott of the 1973 Open unless the prize money was equalized. Her protest was successful, and prize money was eventually equalized. Gender-based differences in prize money persisted, however, in other major tournaments, such as Wimbledon and the French Open. As noted, prize differences in and of themselves are not sufficient for most economists to conclude that discrimination exists. However, in 1998, HBO television ratings went up by over 18 percent after increasing its coverage of women's play at Wimbledon, yet until 2007 women still received less than men for winning the singles title.[55] More

---

[53]"Shirley Muldowney: 2000 Star Tracks Archive," at http://www.nhra.com/drivers/driver.asp?driverid=976.

[54]It should be noted that men and women do not produce equivalent output in tennis matches, because men's matches are typically best of five sets and women's are best of three.

[55]"Not About Money: HBO Declines to Renew Wimbledon Contract After 25 Years," CNN/SI at www.cnnsi.com/tennis/1999/wimbledon/news/1999/06/28/hbo_wimbledon/index.html. Another frequently cited example of women's sports eclipsing men's in popularity is that ratings from television broadcasts of the Olympics show that women's figure skating and gymnastics are consistently among the most watched events.

recently, problems have arisen in women's professional golf and its organization, the LPGA. In 2009, Commissioner Carolyn Bivens was forced to resign amid concerns by top players over the loss of seven tournaments between 2007 and 2009 and a failed attempt to force the players to adopt an English-only policy.[56]

10.3   Title IX and Discrimination in College Sports

Title IX has been the most important measure ever undertaken to promote gender equity in sports. It has completely changed the face of scholastic and collegiate opportunities for women. Some even ascribe the success of the WNBA and the U.S. Women's World Cup soccer team directly to Title IX. It has not, however, been universally praised. Many claim that Title IX has denied opportunities to as many people as it has helped.

Though it stands as a lightning rod for both proponents and detractors of women's athletic rights, it is a seemingly innocuous section of the 1972 Educational Amendments to the 1964 Civil Rights Act. For such an important piece of legislation, Title IX itself is remarkably unimposing, measuring only one sentence in length. It reads:

> No Person in the United States shall, on the basis of sex, be excluded from participation in, be denied the benefits of, or be subjected to discrimination under any educational program or activity receiving federal financial assistance.[57]

Three years later, the Department of Health, Education, and Welfare established three areas of regulatory jurisdiction:

1. Financial aid

2. Other benefits and opportunities

3. Participation in athletics

The third of these areas is directed at accommodating men and women in their efforts to participate in intercollegiate athletics. Congress established compliance guidelines for athletics in a 1979 amendment to the original legislation. Compliance can be achieved in one of three ways: proportionality, program expansion, or accommodating the interests and abilities of the student body.

Proportionality means that the percentage of women who participate in sports at a university should approximate the percentage of female undergraduates enrolled at the school. For example, if women make up 55 percent of a school's undergraduate enrollment, approximately 55 percent of the athletes participating on the school's teams would have to be female. The Office of Civil

---

[56]"Evans Takes Over as Acting Commish," *ESPN Golf,* at http://sports.espn.go.com/golf/news/story?id=4323583. Accessed August 4, 2009.

[57]*Title IX Legal Manual,* U.S. Dept. of Justice, Civil Rights Division, Jan. 11, 2001. Online at http://www.usdoj.gov/crt/cor/coord/IXlegal.htm.

Rights of the Department of Education oversees the enforcement of Title IX and uses a ±5 percentage point rule in its interpretation of this test (e.g., if a school's enrollment is 50 percent female and 45 percent of women are on school teams, the school would be in compliance).

To show program expansion, the college must demonstrate that it has increased and continues to increase opportunities for the underrepresented gender. This criterion is open to interpretation. Depending on how one interprets the word *expansion,* women's sports could achieve proportionality with men in very short order, or it could take an extremely long time to reach equal or proportional programming levels for men and women.

Finally, colleges may show that they have fully accommodated the interests and abilities of the underrepresented sex. It is also difficult to use this criterion to challenge a school, because the school itself can be the judge of a student's ability to participate.

Each of these criteria leaves room for interpretation. Perhaps because it is a numerical measure and thus most easily checked, challenges to schools' compliance with Title IX have generally been based on the proportionality standard.[58]

Like most legislation, Title IX has had both intended and unintended effects. Unless a program can generate enough revenue to support itself, it can gain funding only if the university increases funding to athletics or if another program is cut. The balanced-budget approach to changes in athletic funding has greatly contributed to the controversy over the implementation of Title IX guidelines, as men's sports have at times paid the ultimate price—cancellation of their program—in order to accommodate new women's programs. According to the Independent Women's Forum, which documents the effect of Title IX quotas, over 350 men's programs were discontinued between 1992 and 1997.[59] Among Division I schools, in 54 percent of cases, schools that dropped men's teams cited gender equity as a "great or very great" influence on their decisions.[60] These schools claimed that, by forcing them to cut opportunities for men in order to open opportunities for women, Title IX imposed a **zero-sum game** on them.

Whatever its impact on men's sports, Title IX has clearly increased the number of women taking part in athletics. The participation in sports by high school girls (also covered by Title IX) increased from 294,000 in 1971 to 2.8 million in 2002.[61]

Although Title IX is almost certain to remain a source of ongoing debate, it seems clear that it will remain. After much contentions, the Secretary of Education's Commission on Opportunity in Athletics concluded in its study of Title IX

---

[58] Andrew Zimbalist, *Unpaid Professionals* (Princeton, N.J.: Princeton University Press, 1999), p. 63.

[59] Jessica Gavora, *Tilting the Playing Field* (San Francisco: Encounter Books, 2002), p. 53.

[60] "'Open to All' Title IX at Thirty," Report of the Secretary of Education's Commission on Opportunity in Athletics, p. 19.

[61] "'Open to All' Title IX at Thirty," Report of the Secretary of Education's Commission on Opportunity in Athletics, p. 13.

that it had resulted in 30 years of great progress for women and girls and that it should remain, with the goals of continuing this progress while retaining the opportunities for boys and men. In the words of U.S. Secretary of Education Rod Paige, "Without a doubt, Title IX has opened the doors of opportunity for generations of women and girls to compete, to achieve and pursue their American Dreams. This Administration is committed to building on those successes."[62]

BIOGRAPHICAL SKETCH

BRANCH RICKEY

The greatest proof of Rickey's genius was that you always knew what he was doing—except when he was doing it to you.

—Bill Veeck[1]

Even if Branch Rickey had never broken baseball's color line, he would still be remembered as one of baseball's greatest innovators. In fact, by the time Rickey first joined the Dodgers at the age of 62, he had already experienced a full career in baseball.

Born in 1881, Wesley Branch Rickey was raised in a staunch Methodist family. A budding baseball career pretty much ended one day in 1903 when he refused to play on a Sunday. For the rest of his life—with the exception of a special war bonds drive during World War II—Rickey never attended a ballgame on a Sunday, though—some were quick to point out—that did not stop him from calling the ballpark to check on the day's gate receipts.

Rickey's preoccupation with money probably stemmed from an impoverished upbringing. Rickey was so poor that he had to delay going to college for several years after he graduated from high school. He later recalled that when he finally went to Ohio Wesleyan University, "[d]uring my first term ... I had only one pair of pants, and nobody saw me wear anything else."[2]

Rickey's frugality was to follow him when he assumed a front office job with the St. Louis Cardinals, which had hired him away from their crosstown rivals, the Browns, in 1916. Frustrated that his scouts would frequently identify talented minor league players only to lose them to wealthier teams such as the New York Giants, Rickey began to buy minor league teams so as to keep players within the fold. This was the beginning of baseball's first "farm system." The Cardinals' system became so extensive and so laden with talent (the products of that system included Hall of Famers Dizzy Dean, Joe Medwick, and Stan Musial) that the Cardinals displaced the Giants as the National League's dominant team in the 1930s. Rickey's spending on the team, however, eventually ran afoul of the team's ownership, and in 1943, at the age of 62, he headed east to Brooklyn to become president and 25 percent owner of the Dodgers.

---

[62]"'Open to All' Title IX at Thirty," Report of the Secretary of Education's Commission on Opportunity in Athletics, p. 2.

While rebuilding the Dodgers' farm system in the early and mid-1940s, Rickey also introduced a number of other innovations that are now taken for granted. He was the first to use a pitching machine and to have players practice their slides in sliding pits. Inspired by Dwight Eisenhower's account of preparations for D-Day, Rickey borrowed the philosophy to create "Dodgertown," in Vero Beach, Florida. Dodgertown was a vast complex where the entire Dodger system, minor leaguers and major leaguers alike, could receive instruction at one time.

Rickey became a well-known figure to New York sportswriters, who dubbed him "The Mahatma" because they saw Rickey's image in John Gunther's description of Mohandas "Mahatma" Gandhi as "a combination of God, your father, and Tammany Hall."[3] His double-talk was so renowned that his office in Brooklyn became know as "The House of Winds." One thing about which Rickey was absolutely silent was his plan to break baseball's color line.

One can only speculate about Rickey's motivation for seeking to integrate the Dodgers. Publicly, he spoke of the added fans and higher gate receipts an integrated team would attract. Privately, however, he recounted a different motivation that stemmed from his days at Ohio Wesleyan. While with the baseball team there, he roomed with a black teammate. On one road trip, the team was denied admission to a hotel because of the black player. After making arrangements at another hotel that involved sneaking the player in through the kitchen, Rickey found his roommate in tears, scratching at his hands and asking himself why the color couldn't rub off.

Whatever his reasons, Rickey took great care in finding the right player to integrate the major leagues. With a stealth that befitted a Cold War spy novel, Dodger scouts fanned the nation, ostensibly looking to recruit players for a new Negro League team to be called the "Brooklyn Brown Dodgers." Ruling out established stars such as Satchel Paige or Buck O'Neill as being too old to be able to establish careers in a new league and young stars such as Roy Campanella or Don Newcombe as being too young to withstand the pressures of being the first player to cross the color line, Rickey settled on Jackie Robinson, a rising star with the Kansas City Monarchs.

On October 23, 1945, the Brooklyn Dodgers revealed that they had signed Robinson to a contract with their top farm club, the Montreal Royals. Rickey had carefully chosen both the signing date and the ball club to which he assigned Robinson. The date was early enough that other players would know that they were likely to play with a black ballplayer and could arrange for a trade if they objected to doing so. The Montreal club was far enough out of the limelight and from America's overheated racial environment to allow Robinson some chance of a normal environment. (Even so, he recalled being close to a nervous breakdown by the end of the season.)

Soon after signing Robinson, Rickey had to withstand pressure from other owners—among them the legendary Connie Mack—who called to complain that he was about to ruin the game; they arranged a vote on the Dodgers' move in which Rickey cast the only approving vote. Far from being discouraged at the attitudes of the other owners, Rickey quickly became the one to sign the second, third, fourth, and fifth black baseball players to contracts.

Rickey also had to deal with on-the-field problems. At first he had to reassure the manager in Montreal, a Mississippian named Clay Hopper, who asked, "Mister Rickey, tell me—do you really think a nigra's a human being?"[4] Rickey was so reassuring and Robinson's play and demeanor so exemplary that Hopper eventually became one of Robinson's biggest backers. After Robinson's outstanding year in Montreal, Rickey then had to convince the Dodgers' manager, Leo Durocher, and the team's Mississippi-born broadcaster, Red Barber, to support his move.

In 1950 Walter O'Malley, who also owned 25 percent of the Dodgers and was Rickey's rival for control of the club, gained control of another 25 percent of the Dodgers and forced Rickey out as president. Rickey quickly landed a position as vice president and general manager of the Pittsburgh Pirates, where he built the foundation of a team that won the 1960 World Series (including

continued

stealing a young prospect named Roberto Clemente from the Dodger organization).

Rickey continued to affect baseball well into the 1960s. His attempt to create a rival Continental League forced the National League into its first expansion of the century and led the National League to replace the departed Dodgers and Giants with the New York Mets. In 1963, Rickey returned to the Cardinals as a consultant. He helped oversee the 1964 Cardinals as they appeared in and won the World Series, their first win since the 1946 team, which Rickey also built. Branch Rickey died in 1965, after spending almost 70 years in baseball and living long enough to share the podium at the Baseball Hall of Fame induction of his good friend, Jackie Robinson.

[1]Bill Veeck, *The Hustler's Handbook* (Durham, N.C.: Baseball America Classic Books, 1996), p. 100.
[2]Harvey Frommer, *Rickey and Robinson* (New York: Macmillan, 1982), p. 38.
[3]From Harvey Frommer, *Rickey and Robinson* (New York: Macmillan, 1982), p. 87. Tammany Hall was where New York City's notorious political machine had been headquartered, so that any political boss in New York was dubbed "a Tammany Hall politician."
[4]Harvey Frommer, *Rickey and Robinson*, p. 120.

Sources: John Helyar, *Lords of the Realm* (New York: Ballantine Books, 1994); Harvey Frommer, *Rickey and Robinson* (New York: Macmillan, 1982); and Bill Veeck, *The Hustler's Handbook* (Durham, N.C.: Baseball America Classic Books, 1996).

Summary

This chapter introduced economic theories of discrimination and used them to describe how the tastes and preferences of employers, employees, and consumers can affect wages of athletes. Evidence shows that, although discrimination was overt in the 1940s, it has diminished over time. Examples from baseball in the 1950s support the hypothesis that discriminators will suffer lower profits or at least lower success rates, as measured in wins. There is evidence that some discrimination on the part of consumers still creates wage differentials in sports such as basketball. There is also substantial evidence that positional discrimination still exists in the NFL and in other sports on the playing field as well as in the coaching ranks. The implementation of Title IX in the 1970s stands as a watershed event in the effort to achieve gender equity in college sports.

Discussion Questions

1. Think of recent events from the sports industry that show a taste for discrimination. Do they represent consumer, employer, or employee discrimination?
2. Discuss the role of the media in shaping perceptions about racial and ethnic diversity in professional and amateur sports.
3. How might the development of the NFL and MLB have been different if blacks had not been excluded from these leagues during the years that spanned World War II?

4. Identify specific economic concepts and theories about discrimination in Leo Durocher's statement about Jackie Robinson on page 326.

5. If implementing Title IX means that men's sports must experience a reduction in funding, should it be eliminated?

6. Discuss the implications of a government policy that any network that intends to cover the Olympics must devote equal air time to men's and women's events.

Problems

10.1 Suppose that the competitive wage in independent league baseball is $20,000 per season. One team owner has a taste for discrimination against all nonwhite players. Her coefficient of discrimination against Latinos is 0.20, and her coefficient of discrimination against blacks is 0.18. What would she consider the wages of people who are members of these two groups to be? If the supply of players were perfectly elastic, how many of each group would be hired?

10.2 How can you determine if a running back in the NFL is suffering from wage discrimination? Would the process be the same for a lineman?

10.3 Under what circumstances would an owner be able to practice employer discrimination over a long period of time?

10.4 Suppose that the supply of both Hispanic and white pitchers (of equal quality) were perfectly elastic. Using supply and demand graphs, show the number of each player type hired by an owner with a taste for discrimination against Hispanics and those hired by a nondiscriminating owner.

10.5 Use Becker's model to explain why sponsors who discriminate will likely experience lower profits for doing so.

10.6 Using supply and demand graphs, show how positional segregation can occur even if only the players (including potential future players) believe that such discrimination exists.

10.7 True, false, or uncertain: Title IX compliance requires equal expenditures on men's and women's sports. Explain your answer.

10.8 Use what you know about the prisoner's dilemma to explain why the British Premier League teams such as Arsenal have so many foreign players even when, as a group, the Premier League teams agree that they want to limit the number of foreign-born players.

10.9 Would it be possible to have legislation similar to Title IX that governed professional sports? Why or why not?

10.10 Draw a set of indifference curves (as described in Appendix 2A) depicting an owner with a taste for discrimination against Francophones. Put Anglophones on the horizontal axis.

PART FIVE
Sports in the Not-for-Profit Sector

CHAPTER 11
The Economics of Amateurism and College Sports

CHAPTER 11

The Economics of Amateurism and College Sports

There are 360,000 NCAA student athletes, and each one of us is getting two educations.

—FORMER USC BASKETBALL PLAYER TYLER MURPHY
IN A TELEVISION AD PROMOTING THE DUAL MISSION OF THE NCAA.[1]

Introduction

The preceding chapters discussed a variety of economic theories as they are applied to the sports world, including the following concepts:

- How and whether teams are profitable—and the difficulty in measuring profits

- How monopolies create barriers to entry by potential competitors

- How sports leagues may use their monopsony power to minimize labor costs

- How cities have based economic development on sports franchises

All these factors apply as well to the relationship between colleges and their athletic programs, for it is impossible to deny that college sports are a very big business. The finances of college athletic departments sometimes rival those of professional franchises in both size and complexity. Observers claim that the two profit centers—football and men's basketball—of the most profitable athletic programs compare favorably with the market values of their professional counterparts.[2] At the other end of the scale, some major college programs resemble unprofitable professional franchises in their struggle to keep their

[1]Michelle Jeffers, "Y&R Balances NCAA's Student-Athlete Act," *AllBusiness* at http://www.allbusiness.com/marketing-advertising/4122624-1.html. Accessed August 17, 2009.

[2]See, for example, Richard Sheehan, *Keeping Score* (South Bend, Ind.: Diamond Press, 1996), pp. 70–74, 101, and 272–274.

heads above water both competitively and financially. Unlike a professional market, the incentive structure is difficult to discern. Total 2008–2009 revenues for the nonprofit NCAA, excluding football bowl game revenue, exceed $660 million.[3] Over 90 percent of this total is generated by the annual "March Madness" Division I basketball tournament. In 1999, the NCAA signed a TV contract with CBS for the men's basketball tournament that was worth $6 billion over 11 years. Thus, fewer than 1 percent of NCAA athletes generate almost all NCAA revenue. Huge sums rest on the performance of young men who are not permitted to accept money for playing basketball.

The disproportionate share of revenue generated by big-time basketball is reflected in news coverage. While much of the national media attention on college athletes focuses on Division I football and basketball, the vast majority of student-athletes compete in sports that receive little or no media attention and generate no revenue. Offering these activities can cost even a small college hundreds of thousands of dollars per year. That college-level athletics occupies such a prominent place in the budgets of schools of all sizes indicates that schools see value beyond ticket and television revenue. Although much of our focus in this chapter is on revenue-producing sports, we also discuss strategic reasons for promoting athletics that go beyond revenue generation.

With respect to large-revenue sports, Chapter 4 explained how the NCAA can be regarded as an "incidental cartel," and Chapter 7 showed how cities have attempted to use sports as a vehicle for economic growth. This chapter combines these two forces and demonstrates how they affect colleges. Colleges—like cities—have attempted to use athletics to improve their prestige and bottom line. We also explore how the monopsony power that colleges can exercise over their athletes in revenue-generating sports has depressed the returns to the participants. Since much of the economics in this chapter deals with organizations such as the NCAA and attitudes such as the Olympic ideal, we place the analysis in the appropriate historical and institutional context and explain the following points:

- How profit-maximizing cartels allocate output among their members

- The role of an enforcer in a cartel

- The economic theory of how bureaucracies operate

11.1   The Troublesome Concept of Amateurism

Much of the controversy surrounding college sports and the NCAA centers on the role of amateurism in college sports. In its otherwise critical report on the state of college sports, the Knight Commission claimed in 2001, "At one time . . .

---

[3]"The National Collegiate Athletic Association Revised Budget for Fiscal Year Ending August 31, 2009." At http://www.ncaa.org/wps/wcm/connect/6d3874004e51aadc96e0d622cf56f2f3/2008-09+BUDGET+%28Budget+moves+in+08-09%29_FINAL.pdf?MOD=AJPERES&CACHEID=6d3874004e51aadc96e0d622cf56f2f3. Accessed August 17, 2009.

[a]mateurism was a cherished ideal. In such a context, it made sense to regard athletics as an educational undertaking. Young people were taught values ranging from fitness, cooperation, teamwork and perseverance to sportsmanship as moral endeavor."[4] Many of the regulations that colleges routinely place upon themselves—and violate—stem from the tension created by trying to uphold the notion that student-athletes are students first and athletes second. The idealized image of the past, however, is an illusion. Within the sphere of big-time college athletics, even the term *student-athlete* itself has a checkered history.

A Brief History of Amateurism and "the Olympic Ideal"

Long after the Olympics abandoned amateurism as a condition for competing, American colleges and universities remain wedded to the concept that their athletic teams should consist of students who engage in sports as a pastime rather than as a profession. Those who call for the "deprofessionalization" of college athletics often evoke the image of Olympic purity and sometimes explicitly urge colleges to "return to the Greek notion of amateur competition."[5] However, the historical record shows that the modern view of amateurism has less to do with the Greek Olympic ideal than with 19th-century British class divisions.

The Original Olympic Games   The Olympic Games were actually one of four sets of Greek athletic contests, the other three being the Pythian, Nemean, and Isthmian Games. The Olympics were first held in 776 B.C. (the earliest recorded date in history) and continued every four years for over a millenium to honor the Greek god Zeus. These athletic competitions had a deeper, more spiritual role in the lives of the ancient Greeks than sporting events have in the lives of people today. Athletic contests were an integral part of religious festivals, not a sideshow like the modern Thanksgiving Day football game or the Fourth of July doubleheader. The ancient Olympic Games came about "because Olympia was already an established sacred site, not the other way round."[6]

---

[4]Mark Alesia, "Tourney Money Fuels Pay-to-Play Debate," *Indianapolis Star* online at http://www.indystar.com/apps/pbcs.dll/article?AID=/20060401/SPORTS/604010509.

[5]The University of Colorado's president, Gordon Gee, quoted in Shannon Brownlee and Nancy Linnon, "The Myth of the Student-Athlete," *U.S. News and World Report,* January 8, 1990, p. 50 (from Lexis-Nexis). See also Welch Suggs, "The Demise of the 'Amateur Ideal,'" *Chronicle of Higher Education,* October 29, 1999, pp. A75–A76. The earliest known reference to an athletic contest was the funeral games that Achilles staged for his friend Patroclus in *The Iliad.*

[6]Quotation taken from Moses Finley and H. W. Pleket, *The Olympic Games: The First Thousand Years* (New York: Viking Press, 1976), p. 15. The other games honored Apollo, Herakles, and Poseidon. See Finley and Pleket, *The Olympic Games* (1976), pp. 23–25; Lynn Poole and Gray Poole, *History of Ancient Greek Olympic Games* (New York: Ivan Obolensky, Inc, 1963); B. Kidd, "The Myth of the Ancient Games," in *Five Ring Circus: Money, Power and Politics at the Olympic Games,* ed. by Alan Tomlinson and Garry Whannel (London: Pluto Press, 1984), p. 73; Francis Dealy, *Win at Any Cost: The Sell Out of College Athletics* (New York: Birch Lane Press, 1990), pp. 31–32 and 60; and Lawrence Hatab, "The Greeks and the Meaning of Athletics," in *Rethinking College Athletics,* ed. by Judith Andre and David James (Philadelphia: Temple University Press, 1991), pp. 32–35.

In the worldview of the ancient Greeks, people could rise above the limits of their mortality by defying death and performing heroic deeds in war. When they had no war to fight, the Greeks replaced the battlefield with the athletic field. In their struggles against one another and against adversity, the participants came to resemble the gods they worshipped. Indeed, the word *athlete* comes from the Greek word *athlos,* which means "conflict," or "struggle." Initially, the rewards for success at the Games were crowns of olive sprigs. This practice (which was the original reward even when the modern Olympic Games were revived) was supposed to symbolize the pure motives of the competitors, who sought only the joy and glory of competition as their reward.

Even then, however, the symbol of amateurism had little to do with reality. The practice of awarding an olive crown stems from the same legend that surrounds the origins of the Games. It states that in order to win the hand of the daughter of King Oenomaus and hence inherit the kingdom, Pelops, a young Greek hero, first had to beat Oenomaus in a chariot race. Having won the race—and in the process killing the king by sabotaging his chariot— Pelops wished to dispel the impression that he sought personal gain. He thus turned down the gold that was part of his prize for winning the race and asked instead to mark his victory with a crown made of a branch from a wild olive tree.

Following in this tradition, the olive crown given to the winners of the Olympic Games masked an array of greater rewards. Those selected to compete in the Games were regarded as heroes in their home cities. Honors, favorable marriages, and cash awaited them, especially if they returned victorious. According to Plutarch, Athenian winners at the Olympic Games were awarded 500 drachmai by their grateful city as early as 600 B.C. An Athenian inscription from the fifth century B.C. notes that Athens rewarded citizens who won an Olympic event with a free meal every day for the rest of their lives.[7] As a result of the ever-increasing prizes for victors at the Games, participants became increasingly professional, training full time for the Games. They also began to specialize in certain events, further detaching the Games from their original connection to warfare.[8] Greek athletes of ancient times earned enough to focus full time on athletic endeavors, as they were compensated with money and gifts. "[A] rising young sports star [could] support himself entirely by athletics. . . . Awards in Athens, for example, totaled an estimated $600,000 in today's terms."[9] After the Romans conquered Greece in the second century B.C., taking over Greek customs in the process, the Games turned into flagrant competitions between

---

[7]Finley and Pleket, *The Olympic Games* (1976), pp. 77–78; and University of Pennsylvania Museum of Anthropology and Archeology, "The Real Story of the Ancient Olympic Games," at http://www .upenn.edu/museum/Olympics/olympicathletes.html, 1996.

[8]Finley and Pleket, *The Olympic Games* (1976), pp. 70–71; Dealy, *Win at Any Cost* (1990), p. 60; and Hatab, "The Greeks and the Meaning of Athletics" (1991), pp. 31–35.

[9]Tony Perrotet, *The Naked Olympics* (New York: Random House, 2004), p. 53.

professional athletes, and they slowly degenerated until Christian Emperor Theodosius stopped them in A.D. 393, when he banned all pagan practices.[10]

The British Ethic and the Rise of the Modern Olympics By the 19th century, the Olympic Games of ancient Greece had been forgotten by all but a few historians and archaeologists. However, as the British came to dominate the economics, politics, and culture of Europe, their particular brand of "muscular Christianity" assumed increasing importance in the minds of friends and foes alike. The British, more than any country, took Juvenal's claim *mens sana in copore sano* ("a sound mind in a sound body") to heart. The Duke of Wellington found a practical application of this admonition when he attributed his victory over Napoleon at Waterloo to the sports his soldiers played at British public schools.[11]

For the rest of Europe, the impetus to develop sports programs seems to have sprung from defeat on the battlefield. Humiliated by Napoleon, the German states found a way to express their national sentiments and to combat the popular perception that they were physically inferior to the French through a mass gymnastics program known as the *Turnverein*, or Turner Movement.[12]

When the newly formed German nation turned the tables on the French in the Franco-Prussian War of 1870–1871, the French sought a model for national revival. A wealthy young Frenchman named Pierre de Coubertin looked to England to find a way to restore French youth to the moral and physical vigor associated with the days of Napoleonic glory. Two particular items captured de Coubertin's attention: the British educational system and its emphasis on athletics (probably a result of his lifelong fascination with the book *Tom Brown's School Days*) and the "Wenlock Olympic Games," a festival staged in the town of Wenlock by a physician and fitness advocate named William P. Brookes.

De Coubertin's 1892 proposal to revive the "Olympic" Games thus stems from an attempt to shame and inspire French youth to follow the example of superior athletes from elsewhere in the world, especially from England and the United States. In fact, de Coubertin's choice of the name "Olympic Games" was a mix of public relations gimmickry and his happening upon Dr. Brookes and his festival. De Coubertin found the name of Brookes's contest "more festive and potentially inspiring than any other at hand."[13]

---

[10]Hatab, "The Greeks and the Meaning of Athletics" (1991), p. 35; Richard Mandell, *The Nazi Olympics* (New York: Ballantine Books, 1972), pp. 4–5; Poole and Poole, *History of Ancient Greek Olympic Games* (1963), pp. 24–25 and 33; and Kidd, "The Myth of the Ancient Games" (1984), pp. 72–80.

[11]"The Battle of Waterloo was won on the playing fields of Eton." See Mandell, *The Nazi Olympics* (1972), pp. 8–9.

[12]Mandell, *The Nazi Olympics* (1972), pp. 12–13. Mass gymnastics survive to this day, as in the Czech *Sokol* movement.

[13]Mandell, *The Nazi Olympics* (1972), pp. 12–24; Alan Tomlinson, "De Coubertin and the Modern Olympics," in *Five Ring Circus: Money, Power and Politics at the Olympic Games*, ed. by Alan Tomlinson and Garry Whannel (London: Pluto Press, 1984), pp. 88–90; and David Young, *The Modern Olympics: A Struggle for Revival* (Baltimore: Johns Hopkins University Press, 1996), pp. 24–80.

Given the vital role of the Olympic Games in the history of competitive sports, it is worth noting that early sporting events were limited by gender. At the insistence of de Coubertin, women were prohibited from competing in early Olympic contests. Regrettably, this precedent turned out to be long lived. Women did not compete in the Olympics at all until 1900, and did not compete in track and field events until the 1928 Games.[14]

De Coubertin's aristocratic upbringing, his indifference to the reality of the original Olympic Games, and his worship of the English system of education explain the central part that amateurism plays in the modern Olympic ideal. Since the English schools that de Coubertin visited drew from the upper strata of British society, when he began to develop the foundation for the Olympic Games, he focused largely on attitudes held by the British upper class. As the next section describes, however, the British aristocracy was beginning to feel threatened by, and to react to, the encroachments made by working-class athletes on the "gentlemen's" sporting world.

11.2 Amateurism, Profits, and the NCAA

This section shows how the concept of amateurism is applied to the contemporary American university, revealing the dual nature of many restrictions placed on the collegiate athlete. Depending on one's viewpoint, the restrictions can be seen as either a moral stance in favor of academic ideals or as an exercise of monopsony power. The discussion builds upon the monopsony model described earlier and provides further insights into the relationship between marginal and average costs.

Chapter 2 showed that organized sports first took root among the well-to-do in the United States and England, spreading to other nations as they developed economically. As it expanded geographically, sports also expanded economically, coming within reach of the working class in the United States and England as the benefits of industrialization spread across all segments of these societies. The upper classes viewed the increasing participation—and then dominance—by the working-class teams with alarm. They felt that losing to teams drawn from "lesser" classes upset the natural order of society. In his classic *Theory of the Leisure Class*, Thorstein Veblen singled out sports as one of the "occupations" of a leisure class that studiously abstained from productive behavior. Their defeat at the hands of their social inferiors set dangerous social and political precedents, much as the competition between all-black and all-white teams would in generations to come.[15]

The responses of the upper classes to this challenge varied. Harvard and Yale responded to losses in rowing competitions against "lesser" colleges—such as

---

[14]Perrotet, *The Naked Olympics,* p. 160.

[15]William Baker, *Sports in the Western World* (Totowa, N.J.: Rowman & Littlefield, 1982), p. 125; Robert Burk, *Never Just a Game: Players, Owners, and American Baseball to 1920* (Chapel Hill: University of North Carolina Press, 1994); and Thorstein Veblen, *Theory of the Leisure Class* (New York: The Viking Press, 1967), particularly Chapter 3, "Conspicuous Leisure."

Massachusetts Agricultural College (later renamed the University of Massachusetts)—by withdrawing from intercollegiate competition in 1875. This effectively ended crew's two-decade dominance of intercollegiate athletics in the United States.[16] Crew teams in England—where Oxford and Cambridge Universities had been competing since 1829—took a more proactive approach to restricting competition by lower classes.[17] The British Rowing Association restricted competition to amateurs and defined an "amateur" as one who had never been "by trade or employment for wages a mechanic, artisan, or labourer or engaged in any menial duty."[18] This definition diverged dramatically from the notion held by the ancient Greeks, for whom "professional . . . meant a man who received proper training and devoted himself more or less full-time to an activity."[19] It also effectively excluded all competitors who were not independently wealthy.

The Code of Amateurism: Academic Ideals or Monopsony Power?

The British attitudes toward education and athletics took easy root in American universities, since "[n]ot only was the structure of educational instruction patterned after the English but the form of collegiate living, the collegiate way[,] was borrowed from the English."[20] Central to the "collegiate way" was a preoccupation with building the character of the students. The emphasis on character, which initially took the form of rigidly enforced religious devotions, often competed with intellectual concerns for primacy in American colleges.

While American society steadily moved away from strict religious adherence, colleges' preoccupation with character did not cease but was slowly replaced by the character-building force of athletics, epitomized in the 1940 film *Knute Rockne—All American*, a semibiographical film about the man who, as football coach at Notre Dame from 1918 to 1931, first brought the team to prominence. In the film, Rockne proclaims, "We [coaches] believe the finest work of man is building the character of man. We have tried to build courage and initiative, tolerance and persistence—without which the most educated brain in the head of man is not worth very much."[21]

---

[16]Ronald Smith, *Sports and Freedom: The Rise of Big-Time College Athletics* (New York: Oxford University Press, 1988), pp. 38–51.

[17]Allen Guttman, "The Anomaly of Intercollegiate Athletics," in *Rethinking College Athletics*, ed. by Judith Andre and David James (Philadelphia: Temple University Press, 1991), p. 18; and Ronald Smith, *Sports and Freedom* (1988), pp. 26–29.

[18]Quoted in Dealy, *Win at Any Cost* (1990), p. 60; and Smith, *Sports and Freedom* (1988), p. 166. Baker, *Sports in the Western World* (1982), p. 125, cites similar attitudes in the British Football Association. The class snobbery and ethnic prejudice that accompanied the code of amateurism is eloquently expressed in the 1981 film *Chariots of Fire*.

[19]Finley and Pleket, *The Olympic Games* (1976), p. 71.

[20]Smith, *Sports and Freedom* (1988), p. 11.

[21]Quoted in Murray Sperber, *Onward to Victory: The Crises that Shaped College Sports* (New York: Henry Holt and Co., 1998), p. 18. Sperber makes an intriguing case for claiming that this movie is the most significant American film of the 20th century.

Amateurism today is enshrined in the NCAA manual, which states:

Student-athletes shall be amateurs in an intercollegiate sport, and their participation should be motivated primarily by education and the physical, mental, and social benefits to be derived. Student participation in intercollegiate athletics is an avocation, and student-athletes should be protected from exploitation by professional and commercial enterprises.[22]

The manual goes on to define what aid a college athlete may receive:

A grant-in-aid administered by an educational institution is not considered to be pay or the promise of pay for athletics skill provided it does not exceed the financial aid limitations set by the association's membership.[23]

The limits on scholarship levels have long been criticized as insufficient to meet the total cost of a college education. In February of 2006, three former college athletes filed suit against the NCAA. They sought a $2,500 increase (a figure that the NCAA itself agrees is an accurate measure of the shortfall in expenses) in scholarships in the form of a stipend designed to cover the "full cost of attendance."[24] The case was settled in 2008. Under the settlement, the NCAA will make $218 million available to Division I schools through the 2012–2013 year.[25] The increased funding will be available through preexisting funds (the special assistance fund, the student-athlete opportunity and the academic enhancement fund), though the settlement increases accessibility to the funds. These funds may be used for additional semesters of education, health and safety expenditures, travel and other personal or family expenses, and clothing. In 2008–2009, most of the student-athlete opportunity funds (62 percent) were used for educational purposes, such as funding additional semesters of education. Most of the special assistance funds (68 percent) were used for clothing. Sixty percent of the academic enhancement funds were used for personnel, with another 25 percent used for tutoring.[26] Together, these increases represent a significant rise in the funding directed to Division I athletes. Whether these increases bring the value that

[22]NCAA, *2005–2006 NCAA—Division I Manual,* online at www.ncaa.org/library/division_/ _manual/2005-06/2005-06_ d1_manual.pdf.p5.

[23]NCAA, *Division I Manual,* p. 69.

[24]Quote is from Mark Alesia, "Tourney Money Fuels Pay-to-Play Debate," *IndyStar.com (Indianpolis Star* online edition), April 1, 2006. Available online at http://www.indystar.com/apps/pbcs.dll/ article?Date=20060401&Category=SPORTS&ArtNo=604010509&SectionCat=&Template=printart. Accessed August 22, 2006. See also Doug Lederman, "Court Challenge on Athletic Aid," *insidehighered.com (Inside Higher Ed* online edition) available online at http://www.insidehighered .com/news/2006/02/23/antitrust. Accessed August 22, 2006.

[25]Jack Carrey and Andy Gardiner, "NCAA Settlement Gives Aid to Athletes," *USA Today,* at http://www.usatoday.com/sports/college/2008-01-29-settlement-aid-details_N.htm. Accessed August 17, 2009.

[26]2008–2009 Revenue Distribution Plan. *NCAA,* at http://www.ncaa.org/wps/wcm/connect/ 46f776004e0d547d9ef9fe1ad6fc8b25/Revised+Revenue+Distribution+Summary_012709.pdf?MOD =AJPERES&CACHEID=46f776004e0d547d9ef9fe1ad6fc8b25. Accessed August 17, 2009.

college athletes bring to their institutions in line with the benefits the athletes receive is unclear.

In the cases of major revenue sports such as football and basketball, restrictions on allowable benefits to student-athletes can be viewed in two fundamentally different ways. On one hand, the NCAA can be seen as vigorously defending the academic mission of the university. According to this view, students who participate in athletics should not receive any privileges not accorded to the general student body.

On the other hand, it is possible to conclude that the NCAA—meaning the member schools that make up the NCAA—has subverted the market for athletic talent. Colleges have strict limits on what they can pay to attract a star quarterback or point guard. This restriction has led some to conclude that the NCAA is effectively acting like the enforcer in a cartel.[27] An enforcer can help a cartel to avert prisoner's dilemma problems like the one discussed in Chapter 4, in which some colleges overturned TV restrictions that had proved highly profitable for all colleges in favor of a less restrictive—and less profitable—arrangement. Table 11.1 shows that the same forces could lead colleges to compete for athletes by offering to pay them their market value, an action that some observers forcefully advocate.[28]

Table 11.1 shows a simplified version of the problem facing colleges that want to win but do not want to break the bank doing so. Both schools—Darwin

TABLE 11.1

The Prisoner's Dilemma Leads Colleges to Spend Heavily

	Darwin Spends Heavily	*Darwin Doesn't Spend*
Huxley Spends Heavily	Schools recruit evenly High recruiting costs	Huxley dominates rivalry
Huxley Doesn't Spend	Darwin dominates rivalry	Schools recruit evenly Low recruiting costs

[27]This view is forcefully expressed in Robert W. Brown, "An Estimate of the Rent Generated by a Premium College Football Player," *Economic Inquiry,* vol. 21, no. 4 (October 1993), pp. 671–684; Robert W. Brown, "Measuring Cartel Rents in the College Basketball Player Recruitment Market," *Applied Economics,* vol. 26, no. 1 (January 1994), pp. 27–34; Walter Byers with Charles Hammer, *Unsportsmanlike Conduct: Exploiting College Athletes* (Ann Arbor: University of Michigan Press, 1995); Arthur Fleisher, Brian Goff, and Robert Tollison, *The National Collegiate Athletic Association: A Study in Cartel Behavior* (Chicago: University of Chicago Press, 1992); and Paul Lawrence, *Unsportsmanlike Conduct: The National Collegiate Athletic Association and the Business of College Football* (New York: Praeger, 1987). While we focus on the exploitation of athletes, the NCAA also depressed the pay of assistant coaches, for which it was successfully sued for $54.5 million (see, for example, Welch Suggs, "NCAA to Pay $55-Million to Settle Lawsuit by Assistant Coaches," *Chronicle of Higher Education,* March 19, 1999, p. A47).

[28]See, for example, Gary S. Becker, "College Athletes Should Get Paid What They're Worth," *Business Week,* September 30, 1985, p. 38; and Rick Telander, *The Hundred Yard Lie: The Corruption of College Football and What We Can Do to Stop It* (New York: Simon and Schuster, 1989).

and Huxley—are evenly matched if neither spends money to attract athletes. Each school realizes, however, that it can dominate the other by spending heavily on its athletes. Each school also realizes that it cannot compete with the other school if it fails to match that school's spending. Both schools wind up spending large sums of money to attract students (the upper-left payoff quadrant in Table 11.1), though they would be better off not spending so much money (the lower-right payoff quadrant).

An enforcer can help Darwin and Huxley avoid the prisoner's dilemma by enforcing cooperation. This is accomplished by monitoring the schools' behavior and punishing anyone who deviates from the strategy that maximizes the group's well-being. In a cartel such as OPEC, an enforcer can be a large oil producer that threatens to increase production and drive down prices if the members do not obey their quotas. In college athletics, the NCAA can limit TV appearances, cut scholarships, or impose the "death penalty" described in Chapter 4 to keep schools from stepping out of line.

The goal of the cartel in this case would be to act like a monopsonist and minimize expenditures on athletes. This occurs where marginal expenditure on labor equals the marginal benefit of the last worker employed. Figure 11.1 shows the impact of a typical monopsony. The employer reduces both the number of workers and the level of pay below the competitive level, and a deadweight loss occurs.

The owners of professional teams relied on the reserve clause to ensure their monopsony power, and college athletes face similar types of rules that bind them to the colleges they initially commit to play for. NCAA regulations require that collegiate athletes who have made a written commitment to a

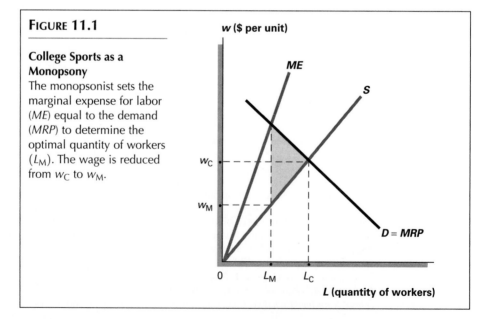

FIGURE 11.1

College Sports as a Monopsony
The monopsonist sets the marginal expense for labor (*ME*) equal to the demand (*MRP*) to determine the optimal quantity of workers (L_M). The wage is reduced from w_C to w_M.

school must sit out a year and lose a year of eligibility if they want to play for another school. For example, when basketball player Jonathan Haynes sought to transfer to Villanova University after spending only a few weeks at Temple University in the 1990–1991 academic year, he had to sacrifice two years, losing his eligibility for the year that he had briefly attended Temple and for the next year as well.

Again, these restrictions can be viewed in a more benign light. Restrictions on movement may help prevent the excesses of the "tramp athlete" of the early 20th century. Like the baseball players who jumped contracts in the days before the reserve clause, the tramp athlete was a mercenary who traveled from school to school, looking for the best deal. Carl Johanson, who spent eight years playing football at Williams, Harvard, and Cornell, may have set the record for such activity in the late 19th century. Some players never even bothered to enroll, as was the case for seven players on the 1893 University of Michigan football team.[29] The restrictions may thus have reinforced the academic mission of the university as well as its monopsony power.

Pay for Play: The Grant-in-Aid

Today, when sports fans across the country eagerly scan the newspapers to find out what blue-chip prospect has accepted a scholarship to play for old State U., it is hard to imagine that athletic scholarships were ever a subject of controversy. As recently as the late 1950s, however, many colleges refused to offer such payments for nonacademic talent.

While some schools openly offered athletic scholarships as early as 1900 (when Penn State began the practice) and a great many more offered money under the table, such practices were largely frowned upon.[30] In 1929, the Carnegie Commission on Education reported with some horror that a "system of recruiting and subsidizing has grown up, under which boys are offered pecuniary and other inducements to enter a particular college." Prior to 1956, the NCAA officially forbade schools from making any distinction in the aid it offered athletes and nonathletes, though the Carnegie Commission reported that as many as three-fourths of the NCAA's members disobeyed the rules they helped promulgate.[31] Officially, if not in practice, all students drew from the same pool of funds, which were awarded on the basis of a uniform set of criteria.

The defeat of the Sanity Code (detailed in Chapter 4) spelled the end of the attempt to treat athletes like other students. Indeed, the Code's defeat stemmed largely from its attempts to formalize the limits on financial aid and on the rampant unofficial support given to athletes by alumni and other boosters. In 1956,

---

[29]Smith, *Sports and Freedom* (1988), p. 177; and Lee Sigelman, "It's Academic—or Is It? Admissions Standards and Big-Time College Football," *Social Science Quarterly*, vol. 76, no. 2 (June 1995), p. 247.

[30]Smith, *Sports and Freedom* (1988), p. 171. In the 1880s Yale supposedly had a secret $100,000 fund to pay its athletes. See Dealy, *Win at Any Cost* (1990), p. 69; and Andrew Zimbalist, *Unpaid Professionals* (Princeton, N.J.: Princeton University Press, 1999), p. 7.

[31]Quote from Guttman, "The Anomaly of Intercollegiate Athletics" (1991), p. 20. See also Zimbalist, *Unpaid Professionals* (1999), p. 8.

the NCAA membership voted to allow schools to provide scholarships to athletes regardless of their financial need or academic merit. The justification for athletic grants-in-aid was essentially, "Everyone is doing it anyway, so we may as well keep it all out in the open where we can regulate things." In fact, the Big 10 conference tried for several years to hold athletes and nonathletes to the same standard for financial aid. Other schools questioned the sincerity of the Big 10's stance and pointed out that, while the schools did not give outright athletic scholarships, they did provide ample compensation for questionable on-campus employment.[32]

What's in a Name? The Lot of the "Student-Athlete"

While the advent of grants-in-aid specifically targeted for athletes may have eliminated hypocrisy in recruiting, it also created a number of philosophical and legal problems for colleges. Philosophically, schools now had to reconcile themselves with their provision of financial assistance to students for participating in activities that often forced them to miss classes. In the 1999–2000 season, West Virginia University's basketball team sought to cope with an asbestos problem in its home arena by scheduling "home games" in Wheeling (75 miles away) and Charleston (155 miles away). Futhermore, the West Virginia coach wanted to practice at the arena the day before a game, meaning that the West Virginia team was on the road for 52 days from December 1999 through February 2000.[33]

More practically, schools had placed themselves in the position of being considered the athletes' employers. This relationship left colleges open to claims for workers' compensation insurance by athletes who were injured "on the job." NCAA Executive Director Walter Byers first coined the term *student-athlete* in an attempt to avoid such claims. In a Kafkaesque twist, athletes who wish to receive an athletic scholarship must now sign an agreement that explicitly rejects the notion that they are being paid for their performance as athletes.[34]

Measuring the Net Value of Athletes to Colleges

By depressing what they pay their athletes, colleges can generate considerable economic rent. **Economic rent** equals the difference between the marginal revenue product (*MRP*) of the athlete and the payment for tuition and fees. Robert Brown has measured the rents that a college generates as a result of attracting a premium athlete to its program.

Brown estimated the *MRP* of premium players by first assuming that a professional franchise drafts a player only if it regards that player as having the

---

[32]See, for example, Byers, *Unsportsmanlike Conduct* (1995), pp. 67–72; and Sperber, *Onward to Victory* (1998), pp. 177–185 and 227–242.

[33]See Seth Davis, "A Blight on the Mountaineers," *Sports Illustrated*, December 6, 1999, pp. 80–81. See also Byers, *Unsportsmanlike Conduct* (1995), p. 103.

[34]Zimbalist, *Unpaid Professionals* (1999), p. 37; and Byers, *Unsportsmanlike Conduct* (1995), pp. 67–70.

potential to be a professional. He then estimated how the number of players the college teams have sent to the professional draft (controlling for overall team quality) affects the teams' revenues.

Brown found that a player with the potential to play in the NFL brought a college football team between $539,000 and $646,000 per year, more than $2 million over a 4-year career. The premium for attracting a blue-chip basketball player was even greater, as he generated between $871,000 and $1 million annually.[35] In both cases, the colleges appear to profit handsomely from an annual commitment of perhaps $30,000 in scholarship money.

Dividing the Profits: The NCAA as an Efficient Cartel

As we showed in Chapter 4, the NCAA has also tried to use its power as an incidental cartel to act as a monopolist. Our simple model of monopoly behavior, however, is inadequate for analyzing how cartels behave. Unlike a monopoly, a cartel is not monolithic. In addition to determining what level of output maximizes profit, a cartel must allocate output and profit among its members. To see how a cartel operates, consider a cartel with only two members (the general conclusions hold for a cartel of any size).

The problem facing a cartel with two members is identical to the problem facing a monopoly that must decide how to allocate its output between two plants. If the plants are identical in every way, the decision is easy: Just allow each plant to produce half the output. This corresponds to an equal division of the monopoly profit between the two members of the cartel.

Generally, however, cartels consist of firms that are not identical. Figure 11.2 shows the marginal cost curves for two heterogeneous firms, A and B. Since the marginal cost curve for Firm A lies below that for Firm B, it is cheaper for Firm A to increase its output a little bit than it is for Firm B if both firms are producing the same level of output. Given the marginal cost curves for the individual firms, we can construct the marginal cost curve for the monopoly by computing the horizontal sum, just as we computed the market demand curve from individual demand curves in Chapter 2. At very low levels of output, the joint marginal cost curve corresponds to the marginal cost curve for Firm A alone (MC_A), since Firm B can produce nothing at such low marginal cost. Until Firm A's output reaches Q_1, the cartel as a whole can increase output most cheaply by letting Firm A produce everything. When Firm A reaches output level Q_1, the cost of increasing its output by one unit is the same as Firm B's cost for producing its first unit of output. At this point, it pays for both firms to produce, and the marginal cost curve of the cartel (MC_C) is the horizontal sum of the individual firms' curves.

If the two firms act like a single firm, then they face a single market demand curve. This effectively says that consumers do not care whether they

---

[35]Brown, "An Estimate of the Rent Generated by a Premium College Football Player" (1993), p. 679; and Brown, "Measuring Cartel Rents in the College Basketball Recruitment Market" (1994), p. 32. Brown's actual estimation is more complex than shown here.

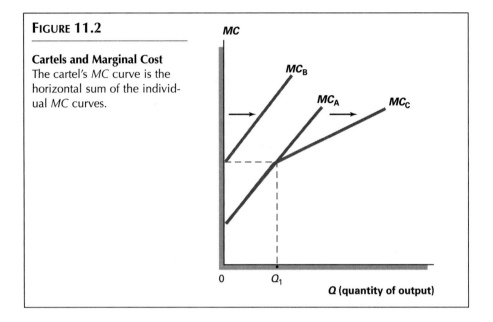

FIGURE 11.2

Cartels and Marginal Cost
The cartel's *MC* curve is the horizontal sum of the individual *MC* curves.

make their purchases from Firm A or Firm B. As a result, the two firms also face a common marginal revenue curve, as seen in Figure 11.3.

The optimal level of output for the cartel occurs where the cartel's marginal cost curve (MC_C) meets the marginal revenue curve (MR). The overall output of the cartel is thus Q_C^*, where $MR^* = MC_C^*$. The division of output that maximizes overall profit allocates production according to the individual firms' marginal costs so that $MC_A = MC_B = MR^*$. In Figure 11.3, this occurs at Q_A^* for Firm A and Q_B^* for Firm B. Because the marginal cost curve for the cartel is the horizontal sum of the individual marginal cost curves, $Q_A^* + Q_B^* = Q_C^*$.

A standard cartel therefore allocates the lion's share of output and profit to its most efficient members. It rewards colleges that generate the greatest net revenue. Colleges cannot allocate resources quite this easily. Athletic conferences and the NCAA itself have traditionally required that schools share their revenues with less profitable members. The need to share revenues means that the NCAA and collegiate conferences may more closely resemble clubs than cartels. Recall that, according to the theory of clubs, a league determines its optimal size by weighing the additional revenue from admitting a new member against the cost of sharing revenue with an additional member. In effect, when a league adds a new member, it increases the size of its pie, but it also increases the number of slices into which the pie must be divided. Leagues therefore seek out those members who contribute the most revenue and weed out members that are a drag on net revenues. This has led to several recent controversies in college sports.

Consider football. College football's Division I-A level was created because the most profitable football programs wanted to stop sharing TV revenue with

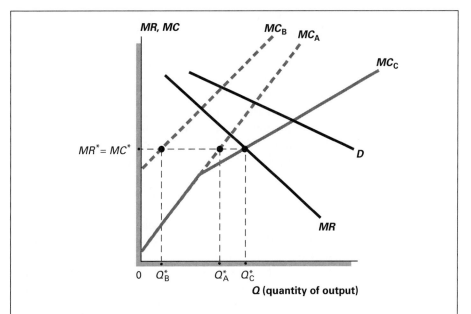

FIGURE 11.3

Optimal Division of Output by a Cartel
The cartel sets the optimal level of output, Q*$_C$, by setting marginal revenue (MR)
equal to the sum of the marginal cost curves (MC$_C$). Firm A produces Q*$_A$ and
firm B produces Q*$_B$.

less profitable programs. The conflict lay behind the antitrust suit by the
Universities of Georgia and Oklahoma discussed in Chapter 4. After losing the
lawsuit, the NCAA recognized that it had to accommodate the major football
powers. Before the lawsuit, the NCAA had sorted all athletic programs into
Divisions I, II, and III according to the number of sports they sponsored and the
size and number of athletic scholarships they offered. In 1978, the NCAA subdivided Division I into Division I-A and I-AA (renamed Football Bowl Subdivision [FBS] and Football Championship Subdivision [FCS] in 2006). While there
are a number of criteria for FBS status, the most controversial criterion relates to
a school's profitability rather than a school's size. Specifically, FBS schools must
have an average home attendance at its football games of at least 15,000.[36]

The FBS has subdivided still further. In the 1990s, the commissioners of
the major football conferences and representatives of the major TV networks
created the Bowl Championship Series (BCS). The avowed aim of the BCS is
to bring order to the mass of postseason bowl games (totaling 34 in
2009–2010) and to create a clear "national champion" collegiate football team.

---

[36]Until 2003, schools had to sell an average of 17,000 tickets. The new requirement refers to actual
attendance.

An additional effect of the consortium has been to restrict participation in the major bowl games largely to teams from the major football conferences. Since the BCS bowl games generate larger TV ratings and, as a result, are far more lucrative than the non–BCS bowl games, the effect has been to increase the disparity between the major football conferences and the lesser conferences. Table 11.2 shows the difference in revenue that existed through 2008 between conferences whose champions automatically qualify for the BCS and conferences without guaranteed access to the BCS. The football programs in conferences in which the champion receives an automatic bid can count on receiving roughly $20 million, while those in other FBS conferences receive much less.

In 2007, the BCS format changed yet again to include a fifth major bowl game under a system called "double hosting." The double hosting format is not a true play-off system. It pits the number 1 and 2 seeds from the final BCS poll against one another, rather than a "plus-one" system that would involve two winners from the four major BCS bowls played the week before. The original four BCS bowls (The Orange, Fiesta, Rose, and Sugar Bowls) plus the national championship game will be populated by winners of the BCS conferences plus four at-large bids. Notre Dame is guaranteed an at-large bid if it finishes in the top eight in the rankings. Despite these changes, some non–BCS schools remain unhappy and have threatened legal action, claiming that the current system unfairly excludes certain teams and potentially disqualifies teams that may, in fact, be the best in the country from the national championship game. In 2009, Utah's Attorney General began investigating the BCS for a possible violation of the Sherman Antitrust Act. At the heart of the complaint is the University of

TABLE 11.2

BCS Revenue Distributions by Conference, 2005–2006 through 2007–2008

Conference	2006–2007	2007–2008
Big 10	$22,588,675	$22,824,992
Southeastern	22,588,675	22,824,992
Big 12	18,088,675	22,824,992
Pacific 10	18,088,675	18,324,992
Atlantic Coast	18,088,675	18,324,992
Big East	18,088,675	18,324,992
Western Athletic	9,008,000	9,170,000
Mountain West	3,529,600	3,724,000
Conference USA	2,486,400	2,616,000
Sunbelt	1,443,200	2,062,000
Mid-American	1,964,800	1,508,000
Notre Dame	4,500,000	1,316,971

Source: "Bowl Championship Series, Five Year Summary of Revenue Distribution 2003–2007," *NCAA* at http://www.ncaa.org/wps/wcm/connect/f54bee004e0b9a869ce0fc1ad6fc8b25/BCS++Revenue+ Distribution+by+Conference+2007-08.pdf?MOD=AJPERES&CACHEID=f54bee004e0b9a869ce0fc1ad6fc8b25. Accessed August 17, 2009.

Utah, whose football team became the first school from a conference without an automatic qualifying bid to win two BCS bowl games. Despite being undefeated in both seasons, Utah was left out of the national championship game in both years. If the suit were successful, the courts could force the BCS to end the current selection process for the national championship game.[37]

11.3   College as an Investment for the Student-Athlete

As explained in Chapter 8, the basic theory of human capital states that workers invest in skills in order to increase their future earnings. When workers invest in on-the-job training that will increase their earning power at competing employers, they "pay" for their training by receiving lower pay than they otherwise would. Therefore, looking solely at their wages or salaries understates the value of their total compensation.

In this section, we examine the claim by Penn State's football coach, Joe Paterno, that "An athlete who . . . graduates is overpaid"[38] from a number of standpoints. Student-athletes who receive a degree see a significant increase in their lifetime earnings thanks to their participation in athletics regardless of whether they play professionally. Even if they do not graduate, student-athletes who go on to professional sports careers may be making such a significant investment in their skills as athletes that their scholarships overcompensate them. This section examines whether intercollegiate athletics is a good investment for athletes.

While in college, student-athletes may invest in their physical human capital and prepare for a career as a professional athlete, or they may invest in their intellectual human capital and work toward a college degree. If one judges success in either area by the likelihood of receiving a degree or making the professional ranks, then playing intercollegiate sports as a scholarship athlete does not appear to be a good investment.

The data in Table 11.3 suggest that professional athletics resembles the winner-take-all environment described in Chapter 8. The payoff to being a professional athlete is very high, but the odds of success are very low. Table 11.3 comes from an NCAA study that used data from 1982 through 2006. The table clearly shows that the chances of moving from the NCAA to the professional ranks in any of the major sports is very small. Other than baseball, in which players rarely move from the NCAA to the major leagues, and hockey, in which players also often are assigned to minor league teams when drafted, the chances are less than 2 percent. Even this estimate is extremely generous, as the study assumed that every drafted player earned a spot on the roster. For example, in baseball, the figures are likely skewed upward by the fact that there are

---

[37]Lester Munson and Paula Lavigne, "Utah has BCS Lawsuit in Mind," ESPN.com at http://sports.espn.go.com/espn/print?id=4030992&type=story. Accessed August 17, 2009.

[38]Quoted in Sheehan, *Keeping Score* (1996), p. 286.

TABLE 11.3

Probability of Moving from NCAA Participation to Professional Career in Sports, 1982–2006

Student-Athletes	Men's Basketball	Women's Basketball	Football	Baseball	Men's Ice Hockey	Men's Soccer
NCAA Senior Student-Athletes	3,682	3,355	13,612	6,393	883	4,398
NCAA Student-Athletes Drafted	44	32	250	600	33	76
Percent High School to NCAA	3.0	3.3	5.7	6.1	11.0	5.5
Percent NCAA to Professional	1.2	1.0	1.8	9.4	3.7	1.7

Source: Estimated Probability of Competing in Athletics Beyond the High School Interscholastic Level. http://www.ncaa.org/wps/ncaa?key=/ncaa/NCAA/Academics%20and%20Athletes/Education%20and%20Research/Probability%20of%20Competing/. Accessed August 19, 2009.

over 20 rounds in the draft, nearly enough to repopulate the roster of every team every year. Most of these drafted players never actually make a major league roster.

A study by James Long and Steven Caudill contradicts the above reasoning and suggests that athletics may be a good investment even if it does not lead to a professional career. They find that men who participate in intercollegiate athletics earn more in later life than men who do not. (They find no statistically significant differential for women.) The study, however, is hampered by limitations imposed by the data. Data sets that identify whether a person participated in interscholastic or intercollegiate athletics and follow his or her earnings history are only recently available and are often imperfect. The data available to Long and Caudill did not permit them to control for either the sport the student played or the school attended. Their study thus treats squash players at Swarthmore and football players at Ohio State as one and the same.[39]

Because of the lack of appropriate data, both researchers and the popular media have generally not tried to measure future earnings and looked at the graduation rates of varsity athletes instead. Overall, the graduation rates of varsity athletes—and of football players and basketball players in particular—do not differ significantly from those of nonathletes and in some cases are marginally higher. However, this observation may be misleading. It does not, for example, account for the fact that, unlike other students, scholarship athletes rarely have to leave school because they cannot pay their tuition bills. Conversely, as noted in Chapter 8, athletes may leave college early for the (sometimes incorrectly) anticipated bonanza of a professional career. Equating

---

[39]James Long and Steven Caudill, "The Impact of Participation in Intercollegiate Athletics on Income and Graduation," *Review of Economics and Statistics,* vol. 73, no. 3 (August 1991), pp. 525–531. See also Zimbalist, *Unpaid Professionals* (1999), p. 51.

the graduation rates of athletes and nonathletes also fails to account for the millions of dollars spent on academic support facilities for athletes, a service mandated by the NCAA. The magnitude of such commitments was made clear by University of Michigan president emeritus James J. Duderstadt, who noted that "the Student Athlete Support Program consists of a director, 6 full-time advisors, 3 assistant advisors, 70 tutors, 10 specialized writing instructors, and 15 proctors for supervised study sessions."[40] Finally, the aggregate statistic obscures the difference between major athletic powers and small, more recreational programs. Football players and basketball players at major programs are less likely to graduate than other athletes and are far less likely to graduate than the typical male undergraduate at their institution. Moreover, this gap is generally larger at the more successful programs.[41]

Table 11.4 shows average graduation success rates (GSR) for all of the BCS major bowl schools, plus schools that competed in selected other bowls for 2008–2009. The **graduation success rate** modifies the federal graduation rate (all first-time full-time students who complete their degree within six years) by excluding students who leave the school in good academic standing from the denominator and including those who transfer in and graduate in the numerator. Thus, GSRs are typically higher than the federal rate.[42] Tables 11.5 and 11.6 show the GSRs for the for the men's and women's teams that reached the 2008 "sweet 16" round of the NCAA basketball tournament. The data show that most men's teams were more successful on the court or field than in the classroom.

For the football teams shown in Table 11.4, the GSR is 10 or more percentage points lower than for all student athletes in all but four cases, and more than 20 percentage points lower in seven cases. Only at Cincinnati do football players graduate at a higher rate than the overall student-athlete average, and the difference is just 2 percentage points. In contrast, football players at Michigan State graduated at a rate nearly 30 percentage points lower than the average for all student athletes.

Tables 11.5 and 11.6 show that the graduation success rates vary dramatically by gender when it comes to basketball. For women's teams that reached the sweet 16, 11 had graduation success rates that were *higher* than the overall student-athlete average. At Tennessee, Connecticut, and Oklahoma State, the GSR for women's basketball players was 14 or more percentage points higher

---

[40]James J. Duderstadt, *Intercollegiate Athletics and the American University: A University President's Perspective* (Ann Arbor, University of Michigan Press, 2000), p. 199.

[41]See, for example, Dean Purdy, D. Stanley Eitzen, and Rick Hufnagel, "Are Athletes Also Students? The Educational Attainment of College Athletes," in *Sports and Higher Education*, ed. by Donald Chu, Jeffrey Segrave, and Beverly Becker (Champaign, Ill.: Human Kinetics Publishers, 1985), pp. 231–234; and Louis Amato, John Gandar, Irvin Tucker, and Richard Zuber, "Bowls Versus Playoffs: The Impact on Football Player Graduation Rates in the National Collegiate Athletic Association," *Economics of Education Review*, vol. 15, no. 2 (April 1996), pp. 187–195. Amato et al. find that the graduation rate for players in Division I-A programs declines by 3 percent per bowl appearance. They find no statistically significant relationship for Division I-AA programs.

[42]"A New Way to Keep Score," *Inside Higher Ed*, online at http://www.insidehighered.com/news/ 2005/12/20/grad. Accessed August 17, 2009.

TABLE 11.4

Academic Progress Rates (APRs) and Graduation Success Rates (GSRs) for Selected Bowl Teams, 2008–2009

Team	APR	Football GSR	Overall Student-Athlete GSR
Florida	963	68	87
Oklahoma	952	46	69
Utah	954	57	75
Alabama	955	55	77
Virginia Tech	932	75	85
Cincinnati	947	73	71
Ohio State	968	52	78
Texas	939	50	72
Penn State	976	78	89
USC	956	54	69
Georgia	976	48	70
Michigan State	931	51	79
LSU	960	54	69
Georgia Tech	957	48	70
Northwestern	973	92	97
Missouri	951	59	71
Vanderbilt	969	91	94
Boston College	970	92	96

Sources: "2009 NCAA Division I Academic Progress Rate (APR) Reports by School," at http://www.ncaa.org/wps/ncaa?key=/ncaa/ ncaa/academics+and+athletes/education+and+research/academic+reform/apr/2009/2007-08_school_apr_data.html; "2008 NCAA Division I Graduation Success Rate (GSR) Data," at http://www.ncaa.org/wps/ncaa?key=/ncaa/ncaa/academics+and+athletes/ education+and+research/academic+reform/gsr/2008/2008_d1_school_gsr_data.html; and "Overall student athlete GSR data: 2008 NCAA Division I Federal Graduation Rate Data," at http://www.wwwncaa.com/wps/ncaa?key=/ncaa/ncaa/academics+and+ athletes/education+and+research/academic+reform/grad+rate/2008/2008_d1_school_grad_rate_data.html.

than the overall rate. Only 5 teams had GSRs below the overall rate and most differences were small. In contrast, 12 of the 16 men's teams had GSRs below the overall rate. Two schools, UCLA and Louisville, were more than 30 percentage points lower, and three schools, Washington State, Tennessee, and Texas, were more than 40 percentage points lower.

Studies cite a variety of reasons for the low graduation rates of football and men's basketball players, such as the fact that athletes are less prepared for college than their fellow students. A case study of students at Colorado State University from 1970 through 1980 showed that athletes there had lower SAT scores, lower grades, and lower high school class rank than the typical Colorado State student. The shortfall in preparation was particularly large for male athletes, black athletes, and members of the football and men's basketball teams. A more recent study of Division I-A football programs showed that similar gaps existed at many schools well into the 1990s: The average entering

TABLE 11.5

Academic Progress Rates (APRs) and Graduation Success Rates (GSRs) for Men's 2008 Sweet 16 Teams

School	APR	Basketball GSR	Overall Student-Athlete GSR
Kansas	1000	64	70
Villanova	985	89	95
Wisconsin	933	86	79
Davidson	1000	100	97
UCLA	968	46	79
Western Kentucky	972	100	80
Xavier	976	82	92
West Virginia	960	41	68
North Carolina	989	86	85
Washington State	946	33	73
Tennessee	924	38	78
Louisville	965	42	75
Memphis	953	55	72
Michigan State	985	60	79
Texas	979	31	72
Stanford	968	67	95

Sources: "2009 NCAA Division I Academic Progress Rate (APR) Reports by School," at http://www.ncaa.org/wps/ncaa?key=/ncaa/ncaa/academics+and+athletes/education+and+research/academic+reform/apr/2009/2007-08_school_apr_data.html; "2008 NCAA Division I Graduation Success Rate (GSR) Data," at http://www.ncaa.org/wps/ncaa?key=/ncaa/ncaa/academics+and+athletes/education+and+research/academic+reform/gsr/2008/2008_d1_school_gsr_data.html; and "Overall student athlete GSR data: 2008 NCAA Division I Federal Graduation Rate Data," at http://www.wwwncaa.com/wps/ncaa?key=/ncaa/ncaa/academics+and+athletes/education+and+research/academic+reform/grad+rate/2008/2008_d1_school_grad_rate_data.html.

student had SAT scores 165 points higher than the average entering student with a football scholarship, and coaches who try to build a team that resembles the student body at large may damage their chances of winning by "unduly" restricting their recruiting, as teams with larger gaps in SAT scores generally had better records.[43]

Another study claims that college athletes choose to not pursue their studies as the result of rationally maximizing their utility. It points out that it makes more sense for a student-athlete to focus on his prospects as a football player at Notre Dame, which sent 76 players to the professional ranks from 1979 through 1993, than at Bucknell, which sent only 1 player to the NFL during the same time period. In light of such differences in professional prospects, the authors of this study suggest that student-athletes make their decisions to attend a specific college—and to become part of a specific athletic program—as part of their

---

[43]See, for example, Purdy et al., "Are Athletes Also Students?" (1985), pp. 221–234; and Sigelman, "It's Academic—or Is It?" (1995), pp. 247–261.

TABLE 11.6

Academic Progress Rates (APRs) and Graduation Success Rates (GSRs) for 2008 Women's Sweet 16 Teams

School	APR	Basketball GSR	Overall Student-Athlete GSR
Connecticut	991	100	81
Old Dominion	962	73	74
George Washington	977	100	94
Rutgers	968	69	80
Maryland	972	67	79
Vanderbilt	979	100	94
Pittsburgh	976	93	84
Stanford	989	100	95
North Carolina	970	90	85
Louisville	954	80	75
Oklahoma State	906	89	75
Louisiana State	967	70	69
Tennessee	973	100	78
Notre Dame	983	100	98
Duke	989	90	97
Texas A&M	956	67	72

Sources: "2009 NCAA Division I Academic Progress Rate (APR) Reports by School," at http://www.ncaa.org/wps/ncaa?key=/ ncaa/ncaa/academics+and+athletes/education+and+research/academic+reform/apr/2009/2007-08_school_apr_data.html; "2008 NCAA Division I Graduation Success Rate (GSR) Data," at http://www.ncaa.org/wps/ncaa?key=/ncaa/ncaa/academics+and+ athletes/education+and+research/academic+reform/gsr/2008/2008_d1_school_gsr_data.html; and "Overall student athlete GSR data: 2008 NCAA Division I Federal Graduation Rate Data," at http://www.wwwncaa.com/ wps/ncaa?key=/ncaa/ncaa/ academics+and+athletes/education+and+research/academic+reform/grad+rate/2008/2008_d1_school_grad_rate_data.html.

broader career choices. It is therefore no more surprising for a football player from a traditional football power such as Tennessee to fail to make the NFL than it is for a premed student at a small liberal arts college to fail to get into medical school.[44]

11.4   The NCAA and the Uneasy Coexistence of Athletics and Academia

In this section, we do not view the NCAA as a profit-maximizing monopolist. Instead, we adopt a more benign interpretation of the NCAA and treat it as a regulatory agency, like the U.S. Food and Drug Administration or the

---

[44]Lawrence DeBrock, Wallace Hendricks, and Roger Koenker, "The Economics of Persistence: Graduation Rates of Athletes as Labor Market Choice," *Journal of Human Resources*, vol. 31, no. 3 (Summer 1996), pp. 513–539.

Occupational Safety and Health Administration, with the goal of ensuring the safety of a product or the workplace. Problems, however, often accompany an agency's attempts to regulate an industry in which members seek to circumvent regulations. This section also discusses how the motives of colleges to build athletic programs—and to avoid or undermine regulation—stem from the same desire for prestige and recognition that motivated cities in Chapter 7.

As you consider this material, keep in mind that the role of athletics within the broader institutional mission of the college or university varies enormously from school to school. Throughout this chapter, much of our focus is on major revenue-producing programs (i.e., football and basketball) at large universities. We should not expect the athletics department at a small, selective liberal arts college to resemble the athletics program at Penn State University, and it does not. Most liberal arts colleges compete in Division III, where no sports, including football and basketball, are expected to earn more than trivial revenues, students are not allowed to receive any form of athletic scholarships, and students do not typically have aspirations of playing beyond the college level. Thus, although there may be a few thousand people at a football game on a Saturday afternoon, athletics exist primarily for the student-athletes themselves as a valued activity. Intercollegiate athletics are important at such schools. It would be wrong, however, to lump all collegiate athletic activities together as we consider their economic implications. In contrast to small-school sports, revenue-producing teams at major universities may be among the highest-profile activities at the university. Such teams play televised games in stadiums filled with tens of thousands of fans and have coaches that earn salaries measured in millions (and may be greater than the salary of the president of the university). In this section, we consider the development of "big-time" athletics and discuss their status in today's universities.

As in baseball a generation or so earlier, the athletes themselves ran intercollegiate athletics during the late 19th century. Students operated sports clubs independent of—and sometimes in defiance of—faculty and administration. Indeed, most university administrations seemed disdainful at best toward the growing popularity of football among their students. In refusing to allow a group of students to travel to Ann Arbor to play a football game at the University of Michigan in 1873, Cornell President Andrew D. White proclaimed, "I will not permit thirty men to travel four hundred miles to agitate a bag of wind."[45] The very size of a football squad may have been determined by such hostility, as the Yale Football Association pushed for team size to be limited to 11 players because it feared that the faculty would oppose allowing a larger group of students to leave campus for away games.[46] While the informal organization of sport in America resembled its British antecedents, differences soon appeared between the British and American models of intercollegiate sport, which reflected the differing social milieux in which the sports took place. Students at the major British universities "were gentlemen first and students

---

[45]Smith, *Sports and Freedom* (1988), p. 74

[46]Smith, *Sports and Freedom* (1988), pp. 73–77.

and athletes only incidentally."[47] While aristocratic Englishmen felt they were above engaging in intense competition on the playing fields, the more egalitarian Americans soon progressed from viewing intercollegiate athletics as an opportunity for friendly competition between schools to viewing them as sporting contests to be won.[48] The pressure to win increased when the control of college sports passed out of the hands of students and into those of faculty and administrators.

The shift of control began in the early 1880s, when many colleges established faculty oversight committees.[49] The rationale for such committees was concern over the growing violence in football.

Attitudes, however, soon changed. In the eyes of faculty, administrators, and alumni, teams came to represent the entire school. Just as a city could not be a "world-class" city without a winning professional franchise, colleges came to believe that a winning team was part of a top-flight university. Schools, like cities, saw sports as a way to raise their profiles to the national level. Instead of attracting business, however, schools sought to attract students, prestige, and funds.[50]

Why Schools Promote Big-Time Athletic Programs

As early as the 1880s, colleges faced the same forces that cities did decades later when they began to bid against one another for sports franchises. At first, the two situations do not appear at all similar. Unlike professional franchises, intercollegiate athletic programs are inextricably linked to the universities that house them. While the NFL's Rams left southern California for a better deal in St. Louis, one could hardly imagine UCLA's football team making a similar move. Indeed, the NCAA discourages such moves even on an individual level, let alone a team level. As with cities, however, public goods and financial spillovers play a major role in motivating colleges to invest in big-time athletic programs. College teams give students a sense of identity and belonging that they do not seem to get in the classroom. Paul "Bear" Bryant, former football coach at the University of Alabama, justified the prominence of his program by claiming that "it was unlikely that 50,000 people would show up to watch an English professor give a final exam."[51]

The consumption of the public good may extend beyond the campus, as several studies have shown that colleges with "big-time" athletic departments attract more and better students.[52] Studies suggest, for example, that schools that

---

[47]Dealy, *Win at Any Cost* (1990), p. 60.

[48]Dealy, *Win at Any Cost* (1990), pp. 60–61; and Smith, *Sports and Freedom* (1988), p. 34.

[49]Princeton formed the first such committee in 1881. See Dealy, *Win at Any Cost* (1990), p. 68.

[50]Dealy, *Win at Any Cost* (1990), pp. 51 and 68; Guttman, "The Anomaly of Intercollegiate Athletics" (1991), p. 21; and Lawrence, *Unsportsmanlike Conduct* (1987), pp. 6–7.

[51]Quoted in Zimbalist, *Unpaid Professionals* (1999), p. 223.

[52]For a particularly cynical view of "mission-driven athletics," see Murray Sperber, *Beer and Circus: How Big-Time College Sports Is Crippling Undergraduate Education* (New York: Henry Holt, 2000).

belong to major athletic conferences attract freshmen with higher SAT scores, and that the more successful a school's football program is, the higher the scores rise. The reason for the higher SATs appears to be that success on the football field expands a school's overall applicant pool (at least for Division I-A programs), allowing the school to generate more revenue by admitting more students or to generate greater prestige by being more selective in its admissions process.[53]

The studies, however, rely on assumptions that may invalidate their conclusions. For example, when a study equates a big-time football program with one that belongs to a major athletic conference, it includes many of the nation's premier state universities.[54] Finding that such programs attract more and better students may reflect the impact of the school's position in the state rather than the prominence of its football team.

A survey of 500 college-bound high school seniors in the spring of 2000 provides support to both proponents and opponents of college sports. The survey found that "73 percent of the respondents said their decision to attend a given college was not influenced by its position in the divisional hierarchy of the National Collegiate Athletic Association. And more than a third—37 percent— said they did not know whether their college of choice belonged to Division I, II, or III."[55] This result can be interpreted in several ways. On one hand, the vast majority of students do not care about college sports. On the other hand, over one-fourth of college applicants admitted to taking the success of Duke's basketball team or Florida State's football team into account when deciding whether to attend those colleges. Implicitly, if 73 percent do not care, then 27 percent do care. Whether success on the field brings success in the admissions office remains an open question.

Even if it is possible to attribute successful recruiting to successful athletic departments, these same studies also have a dark side. They assert that the key to success lies in having a winning program in high-visibility sports such as football and men's basketball. Success in these sports is **a zero-sum game** in which one team's success is another team's failure. The expenditures the college must expend to establish and maintain a winning program may offset the benefits of a winning program to the student body as a whole.[56]

---

[53]See Melvin Borland, Brian Goff, and Robert Pulsinelli, "College Athletics: Financial Burden or Boon?" in *Advances in the Economics of Sport*, vol. 1 (New York: JAI Press, 1992), p. 218; Robert McCormick and Maurice Tinsley, "Athletics Versus Academics? Evidence from SAT Scores," *Journal of Political Economy*, vol. 95, no. 5 (October 1987), pp. 1103–1116; and Robert Murphy and Gregory Trandel, "The Relation Between a University's Football Record and the Size of Its Applicant Pool," *Economics of Education Review*, vol. 13, no. 3 (September 1994), pp. 265–270.

[54]This opens the door to the question of what constitutes a "major" conference. Robert McCormick and Maurice Tinsley, "Athletics and Academics: A Model of University Contributions," *Sportometics*, ed. by Brian Goff and Robert Tollison (College Station: Texas A&M University Press, 1990), pp. 193–204, used the Atlantic Coast, Southeastern, Southwest, Big 10, Big 8, and Pacific 10 conferences.

[55]Welch Suggs, "In Choosing Colleges, Students Give Little Weight to the Quality of Sports Teams, Poll Finds," *Chronicle of Higher Education*, March 14, 2001.

[56]See Borland et al., "College Athletics: Financial Burden or Boon?" (1992), pp. 218 and 227–230; and McCormick and Tinsley, "Athletics Versus Academics?" (1987), pp. 1103–1116.

Identifying with a school's athletic program can extend beyond current or potential students to the institution's alumni and sometimes to the residents of a state or region or to members of a particular ethnic group. The devotion of alumni and other outsiders—in particular, those who can make sizable donations or allocate state funds—can cause schools to see athletics as a vital source of funds.

As explained in Chapter 7, state and local governments may choose to subsidize facilities that fail to make a profit if the spillovers into the overall economy lead the city as a whole to benefit. Like cities, schools may benefit from victorious athletic programs even if the programs do not show a profit themselves. The academic side of the university may realize spillovers from gifts proud alumni or state legislators make, prompted by a winning, if unprofitable, athletic program. The evidence regarding the impact of athletics on such giving, however, is decidedly mixed.

Most studies of alumni refer to specific schools, which are difficult to generalize to different schools at different times. Moreover, the case studies provide contradictory evidence. Studies of Clemson and Mississippi State showed that successful athletic teams lead to greater alumni giving, but a case study of Washington State and a broader study by the Council for Financial Aid to Education showed that athletic performance has no significant impact. Moreover, a study commissioned by the NCAA found no statistically significant relationship between either a school's expenditure on its football program or the success its football program enjoyed and the amount of alumni giving.[57]

While studies fail to agree on the impact of athletic success on alumni donations in general, they have found an unambiguously positive impact on alumni donations to the athletic department itself. Numerous studies show that alumni donations to athletic departments and booster clubs rise with performance. Moreover, some studies find evidence that donations to the academic and athletic sides of the university are positively correlated. However, schools that depend on athletic success to bring alumni donations are under continual pressure to field winning teams, which brings the need to spend money to ensure athletic success. Schools must therefore spend money in order to make money, and these increasing costs may offset the benefits of the additional donations.[58]

---

[57]Robert E. Litan, Jonathan M. Orszag, and Peter R. Orszag, "The Empirical Effects of Collegiate Athletics: An Interim Report," Report Commissioned by the National Collegiate Athletic Association, August 2003.

[58]See, for example, Paul Grimes and George Chressanthis, "The Role of Intercollegiate Sports and NCAA Sanctions in Alumni Contributions," *American Journal of Economics and Sociology,* vol. 53, no. 1 (January 1994), pp. 27–40; Guttman, "The Anomaly of Intercollegiate Athletics" (1991), p. 22; McCormick and Tinsley, "Athletics and Academics" (1990); Murray Sperber, *College Sports Inc.* (New York: Henry Holt and Co., 1990), pp. 70–81; Shulman and Bowen, *The Game of Life* (2001), pp. 220–226; Brownlee and Linnon, "The Myth of the Student-Athlete" (1990); Cletus C. Coughlin and O. Homer Erekson, "An Examination of Contributions to Support Intercollegiate Athletics," *Southern Economic Journal,* vol. 50, no. 1 (July 1984), pp. 180–195; and Lee Sigelman and Samuel Bookheimer, "Is It Whether You Win or Lose? Monetary Contributions to Big-Time College Athletic Programs," *Social Science Quarterly,* vol. 64, no. 2 (June 1983), pp. 347–359.

The Difficulty in Regulating College Sports

Shortly before he disbanded the football team at the University of Chicago in 1939, President Robert Hutchins suggested, "A college racing stable makes as much sense as college football. The jockey could carry the college colors; the students could cheer; the alumni could bet; and the horse wouldn't have to pass a history test."[59] Today, Dr. Hutchins's words seem almost innocent. In their desire to build or maintain winning programs, universities have sometimes admitted marginal students and then gone to extraordinary lengths to keep them eligible.

The behavior of these schools resembles that of firms battling for market share. Firms have frequently turned to providing additional amenities when price competition has been suppressed by either regulation or cartel agreements. For example, prior to deregulation in the late 1970s, the airlines competed largely on the basis of punctuality, decor, and in-flight amenities. Unable to compete for athletes based on price (wages), colleges have also used amenities as a lure. In the 1970s, the NCAA engaged in protracted negotiations with the University of Kentucky over "Wildcat Lodge," a mansion the university had converted into an athletic dormitory. The negotiations covered everything from the number of people to a bedroom (at least two) to the composition of bathroom faucets (no gold allowed). Eventually, "the NCAA forced the university to stop the cooked-to-order breakfasts and remove some of the $200,000 in furnishings, to bring the place more in line with the facilities in which the typical undergraduate lived."[60]

Schools have also tried to build winning teams by admitting talented athletes who do not meet their normal academic standards. In one extreme example from the early 1980s, more than 150 colleges pursued a star basketball player despite his having a combined (math plus verbal) SAT score of 470. His verbal score of 200 reflected his failure to answer a single question correctly.[61] In 2003, St. Bonaventure University was forced to withdraw from the Atlantic 10 postseason basketball tournament when it was revealed that the president of the university had approved the transfer of a basketball player who had not completed the requisite junior college courses.[62]

Academic violations date to the very beginning of the intercollegiate competition. In the first intercollegiate football game, an 1869 match between Rutgers and Princeton, the victorious Rutgers squad had the services of three students who were failing algebra and a fourth who was failing geometry.[63]

---

[59]Quoted in Sheehan, *Keeping Score: The Economics of Big-Time Sports* (South Bend, Ind.: Diamond Press, 1996), p. 261.

[60]Quoted in Alexander Wolff and Armen Keteyian, *Raw Recruits* (New York: Pocket Books, 1991), p. 107. See also Byers, *Unsportsmanlike Conduct* (1995), p. 101.

[61]Guttman, "The Anomaly of Intercollegiate Athletics" (1991), p. 22; and Zimbalist, *Unpaid Professionals* (1999).

[62]Instead of an Associate of Arts degree, the student had earned a certificate in welding.

[63]Zimbalist, *Unpaid Professionals* (1999), pp. 6–7 and 20; and Smith, *Sports and Freedom* (1988), pp. 30 and 71.

Admitting athletes who are academically unprepared brings with it the need to find ways to keep them eligible. Colleges have found a number of creative methods. A lawsuit brought in the early 1980s by Jan Kemp, an instructor in the Developmental Studies Program at the University of Georgia, revealed a veritable school within a school, in which students could "never pass a remedial course, never take a college-level course, and still maintain their playing eligibility for two years."[64] Georgia again found itself in hot water in 2003 when it was revealed that several basketball players had enrolled in a course that never met. The instructor in the phantom course was none other than the basketball coach's son.

Some schools have also allowed students to maintain their eligibility—if not progress toward a degree—by "cherry-picking" dead-end courses such as golf, billiards, and slo-pitch softball. One All-American football player reportedly took summer courses in golf, music, and AIDS awareness, as well as a mass communications course in which every student in the class received a grade of either A or A−, to increase his grade point average.[65] Even legitimate courses have sometimes been compromised. During the 2003 season, another star football player passed a course in African American Studies without taking the midterm or final examination. Instead, he took two oral exams, an option not offered to the other students in the class.[66]

The many responses of schools to the attempt to suppress price competition have led the NCAA to issue a regulations manual that rivals the size of a major city's phone book. The NCAA, like any regulator, must deal with the fact that the institutions being regulated will go to great lengths to avoid regulations that limit the pursuit of their goals. As a result, the regulator may find itself bogged down in minutiae that seem to have nothing to do with its original reason for being.

The Knight Commission on Intercollegiate Athletics

The continuing struggles of the NCAA and major college athletic programs to create an appropriate environment for student-athletes have been borne out at least in part by the lack of an independent voice. Such a voice appeared in the Knight Commission report of 1991. The goal of the Commission was to pressure colleges and universities to take institutional control of athletics away from athletic directors and to return it to the presidents and faculty, thereby restoring academic integrity.

The members of the commission, which included current and retired college presidents, professional athletes, and journalists, called for a "one plus three" strategy for improvement. The "one" was the president of the university.

---

[64]Dealy, *Win at Any Cost* (1990), pp. 86–92.

[65]In "Black Eye for the Buckeyes," *Sports Illustrated,* June 16, 1999, the All-American football player denied receiving special treatment; and Zimbalist, *Unpaid Professionals* (1999), p. 35.

[66]Mike Freeman, "When Values Collide: Clarett Got Unusual Aid in Ohio State Class," *New York Times,* July 13, 2003, Section 8, p. 1.

The commission called for trustees to explicitly grant control of athletic programs to the president of the university, ahead of athletic directors, coaches, and boosters. The "three" represented academic integrity, financial integrity, and independent certification of finances and academics.[67] The original report was issued in 1991, with a follow-up report in 2001. According to the 2001 report, *A Call to Action: Reconnecting the College Sports and Higher Education*, 52 percent of Division I-A colleges and universities had been penalized in the 1990s. Thus, more than half of the nation's biggest athletic programs were guilty of violating rules that they—as members of the NCAA—had helped to create. Such a poor record of compliance is clear evidence of the powerful incentives for coaches and athletic directors to succeed at any cost. To curb the growing trend toward professionalization of college sports, the Knight Commission's 2001 report urged that athletes be "mainstreamed" into the same academic experience as the general student body, that scholarships be tied to specific individuals until they or their class graduate, that graduation rates improve, that playing and practice time be reduced, and that the NFL and NBA develop minor leagues independent of colleges.[68] Although it argues that there is still much work to be done, the 2001 report indicates that progress has been made in a number of areas, most notably in the area of academic integrity, a topic we address in the following section.

Academic Standards: Bulwarks of Integrity or Barriers to Entry?

Since the 1960s, the NCAA has attempted to prevent schools from jeopardizing their academic standards in pursuit of victory on the playing field by setting minimum academic standards for athletes. Again, however, these standards can be viewed in either of two ways: as an attempt by educators to maintain their academic integrity, or as an attempt by established athletic powers to erect an entry barrier that will prevent other schools from becoming competitive. Still others see the regulations as yet another barrier placed in the path of the black student-athlete. This section summarizes the NCAA's attempts to establish academic criteria for participating in intercollegiate athletics.

Attempts at Reform   As part of its attempt to reform college athletics in the early 1950s, the NCAA tried to require that athletes have the same academic credentials as the typical student at the schools they attended. The NCAA could not agree on a standard, however, until 1965, when it adopted the "1.600 Rule." This rule required that incoming freshmen who wished to participate in intercollegiate athletics have a predicted grade point average (GPA) of at least a

---

[67]*Keeping Faith with the Student-Athlete: A New Model for Intercollegiate Athletics—The Knight Commission's March 1991 Report*, Introduction. At http://www.knightcommission.org/about/keeping_faith_introduction. Accessed August 6, 2006.

[68]*A Call to Action*, at http://www.knightcommission.org/about/a_call_to_action/. Accessed August 6, 2006.

C− (numerically a 1.6, hence the name of the rule). The NCAA predicted the GPA by comparing the athletes' class rank in high school and SAT scores with data from almost 41,000 students at 80 different colleges.

In 1971 the colleges in the Ivy League sought to have the NCAA tighten the provisions of the 1.600 Rule. They were upset that the rule was lower than the standard they had set for themselves, giving other schools an advantage in recruiting. Reopening the issue, however, did not bring the result the Ivy League desired. In 1973, athletic directors pushed through the "2.000 Rule." The name implied that students would be held to a higher grade standard. In fact, it was a significant dilution of the existing rules, as students simply had to earn a C+ average in any high school courses whatever. Many of the abuses cited earlier in this section, in which students were admitted to reputable schools despite glaring academic deficiencies, occurred in the 1970s and 1980s when the 2.000 Rule was in effect.

In an attempt to prevent academic scandals, such as those that arose in the early 1980s, the NCAA has formulated a series of reforms. The NCAA adopted the first of these, Proposition 48, in 1983 and began enforcing it in 1986. It set the pattern that has continued to this day.

Proposition 48 required that students earn a score of at least 700 out of a possible 1600 on their SATs (or 15 out of 36 on the ACT) and have a GPA of at least 2.0 in 11 core high school courses in order to receive an athletic grant-in-aid. The last provision was intended to prevent students from maintaining acceptable grades by taking courses with minimal academic merit. A subsequent revision allowed students who met one standard but not the other to be "partial qualifiers," receiving financial aid but unable to play or practice with the team for one year. The idea was to allow such students to establish themselves academically before engaging in athletics. Partial qualifiers also lost one year of eligibility.[69]

Some schools attempted to eliminate the partial-qualifier provision at the NCAA's 1989 convention. The result was Proposition 42, which, when amended at the 1990 convention, actually broadened the provision. Proposition 42 allowed a partial qualifier to be offered a scholarship from the school's general scholarship fund. The change allowed schools to circumvent the NCAA's limit on scholarships and to stockpile talented players.[70]

Following the publication of the first Knight Commission report in 1991, the NCAA again tried to toughen standards at its 1992 convention by approving Proposition 16. As later amended in 1995 and 1996, Proposition 16 created a sliding scale of SAT scores and grades, so a student could qualify with a 2.0 GPA and a 900 SAT or with a 2.5 GPA and a 600 SAT. The NCAA also raised the number of core courses from 11 to 13 and created a clearinghouse to evaluate the merit of the courses.

All of the propositions have generated controversy. In particular, opponents note the disproportionate impact of the rules on black athletes. They have

---

[69]Fleisher et al., *The NCAA* (1992), p. 61; Dealy, *Win at Any Cost* (1990), p. 115; and Zimbalist, *Unpaid Professionals* (1999), p. 30.

[70]Dealy, *Win at Any Cost* (1990), pp. 120–121; and Zimbalist, *Unpaid Professionals* (1999), p. 29.

charged that SAT tests are racially biased and that they reflect poor school systems rather than personal failings by the student. They conclude that any requirement that places weight on the SAT discriminates against black athletes.[71]

Proponents of the reforms regard them as a necessary counterweight to the emphasis on athletics. Sociologist and activist Harry Edwards supported the proposals, claiming, "[B]lack parents, black educators, and the black community must insist that black children be taught and that they learn whatever subject matter is necessary to excel on diagnostic and all other skills tests."[72] Those in favor of reform note that, while Propositions 48, 42, and 16 disproportionately affected black athletes, graduation rates of black athletes have risen as a result of the new standards.[73]

In response to both the legal challenge to Proposition 16 and the concern over low graduation rates, the NCAA passed the most sweeping changes to academic standards since Proposition 48. The new standards, which went into effect August 1, 2003, place less emphasis on test scores and more emphasis on academic progress in college. The latest rules retain the sliding scale with two important changes. First, the number of required core courses increases from 13 to 14. More importantly, the role of the SAT has been reduced. Athletes can now be eligible to compete as freshmen with a cumulative SAT of 400 if they have a grade point average of at least 3.55. While it is easier to qualify as a freshman, it is now harder to maintain eligibility. Prior to this, students were able to maintain eligibility by finishing only 25 percent of the work needed to complete a degree after 2 years, 50 percent after 3 years, and 75 percent after 4 years. Now, students will have to have completed 40 percent of their work after 2 years, 60 percent after 3 years, and 80 percent after 4 years.

Although the sliding SAT and grade point average increases fairness in the sense that it gives students who perform poorly on standardized tests a chance to qualify, there is evidence that it has at the same time created a new problem. Pete Thamel of the *New York Times* found that at some prep academies, eligibility, rather than academics, was the primary focus. He noted that "[T]hese athletes were trying to raise their grades to compensate for poor College Board scores or trying to gain attention from major-college coaches."[74] At these

---

[71]See, for example, "What's Wrong with the NCAA's Test Core Requirements?" Fair Test: The National Center for Fair and Open Testing, at http://www.fairtest.org/facts/prop48.htm; College Board Online, "Students and Parents—SAT Information—Frequently Asked Questions. SAT Program—Is the SAT Fair? Aren't Minority Students at a Disadvantage?" at http://www.collegeboard.org/sat/html/students/mofaq013.html; and James P. Smith and Finis Welch, "Black Economic Progress After Myrdal," *Journal of Economic Literature*, vol. 27, no. 2 (June 1989), pp. 519–564.

[72]Simon, "Intercollegiate Athletics" (1991), p. 62.

[73]Anonymous, "March Madness," *The New Republic*, March 29, 1999, pp. 10–11; and David Goldfield, "Weaker NCAA Standards Won't Help Black Athletes," *Chronicle of Higher Education*, April 9, 1999, p. A64.

[74]Pete Thamel, "Schools Where the Only Real Test Is Basketball," *New York Times*, February 25, 2006. Available online at http://www.nytimes.com/2006/02/25/sports/ncaabasketball/25preps.html?pagewanted=1&ei=5088&en=b4408741cba1781f&ex=1298523600&partner=rssnyt&emc=rss. Accessed August 22, 2006.

academies, there was concern that students spent much of their time focusing on basketball and very little time on academics. According to Thamel, over 200 players have attended such schools over a 10-year period, many going on to play in top Division I programs. Because the NCAA has not historically evaluated high schools, transcripts are not scrutinized for academic content. To address the problem, the NCAA created a task force to begin the process of reviewing high schools and their academic curricula, but with 5,000 private high schools, the magnitude of the regulatory effort required was huge. Perhaps as a reflection of the scale of the effort required, *Washington Post* reporter Eli Saslow reported in 2007 that the NCAA's efforts to crackdown on diploma mill academies was not proceeding as smoothly as hoped. After initially announcing that it had found "... more than 30 problematic private high schools, the NCAA impugned schools that never have fielded basketball teams, and punished schools that do not exist ..." In addition, "(I)t confused two schools with the same name."[75]

At the same time that the NCAA has had to deal with the academic legitimacy of private high schools, it has made substantial changes in academic requirements at the collegiate level that turn the focus from the athlete to the athletic program. In 2005, the NCAA introduced one of the most sweeping changes in academic standards monitoring in the last 50 years. Rather than focus on initial eligibility for freshmen, the NCAA began to focus on schools' ability to graduate their athletes. Also, rather than simply punishing individual athletes for lack of progress, the NCAA created penalties that impact teams and even entire programs. Division I scholarship-granting institutions must now track **academic progress rates** and can be penalized if too few athletes are making adequate progress towards graduation.[76] Academic progress rates are calculated by awarding student-athletes one point for remaining enrolled at the institution and one point for remaining academically eligible. For example, "[A] men's basketball team offering the full complement of 13 scholarships could accumulate a maximum of 52 points (13 × 2 points × 2 semesters) each year. Losing four points would lower its APR from 1,000 to 923 (92.3%)."[77] Scores are calculated and penalties are assessed on a team-by-team basis. Once a team's score falls below 925, it may be subject to sanctions. Tables 11.4 through 11.6 show the APRs for the selected football bowl teams and men's and women's Sweet 16 teams for 2007–2008. In that year, the only teams listed that

---

[75]Eli Saslow, "School Administrators Say NCAA Crackdown on 'Diploma Mills' Is Flawed," *The Washington Post*, March 7, 2007, at http://www.washingtonpost.com/wp-dyn/content/article/2007/03/06/AR2007030602600 pf.html. Accessed August 18, 2009.

[76]For institutions that do not offer scholarship athletes, the measure applies to recruited athletes. See Welch Suggs, "New Grades on Academic Progress Show Widespread Failings Among Teams," *The Chronicle of Higher Education*, March 11, 2005, at http://chronicle.com/free/v51/i27/27a04001.htm. Accessed August 6, 2006.

[77]Steve Wieberg, "Academic progress rates analyzed," *USA Today*, March 1, 2005. At http://www.usatoday.com/sports/college/2005-03-01-apr-analysis_x.htm. Accessed August 6, 2006.

did not reach the 925 minimum were the Oklahoma State women's team (905) and the University of Tennessee men's team (924). The 925 minimum implies a projected graduation rate of 50 percent. Sanctions are severe. They include the loss of scholarships and bans from postseason play. The most chronic offenders could even have their membership status in the NCAA reduced, which would bar all teams from that school from postseason play. The Knight Commission reported that in 2008, 218 teams (3.5 percent of the Division I total) at 123 different schools had received penalties, up from 2 percent the year before. Another 507 teams had APRs below 925 but did not receive penalties.[78] As of July 2009, the NCAA listed 19 men's baseball, 33 football, 42 men's basketball (including Tennessee) and 10 women's basketball (including Oklahoma State) teams as subject to penalties for 2008–2009.[79] Severe penalties should provide a powerful incentive for colleges and universities that offer athletic scholarships to only recruit athletes that have a reasonable chance of graduating.

Academic Standards as a Barrier to Entry

As was the case for athletic scholarships, it is possible to view the restrictions put in place by the NCAA's reforms in one of two ways. Defenders of these standards, such as coach Joe Paterno of Penn State, fear that abolishing them would return colleges to the "win at all costs" atmosphere that characterized the 1970s and 1980s.[80] Former NCAA Commissioner Walter Byers went further and questioned the motives of the schools opposing standards. He believed that administrators of these schools did not feel that they could compete with the major athletic programs for athletes if their schools were held to the same academic standard as the established athletic powers.[81]

Some opponents of the eligibility requirements have accused the established football powers of erecting barriers to entry by other schools seeking to create powerful programs by denying schools the chance to admit superior athletes who cannot meet specific academic standards. Unable to pay students more and unable to admit weaker students, the less-established athletic programs find it difficult to break into the ring of successful programs, because successful programs would have an advantage recruiting athletes who meet the higher academic standards. In his study of competitive balance and eligibility requirements, E. Woodrow Eckard finds that, whatever their benefits, the restrictions on recruiting imposed by the NCAA have worsened competitive balance among the big-time football schools, with conference standings and

---

[78]"NCAA issues penalties and waivers for APR failures" at http://www.knightcommission.org/index.php?option=com_content&view=article&id=91%3A-may-06-2008-ncaa-issues-penalties-and-waivers-for-apr-failures&catid=7%3Aacademic-integrity&Itemid=63. Accessed August 18, 2009.

[79]"Teams Subject to Penalties 2008-09 by Sport," *NCAA,* at http://www.ncaa.org/wps/ncaa?ContentID=49706. Accessed August 18, 2009.

[80]Joe Paterno, "Score on the SAT to Score on the Field," *Wall Street Journal,* March 16, 1999, p. A26.

[81]Byers, *Unsportsmanlike Conduct* (1995), pp. 73–74.

national rankings becoming increasingly predictable.[82] A more recent study by Depken and Wilson (2006) finds conflicting evidence regarding the effects of standards and enforcement. They find that, while increases in enforcement efforts increase competitive balance, increases in penalties for violations of those standards decrease it.[83] Given these apparently conflicting effects, it will be interesting to see the effects of the academic progress rate requirements. For example, once a school is sanctioned for a poor academic progress rating, it may find it more difficult to attract top recruits who are also well qualified academically. In that case, repeated sanctions may lead to reduced ability to field a competitive team.

The use of entry barriers to reduce supply and maintain monopoly power occurs in many professional fields. Doctors, lawyers, accountants, and other professionals also benefit from rigorous accreditation standards. Accreditation requirements, for example, limit the number of law schools permitted to provide the necessary training, while the bar exams limit the number of law school graduates who are permitted to practice the craft. Such standards may protect the public by winnowing out unqualified practitioners and ensuring that capable students receive adequate training. In so doing, however, they limit the degree of competition in the market and inflate the pay of workers already in the field.

11.5   The Finances of College Athletics

A persistent source of contention in intercollegiate athletics is the extent to which major university athletics programs represent, or should represent, a profit center. We specifically narrow our focus here to major university programs. On one level, the entire argument demonstrates the peculiar position of athletics. After all, universities seldom publicly debate the profitability of their departments of physics or economics, even though these departments play a central role in the school's academic mission. The debate over athletics, however, shows the discomfort that many feel with the role it plays in academe. At schools with unprofitable athletic departments, the faculty members often complain that athletics drain resources away from "more deserving" activities. At schools with highly profitable athletic departments, faculty members often complain that the profits show the misplaced values of the institution.

Do Colleges Make a Profit from Athletics?

In one sense, whether or not colleges earn a profit from athletics seems like a strange question. After all, most colleges and universities are chartered as

---

[82]E. Woodrow Eckard, "The NCAA Cartel and Competitive Balance in College Football," *Review of Industrial Organization*, vol. 13, pp. 347–369.

[83]Craig A. Depken, II, and Dennis P. Wilson, "NCAA Enforcement and Competitive Balance in College Football," *Southern Economic Journal*, vol. 72, no. 4, pp. 826–845.

nonprofit organizations. As such, they are prohibited from earning profits. Yet the NCAA's own reports on the economic status of intercollegiate sports frequently refer to surpluses or net revenues as profits. To parallel the NCAA's language, we do so as well throughout this section, but keep in mind that "profits" in any given sport are actually surplus net revenues that must be then spent on some other sport or administrative expense, or within some other area at the institution. In the terminology of the NCAA, profits within a given sport, department, conference, or division exist whenever net revenues are positive.

The short answer to whether colleges earn a profit from athletics is "no." With very few exceptions, athletics constitute a net drain on resources—often a very substantial one. The NCAA tracks and reports the revenues and expenses of its member teams for all divisions, and importantly, subsets within Division I. In doing so, it makes an important distinction regarding the source of revenues. **Generated revenues** are brought in by the athletics department through ticket sales, radio and television contracts alumni contributions to athletics and other payments that are directly the result of the athletic endeavor. **Allocated revenues** represent an internal transfer within the institution from sources outside athletics to the athletic department. These consist of student activity fees, institutional support (direct budget transfers or payment of expenses) and government support.[84] This distinction is important as it directly impacts the conclusion as to whether athletics programs are self-sustaining. If programs are only "profitable" after including institutional support, then they represent a drain on the assets of the institution rather than a contribution.

Table 11.7a through 11.7c show the median generated revenue, median total revenue including allocations, median expenses, and median net generated revenue for FBS schools, FCS schools, and other Division I schools without football. The data clearly show that, with a median loss of over $7 million, the typical school has expenses that far outpace generated revenues. In fact, only 19 FBS schools generated positive net revenue in that year. The 2004–2006 *NCAA Revenue and Expenses Report* (hereafter, The NCAA Report) notes that while at the median, basketball and FBS football teams generate positive net

TABLE 11.7a

Median Revenue, Expenses, and Net Surplus for FBS Schools, 2006 (in $000s)

Category	Generated Revenue	Total Revenue	Total Expenses	Net Generated Revenue
Men	17,003	18,824	15,196	731
Women	641	1,702	6,143	(4,981)
Coed	6,917	13,590	11,867	(3,315)
Total	26,432	35,400	35,756	(7,625)

[84]*2004–2006 NCAA Revenues and Expenses of Division I Intercollegiate Athletics Programs Report.* 2008. The National Collegiate Athletic Association. All data reported and discussed in this section concerning revenue, expenses, surpluses, and losses are from this report.

TABLE 11.7b

Median Revenue, Expenses, and Net Surplus for FCS Schools, 2006 (in $000s)

Category	Generated Revenue	Total Revenue	Total Expenses	Net Generated Revenue
Men	1,072	3,028	4,024	(2,714)
Women	171	1,441	2,701	(2,336)
Coed	928	4,427	2,807	(1,681)
Total	2,345	9,642	9,485	(7,121)

TABLE 11.7c

Median Revenue, Expenses, and Net Surplus for Non-Football Division I Schools, 2006 (in $000s)

Category	Generated Revenue	Total Revenue	Total Expenses	Net Generated Revenue
Men	615	2,791	3,003	(2,178)
Women	152	2,235	2,949	(2,680)
Coed	704	3,518	2,564	(1,701)
Total	1,828	8,771	8,918	(6,607)

Source: 2004–2006 NCAA Revenues and Expenses of Division I Intercollegiate Athletics Programs Report. 2008. The National Collegiate Athletic Association.

revenue, just 19 of the 119 FBS athletic programs generated positive net revenues for 2006. In the FCS, and at Division I schools without football, the median school again has negative net revenue in the range of $6 to $7 million for 2006. The loss for these schools is proportionally larger given that their programs typically operate with much lower revenues than FBS schools. Also note that at non-FBS schools, even men's sports have expenses that exceed revenues at the median.

Beyond the negative net revenues that athletics generate at most schools, another major area of concern is the gap between those programs that generate the most revenue and highest surpluses and those that generate the largest losses. The NCAA report notes that while a very small number of schools had net generated revenues in excess of $10 million, more than a third of the FBS schools had losses in excess $10 million dollars. A similar disparity exists in the FCS, where the difference between the largest generated revenue and the smallest is in excess of $12 million. More alarming is the difference between the largest expenditure (almost $35 million) and the smallest (less than $12 million) at FCS schools. Unfortunately, the problem of negative net generated revenues is likely to continue to get worse, as the growth in revenue from 2004 to 2006 is far less than the growth in expenses. For FBS schools, revenues increased by 16 percent from 2004 to 2006 while expenses increased by 23 percent. At FCS schools revenues increased by 13 percent and expenses increased by 23 percent over the same period.

Such a disparity is likely to create tension between big-budget and small-budget schools. As we noted earlier, it is also likely to create tensions between athletic departments and faculty on campuses where expenses are viewed as too high. Yet, we cannot draw any conclusions about whether any given sport or group of sports are a "good thing" or a "bad thing" for an institution without understanding the desired role for sports within the mission of the specific college. To close any program—men's or women's—simply because it does not cover its expenses would mean canceling virtually every sport in all of Divisions II and III.

College Athletics and Profit Maximization

As we noted in the previous section, most colleges are organized as nonprofit institutions and so are legally prohibited from earning profits. The athletic departments within those schools are thus bound by the same constraint. While this may seem like a trivial detail, it dramatically alters the incentives of the administrators who run the programs. In a for-profit institution, the principals, or owners, have a powerful incentive to maximize profits because they are the beneficiaries. Strategies that are personally satisfying or win favor with cowork-ers or subordinates (such as overly generous vacation allowances) come at a well-defined cost. In fact, as Adam Smith pointed out over 200 years ago, the desire to pursue profits creates a powerful engine of efficiency that drives managers to do their best for the good of the firm. In contrast, those who lead nonprofit institutions do not have these same incentives. Managers of nonprofit agencies and institutions—including university athletic directors (ADs) and presidents—have no claim to any residual profits that remain once expenses are paid. Thus, if ADs are in a position to generate surpluses, they may also have the power and the will to generate expenses that exhaust those surpluses in ways that are not consistent with broader university goals. For example, an AD who is more interested in seeking power and control over a large program than finan-cial stability may push to add sports that are expensive to offer and garner little student interest. Economists refer to this as the **principal–agent** problem.

The principal–agent problem occurs when the actions of one party (the agent) affect the well-being of another (the principal). In the case of intercolle-giate sports, the agent is the individual with budgetary control in the athletics department. We can think of the principal as the president of the university. The problem for the university is that the actions of the AD impact the well-being of the university (and so the president), but, historically, university presidents have not had sufficient authority to control the decision-making power of ADs.[85] This is reflected in the primary directive of the Knight

[85]In fact, identifying the principal is a bit more difficult. We could also assume that collectively, the students represent the principal. Placing the president in the role of the principal assumes that the president acts as a representative for all interest groups and can be placed in this role because it is relatively straightforward to hold presidents accountable for their actions. For more on the actions of individuals in nonprofit organizations, see William Niskanen, *Bureaucracy and Representative Government* (Chicago: Aldine Atherton, 1971).

Commission: presidential control. In its landmark 1991 report, the Commission recommended the following.

1. Trustees will delegate to the president—not reserve for the board or individual members of the board—the administrative authority to govern the athletics program.

2. Presidents will have the same degree of control over athletics that they exercise elsewhere in the university, including the authority to hire, evaluate and terminate athletics directors and coaches, and to oversee all financial matters in their athletics departments.

3. The policy role of presidents will be enhanced throughout the decision-making structures of the NCAA.

4. Trustees, alumni and local boosters will defer to presidential control.[86]

Even with presidential control, intercollegiate athletics at most schools will never generate net surpluses. The recommendation of the Knight Commission is simply to bring the control over the decision making into the president's office such that expenditures on athletics can be appropriately weighed against expenditures on other activities. One area of particular concern is salaries.

Rising payrolls have made labor costs the largest single expense for athletic departments. As Table 11.8 shows, at 32 percent of total expenditure, they are more than twice the size of the next highest expense, grants-in-aid. In contrast, professional baseball, football, basketball, and hockey all have labor costs that

TABLE 11.8

Operating Expenses by FBS Athletic Departments (%) for 2006

Salaries and benefits	32
Grants-in-aid	16
Facilities maintenance and rental	14
Team travel	7
Game expenses	4
Guarantees and options	3
Fund raising	3
Equipment and supplies	3
Recruiting	2
Other	28

Source: 2004–2006 *NCAA Revenues and Expenses of Division I Intercollegiate Athletics Programs Report* (March 2008).

---

[86]*Keeping Faith with the Student-Athlete: A New Model for Intercollegiate Athletics—The Knight Commission's March 1991 Report,* Introduction. At http://www.knightcommission.org/about/keeping_faith_introduction. Accessed August 9, 2006.

account for over 50 percent of included revenues. As we explained earlier in this chapter, the reason for the disparity stems from the monopsony power of the NCAA, which allows its members to depress the "pay" of their most valuable resource—the athletes themselves—well below their market value.

BIOGRAPHICAL SKETCH

ANITA DEFRANTZ

Without Anita DeFrantz, the corruption and the image of corruption will run unabated. With her, I have a genuine hope for our Olympic athletes inspiring young people that they can all live within that one circle of humanity.
— *Richard E. Lapchick*[1]

One of the most powerful women in the sports industry had little intention of following a career in sports. Instead, she came to her position as the result of a couple of fortuitous accidents. Born and raised in Indiana, Anita DeFrantz attended Connecticut College, a small school better known for its academics than for its Division III athletics. While a sophomore, the first accident occurred. One day, she saw the school's crew coach carrying a boat and asked him what it was for. The coach noticed that DeFrantz, at 5'11", looked strong and athletic, and he soon had her on the water with the team. DeFrantz went on to be a six-time national champion and, three years after her chance encounter with the crew coach, she captained the eight-woman boat to a bronze medal in the 1976 Summer Olympic Games in Montreal, the first Olympics to feature women's rowing.

An accident of timing led her from athletic success to a professional career in sports administration. While preparing for the 1980 Games, DeFrantz got a law degree from the University of Pennsylvania and passed the bar exam. Her hopes for a gold medal were dashed, however, when President Jimmy Carter declared that the United States would boycott the 1980 Moscow Games to protest the Soviet Union's invasion of Afghanistan. DeFrantz then took a step that helped define the future course of her career. She put her legal training to use by suing the United States Olympic Committee (USOC). Her lawsuit claimed that the government could not declare a boycott of the Olympics and that America's Olympic athletes had the right to make their own decision about whether they attended the Games.

DeFrantz's lawsuit proved politically unpopular—some critics suggested that she join the Communist Party—and, ultimately, unsuccessful. Although DeFrantz lost her suit, she succeeded in catching the attention of the International Olympic Committee (IOC). It awarded her a medal for her effort to put Olympic competition above politics and helped her to begin a career in the Olympic movement. In 1984, while still in her early 30s, DeFrantz was named vice president of the Los Angeles Olympic Organizing Committee. After the Los Angeles Olympics were held, she joined the Amateur Athletic Foundation (AAF) and the USOC, rapidly rising in each to become the

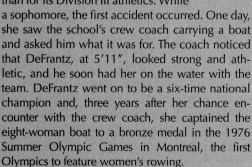

continued

president of the AAF and a member of the executive committee of the USOC. Recognizing her talents, the IOC named her as a lifetime member.

DeFrantz's appointment again made her a pioneer. She became the first American woman and only the fifth woman ever invited to join the IOC. Since her appointment, DeFrantz has become an extremely influential member of the IOC, especially in matters related to women's sports and developing countries. She has been a leading advocate of funding for training facilities in countries that cannot afford to build them. In 1992, she became the chair of the IOC's committee on women's sports and played a critical role in having women's softball and soccer added to the 2000 Olympic Games in Atlanta.

DeFrantz's reputation for integrity and fairness helped her become the first woman to be elected vice president of the IOC's Executive Committee in 1997. After IOC President Juan Antonio Samaranch retired, DeFrantz ran unsuccessfully to succeed him. Despite this setback, she has continued to use her position to speak out as a voice for athletes.

[1]Richard E. Lapchick, "A New Vision for the IOC: Anita L. DeFrantz," *Sport in Society,* http://www.sportinsociety .org/rel-article19.html.

Sources: Sarah J. Murray, "Anita DeFrantz: Setting the Standard," online at http://www .womenssportsfoundation.org/cgi-bin/iowa/athletes/ article.html?record=68; Richard E. Lapchick, "A New Vision for the IOC: Anita L. DeFrantz," *Sport in Society,* at http://www.sportinsociety.org/rel-article19.html; and "Olympian Rise" *Houston Chronicle,* online at http:// www.chron.com/content/chronicle/sports/special/ barriers/defrantz.html.

Summary

This chapter used the tools of economics to analyze the behavior of the NCAA, its member schools, and the athletes who participate in collegiate sports. At the outset, we noted that amateurism is a troublesome concept with a history that may be more mythologically than factually based. For a university, the tension between fielding the best possible team and maintaining academic standards can be difficult to manage effectively, especially given that there are economic, sociological, and ethical dimensions that may be impossible to balance simultaneously.

The NCAA also functions as a cartel in the college sports market. To gain access to the lucrative television contracts and big-name opponents, schools must join the NCAA. Unlike most cartels, however, individual athletic programs, such as football at member schools, are not permitted to earn profits, and they are limited in their ability to maintain control over residual revenues generated by their programs.

Discussion Questions

1. Discuss the viability of amateurism in the United States today. Is it possible, given the attention that elite athletes receive, to have "pure" amateurs?

2. In 2004, Jeremy Bloom, a University of Colorado football player, was ruled permanently ineligible by the NCAA for accepting endorsement income

related to his Olympic skiing career. Should the NCAA allow student-athletes to receive endorsement income unrelated to their collegiate athletic activity?

3. Discuss the possible implications of allowing schools to pay student-athletes whatever level of compensation necessary to attract them to their programs.

4. Discuss the positive and negative implications of removing all entrance standards for college athletes, assuming that they must also enroll as full-time students.

5. Discuss the positive and negative implications of permitting colleges to use paid players who are not students.

6. Discuss the factors that should be included in the decision process by an elite high school senior baseball player of attending a Division I baseball school versus reporting directly to the minor professional leagues.

7. Discuss the use of student activity fees (charged to all students) that are used to support athletics. Should students have the right to decide how such fees are allocated?

Problems

11.1 Show, using supply and demand for labor diagrams for Divisions I and III, the effect of a new rule allowing Division III schools to pay athletes a one-time bonus for enrolling at their schools.

11.2 Use MC and MR curves to show why the NCAA allows major football programs to have a larger share of bowl and TV revenues.

11.3 Use human capital theory to explain why colleges might not pay students their full marginal product.

11.4 Assume that you are the newly appointed head of the NCAA. Construct a framework for a new scholarship program that would entirely replace the existing system. Describe what should be its fundamental tenets if:

   a. The primary goal is to ensure that athletes were not exploited.

   b. The primary goal is to ensure that student-athletes receive degrees.

   c. The primary goal is to simplify the system and reduce violations.

   d. Your primary goal is to be reappointed.

11.5 What effect do the following have on a person's decision to invest in athletic training versus academic training? In each case, explain the direction and likely significance of the effect.

   a. Risk of career-ending injury

   b. The probability of success in athletics

   c. An increase in the cost of college tuition

   d. An increase in the demand for professional sports

11.6 Use game theory to describe how an effort by two universities to recruit a top basketball player might result in both committing NCAA recruiting violations.

11.7 What unselfish and selfish motives might be behind the attempts by some schools to set academic standards for student-athletes?

11.8 Use supply and demand analysis to show and describe the dramatic increase in "basketball academy" prep schools following the creation of Proposition 16.

11.9 How might failing to graduate from college be an optimal investment in one's human capital?

11.10 Use human capital theory to explain why graduation rates for women's basketball players are so much higher than those for men's basketball players.

WORKS CITED

"1984 Los Angeles Olympic Games Surplus Continues to Benefit Southern California Youth," *LA84 Foundation,* June 23, 2004, online at http://www.la84foundation .org/10ap/NewsRelease06232004_frmst.htm.

2004–2006 NCAA Revenues and Expenses of Division I Intercollegiate Athletics Programs Report, Indianapolis: The National Collegiate Athletic Association, 2008.

"2008 NCAA Division I Graduation Success Rate (GSR) Data," *National Collegiate Athletic Association,* online at http://www.ncaa.org/wps/ncaa?key=/ncaa/ncaa/ academics+and+athletes/education+and+research/academic+reform/gsr/2008/ 2008_d1_school_gsr_data.html.

"2008–2009 Revenue Distribution Plan," *NCAA.org,* online at http://www.ncaa.org/ wps/wcm/connect/46f776004e0d547d9ef9fe1ad6fc8b25/Revised+Revenue+ Distribution+Summary_012709.pdf?MOD=AJPERES&CACHEID=46f776004e0d54 7d9ef9fe1ad6fc8b25

"2008–09 Variable Pricing Schedule," *NHL.com Network,* July 28, 2008, online at http://sabres.nhl.com/club/news.htm?bcid=369062.

"2009 NCAA Division I Academic Progress Rate (APR) Reports by School," *National Collegiate Athletic Association,* online at http://www.ncaa.org/wps/ncaa?key=/ ncaa/ncaa/academics+and+athletes/education+and+research/academic+reform/ apr/2009/2007-08_school_apr_data.html.

Abrams, Roger. *Legal Bases: Baseball and the Law.* Philadelphia: Temple University Press, 1998.

Ahles, Andrea. "Dallas Cowboys Stadium Funding from a Variety of Sources," Star-Telegraph.com, September 28, 2008, online at http://www.star-telegram.com/ stadium/story/937327.html.

Alesia, Mark. "Tourney Money Fuels Pay-to-Play Debate," *IndyStar.com* (*Indianapolis Star* online edition). April 1, 2006, online at http://www.indystar.com/apps/ pbcs.dll/article?Date=20060401&Category=SPORTS&ArtNo=604010509& SectionCat=&Template=printart.

Amato, Louis, John Gandar, Irvin Tucker, and Richard Zuber. "Bowls Versus Playoffs: The Impact on Football Player Graduation Rates in the National Collegiate Athletic Association," *Economics of Education Review,* vol. 15, no. 2 (April 1996), pp. 187–195.

American Association of University Women. "Equity in School Athletics," 2006, online at http://www.aauw.org/issue_advocacy/actionpages/positionpapers/titleix_ athletics.cfm.

Anderson, Torben, and Sumner J. La Croix. "Customer Discrimination in Major League Baseball," *Economic Inquiry,* vol. 29, no. 4 (October 1991), pp. 665–677.

Andreff, Wladimir, and Paul Staudohar. "European and U.S. Business Sports Models," in C. Barros, M. Ibrahimo, and S. Szymanski (eds.), *Transatlantic Sport: The Comparative Economics of North American and European Sport* (Cheltenham: Edward Elgar, 2002).

Andrews, Geoff. *Not a Normal Country: Italy After Berlusconi,* London: Pluto Press, 2005.

"Answers Please," *The Economist,* August 2, 2003, pp. 23–27.

"AOL Kills Goodwill Games after $150 Million in Losses," *Wall Street Journal,* December 21, 2001, p. B7.

Aronson, Eliot, Timothy D. Wilson, and Robin M. Akert. *Social Psychology: The Heart and Mind.* New York: HarperCollins College Publishers, 1994.

Associated Press. "Court Backs N.C.A.A. on Proposition 16." *New York Times,* December 23, 1999, p. D5.

———. "New Ballparks Mean Higher Ticket Prices." *Sporting News,* April 4, 2000, online at http://www.tsn.sportingnews.com/baseball/articles/2000404/228259.html.

———. "Commissioner Spent $1.2 Million on Lobbying in 2001." *ESPN.com,* May 15, 2002, online at http://www.espn.com.

———. "Manchester United Signs up Aon as New Jersey Sponsor," *USAToday.com,* June 4, 2009, online at http://www.usatoday.com/sports/soccer/europe/2009-06-03-manchester-united-aon-sponsorship_N.htm?csp=34.

———. "Yanks Cut Some Premium Ticket Prices," ESPN.com, April 28, 2009, online at http://sports.espn.go.com/mlb/news/story?id=4108293.

Athens News Agency. "Cost of 2004 Olympics," *Hellenic Republic Embassy of Greece,* November 13, 2004, online at http://www.greekembassy.org/Embassy/content/en/Article.aspx?office=3&folder=200&article=14269.

Austrian, Ziona, and Mark Rosentraub. "Cleveland's Gateway to the Future," in *Sports, Jobs, and Taxes,* ed. by Roger Noll and Andrew Zimbalist. Washington, D.C.: Brookings Institution Press, 1997, pp. 355–384.

Aynsworth, Hugh. "Owner of Dallas Cowboys Seeks $1 Billion in Tax Funds," *Washington Times,* February 2, 2004, online at http://www.washingtontimes.com/national/20040202-120350-8901r.htm.

Baade, Robert. "Professional Sports as Catalysts for Metropolitan Economic Development," *Journal of Urban Affairs,* vol. 18, no. 1 (1996), pp. 1–17.

———. "Should Congress Stop the Bidding War for Sports Franchises?" Hearing Before the Subcommittee on Antitrust, Business Rights, and Compensation, Senate Committee on the Judiciary. "Academics," *Heartland Policy,* vol. 4 (November 29, 1995), online at http://www.heartland.org/stadps4.html.

Baade, Robert, and Richard Dye. "The Impact of Stadiums and Professional Sports on Metropolitan Area Development," *Growth and Change,* vol. 21, no. 2 (Spring 1990), pp. 1–14.

Baade, Robert A., and Victor A. Matheson. "The Quest for the Cup: Assessing the Economic Impact of the World Cup," *Regional Science,* vol. 38, no. 4 (June 2004), pp. 343–354.

Baade, Robert A., and Allen Sanderson. "The Employment Effect of Teams and Sports Facilities." In *Sports, Jobs, and Taxes,* ed. by Roger Noll and Andrew Zimbalist. Washington, D.C.: Brookings Institution Press, 1997, pp. 55–91.

———. "Field of Fantasies," *Intellectual Ammunition,* March/April 1996, online at http://www.heartland.org/01maap96.htm.

Badenhausen, Kurt, Michael K. Ozanian, and Christina Settimi, "NFL Team Valuations," *Forbes Magazine,* online at www.forbes.com/lists/2008/30/nfl08_NFL-Team-Valuations_Rank.html.

Baker, Nick. "New Indianapolis Stadium May Already Need Bailout," *The Heartland Institute,* January 1, 2009, online at http://www.heartland.org/publications/budget%20tax/article/24305/New_Indianapolis_Stadium_May_Already_Need_Bailout.html.

Baker, William. *Sports in the Western World.* Totowa, N.J.: Rowman & Littlefield, 1982.

"Baltimore Orioles Attendance Analysis" and "Cleveland Indians Attendance Analysis," *Baseball Almanac,* June 18, 2009, online at www.baseball-almanac.com.

Baltzell, E. Digby. *Sporting Gentlemen: Men's Tennis from the Age of Honor to the Cult of the Superstar.* New York: The Free Press, 1995.

Bamberger, Michael, and Don Yaeger. "Over the Edge," *Sports Illustrated,* April 14, 1997, pp. 61–70.

Bandini, Paolo. "Barca Take the Moral High Ground," *guardian.co.uk,* September 13, 2006, online at http://www.guardian.co.uk/football/2006/sep/13/barcelona.

Baroncelli, Alessandro, and Umberto Lago. "Italian Football," *Journal of Sports Economics,* vol. 7, no. 1 (February 2006), pp. 13–28.

Barra, Allen. *The Last Coach: A Life of Paul "Bear" Bryant.* New York: W. W. Norton, 2005.

Barra, Allen. "In Anti-trust We Trust," *Salon Magazine,* May 19, 2000, online at http://www.salon.com/news/feature/2000/05/19/antitrust/index.html.

Barry, Dave. *Dave Barry Turns Fifty.* New York: Random House, 1999.

Bartlett, Donald, and James Steele. "Snow Job," *Sports Illustrated,* December 10, 2001, pp. 79–97.

"Baseball Agreement to Extend Through 2003," online at http://www.theolympian.com/home/specialsections/Mariners2002/20020831/41339.shtml.

Becker, Gary S. "College Athletes Should Get Paid What They're Worth," *Business Week,* September 30, 1985, p. 38.

———. *The Economics of Discrimination,* 2nd ed. Chicago: University of Chicago Press, 1971.

———. *Human Capital,* 3rd ed. Chicago: University of Chicago Press, 1993.

———. "A Theory of Competition Among Pressure Groups for Political Influence," *Quarterly Journal of Economics,* vol. 97, no. 3 (August 1983), pp. 371–400.

Beckett's Baseball Card Plus. Beckett Publications, June/July 2006.

"Beijing Enters Play-Offs to Be Olympics Host," *People's Daily Online,* March 24, 2000, online at http://www.english.peopledaily.com.cn/200003/24/eng20000324S101.html.

Belson, Ken. "Tickets Cost Too Much? Check Back Tomorrow," *New York Times,* May 18, 2009, p. D-2.

Benson, Marty. *1999 NCAA Division I Graduation Rates Report.* Indianapolis: NCAA, 1999.

Berentsen, Aleksander. "The Economics of Doping," *European Journal of Political Economy,* vol. 18 (March 2002), pp. 109–127.

Berk, Sheryl. "Golden Girl," *McCalls,* December 1998, pp. 110–112.

Bernstein, Andy. "Flexibility a Key in the New MLB-ESPN Deal," *Street and Smith's Sports Journal,* online at www.sportsbusinessjournal.com.

———. "Inside the Complex NHL Deal," June 4, 2009, at www.sportsbusinessjournal.com/index.cfm?fuseaction=article.printArticle%articleid=46287.

Berri, David J. "What Do Chris Paul, Dwight Howard, LeBron James, and Tim Duncan Have in Common" *The Wages of Wins Journal,* May 22, 2008, online at http://dberri

.wordpress.com/2008/05/22/what-do-chris-paul-dwight-howard-lebron-james-and-tim-duncan-have-in-common/.

Berri, David, Stacey Brook, Bernd Frick, Aju Fenn, and Roberto Vicente-Mayoral. "The Short Supply of Tall People: Explaining Competitive Imbalance in the National Basketball Association," *Journal of Economic Issues,* vol. 39, no. 4 (December 2005), pp. 1029–1041.

Berri, David J., and Martin B. Schmidt. "On the Road with the National Basketball Association's Superstar Externality," *Journal of Sports Economics*, vol. 7, no. 4 (November 2006), pp. 347–358.

Berri, David, Martin Schmidt, and Stacey Brook. *The Wages of Wins.* Stanford, Calif.: Stanford University Press, 2006.

Berri, David J., and Rob Simmons. "Race and the Evaluation of Signal Callers in the National Football League," *Journal of Sports Economics*, vol. 10, no. 1 (February 2009), pp. 23–43

Betzold, Michael, and Ethan Casey. *Queen of Diamonds: The Tiger Stadium Story.* West Bloomfield, Mich.: Northfield Publishing Co., 1992.

Birger, Jon. "Baseball Battles the Sulum," *CNNMoney.com*, online at http://money.cnn.com/2009/02/18/magazines/fortune/birger_baseball.fortune/index.htm.

Bissinger, H. G. *Friday Night Lights.* Reading, Mass.: Addison-Wesley, 1990.

Blass, Asher C. "Does the Baseball Labor Market Contradict the Human Capital Model of Investment?"*Review of Economics and Statistics*, vol. 71, no. 2 (May 1992), pp. 261–268.

Bloom, Barry M. "Yanks, Red Sox Hit with Luxury Tax Bills" MLB.com, online at http://mlb.mlb.com/NASApp/mlb/news/article.jsp?ymd=20051221&content_id=1286225&vkey=news_mlb&fext=.jsp&c_id=mlb.

Bovarsson, Orn B. "A Test of Employer Discrimination in the NBA," *Contemporary Economic Policy,* vol. 17, no. 2 (April 1999), pp. 243–256.

"Bowl Championship Series, Five Year Summary of Revenue Distribution 2003–2007," *National Collegiate Athletic Association*, April 11, 2008, online at http://www.ncaa.org/wps/wcm/connect/f54bee004e0b9a869ce0fc1ad6fc8b25/BCS++Revenue+Distribution+by+Conference+2007-08.pdf?MOD=AJPERES&CACHEID=f54bee004e0b9a869ce0fc1ad6fc8b25.

Briggs, Lindsey Valaine. "UEFA v The European Community: Attempts of the Governing Body of European Soccer to Circumvent EU Freedom of Movement and Antidiscrimination Labor Law," *Chicago Journal of International Law,* vol. 6, no. 1 (Summer 2005), pp. 439–454.

Brown, Maury. "2009 MLB Salary Arbitration Vital Stats," *The Biz of Baseball,* February 20, 2009, online at http://www.bizofbaseball.com/index.php?option=com_ content&view=article&id=2974:2009-mlb-salary-arbitration-vital-stats&catid=66: free-agency-and-trades&Itemid=153.

Brown, Robert W. "An Estimate of the Rent Generated by a Premium College Football Player," *Economic Inquiry,* vol. 21, no. 4 (October 1993), pp. 671–684.

———. "Measuring Cartel Rents in the College Basketball Player Recruitment Market," *Applied Economics,* vol. 26, no. 1 (January 1994), pp. 27–34.

Brown, Robert W., and R. Todd Jewell. "Is There Customer Discrimination in College Basketball? The Premium Fans Pay for White Players," *Social Science Quarterly,* vol. 75, no. 2 (June 1994), pp. 401–412.

Brownlee, Shannon, and Nancy Linnon. "The Myth of the Student-Athlete," *U.S. News and World Report*, January 8, 1990, p. 50.

Buchanan, James. "An Economic Theory of Clubs," *Economica*, vol. 32, no. 125 (February 1965), pp. 1–14.

Buraimo, Babatunde, and Rob Simmons. "Do Sports Fans Really Value Uncertainty of Outcome? Evidence from the English Premier League," *International Journal of Sport Finance*, vol. 3, no. 3 (August 2008), pp. 146–155.

Bureau of Economic Analysis. "Personal Income and Per Capita Personal Income by Metropolitan Area, 2005–2007," June 23, 2009 online at http://www.bea.gov/ newsreleases/regional/mpi/mpi_newsrelease.htm.

Burger, John D., and Stephen J. K. Walters. "Market Size, Pay, and Performance: A General Model and Application to Major League Baseball," *Journal of Sports Economics*, vol. 4, no. 2 (May 2003), pp. 108–125.

Burk, Robert. *Never Just a Game: Players, Owners, and American Baseball to 1920*. Chapel Hill: University of North Carolina Press, 1994.

Burns, Ken. *Baseball* (film). PBS Video, 1994.

"Business of 1999 Bowl Games." *Fox Sports Biz.com* online at http://www.foxsports .com/business/resources/bowls.

"The Business of Baseball," *Forbes.com*, April 22, 2009, online at http://www.forbes .com/lists/2009/33/baseball-values-09_The-Business-Of-Baseball_MetroArea.html.

Butler, Michael R. "Competitive Balance in Major League Baseball," *American Economist*, vol. 39, no. 2 (Fall 1995), pp. 46–50.

Byers, Walter, with Charles Hammer. *Unsportsmanlike Conduct: Exploiting College Athletes*. Ann Arbor: University of Michigan Press, 1995.

Byrne, Jim. *The $1 League: The Rise and Fall of the USFL*. New York: Prentice Hall, 1986.

Cagan, Joanna, and Neil deMause. *Field of Schemes*. Monroe, Maine: Common Courage Press, 1998.

Carrey, Jack, and Andy Gardiner. "NCAA Settlement Gives Aid to Athletes," *USA Today*, online at http://www.usatoday.com/sports/college/2008-01-29-settlement-aid-details_N.htm

Cassing, James, and Richard Douglas. "Implications of the Auction Mechanism in Baseball's Free Agent Draft," *Southern Economic Journal*, vol. 47, no. 1 (July 1980), pp. 110–121.

Cayleff, Susan. *Babe: The Life and Times of Babe Didrickson Zaharias*. Urbana: University of Illinois Press, 1995.

"CBA—Complete," *National Football League Players Association*, online at www .nflpa.org/CBA/CBA_Complete.aspx, 2002.

"CBA—Extension," *National Football League Players Association*, online at www .nflpa.org/CBA/CBA_Extension.aspx, 2006.

CBC News. "Quebec's Big Owe Stadium Debt Is Over," *CBCnews.ca*, December 19, 2006, online at http://www.cbc.ca/canada/montreal/story/2006/12/19/ qc-olympicstadium.html.

Chan, Sewell. "Comptroller Assails Mayor on New Yankee Stadium," New York Times: City Room, January 13, 2009, online at http://cityroom.blogs.nytimes.com/2009/ 01/13/comptroller-assails-mayor-on-new-yankee-stadium.

Channel Sports. "Beijing Welcomes Inclusion on Shortlist to Hold 2008 Olympics," *China Daily Information*, August 29, 2000, online at http://www.chinadaily.net/cover/storydb/2000/08/29/sp-beiji.829.html.

Chema, Thomas. "When Professional Sports Justify the Subsidy," *Journal of Urban Affairs*, vol. 18, no. 1 (February 1996), pp. 19–22.

Clapp, Christopher M., and Jahn K. Hakes. "How Long a Honeymoon? The Effect of New Stadiums on Attendance in Major League Baseball," *Journal of Sports Economics*, vol. 6, no. 3 (August 2005), pp. 237–263.

Coase, Ronald. "The Problem of Social Cost," *Journal of Law and Economics*, vol. 3, no. 1 (October 1960), pp. 1–44.

Coates, Dennis, and Bradley R. Humphreys. "The Effect of Professional Sports on Earnings and Employment in U.S. Cities," *Regional Science and Urban Economics*, vol. 33, no. 2 (March 2003), pp. 175–198.

———. "Professional Sports Facilities, Franchises, and Urban Economic Development." *Public Finance and Management*, vol. 3, no. 3 (September 2003), pp. 335–357.

Cohen, Rachel. "NBA Extends TV Deals with ESPN/ABC, TNT," June 27, 2007, at http://www.usatoday.com/sports/basketball/2007-06-27-3096131424_x.htm.

College Board Online. Students and Parents—"SAT Information—Frequently Asked Questions; SAT Program—Is the SAT Fair? Aren't Minority Students at a Disadvantage?" February 15, 2001, online at http://www.collegeboard.org/sat/html/students/mofaq013.html.

Coon, Larry. "NBA Salary Cap FAQ," http://members.cox.net/lmcoon/salarycap.htm. August 8 2009.

Cot's Baseball Contracts online at http://mlbcontracts.blogspot.com.

Coughlin, Cletus C., and O. Homer Erekson. "An Examination of Contributions to Support Intercollegiate Athletics," *Southern Economic Journal*, vol. 50, no. 1 (July 1984), pp. 180–195.

Covington, Robert N. "How Much Is the Law to Blame for Baseball's Turbulent Labor Relations?" *Journal of Sports Economics*, vol. 4, no. 4 (November 2003), pp. 357–361.

Danielson, Michael. *Home Team: Professional Sport and the American Metropolis.* Princeton, NJ: Princeton University Press, 1997.

Davis, Seth. "A Blight on the Mountaineers," *Sports Illustrated*, December 6, 1999, pp. 80–81.

DeBrock, Lawrence, Wallace Hendricks, and Roger Koenker. "The Economics of Persistence: Graduation Rates of Athletes as Labor Market Choice," *Journal of Human Resources*, vol. 31, no. 3 (Summer 1996), pp. 513–539.

Depken, Craig A. II, "Fan Loyalty and Stadium Funding in Professional Baseball," *Journal of Sports Economics*, vol. 1, no. 2 (May 2000), pp. 124–138.

———. "Free-Agency and the Competitiveness of Major League Baseball," *Review of Industrial Organization*, vol. 14, no. 3 (May 1999), pp. 205–217.

Depken, Craig A. II, David R. Kamerschen, and Arthur Snow. "Generic Advertising of Intermediate Goods: Theory and Evidence," *The Review of Industrial Organization*, vol. 20, no. 3 (May 2002), pp. 205–220.

Depken, Craig A. II, and Dennis P. Wilson. "NCAA Enforcement and Competitive Balance in College Football," *Southern Economic Journal*, vol. 72, no. 4 (April 2005), pp. 826–845.

Dey, Matthew S. "Racial Differences in National Basketball Association Salaries: A New Look," *American Economist*, vol. 41, no. 2 (Fall 1997), pp. 84–90.

Dickey, Glenn. *Just Win, Baby: Al Davis and His Raiders.* New York: Harcourt, Brace, Jovanovich, 1991.

Dienhart, Tom. "New NCAA Rules Make It Tough on Small Schools," *SportingNews.com,* June 3, 2002, online at http://www.sportingnews.com/voices/tom_dienhart/20020603-p.html.

Dodd, Scott. "Winston Kelley to Run NASCAR Hall," *Charlotte Observer,* July 6, 2006, online at http://www.charlotteobserver.com.

Donadio, Rachel. "Berlusconi's Wife Says She Wants a Divorce," *New York Times,* online at www.nytimes.com/2009/05/04/world/europe/04iht-italy.html.

Dorian, P. Owen, Michael Ryan, and Clayton R. Weatherston. "Measuring Competitive Balance in Professional Team Sports Using the Herfindahl-Hirschman Index," *Journal of Industrial Organization,* vol. 31, no. 4 (December 2007), pp. 289–302.

Dubow, Josh. "Non-BCS Schools Allege Antitrust Violations," *CollegeSports.com,* July 22, 2003, online at http://www.collegesports.com/sports/m-footbl/stories/072203aax.html.

"The Ducks Look," June 8, 2009, online at http://ducks.nhl.com/team/app/?service=page&page=NHLPage&id=16478.

Duderstadt, James J. *Intercollegiate Athletics and the American University: A University President's Perspective.* Ann Arbor: University of Michigan Press, 2000.

Eckard, E. Woodrow. "The ANOVA-Based Competitive Balance Measure: A Defense," *Journal of Sports Economics,* vol. 4, no. 1 (February 2003), pp. 74–80.

Ehrenberg, Ronald G., and Michael Bognanno. "Do Tournaments Have Incentive Effects?" *Journal of Political Economy,* vol. 98, no. 6 (December 1990), pp. 1307–1324.

Ehrenberg, Ronald G., and Robert Smith. *Modern Labor Economics: Theory and Public Policy,* 9th ed. Reading, Mass.: Addison Wesley Longman, 2008.

El-Hodiri, Mohamed, and James Quirk. "An Economic Model of a Professional Sports League," *Journal of Political Economy,* vol. 79, no. 6 (Nov.–Dec. 1971), pp. 1302–1319.

"Estimated Probability of Competing in Athletics beyond the High School Interscholastic Level," http://www.ncaa.org/wps/ncaa?key=/ncaa/NCAA/Academics%20and%20Athletes/Education%20and%20Research/ Probability%20of%20Competing. August 1, 2009.

"Evans Takes Over as Acting Commish," *ESPN Golf,* July 13, 2009, at http://sports.espn.go.com/golf/news/story?id=4323583.

Euchner, Charles. *Playing the Field.* Baltimore: Johns Hopkins University Press, 1993.

Ewing, Jack, Laura Cohn, Maureen Kline, and Rachel Tiplady. "Can Football Be Saved?" *BusinessWeek* online (July 19, 2004), online at www.businessweek.com.

Fainaru-Wade, Mark, and Lance Williams. *Game of Shadows: Barry Bonds, BALCO, and the Steroids Scandal That Rocked Professional Sports.* New York: Gotham Books, 2006.

Farber, Michael. "Giant Sucking Sound," *Sports Illustrated,* March 20, 1995, p. 104.

Ferguson, D. W., Kenneth G. Stewart, J. C. H. Jones, and Andre Le Dressay. "The Pricing of Sports Events: Do Teams Maximize Profits?" *Journal of Industrial Economics,* vol. 39, no. 3 (March 1991), pp. 297–310.

Fernandez, Bob. "Comcast to Put NBA on 'Digital Classic' Tier," June 4, 2009, at www.philly.com/philly/business/technology/46890407.html.

"FIFA Thumbs-up for 'Six-Plus-Five' Player Rule," *ESPN.com,* May 30, 2008, online at http://soccernet.espn.go.com/news/story?id=540901&cc=5901.

Finley, Moses, and H. W. Pleket. *The Olympic Games: The First Thousand Years*. New York: Viking Press, 1976.

Foer, Franklin. *How Soccer Explains the World: An Unlikely Theory of Globalization*. New York: HarperCollins, 2004.

"Forbes Celebrity 100" at http://www.forbes.com/lists/53/compen_salary.html.

Fort, Rodney, and Andrew Gill. "Race and Ethnicity Assessment in Baseball Card Markets," *Journal of Sports Economics*, vol. 1, no. 1 (February 2000), pp. 21–38.

Fort, Rodney, and James Quirk. "The College Football Industry." In *Sports Economics: Current Research*, ed. by John Fizel, Elizabeth Gustafson, and Lawrence Hadley. Westport, Conn.: Praeger, 1999, pp. 11–26.

Foy, Paul. "Romney Just Glad Olympics Worked," *2002 Winter Olympic Games*, online at http://www.olympics.hiasys.com/olympics_main/news/ ap_olynewsscene02252002.htm.

Frank, Robert, and Philip Cook. *The Winner-Take-All Society*. New York: The Free Press, 1995.

Frederick, David M., William H. Kaempfer, and Richard L. Wobbekind. "Salary Arbitration as a Market Substitute." In *Diamonds Are Forever: The Business of Baseball*, ed. by Paul M. Sommers. Washington, D.C.: The Brookings Institution, 1992, pp. 29–49.

Freedman, Matthew (Ed). *2000 Inside the Ownership of Professional Sports Teams*. Chicago: Team Marketing Report, 2000.

Freeman, Mike. "When Values Collide: Clarett Got Unusual Aid in Ohio State Class," *New York Times*, July 13, 2003, p. 8–1.

———. "Pursuit of Victories Presses on Colleges," *New York Times*, July 18, 2003, p. 8–4.

Freeman, Richard, and James Medoff. *What Do Unions Do?* New York: Basic Books, 1984.

Friedman, Milton. *Essays on Positive Economics*. Chicago: University of Chicago Press, 1953.

Frommer, Harvey. *Rickey and Robinson*. New York: Macmillan, 1982.

Gabriel, Paul E., Curtis D. Johnson, and Timothy J. Stanton. "Customer Racial Discrimination for Baseball Memorabilia," *Applied Economics*, vol. 31, no. 11, pp. 1331–1335.

Gavora, Jessica, *Tilting the Playing Field*. San Francisco: Encounter Books, 2002.

Gilbert, Susan. "The Smallest Olympians Face the Biggest Risk," *New York Times*, July 28, 1996, p. E4.

Ginsborg, Paul. *Silvio Berlusconi: Television, Power and Patrimony*. London: Verso, 2004.

Gius, Mark, and Donn Johnson. "An Empirical Investigation of Wage Discrimination in Professional Basketball," *Applied Economics Letters*, vol. 5, no. 11 (November 1998), pp. 703–705.

Goldfield, David. "Weaker NCAA Standards Won't Help Black Athletes," *Chronicle of Higher Education*, April 9, 1999, p. A64.

Goldman, William. *The Princess Bride*. New York: Ballantine Books, 1974.

"Governor Mitt Romney," *Massachusetts Office of the Governor*, online at http://www .mass.gov/portal/index.jsp?pageID=agcc&agid=gov&agca=biographies&agcc= mittromneybiom.

Gramm, Cynthia, and John Schnell. "Difficult Choices: Crossing the Picket Line During the 1987 National Football League Strike," *Journal of Labor Economics*, vol. 12, no. 1 (January 1994), pp. 41–71.

"Grand Slam Four Packs," at http://philadelphia.phillies.mlb.com/phi/ticketing/ fourpacks.jsp.

Gregory, Sean, and Steve Goldberg. "Daytona Drag: NASCAR Tries to Outrace the Recession," *Time,* online at www.time.com/time/business/article/ 0,8599,1879136,00.html.

Grimaldi, James. "Olympics File Suit Over Web Domain," *Washington Post,* July 14, 2000, p. E4, online at http://www.washingtonpost.com/wp-dyn/articles/A404762000 July13.html.

Grimes, Paul, and George Chressanthis. "The Role of Intercollegiate Sports and NCAA Sanctions in Alumni Contributions," *American Journal of Economics and Sociology,* vol. 53, no. 1 (January 1994), pp. 27–40.

Guttman, Allen. "The Anomaly of Intercollegiate Athletics." In *Rethinking College Athletics,* ed. by Judith Andre and David James. Philadelphia: Temple University Press, 1991, pp. 17–30.

Gwartney, James A., and Charles Haworth. "Employer Costs and Discrimination: The Case of Baseball," *Journal of Political Economy,* vol. 82, no. 4 (July/August 1974), pp. 873–881.

Hadley, Lawrence, James Ciecka, and Anthony Krautmann. "Competitive Balance in the Aftermath of the 1994 Players' Strike." *Journal of Sports Economics,* vol. 6, no. 4 (November 2005), pp. 379–389.

Hakes, Jahn, and Raymond Sauer. "An Economic Evaluation of the *Moneyball* Hypothesis," *Journal of Economic Perspectives,* vol. 20, no. 3 (Summer 2006), pp. 173–185.

Hamilton, Barton H. "Racial Discrimination and Professional Basketball Salaries in the 1990s," *Applied Economics,* vol. 29, no. 3 (March 1997), pp. 287–296.

Hamilton, Bruce, and Peter Kahn. "Baltimore's Camden Yards Ballparks," In *Sports, Jobs, and Taxes,* ed. by Roger Noll and Andrew Zimbalist. Washington, D.C.: Brookings Institution Press, 1997, pp. 245–281.

Hanssen, Andrew F., and Torben Anderson. "Has Discrimination Lessened over Time? A Test Using Baseball's All-Star Vote," *Economic Inquiry,* vol. 37, no. 2 (April 1999), pp. 326–352.

Harasta, Cathy. "Romney Shows His Mettle," *Dallas Morning News,* February 17, 2002.

Harris, David. *The League: The Rise and Decline of the NFL.* New York: Bantam Books, 1986.

Hart-Davis, Duff. *Hitler's Games.* London: Century, 1986.

Hatab, Lawrence. "The Greeks and the Meaning of Athletics." In *Rethinking College Athletics,* ed. by Judith Andre and David James. Philadelphia: Temple University Press, 1991, pp. 31–42.

Haugen, Kjetil K. "The Performance Enhancing Drug Game," *Journal of Sports Economics,* vol. 5, no. 1 (February 2004), pp. 67–86.

Hausman, Jerry A., and Gregory K. Leonard. "Superstars in the National Basketball League: Economic Value and Policy," *Journal of Labor Economics,* vol. 15, no. 4 (October 1997), pp. 586–624.

Hayes, Beth. "Unions and Strikes with Asymmetric Information," *Journal of Labor Economics,* vol. 2, no. 1 (January 1984), pp. 57–84.

Heintel, Robert. "The Need for an Alternative to Antitrust Regulation of the National Football League," *Case Western Reserve Law Review,* vol. 46, no. 4 (Summer 1996), pp. 1033–1069.

Helyar, John. *Lords of the Realm.* New York: Villard Books, 1994.

Hepp, Christopher. "Near Fabled Park, Ambience a Lure," *Philadelphia Inquirer,* September 29, 1999, pp. A1 and A6.

"History of the Goodwill Games," *Courier Mail* (Queensland, Australia), July 17, 2001, p. H4.

"Hockey Schedule a Bow to NBC," June 4, 2009, at www.pittsburghlive.com/x/pittsburghtrib/sports/s_627457.html.

Hodgson, Andrew. "Blatter Bid to Put Limit on Foreign Players Wins FIFA Backing," *London Evening Standard,* May 30, 2008, online at http://www.thisislondon.co.uk/standard-sport/article-23488572-details/Blatter+bid+to+put+limit+on+foreign+players+wins+FIFA+backing/article.do.

"How They Bring in the Gold," *U.S. News and World Report,* January 31, 1994, p. 16.

Hudson, Ian. "Bright Lights, Big City: Do Professional Sports Teams Increase Employment?" *Journal of Urban Affairs,* vol. 21, no. 4 (October 1999), pp. 397–407.

Humphreys, Bradley R. "Alternative Measures of Competitive Balance," *Journal of Sports Economics,* vol. 3, no. 2 (May 2002), pp. 133–148.

———. "The ANOVA-Based Competitive Balance Measure: A Reply," *Journal of Sports Economics,* vol. 4, no. 1 (February, 2003), pp. 81–82.

Isadore, Chris. "Baseball Close to Catching NFL as Top $ Sport," October 25, 2007, at http://money.cnn.com/2007/10/25/commentary/sportsbiz/index.htm.

Itano, Nicole. "As Olympic Glow Fades, Athens Questions $15 Billion Cost," *Christian Science Monitor,* July 21, 2008, online at http://www.csmonitor.com/2008/0721/p04s01-wogn.html.

"Jazz Announces Variable Ticket Pricing Plan for Upcoming Season," *NBA.com,* September 19, 2008, online at http://www.nba.com/jazz/tickets/0809_tickets_variablepricing.html.

Jeffers, Michelle. "Y&R Balances NCAA's Student-Athlete Act," *AllBusiness,* March 17, 2003, online at http://www.allbusiness.com/marketing-advertising/4122624-1.html.

Jenkins, Jeffrey A. "A Reexamination of Salary Determination in Professional Basketball," *Social Science Quarterly,* vol. 77, no. 3 (September 1996), pp. 594–608.

Jenson, Mike. "Start of Women's Pro Soccer League Not Just Around the Corner," *Philadelphia Inquirer,* July 8, 1999, p. E1.

"Joe Louis (Barrow)," *Arlington National Cemetery Website,* July 27, 2009, online at http://www.arlingtoncemetery.net/joelouis.htm.

Johnson, Arthur. *Minor League Baseball and Local Economic Development.* Urbana: University of Illinois Press, 1995.

Johnson, John. "When a Professional Sport Is Not a Business: Baseball's Infamous Antitrust Exemption," In *Sports and the Law,* ed. by Charles Quirk. New York: Garland, 1996, pp. 149–165.

Johnson, Roy. "We Got Game (Finally)," *Fortune,* February 1, 1999, pp. 28–29.

Jones, J. C. H., and W. D. Walsh. "Salary Determination in the National Hockey League: The Effects of Skills, Franchise Characteristics, and Discrimination," *Industrial and Labor Relations Review,* vol. 41, no. 4 (July 1988), pp. 592–604.

———. "The World Hockey Association and Player Exploitation in the National Hockey League," *Quarterly Review of Economics and Business,* vol. 27, no. 2 (Summer 1987), pp. 87–101.

Jones, Richard, and Don Walker. "Packer Boss Warns of Move if Stadium Doesn't Get Upgrade," *Milwaukee Sentinel Journal,* March 1, 2000, online at http://www.jsonline.com/packer/news/feb00/lambeau01022900.asp.

Kahn, Lawrence M. "Discrimination in Professional Sports: A Survey of the Literature," *Industrial and Labor Relations Review,* vol. 44, no. 3 (April 1991), pp. 395–418.

———. "The Effects of Race on Professional Football Players' Compensation," *Industrial Labor Relations Review,* vol. 45, no. 2 (January 1992), pp. 295–310.

———. "The Sports Business as a Labor Market Laboratory," *Journal of Economic Perspectives,* vol. 14, no. 3 (Summer 2000), pp. 75–94.

Kahn, Lawrence M., and Peter Sherer. "Racial Differences in Professional Basketball Players' Compensation," *Journal of Labor Economics,* vol. 6, no. 1 (January 1988), pp. 40–61.

Kahn, Roger. *The Era: 1947–1957.* New York: Ticknor and Fields, 1993.

Kanazawa, Mark T., and Jonas P. Funk. "Racial Discrimination in Professional Basketball: Evidence from Nielsen Ratings," *Economics Inquiry,* vol. 39, no. 4 (October 2001), pp. 599–608.

Kantorczyk, Todd. "How to Stop the Fast Break: An Evaluation of the 'Three-Peat' Trademark and the FTC's Role in Trademark Law Enforcement," *UCLA Entertainment Law Review,* vol. 2, no. 1 (Winter 1995), pp. 195–228.

Keating, Raymond. "Sports Pork: The Costly Relationship Between Major League Sports and Government." *Policy Analysis,* no. 339. Washington, D.C.: Cato Institute, 1999.

Kesenne, Stefan. "Revenue Sharing and Competitive Balance: Does the Invariance Proposition Hold?" *Journal of Sports Economics,* vol. 6, no. 1 (February 2005), pp. 98–106.

Kidd, Bruce. "The Myth of the Ancient Games." In *Five Ring Circus: Money, Power and Politics at the Olympic Games,* ed. by Alan Tomlinson and Garry Whannel. London: Pluto Press, 1984, pp. 71–83.

King, Bill. "New Ballparks Sport Old Look: Empty Seats," *Street & Smith's SportsBusiness Journal,* May 26–June 1, 2003, p. 37.

———. "Passion That Can't Be Counted Puts Billions of Dollars in Play," *Street & Smith's SportsBusiness Journal: By the Numbers,* May 26–June 1, 2003, pp. 148–149.

Klein, Eugene. *First Down and a Billion: The Funny Business of Pro Football.* New York: Morrow, 1987.

Knapple, Jeffrey S. "Naming Rights Industry." In *Naming Rights Deals.* Chicago: Team Marketing Report, 2001.

Knight Foundation Commission on Intercollegiate Athletics. *A Call to Action: Reconnecting College Sports and Higher Education.* Miami, FL: John S. and James L. Knight Foundation, June 2001.

Knight Commission. "Keeping Faith with the Student-Athlete: A New Model for Intercollegiate Athletics: The Knight Commission's March 1991 Report," *Knight Commission Reports,* March 1991, online at http://www.knightcommission.org/images/pdfs/1991-93_KCIA_report.pdf.

Knowles, Glenn, Keith Sherony, and Mike Haupert. "The Demand for Major League Baseball: A Test of the Uncertainty of Outcome Hypothesis," *American Economist,* vol. 36, no. 2 (Fall 1992), pp. 72–80.

Koch, James. "Intercollegiate Athletics: An Economic Explanation," *Social Science Quarterly,* vol. 64, no. 2 (June 1983), pp. 360–374.

Korr, Charles. "Marvin Miller and the New Unionism in Baseball." In *The Business of Professional Sports,* ed. by Paul Staudohar and James Mangan. Urbana: University of Illinois Press, 1991, pp. 115–134.

Kowalewski, Sandra, and Michael Leeds. "The Impact of the Salary Cap and Free Agency on the Structure and Distribution of Salaries in the NFL." In *Sports Economics: Current Research,* ed. by John Fizel, Elizabeth Gustafson, and Lawrence Hadley. Westport, Conn.: Praeger, 1999, pp. 213–226.

Krashinsky, Michael, and Harry D. Krashinsky. "Do English Canadian Hockey Teams Discriminate Against French Canadian Players?" *Canadian Public Policy—Analyse de Politiques,* vol. 23, no. 2 (June 1997), pp. 212–216.

Krautmann, Anthony. "What's Wrong with Scully Estimates of a Player's Marginal Revenue Product," *Economic Inquiry,* vol. 37, no. 2 (April 1999), pp. 369–381.

Krautmann, Anthony C., Peter von Allmen, and David Berri. "The Underpayment of Restricted Players in North American Sports Leagues," *International Journal of Sport Finance,* vol. 4, no. 3 (August 2009), pp. 75–93.

Kuklick, Bruce. *To Everything a Season: Shibe Park and Urban Philadelphia, 1909–1976.* Princeton, N.J.: Princeton University Press, 1991.

Laband, David L. "How the Structure of Competition Influences Performance in Professional Sports: The Case of Tennis and Golf." In *Sportometrics,* ed. by Brian L. Goff and Robert D. Tollison. College Station: Texas A&M University Press, 1990, pp. 133–150.

Lago, Umberto, Rob Simmons, and Stefan Szymanski. "The Financial Crisis in European Football," *Journal of Sports Economics,* vol. 7 no. 1 (February 2006), pp. 3–12.

Lambrinos, James, and Thomas D. Ashman. "Salary Determination in the National Hockey League: Is Arbitration Efficient?" *Journal of Sports Economics,* vol. 8, no. 2 (April 2007), pp. 192–201.

Landes, William, and Richard Posner. "Adjudication as a Private Good," *Journal of Legal Studies,* vol. 8, no. 235 (July 1979), pp. 77–94.

Landsburg, Steven E. *The Armchair Economist: Economics and Everyday Life.* New York: Free Press, 1993.

Lapchick, Richard E. "A New Vision for the IOC: Anita L. DeFrantz," online at http://www.sportinsociety.org/rel-article19.html.

Lapchick, Richard E., Eric Little, Colleen Lerner, and Ray Mathew. "The 2008 Racial and Gender Report Card: College Sport," *The Institute for Ethics and Diversity in Sport,* February 19, 2009, online at http://www.tidesport.org/racialgenderreportcard.html.

Lapchick, Richard E., Alejandra Diaz-Calderon, and Derek McMechan. "The 2009 Major League Baseball Racial and Gender Report Card," *The Institute for Ethics and Diversity in Sport,* April 15, 2009, online at http://www.tidesport.org/racialgenderreportcard.html.

Lapchick, Richard E., Nicole Bowey, and Jessica Zahn. "The 2008 Major League Soccer Racial and Gender Report Card," *The Institute for Ethics and Diversity in Sport,* September 24, 2008, online at http://www.tidesport.org/racialgenderreportcard.html.

Lapchick, Richard E., Eric Little, and Colleen Lerner. "The 2008 National Football League Racial and Gender Report Card," *The Institute for Ethics and Diversity in Sport,* August 27, 2008, online at http://www.tidesport.org/racialgenderreportcard.html.

Lapchick, Richard E., Jessica Hanson, Charles Harless, and William Johnson. "The 2009 National Basketball Association Racial and Gender Report Card," *The Institute for Ethics and Diversity in Sport*, June 10, 2009, online at http://www.tidesport.org/racialgenderreportcard.html.

Lapchick, Richard E., Cara-Lynn Lopresti, and Nathalie Reshard. "The 2009 Women's National Basketball Association Racial and Gender Report Card," *The Institute for Ethics and Diversity in Sport*, July 23, 2009, online at http://www.tidesport.org/racialgenderreportcard.html.

Lawrence, Paul. *Unsportsmanlike Conduct: The National Collegiate Athletic Association and the Business of College Football*. New York: Praeger, 1987.

Lawson, M. J. "Going for Gold," *Accountancy*, vol. 117, no. 1234 (June 1996), pp. 30–32.

Leadley, John C., and Zenon X. Zygmont. "When Is the Honeymoon Over? Major League Baseball Attendance 1970–2000," *Journal of Sport Mangement*, vol. 19, no. 3 (July 2005), pp. 278–299.

———. "When Is the Honeymoon Over? National Hockey League Attendance 1970–2003," *Canadian Public Policy*, vol. 32, no. 2 (June 2006), pp. 213–232.

———. "When Is the Honeymoon Over? National Basketball Association Attendance 1971–2000," *Journal of Sports Economics*, vol. 6, no. 2 (May 2005), pp. 203–221.

Lederman, Doug. "Court Challenge on Athletic Aid," insidehighered.com (*Inside Higher Ed* online edition), online at http://www.insidehighered.com/news/2006/02/23/antitrust.

Leeds, Eva Marikova, Michael A. Leeds, and Irina Pistolet. "A Stadium by Any Other Name," *Journal of Sports Economics*, vol. 8, no. 6 (December 2007), pp. 585–595.

Leeds, Michael A. "Bargaining as Search Behavior Under Mutual Uncertainty," *Southern Economic Journal*, vol. 53, no. 3 (January 1987), pp. 677–684.

———. "Salary Caps and Luxury Taxes in Professional Sports Leagues." In *The Business of Sports*, vol. 2. ed. by Brad R. Humphreys and Dennis R. Howard. Westport, Conn.: Praeger, 2008, pp. 181–206.

Leeds, Michael A., and Sandra Kowaleski. "Winner Take All in the NFL: The Effect of the Salary Cap on Compensation of the Skill Position Players," *Journal of Sports Economics*, vol. 2, no. 3 (August 2001), pp. 244–256.

Leifer, Eric. *Making the Majors: The Transformation of Team Sports in America*. Cambridge, Mass.: Harvard University Press, 1995.

Lewis, Michael. *The Blind Side: Evolution of a Game*, New York: W.W. Norton, 2006.

———. *Moneyball*, New York: Norton, 2003.

Lo Franco, Robert. "Profits on Ice," *Forbes*, May 5, 1997, pp. 86–89.

Long, James, and Steven Caudill. "The Impact of Participation in Intercollegiate Athletics on Income and Graduation," *Review of Economics and Statistics*, vol. 73, no. 3 (August 1991), pp. 525–531.

Long, Judith Grant. "Full Count: The Real Cost of Public Funding for Major League Sports Facilities," *Journal of Sports Economics*, vol. 6, no. 2 (May 2005), pp. 119–143.

Longley, Neil. "Salary Discrimination in the National Hockey League: The Effects of Location," *Canadian Public Policy—Analyse de Politiques*, vol. 21, no. 4 (December 1995), pp. 413–422.

———. "The Underrepresentation of French Canadians on English Canadian Teams," *Journal of Sports Economics*, vol. 1, no. 3 (August 2000), pp. 236–256.

Lorge, Barry. "Kroc Wanted to Give Padres to City," *San Diego Union-Tribune,* July 29, 1990, p. H1.

MacCambridge, Michael. *America's Game.* New York: Random House, 2004, p. 44.

MacDonald, Don N., and Morgan O. Reynolds. "Are Baseball Players Paid Their Marginal Products?" *Managerial and Decision Economics,* vol. 15 (September/October 1994), pp. 443–457.

Madden, Janice Fanning. "Differences in the Success of NFL Coaches by Race, 1990–2002: Evidence of Last Hire, First Fire," *Journal of Sports Economics,* vol. 5, no. 1 (February 2004), pp. 6–19.

Maidment, Paul. "Rich Spoils from Soccer's Biggest Match," June 5, 2009, at www.forbes.com/2009/05/26/manchester-barcelona-uefa-business-sports-football.html.

"Major League Baseball Average Ticket Price Rises 10.9 Percent to $25.40," June 5, 2009, at http://sports.espn.co.com/espn/wire?section=mlb&id=3317969.

Malone, Andrew. "Abandoned, Derelict, Covered in Graffiti and Rubbish: What Remains of Athens' £9 Billion Olympic 'Glory'?" *Mail Online,* July 18, 2008, online at http://www.dailymail.co.uk/news/worldnews/article-1036373/Abandoned-derelict-covered-graffiti-rubbish-What-left-Athens-9billion-Olympic-glory.html.

Mandell, Richard. *The Nazi Olympics.* New York: Ballantine Books, 1972.

"March Madness," *New Republic,* March 29, 1999, pp. 10–11.

Margolick, David. *Beyond Glory: Joe Louis vs. Max Schmeling, and a World on the Brink.* New York: Alfred A. Knopf, 2005.

McCallum, Jack. "A Cut Above," *Sports Illustrated,* March 10, 1997, pp. 24–29.

McCormick, Robert, and Maurice Tinsley. "Athletics and Academics: A Model of University Contributions." In *Sportometrics,* ed. by Brian Goff and Robert Tollison. College Station: Texas A&M University Press, 1990, pp. 193–204.

———. "Athletics Versus Academics? Evidence from SAT Scores," *Journal of Political Economy,* vol. 95, no. 5 (October 1987), pp. 1103–1116.

McDonald, Mark, and Daniel Rascher. "Does Bat Day Make Cents? The Effect of Promotions on the Demand for Major League Baseball," *Journal of Sport Management,* vol. 14, no. 1 (January 2000), pp. 8–27.

McGrath, Ben. "The Extortionist," *The New Yorker,* October 29, 2009, online at http://www.newyorker.com/reporting/2007/10/29/071029fa_fact_mcgrath.

McGraw, Dan. "The Foreign Invasion of the American Game," *The Village Voice* online May 28–June 3, 2003, online at http://www.villagevoice.com/news/0322,mcgraw,44409,1.html.

Mead, Chris. "Triumphs and Trials," *SIVault,* September 23, 1985, online at http://vault.sportsillustrated.cnn.com/vault/article/magazine/MAG1119926/4/index.htm.

Media, Peter S. Battin. *Television Sports Rights 2003,* June 18, 2003, online at http://www.gouldmedia.com/nv_rpt_tsr03.php.

Metropolitan and Micropolitan Statistical Area Estimates, at www.census.gov/popest/metro/cbsa0est2008-pop-chg.html.

Mickle, Tripp, and Terry Lefton. "Several Leagues Later, Debate on Single Entity Model Still Lively," *SportsBusinessJournal.com,* June 8, 2009, online at http://www.sportsbusinessjournal.com/article59720.

Miller, James. *The Baseball Business: Pursuing Pennants and Profits in Baltimore.* Chapel Hill: University of North Carolina Press, 1990.

Miller, Matthew, Dorothy Pomerantz, and Lacey Rose. "The Celebrity 100," *Forbes.com*, June 3, 2009, online at www.forbes.com/2009/06/03/forbes-100-celebrity-09-jolie-oprah-madonna-land.html.

"MLB Attendance Report—2008," June 5, 2009, online at http://sports.espn.go.com/mlb/attendance?sort=home_avg&year=2008&seasonType=2.

"MLB Team Valuations," *Forbes Magazine*, online at www.forbes.com/lists/2009/33/baseball-values-09_The-Business-Of-Baseball_Rank.html.

Morgan, Jon. *Glory for Sale: Fans, Dollars, and the New NFL.* Baltimore: Bancroft Press, 1997.

MSC Sports. "New Park Financing: How the Deals Got Done," 1999, online at http://www.wcco.com/sports/stadiums.html.

Munsey, Paul, and Corey Suppes. "Ballparks," 2009, online at http://www.ballparks.com.

Munson, Lester, and Paula Lavigne. "Utah has BCS Lawsuit in Mind," *ESPN College Football* March 31, 2009, online at http://sports.espn.go.com/ncf/news/story?id=4030992.

Murphy, Robert, and Gregory Trandel. "The Relation Between a University's Football Record and the Size of Its Applicant Pool," *Economics of Education Review,* vol. 13, no. 3 (September 1994), pp. 265–270.

Nack, William. "This Old House," *Sports Illustrated,* June 7, 1999, pp. 100–116.

Nardinelli, Curtis, and Clark Simon. "Customer Discrimination in the Market for Memorabilia: The Case of Baseball," *Quarterly Journal of Economics,* vol. 105, no. 3 (August 1990), p. 575–595.

"The National Collegiate Athletic Association Revised Budget for Fiscal Year Ending August 31, 2009," *NCAA.org,* online at http://www.ncaa.org/wps/wcm/connect/6d3874004e51aadc96e0d622cf56f2f3/2008-09+BUDGET+(Budget+moves+in+08-09)_FINAL.pdf?MOD=AJPERES&CACHEID=6d3874004e51 aadc96e0d622cf56f2f3.

"NBA Team Valuations," *Forbes Magazine,* online at www.forbes.com/lists/2008/32/nba08_NBA-Team-Valuations_Rank.html.

NCAA. "NCAA Division I, II, and III Membership Criteria," 1999, online at http://www.ncaa.org/about/div_criteria.html.

———. *2005–2006 NCAA Division I Manual,* online at www.ncaa.org/library/division_1_manual/2005-06/2005-06_dl_manual.pdf.

"NCAA Issues Penalties and Waivers for APR Failures," *Knight Commission on Intercollegiate Athletics*, May 6, 2008, online at http://www.knightcommission.org/index.php?option=com_content&view=article&id=91%3A-may-06-2008-ncaa-issues-penalties-and-waivers-for-apr-failures&catid=7%3Aacademic-integrity&Itemid=63.

Neale, Walter. "The Peculiar Economics of Professional Sports," *Quarterly Journal of Economics,* vol. 78, no. 1 (February 1964), pp. 1–14.

"NHL FAQ: Article 10 Free Agency," online at http://nhl.comnhlhq/cba/archive/cba/article10.html.

"NHL Team Valuations," *Forbes Magazine,* online at www.forbes.com/lists/2008/31/nhl08_NHL-Team-Valuations_Rank.html.

"A New Way to Keep Score," *Inside Higher Ed,* December 20, 2005, online at http://www.insidehighered.com/news/2005/12/20/grad.

Nightengale, Bob. "Boras Is Baseball's Bigger Deal Man," *USA Today,* November 14, 2006, online at http://www.usatoday.com/sports/baseball/2006-11-14-boras-cover_x.htm.

Niskanen, William. *Bureaucracy and Representative Government.* Chicago: Aldine Atherton, 1971.

Noden, Merrell. "Dying to Win," *Sports Illustrated,* August 8, 1994, pp. 52–59.

Noll, Roger. "The Economics of Intercollegiate Sports." In *Rethinking College Athletics,* ed. by Judith Andre and David James. Philadelphia: Temple University Press, 1992, pp. 197–209.

———. "The Economic Impact of Sports Teams and Facilities." In *Sports, Jobs, and Taxes,* ed. by Roger Noll and Andrew Zimbalist. Washington, D.C.: Brookings Institution Press, 1997, pp. 55–91.

Noll, Roger G. "The Organization of Sports Leagues," *Oxford Review of Economic Policy,* vol. 19, no. 4 (Winter 2003), pp. 530–551.

Noll, Roger, and Andrew Zimbalist. "Build the Stadium—Create the Jobs!" In *Sports, Jobs, and Taxes,* ed. by Roger Noll and Andrew Zimbalist. Washington, D.C.: Brookings Institution Press, 1997, pp. 1–54.

———. "The Economics of Sports Leagues." In *Law of Professional and Amateur Sports,* ed. by Gary A. Uberstine and Richard J. Grad. New York: Boardman, 1988, pp. 17-1–17-37.

"Not About Money: HBO Declines to Renew Wimbledon Contract After 25 Years," June 28, 1999, CNN/SI, online at http://www.cnnsi.com/tennis/1999/wimbledon/news/1999/06/28/hbo_wimbledon/index.html.

O'Hara, Jane, et al. "In the Name of Greed," *Maclean's,* January 19, 1998, pp. 22–24.

"Olympian Rise," *Houston Chronicle,* online at http://www.chron.com/content/chronicle/sports/special/barriers/defrantz.html.

"Open to All: Title IX at Thirty." The Secretary of Education's Commision on Opportunity in Athletics, online at http://www.nacua.org/documents/TitleIX_Report_022703.pdf.

"Osaka Vows to Battle On to Host 2008 Olympics," Reuters, Ltd., August 28, 2000, online at http://www.web4.sportsline.com/u/wire/stories/0,1169,2712403_15,00.html.

"Overall Student Athlete GSR Data: 2008 NCAA Division I Federal Graduation Rate Data," National Collegiate Athletic Association, online at http://www.wwwncaa.com/wps/ncaa?key=/ncaa/ncaa/academics+and+athletes/education+and+research/academic+reform/grad+rate/2008/2008_d1_school_grad_rate_data.html

Pappas, Doug. "The Numbers (Part 2): Local Media Revenues," *The Baseball Prospectus,* online at http://www.baseballprospectus.com/news/20011212pappas.html, December 12, 2001.

Parrish, Paula. "Leap of Faith: Mitt Romney Embraces Challenges, and This Might Be His Biggest One," *Rocky Mountain News,* February 4, 2002, p. 8S.

Pastier, John. "Diamonds in the Rough: Two Cheers for the New Baseball Palaces," *Slate,* July 31, 1996, online at http://www.slate.msn.com/feature2/96-07-31/feature2.asp.

Paterno, Joe. "Score on the SAT to Score on the Field," *Wall Street Journal,* March 16, 1999, p. A26.

Patrick, Aaron O., and Dana Cimilluca. "English Soccer's Morning After," June 5, 2009, online at http://online.wsj.com/article/SB124346762522860417.html.

Patrick, Dick. "White's Words Key in Montgomery, Gaines Cases," *USA Today,* December 13, 2005, online at http://www.usatoday.com/sports/olympics/summer/track/2005-12-13-montgomery-gaines-suspended_x.htm.

Pearce, David W. (Ed). *The MIT Dictionary of Modern Economics,* 3rd ed. Cambridge, Mass.: The MIT Press, 1986.

Pearlman, Jeff. "At Full Blast," *Sports Illustrated,* December 27, 1999–January 3, 2000, pp. 62–64.

Perrotet, Tony. *The Naked Olympics.* New York: Random House, 2004.

"Personal Income and Per Capita Personal Income by Metropolitan Area, 2005–2007," online at www.bea.gov/newsreleases/regional/mpi/mpi_newsrelease.htm.

Peterson, Robert. *Only the Ball Was White: A History of Legendary Black Players and All-Black Professional Teams.* New York: Gramercy Books, 1970.

"A Plucky Proposition," *Sports Illustrated,* February 16, 1998, p. 28.

Pluto, Terry. *Loose Balls: The Short, Wild Life of the American Basketball Association.* Upper Saddle River, N.J.: Simon & Schuster, 1990.

Poole, Lynn, and Gray Poole. *History of Ancient Greek Olympic Games.* New York: Ivan Obolensky, Inc., 1963.

Porter, Philip. "Mega-Sporting Events as Municipal Investments: A Critique of Impact Analysis." In *Sports Economics: Current Research,* ed. by John Fizel, Elizabeth Gustafson, and Larry Hadley. Westport, Conn.: Praeger Publishers, 1999.

Posner, Richard. "The Social Costs of Monopoly and Regulation," *Journal of Political Economy,* vol. 83, no. 4 (August 1975), pp. 807–827.

Preston, Ian, and Stefan Szymanski. "Racial Discrimination in English Football," *Scottish Journal of Political Economy,* vol. 47, no. 4 (September 2000), pp. 342–363.

"Prize Money," at *Wimbledon: The Official Site,* online at http://aeltc.wimbledon.org/en_GB/about/history/prizemoney_history.html.

Purdy, Dean D., Stanley Eitzen, and Rick Hufnagel. "Are Athletes Also Students? The Educational Attainment of College Athletes." In *Sport and Higher Education,* ed. by Donald Chu, Jeffrey Segrave, and Beverly Becker. Champaign, Ill.: Human Kinetics Publishers, 1985, pp. 221–234.

Quinn, Kevin, Paul B. Bursik, Christopher Borick, and Lisa Raethz. "Do New Digs Mean More Wins? The Relationship Between a New Venue and a Professional Sports Team's Success," *Journal of Sports Economics,* vol. 4, no. 3 (August 2003), pp. 167–182.

Quirk, James, and Rodney Fort. *Hardball.* Princeton, N.J.: Princeton University Press, 1999.

———. *Pay Dirt.* Princeton, N.J.: Princeton University Press, 1992.

Rader, Benjamin G. *In Its Own Image: How Television Has Transformed Sports.* New York: The Free Press, 1984.

Ralph, Dan. "Toronto Among Finalists to Host 2008 Olympics," *Canadian Press,* August 29, 2000, online at http://www.herald.ns.ca/stories/2000/08/29/f161.raw.html.

Rappoport, Jordan, and Chad Wilkerson. "What Are the Benefits of Hosting a Major League Sports Franchise?" *Federal Reserve Bank of Kansas City Economic Review,* First Quarter, 2001, pp. 55–85.

Rascher, Daniel. "A Test of Optimal Positive Production Network Externality in Major League Baseball." In *Sports Economics: Current Research,* ed. by John Fizel, Elizabeth Gustafson, and Larry Hadley. Westport, Conn.: Praeger Publishers, 1999, pp. 27–45.

Rascher, Dan, Chad McEvoy, Mark Nagel, and Matthew Brown. "Variable Ticket Pricing in Major League Baseball," *Journal of Sport Management,* vol. 21, no. 3 (July 2007), pp. 407–437.

Ray, Margaret A., and Paul W. Grimes. "Jockeying for Position: Winnings and Gender Discrimination on the Thoroughbred Track," *Social Science Quarterly,* vol. 74, no. 1 (March 1993), pp. 46–61.

Reaves, Joseph A. *Taking in a Game: The History of Baseball in Asia,* Lincoln: University of Nebraska Press, 2002.

Ribowsky, Mark. *Slick: The Silver and Black Life of Al Davis.* New York: Macmillan, 1991.

Rice, Lewis. "Games Saver." *Harvard Law Bulletin,* Spring 2002, online at http://www .law.harvard.edu/alumni/bulletin/2002/spring/feature_1-1.html.

Riddell, Kelly. "Comcast, NFL Agree to New Contract, End Legal Fights," at www .bloomberg.com/aps/news?pid=email_en&sid=aOsV2TLja8jU.

Roberts, Gary. "Antitrust Issues in Professional Sports." In *Law of Professional and Amateur Sports,* ed. by Gary Uberstine. Deerfield, Ill.: Clark, Boardman, and Callaghan, 1992, pp. 19-1–19-45.

———. "*Brown v. Pro Football, Inc.:* The Supreme Court Gets It Right for the Wrong Reasons," *Antitrust Bulletin,* vol. 42, no. 3 (Fall 1997), pp. 595–639.

———. "Should Congress Stop the Bidding War for Sports Franchises?" Hearing Before the Subcommittee on Antitrust, Business Rights, and Compensation, Senate Committee on the Judiciary. "Academics," *Heartland Policy,* vol. 4 (November 29, 1995), online at http://www.heartland.org/stadps4.html.

Rosen, Harvey. *Public Finance.* Chicago: Irwin, 1995.

Rosen, Sherwin. "The Economics of Superstars," *American Economic Review,* vol. 71, no. 5 (December 1981), pp. 845–858.

Rosentraub, Mark. *Major League Losers.* New York: Basic Books, 1997.

———. "Stadiums and Urban Space." In *Sports, Jobs, and Taxes,* ed. by Roger Noll and Andrew Zimbalist. Washington, D.C.: Brookings Institution Press, 1997, pp. 178–207.

Ross, Sonya. "Clinton Signs Bill Removing Baseball Antitrust Exemption for Labor Matters," *Associated Press,* October 28, 1998, online at http://www.fl.milive.com/ tigers/stories/19981028antitrust.html.

Ross, Stephen. "Should Congress Stop the Bidding War for Sports Franchises?" Hearing Before the Subcommittee on Antitrust, Business Rights, and Compensation, Senate Committee on the Judiciary. "Academics," *Heartland Policy,* vol. 4 (November 29, 1995), online at http://www.heartland.org/stadps4.html, volume 2.

Rother, Caitlin. "Tab Climbs in Charger Ticket Deal with City," *San Diego Union-Tribune,* September 12, 2000, p. B1.

Rottenberg, Simon. "The Baseball Players Labor Market," *Journal of Political Economy,* vol. 64, no. 3 (June 1956), pp. 242–258.

Rovell, Darren. "Branded Jerseys Come to the WNBA," June 4, 2009 at www.cnbc .com/id/31034379.

———. "What's the Lease You Can Do?" *ESPN: Sports Business,* September 20, 2002, online at http://www.ESPN.com.

———. "Sports Fans Feel Pinch in Seat (Prices)," *ESPN Sports Business,* June 21, 2002, online at http://espn.go.com/sportsbusiness/s/2002/0621/1397693.html.

Rushin, Steve. "Inside the Moat," *Sports Illustrated,* March 3, 1997, pp. 69–83.

Ryan, Joan. *Little Girls in Pretty Boxes.* New York: Doubleday, 1995.

Sandomir, Richard. "Yankees Slash the Price of Top Tickets," *The New York Times,* online at www.nytimes.com/2009/04/29/sports/baseball/29tickts.html?_r=1&scp=4& sg=+%20yankees%20+%%22ticket%20prices%22&st=cse.

———. "NBC Confronts the Departure of Its Must-See N.B.A. Star," *New York Times,* January 13, 1999, p. D3.

Saslow, Eli. "School Administrators Say NCAA Crackdown on 'Diploma Mills' Is Flawed," *The Washington Post,* March 7, 2007, online at http://www.washingtonpost .com/wp-dyn/content/article/2007/03/06/AR2007030602600_pf.html.

Scahill, Edward. "Did Babe Ruth Have a Comparative Advantage as a Pitcher?" *Journal of Economic Education,* vol. 21, no. 4 (Fall 1990), pp. 402–410.

Schmuckler, Eric. "Is the NFL Still Worth It?" *Mediaweek,* September 28, 1998, pp. 26–32.

Schoenfeld, Bruce. "Hockey-Mad Canadians Hard-Pressed to Afford NHL Teams." *Street & Smith's Sports Business Journal,* April 24, 2000, p. 1.

Scully, Gerald W. *The Business of Major League Baseball.* Chicago: University of Chicago Press, 1989.

———. *The Market Structure of Sports.* Chicago: University of Chicago Press, 1995.

———. "Pay and Performance in Major League Baseball," *American Economic Review,* vol. 64, no. 5 (December 1974), pp. 915–930.

Seiken, Eric. "The NCAA and the Courts: College Football on Television." In *Sports and the Law,* ed. by Charles Quirk. New York: Garland, 1996, pp. 56–62.

Seldon, Arthur. "Public Choice and the Choices of the Public." In *Democracy and Public Choice,* ed. by Charles Rowley. London: Basil Blackwell, 1987, pp. 122–134.

"Serie A Clubs Form Their Own Premiership," June 5, 2009, at www.footballeconomy .com/world.htm.

Seymour, Harold. *Baseball: The Early Years.* New York: Oxford University Press, 1960.

———. *Baseball: The Golden Years.* New York: Oxford University Press, 1971.

Shapiro, Leonard, and Mark Maske. "Monday Night Football Changes the Channel," *Washington Post,* April 19, 2005, p. A01.

Sheehan, Richard. *Keeping Score: The Economics of Big-Time Sports.* South Bend, Ind.: Diamond Press, 1996.

"Shirley Muldowney: 2000 Star Tracks Archive," online at http://www.nhra.com/ drivers/driver.asp?driverid=976.

Shropshire, Kenneth. *The Sports Franchise Game.* Philadelphia: University of Pennsylvania Press, 1995.

Shulman, James L., and William G. Bowen. *The Game of Life.* Princeton, N.J.: Princeton University Press, 2001.

Siegfried, John, and Andrew Zimbalist. "The Economics of Sports Facilities and Their Construction," *Journal of Economic Perspectives,* vol. 14, no. 3 (Summer 2000), pp. 95–114.

———. "A Note on the Local Economic Impact of Sports Expenditures," *Journal of Sports Economics,* vol. 3, no. 4 (November 2002), pp. 361–366.

Sigelman, Lee. "It's Academic—or Is It? Admissions Standards and Big-Time College Football," *Social Science Quarterly,* vol. 76, no. 2 (June 1995), pp. 247–261.

Sigelman, Lee, and Samuel Bookheimer. "Is It Whether You Win or Lose? Monetary Contributions to Big-Time College Athletic Programs," *Social Science Quarterly,* vol. 64, no. 2 (June 1983), pp. 347–359.

"Silvio Berlusconi and Family," *The World's Billionaires,* online at www.forbes.com/lists/2009/10/billionaires-2009-richest-people_Silvio-Berlusconi-family_EEPT.html.

Simmons, Bill. "Welcome to the No Benjamins Association," *ESPN.com* online at http://espn.com.

Simon, Robert. "Intercollegiate Athletics: Do They Belong on Campus?" In *Rethinking College Athletics,* ed. by Judith Andre and David James. Philadelphia: Temple University Press, 1991, pp. 43–68.

Singell, Larry D., Jr. "Baseball-Specific Human Capital: Why Good but Not Great Players Are More Likely to Coach in the Major Leagues," *Southern Economic Journal,* vol. 58, no. 1 (July 1991), pp. 77–86.

Singer, Tom. "Yankees, Tigers Hit with Luxury Tax," *Yankees.com,* December 22, 2008, online at http://mlb.mlb.com/news/article.jsp?ymd=20081222&content_id=3726222&vkey=news_nyy&fext=.jsp&c_id=nyy&partnerId=rss_nyy.

Smith, Gary. "A New Life," *Sports Illustrated,* March 28, 1983, pp. 60–67.

Smith, James P., and Finis Welch. "Black Economic Progress After Myrdal," *Journal of Economic Literature,* vol. 27, no. 2 (June 1989), pp. 519–564.

Smith, Ronald. *Sports and Freedom: The Rise of Big-Time College Athletics.* New York: Oxford University Press, 1988.

Smith, Stephen A. "Phenom Works to Capture His Lost Dream," *Philadelphia Inquirer,* January 14, 2000, pp. D1–D2.

"Soccer Team Valuations," *Forbes Magazine,* June 4, 2009, online at www.forbes.com/lists/2009/34/soccer-values-09_Soccer-Team-Valuations_Rank.html.

"The Sony Ericsson WTA Tour 2006 Official Rulebook," *Sony Ericsson WTA Tour,* online at http://www.sonyercissonwtatour.com/global/pdfs/shared/thewtatour/officialrules.rules.pdf.

"Sony Ericsson WTA Tour Prize Money," *Sony Ericsson WTA Tour,* July 27, 2009, online at http://www.sonyericssonwtatour.com/page/PrizeMoneyRankings/0,,12781~0~1~100,00.html.

Spence, A. Michael. "Job Market Signaling," *Quarterly Journal of Economics,* vol. 87, no. 3 (August 1973), pp. 355–374.

Sperber, Murray. *Beer and Circus: How Big-Time College Sports Is Crippling Undergraduate Education.* New York: Henry Holt, 2000.

———. *Onward to Victory: The Crises That Shaped College Sports.* New York: Henry Holt, 1998.

"Sports Quotes—Another 'Top 10' List of Favorites . . ." online at http://www.famous-quotes-and-quotations.com/sports-quotes.html.

Staudohar, Paul. "The Football Strike of 1987: The Question of Free Agency," *Monthly Labor Review,* vol. 111, no. 8 (August 1988), pp. 3–9.

———. "Labor Relations in Basketball: The Lockout of 1998–99," *Monthly Labor Review,* vol. 122, no. 4 (April 1999), pp. 3–9.

———. *Playing for Dollars: Labor Relations and the Sports Business.* Ithaca, N.Y.: ILR Press, 1996.

———. "Salary Caps in Professional Team Sports." Compensation and Working Conditions, U.S. Department of Labor, Spring 1998, pp. 3–11.

———. "The Hockey Lockout of 2004–2005," *Monthly Labor Report,* December 2005, pp. 23–29.

————. "Why No Baseball Work Stoppage?" *Journal of Sports Economics*, vol. 4, no. 4 (November 2003), pp. 362–366.

————. "Professional Football and the Great Salary Dispute," *Personnel Journal*, vol. 61, no. 9 (Septemper 1982), p. 675.

Steptoe, Sonja, and E. M. Swift. "A Done Deal," *Sports Illustrated*, March 28, 1994, pp. 32–36.

Stern, Sam. "Olympic Soccer Limits Age, Not Talent," *New York Sun*, August 5, 2008, online at http://www.nysun.com/sports/olympic-soccer-limits-age-not-talent/83209.

Stigler, George, and Gary Becker. "De Gustibus Non Est Disputandum," *American Economic Review*, vol. 67, no. 1 (March 1977), pp. 76–90.

Stratmann, Thomas. "Logrolling." In *Perspectives on Public Choice: A Handbook*, ed. by Dennis Mueller. Cambridge, U.K.: Cambridge University Press, 1997, pp. 322–341.

Street & Smith's SportsBusiness Journal, By the Numbers, vol. 5, no. 6, December 30, 2002.

Struck, Doug. "Hosts Left to Foot World Cup Bill," *Washington Post*, June 29, 2002, p. A1.

Suellentrop, Chris. "Mark Cuban: How to Meddle with Your Sports Team—The Right Way," *Slate* magazine online, December 4, 2002, at www.slate.com.

Suggs, Welch. "Fight Over NCAA Standards Reflects Long-Standing Dilemma," *The Chronicle of Higher Education*, April 9, 1999, pp. A48–A49.

————. "New Grades on Academic Progress Show Widespread Failings Among Teams," *The Chronicle of Higher Education*, March 11, 2005, online at http://chronicle.com/free/v51/i27/27a04001.htm.

————. "NCAA to Pay $55-Million to Settle Lawsuit by Assistant Coaches," *The Chronicle of Higher Education*, March 19, 1999, p. A47.

Sullivan, Neil J. *The Dodgers Move West*. New York: Oxford University Press, 1987.

"Summary of New 2002–2006 CBA," online at http://www.roadsidephotos.com/baseball/laborstatus.htm.

Swift, E. M. "The $40 Million Man," *Sports Illustrated*, June 10, 1996, pp. 44–45.

————. "Anatomy of a Plot: The Kerrigan Assault," *Sports Illustrated*, February 14, 1994, pp. 28–38.

Swindell, David, and Mark Rosentraub. "Who Benefits from the Presence of Professional Sports Teams? The Implications for Public Funding of Stadiums and Arenas," *Public Administration Review*, vol. 58, no. 1 (January/February 1998), pp. 11–20.

Szymanski, Stefan. "A Market Test for Discrimination in the English Professional Soccer Leagues," *Journal of Political Economy*, vol. 108, no. 3 (June 2000), pp. 590–603.

Szymanski, Stefan, and Andrew Zimbalist. *National Pastime: How Americans Play Baseball and the Rest of the World Plays Soccer*. Washington, D.C.: Brookings Institution Press, 2005.

Taibbi, Matt. "The Devil's Doorstep: A Visit with Scott Boras," *Men's Journal*, February 23, 2009, online at http://www.mensjournal.com/the-devil%E2%80%99s-doorstep.

Taylor, Beck A., and Justin G. Trogdon. "Losing to Win: Tournament Incentives in the National Basketball Association," *Journal of Labor Economics*, vol. 20, no. 1 (January, 2002), pp. 23–41.

Taylor, Phil. "To the Victor Belongs the Spoils." *Sports Illustrated*, January 18, 1999, pp. 48–52.

"Teams Subject to Penalties 2008–09 by Sport," National Collegiate Athletic Association, July 30, 2009, online at http://www.ncaa.org/wps/ncaa?ContentID=49706.

Telander, Rick. *The Hundred-Yard Lie: The Corruption of College Football and What We Can Do to Stop It.* New York: Simon & Schuster, 1989.

"Tennis: WTA Money Leaders," *USA Today,* online at http://usatoday.com/sports/tennis/money.tnwn.htm.

Terry, Richard. "Tight End Mackey Blocks Commissioner Rozelle." In *Sports and the Law,* ed. by Charles Quirk. New York: Garland, 1996, pp. 187–189.

Thaler, Richard. "The Winner's Curse," *Journal of Economic Perspectives,* vol. 2, no. 1 (Winter 1988), pp. 191–202.

Thamel, Pete. "Schools Where the Only Real Test Is Basketball," *New York Times,* February 25, 2006, available online at http://www.nytimes.com/2006/02/25/sports/ncaabasketball/25preps.html?pagewanted=1&ei=5088&en=b4408741cbal781f&ex=1298523600&partner=rssnyt&emc=rss.

"The Business of Football," *Forbes.com,* September 1, 2005, online at http://www.forbes.com/2005/09/01/sports-football-gambling-cz_05nfland.html.

"The Baseball Archive," 2000, online at http://www.baseball1.com.

"The Forbes 400 Richest People in America," *Forbes Online* at http://www.Forbes.com.

Thomas, G. Scott. "Surhoff Proves to Be '99s Best Investment," *Street & Smith's SportsBusiness Journal,* October 25–31, 1999, p. 1.

Thornley, Stew. *Land of the Giants: New York's Polo Grounds.* Philadelphia: Temple University Press, 2000.

Thurow, Roger. "Thrown for a Curve," *Wall Street Journal,* August 28, 1998, pp. A1 and A6.

Tofler, Ian, Barri Katz Stryer, Lyle J. Micheli, and Lisa Herman. "Physical and Emotional Problems of Elite Female Gymnasts," *New England Journal of Medicine,* vol. 335, no. 4 (July 25, 1996), pp. 281–283.

Tollison, Robert. "Rent Seeking." In *Perspectives on Public Choice: A Handbook,* ed. by Dennis Mueller. Cambridge, U.K.: Cambridge University Press, 1997, pp. 506–525.

Tomlinson, Alan. "De Coubertin and the Modern Olympics," In *Five Ring Circus: Money, Power and Politics at the Olympic Games,* ed. by Alan Tomlinson and Garry Whannel. London: Pluto Press, 1984, pp. 84–97.

Ungerleider, Steven. *Faust's Gold: Inside the East German Doping Machine.* New York: Thomas Dunne Books, 2001.

University of Pennsylvania Museum of Anthropology and Archeology. "The Real Story of the Ancient Olympic Games," 1996, online at http://www.upenn.edu/museum/Olympics/olympicathletes.html.

"U.S. v. International Boxing Club of N.Y.," online at http://www.ripon.edu/faculty/bowenj/antitrust/ibcofny1.htm.

"USA Today Salaries Database," June 10, 2009, online at http://content.usatoday.com/sports/baseball/salaries/default.aspx.

Vamplew, Wray. *Pay Up and Play the Game: Professional Sport in Britain, 1875–1914.* Cambridge, U.K.: Cambridge University Press, 1988.

van Riper, Tom. "Boxing's Last Golden Boy?" *Forbes.com,* January 15, 2009, online at http://www.forbes.com/2009/01/14/boxing-oscar-de-la-hoya-biz-sports_cx_tvr_0115delahoya.html?partner=whiteglove_google.

———. "Strike Risk Grows for NFL," *Forbes.com,* June 9, 2009, online at http://www .forbes.com/2009/06/09/nfl-players-union-business-sports-football.html.

Veblen, Thorstein. *Theory of the Leisure Class.* New York: The Viking Press, 1967.

Veeck, Bill, with Ed Linn. *The Hustler's Handbook.* Durham, N.C.: Baseball America Classic Books, 1996.

———. *Veeck as in Wreck.* Chicago: University of Chicago Press, 1962.

von Allmen, Peter. "Is the Reward System in NASCAR Efficient?" *Journal of Sports Economics,* vol. 2, no. 1 (February 2000), pp. 62–79.

Vrooman, John. "Franchise Free Agency in Professional Sports Leagues," *Southern Journal of Economics,* vol. 64, no. 1 (July 1997), pp. 191–219.

———. "NBA Average Salaries and Salary Caps," online at http://www.ea.grolier .com/ea-online/wsja/text/ch10/tables/sp012.htm.

Waldman, Don E. *Microeconomics.* Boston: Pearson, 2004.

Walsh, William D. "The Entry Problem of Francophones in the National Hockey League: A Systematic Interpretation," *Canadian Public Policy—Analyse de Politiques,* vol. 18, no. 4 (December 1992), pp. 443–460.

Ward, Geoffrey, and Kenneth Burns. *Baseball: An Illustrated History.* New York: Alfred A. Knopf, 1994.

Warner, Gene. "Hockey Team Has $65 Million Impact, Hevesi Says," *Buffalo News* online, February 26, 2003, at http://www.Buffalo.com.

Weaver, Jane. "Steroid Addiction a Risk for Young Athletes," *MSNBC,* April 5, 2005, online at http://www.msnbc.msn.com/id/7348758.

Weiler, Paul, and Gary Roberts. *Sports and the Law: Cases, Materials, and Problems.* St. Paul, Minn.: West Publishing, 1993.

Weiner, Jay. "Investigating the 'U': A Year Later," *Minneapolis Star-Tribune,* March 10, 2000.

Westcott, Rich. *Philadelphia's Old Ballparks.* Philadelphia: Temple University Press, 1996.

"What's Wrong with the NCAA's Test Score Requirements?" FairTest: The National Center for Fair and Open Testing, February 2001, online at http://www.fairtest .org/facts/prop48.htm.

Wheatcroft, Geoffrey. "Non-Native Sons," *Atlantic Monthly,* June 2006, pp. 133–135.

Whitson, Jennifer. "Lucas Oil Stadium Begins in the Red," *Indianapolis Business Journal,* August 09, 2008, online at http://www.ibj.com/html/detail_ page_Full .asp?content=18441.

Wicksell, Knute. "On the Theory of Interest." In *Selected Essays in Economics: Volume I,* ed. by Bo Sandelin. London: Routledge, 1997, pp. 41–53.

Wieberg, Steve, "Academic Progress Rates Analyzed," *USA Today* online edition at http://www.usatoday.com/sports/college/2005-03-01-apr-analysis_x.htm.

Will, George. *Bunts.* New York: Scribner, 1998.

Wolf, Jason. "Haskins Lied, Told Players to Lie in Minnesota Basketball Scandal," *Associated Press,* November 19, 1999.

Wolff, Alexander, and Armen Keteyian. *Raw Recruits.* New York: Pocket Books, 1991.

"Yanks Cut Some Premium Ticket Prices," at http://sports.espn.go.com/espn/print ?id=4108293&type=HeadlineNews&imagesPrint=off.

Yeager, Don. "Black Eye for the Buckeyes," *Sports Illustrated,* June 16, 1999, p. 96.

Young, David. *The Modern Olympics: A Struggle for Revival.* Baltimore: Johns Hopkins University Press, 1996.

Young, Scott. *100 Years of Dropping the Puck: A History of the OHA.* Toronto: McClelland and Stewart, 1989.

Zimbalist, Andrew. *Baseball and Billions.* New York: Basic Books, 1992.

———. "Competitive Balance in Sports Leagues: An Introduction," *Journal of Sports Economics,* vol. 3, no. 2 (May 2002), pp. 111–121.

———. "Labor Relations in Major League Baseball," *Journal of Sports Economics,* vol. 4, no. 4 (November 2003), pp. 332–355.

———. "Salaries and Performance: Beyond the Scully Model." In *Diamonds Are Forever: The Business of Baseball,* ed. by Paul M. Sommers. Washington, D.C.: The Brookings Institution, 1992, pp. 109–133.

——— "There's More Than Meets the Eye in Determining Players' Salary Shares," *SportsbusinessJournal.com,* June 4, 2009, online at http://www.sportsbusinessjournal.com/article/58351.

———. *Unpaid Professionals.* Princeton, N.J.: Princeton University Press, 1999.

PHOTO CREDITS

INDEX

Note: Page numbers followed by the letters *f* and *t* refer to figures and tables, respectively.

A

AAF. *See* Amateur Athletic Foundation (AAF)
AAFC. *See* All-American Football Conference (AAFC)
Aaron, Hank, 14, 16, 17, 23, 24–27, 234, 264
ABA. *See* American Basketball Association (ABA)
Abramovich, Roman, 98
Academic progress rates (APR), 366*t*, 367*t*, 368*t*, 378
Academics, college
    athletics and, 368–80
    attempts to reform, 375–79
    as barrier to entry, 375–80
Accounting profits, 177
AC Milan, 97, 99, 100, 131
Advantage
    absolute, 6–8
    comparative, 5–9
Advertising, 74*f*
    broadcasting rights and, 81–82
AFL. *See* American Football League (AFL)
African American coaches and managers
    percentage of, in MLB, 335*t*
    percentage of, in NBA, 335*t*
    percentage of, in NFL, 335*t*
African-American players
    in American Association, 326
    antitrust exemption and, 129–30
    discrimination against, 311–12, 317–28
    employee discrimination, 326–28
    employer discrimination, 315–25
    Negro League and, 321
    positions in MLB, 333, 333*t*
    treatment of, 129–30

All-American Football Conference (AAFC), 128, 146, 183
Allen, Paul, 228
Allocated revenues, 381
All-or-nothing demand curve, 185–87
Amateur Athletic Foundation (AAF), 385
Amateurism, 347–88
    British influence on, 351–52
    code of, 353–57
    concept of, 348–52
    history of, 349–52
    NCAA and, 354–55
    Olympic ideal and, 349–51
    profits and, 359–63
American Association
    African-American players in, 326
    demise of, 176
American Baseball League (ABL), 67, 275
American Basketball Association (ABA), 67
    antitrust laws and, 131
American Football League (AFL), 71
    expansion of, 184
    merger with NFL, 131
    monopoly and, 123–24
American Jobs Creation Act, 96
American League (AL), 95, 146
    attendance, 146*t*
    baseball antitrust exemption and, 126
    color barrier and, 311
    discrimination and, 317
    establishment of, 68–69
    as rival to National League, 290
Anaheim Angels, 73
Anaheim Ducks, 94
Anson, Cap, 326
Antitrust laws, 124–26
    African-American players and, 129–30
    baseball's exemption from, 126–30
    boxing and, 128

Antitrust laws (*continued*)
  economic impact of, 130–31
  government regulation of, 127–28
  NCAA and, 132–35
  NFL and, 128
  NHL and, 283
Apprentices, productivity salary and, 292
Arbitration
  binding, 285
  definition of, 285
  final offer, 285
  in MLB, 284, 285–86
  in NHL, 284, 285
  salary, 284–86
Arbitrator, 285
Arizona Diamondbacks, 221
Ashe, Arthur, 311
Association of Intercollegiate Athletics
  for Women (AIAW), 133
Association of Tennis Professionals (ATP),
  305
Assumption
  strong, 23
  weak, 23
Astrodome, 193, 196, 196f, 197f
Athletic directors (AD), 382
Atlanta Braves, ownership of, 90
Atlanta Falcons, 277
Atlantic Division of the Eastern Conference,
  152–53
Attendance
  Negro League and, 321, 322f
  new facilities and, 181–82
  revenues, 79
  television, impact on, 82–83
AT&T Park, 234
Australian Football League, 68
Auto racing, women in, 336–37
Average cost, 122
Average propensity to consume (APC),
  211

B
Baade, Robert, 190, 201, 212, 218
Baker Bowl, 198
BALCO. *See* Bay Area Laboratory Co-Operative
  (BALCO)

Baltimore Colts, 131
  move to Indianapolis, 90
Baltimore Orioles, 176, 181
  ownership of, 90
Baltimore Ravens, 203, 221
  stadium arrangements for, 210
Baltimore Terrapins, 127
Bank of America Stadium, construction of,
  118–19
Bargaining, collective, 293
Barriers to entry
  academic standards as, 375–80
  as cooperative behavior, 71–72
  into leagues, 68–71
  monopoly and, 123–24
Barry, Dave, 175
Baseball
  competitive balance in, 159–60
  exemption from antitrust laws, 126–30
  golden age of, 176, 192
  history of, 39
  luxury tax and, 165
  professionalization of, 37–40, 50–51
  standardized rules, 66–67
Baseball Card Plus (Beckett), 17
Baseball cards, pricing of, 14–27, 15f, 16f,
  17f, 19f
Basketball, 101. *See also* College basketball;
  National Basketball Association (NBA)
Basso, Ivan, 265
Bay Area Laboratory Co-Operative (BALCO),
  264
Beane, Billy, 167, 168
Becker, Gary, 253, 254, 313
Becker's theory of labor discrimination, 313–15,
  322, 324
Beeston, Paul, 93
Beijing Games, 190
Bell, Bert, 131, 166
Benefits
  of debt, 235–36
  direct, for cities, 211–18
  of franchise to cities, 207–40
  maximizing, of major league teams,
  222–25
Berlin Games, 190
Berlusconi, Silvio, 40–41, 99
Berra, Yogi, 19

Berri, David, 155, 249, 250, 292, 334
Bettman, Gary, 301
Between-season variation, 155–57
    frequency of championships, 156
Bicycling, doping and, 265
Big 10 Conference, 148
Bilateral monopoly, 294, 295*f*
Binding arbitration, 285
Biographies
    Berlusconi, Silvio, 40–41
    Boras, Scott, 267–68
    Davis, Al, 202–203
    DeFrantz, Anita, 385–86
    Miller, Marvin, 307–308
    Rickey, Branch, 340–42
    Romney, Mitt, 237–38
    Rozelle, Pete, 138–40
    Selig, Bud, 169–70
    Veeck, Bill, 102–103
    Zaharias, Babe Didrikson, 8–10
Bird, Larry, 164, 251
Bivens, Carolyn, 338
Blackmum, Harry, 130
Blackouts, in television, 82
"Black Sox" scandal of 1919, 67, 127
Blue Ribbon Panel, 159
Boggs, Hale, 184
Bonaparte, Napoleon, 351
Bonds, 235–36
    face value of, 235
Bonds, Barry, 234
    doping and, 264
Bonuses, 287–88
    likely to be earned, 288
    not likely to be earned, 288
Book profit, 94
Booster clubs, 372
Boras, Scott, 267–68
Bosman, Jean-Marc, 331
Boston Braves, 176
Boston Celtics, 158
    dominance of, 147, 152, 152*f*
    salary caps and, 164–65
    ticket prices, 113
Boston Red Sox, 176
    cable broadcasting revenues, 78
    Herfindahl-Hirschman Index (HHI) and,
        157

operating income of, 88
    Ruth, George Herman "Babe" and, 6–8, 161
    ticket prices and, 20, 112
Boston Red Stockings, 281
Bowl Championship Series (BCS), 361
    revenue distributions from, 362*t*
Boxing, 243–44, 245
    discrimination and, 327
    labor supply curve for, 247*f*
Brady, Tom, 266
British Rowing Association, 353
British Sky Broadcasting Group, 99
Broadcast rights. *See* Television
Brook, Stacey, 155, 250
Brookes, William P., 351
Brooklyn Dodgers, 341
    move to Los Angeles, 176–77, 183
    origin of draft and, 165
    ownership of, 127
    racial integration and, 323
    Robinson, Jackie and, 311
    stadium, 199
    success of, 176–77
Brown, Robert, 358
Brown University, 151, 152
Brown v. Prof Football, Inc., 130
Bryant, Kobe, 149, 258, 261
Bryant, Paul "Bear," 323, 370
Buchanan, James, 68, 226
Budget constraint, 48*f*, 49*f*
Budget constraints, indifference curves and,
    50–51
Buffalo Bills, 277
    naming rights and, 84
    operating income of, 88
Buffalo Sabres
    benefits of, 217
    direct benefits from, 211–12
    gross revenues of, 213
    multiplier effects and, 218–19
    negative externalities and, 214–15
    ticket prices, 113
Bundesliga, 168
Bundling, 115
Burciaga, Juan, 136
Busch, Augustus, 129
Byers, Walter, 132
Byers, Wayne, 358

C

Cable broadcasting, television revenue and, 81

A Call to Action: Reconnecting the College Sports and Higher Education, 375

Campanella, Roy, 341

Cannon, Robert W., 307

Capital, human, 253–54

Carnegie Commission on Education, 357

Carolina Hurricanes, 131

Carolina Panthers, 110
    personal seat licenses and, 118–20
    ticket prices, 116–18

Cartels, 124, 133
    incidental, 132–35, 348
    marginal cost and, 360*f*
    NCAA as, 348, 359–63

Caudill, Steven, 364

Cellar, Emmanuel, 129

Cellar Committee, 129

Central business district, 200

Championships, frequency of, 156

Change in demand, 18, 19*f*, 37*f*

Change in quantity
    demanded, 14
    supplied, 15

Change in supply, 19*f*, 20, 21*f*

Chapman, Ben, 327

Charles, Ezzard, 243

Chicago, Illinois, importance of sports teams on local economies, 213*t*

Chicago Bears, 139, 166

Chicago Blackhawks
    ticket prices, 112
    ticket sales policy of, 34–35

Chicago "Black Sox," 67, 127

Chicago Bulls, 90, 100
    profitability of, 78–79
    revenue sharing and, 87

Chicago Cubs, 76
    operating income of, 88
    ownership of, 90, 127

Chicago White Sox, 102, 183
    aborted move of, 123
    baseball antitrust exemption and, 127
    ownership of, 90
    stadium construction and, 224
    ticket sales policy of, 34–35

Chicago White Stockings, 281

Child abuse, 261–62

Cincinnati Bengals, revenue sharing and, 87–88

Cincinnati Red Stockings, 64, 65, 66, 67

Cities
    all-or-nothing demand curve, 185–87
    costs and benefits of major league teams, 207–40
    direct benefits of franchise, 211–18
    importance of sport teams on local economies, 213*t*
    market power and, 183–85
    maximizing benefits of major league teams, 222–25
    multiplier effects, 218–22
    overspending on Olympics, 190
    public choice theory and, 226–28
    special events, impact of, 225–26
    sports teams and, 69*t*
    stadium construction, profits and costs in, 176
    underwriting facilities, 177–81

Citi Field, 85, 199, 209

Civil Rights Act, 338

Clayton Act, 124

Clemens, Roger, 265

Clemson University, 372

Cleveland Browns, 86, 120, 121, 183

Cleveland Cavaliers, 158, 161

Cleveland Indians, 102, 217, 307
    Doby, Larry and, 311
    ownership of, 95

Cleveland Rams, 131

Cleveland's Municipal Stadium, 176, 192

Coaches, discrimination and, 334–36

Coates, Dennis, 218

Collective bargaining, 293

College athletes
    eligibility of, 373–74
    net value of, 358–59
    tramp, 357

College athletics
    academics and, 368–80
    amateurism and, 347–88
    big-time programs, 370–72
    difficulty in regulating, 373–74
    finances of, 380–85
    graduation rates and, 365

grant-in-aid and, 357–58
Knight Commission, 348, 374–75
measuring net value to college, 358–59
as monopsony, 356f
prisoner's dilemma in, 355t
profit maximization and, 382–85
profits and, 380–83
student-athlete and, 363–68
Title IX, 338–40
College basketball
gambling and, 135
graduation rates and, 365
March madness, 348
College football
Bowl Championship Series and, 361
divisions of, 136
eligibility for, 373–74
gambling and, 135
graduation rates and, 365
prisoner's dilemma and, 136–38, 138t
television contracts, 138–39
zero-sum game and, 371
College Football Association (CFA), 136
Collusion, 125
Colorado Avalanche, 131
Colorado Rockies, 99
ownership of, 90
ticket sales policy of, 32–33, 34f
Colorado State, graduation
rates for, 366
Color line
in baseball, 311
marginal revenue product and, 324
Rickey, Branch, and, 311
Comiskey, Charles, 127
Comiskey Park, 176
Comparative advantage, 5–9
Ruth, George Herman "Babe," and, 5–9
Competition
cities underwriting facilities, 177–81
eliminating discrimination with, 321–23
imperfect, 250–51
perfect, 30–32
for professional sports teams, 177–82
Competitive balance, 145–72
attempts to alter, 162–68
between-season variation, 155–57
definition of, 145

economic theories of, 160–62
fan's perspective, 146–48
Herfindahl-Hirschman Index, 157
in Major League Baseball, 159–60
market size, effect of, 149–51, 150f
measuring, 151–62
owner's perspective, 148–51
promotion and regulation, 168
revenue sharing and, 162–63
reverse-order entry draft, 165–68
salary caps and luxury taxes, 164–65
schedule adjustment in NFL, 168
within-season variation, 151–55
Competitive imbalance, 147
illustrating, 157–59
Competitive markets, 29
Connie Mack Stadium, 199
Constrained maximum, 44–50
Constraints
budget, 48f, 49f
effect of, on work hours, 276f
income, 48–50, 271
time, 271
Consumer discrimination, 328–31
Consumer surplus, 109–10, 110f, 186f
personal seat licenses and, 118–20, 120f
in second-degree price discrimination, 117f
Consumption
constraints and, 271
limits of (See Constraints)
Continental League, 129
Contract zone, 298f, 299f
definition of, 298
Cooperative behavior, controlling entry as,
71–72
Copyright laws, monopoly and, 124–26
Cornell University, 357, 369
Corner solution, 273
Costs
average, 122
fixed, 36
of franchise to cities, 207–40
impact of increase in, 36
marginal, 31, 31f, 37, 38f, 73, 91
marketing, 89
of monopoly, 109f
opportunity, 6, 89–90
of professional sports teams, 88–89

Costs (*continued*)
  stadium, 228–36
  transaction, 162
  venue, 89
Craft unions, 292
Crisler, Fritz, 136
Crosby, Sidney, 53, 54, 55, 57, 266
Cross subsidization, 91
Crothers, Douglas, 326
Cuban, Mark, 63, 64, 78, 98, 151
Curd, Ed, 135
Currency market, 223
Curt Flood Act (1998), 130
Customer choice, 45*f*

D

Dallas Cowboys, 40, 78
  operating income, 77*f*
  ownership of, 90
  sales tax and, 232
  stadium agreements and, 83–84
  television and, 82–83
  ticket prices, 113
Dallas Mavericks, 63–64, 78, 98
  competitive balance and, 148
da Silva, Luis Inácio Lula, 160
Davis, Al, 140, 202–203
Deadweight loss
  definition of, 111
  monopoly and, 108–11, 227
  taxes and, 230, 231*f*
Dean, Dizzy, 340
"Death penalty" of NCAA, 135, 356
Debt, benefits of, 235–36
de Coubertin, Pierre, 351, 352
DeFrantz, Anita, 385–86
de la Hoya, Oscar, 243, 245, 246
  labor-leisure choice model and, 275
Demand, 26*f*, 33*f*. *See also* Supply and
  demand
  of baseball cards, 25*f*
  change in, 14, 18, 19*f*, 37*f*
  definition of, 14
  effect of entry on, 70*f*
  elastic, 24
  elasticity of, 23–24, 24*f*
  excess, 16

inelastic, 24
  labor, 248–51
  law of, 14
Demand curve, 14
  all-or-nothing, 185–87
  individual, price discrimination and,
    117–18
  labor, 249*f*
  price of baseball cards and, 18–27
Denver, Colorado
  hosting teams, 222–23
  importance of sport teams on local
    economies, 213*t*
Denver Broncos, ticket sales policy of, 32
Denver Nuggets, 131
Dependent variable, 54
Depreciation
  allowances, 95–97
  straight-line, 95, 96*f*
Designated gross revenue (DGR), 164, 287
Detroit Lions, 67, 78
  draft picks and, 166
  monopoly power and, 121–23
Detroit Red Wings
  sharing facility, 199
  ticket prices, 112
Detroit Tigers
  luxury tax and, 165
  ownership of, 90
DiMaggio, Joe, 183
Diminishing marginal rate of substitution,
  46, 47*f*
Diminishing marginal returns, 149
DirecTV, 83
Discrimination, 311–43, 321*f*
  Becker's theory of labor, 313–15
  in coaching and administrative ranks, 334–36
  coefficient, 317
  competition and, 321–23
  consumer, 328–31
  definition of, 312
  employee, 326–28
  employer, 315–25
  against French-speaking hockey players,
    313, 315–19
  gender, 336–38
  by national origin in European soccer, 331–32
  positional or hiring, 332–36

prejudice *versus,* 312
in professional sports, 315–38
race and, 311–12, 317–25
role, 333
statistical, 319–20
taste for, 314
Title IX and, 338–40
Disequilibrium, 16
Distribution, of income, 265–66
Divisions, of college football, 136
Division Series (DS), 72
Doby, Larry, 95, 103, 311, 312, 326
"Dodgertown," 341
Dominant strategy, 138
Doping, 262–65
Double hosting, 362
Downstream firm, 91, 92*f*
Drugs, performance-enhancing, 262–65
Duderstadt, James J., 365
Dummy variables, 58
Durocher, Leo, 326
Dye, Richard, 218

E
Eagleson, Alan, 300, 308
Earned run average (ERA), 7
Eating disorders, in athletes, 262
Ebbets, Charles, 127, 210
Ebbets Field, 199, 209, 307
Eckard, E. Woodrow, 379
Economic models, 14
Economic profit, 177
Economic rent, 358
Economics
of competitive balance, 160–62
labor, 5
of monopsony, 280–81
normative, 29
positive, 28
role of, in sports, 3–11
of tournaments and superstars, 255–60
of unions, 292–96
Economic theory, labor conflict and, 297–98
Edmonton Oilers, 82, 131
Edward Jones Dome, 86
Edwards, Harry, 377
Effectively efficient markets, 32

Eisenhower, Dwight, 341
Elastic demand, 24
Elasticity of demand, 23–24, 24*f*
Elasticity of supply, 22–23, 22*f*
Eligibility
for college football, 373–74
SAT scores and, 373
Employee discrimination, 326–28
Employer discrimination, 315–25
effects of, 320–25
against French-speaking hockey players,
313, 315–19
English Professional League, 159
Entry, barriers to. *See* Barriers to entry
Equilibrium, 17, 214
exchange rate, impact of change in, 224*f*
labor market, 251–55, 255
point, 16, 68
wage, 252*f*, 317*f*
Equity, 230
gender, 336–38
horizontal, 230
vertical, 230
Ericcson Stadium, construction of, 118–19
Excess demand, 16
Excess supply, 16
Exchange rate, 223
impact of change in equilibrium, 224*f*
Exports, net, 211
Externality, 208
negative, 214, 215*f*
positive, 214, 216*f*
Extreme Football League (XFL), 71, 303

F
Face value
of bond, 235
of tickets, 27
Facilities. *See* Stadiums and arenas
Fallacy of composition, 182
"Fan friendly" stadiums, 195
Fans. *See* Spectators, competitive balance and
FC Barcelona, 148
as symbol, 218
*Federal Baseball Club of Baltimore, Inc. v. National
League of Professional Baseball Clubs,* 127–28,
130, 137, 283

Federal League, 126–27
  antitrust exemption and, 129
Federation Internationale de Football
  Association (FIFA), 100, 188, 189, 331
Federer, Roger, 255
FedEx Forum, 193, 209
Fenway Park, 192
FIFA. *See* Federation Internationale de Football
  Association (FIFA)
Figure skating, 261
  adolescent girls in, 262
  productivity in, 255
Final offer arbitration (FOA), 285
Finances, of college athletics, 380–85
Financing
  incremental, 234
  of stadiums, 228–36
First-degree price discrimination, 116
Fixed costs, 36
Flood, Curt, 129
Flood v. Kuhn, 283
Florida Marlins, 77, 78, 79, 163
Florida State, 371
Florida State University (FSU), 138
Football Association (FA), 65, 66, 121, 369
Football Bowl Subdivision (FBS), 121, 361
Football Championship Subdivision (FCS),
  361
Football League (FL), 66, 98
  discrimination in, 323
Forbes Field, 176, 192
Forbes Magazine, 3, 73, 76, 78, 213, 258
Ford Field, 192
Forsberg, Peter, 333
Fox Broadcasting, 83
"Franchise player," 303
Franchises. *See* Major league franchises
Frazee, Harry, 161
Free agency, 159
  advent of, 282–84
  forms of, 284
  NFL and, 302
  origins of, 301
  restricted, 284
  unrestricted, 284
Free agents, 36
Free rider problem, definition of, 74
French Open, 337

French-speaking hockey players,
  discrimination against, 313, 315–19
Furillo, Carl, 326
Future value, 187

G
Gambling, college football and, 135
Game theory, 138, 142–44
Gasol, Pau, 328
Gate revenue, 79
  television and, 82–83
Gates, Bill, 228
Gateway Project, 225
Gender equity, 336–38
Generated revenues, 381
"Gentlemen's agreement"
  in MLB, 320
  in NFL, 128, 282, 283
Ginobili, Manu, 328
Glasgow Rangers, 97
Goals scored, player salaries and, 53–58, 54*f*,
  55*f*, 56*f*, 57*f*
Golf, women in, 336
Goodenow, Bob, 301
Goods
  inferior, 18
  normal, 18
  public, 74
  trade-off between leisure and, 51*f*
Goodwill Games, 189
Graduation success rate (GSR), 365, 366*t*, 367*t*,
  368*t*
Graf, Steffi, 145
Graham, Otto, 120
Grand Slam events, 305
Grant, Frank, 326
Grant-in-aid, 357–58
Great Depression, 183
Greek Olympic ideal, 349–51
Green Bay Packers, 67, 131
  cable broadcasting revenue, 82
  cities underwriting facilities and, 177–78
  operating income of, 88

H
Hamill, Pete, 175
Hamm, Mia, 337

Hanlon, Ned, 127
Hard cap, 164
Harding, Tonya, 261
Hartford, Connecticut, 222
Hartford Whalers, 131
Harvard University, 134, 151, 152, 237, 352, 357
Haynes, Jonathan, 357
Heffelfinger, William, 64
Heinz Field, 84
Henrich, Christy, 262
Herfindahl-Hirschman Index (HHI), 157
Hiring discrimination, 332–36
Hollywood Games, 9
Hollywood Olympics, 190
Holmes Jr., Oliver Wendall, 127
"Homegrown Rule," 332
Honda Center, 192
Hoosier Dome, 225
Horizontal equity, 230
Hornung, Paul, 67
Hotels, objection to tax increase, 229, 230*f*
Houston Astros, 193
Houston Rockets, marketing efforts of, 73–74, 74*f*
Houston Texans, 194
Howard, Ryan, 266
Hulbert, William, 281
Human capital theory, 253–54
    general training, 253
    specific training, 253
Humphreys, Brad, 218
Hutchins, Robert, 373

IAAUS. *See* Intercollegiate Athletic Association of the United States (IAAUS)
Imperfect competition, labor demand and, 250–51
Incidental cartel, 132–35, 348
Income
    constraints, 48–50, 271
    distribution of, 265–66
    effects, 15, 274
    operating, 77, 94–96
    subsistence level of, 52*f*
    time constraints and, 272*f*
Incremental financing, 234

Independent variable, 54
Independent Women's Forum, 339
Indiana Pacers, 131, 217
Indianapolis Colts, 90, 203
Indifference curves, 45, 46*f*, 271*f*
    budget constraints and, 50–51
    labor-leisure choice model of, 270–77
Indifferent, definition of, 45
Industrial organization, 4
Industrial Revolution
    development of professional sports and, 37–40
    leisure and consumption and, 51
Industrial unions, 292
Inelastic demand, 24
Inferior goods, 18
Integration, vertical, 91, 93*f*
Intercept term, in ordinary least squares estimate, 57
Intercollegiate Athletic Association of the United States (IAAUS), 134
Interest rate, 235
International Boxing Club, 128
International League, 326
International Olympic Committee (IOC), 185, 187
Invariance principle, 160
IOC. *See* International Olympic Committee (IOC)

Jacobs Field, 184, 225
Jagr, Jaromir, 333
James, LeBron, 4, 113, 161, 266
Japan
    baseball in, 6, 8, 20, 68, 253
    profit maximization in, 94
Jobing.com Arena, 193
Jockeys, gender inequity and, 336
Johanson, Carl, 357
Johnson, Jack, 327
Johnson, Magic, 251
Jones, Jerry, 40, 90, 151, 203
Jones, Marion, 264
Jones, Stephen, 113
Jordan, Michael, 244, 250, 251, 258
    retirement of, 258
    as superstar, 258

K

Kansas City Chiefs, 82
Kansas City Royals, 79, 300
    cable broadcasting revenue, 81–82
Karras, Alex, 67
Kemp, Jan, 374
Kerrigan, Nancy, 261
King, Billie Jean, 337
Kingdome, 192
Knapple, Jeffrey, 85
Knickerbocker Rules, of baseball, 66
Knight Commission, 348, 374–75, 384
Kostka, Stan, 165
Krautmann, Anthony, 291
Krock, Joan, 177
Kuhn, Bowie, 284
Kuznetsova, Svetlana, 265

L

Labor conflict
    economic theory and, 297–98
    in professional sports, 296–301, 297t
Labor demand
    imperfect competition and, 250–51
    marginal revenue product, 248–49
    measuring player MRP, 249–50
Labor economics, 5
Labor-leisure choice model
    with fixed hours, 275–77
    of indifference curves, 270–77
Labor market equilibrium, 251–55, 255
Labor market imperfections, 279–309
    rival leagues, impact of, 290–91, 290f
    salary arbitration, 284–86
Labor markets
    in professional sports, 243–69
    supply and demand in, 245–55
Labor supply, 246–48
    changes in, 273f
Labor supply and demand. See Supply and
    demand
Ladies' Professional Golf Association (LPGA),
    10, 338
Landis, Floyd, 265
Landis, Kenesaw Mountain, 103, 126, 127,
    129

Large efficient size, 122
Latino athletes, in baseball, 328–29
Laws
    law of demand, 14
    law of supply, 15
League Championship Series (LCS), 72
Leagues
    contraction of, 72–73
    determining size of, 69f
    entry control, 68–72
    history of, 64–65
    marketing, 73–75
    rule setting, 66–67
    television contracts and, 71, 72
Leeds United, 101
Leisure time, goods consumption and, 51f
Leonard, Dutch, 7
Lewis, Michael, 167
Likely to be earned (LTBE) bonus, 288
Location, of stadiums, 199–202
Lockout. See Strikes and lockouts
Logrolling, 227, 227t
Long, James, 364
Long, Judith Grant, 180
Long, Russell, 184
Lorenz curve, 157–58, 158f
    tennis and, 265, 266f
Los Angeles Clippers, 158
    territorial rights of team and, 72
Los Angeles Coliseum, 192
Los Angeles Dodgers, 88
    dominance of, 159
    labor conflict and, 300
    market size and, 150
    move from Brooklyn, 90
    move to Los Angeles, 176–77
    suspension of players on, 67
Los Angeles Lakers, 72, 75, 158
    diminishing returns and, 149
    dominance of, 125–26
    profitability of, 79
    superstars on, 261
Los Angeles Raiders, 86
Los Angeles Rams, 86, 203, 370
    management of, 139
Louis, Joe, 243, 244, 245, 246, 327
Luxury tax, 165

M

Mack, Connie, 290, 341
Mackey, John, 128
Mackey v. National Football League, 302
Madden, Janice, 336
Madison Square Garden, 199
Major League Baseball (MLB)
    antitrust exemption and, 129
    breakdown of players in, 333*t*
    championships, 156, 156*t*
    competitive balance in, 159–60
    employee discrimination and, 312
    expansion of, 183
    facilities built for, 179*t*
    founding principles of, 107
    gate revenue and, 80
    "gentlemen's agreement" in, 320
    limiting entry in, 68
    luxury tax and, 165
    revenue sharing and, 87–88, 163
    salaries of players in, 279
    salary arbitration in, 284, 285–86
    salary caps and, 164, 288
    stacking in, 332
    1994–1995 strike, 169, 300
    ticket prices in, 20
    variable ticket pricing and, 114
    winning percentages in, 153–54
Major League Baseball Players Association
    (MLBPA), 129, 183, 279, 283, 284, 300,
    301, 303
    Miller, Marvin and, 307
Major league franchises
    costs and benefits to cities, 207–40
    importance in local economies, 64–75
    as profit-maximizing firms, 63–102
Major League Soccer (MLS), employee
    discrimination and, 312
Managers, discrimination and, 334–36
Manchester United, 97
Mantle, Mickey, 14, 16, 17, 19, 23, 24–27
Mara, Tim, 166
Mara, Wellington, 139
March madness, 348
Marciano, Rocky, 243
Marginal benefit (MB), 73, 75*f*
Marginal consumer, 110

Marginal cost curve, in monopoly, 35*f*
Marginal cost (MC), 31, 31*f*, 37, 38*f*, 73, 91
    cartels and, 360*f*
    of effort, 256*f*
Marginal expenditure, 281
    curve, 281
Marginal propensity to consume (MPC), 219
Marginal propensity to save (MPS), 219
Marginal rate of substitution, 270
Marginal revenue (MR), 31, 31*f*, 33*f*
Marginal revenue product (MRP), 248–49,
    324, 358
    curve, 251*f*
    measuring player, 249–50
Marginal utility, 38*f*
Market
    currency, 223
    demand, 30
    failure, 208
    forces, exploitation of, 182–88
    size, effect of, 149–51, 150*f*
    for teams, 175–205
    for World Cup, 160, 161*f*
Marketing
    costs, 89
    league-level, for public good, 73–75
Market power
    cities and, 183–85
    leagues and, 183–85
Markets
    competitive, 29
    effectively efficient, 32
    labor, 243–69
    noncompetitive, 324–25
Market structures, 29–36
    monopoly, 32–36
Mary Kay Cosmetics, 232
Massachusetts Rules, of baseball, 66
Matheson, Victor, 190
Mays, Willie, 198
McCray, Nikki, 275, 277
McGill University, 134
McGwire, Mark, 265
McNamee, Frank, 139
McNeil, Freeman, 302
McNeil et al. v. NFL, 283
McNeil v. Pro Football, Inc., 302

McPhail, Bill, 139

Measurement, of competitive balance, 151–62

Median revenue, 381*t*, 382*t*

Medwick, Joe, 340

Memorial Stadium (Baltimore), 193

Memphis Grizzlies, 18

Merger, of AFL and NFL, 131

Mexican League, 129

Miami Dolphins, 82

Michigan State University, 121

Miller, Marvin, 283, 284, 286, 307–308

Miller Park, 209, 234

Milwaukee Braves, 169
    ownership of, 95

Milwaukee Brewers, 181–82, 300
    stadium, 234

Milwaukee Bucks, stadium arrangements for, 210

Minnesota Twins
    cable broadcasting revenue, 81
    financial viability of, 72–73
    lockout and, 303

Minnesota Vikings, 78
    television revenue and, 80

Minute Maid Park, 193, 195, 195*f*

Mississippi State, 372

Mixed strategy, in tennis, 143*t*

MLB. *See* Major League Baseball (MLB)

Models. *See* Economic models

Moneyball (Lewis), 167

Monopoly, 32–36, 107–44
    advantages of, 121–23
    barriers to entry and, 123–24
    bilateral, 294, 295*f*
    copyright laws and, 124–26
    cost of, 109*f*
    deadweight loss and, 108–11
    definition of, 32
    marginal cost curve in, 35*f*
    monopsony and, 120–21
    natural, 121, 122*f*
    power, 107
    price discrimination and, 112–18
    problems with, 108–21
    promotion and regulation system, 111–12
    rent seeking behavior and, 111
    vertically integrated, 91

Monopsony, 324*f*, 325*f*
    college sports as, 356*f*
    definition of, 120–21
    economics of, 280–81
    measuring power, 291–92
    power, 107
    reserve clause system and, 120–21, 281–84
    rival leagues and, 283, 290, 290*f*
    unions and, 295*f*
    wages and, 280*f*

Montreal Canadiens
    dominance of, 147
    sharing facility, 199
    as symbol, 218
    tax rates and, 223
    ticket prices, 113

Montreal Expos
    financial viability of, 72–73
    lockout and, 303

Montreal Royals, 311

Moore, Bernie H., 135

M&T Bank Stadium, 225

Muldowney, Shirley, 336

Multiple regression, 58–59

Multiplier, simple, 220

Multiplier effects
    definition of, 219
    of sports franchises, 218–22

Multipurpose facilities, 193–98

Municipal ownership, opposition to, 178

Murphy, Tyler, 347

Musial, Stan, 340

N

NABBP. *See* National Association of Baseball Players (NABBP)

Naming
    rights, 84–85
    of stadiums and arenas, 192–93

NASCAR, 19
    broadcasting rights, revenue from, 81
    competitive balance and, 148
    Hall of Fame location for, 185–86, 187–88, 229
    reward scheme for, 259–60, 259*f*

Nash, John, 295, 296

National Association of Baseball Players (NABBP), 66

National Association of Professional Base Ball Players, 281
National Basketball Association (NBA), 154
  championships, 156, 156t
  competitive imbalance, 157–58
  consumer discrimination in, 330
  employee discrimination and, 312
  facilities built for, 179t
  gate revenue and, 79–80
  labor market equilibrium in, 251
  limiting entry in, 68
  lockout of 1998–1999, 296, 303
  multiplier, 220
  revenue sharing, 87–88
  reverse-order entry draft and, 166
  salary caps and, 164, 286–87
  sharing arena with NHL, 198–99
  wage increases in, 252f
National Basketball League (NBL), 176
National Basketball Players Association (NBPA), 283
National Car Rental Arena, 192
National Collegiate Athletic Association (NCAA), 5, 9
  amateurism and, 354–55
  antitrust laws and, 132–35
  athletics and academics, 368–80
  as cartel, 348, 359–63
  child abuse and, 261–62
  "death penalty" of, 135, 356
  divisional hierarchy of, 371
  divisions of, 136
  grant-in-aid, 357–58
  Knight Commission, 348, 374–75
  market power and, 182
  move to professional sports from, 364t
  origins of, 134
  Proposition 16, 376–77
  Proposition 42, 376–77
  Proposition 48, 376–77
  revenue generated for, 348
  2000 rule, 376
  Sanity Code regulations, 134, 357
  tramp athletes and, 357
  women's sports and, 133
National Football League (NFL)
  championships, 156, 156t
  employee discrimination and, 312
  entry into, 68
  establishment of, 64–65
  expansion of, 184
  facilities built for, 179t
  gate revenue and, 79–80
  "gentlemen's agreement" in, 128, 282, 283
  merger with AFL, 131
  monopoly and, 108, 123–24
  revenue sharing and, 87–88, 163
  reverse-order entry draft and, 165–68
  salaries of players in, 279, 301–304
  salary caps and, 164, 287–88
  schedule adjustments in, 168
  stacking in, 332
  stadium agreements, 83–86
  strikes in, 298–99
  team moves in, 176–77
  television blackouts, 82
  television contracts, antitrust exemption and, 131–32
  television revenue and, 80–81, 80–86
  tragedy of the commons, 86
  winning percentages in, 153–54
National Football League Players Association (NFLPA), 128, 279, 287, 298
  missteps by, 302–303
  structural problems facing, 301–302
National Hockey League (NHL)
  antitrust laws and, 283
  cancellation of 2004–2005 season, 287, 296
  championships, 156, 156t
  discrimination against French-speaking players, 313, 315–19
  Eastern European players in, 333–34
  expansion of, 183
  facilities built for, 179t
  free agency and, 284
  gate revenue and, 79–80
  limiting entry in, 68
  profit maximization and, 214
  revenue sharing, 87–88
  reverse-order entry draft and, 166
  salary arbitration in, 284, 285
  salary caps and, 164, 287
  sharing arena with NBA, 198–99
  team payroll of, 289f
  television revenue and, 80–81

National Hockey League Players Association (NHLPA), 301

National Hot Rod Association (NHRD), 336

National League, 67, 68, 69, 90, 99, 176, 342
attendance, 146*t*
baseball antitrust exemption and, 126
color barrier and, 311
discrimination and, 317
establishment of, 64–65
market power, 183
racial integration and, 323
as rival to American League, 290

National League of Professional Baseball Clubs, 281

Nationwide Arena, 180

Natural monopoly, 121, 122*f*
regulation of, 125

NBA. *See* National Basketball Association (NBA)

NBL. *See* National Basketball League (NBL)

NBPA. *See* National Basketball Players Association (NBPA)

NCAA. *See* National Collegiate Athletic Association (NCAA)

NCAA Revenue and Expenses Report, 381

Negative externalities, 214, 215*f*

Negro Leagues, 103, 321
attendance and, 321, 322*f*

Net exports, 211

Net value, of athletes to colleges, 358–59

Newcombe, Don, 341

New England Patriots
draft picks and, 166
stadium, 209
television and, 82–83

Newfield, Jack, 175

New Jersey Devils, 156

New Jersey Nets, 131

New Orleans Hornets, 250

New Orleans Saints, 184

New York Giants, 112, 131, 166, 183
discrimination and, 326
stadium, 198

New York Islanders, 147

New York Jets, 112

New York Knickerbocker Club, 39

New York Knicks, 152, 161, 162, 217
salary cap and, 288

New York Mets
attendance revenue, 79
bundling and, 115
cable broadcasting revenues, 78, 81
construction of stadium, 228
ticket prices, 113

New York Rangers, sharing facility, 199

New York Yankees, 146
antitrust laws and, 129
attendance revenue, 79
cable broadcasting revenues, 78, 81
championships, 156, 156*t*
color barrier and, 323
competitive balance and, 148
construction of stadium, 228
dominance of, 147, 159, 232
Herfindahl-Hirschman Index (HHI) and, 157
labor conflict and, 300
luxury tax and, 165
market size and, 150
operating income, 97
Ruth, George Herman "Babe," and, 6, 161
salary cap and, 288
ticket prices and, 20

NFL. *See* National Football League (NFL)

NFLPA. *See* National Football League Players Association (NFLPA)

NHL. *See* National Hockey League (NHL)

NHLPA. *See* National Hockey League Players Association (NHLPA)

Nippon Professional Baseball League (NPB), 68

Niskanen, William, 226

Nonexclusion, 74

Nonrivalry, 74

Normal goods, 18

Normative economics, 29

Not likely to be earned (NLTBE) bonus, 288

Notre Dame University, 353
graduation rates for, 367
television contract and, 138

O

Oakland-Alameda County Stadium, 192

Oakland Athletics, 159, 167–68

Oakland Raiders, 202, 203
  salary cap and, 288
Occupational Safety and Health
  Administration (OSHA), 369
Oklahoma City Thunder, 80
Oklahoma State, 379
Oklahoma University, 136
Olympics. *See also* International Olympic
  Committee (IOC)
  in Beijing, 190
  in Berlin, 190
  child abuse and, 261–62
  doping and, 264–65
  East German women in, 263
  figure skating and, 261
  Greek ideal, 349–51
  impact of, 225–26
  in Los Angeles, 190
  in Montreal, 190
  overspending and, 188–91
  rise of modern, 351–52
  selecting location for, 188–91
  in Sydney, 264
O'Malley, Walter, 175, 341
O'Neal, Shaquille, 261
O'Neill, Buck, 341
Open system, dangers of, 101
Operating income, 77, 88, 94–96
  for soccer, 97t
Opportunity costs, 6, 89–90
Ordinary least squares (OLS), 55, 55f
Oriole Park, 181, 199, 209, 225
OSHA. *See* Occupational Safety and Health
  Administration (OSHA)
Ottawa Senators, 64, 82
Output, defining and measuring in sports, 29
Overspending, Olympics and World Cup and,
  188–91
Ownership
  municipal, opposition to, 178
  resurgent, 303–304
  single entity, 101–102
  subchapter S corporation, 95
Owners of sports franchises
  behavior of, 90–93
  perspectives on competitive balance,
    148–51

P
Pacific Division of the Western Conference,
  152–53
Paige, Rod, 340
Paige, Satchel, 103, 341
Palmiero, Raphael, 265
Pan American Games, 188
Papa John's Cardinal Stadium, 85
Patents, 125
Paterno, Joe, 379
Patrick, Danica, 337
Paul, Chris, 250
Payoff matrix, 138
Payroll, team, 289f
  of NHL, 289f
Payton, Walter, 302
Penn State University, 363, 369, 379
Perfect competition, 30–32
Perfectly inelastic, 23, 24f
Performance-enhancing drugs (PED), 262–65
  as prisoner's dilemma, 264f
Personal seat license (PSL), consumer surplus
  and, 118–20, 120f
PETCO park, 234
Philadelphia, Pennsylvania, importance of
  sport teams on local economies, 213t
Philadelphia Athletics, 176, 290–91
Philadelphia Eagles, 275
  attendance and, 82
  origin of draft and, 165
  ownership of, 139, 166
Philadelphia Flyers, 148, 156
  sharing facility, 199
Philadelphia Phillies, 3, 129, 146
  bundling and, 115
  discrimination and, 327
  Negro League and, 323
  ownership of, 90
  ticket sales policy of, 29
*Philadelphia World Hockey Club v. Philadelphia
  Hockey Club*, 283
Phoenix Coyotes, 131
Phoenix Mercury, 84
Phoenix Suns, stadium arrangements for, 210
Pittsburgh Penguins, 53
Pittsburgh Pirates, aborted move of, 123
Player development, costs of, 89

Player salaries. *See* Salaries of players
Point shaving, 135
Porter, Philip, 226
Positional discrimination, 332–36
Positive economics, 28
Positive externalities, 214, 216f
Prejudice, discrimination *versus*, 312
Premier League, 98, 99, 100, 101, 131, 148, 154,
    168
    championships, 156, 156t
Present value, 186, 187
Price
    of baseball cards, 14–27
    equilibrium, 17
    future, expectations of, supply and demand,
        21
    transfer, 92
Price ceiling, on tickets, effects of, 27–29,
    28f
Price discrimination
    definition of, 116
    first-degree, 116
    monopoly and, 112–18
    second-degree, 117, 117f
    third-degree, 118
Price-takers, 31
Princeton University, 134, 373
Principal-agent problem, 382
Prisoner's dilemma
    in college athletics, 136–38, 138t
    college spending and, 355t
    definition of, 138
    game theory and, 142–44
    performance-enhancing drugs as, 264f
Privately built facilities, 209–10
Prize winnings, disparity in, 259
Producer surplus, 109
Production possibilities frontier (PPF), 212,
    213f
Productivity, relative, 255
Professional sports, development of, 37–40
Professional tennis associations, 304–306
Profit maximization, 63–102
    college athletics and, 382–85
    in soccer, 98–99
Profits
    accounting, 177
    amateurism and, 359–63

book, 94
    from college athletics, 359–63, 380–83
    definition of, 75–76
    economic, 177
    manipulation of, 93–96
    from stadiums and arenas, 83–86
    turning losses into, 93–96
Progressive Field, 181, 225
Promotion
    competitive balance and, 168
    monopoly power and, 111–12
    for soccer franchises, 99–100
Property rights, 160
Proposition 16, 376–77
Proposition 42, 376–77
Proposition 48, 376–77
Providence Bruins, hockey cards and, 18
Public choice theory, 111, 226–28, 233
Public finance, 4, 175–205
Public good, 74
Publicly built facilities, 210–22
Pujols, Albert, 282
Purchasing power effect, 15

Q
Qualcomm Stadium, 210
Quebec, Canada, 222
Quebec Nordiques, 131

R
The 2008 Racial and Gender Report Card, 312, 333,
    335
Radovich, George, 128
Radovich v. National Football League, 282
Ramirez, Manny, 67, 265
Ramsey rule, 229
Rank-order tournaments, 255
Rational choice, 44
Real Madrid, 97, 148
Reese, Pee Wee, 327
Reeves, Dan, 139
Regression
    analysis, 53–59
    multiple, 58–59
    simple, 56

Regulation
  of college sports, 373–74
  competitive balance and, 168
  monopoly power and, 111–12
  of natural monopolies, 125
  for soccer franchises, 99–100
Reinsdorf, Jerry, 90, 183
Relative productivity, 255
Reliant Stadium, 194, 194f
Rent gradient, 200, 201f
Rent seeking
  definition of, 111
  in monopoly, 111
Reserve clause system, 120
  monopsony and, 281–84
Restricted free agent, 284
Resurgent ownership, 303–304
Retro stadiums, 181
Returns, diminishing marginal, 149
Revenue
  allocated, 381
  BCS, 362t
  designated gross, 164, 287
  gate, 79
  generated, 381
  marginal, 31, 31f
  median, 381t, 382t
  sharing of, 87–88
  soccer, 97t
  television, 80–86, 80t
  total, 76–79
  venue, 181
Revenue sharing
  competitive balance and, 162–63
  effects of, 87–88
Reverse-order entry draft, 165–68
  evaluation of, 166–67
  evaluation of talent and, 167–68
  origins of, 165
Ricardo, David, 235
"Richard Riot," 218
Richfield Coliseum, 184
Rickey, Branch, 184, 311, 340–42
Right of first refusal, 284
Riley, Pat, 125
Rival leagues, impact of, 290–91, 290f
Robertson, Oscar, 283
Robertson v. NBA, 283

Robinson, Jackie, 103, 282, 311, 312, 321, 326, 341
Roddick, Andy, 255
Rodriguez, Alex, 4, 36, 267, 268
  doping and, 265
Role discrimination, 333
Romney, Dick, 136
Romney, Mitt, 237–38
Roosevelt, Theodore, 134
Rose, Pete, 67
Rottenberg, Simon, 249
Rowing, women in, 385–86
Rozelle, Pete, 128, 131, 138–40, 203, 283
Rozelle rule, 128, 283, 302
Rules, setting, as league function, 66–67
Runs batted in (RBIs), 17
Rupp, Adolph, 135
Ruppert, Jacob, 192
Rutgers University, 373
Ruth, George Herman "Babe," 5–9, 147, 198
  Boston Red Sox and, 161
R-value, 154
Rypien, Mark, 277

S
Sacramento Kings, 152, 158, 182
Safina, Dinara, 265
Salaries of players
  arbitration-eligible, 284–86
  average annual, 245f
  Canadian exchange rate, 223–24
  goals scored and, 53–58, 54f, 55f, 56f, 57f
  human capital and, 253–54
  in NFL, 301–304
  profits, impact on, 88
  ticket prices and, 36
Salary arbitration, 284–86
Salary caps, 164, 286–90
  hard cap, 164
  impact of, 288, 290
  in NBA, 286–87
  in NFL, 287–88
  in NHL, 287
  soft cap, 164
Sales tax, 232–34
  supply curve and, 21
Salhany, Lucy, 83
Salt Lake Organizing Committee (SLOC), 237

Samaranch, Juan Antonio, 386
San Antonio Spurs, 131
San Diego Chargers, stadium arrangements for, 210–11
San Diego Padres, 81, 177
    attendance, 234
San Francisco Giants, 73, 88
    operating income of, 88
    ticket prices, 113
Sanity Code, 134, 357
Scalping, price ceilings and, 27–29
Schedules adjustments, in NFL, 168
Schmidt, Martin, 155, 250
Scholastic Aptitude Test (SAT), 377
    big-time programs and, 370–72
    college athletes and, 367
    student-athlete eligibility of, 373
Schramm, Tex, 139
Schwartzwalder, Ben, 202
Scottish Football League, 218
Second-degree price discrimination, 117, 117f
Secretary of Education's Commission on Opportunity in Athletics, 339
Seibu Lions, 94
Selig, Bud, 72, 169–70, 300
Selig-Preib, Wendy, 169
Sharapova, Maria, 258
Sherman Antitrust Act, 124, 126, 136, 140, 362
Shibe Park, 176, 192, 199
Shortage, 16
Simple regression, 56
Single entity ownership model, 101–102
Sin tax, 233
Slope term, in ordinary least squares estimate, 57
Smith, DeMaurice, 303
Soccer
    club values, 97t
    discrimination in, 331–32
    expansion of, 185
    history of, 39
    open system and, 101
    operating income, 97t
    organizational structure of, 99t
    professionalization of, 37–40, 50–51
    profit maximization in, 98–99
    promotion and regulation in, 99–100
    revenues, 97t
    single-entity league of, 101–102

women in, 337
Soft cap, 164
Sorenstam, Annika, 336
Sosa, Sammy, 265
Southeastern Conference (SEC), 135
Spectators, competitive balance and, 146–48
Spielman, Chris, 277
St. Bonaventure University, 373
St. Louis Browns, 176
    ownership of, 90
    Veeck, Bill and, 103
St. Louis Cardinals, 129, 146, 176, 267
    discrimination and, 327
St. Louis Rams, Super Bowl and, 275
Stacking, 332
Stadiums and arenas
    agreements, 83–86
    attendance and, 181–82
    cities underwriting, 177–81, 179t
    construction of, 176
    costs and financing of, 228–36
    "fan friendly," 195
    form and function of, 191–202
    location of, 199–202
    multipurpose facilities, 193–98
    naming rights, 84–85, 192–93
    privately built, 209–10
    publicly built, 210–22
    public support for, 180t
    retro, 181
    size and shape of, 193–99
Standard deviation, 152
Standard error, 57
Stankey, Eddie, 326
Statistical discrimination, 319–20
Staudohar, Paul, 297
Stereotypes, definition of, 314
Stern, David, 138
Stovey, George, 326
Straight-line depreciation, 95, 96f
Strikes and lockouts
    arbitration and, 284–86
    lockout, definition of, 293
    MLB strike of 1994–1995, 169, 300
    NBA lockout of 1998–1999, 296, 303
    NFL strikes, 298–99
    NHL lockout of 2004–2005, 287, 296
    strike, definition of, 293

Strong assumption, 23
Student-athletes, 349, 358, 367
　college as investment for, 363–68
Subchapter S corporation, 95
Substitution
　diminishing marginal rate of, 46, 47*f*
　effect, 14
　effects, 274
　marginal rate of, 270
Sunny Day Fund, 221
Super Bowl, 98, 147, 275
　impact of, 225–26
Superstars
　economics of, 255–60
　highest paid, 258*t*
Supply
　change in, 15, 19*f*, 20, 21*f*
　definition of, 15
　elasticity of, 22–23, 22*f*
　excess, 16
　labor, 246–48, 273*f*
　law of, 15
Supply and demand, 14–27
　of baseball cards, 14–27
　in labor markets, 245–55
Supply curve, 15
　individual, 274*f*
　labor, 247*f*, 274*f*
　price of baseball cards and, 18–27
　sales tax and, 21
　social, 214
Surplus, 16
　consumer, 109–10, 110*f*, 118–20, 120*f*, 186*f*
　producer, 109
Suspension of players, for drug use, 67
Sweet 16 teams, 368*t*, 378
Sydney Olympics, 264
Syracuse Stars, 326
Szymanski, Stefan, 323

T
Taft, William Howard, 127
Tagliabue, Paul, 138
Talent, evaluating, 167–68
Tampa Bay Devil Rays, 88
Tampa Bay Rays, 163
Taste for discrimination, 314

Taxes
　breaks favoring municipal bonds,
　　235*f*
　broadening burden, 234–35
　deadweight loss and, 230, 231*f*
　economic view of, 229–32
　luxury, 165
　rates in Canada, 223
　sales, 232–34
　sin, 233
Teixeira, Mark, 267
Television
　blackouts, 82
　college football contracts, 138–39
　contracts, leagues and, 71, 72
　contracts, NFL antitrust exemption and,
　　131–32
　gate receipts and, 82–83
　revenue, 80–86, 80*t*
　"timeouts," 83
Tennessee Titans, 203
Tennis
　mixed strategy in, 143*t*
　productivity in, 255
　professional associations, 304–306
　women in, 265, 304–305, 337–38
Texas Stadium, 84, 192
Texas Women's Open, 9
Theory of the Leisure Class (Veblen), 352
Third-degree price discrimination, 118
Thompson, Bobby, 198
Threat point, 296
Three Rivers Stadium, 193
Ticket prices
　Major League Baseball, 20
　in monopoly market, 32–36
　player salaries and, 36
　price ceiling, effect on, 27–29, 28*f*
　variable, 112–15, 114*f*
Time constraint, 271
　income and, 272*f*
Time Warner Cable, 91
Title IX, 338–40
　zero-sum game and, 339
Toolson, George, 129
Toolson v. New York Yankees, 283
Toronto Blue Jays, 93
　ownership of, 90

Toronto Maple Leafs, 78, 113, 223
  sharing facility, 199
  training and, 254
Total revenue, 76–79
Total utility, 44
Tour de France, 265
Tournaments
  child abuse, 261–62
  creating incentive for, 257f
  doping, 262–65
  economics of, 255–60
  rank-order, 255
Toyota Center, 193
Tragedy of the commons, 86
Training
  general, 253–54
  paying for, 254–55
  specific, 253–54
Tramp athlete, 357
Transaction cost, 162
Transfer price, 92
TransWorld Dome, 86
Treaty of Rome, 331, 332
Tribune Company, 91
T-statistic, 57
Tullock, Gordon, 226
Turner Movement, 351
Turnover, 155. *See also* Competitive balance
Turnverein. See Turner Movement

U
UEFA. *See* Union of European Football
  Associations (UEFA)
Ullrich, Jan, 265
Union League, 129
Union of European Football Associations
  (UEFA), 100, 331, 332
Unions. *See also* Strikes and lockouts
  bilateral monopoly and, 294, 295f
  craft, 292
  economics of, 292–96
  effect of, on wages, 293f
  free agency and, 282
  industrial, 292
  labor conflict in professional sports, 296–301
  monopsony and, 295f
  of professional sports, 304–306

resurgent ownership and, 303–304
United Center, 35, 36, 216
United Nation's Children Fund (UNICEF), 85
United States Football League (USFL), 71, 203,
  291, 303
  antitrust laws and, 131
United States Olympic Committee
  (USOC), 385
University of California at Los Angeles
  (UCLA), graduation rates for, 366
University of Chicago, 148
University of Colorado, 136
University of Georgia, 136, 374
University of Kentucky, 135, 373
  "Wildcat Lodge," 373
University of Maryland, naming rights
  and, 85
University of Massachusetts, 353
University of Miami, 138
University of Michigan, 27, 121, 136, 148
  popularity of football at, 365
  tramp athletes at, 357
University of Minnesota, 165
University of Tennessee, 379
University of Utah, 362–63
Unrestricted free agent, 284
Upshaw, Gene, 301, 303
Upstream firm, 91, 92f
U.S. Cellular Field, 224
U.S. Food and Drug Administration
  (FDA), 368
U.S. Treasury's Troubled Asset Relief
  Program, 85
User fee, 231
USFL. *See* United States Football League (USFL)
USOC. *See* United States Olympic Committee
  (USOC)
Utility, 38
  function, 44, 270
  maximizing, 50f, 52f
  total, 44
Utility-maximizing curves, 273f

V
Variables
  dependent, 54
  dummy, 58

independent, 54
Variable ticket pricing (VTP), 112, 114*f*
Variation
    between-season, 155–57
    within-season, 151–55
Veblen, Thorstein, 352
Veeck, Bill, 95, 96, 102–103, 217, 221, 311, 323
Venue revenue, 181
Vermeil, Dick, 275
Vertical equity, 230
Vertical integration, 91, 93*f*
Veterans Stadium, 193
Villanova University, 357
Vincent, Fay, 169
von der Ahe, Chris, 90

W

Wachovia Center, 199
Wade, Dwayne, 149
Wage, 246
    effect of unions on, 293*f*
    equilibrium, 252*f*, 317*f*
    monopsony and, 280*f*
Walker, Dixie, 326
Walker, Moses Fleetwood, 326
Walker, Tilly, 7
Walt Disney Corporation, 94
Washington Nationals, 73, 78, 146, 163
    construction of stadium, 228
Washington Redskins, operating income, 97
Washington Senators, 184
Washington Wizards, 158
Weak assumption, 23
Wenlock Olympic Games, 351
Wertz, Vic, 198
WFL. *See* World Football League (WFL)
WHA. *See* World Hockey Association (WHA)
White, Andrew D., 369
White, Byron "Whizzer," 136
Wie, Michelle, 336
"Wildcat Lodge," 373
Williams, Serena, 143–44, 265
Williams, Ted, 183
Williams College, 357

Wimbledon, 255
    child abuse and, 261–62
    women in, 337
Winnepeg Jets, 131
Winner's curse, 187–88
Winning percentages
    dispersion of, 153*t*
    in MLB, 153–54
    in NFL, 153–54
Within-season variation, 151–55
Women athletes
    in auto racing, 336–37
    discrimination against, 336–38
    in golf, 336
    as jockeys, 336
    in rowing, 385–86
    in soccer, 337
    in tennis, 265, 337–38
    Title IX and, 338–40
Women's American Basketball League, 176
Women's athletics, NCAA and, 133
Women's National Basketball Association (WNBA), 70, 73
    employee discrimination and, 312
    labor-leisure choice model and, 275
    Title IX and, 338
Women's Tennis Association (WTA), 265, 266*f*, 305
Women's U.S. Open, 337
Women's World Cup, 337, 338
Woods, Tiger, 258
World Chess Federation, 265
World Cup, 160
    impact of, 225–26
    market for, 160, 161*f*
    overspending and, 188–91
World Football League (WFL), 71, 291, 303
World Hockey Association (WHA), 71, 131
    rival leagues and, 283
World Series, 146
World University Games, 188
World War II, baseball and, 183
Wrigley, Philip, 127
Wrigley Field, 192, 216
WTA. *See* Women's Tennis Association (WTA)

X

Xcel Energy Center, 178, 180

Y

Yale University, 352
   Football Association, 369
Yankee Stadium, 176, 180, 192, 199, 210

Z

Zaharias, Babe Didrikson, 8–10, 262
Zero-sum game, 339, 371
Zimbalist, Andrew, 89
Zito, Barry, 267, 268